Hitler, the Holocaust, and the Bible:
A Scriptural Analysis
of Anti-Semitism, National Socialism,
and the Churches in Nazi Germany

by

Joseph Keysor

Published by

ATHANATOS
PUBLISHING GROUP

Hitler, the Holocaust, and the Bible:
A Scriptural Analysis of Anti-Semitism, National Socialism, and the Churches in Nazi Germany

by

Joseph Keysor

Published by

ATHANATOS
PUBLISHING GROUP

Hitler, the Holocaust, and the Bible: *A Scriptural Analysis of Anti-Semitism, National Socialism, and the Churches in Nazi Germany*

Copyright 2010, 2011, 2012, by Joseph Keysor
www.hitlerandchristianity.com

Published by the Athanatos Publishing Company
www.athanatosministries.org/group

Cover by Luke Thompson
www.sojournerdesign.org

3rd Edition, Hard Cover.

ISBN: 978-0-9822776-4-5

Soft Cover ISBN: 978-0-9822776-5-2
E-Book ISBN: 978-1-9368302-2-0

Printed in the United States of America.

A word from the author about quotations:
Some of the sources used in this book are in the public domain. Some have been quoted with permission from the authors or publishers. I have relied on "fair use." If any possessors of copyright feel I have transgressed the boundaries of fair use (I often use less than 100 words) they may contact the publisher and we will take necessary steps to rectify any perceived violation of copyright. I was unable after repeated attempts to locate the source of the internet translation of *Mein Kampf.*

Table of Contents

Part I: Christianity and National Socialism

The Hep riots ... A great and terrible mystery ... The biblical concept of Satan ... The devilish nature of anti-Semitism ... Original sin ... Christian servants of the devil ... What is a Christian? ... Did Hitler or the Nazi Christians bear good fruit? ... The Bible as the source of anti-Semitism ... Paul's teaching of salvation by grace through faith—an attack on Judaism? ... The New Testament's description of Jews ... The crucifixion of Christ ... Pontius Pilate and the guilt of the Gentiles ... "His blood be on us" ... Has God rejected the Jews? ... Who are the children of the devil? ... The Holocaust and the Old Testament ... The massacres of the Canaanites ... The Nuremberg racial laws ... Hitler's study notes on the Bible ... The Christian way of holiness

Introduction ... An analogy ... The Jewish experience in the Middle Ages ... Christian limitations ... Concepts of the Jews ... Christian doctrinal criticisms of Judaism ... Concepts of government ... Moral doctrines ... The restraints in practice ... Government protection of Jews ... The Crusades ... The Church of Rome and the Jews ... John Chrysostom ... The apostles' attitudes toward the Jews ... Chrysostom's motive ... Martin Luther ... Some misconceptions about Luther ... Luther and the Nazis ... Luther in perspective ... A secular evaluation of Luther ... Luther's goal ... Matthew Henry and Romans 11 ... A glimpse ahead ... Conclusion

Hitler in the light of scripture ... A blatant absence of Christian doctrines ... Hitler's unbiblical principles (i) ... Hitler's unbiblical principles (ii) ... Hostility to Christianity in *Mein Kampf* ... An honest liar ... Hitler the Catholic? ... Honest Adolf strikes again ... Christ in *Mein Kampf* ... Hitler's last will and testament ... Hitler's references to God ... Hitler's references to the Bible ... Hitler's expressions of support for Christianity and the German churches ... The example of the trade unions ... The Nazi party platform supported "positive" Christianity ... Hitler's policy toward the churches – words contradicted by deeds ... A blueprint for the future ... Nazi church policies in Austria ... Nazi church policies in the Warthegau ... Hitler linked to Christianity ... A. Hatred and fear of Christianity ... A bias revealed ... B. A lack of information ... C. Illogical arguments ... D. Misstatements of fact ... *Hitler's Table Talk* ... Quotes from Hitler's followers ... Nazi photos ... Nazi artifacts ... E. Ignorance of Christianity ... Paul's letter to the Galatians ... What was Hitler?

Part II: The Origins of National Socialism

intensification of Folkish tendencies ... Julius Langbehn ... The Pan-German Association ... The Folkish movement and Christianity

Preface to the second edition

Some changes have been made to the first edition. With the help of some constructive criticisms, as well as more research materials obtained from the States, I have been able to strengthen the bibliography and add more historical detail and accuracy to the work. Some of the Christian polemics have been deleted from the second part, which is after all more academic in nature (as well as from chapter 4). The sections on Luther, Bonhoeffer, Kant, Schopenhauer, and Wagner in particular have been added to and revised.

Whatever flaws there might be in the book—and no book on these topics will satisfy everyone—I am confident that the main points are unassailable. Biblical Christianity, as taught by Christ and the apostles, and as practiced by many sincere Christians over the centuries, has nothing whatever to do with modern secular hallucinations such as National Socialism or Communism. Criticisms which do not touch upon these points may be interesting and useful, but cannot I think be anything other than secondary.

Finally, it should be pointed out that this book is a work of Christian apologetics, not of secular academic scholarship. As such, it legitimately deals with aspects of the human experience beyond the confines of conventional studies of Hitler.

Introduction

The present situation

Christianity is being attacked in America today as never before. On TV shows and in movies, in the news media, in academia, in books of pop philosophy and pop science, Christians are being increasingly portrayed as narrow-minded, intolerant, ignorant, hypocritical, and even evil. This goes beyond mere ridicule. The basic teachings of Christianity are being condemned to an extent previously unimagined in this country.

It is being increasingly said that Christianity has had a negative impact on America's history and culture—not just because of abuses, but because of fundamental characteristics of the religion. It was the Christians, it is argued, who enslaved the blacks, exterminated the Indians, oppressed women, burdened people with guilt and denied them sexual freedom, and forced the gays to stay in the closet.

Christianity has even been blamed for pollution and the destruction of the environment. God's commandment in Genesis to "subdue" the earth and "have dominion" over the creatures is said to be a license for ecological plundering and pillaging. Never mind that the destruction of the environment only emerged as a serious problem in the modern era, nearly two thousand years after Christ died and rose again. Never mind that those who make the most noise about the destruction of the environment continue to enjoy their wasteful and environmentally destructive modern lifestyles while they attack the Bible.

Part of this negative trend has been increasing attempts to link Christianity and the Bible to Adolf Hitler and the crimes of the Nazis. While it will seem incredible to some that the teachings of Christ and the Bible should be linked to Aryan supremacy, German militarism, the horrors of the death camps, and the extermination of six million Jews, such is sadly the case.

Christianity linked to Naziism

In the recent past, it was much more commonly assumed that Christianity had nothing to do with National Socialism. It was believed that Christianity was basically benevolent, while National Socialism was basically evil, that Hitler was as far removed from the Sermon on the Mount as it is humanly possible to get. The great majority of Americans would have assumed that the Jewish experience in America was the norm, the result of the Christian influence on American culture.

The cultural climate has changed in the last fifty years, however, and the growing power of secularism makes people less inclined to view Christianity so tolerantly. The well-known support of German Christians for Hitler; statements about God, Christianity, and the churches by Hitler and by leading Nazis, including strong opposition to atheism; Hitler's Catholic upbringing and his Concordat with the Vatican; the fact that Hitler never officially withdrew from the Catholic Church; the official support for "positive Christianity" in the Nazi party platform; the supposed fact that Hitler came to power in an overwhelmingly Christian country; centuries of Christian anti-Semitism; verses in the New Testament that seem hostile to Jews; the massacres of the Canaanites in the Old Testament—all of these and even other arguments have been emphasized by those who see more and more evidence of connections between Hitler and Christianity. Hitler's opposition to birth control, abortion, and homosexuality are easily connected to the family values of the religious right.

Reputable scholars and historians have studied Hitler's ideology more objectively. George Mosse's *The Crisis of German Ideology: Intellectual Origins of the Third Reich*; Daniel Gasman's *The Scientific Origins of National Socialism*; Peter Viereck's *Metapolitics: The Roots of the Nazi Mind*; Richard Weikart's *From Darwin to Hitler: Evolutionary Ethics, Eugenics, and Racism in Germany*; Michael Mack's *German Idealism and the Jew: The Inner Anti-Semitism of Philosophy and German Jewish Responses*; Paul Lawrence Rose's *German Question / Jewish Question: Revolutionary Antisemitism in Germany from Kant to Wagner*—these all show from different perspectives and with different emphases how the 19th century's secular philosophies opened the door to the emergence of horrors unprecedented in the history of the human race. John Conway's *The Nazi Persecution of the Churches 1933-1945* does not deal with the origins of National Socialism, but it demonstrates that Hitler viewed Christianity as a rival for the allegiance of the German people and sought to eliminate its influence as much as possible, his devious political rhetoric notwithstanding.

The works of these and other authors too numerous to name have had a significant impact, but unfortunately there remain those who seem to relish attacking Christianity. Oblivious to historical realities and misinformed or even hopelessly ignorant of biblical teachings, they continue to try to link Christianity to Hitler. They have had an impact as well, and we should not underestimate them. Too few Christians understand the extent to which what they perceive as a beneficent religion of grace, peace, and forgiveness is increasingly associated by many with the cruelties of the Third Reich.

A Holocaust video checked out from the local library asserts that centuries of Christian anti-Semitism made Jews Hitler's natural target (completely omitting all of 19th-century secular and racial anti-Semitism). A history of the Third Reich compares Hitler's Nazi party rallies to religious revival meetings, and a popular biography of Hitler agrees with a Holocaust scholar that Hitler was just carrying out the policies of the Roman Catholic Church when he slaughtered the Jews. An in-depth academic analysis of the Holocaust published by a prestigious university press and acclaimed by scholars from top American universities refers to the false and "venomous" anti-Jewish teachings of the New Testament and asserts that by demonizing the Jews Christianity played a significant role in laying the foundations for the Holocaust.[1]

The debate over what Hitler believed and where he got his ideas has not merely continued over the years, it has intensified. This is true to such an extent that Richard Evans, editor of the prestigious *Journal of Contemporary History* has written, "The relationship of German National Socialism to religion in general, and Christianity in particular, has recently moved to the forefront of historical inquiry."[2] Partly this is due to a natural human desire for deeper spiritual understanding that the countless secular books about Hitler have not satisfied and will never satisfy. Partly it is due to the fact that linking Hitler to Christianity is an increasingly common tactic in the culture wars. If Naziism can be convincingly blamed on Christian influence, then obviously Christians are potentially dangerous fanatics who deserve to be marginalized or even excluded from the political process as much as possible. This reasoning explains why some believe they are protecting American liberty and democracy by working to eliminate Christian influence. There are those who sincerely believe that they are defending democracy by attacking and marginalizing Christianity.

A notable advocate of this "Christians-are-dangerous-potential-fascists" line of thought is one Mr. Jim Walker. He has put up a website called "Hitler's Christianity" at http://www.nobeliefs.com/Hitler1.htm, arguing that Hitler was a Christian and acted like a Christian. From this he draws the inevitable conclusion that American Christians today are a menace to society. One wonders what Christians he has met who want to exterminate the Jews or who believe that the Americans are the master race whose destiny it is to rule the world, but we can examine his arguments later.

As groundless as such arguments are, they are effective with people who know little about history and nothing about Christianity. In more than one internet debate, I have been referred to Walker's website for proof that Christianity leads to hatred, cruelty, and fascism. Such accusations have gone for far too long without a direct response. As was the case in Germany, the Christians in America have been too passive and inert while the forces of darkness grow in strength and intensity. The spread of such ideas will affect us directly and has already begun to affect us. We are mistaken if we think that because God has blessed America with liberty in the past, we are therefore guaranteed of this blessing forever.

A more academic attempt to directly link Christianity to Naziism is Richard Steigmann-Gall's *The Holy Reich* (Cambridge University Press). Reflecting views increasingly popular among secular scholars, the book argues that many Nazis were not anti-Christian at all, but thought themselves to be Christians, "understood their movement (among other ways) within a Christian frame of reference" and "drew on Christian traditions to articulate their vision of Naziism."[3] The book even goes so far as to assert that Hitler "regarded Christ's struggle as direct inspiration for his own"[4] and claims "Hitler insists that Christianity is at the center of Nazi social thought" and "regards the teachings of Christ as direct inspiration for the 'German' socialism advanced by the party."[5] This explains why Hitler cared nothing for political power, was a pacifist, and commanded his followers not to fight on his behalf.

Walker and Steigmann-Gall are by no means the only ones presenting such theories. *The Holy Reich* has been called (on its back-cover promotion at least) a "thought-provoking work of admirable scholarship . . . deeply researched and thoughtfully argued . . . brilliant . . . important and original" and so on. This sounds impressive, but back-cover blurbs always do. Some recent critiques of Steigmann-Gall in the same issue of the *Journal of Contemporary History* quoted above were considerably less flattering.[6] These point out some of the many historical and scholarly errors in Steigmann-Gall's work, but unfortunately don't address the central problem of his total indifference to the meaning, spirit, and essence of Christianity as taught by Christ and the apostles.

Non-Christians with more insight into Christianity don't base their ideas on a total or near total ignorance of essential Christian beliefs. They recognize that Christianity is profoundly different from Naziism, but still claim that Christianity contributed significantly to the Holocaust by creating a deep reservoir of anti-Jewish hate that Hitler tapped into. Scholars debate the exact nature of the relationship between Christianity and National Socialism. Some see more of a connection, others less, but the fact of some sort of connection is accepted as a given among non-Christians—and it is non-Christians who now dominate academia, the courts, the government, and the media. They are increasingly receptive to the view that Christians are dangerous.

A huge amount of literature has been generated on the origins of the Nazi ideology and on the resultant Holocaust, and Holocaust studies has become a significant field with notable figures and competing schools of thought. It is a field which has been too much ignored by those who believe in the Bible as the word of God. Those who do not believe in the Bible and have little understanding of its teachings too often dominate the discussion—as a result there is growing agreement among secular scholars, historians, and experts, that Christianity is to blame (to a disputed but always significant degree) for the emergence of Naziism, and for the crimes of the Nazis.

The Christian response

It is easy for Christians to dismiss such attacks as being too absurd to dignify with a response—but given that a growing chorus of unbelievers has been attacking our beliefs, silence is a serious mistake. When the slaughter of six million Jews is laid at the feet of Christ and the apostles and at the door of the church, we do not honor or serve our Saviour by saying nothing. More people than we would like to think really do not know what Christianity is, and find it easy to conclude from photographs of church leaders saluting Hitler that "Christianity is compatible with Naziism," and "the religious right is a menace to democracy."

When serious academic publishers make a direct assault on Christianity as an evil religion and present historical information to support their claims, and when such ideas are given credit in American universities and taught as fact, there is little or no Christian response. Unbelievers are too often allowed to dominate discussions about Christianity and Hitler, and spread distortions and lies unopposed.

From the vantage point of faith in the Bible as the divinely inspired and inerrant word of God, this essay will examine the charge that biblical Christianity was in some way involved with the emergence of Naziism. It will assert that all forms of hatred and persecution are directly contrary to the message of Christ and the apostles; that supposedly Christian anti-Semitism was a result of ignorance of the Christian message; that medieval cruelties (nowhere mentioned or sanctioned by the New Testament) and modern racial anti-Semitism were the result not of the Bible, but of rebellion against the Bible; that the common and unifying factors between medieval or Czarist pogroms and the Nazi persecutions are not biblical teachings, but sin and evil in the human heart, manipulated by Satan and by invisible spiritual powers of wickedness. This was also the motivating force behind Pharaoh's and Haman's attempts to exterminate the Jews long before the introduction of any Christian or modern racial elements—the power of Satan, the prince of darkness, working through cruel, ignorant, and evil men, void of the Spirit of Christ.

I have had some experience of scholars and intellectuals who are incapable of even understanding, let alone responding fairly to, the biblical viewpoints I hope to articulate. I know that if this writing should ever come into public view it will be dismissed by dogmatic secularists. Their beliefs that the invisible and eternal truths of God are non-existent will inhibit objective analysis. People of other faiths will also find my presuppositions and conclusions unacceptable. I haven't tiptoed delicately around such things so as to avoid causing disagreement.

The plan of this essay
The nature of Hitler's relationship to Christianity can be seen in the answers to two questions: "Which teachings of the Sermon on the Mount did Hitler follow?" and "Where in the New Testament does it say that the blond, blue-eyed Aryans are the master race, that it is their destiny to rule the world, or that Jews are subhuman vermin who should be exterminated?" Anyone who answers these questions knowledgeably and fairly will have a correct understanding of the point at issue. Since, however, there are those who do not have an adequate understanding of and are sometimes even openly hostile to biblical Christianity, further explanation is necessary.

Attempts to link Christianity to Naziism rely on a few key points: (a) teachings in the Bible itself; (b) teachings and actions of Christian anti-Semites in the centuries preceding the modern era; (c) statements by Hitler and his followers; and (d) the support of the churches and of different varieties of Christians for Hitler. After having responded to those arguments, it will also be necessary to consider (e) the origins of Hitler's ideology. After all, if National Socialism did not arise out of a Christian context, the question logically arises as to where it did come from. The essay, then, will have five main parts:

An overview of the five parts: Part I

This will have to include a brief discussion of the biblical concepts of Satan and original sin. These are out of fashion in our secular age, but the failure to take these basic truths of existence into account has led to the superficiality of many attempts to understand Hitler and the Holocaust. The idea that Hitler received his mysterious power from the devil himself is irrelevant to many, but it explains his destructive power on the deepest level.

A definition of the term "Christian" is also needed. Since so many have assumed that all non-Jewish Poles were automatically Christians; that German soldiers who wore "God with us" belt buckles were Christians; that anyone who had been baptized as an infant, attended church once every five or ten years, or used the words "God" and "Jesus" on occasion was a Christian, we need some rudimentary definition of what a Christian is.

That there are plain biblical warnings about false Christians and false teachers will need to be mentioned. We also need to remember Paul's admonition in I Corinthians that Christianity without love is worthless. Too many people are discussing Christianity in hostility and ignorance with no knowledge of its essence, spirit, or purpose.

It will then be necessary to look at verses in the New Testament that supposedly show hostility toward Jews. It will be shown that Paul's statements on the inability of the Jews to obtain salvation by the law or teachings on the Jewish rejection of Christ and the subsequent adoption of the Gentiles into the covenant relationship formerly occupied by the Jews provide no license or incentive for hatred and killing. The participation of the Gentiles with the Jews in the crucifixion of Christ and their shared guilt will be elaborated on. Understanding that Christ died according to the will of the Father; that his death and resurrection were for our redemption; that insofar as we have all sinned we all were involved to some degree in Christ's death—these and yet other factors forbid anger and malice toward Jews on the part of sincere Christians.

Having completed a brief survey of passages in the New Testament, it will then be necessary to look at the Old Testament as well. The Jewish massacres of the Canaanites have sometimes been compared to Hitler's crimes. Christians have even been publicly challenged to show that Hitler's massacres were any different from those commanded by God in the Bible. Similarly, the Nuremberg Laws that were designed to exclude Jews from German life have been compared to the Old Testament prohibition of intermarriage between Jews and non-Jews.

Part II

Many or all of the comments in Part I can be dismissed as nothing but spin-doctoring—attempts to put a favorable interpretation on unpleasant facts. We Christians can put the best possible face on disputed verses—the fact remains that many Christians over the centuries have hated and persecuted Jews. This, it will be argued, is proof of the inherent anti-Semitism in Christianity.

That many Christians have never persecuted Jews and that many Jews have had decent lives in western countries are also facts, however. Jews have not been subjected to an unending succession of pogroms and hate. We have to look beyond the Middle Ages and consider the Jewish experience not only in medieval Europe or Czarist Russia, but in the New World and in western Europe in the centuries between the Protestant Reformation and World War I. Surely if medieval pogroms and hatred were inherent in Christianity the Jews in America, Canada, England, Denmark etc. would have experienced at least one pogrom in the last few centuries. The fact that western Baptists, Methodists, and Lutherans have not been rampaging through Jewish neighborhoods killing Jews shows that serious faith in the Bible does not inevitably lead to violent anti-Semitism.

Moral restraints inherent in Christianity ensured that centuries of Christian cultural domination never gave birth to any mad schemes to exterminate all Jews. Biblical concepts of ethics and law ensured that they were never reduced to the arbitrary will of a Fuhrer. Examples of these restraints, ensuring that the Jews were more widely tolerated and even protected in the medieval period than is commonly known, will be presented. The totally unbiblical Crusades and Inquisition will be taken into account and shown to be radically different, both in nature and in degree, from the institutionalized and industrialized madness of Nazi Germany. Medieval theological criticisms and condemnations of Judaism were far removed from the hallucinations of German racial theorists.

It will then be necessary to look at the writings of two Christian authors whose names regularly come up in these discussions: John Chrysostom and Martin Luther. Luther's attacks on the Jews in particular will be analyzed carefully, given the fact that he was a German, and the Nazis (including Hitler) professed to have admiration for him. Luther's case is doubly important because he is still rightly respected by many Christians today as a deeply spiritual man who accomplished a great deal of good. A careful study of his comments against the Jews will reveal them to be different from what is usually claimed, and nothing like the modern racial anti-Semitism of the Nazis. They were also a distraction and a diversion from the basic principles of the Reformation.

Finally, an examination of Matthew Henry's 18th-century commentaries will show how the Evangelical understanding of the Jews that emerged from the Reformation leads to toleration, not anti-Semitism.

Part III

This part will examine seemingly religious statements uttered by Hitler. Does mere use of words like "God," "Providence," or "the Lord" make one a Christian, or does even a casual glance at 19th-century German philosophy and religion show the frequent use of spiritual terms in a non-Christian context? Were Hitler's public statements about respecting and supporting the churches truthful (like his expressed desire to expand to the east), or were they politically motivated deceptions (like his feigned desire for peace and cooperation with other nations)? If a reference to God proves Hitler was a Christian, do references in *Mein Kampf* to gods and goddesses, or to evolution and to survival of the fittest, show that Hitler was a Christian-Darwinist-polytheist?

A notable feature of Hitler's combined comments about the meaning of life is a complete absence of any reference to essential Christian doctrines. Did Hitler even once refer to Jesus Christ as the son of God who died on the cross as a sacrifice for the sins of the world, and then rose from the dead? Did this supposed Catholic mention the Virgin Mary one single time? The idea of Chancellor Hitler counting rosary beads or going to confession is ludicrous. Does anyone think Hitler believed that eternal life through faith in Christ made political affairs of secondary importance, or that there is one passage in the Sermon on the Mount that can be even remotely connected to Hitler?

Hitler not only avoided essential biblical teachings. He also expressed in *Mein Kampf* ideas totally foreign to biblical Christianity. Christ is referred to briefly as a teacher of ethics (a common secular view) and also as an anti-Semite who drove the Jews out of the temple. The origin of the human race is attributed solely to secular causes. Biblical ethics are dismissed and replaced by a social Darwinist emphasis on survival of the fittest. Nearly all of the Old Testament is rejected as unhistorical, sin is described as racial impurity, happiness and the true meaning of life are achieved by racial purity.

Hitler also expressed overt hostility to Christianity. Africans who converted to Christianity are described in *Mein Kampf* as "a rotten brood of bastards."[7] Christianity is condemned as intolerant—a common argument of secularists today—and its undeniable and well-known Jewish origins are referred to with open hostility. The failure of the churches to understand the Jewish problem is pointed out, and a future blueprint for the elimination of the churches' influence is laid out (this was to be achieved by carefully controlled repression combined with educating the young in Hitler's new faith).

Next it will be necessary to look at a couple of rare occasions (one of them quoted second-hand) when Hitler claimed to be a Christian. Not surprisingly, they contain no doctrinal substance and prove nothing but Hitler's dishonesty. Some of Hitler's references to God and to the Bible will be examined, as will his promises to support the churches and protect them. The Nazi party platform and Hitler's policy toward the churches—not only in Germany but also in Austria and Poland—require consideration.

Jim Walker's aforementioned "Hitler's Christianity" website will then be examined in detail. Some of the numerous errors of logic and fact will be emphasized, and the paganism underlying even Hitler's seemingly religious statements will be exposed. Nazi support for "positive" Christianity, Nazi violations of the Concordat with the Vatican, and church policies of the Nazi government are some of the topics that will be discussed to show the value of Hitler's religious rhetoric—rhetoric that is still deceiving people today. It is necessary to look not only at Hitler's words, but also at his actions. The treatment of the churches in Nazi Germany reveals Hitler's "Christianity" clearly enough.

Part IV

The support of German Christians for Hitler—or at least their failure to oppose him—is commonly pointed to by unbelievers as proof of a Nazi-Christian connection of some kind. It is also said that Hitler emerged in a Christian country; that Christianity was easily harmonized with National Socialism; that the Christians in Germany were silent about the persecution of the Jews because their theology led them to approve of it.

To deal with these arguments, it is not sufficient merely to state that Christianity is defined by Christ and by the apostles, not by the churches of Germany. True as that is, it is also necessary to give some historical background information, followed by an examination of the churches in Nazi Germany. It will be demonstrated that Germany was not a Christian country and that Hitler did not, as is so often falsely claimed, arise out of a Christian environment. Germany was in many ways a deeply secular country, and the churches did not have sufficient power or influence to prevent Hitler's rise.

Nevertheless, while the extent of Christian influence in Germany is usually overstated, it must be said that much more could have been done by the churches than was done. Hitler and the lies of National Socialism were not sufficiently opposed from church pulpits and presses with the spiritual sword of biblical truth. There were several reasons for this. German Christians who claimed National Socialism was compatible with Christianity and supported Hitler for "theological" reasons had totally abandoned biblical Christianity. Those more orthodox who supported Hitler for political reasons and hoped he would bring stability to Germany were gullible and deceived. Much of the failure to oppose Hitler was due not to Christian teachings, but to fear. Too many Christians kept silent and went along because they did not want to be sent to a concentration camp.

The few exceptions who showed extraordinary courage and did speak out should not be forgotten. They represented the potential opposition that Hitler was mindful of in formulating his church policies. These policies were a careful combination of administrative challenges aimed at making the churches entirely subordinate to the state; of an ideological campaign to draw people away from the churches; and naked repression where extreme cases made it necessary. This has been described in scholarly detail in Conway's book *The Nazi Persecution of the Churches 1933-1945*.

Having completed this brief overview of the churches in Germany, it is necessary to say more about the failure of the churches to speak out for the Jews. Was this due to anti-Semitism inherent in Christianity, or were there Christians who knew that the Nazi policies were wrong but said nothing because of fear? There is ample evidence to show that many German Christians said nothing because of the latter rather than because of the former reason. After all, the churches said little or nothing about the torture and murder of other Germans either. Even the well-known opposition to Hitler's euthanasia program was limited to a very small number of heroic individuals while most remained silent. Those who did hold to some kind of traditionally anti-Semitic views were not necessarily in favor of shoving Jews into gas chambers.

What, then, should the churches have done? To what extent were they responsible for Hitler coming to power? To what extent did Christian beliefs about obedience to authority obligate them to support Hitler, or refrain from opposing him? These questions need to be answered by biblical teaching within the context of historical realities.

Part V

Hitler's ideas seem preposterous to us, but they did not seem so to many in Hitler's day, and were in fact the product of a long tradition going back well over a century before 1933. After commenting on such aspects of the Hitler riddle as the importance of technology, or the question "Do we all have something of Hitler in us, or was he so far off the map as to be totally unique?", it will be necessary to try and untangle the roots of that tradition.

Various attempts have been made to analyze that tradition, and attention has been drawn to ideas similar and even identical to Hitler's in the philosophies of Kant, Fichte, and Hegel. Other thinkers such as Gobineau, Jahn, Lagarde, Langbehn, Wagner, Chamberlain, Haeckel, and Nietzsche have also been pointed to as sources of National Socialism.

Ideas of extreme nationalism, political authoritarianism, and secular anti-Semitism emerged out of the so-called Enlightenment, grew in popularity over some decades, and coalesced to form what became known as the Folkish ideology (or movement). Advocated by a significant minority of German intellectuals—including scientists, doctors, professors, journalists, sociologists, politicians, and educators—it came to have a disproportionately large influence in the second half of the nineteenth century.

This study will examine the roots of the Folkish movement, especially as finally expressed in the writings of Richard Wagner and Houston Stewart Chamberlain, and will point to those ideas as important sources of many of the essential ingredients of the toxic brew of National Socialist ideology. It will also argue that it was the combination of a pre-existing Folkish tradition with uniquely German interpretations of Darwinism that added immensely to the appeal and respectability of the movement. This combination is most clearly articulated in the writings of the eminent German Darwinist Ernst Haeckel—though many others had similar or identical ideas.

Given the "scientific facts" that life was nothing more than a pitiless and amoral struggle for survival, and that the more advanced human "races" were higher on the evolutionary scale than lower "races," previous concepts of Aryan supremacy and enthusiastic militarism could be seen (and were seen) as scientifically based, and objectively factual. The belief that we are in essence only animals of a higher sort with no immortal soul contributed greatly to the devaluation of human life that made mass extermination more acceptable as a matter not of crime, but of rational policy.

After looking at the historical background in German romantic and idealistic philosophy going back as far as Kant and the "Enlightenment," I will focus on four writers—not as causes of National Socialism, but as representatives of social and intellectual currents that converged in a unique set of circumstances to make Hitler's ideas acceptable. Those four are Wagner, Chamberlain, Haeckel, and Nietzsche. Given the importance of these four, their writings will be examined in some detail.

Also not to be forgotten is the unique genius of Hitler. Far from dismissing Hitler as an idiot incapable of reading a book, or a crazy man (though he was mad in the end), I will seek to demonstrate that Hitler had a good though selective understanding of the above-mentioned thinkers, and consciously drew on their ideas to forge an exceedingly powerful and compelling ideology. Neither a nihilist nor an opportunist who believed in nothing but his own power, Hitler was passionately committed to a coherent and consistent (though false and ugly) world view. He believed that by leading the Aryan race to its rightful position of world dominance, by subordinating inferior races such as the Slavs and exterminating the Jews, he was benefiting the human race and guiding it to a better future.

A question of presuppositions

If doctors are puzzled by a new disease, they gather a lot of information and eventually understanding emerges. If the police want to solve a crime, they gather a lot of data and eventually a suspect can be identified. But, if one wants to understand how the most hideous evil could explode with volcanic force in the heart of supposedly civilized Europe, merely amassing a lot of data will not lead to a deeper understanding.

Can we explain why a man would kidnap a little child, sexually molest it, torture it, and kill it? If we can, we might have a concept of evil that would extend not only to National Socialism and the Holocaust but also to all of the horrors of World War II and beyond. If, however, we cannot even explain one murder, can we explain millions? If there is no higher moral understanding at all, then there is nothing left to do but record the facts and abandon all hope of going further. We cannot even say with confidence that what the Nazis did was wrong. If on the other hand there is a higher understanding, then it is only in the light of this that the evils of Naziism can be understood. It is a deficient understanding of morality and spirituality that leads so many to place the blame for the crimes of the Nazis wrongly, while the most immediately and obviously guilty parties are exonerated.

It is a common error to assume that a rejection of religion guarantees objectivity. Many take it as a given that those who believe in the Bible are hopelessly subjective and incapable of seeing life as it is, while those who reject the Bible are—this is supposedly an infallible and eternal truth—clear-sighted, rational, objective, unbiased. But this is itself only another kind of subjectivity and bias, more powerful because it is unrecognized. Approaching the subject of Hitler's relationship to Christianity under the assumption of the non-existence or the irrelevance of God and the falsehood of the Bible, secularists miss an entire dimension of the problem—and the most crucial one at that. Then, attempting to understand the relationship of Christianity to Naziism, they seriously misinterpret the Bible because they do not know what it means. They leave out very important teachings completely, seriously distort others, and arrive at misguided conclusions—all the while complacently resting in their imaginary objectivity.

This is why so many will point to the Bible, Christian anti-Semitism, and Martin Luther to show the Christian origins of the Holocaust, while they ignore or lightly pass over 19th-century German thinkers who explicitly rejected the Bible and introduced new concepts and new ways of hating Jews that are much closer to the death camps both chronologically and spiritually. It is necessary to show that religious belief is ignorant and misguided, and leads to catastrophe, so that one can reject the claims of religion. That men can reject the Bible, assert their freedom from the need for divine revelation, and then with their secular human reason and logic come to the conclusions that the Aryans are the master race and Jews are vermin to be exterminated—this is a troubling fact that must be covered up at all costs. It is too frightening to consider that human reason without God can lead to such horrifying disasters, so the truth is avoided.

This is why we are constantly given the examples of the Crusades and the Inquisition to show the dangers of religious fanaticism. The atrocities of Lenin, Stalin, Mao, Castro, and Pol Pot, much more relevant to our own times than events of centuries ago, and much greater in terms of numbers slain—these are not held up as examples of the dangers inherent in trying to organize society by reason alone, without regard to a higher and superior power whom we must obey.

True belief in God imposes limits—the rejection of biblical values and the lowering of man to the level of a beast open the door to the most hideous and unbridled atrocities.

That the human mind once freed from the restraints of God's law is capable of devising bizarre ideologies and inflicting merciless cruelties; that there is innate evil in the human soul which does not need to be encouraged but which rather needs to be limited and restrained—these are truths which many will reject. Nevertheless, it should be evident, and will be evident to an impartial observer, that it is not the fault of the Bible if secular human reasoning without divine revelation comes to the conclusions that life is only a pitiless struggle in which the strong survive and the weak die; that this struggle is the most fundamental law of life, the very source of our being; that heaven and hell are useless deceptions; that materially speaking the Europeans are superior to other racial and ethnic groups and "materially superior" means "superior" because the material reality is the only real criterion; that the Jews through Christianity have corrupted western civilization with false values; that kindness, forgiveness, and mercy are vices, while cold and pitiless cruelty is a virtue, and healthy; that man is only an animal, nothing more; that the Europeans lead the world, and the northern Europeans, the Germanic peoples, lead Europe, making the Germans the elite of the elite.

These ideas did not come from Christ, the apostles, or Roman Palestine. They didn't come from the anti-Jewish sermons of Chrysostom, the Vatican, or from the Protestant Reformation. They came from modern man in the modern age. They gave birth to a philosophy that was nothing but the elementary evils of pride, vanity, and cruelty bolstered and intensified by pseudo-science, secular philosophy, and modern technology without the salutary restraints of Christianity, animated by the invisible but real powers of Satan and of human sin.

A final note

Except for brief periods in America and Canada, this essay was written while I was working as an English teacher in the Sultanate of Oman, and I would like to express my gratitude to the authorities of Oman for giving me the privilege of peacefully living and working in their beautiful country. I have been deeply impressed by the friendliness of the Omani people and have never been made to feel unwelcome as a Christian or as an American.

I would especially like to thank Prof. John Conway, Prof. Daniel Gasman, Simon Weil, and Walter S. Frank for permission to quote at length from their books and websites. My views are in many ways different from theirs, but in the material which I use pertaining to Hitler's relationship to the churches; Ernst Haeckel's basic ideas; Wagner's anti-Semitism; and Hitler's early life, I am in agreement with them and have used their material in accordance with their own purposes. I am indebted to Profs. Conway, Gasman, and Richard Weikart for instructive criticisms and comments, and to Prof. Weikart specifically for sending me chapter 2 of his work in progress, *Hitler's Ethic*.

Have the gates of death been opened unto thee?
or hast thou seen the doors of the shadow of death?
Hast thou perceived the breadth of the earth? declare if thou knowest it all.
Where is the way where light dwelleth? and as for darkness, where is the place thereof,

That thou shouldest take it to the bound thereof, and that thou shouldest know the paths to the house thereof? (Job)

---

[1] Steven Katz, *The Holocaust in Historical Context* (Oxford University Press 1994), pp. 235-236.

[2] Richard Evans, "Naziism, Christianity and Political Religion: A Debate," *Journal of Contemporary History* 42, no. 1 (2007), p. 5.

[3] Richard Steigmann-Gall, *The Holy Reich: Nazi Conceptions of Christianity, 1919-1945* (Cambridge 2004), p. 3. Steigmann-Gall's analysis is notable for its complete indifference to Christian primary sources—the teachings of Christ and the apostles as contained in the New Testament—as well as for its indifference to secular German thinkers who expressed ideas similar or identical to Hitler's while openly rejecting biblical Christianity.

[4] Ibid., p. 27.

[5] Ibid., p. 46.

[6] See Manfred Gailus ("A Strange Obsession with Nazi Christianity: A Critical Comment on Richard Steigmann-Gall's *The Holy Reich*"); Ernst Piper ("Steigmann-Gall, *The Holy Reich*"); and Irving Hexham ("Inventing 'Paganists': A Close Reading of Richard Steigmann-Gall's *The Holy Reich*").

[7] Adolf Hitler, *Mein Kampf*, trans. Ralph Manheim (Boston / New York 1999), p. 403.
The passage from the online version of *Mein Kampf* reads:
> . . . the pious missionary goes out to Central Africa and establishes missionary stations for negroes. Finally, sound and healthy—though primitive and backward—people will be transformed, under the name of our 'higher civilization', into a motley of lazy and brutalized mongrels.
> It would better accord with noble human aspirations if our two Christian denominations would cease to bother the negroes with their preaching, which the negroes neither desire nor understand. [vol. II chapt. 2 "The State"] http://www.hitler.org/writings/ Mein_Kampf/mkv2ch02.html; accessed September 2007.

Future quotations from the online version will not be noted. Book and chapter numbers will be given so the quotes can be located. Click on "Edit," select "Find," and enter the appropriate word or phrase. Endnotes to *Mein Kampf* indicating page numbers refer to the printed source translated by Manheim indicated above.

Part I: Christianity and National Socialism

Chapter 1. The New Testament and the Jews

The Hep Riots

In 1819 a series of anti-Jewish disturbances called the Hep (or Hep! Hep!) Riots broke out in Germany. They lasted for a short time, and various sources mention no loss of life. Local authorities used police and in some cases the army to suppress the riots. The violence spread to various parts of Germany and even to Denmark and Poland, but there was none in Protestant Prussia (except for Danzig) and little in Catholic Austria.

The cause of the riots is attributed not to pastors quoting a tract from Luther, or to Paul's comments on the Jews in Romans, or to the Jewish rejection of Christ. The immediate causes are described as political and economic: resentment over Jewish demands for emancipation at the Congress of Vienna in 1815; the conspicuous wealth of some Jewish families; indebtedness of peasants to Jews; rumors of Jewish financial domination; perceptions of Jews as being "conservative and anti-nationalist."[1]

Academics, politicians, and nationalist student associations were particularly active in the riots—and the inclinations of these sectors of society were more modern, liberal, and secular, more open to the influences of the "Enlightenment," than traditionally Christian. The New Testament has zero emphasis on nationalism. People who view themselves as temporarily passing through this world on the way to a better place have some natural concern for their country, but are not going to center their hopes and dreams on it.

Whatever the cause of the Hep riots, we see various governments of a divided Germany using the police and the army to protect Jews. Something obviously changed between 1819 and 1933. At the beginning of the 19th century, when secular forces were on the rise but the old moral, religious, social, philosophical, and political order was inarguably much more intact, the Jews were discriminated against, but protected—what happened in the succeeding century? As is well known, Germany's defeat in World War I, the destruction of the old order politically and economically, and the tribulations of the Weimar era had much to do with it. There were, however, also major moral, philosophical, and spiritual changes. These are often neglected or superficially studied by those who try to explain Hitler without due regard for the cultural background out of which he emerged.

An understanding of these changes will bring us much closer to the essence of Naziism than will studies of the four Gospels or the Protestant Reformation. That the Jews were scheming to control Europe; that they controlled the banking system; that their rigid adherence to laws and traditions was directly contrary to the dynamic life-force of new secular philosophies; that their lack of a homeland (rootless cosmopolitanism) demonstrated them to be less than fully human; that they opposed German unification or were a threat to racial purity—these and other ideas are not found in the New Testament or in 16th-century Protestantism. They were themes of a new kind of anti-Semitism with secular and often overtly anti-Christian philosophical origins.

Some may counter that it was biblical teaching which isolated the Jews in the first place, and set them up as natural targets for fanaticism and bigotry—so we need to examine the Bible and see if it does in fact teach hatred of Jews. If it does, then the nature of the relationship between Christian anti-Semitism (or anti-Judaism, "anti-Semitism" being a 19th-century coinage) and modern racial anti-Semitism can be explored in scholarly detail. If, however, the Bible does not in any way, shape, or form encourage hatred of Jews or of anyone else; if medieval anti-Semitism was in no sense the result of the Bible but was the result of direct disobedience to the Bible—then it will be necessary to look not at scriptural Christianity but elsewhere for an explanation of Hitler.

A great and terrible mystery

Anyone can imagine a few lonely eccentrics with Hitler's pitiful pseudo-philosophy, but that a man such as Hitler should swiftly rise from utter obscurity and ignominy to seize power in a fully industrialized and advanced modern state defies ordinary understanding. It does not defy spiritual understanding. Can it be that refusal to recognize the existence of an invisible spiritual realm guarantees from the outset that all secular attempts to resolve the riddle of Hitler are necessarily and inevitably flawed?

Hitler's life continues to exert fascination. There was something more than merely human about the man, about his life, his power over people. There is a glimpse of something invisible and larger than we are working behind the scenes. There is also a sense of the literally demonic in Hitler. His hatred, his wrath, the devastating effects of his poisonous ideology—Hitler and his myriads of devoted followers made a mockery of the optimism expressed by many secular thinkers who were far too clever to believe in the Bible. The rejection of all of the accepted truisms of modern secular humanism; the glorification of war and the contempt for peace; the hatred of democracy; the piles of emaciated corpses; the terrible power of a modern industrial state put at the service of a devious maniac—these prove, or should prove, that there is something terribly wrong with the world, and with human nature. Hitler's triumphs over diplomacy, law, democracy, international cooperation and even over ordinary human reason dramatically highlight the fragility of civilized norms.

The fact that many professional experts on Hitler and the Third Reich have no more understanding of the spiritual dimensions of the Hitler problem than the average man on the street has greatly hindered a deeper understanding of Hitler. This does not mean that Hitler should be demonized to such an extent that he ceases to be a historical figure. Recognizing the spiritual dimension, we can then see it at work in a specific cultural and historical context. Both the spiritual and the historical dimensions can then be considered, not the historical dimension only. There have been more than enough boring, lifeless, one-dimensional secular materialistic studies of Hitler.

An ultimate understanding of Hitler and his crimes is beyond the reach of conventional history and ordinary secular understanding. To go farther we need, I believe, not psychology, sociology, safely conventional history, or more statistical data. Hitler was out of the ordinary, and so we need something out of the ordinary to explain him. We need biblical insight and biblical wisdom to deal with what are, at bottom, spiritual questions, not material ones. Studies of what percentage of which social class in which region voted for Hitler have not gotten anywhere near to the heart of the Hitler problem and will never do so. Marxist analyses in particular with their crippling materialism can never get beyond secondary considerations.

One German, after having seen Hitler go by in a car, described him in this way: "I am neither an occult nor a mystic. I am a child of my time . . . and I hold strictly to what I can see. But there is a frightful riddle . . .What I saw gliding by there, behind the fence of his Mamelukes, like the Prince of Darkness himself, was no human being. That was a figure out of a ghost story."[2] Even if one accepts this description at face value (though "ghost story" is far too trivial for what we are discussing here, and highlights the secular character of the observation), a belief in the reality of invisible spiritual powers of evil of which Hitler was only an agent (an eagerly willing agent) does not mean that he was superhuman, or that he was a totally incomprehensible phenomenon that just materialized out of nowhere with no reference to his environment. He was very much a product of the world in which he lived—and hence a suitable instrument in the service of higher purposes of which he himself was not fully aware.

The biblical concept of Satan

Within the colossal framework of biblical teaching, the spiritual dimensions of evil have two aspects, both of them confined within the boundaries of God's sovereign control. One of these is the existence of higher spiritual powers of wickedness—Satan and the demons. The other is the power of sin that works in the human heart. Without taking these into consideration there can be no final understanding of Hitler and of the people who followed him.

Few are willing to even consider, let alone write about, the idea that Hitler was an instrument of Satan. The idea that the devil has an undying hatred against the Jews because God has used them to shed his light into the world through Moses, the prophets, Christ, and the apostles, will seem incredible, even preposterous to many, and will in the eyes of some reduce or eliminate the credibility of this book, but it does explain a great deal about Hitler. Otherwise baffling aspects of the Hitler mystery become more comprehensible if we consider that there was a greater spiritual power of darkness behind him. The "rulers of the darkness of this world," the "spiritual wickedness in high places" (Ephesians 6:12), "the prince of the power of the air, the spirit that now works in the children of disobedience" (Ephesians 2:2)—these gave Hitler his unique and more than ordinary powers.

Of course, many will think the idea of Satan is irrelevant, but we are not examining Hitler from their non-falsifiable, non-testable, non-empirical faith assumption of the non-existence of Satan. In order to understand biblical Christianity and its relationship to anti-Semitism, we need to consider what the Bible says about this old-fashioned concept of the devil. Apart from whether or not the devil really exists, what is the Christian view of this important subject? Looking at the Bible's teachings will reveal that supposedly Christian concepts of the Jew as the embodiment of evil, the personification of Satan, the focus of the struggle between darkness and light, all have no biblical basis.

The scriptural concept of evil is centered not on the Jews, but on sin in the hearts of both Jews and Gentiles, and on Satan as a lofty spiritual power of wickedness. There is much that is mysterious about Satan—but the use of the word "mysterious" does not automatically negate a concept or relegate it to the level of superstition. There are many mysteries even in the realm of science, many things we do not understand. Until fairly recently the workings of the sun were a complete mystery, and even today the vast majority of people don't understand the sun's inner processes—yet they produce heat and light nonetheless. Our failure to understand something does not negate its existence. Still, while Satan is a mystery, the Bible does give us some information about him.

Jesus referred to Satan as the father of lies and murder (John 8:44), and said he saw Satan fall like lightning from heaven (Luke 10:18). The devil is described in II Corinthians as "an angel of light." Revelation describes the devil, Satan, as the old serpent that deceives the world. He has numerous lesser spirits of evil devils and demons that serve him. In Ephesians he is described as being not of "flesh and blood" (6:12) but as a spiritual power who should be resisted with spiritual weapons of truth, righteousness, faith, the word of God, and prayer—not with pogroms, murders, hatred, tortures, and lies.

As a fallen angel in opposition to God, Satan has a hatred of truth, and is supernaturally skilled at concocting the numerous deceptions that have led countless people astray since the beginning of human history. He also has a hatred of mankind in general, and delights in the misery and suffering of the human race. That Satan has a hatred of the Jewish people in particular is demonstrated in the twelfth chapter of Revelation. To say that this is not subject to empirical investigation and hence beyond the realm of consideration is, in my view, a bad mistake that illustrates a profound confusion about the nature and the limitations of the scientific method.

The devilish nature of anti-Semitism

The Bible records that Pharaoh wanted to exterminate the Jews. He saw them as a threat, and planned their extinction. Later in Jewish history, the Old Testament records that Haman also wanted to massacre the Jews. Needless to say, these attempts at genocide were not the result of Christian values. Any attempt to fully explain anti-Semitism has to go beyond New Testament teachings or medieval anti-Judaism. Experts on the problem of Christian anti-Semitism have to explain pre-Christian as well as post-Christian anti-Semitism.

Why is it that the Iranian government today has such a virulent hatred of Israel? What is this mysterious power of hatred that persists in essence unchanged over thousands of years but manifests itself in different forms according to the prevailing cultural conditions? It appears as one form in medieval Europe, in another form in modern Germany, in yet another form in present-day Iran, yet differently in leftist political circles—so many variations on the same persistent theme: hatred of Jews. There is no secular explanation which can cover such a vast field.

To the secularist, this subject must forever be an impenetrable mystery. From the biblical point of view, however, it all fits into place. From Pharaoh to 19th-century German "philosophers" to Nazis to Iranian mullahs and to loony left-wing college kids, there is definitely a continuity underlying the many significant variations of anti-Semitism in world history. This underlying continuity comes, according to the Christian understanding, from the devil himself and from human sin. It is Satan, the prince of darkness, who manipulates sinful people to do his will. He has a deep and undying hatred of the Jews, yet adapts it to suit the changing historical contexts within which he works. Viewed in this light, National

Socialism can be seen as a lie concocted by the devil, and carried out by blind, foolish, hateful, ignorant and evil people who were thus by nature.

Describing National Socialism as "a lie of the devil" does not preclude further analysis. False philosophies that emerged out of the so-called Enlightenment's reliance on human reason and rejection of divine revelation contributed to new concepts of nation, race, and "the Jew" unheard of in nearly 2,000 years of Christianity. Jews as a threat to racial purity; as scheming to control the world; as selfish and egotistical materialists inherently alienated from the mystic life force that had destined the German people for greatness; as the source of diverse and disconnected social evils—these and other aspects of a new and more virulent form of anti-Semitism than anything seen before can still be traced historically, even as we attribute them to Satan and to human sin.

The New Testament by no means focuses on "the Jews" as the living embodiments of Satan. The Bible does not warn us of Jews poisoning wells, torturing communion wafers, or using Christian blood for ritual purposes. Neither does it warn of Jewish conspiracies to control the banking system, take over the world, or destroy the purity of a non-existent master race. That Christianity makes Jews the embodiment of evil is a fiction presented by people who do not understand its character or its teachings (or else who deliberately state what they know to be false).

The fiercest attempts to destroy the church in the first few centuries came from the Gentiles, not from the Jews, and I Corinthians says that the Gentiles sacrificed to devils (10:20). Acts says that the people healed by Jesus had been "oppressed of the devil" (10:38), without indicating that it was "the Jews" who made other Jews blind, lame, and leprous. I John says "He that committeth sin is of the devil" (3:8). That this extends to the entire world, not just the Jews, is clear from many passages. Revelation says that Satan "deceives the whole world" (12:9), and we can see the sins described in Romans chapter 1 (hatred, lying, murder, immorality) clearly manifest in the world, not just in Israel or in Jewish neighborhoods. As John said, the world truly does lie in wickedness (I John 5:19).

When someone discovered that malaria was transmitted by mosquitoes, the mere discovery of a cause did not terminate further inquiry—quite the contrary. It opened up many new avenues of research. Similarly, if we say that Satan was behind Hitler and gave him not only his philosophy but also his remarkable powers, this not only opens up new avenues of exploration. It also allows previously gained knowledge of Hitler's background and methods to be viewed in an entirely different light.

Jesus called Satan the father of lies and murder, and said that murderers were children of the devil. There is no more concise and insightful description of the true nature of National Socialism than this. Here is the source not only of the Holocaust, the massacres of the Crusades, the Inquisition, and the pogroms of eastern Europe, but of every kind of deviltry and sin: the wickedness of the unregenerate human heart, played upon and manipulated by Satan and the devils beneath him. This would account for an anti-Semitism that is above and beyond history, yet is within it as well, and is consistently adjusted to fit various historical situations. It harmonizes perfectly with Paul Rose's idea that "Christian and revolutionary antisemitisms both reflect the same kind of inner psychological structure, albeit one whose formal expression mutates as intellectual and religious systems change."[3]

What secular or materialist explanation fits these facts so precisely? What else so exactly explains the singularity of Nazi anti-Semitism, yet also sees the connection with many other historical situations? We can as Christians agree with Rose's statement that "there is a universal essence of 'antisemitism' that pervades all its various manifestations."[4] This essence includes, as he points out, resentment against Jews for remaining apart. This essence of antisemitism also includes (a point Rose does not make) hostility toward the clear statement by the continued existence of the Jewish nation that God exists, and he has rules for us to follow. Neither of these essential aspects of Judaism are a problem for decent and honest people who have happiness and peace of mind within themselves. The hidden, underlying common denominator Rose is seeking is sin—not Christian teaching, but disobedience to or ignorance of Christian teaching.

Original sin

A second essential factor behind the extraordinary manifestations of humanly inexplicable cruelty described in so many narratives of the Nazi era is the reality of original sin. The terrible crimes of that period do not destroy the eternal truths of the Bible. They do destroy the ephemeral secular fantasy of man as being basically good.

A defense of biblical teachings on original sin is beyond the scope of this essay. That sin entered the world through the fall of Adam and Eve will only be stated here as a fact presented in Romans: ". . . as by one man sin entered into the world, and death by sin; and so death passed upon all men, for that all have sinned . . ." (5:12). There are more teachings about the power of sin that dwells in us, and drives us to do things contrary to the will of God.

Sin has little meaning as an abstract concept. It has meaning only relative to God's eternal and unchanging standards of holiness as revealed in scripture, and it consists of rebellion against those standards. Without God's law, nothing is finally and ultimately wrong—everything is only relative. One man thinks slaughtering Jews is right and proper, another thinks it is evil—who can say which is right? Conscience is inadequate. We need standards and we need rules. Those rules are derived from God, and sin resists them, rejects them, and puts false concepts of good and evil in their place.

It is this sin that underlies all of the various manifestations of evil in the entire history of the human race. Walking in darkness, enslaved to sin, wicked men imagine that their evil deeds are right, and in some cases even pleasing to God. In reality, however, far from pleasing God, they are treasuring up unto themselves wrath "against the day of wrath and revelation of the righteous judgment of God; who will render to every man according to his deeds. . ." (Romans 2:5-11).

The failure to understand the dark reality of original sin has nullified from the outset the vast majority of attempts to come to grips with the evils of the Third Reich. People with no firm convictions concerning righteousness, holiness, sin, or evil wander in a maze when they try to understand these matters. They are certain that the Nazis were evil, but are unable to provide any convincing or coherent explanation of the delight in cruelty that is one of the most outstanding features of the Holocaust. A real explanation is possible within a biblical framework. For those who see human nature as basically good, Hitler will forever remain an insoluble riddle—as will many of life's other problems.

For example, in Daniel Goldhagen's book *Hitler's Willing Executioners: Ordinary Germans and the Holocaust*, a scholar who tries to understand these things without reference to that reality of God which alone gives meaning to ethics and moral standards lists conventional secular explanations for the cruelty of the Nazis.[5] Those who persecuted Jews were (a) coerced, forced to go along to avoid death or imprisonment; (b) blindly following orders with no moral sense; (c) conforming to peer pressure; (d) petty bureaucrats concerned only with their careers; (e) unaware of the big picture, committing individual acts without having a sense of the enormity of the whole.

Goldhagen rightly senses that although these explanations apply to varying degrees in individual cases, they are all somehow inadequate. He suggests that the criminals did evil because they wanted to do so. This is getting closer to the truth—but what is it that makes some people enjoy evil, revel in it, and pursue it to the farthest possible extremes? This question is totally beyond the reach of conventional secular scholarship. It is the problem of sin and evil in the human heart, and the Bible says the human heart is wicked by nature. Thus, any serious attempt to explain the Holocaust must take into account not only its uniquely German characteristics, but also evil itself.[6]

Parenthetically, the title of Goldhagen's book—*Hitler's Willing Executioners: Ordinary Germans and the Holocaust*—implies that ordinary Germans were slaughtering Jews. This omits the fact that the majority of Germans never voted for Hitler and in fact voted against him. Finding themselves in a dictatorship not of their making, they went along to varying degrees (with rare exceptions), but only a small percentage of Germans were directly involved in the Holocaust.

Victor Klemperer, a Jew who was able to remain in Germany due to his Aryan wife, does not in any way minimize the cruelties of the Third Reich, but also records examples of Germans who went out of their way to demonstrate that they had nothing against him personally. In the second volume of his diary, *I Will Bear Witness: A Diary of the Nazi Years 1942-1945*, Klemperer states that in the factory where he was forced to work, "ninety-nine percent of the male and female workers are undoubtedly more or less extremely anti-Nazi, well-disposed to the Jews, opposed to the war, weary of tyranny . . ." He adds "but fear of the one percent loyal to the regime, fear of prison, ax, and bullet binds them."[7]

To really understand the crimes of the Nazis we need more than stereotypes about Germans. We need coherent concepts of sin and evil. These are provided by biblical teaching. Satan and human wickedness are spiritual realities, not just Bible words, and these powers of sin and evil that drove Hitler and his followers did not disappear when Hitler killed himself. I knew an American years ago who enjoyed bullying people beneath him and then presented a false front of injured innocence when people objected. He once told me "I wish I could have been in the SS," and I had the distinct impression he wasn't joking. Those who do not have a convincing explanation for human evil in general can never have a convincing explanation for any particular manifestation of evil—be it Auschwitz, the Soviet Gulag, the Cambodian killing fields, or the abduction and murder of a single child by a random serial killer. Those who are nothing more than indifferent to others also show the power of sin, as do those who knowingly do what is wrong, or even just keep silent because they are afraid of persecution or disapproval.

Sin manifested itself greatly in Hitler. There is no more overt denial of Christ's Sermon on the Mount than the philosophy and actions of Hitler. To what extent, since we all have sin, do we share Hitler's evil? Is there a little bit of Hitler in all of us, or is he so far off the map as to be truly unique? Perhaps this question can be clarified by elevating Hitler's gift for lies and murder to the level of genius. We all have some mathematical ability—any ordinary person can do some simple sums—but Einstein's genius is far beyond us. We all have some artistic ability, and could at least make a picture of a house or a tree, even if clumsily—but Rembrandt's genius is far beyond us. If we consider that Hitler was a criminal genius, then we can say that all of us have the capacity to lie, to be egotistical, to do wrong, even to hate someone in our hearts (without acting on it)—but we don't have it to such an extreme degree. Thus, we can say that Hitler was like us, but different from us at the same time.

I can easily imagine myself keeping silent out of fear while others were being persecuted. Most of those who criticize the Germans for not speaking out would do the same if their lives were in danger. I can imagine myself going along with the crowd and saying things I did not believe just to stay out of trouble. I can imagine myself shouting "Heil Hitler!" and rejoicing in his conquests. I cannot see myself tossing a baby out of a hospital window or kicking someone to death— but if I had come to believe (as Nietzsche taught in *The Antichrist*) that patience and kindness were vices while pitiless cruelty was a virtue, why not? If my sole concern was my own will to power, it would give me an extraordinary feeling of power and even make me feel like some kind of a little god if I could make starving and sick people jump up and lie down repeatedly with a wave of my hand until they collapsed from exhaustion. I can also see myself, if God gave me strength, as a real hero, suffering death and torture rather than committing evil.

The problem is not with German nature but with human nature. The rejection of shallow, complacent, and dull liberal doctrines of peace and prosperity, as if people were nothing more than hamsters; the glorification of power; contempt for others and the elimination of moral limits; the need for struggle, for sacrifice, for commitment to a cause; many potentially good qualities put to the wrong uses— the biblical concept of human nature can account for all of this and more in a way that a secular world-view cannot.

From the traditionally Christian point of view we can describe the essence of National Socialism as human sin following a false, ugly, and literally devilish philosophy of rebellion against God. Hitler was serving Satan in direct opposition to God. A striking expression of this was made by Hugo Gryn, a Holocaust survivor who pointed out the great extent to which Naziism was a violation of the Ten Commandments.[8] Elaborating on his deep insight, we can look at the first commandment—"Thou shalt have no other Gods before me."

Is it necessary to point out that the Nazis did not believe in the God of Abraham, Isaac, and Jacob, the God who called the Jews and used them to bless the world with his truths? The God who sent his Son Jesus into the world to die for the sins of mankind and rise again for our deliverance? The Nazis worshipped Hitler as a god; or, it may be said that Germany was their god; or, it may be said that their god was a vast impersonal process that moved life on earth, from the lowest species to the most advanced nations, through a pitiless process of struggle in which death through starvation, disease, or violence was an everyday fact of life.

The Ten Commandments also prohibit killing. That this refers to criminal murder is evident since the same book which presents them also allows for killing in war and as punishment for certain crimes. Stealing is forbidden, as are bearing false witness—"The Jews are plotting to take over the world"—and sexual immorality. The Nazi philosophy encouraged these things and saw them as normal. This was the logical result of the complete revaluation of values that resulted from certain secular philosophies. The third commandment forbids taking God's name in vain. Hitler and the Nazis broke this one every time they said "God," "the Lord," "the Almighty."

The tenth commandment, not to covet, to desire anything excessively, is one of the most important here. Why did Hitler desire more and more territory? The Germans could have lived decent lives without adding Austria, the Sudetenland, or much of Poland to their already adequate territory. The lust for others' possessions was one of the prime causes of WWII. People who are ignorant of history say that religion has caused many wars, without considering that it is covetousness, the lust for more territory, more power, more wealth, more glory that has been a much greater cause.

If Hitler had devoted his life to sincerely following the Ten Commandments, Europe would have been spared unspeakable suffering. Any attempt to explain the man without taking his sin against God and disobedience to God's laws into account is necessarily defective from the outset and will never attain to the deeper understanding permanently denied to those who refuse to consider invisible spiritual realities.

Christian servants of the devil

Unfortunately, people who have an outward appearance of Christianity can also serve sin and the devil. The same passage in II Corinthians that described Satan as an angel of light also described his followers. In this passage they are not "the Jews." They are "false apostles, deceitful workers, transforming themselves into the apostles of Christ" (11:13-14).

This describes bishops, pastors, and theologians who believed that God had given the German people a new revelation in Adolf Hitler. They advocated a "Germanic Christianity" purged of Jewish elements, including all of the teachings of the arch-rabbi Paul. They thought Hitler would bring a spiritual renewal to Germany—deceitful workers, servants of the devil. The failure of the German church to follow elementary warnings about false teachers needs to be examined in another chapter. We have some such deceitful workers in America today, altering the message of Christ to make it conform to the world.

An understanding of this principle exposes one of the major errors that runs through all of a book referred to in the Introduction—Steigmann-Gall's *The Holy Reich*. Trying to prove that the Nazis were Christians and developed their ideology in a Christian framework, he sees every reference to Christ as a proof of Christianity. That false teachers might disguise themselves as servants of Christ to deceive people is completely beyond his comprehension. His extremely limited understanding of biblical teaching permeates his entire analysis. If people want to understand the relationship between A and B, they need an understanding of both A and B, not of A only.

One example given by Steigmann-Gall of deceitful workers presenting a false image of Christ is Walter Buch. Martin Bormann's father-in-law, a member of

Hitler's inner circle and head of the Nazi Party court, Buch is quoted as saying "Christ preached struggle as did no other."[9] That Christ did not resist but passively allowed himself to be taken and killed; that he told his disciples not to fight on his behalf; that he said people should return good for evil, even to the extent of turning the other cheek when struck—these simple facts were ignored for some reason by Steigmann-Gall. Buch's comments reveal not the Christian origins of Naziism, but rather a false image of Christ.

What is a Christian?

Having looked at some biblical teachings on sin and evil, we also need to give a brief description of the Bible's definition of a Christian. This is especially important because so many have tried to discuss Christianity and Hitler without even knowing what a Christian is. For some a Christian is "a non-Jew who was born in Europe" or "anyone who was baptized as an infant" or "anyone who calls himself a Christian no matter what he believes or how he acts" or "a less than fully honest politician who uses God-words on occasion."

It is true, an understanding of Christianity has been made much more difficult by so many different interpretations. Protestant, Catholic, Orthodox, Liberal, Fundamentalist, Evangelical, Pentecostal, so many centuries, so many cultures— yet which of these interpretations of Christianity have ever included the ideas that the Germans were the master race and Germany should rule the world? That the basic law of life was pitiless struggle? That the entire Jewish nation should be exterminated? Where are these doctrines found in the Bible? The fact that these doctrines took root in one country and in one period shows this to be a German problem and a modern one.

How, though, given all of this confusion, can we define a Christian? It is not necessary to give a lengthy definition that covers all different theoretical perspectives. It is only necessary to distinguish here between black and white, not between all the many different shades of gray that lie between those extremes. At the very least, a Christian should have some core beliefs about Christ, and also make a sincere effort to live by his teachings—just as a Marxist or a Freudian should have some core beliefs derived from their masters' teachings, and make a real effort to apply them.

Paul's definition of a Christian in Romans chapter 8 is essential to an understanding of this question. He states that a Christian is someone who has the Spirit of God, the Spirit of Christ, dwelling in him. Someone who does not have the Spirit of Christ, the Spirit of God, is not a Christian. As it says in that chapter: "But ye are not in the flesh, but in the Spirit, if so be that the Spirit of God dwell in you. Now if any man have not the Spirit of Christ, he is none of his . . . ." Those who do not have the Spirit of Christ are said to be "in the flesh," that is, living according to the natural powers of man apart from God—and "they that are in the flesh cannot please God."

Those that have the Spirit of Christ in them are Christians. How is this Spirit received? It is not earned by a baptismal ceremony or by following man-made church rules, by going to church, by becoming a seminary professor, by being elected to a high position in the church bureaucracy, or by merely appearing to the world as a Christian. Scriptural Christianity is a matter of the heart, not of outward appearance only. It requires a Spirit from above, and this Spirit is given by God through faith in Christ. It is "the gift of God: not of works, lest any man should boast" (Ephesians 2:8-9).

Once received, the Spirit of Christ is not merely theoretical, passive, inert. It works in the believer, and those who have received it will show some evidence of it in their lives. Christians can certainly stumble, err, have wrong ideas, say wrong things—the Bible allows for that. But, when their lives are considered overall, there will be some evidence of what is called "the fruit of the Spirit." This fruit is described in Galatians. It includes "love, joy, peace, longsuffering, gentleness, goodness, faith, meekness, temperance . . . ."

The same passage also describes the fruits of those who are without the Spirit, who live according to the flesh (that is, according to the natural powers of man). These fruits include such qualities and actions as hatred, wrath, strife, and murders. These and many other sins are followed by a clear warning: " . . . they which do such things shall not inherit the kingdom of God."

Pausing in our definition of a Christian for a moment, is there any doubt which of these two categories Hitler falls into? No reasonable person would argue that Hitler's life was on balance characterized more by "love, joy, and peace" than by "hatred, wrath, and murder." By the Bible's own definition of a Christian, Hitler is excluded. If many other Christians are excluded by it as well, that will be too bad for them on the day of judgment. Jesus said, ". . . strait is the gate, and narrow is the way, which leadeth unto life, and few there be that find it."

Another passage in James describes two kinds of wisdom. One descends from above, from God—". . . the wisdom that is from above is first pure, then peaceable, gentle, and easy to be intreated, full of mercy and good fruits, without partiality, and without hypocrisy." Another is not from God but is of this world. It is characterized by "bitter envying and strife" and "is earthly, sensual, devilish. For where envying and strife is, there is confusion and every evil work" (3:14-17). Again, there is no question which of these two kinds of wisdom Hitler lived by.

Someone can legitimately ask "If the Holy Spirit gives such wonderful qualities, why aren't they evident in Christians today?" There are two answers to this. Sadly, one of them is that the churches definitely lack those qualities. Too many Christians are lazy, dull, complacent, soft, weak, thoroughly conformed to the culture around them. Their lives are full of sin and disobedience, as are their churches, many of which are only worldly social clubs. Secondly, the few Christians who do have those qualities are ignored and/or rejected by the world. True biblical holiness is anathema to the world, when it is noticed at all.

Returning to the question "What is a Christian?", it is necessary to emphasize that the Bible does lay down some definite limits. Those who claim to be Christians are not automatically guaranteed of a place in heaven no matter what they do. There are several passages in the New Testament that clearly state: murderers will not go to heaven. In addition to the passage just cited in Galatians, there are others: ". . . no murderer hath eternal life abiding in him" (I John 3:15), and " . . . the fearful, and unbelieving, and the abominable, and murderers, and whoremongers, and sorcerers, and idolaters, and all liars, shall have their part in the lake which burneth with fire and brimstone: which is the second death" (Revelation 21:8). No matter if they go to church every week, were baptized, or refer to God or Jesus once in a while—murderers and liars will go to the place of eternal punishment, unless they repent and are saved by Christ.

Contrary to the misconceptions of some, this does not allow people to murder, repent, murder again, repent again indefinitely. Sincere repentance brings with it abhorrence of the sin. Moreover, the vast majority of murderers have no concern for such things. Their hearts are hardened, they feel no need for repentance, and so die in their sins. Christianity does allow, theoretically, for repentance just before death, but this is even rarer. Adolf Eichmann, for example, in his interrogation and trial, showed not the slightest iota of remorse, and presented only lies, equivocations, and self-justification instead.[10]

Also essential is love. Paul describes love in a famous passage in I Corinthians. He says love is, among other things, patient, kind, humble, well-behaved, does not even think evil (let alone do evil), and rejoices not in iniquity but in truth. Paul also says in this passage that if Christians have all faith and all knowledge but do not have love, their Christianity is worthless. I John says "He that loveth not knoweth not God; for God is love," and "God is love; and he that dwelleth in love dwelleth in God, and God in him."

We Christians really need to ask ourselves—does this apply to us? Do we have love and the fruits of the Spirit? We do not need to ask if Hitler had love. He claimed to love the German people, but the biblical love of God as manifested in Christ was totally, conspicuously, glaringly absent. This one fact alone should be sufficient to end the entire debate about Hitler's relationship to Christianity.

There are not only moral limits—there are also doctrinal limits. Christians may disagree on exactly where to draw the lines, but this does not refute the fact that some limits do exist. II John says that those "who confess not that Jesus Christ is come in the flesh" (v.7) are deceivers and antichrists. This means more than just "saying something positive about Jesus" or "never condemning Jesus," worldly criteria which have been used to feebly argue that Hitler was a Christian. From the entire context of John's Gospel and letters, this is Christ the Son of God come in the flesh—a belief Hitler never asserted in his many comments on the meaning of life. That "the Father sent the Son to be the Saviour of the world" (I John 4:14) was never stated by Hitler or any leading Nazis—"And every spirit that confesseth not that Jesus Christ is come in the flesh is not of God: and this is that spirit of antichrist . . ." (I John 4:3). By the Bible's standards, Hitler was not a Christian but a false prophet, a deceiver, and an antichrist.

The Bible teaches that there are false Christians. As James says, "But be ye doers of the word, and not hearers only, deceiving your own selves" (1:22). He even says that those who seem to be religious but whose tongues are out of control deceive their own hearts, and their religion is vain (1:26). Paul refers to those "having a form of godliness, but denying the power thereof." He describes them as "Without natural affection, trucebreakers, false accusers, incontinent, fierce, despisers of those that are good," and also "covetous, boasters, proud" (II Timothy 3:2-5). These have a form of godliness, and appear to be Christians—but in the same passage Christians are told to turn away from people who thus make a mockery of religion.

A passage in II Peter well describes German "Christians" like Hans Kerrl, the Nazi Minister for Church Affairs. Kerrl stated "A new authority has arisen as to what Christ and Christianity really are—Adolf Hitler . . . ."[11] II Peter says:

> But there were false prophets also among the people, even as
> there shall be false teachers among you, who privily shall bring

in damnable heresies, even denying the Lord that bought them, and bring upon themselves swift destruction.

And many shall follow their pernicious ways; by reason of whom the way of truth shall be evil spoken of (2:1-3).

I John also refers to "many false prophets" (4:1) and warns the believers not to believe every spirit. That John says the prophets need to be tried and tested shows that some have a deceptive outward appearance of Christianity—there is no need for believers to test those who openly admit they are not Christians. Revelation also refers to those who even claimed to be apostles but were liars (2:2). Surely they must have maintained a facade of Christianity in order to pass themselves off as apostles. The 16th-century English reformer William Tyndale, indicting the common Christianity of his own time, wrote "And thus are we become an hundred times worse than the wicked Jews which believed that the very work of their sacrifice justified them."[12]

Those who think anyone is a Christian just because they claim to be are ignorant of the Bible's teachings. They are even more foolish than someone would be who tried to talk about Marxism without any reference to the ideas of the Communist Manifesto. Revelation refers to a false prophetess who seduced Christians (2:20), and Jude refers to men who creep in secretly, corrupting the grace of God (v. 4). Finally, there is Jesus' famous warning about false prophets, wolves in sheep's clothing:

> Beware of false prophets, which come to you in sheep's clothing, but inwardly they are ravening wolves. Ye shall know them by their fruits. Do men gather grapes of thorns, or figs of thistles? . . . Wherefore by their fruits ye shall know them (Matthew 7:15-20).

Did Hitler or the Nazi Christians bear good fruit?

There are false Christians who have the appearance of being Christians but are not. This is a basic Bible teaching that is also agreeable to common sense, not a trick devised to dishonestly evade legitimate criticisms. There are people who claim to be honest but lie to and deceive their own wives, children, colleagues, or customers. There is a great deal of deception in the world, and the church is not immune to this, unfortunately. In the church there are deceiving and deceived. This is why Jesus warned us to be "wise as serpents, and harmless as doves" (Matthew 10:16).

Examples of evildoers with an outward appearance of Christianity are given in Acts. In one instance, Satan entered into the heart of Ananias and persuaded him and his wife to lie. Being members of the Christian community, they had all the outward appearance of being Christians, yet Satan was at work in them. Simon Magus is another example of a Christian who could believe in the basic doctrines and even be baptized, but still be "in the gall of bitterness, and in the bond of iniquity," his heart "not right in the sight of God." How many Christians, not only in the Third Reich or the Middle Ages, but in America today, have been baptized and given intellectual assent to doctrine, but have never been delivered from the power of sin? They then lend themselves to evil deeds and evil works, appearing to themselves and to others as "Christians."

There are not merely mistaken and imperfect Christians and Christian teachers, but also false Christians who hide behind a plausible outward appearance of religion. This is confusing to naive Christians, and doubly confusing to those who are not Christians at all. Understanding this helps to explain what one scholar described in personal correspondence to me as the "disjunction between the magnificent message of Christianity and its institutional history." That a powerful church structure supported by the state, or a state unto itself, is something not described or envisioned in the New Testament is one factor. Another factor is human sin and disobedience.

If a father lends his son the family car and tells him "Drive carefully," and the son goes out, robs a bank, gets in a high-speed chase with the police and crashes head-on into a school bus, killing twenty children—isn't this something more than a "disjuncture"? Christians are called to a life of holiness and obedience. "But whoso keepeth his word, in him verily is the love of God perfected: hereby know we that we are in him" (I John 2:5). "Beloved, follow not that which is evil, but that which is good. He that doeth good is of God: but he that doeth evil hath not seen God" (III John 11). There are many verses to this effect. The Sermon on the Mount refers to the wise man who hears the word of God and does it, and the foolish man who hears the word of God and does not do it.

Setting some minimal standards of Christian conduct is not just "raising the bar" to exclude the Nazis, as some have claimed. It is Christ, not man, who sets the bar, and he said ". . . strait is the gate, and narrow is the way, which leadeth unto life, and few there be that find it." Speaking to us through the apostles Christ gave many other standards, statements, and instructions. Paul said wicked people who claimed to be Christians should be put out of the church.

There are some who lower the bar so much that any evildoer can stumble across it effortlessly in his sleep. Someone who wants to enslave blacks or persecute Jews represents not Christianity but disobedience to Christianity. By the way, an atheist who slaughters or enslaves millions does not demonstrate disobedience to any principles inherent in atheism. Critics of Christianity who overlook the crimes of atheism are highly subjective.

Countless people try to discuss Christianity and National Socialism without any understanding of these points. A good example of this is provided by Steigmann-Gall. Trying to prove that many of the Nazis were Christians, he refers to Nazis who "adhered to all the requisite criteria for Christian religiosity—church attendance, baptism, communion."[13] Anyone who thinks that these are all of the requisite criteria for being a Christian, that a Christian has only to be baptized, go to church, take communion, has no real understanding of the New Testament.

Another example of the failure to understand Christianity that inspires Steigmann-Gall's argument is found in his brief study of Erich Koch, a Nazi official (*Gauleiter*) and later wartime Governor of the Ukraine.[14] In this latter capacity Koch was directly involved in the worst Nazi atrocities. This places him under the strongest biblical condemnation. Hatred, wrath, murder, deceit—"they which do such things shall not inherit the kingdom of God." But, Steigmann-Gall points out, before the war Koch was elected president of a provincial church synod.

His detailed analysis curiously neglects to point out that the church elections were rigged, that unfair means were used to ensure that opponents of Naziism would not be elected. It doesn't explain that holding a bureaucratic position nowhere described in the Bible has nothing to do with the teachings of Christ and the apostles. The fact that Koch later resigned his church membership is not elaborated on, but much attention is paid to his rhetoric. For example, after the war he claimed that Naziism came out of Protestantism and the Reformation—as if Nazi war criminals did not consistently try to whitewash their crimes, and try to make themselves seem as normal and innocent as possible.

Koch's religious words are presented at face value, with no insight or deeper understanding. What needs to be explained to Steigmann-Gall's overly credulous admirers is that for a man like Koch, "love" meant "love for Germany, for Hitler, and for the Aryan race"; "truth" meant "whatever Hitler says"; "righteousness" meant "racial purity"; "Joyful and active struggle for the Protestant faith" meant "eliminating opposition to Hitler."

Those who are familiar with the teachings of Christianity and with the historical context in which those remarks were made, know that Koch was either (a) lying in order to persuade Germans to follow the Fuhrer, or (b) sincerely deceived by gross German perversions of Christianity unknown until more than 1800 years after Christ.

The Bible as the source of anti-Semitism

While the above-mentioned points may seem obvious to Bible-believing Christians, many who are outside of the faith will continue to maintain that hatred of Jews is inherent in biblical teaching. It is necessary, therefore, to examine in detail specific accusations.

A good overview of this aspect of the debate is provided by Prof. Steven Katz. In a very long and scholarly book called *The Holocaust in Historical Context*, Katz examines many philosophical, historical, and theological aspects of the Shoah ("Shoah" being the Hebrew word for "Holocaust"). He argues that anti-Judaism is an integral part of the New Testament. He concedes that Naziism was very different from Christianity, and makes the point that an attempt to completely exterminate the Jews did not occur during centuries of Christian domination. He recognizes the existence of moral limits inherent in Christianity that precluded the idea of complete extermination (these will be examined in chapter two of this essay). He even sees Auschwitz as an overthrow rather than a fulfillment of Christian teaching.[15]

Nevertheless, while rejecting the theory of some that Naziism was the natural offshoot of Christianity, Katz still sees a significant connection. This connection between biblical teachings about Jews and the crimes of the Nazis is not simple or direct. Katz recognizes the development of National Socialism was far more complex than that, yet claims that even if we take into account the addition of modern elements, centuries of Christian anti-Semitism still contributed greatly to the conditions out of which Naziism arose.

He goes on to say that these millennia of "Christian" violence were not the result of disobedience to the Bible. He argues that they were the direct result of New Testament teachings; that there is a deep hostility toward Jews expressed throughout the New Testament; and that this emerged from the New Testament with disastrous consequences that contributed to the Holocaust, even if they did not directly cause it.[16]

Katz has studied the New Testament too carefully to make the simple-minded error (if it is an error and not a deliberate falsehood) of equating Naziism with

Christianity. He refers to many different verses, and his arguments will seem plausible to those ignorant of biblical teachings. Before examining them, however, it is necessary to consider the critical question of presuppositions.

Katz considers the New Testament to be a historically inaccurate book. This is evident not only from the entire tone of his argument, but from certain assertions, such as the faith-claim (presented as unquestionable fact) that Paul is inventing words, making up a message from God, rather than giving us what he received from Christ.[17] Similarly, the teaching that Jews who do not believe in Christ are Jews physically but not spiritually, while the Gentiles who believe in Christ are Jews spiritually but not physically, is dismissed as the result of hostility between Jewish Christians and Jews. The terrible cry of the mob, "His blood be on us" is dismissed as fictional.

Those who like myself consider the New Testament narratives concerning the death and resurrection of Christ to be historically accurate to the last detail, and who see Paul and other apostles as having faithfully delivered the message they received from Christ himself, will interpret these books differently from someone who does not. Both points of view represent beliefs that cannot be corroborated or refuted by scientific evidence. A lengthy defense of the historical accuracy of scripture would be out of place here. What is at issue is whether or not Katz in his unbelieving analysis has misinterpreted key passages and wholly omitted others; whether or not acts of hatred done in the name of Christianity are the result of Christian teachings, or of disobedience to Christian teachings.

To support his contentions Katz makes five main points:

A. Paul's teaching that the Jews cannot be saved by keeping the law is described as a radical nullification of Judaism leading to the conclusion that Judaism is not only worthless, but dark and deadly as well.[18] The Jewish law is a "ministration of death . . . the ministration of condemnation" (II Corinthians 3:7,9), and all who rely on it are under a curse (Galatians 3:10-13).

B. The New Testament describes the Jews as sinful and wicked. This is seen in Romans—"But to Israel he saith, All day long I have stretched forth my hands unto a disobedient and gainsaying people" (10:21)—and also in Acts, where Stephen denounces the Jewish council, saying "Ye stiffnecked and uncircumcised in heart and ears, ye do always resist the Holy Ghost . . ." (7:51-53). Paul's comments about Jews in I Thessalonians are not overlooked: " . . . they please not God, and are contrary to all men . . . for the wrath is come upon them to the uttermost" (2:15-16). Jesus' denunciations of the Pharisees are understood to include the Jewish nation in its entirety forever, not just the religious leadership.

This wickedness of the Jews reaches a terrible climax in the killing of Christ, which is referred to as a "consummate, metahuman act of terror."[19] The "sinister" Gospel narratives[20] emphasize Jewish guilt, which is highlighted by Pilate's hand washing (supposedly showing the innocence of the Gentiles) and by the cry of the mob, "His blood be on us, and on our children" (Matthew 27:25).

C. Because of their wickedness, God has rejected the Jews. This is seen in Jesus' words "Behold, your house is left unto you desolate," coming after a long denunciation of the Pharisees (Matthew 23:27-39). Other statements of Christ's are also cited, such as "The kingdom of God shall be taken from you, and given to a nation bringing forth the fruits thereof" (Matthew 21:43), and "that which is highly esteemed among men is abomination in the sight of God" (Luke 16:15).

D. The church has replaced Israel in the covenantal relationship with God. This is seen in Galatians—"And if ye be Christ's, then are ye Abraham's seed, and heirs according to the promise" (3:29)—and in Romans: "For he is not a Jew, which is one outwardly; neither is that circumcision, which is outward in the flesh: But he is a Jew, which is one inwardly; and circumcision is that of the heart, in the spirit, and not in the letter" (2:28-29). Hebrews also asserts that Christians have a new and a better covenant, "which was established upon better promises" (8:6).

E. The Jews are exalted (or debased) to something more (or less) than merely human. They are now "children of the devil" and "not of God" (John 8:44, 47).

An examination of these ideas and verses, as well as other verses omitted by Katz, will show that it is possible to consider the problem of Christian anti-Semitism in a different light. That many Christians have interpreted the New Testament in this different light is proven by the fact that Crusades, pogroms, and massacres are by no means characteristic of the great majority of Christians that have lived in the past nearly two thousand years.

Let's now consider Katz's points, remembering that he is a highly erudite, articulate, and philosophically sophisticated spokesman for a very common approach. His is a common understanding among non-Christians of the relationship between Christianity and the crimes of the Nazis (though this point of view is seldom articulated so thoroughly).

A. Paul's teaching of salvation by grace through faith—an attack on Judaism?

Looking at the first point, the inability of Jews to be saved by keeping the law, it must be said that this is the teaching of Paul, and it is central to Christianity. The Jews cannot earn favor with God merely by following the rules, the laws of Torah. This is however in no sense anti-Jewish for the simple reason that it applies equally and without distinction to the entire human race. Everyone in the world, even Christians who feel that following church rules entitles them to God's favor—none of us can earn salvation from sin by doing good deeds.

Although this general teaching applies to all of us, the Jews are most frequently mentioned in biblical discussions of this for two reasons. First, Christianity was of course introduced into a Jewish setting. Secondly, if even the Jews, with their glorious revelations of God through Moses and the prophets, being far ahead of all other nations in the quest for God, should in spite of all of their advantages be in need of the new sacrifice and the new priesthood ordained by God in the person of Jesus Christ, how much more is this true of those who adhere to other wholly pagan religions and philosophies?

That this inability to earn God's favor by our good deeds applies to the entire human race, not just the Jews, is very plain. Paul writes in Romans: ". . . are we better than they? No, in no wise: for we have before proved both Jews and Gentiles, that they are all under sin; As it is written, There is none righteous, no, not one . . . that every mouth may be stopped, and all the world may become guilty before God."

Paul then offers a different way to obtain the righteousness of God—a righteousness that is outside the ceremonial and sacrificial regulations of Old Testament law (which regulations, being valid in their time, were not intended to endure eternally, but were shadows of better things to come, as it says in Hebrews). This righteousness without the law is referred to in the same chapter of Romans: "But now the righteousness of God without the law is manifested . . . Even the righteousness of God which is by faith of Jesus Christ unto all and upon all them that believe: for there is no difference: For all have sinned, and come short of the glory of God." This redemption is offered to all, Jew or Gentile, without distinction.

Thus, the condemnation that lies upon those who seek salvation from sin through good works lies upon everyone, not only Jews. This includes many people who have the name and outward appearance of "Christian," but have not yet submitted to the righteousness of God and are still laboring to establish their own holiness. This is of course not agreeable to those of the Jewish community who reject Christ as the Messiah, but it is not in and of itself anti-Semitic. That some have abused this concept—and this and other Christian teachings have been abused—should not reflect negatively on the concept itself.

Incidentally, if anyone says that Jesus was not a divine sacrifice for the sins of the world, and did not die for the human race and rise from the dead, this is not an "attack" on Christianity. It is a legitimate statement of belief that falls well within the boundaries of civilized discourse. Similarly, if Christians say that without Christ's sacrifice there can be no remission of sin, this is a legitimate faith statement, not an "attack" on Judaism that can be linked to the *Einsatzgruppen* or to the gas chambers.

But it was claimed above that Galatians 3:10-14 places the Jewish people under a curse. Not only does this apply equally to Jews and to Gentiles—"no man is justified by the law in the sight of God"—but it is based on Torah itself. It was Moses who wrote in Deuteronomy "Cursed be he that confirmeth not all the words of this law to do them" (27:26). Since the law includes loving God with all the heart and soul and mind, and no one can fulfill this, we are all under condemnation.

II Corinthians 3:6-11 was also mentioned. This refers to the Old Testament law as the letter which kills, a ministration of death, "the ministration of condemnation," while the New Testament is called "the ministration of the Spirit" and is described as "glorious." This is, to some, clearly a condemnation of Judaism—yet Moses' face is described in this passage as shining with glory, which is a peculiar form of anti-Semitism. Moreover, while it is a central Christian teaching that in Christ we do have "a better covenant, which was established upon better promises" (Hebrews 8:6), the old covenant is also described in the same passage in II Corinthians as itself glorious (v. 11), yet done away with and replaced by a more excellent glory.

Here it is necessary to add that, contrary to what some might think after reading the verses above, Paul does not dismiss the Old Testament law as bad. In fact, he specifically praises it as good. "What shall we say then? Is the law sin? God forbid. Nay, I had not known sin, but by the law . . . Wherefore the law is holy, and the commandment holy, and just, and good" (Romans 7:7, 12). The problem is not with the law, which is good and from God. The problem is with our sinful natures, which make it impossible for us to live up to the demands of the law. This is why the law is a "ministration of death"—its very goodness and holiness condemn our sinful natures.

Also, the fact that the old covenant of law has been replaced by a new covenant of grace is not meant as a license or a calling to hate and kill those who do not accept the new covenant. Paul writes of this specifically, and says that even though the Jews are enemies of the gospel of Christ (this at a time when the Jewish leadership was actively persecuting Christians), yet nevertheless "they are beloved for the fathers' sakes" (Romans 11:28).

Finally, let's also be sure to notice what Paul does not say. He does not say that Jews are vermin who should be exterminated, nor does he say that blond blue-eyed Aryans are the master race, nor does he say that life is only a struggle in which the strong survive and the weak die, nor does he say anything that even remotely supports the basic tenets of Naziism. He does not teach that the Germans are a unique people favored by destiny, and he does not support Hitler's and Nietzsche's shared view that mercy, kindness, forgiveness, and pity are vices, while cruelty, brutality, and indifference to the suffering of the weak and the unfit are virtues. Significantly, the Nazis never appealed to the writings of Paul in their attacks on the Jews. After all, Paul was a Jew. Nietzsche, in his furious attacks on Christianity in *The Antichrist*, elaborated at length on Paul "the arch rabbi."[21]

B. The New Testament's description of Jews

In Romans, Paul cites a passage from the Jewish prophet Isaiah and refers to the Jews as "a disobedient and gainsaying people" (10:21). This is given by Katz as evidence of Christian hostility to Jews—but Paul is repeating here what was first said about the Jews by a Jew. The first chapter of Isaiah contains a description of the wickedness of the Jews far greater than anything found in the writings of Paul. There we read that the Jews are a "sinful nation, a people laden with iniquity, a seed of evildoers, children that are corrupters: they have forsaken the Lord . . ." (1:4).

Does anti-Semitism begin here? If anything like this were found in the writings of Paul we would never hear the end of it. It would be nonsensical to suggest that the road to the Holocaust begins with Isaiah, but it is significant that there are many statements in the Old Testament about the wickedness of the Jewish people. After the Jews personally experienced God's great deliverance from Egypt, while Moses their famed lawgiver was still alive, they made a golden calf and danced naked around it. They gave a lifeless idol glory for their deliverance from Egypt and turned away from God. What greater example of spiritual blindness could there be? Torah itself says that God was so angry with the Jews that he wanted to eliminate them and begin again with Moses.

Hosea refers to the "whoredom" of the Jews, their spiritual immorality in departing from God (Hosea 1:2). Daniel also confessed the sins of the Jewish people: ". . . therefore the curse is poured upon us, and the oath that is written in the law of Moses the servant of God, because we have sinned against him" (Daniel 9:11). Jeremiah said that God sent the Babylonians in his anger at the wickedness of the Jewish nation, and their beautiful temple was destroyed because of their sin.

When Paul refers to the wickedness of the Jews he is stating a fact, and as a Christian I believe that the Jews are indeed sinful and wicked people. However, we have already seen Paul's teaching in Romans that the entire human race is under sin and guilty before God. I know that I also am a sinful and wicked person. The Jewish problem here is a human problem. All the world is guilty before God (Romans 3:19), not just the Jews. "For all have sinned, and come short of the glory of God" (Romans 3:23). For this reason it says that "The whole world lieth in wickedness" (I John 5:19), not just Israel or Jewish neighborhoods.

The same can be said of other passages presented to show that the Bible teaches hatred of Jews. One is found in I Thessalonians. Writing to the Christians in Thessalonica, Paul says of the Jews that they "both killed the Lord Jesus, and their own prophets, and have persecuted us; and they please not God, and are contrary to all men . . . for the wrath is come upon them to the uttermost" (2:15-16). This surely condemns the Jews—but it condemns the Greeks also, saying to them that "ye also have suffered like things of your own countrymen" (2:14). This shows that the rejection of Christ and hostility to Christians is a human problem, not a Jewish one. Moreover, Paul says in the same letter, "See that none render evil for evil unto any man; but ever follow that which is good, both among yourselves, and to all men" (5:15).

That many Christians have sincerely tried to follow this commandment is one reason why violence, pogroms, and massacres have been isolated incidents in the whole of Christian history. They are not the typical or average Christian response to Jews. Paul said, in agreement with Christ and the other apostles, that we should do good to all. He did not say, "Do good to all except for the Jews because they killed Christ, control the international banking system, and will cause you to fall in the Darwinian struggle for survival of the fittest by corrupting your racial purity."

Also mentioned are Stephen's words to the Jewish council shortly before he was stoned to death:

> Ye stiffnecked and uncircumcised in heart and ears, ye do always resist the Holy Ghost: as your fathers did, so do ye. Which of the prophets have not your fathers persecuted? and they have slain them which shewed before of the coming of the Just One; of whom ye have been now the betrayers and murderers: Who have received the law by the disposition of angels, and have not kept it (Acts 7:51-53).

Apart from the fact that he was speaking to evil people who then killed him for his religious beliefs (and religious persecution is not blameworthy in Christians but acceptable in Jews); apart from the fact that he followed Christ's example of non-resistance to evil and forgave his enemies; apart from the fact that neither he nor any of the apostles said "The Jews killed Christ! Death to the Jews!" but reached out to them instead; in addition to these obvious facts we have to consider that rejecting the Son of God and resisting the Holy Spirit are human sins, not Jewish ones.

When a Jew or a Gentile rejects Christ, it is the same spirit of unbelief. When the Jewish leaders, or the Romans, or the Stalinists tried to eliminate the church, it was the same spirit of unbelief. This unbelief should not be responded to with hatred and evil. The response of Stephen and the early Christians to persecution was in keeping with the example of Christ.

The crucifixion of Christ

The crucifixion of Christ is such a vast subject, and so essential to understanding the wicked and unbiblical nature of medieval anti-Semitism, that the remainder of this part will be divided into several subsections: (1) The crucifixion of Christ; (2) Pontius Pilate and the guilt of the Gentiles; and (3) the terrible cry of "His blood be on us."

It has already been said that the Jewish rejection of Christ is evidence of human sin, not Jewish sin. I know, and every sincere Christian knows—if we have a real experience of the work of grace, and an accompanying awareness of our sinful natures—that we also could have cried "Crucify him! Crucify him!" had we been there. We know that we also, like the Jewish mob, "were dead in trespasses and sins . . . by nature the children of wrath, even as others" (Ephesians 2:1,3).

Moreover, Jesus said "Inasmuch as ye have done it unto one of the least of these my brethren, ye have done it unto me" (Matthew 25:40). This means that those who have beaten, tortured, and killed the least Christian have done it unto Christ. Whether at Golgotha, or in the Soviet Gulag, or in the torture chambers of the Inquisition—any place where Christians are martyred, it is the same. Spiritually aware Christians know that the darkness of Golgotha is satanic evil and human evil, not "Jewish" evil.

At this point it bears repeating that the total percentage of "Christians" who have actively persecuted Jews in nearly 2,000 years of Christianity is a small one. Random mobs in the Middle Ages or in eastern Europe, a cruel Inquisition in only a small handful of countries out of the many in which Christianity has flourished—these denials of Christianity were nothing but sin and evil, directly contrary to the New Testament's calling for the Christian.

There are some more elementary considerations that need to be mentioned. They are obvious to those who have the Spirit of Christ, but are all too often passively assumed and not explained to those who do not understand the Christian message. To begin with, Christ laid down his life voluntarily. A single angel who appeared at the tomb after the crucifixion so struck the guards with the radiance of his glory that they became like dead men. Had God sent even one such angel the mob that came to arrest Christ would have been paralyzed with guilty horror—yet Christ had the authority to summon not one angel, but legions of them. Moreover, Christ contained within himself such astonishing power that when he merely said the words "I am," the cruel and wicked mob was knocked to the ground. Christ could have walked away, but he submitted, and allowed himself to be taken.

Not only did Christ voluntarily lay down his life, but he did so in obedience to the express will of God. This was plainly stated by Peter in the first sermon at Pentecost: "Him, being delivered by the determinate counsel and foreknowledge of God, ye have taken, and by wicked hands have crucified and slain" (Acts 2:23).

Thirdly, Christ died for the sins of the world, meaning that all who sin in any way, be it never so slight, have their part in causing Christ's suffering. All true Christians that have received God's Spirit in living faith know that it was for their sins also that Christ suffered. Christ's death was the result of the sin of the human race. It was not merely the result of the sin of the Jews. This is why John says: "And he is the propitiation for our sins: and not for ours only, but also for the sins of the whole world" (I John 2:2).

Also, not all Jews approved of the act. Luke says that there was "a great company of people, and of women, which also bewailed and lamented him"

(23:27). Other Jews were not even aware of the events at all, being in other places, even other regions—are they to be condemned?

This deep and marvelous topic, that God should die for us, is far from exhausted. Another point is, that Jesus dying on the cross said "Father, forgive them, for they know not what they do." If Christ, our teacher and master, desired only forgiveness and mercy for those who killed him, what shall we say of those supposed Christians who, totally void of the grace of Christ and acting in hatred and malice, withheld the mercy that Christ himself desired?

That this statement of Christ's was not merely abstract theology is evident from Peter's first sermon at Pentecost. Speaking to those who were directly involved and were most clearly guilty, did Peter say "Your sin has doomed you! You are under an iron and irremediable curse"? Quite the contrary. He briefly told them of their guilt and sin in no uncertain terms, and then offered them forgiveness of sins and eternal life.

This is the biblical way and the Christian message. God has not appointed Christians to be agents of his wrath. God has called Christians to be agents of reconciliation, their feet "shod with the preparation of the gospel of peace." That this is so—if any confirmation is needed—is evident from the apostles themselves. They went to the Jews, even into the synagogues, and offered not hatred but blessing and the hope of eternal life. Some of the Jews accepted; those Jews who did not accept were allowed to go their way.

A final point that needs to be mentioned is that God brought the possibility of redemption and forgiveness of sin out of the darkness and unspeakable evil of the crucifixion. According to the determinate foreknowledge and will of God, Christ "redeemed us with his precious blood" and "obtained eternal redemption for us" by the crucifixion. "We were reconciled to God by the death of his Son" and "being justified by his blood, we shall be saved from wrath through him."

That some should take the death of Christ as an occasion for viciousness and brutality shows a complete ignorance of the Spirit and substance of scriptural Christianity. Are they even Christians at all, who are so unmindful of the benefits made available to us by Christ's divine and sinless sacrifice? Are not they also children of the devil, enemies of Christ, doing despite to the Spirit of grace? Are they not even worse than the Jews who cried out for Christ's death? Those Jews were ignorant, and did not know what they were doing—but for those who claim to have knowledge of Christ, and even boast of their knowledge with haughty superiority, and look down on those without such knowledge, for them to pervert their knowledge into a complete reversal of the Sermon on the Mount is surely nothing but the most abysmal wickedness. That they practice evil in the name of Christ does not justify them, but rather intensifies their guilt.

When we consider Christ's divine sacrifice in the light of scripture, it cannot be seen only as an act of evil, though it was that. Because of the cross, we can have "joy unspeakable, and full of glory." Along with the manger, the empty tomb, Christ's reign at the right hand of the Father, and his final return as God revealed, the cross stands at the center and heart of our faith.

Pontius Pilate and the guilt of the Gentiles

Discussing Pilate's role in Christ's death, Katz refers to Pilate's hand washing to show that the New Testament exonerates the Gentiles and shows them to be innocent, placing all of the blame on the wicked Jews. That not the Romans or the

Gentiles but the Jews alone were responsible for the crucifixion has been, according to Katz, "recognized by almost every Christian commentator on Matthew from patristic to modern times."[22]

What sort of commentators think that a judge can knowingly sentence an innocent man to be tortured to death and then clear himself by a simple theatrical gesture? There are other more genuinely spiritual students of scripture whose judgments are not so surprisingly wide of the mark. One example is Matthew Henry. A renowned English biblical commentator from the 18th century whose works are still studied today, he stated Pilate's guilt and the reality of Gentile participation in the Crucifixion very well:

> They delivered him to Pontius Pilate; according to that which Christ had often said, that he should be delivered to the Gentiles. Both Jews and Gentiles were obnoxious to the judgment of God, and concluded under sin, and Christ was to be the Saviour both of Jews and Gentiles; and therefore Christ was brought into the judgment both of Jews and Gentiles, and both had a hand in his death. See how these corrupt church-rulers abused the civil magistrate, making use of him to execute their unrighteous decrees, and inflict the grievance which they had prescribed, Isa. x.1. Thus have the kings of the earth been wretchedly imposed upon by the papal powers, and condemned to the drudgery of extirpating with the sword of war, as well as that of justice, those whom they have marked for heretics, right or wrong, to the great prejudice of their own interests . . . [23]

Notice that he rightly compares the later execution of Christian martyrs to the death of Christ. Returning to the subject of Pilate, we find that Henry says of him:

> (2.) This puts him into a great strait, betwixt the peace of his own mind, and the peace of the city; he is loth to condemn an innocent man, and yet loth to disoblige the people, and raise a devil that would not be soon laid. Had he steadily and resolutely adhered to the sacred laws of justice, as a judge ought to do, he had not been in any perplexity; the matter was plain and past dispute, that a man in whom was found no fault, ought not to be crucified, upon any pretence whatsoever, nor must an unjust thing be done, to gratify any man or company of men in the world; the cause is soon decided; Let justice be done, though heaven and earth come together--*Fiat justitia, ruat cælum* . . .
> (3.) Pilate thinks to trim the matter, and to pacify both the people and his own conscience too, by doing it, and yet disowning it, acting the thing, and yet acquitting himself from it at the same time. Such absurdities and self-contradictions do they run upon, whose convictions are strong, but their corruptions stronger. Happy is he (saith the apostle, Rom. xiv. 22) that condemneth not himself in that thing which he alloweth; or, which is all one, that allows not himself in that thing which he condemns.
> Now Pilate endeavours to clear himself from the guilt,

[1.] By a sign; He took water, and washed his hands before the multitude; not as if he thought thereby to cleanse himself from any guilt contracted before God, but to acquit himself before the people, from so much as contracting any guilt in this matter; as if he had said, "If it be done, bear witness that it is none of my doing." He borrowed the ceremony from that law which appointed it to be used for the clearing of the country from the guilt of an undiscovered murder (Deut. xxi. 6, 7); and he used it the more to affect the people with the conviction he was under of the prisoner's innocency; and, probably, such was the noise of the rabble, that, if he had not used some such surprising sign, in the view of them all, he could not have been heard.

[2.] By a saying; in which, First, He clears himself; I am innocent of the blood of this just person. What nonsense was this, to condemn him, and yet protest that he was innocent of his blood! For men to protest against a thing, and yet to practise it, is only to proclaim that they sin against their consciences. Though Pilate professed his innocency, God charges him with guilt, Acts iv. 27. Some think to justify themselves, by pleading that their hands were not in the sin; but David kills by the sword of the children of Ammon, and Ahab by the elders of Jezreel. Pilate here thinks to justify himself, by pleading that his heart was not in the action; but here is an averment which will never be admitted. *Protestatio non valet contra factum*--In vain does he protest against the deed which at the same time he perpetrates. Secondly, He casts it upon the priests and people; "See ye to it; if it must be done, I cannot help it, do you answer it before God and the world." Note, Sin is a brat that nobody is willing to own; and many deceive themselves with this, that they shall bear no blame if they can but find any to lay the blame upon; but it is not so easy a thing to transfer the guilt of sin as many think it is . . .

Observe, 1. Where this was done--in the common hall. The governor's house, which should have been a shelter to the wronged and abused, is made the theatre of this barbarity. I wonder that the governor, who was so desirous to acquit himself from the blood of this just person, would suffer this to be done in his house. Perhaps he did not order it to be done, but he connived at it; and those in authority will be accountable, not only for the wickedness which they do, or appoint, but for that which they do not restrain, when it is in the power of their hands...

The verse in Acts that Matthew Henry refers to expressly mentions not only Herod and the Jews, but also Pilate and the Gentiles:

The kings of the earth stood up, and the rulers were gathered together against the Lord, and against his Christ.

For of a truth against thy holy child Jesus, whom thou hast anointed, both Herod, and Pontius Pilate, with the Gentiles, and the people of Israel, were gathered together,

For to do whatsoever thy hand and thy counsel determined
before to be done (4:26-28).

If there is a vast amount of literature claiming that the Bible asserts the
innocence of Pilate and the guilt of the wicked Jews, it is contrary not only to
common sense but to the plain teachings of scripture. "Who is this that darkeneth
counsel by words without knowledge?" as it says in Job.

"His blood be on us"

Referring to the cry of the mob "His blood be on us, and on our children"
(Matthew 27:25), Katz calls this fictional, and adds that it "has become a death
sentence for untold thousands of Jews."[24] The dramatic and rhetorical use of the
present perfect tense "has become" is not appropriate here, by the way—it makes
it sound as if Jews are being killed today due to someone reading the Gospel of
Matthew. More importantly, whether this is a fictional narrative or a historically
accurate one is purely a matter of faith. There is no scientific evidence to prove
that it did or did not occur. Certainly there is no evidence against it. It is not
implausible that corrupt and dishonest religious leaders should conspire to kill
someone who exposed their false teachings and was drawing too many people
away from them.

We see a similar case in the execution of John Huss in the 1400's. His biblical
teachings exposed the falsehood and errors of the spiritually corrupt religious
authorities, and there was a real possibility that the spread of his teachings would
undermine their power. So, they had him killed, for the same reasons that the
Pharisees had Christ killed. Once again, we remember those words of Christ,
"Inasmuch as ye have done it to the least of my brethren, ye have done it to me."

It is not Jewish sin that Matthew is describing here, but human sin. The same
spirit that animated the Pharisees and their mob of supporters also animated the
medieval Christian religious authorities who killed John Huss and many other
Christian martyrs. It animated the ancient Romans and the Chinese and Russian
Communists in their futile attempts to eliminate the church. It also works in
today's American Civil Liberties Union, and in everyone else that wants to
eliminate Christianity. Hatred of the truths of Christ that the Bible teaches is
endemic to the world and to fallen man, not just to the Pharisees or the Jews. The
Jewish rejection of Christ is the same in essence as Gentile rejection of Christ.

Moreover, it is evident from the teachings and actions of the apostles after
Christ's resurrection that those terrible words of the Jewish mob were not
considered binding on all Jews for all time. The apostles did not teach that the
Jews were under a curse. As was said a few pages ago but merits repeating, they
shared the message of Christ with both Jews and Gentiles, freely and without
distinction.

It also needs to be pointed out that God is not bound by the foolish words of
wicked men. He is not bound to apply those words to people who were not present
and had no knowledge of them. When the Jews gave up after the Exodus and
wanted to return to Egypt, saying, "Let us make a captain, and let us return into
Egypt" (Numbers 14:4), was God obligated to honor their foolish and wicked
words? His hidden and secret purposes are not slight things to be altered by
whims of human error. His purpose for the Jewish people was not changed by
cowardly Jews in the Old Testament or by evil ones in the New.

If the idea that Christians were appointed to be agents of God's wrath and to slaughter the Jews were truly inherent in Christianity, it would have been carried out in all or most places and at all or most times where Christianity was the predominant religion. The fact that it was not and is not shows it to be one of the many superstitions and false beliefs of the medieval era that has never been taught or practiced by the vast majority of Christians.

C-D. Has God rejected the Jews?

Katz cites two passages about Christians taking the place of Jews in a covenantal relationship with God—one in Hebrews and the other in Galatians. The first says that Jesus had a more excellent ministry than Moses, and that he is "the mediator of a better covenant, which was established upon better promises" (8:6). This same book also asserts that Christ's sacrifice on the cross, which was offered once for all, is infinitely superior to the Old Testament sacrifices of animals. The blood of bulls and goats offered not once for all but repeatedly by fallible human priests was "a shadow of good things to come . . . For it is not possible that the blood of bulls and of goats should take away sins" (10:1,4).

Galatians also teaches that we who have faith in Christ are the children of Abraham (3:7): "And if ye be Christ's, then are ye Abraham's seed, and heirs according to the promise" (3:29). Paul even states that they are not Jews who are Jews outwardly, but they are true Jews who are Jews in spirit (Romans 2:28-29)—and it is evident that Paul is referring to those who have the Spirit of Christ (Romans 9:6,8).

So, the New Testament does teach that those who are in Christ are in the special covenant relationship with God that the Jews used to occupy—but several very important qualifications need to be made at this point. First, "the church" is not synonymous with "the visible church." The buildings, seminaries, ecclesiastical dignitaries and common church-goers are obvious to the world. They are considered by the world to be "the church," "Christians"—but the Bible's concept of the church is radically different. "The church" meant in scripture is different from popular misconceptions of it. The true church, the spiritual church, the body of Christ in this world, is composed of people who have the Spirit of Christ, who love Christ, serve him, and can meet him with joy at his appearing.

Such a definition excludes many whom the world considers Christians—and this inability to distinguish between the spiritual church and the worldly church (which are sometimes one and the same, but at other times are very different) has caused a great deal of confusion among those who try to understand the relationship between the Bible and anti-Semitism. Thieves, liars, drunkards, murderers who teach and practice hatred and cruelty, who openly deny basic teachings of the faith (even if they preserve an outward facade of decency)—they are not "the church," heirs of Abraham by faith in Christ, even if they go to church fifty times a day.

A second important qualification is that many Christians believe God has not completely cast away the Jewish people. He still has a role for them to play in the grand scheme of things. Some of the teachings about this in Romans are disputed and sincere Christians may differ on them, but it seems evident to many that Paul does teach a final restoration of the Jews to God's favor.

Katz points to the belief that a reconciliation of the Jews to God will come through faith in Christ, but mistakenly asserts that this is evidence of deep hostility to Judaism.[25] On the contrary, it is one of the several inherent restraints in Christianity which ensured that the mad dream of exterminating the entire Jewish nation never appeared in Europe before the modern era. After all, if God has a final purpose for the Jews we don't want to eliminate them, do we? This reasoning was actually followed and served as a moderating influence even in the depths of the Middle Ages.

This belief in the fundamental humanity of Jew and Gentile was not merely taught—it was lived by the apostles. They shared the gospel equally with Jew and Gentile. Paul went to the synagogues of the Jews and the markets of the Greeks, sharing the truth with all, and receiving all who believed without distinction. Jews and Gentiles accepted the gospel by the same gift of faith, or rejected it by the same spirit of unbelief.

What shall we say then about the examples of God's anger at the Jews given by Katz? There are two passages from Matthew which he cites verbatim. These contain Jesus' well-known denunciations of the Pharisees. He refers to them as hypocrites, whitewashed tombs, serpents, and as a generation of vipers. They do not enter the kingdom of heaven themselves, and they keep others from going in. They are guilty of the blood of righteous men and will receive a greater condemnation because of their pretense of holiness (Matthew 23:13-15, 27-39).

I would like to re-emphasize that I consider this to be an accurate record of Christ's own words. I do not believe any part of scripture to have been made up after the fact in order to argue for the superiority of the new religion. I also consider the words to be not merely an historically accurate record of what Christ said, but truthful as well, since Christ was Truth incarnate.

Considering the passages, we notice that they are a denunciation of the Jewish religious leadership, not of "the Jews." Of course, leaders of various types like to imagine that they represent "the people" and that any criticism of them is a criticism of "the people," but that is not the case. John the Baptist also had hard words for the religious leaders, not for all of the people who came to him. This will be considered by some to be an evasive tactic, but Matthew 23:1 says Jesus spoke "to the multitude, and to his disciples." He refers to the scribes and the Pharisees in the third person, "they." Then in verse 13 he speaks directly to the scribes and the Pharisees, using the second person, "you." Is making this elementary distinction an apologetic trick, or is refusing to recognize the distinction a distortion? No doubt some Israelis could criticize extremely conservative Jews for evading military service while demanding more and more benefits from the government, only to be told "We represent Judaism! In criticizing us you are criticizing Judaism!"

Some Jews today would be less offended by Christ's criticisms if they were informed that such comments could with equal justice be applied to many leaders in the Christian church. How many church leaders, pastors, theologians, bishops, and popes, whether in the Middle Ages or in recent German history or even in our own times, have "shut up the kingdom of heaven against men" with their false teachings? There are Christian leaders and teachers who do not enter eternal life themselves and keep others from going in. They are blind guides who make a pretense of religion and outwardly may appear good but are full of sin and false teachings within. In the words of the 18th-century evangelist George Whitefield (speaking of the Anglican Church), "Though it may seem a hard saying to many, yet our people need to be cautioned against the scribes and Pharisees of our communion, as much as the Jews were cautioned to beware of the scribes and Pharisees by our Lord Jesus."[26]

Returning to the passage in Matthew, it is worth pointing out that Christ's condemnations did not mean that hypocrisy on the part of Jewish religious leaders was a sin, while hypocrisy on the part of others (including Christian leaders) was pleasing and acceptable to God. If for example a Christian church condemns Israel for its real or alleged abuses while ignoring the persecution of Palestinian Christians by other Palestinians, isn't this the most flagrant and contemptible hypocrisy? When Christian leaders piously intone that abortion and sexual immorality, even homosexuality are acceptable to God, isn't this nothing but dead men's bones and all uncleanness concealed behind a whitewashed facade of empty religiosity?

There are at the end of the second passage from Matthew some words that do pertain more directly to the rejection of the nation of Israel—Jesus' words "Behold, your house is left unto you desolate." Shortly after this prophecy, Israel was destroyed by the Romans, making it a prophetic statement of fact. Of course, it has been said that this prophecy was written after the fact, made up by the New Testament writers. Needless to say, there is not a scrap of evidence to support this assertion.

Whatever the case, prophesying that Jerusalem will be destroyed should not be linked to National Socialism, unless one wants to link Jeremiah to National Socialism as well. Does anyone want to say that Jeremiah's "poisonous" and "venomous" condemnations of the Jews and his prophecy of coming wrath on Jerusalem laid the foundation of Jew hatred that was to bear such dark and terrible fruit first in Christianity and then in the Holocaust? Jews would find that ridiculous, just as sincere Christians find dark mutterings about the harmful effects of Christ's prophecies to be ridiculous. Any persecution of others derives not from the teachings of Christ but from ignorance of and disobedience to the teachings of Christ.

If this prophecy is related not merely to the destruction of Jerusalem but also to the covenantal displacement of the Jewish people, it can be related to another verse from Matthew cited by Katz, "The kingdom of God shall be taken from you, and given to a nation bringing forth the fruits thereof" (Matthew 21:43). That the covenant relationship has passed from Israel to all who are in Christ is a basic teaching of Christianity as has been said, but it does not place the Jews outside the boundaries of a shared humanity. Jews who reject Christ are in essence no different from Gentiles who reject Christ.

Finally, another reference from Luke is given to show that, according to the Christian view, God has cast off the wicked Jews (and therefore they are less than human, to be treated like dirt and finally in the end shoved into the gas chambers?). That is in Luke: ". . . that which is highly esteemed among men is abomination in the sight of God" (16:15). Once again, it plainly says here that Jesus is talking to the Pharisees: "And the Pharisees also, who were covetous, heard all these things: and they derided him. And he said unto them . . ." followed by the words cited above.

"Pharisees" is not synonymous with "the entire Jewish people forever." Besides, Christian leaders can be and certainly have been guilty of covetousness and other sins. Are Jewish leaders such infallible and holy saints that they never experience common human sins? And if they do experience sins and failings, are they to be exempt from criticism lest criticism of Jewish religious leaders lead to a Holocaust two thousand years later? Anyway, what does this have to do with the Weimar Republic, WWI, and the Third Reich? Is any and every criticism of Jews and Judaism now to be automatically linked to Hitler and Auschwitz? I wish some people would study the writings of 19th-century German writers looking for every single scrap or clue linking their ideas to Hitler as diligently as they study the New Testament.

Also, there is a general spiritual principle in this verse that applies not only to the Jews and to Roman Palestine in the 1st century A.D. It applies to humanity as a whole. How many of the people and things highly esteemed in our culture are nothing but abominations to God? Religious leaders, pop stars, movie stars, celebrities, politicians, adored by the masses while their private lives are full of every kind of filthiness and iniquity—how much of what is greatly admired by the lost and sinful world is really an abomination to God? Pride, conceit, immorality, heartlessness, unbelief—how much sin lies behind the facades of glamour and virtue that seem so appealing to the world? And, if the truth were known, it would be found that many of the "Protestant" churches in America today are well described by Christ's denunciations.

Jesus warned his disciples "Beware of the leaven of the Pharisees and of the Sadducees." He wouldn't have warned them of the problem if it had not been a real one. This commandment has, along with many other Bible teachings, been ignored. As a result, many Christians are full of the leaven of the Pharisees (an outward appearance of righteousness that conceals sin) and of the Sadducees (denying the reality of the judgment and the world to come, and so living as if there were nothing more than the things of this world). Anyway, the message that "The Jews as a nation are an abomination to God" is found nowhere in any of the teachings of the apostles.

E. Who are the children of the devil?

Jesus' saying to some Jews "Ye are of your father the devil, and the lusts of your father ye will do" (John 8:44) is constantly referred to as an example of how Christianity demonizes Jews. However, it is clear from two verses (37 & 40) that Jesus is speaking to people that were seeking to kill him. Looking at the whole verse, we can see that it has considerably more depth than "All Jews are children of the devil," which is what some wrongly make it sound like saying. The whole verse is, "Ye are of your father the devil, and the lusts of your father ye will do. He was a murderer from the beginning, and abode not in the truth, because there is no truth in him. When he speaketh a lie, he speaketh of his own: for he is a liar, and the father of it."

Jesus says here that liars and murderers are from the devil. This is a general spiritual truth that applies to everyone, not only to Jews. The torturers of the Inquisition—children of the devil; Crusaders who massacred innocent people—children of the devil; Communist persecutors of the church and people who shoved Jews into gas chambers—children of the devil; mothers, doctors, and nurses who kill unborn children; ordinary murderers; child murderers and serial killers—all of them children of the devil.

Let's not forget the liars. Medieval superstitions about Jews as well-poisoners or ritual murderers; fantasies about the paradise to be established after the dictatorship of the proletariat; the myth of Aryan supremacy; the belief that differences between men and women should be obliterated, or that homosexuality is normal and acceptable—these lies also come from the devil. That is why Revelation says that liars and murderers "shall have their part in the lake which burneth with fire and brimstone" (21:8).

In discussing this passage in John chapter 8, Katz also mentions verses 43 & 47: "Why do ye not understand my speech? even because ye cannot hear my word . . . He that is of God heareth God's words: ye therefore hear them not, because ye are not of God." This is pointed at to show God's rejection of the Jews, but, once again, this is a general truth that applies to everyone in the world, not just Jews.

According to Christian belief, the words of Jesus are words from God. Those who are of God, who have received the gift of faith from God, can hear these words of God. Those who do not hear them are not of God, but are of the world. This is also stated in I John: "They are of the world: therefore speak they of the world, and the world hears them. We are of God: he that knoweth God heareth us; he that is not of God heareth not us. Hereby know we the spirit of truth, and the spirit of error."

It is not only Jews who hear the words of Jesus and reject them. Many people do not believe the message of Christ and do not hear it. This is because they are not of God. Speaking of Jesus, John also says, "In him was life; and the life was the light of men. And the light shineth in darkness; and the darkness comprehended it not." As was said before, this is the darkness of the world, not the darkness of the Jews—for "the whole world lieth in wickedness."

In their rejection of Christ's message and in their crucifixion of him the Jews were fully, essentially, completely human. And, of course, many Jews did not reject Christ and did not crucify him. John's account, far from being "venomous," shows the human sin and evil that has been the spiritual legacy of the entire human race since the fall in the Garden of Eden. That many with the outward appearance of Christianity but not the Spirit have debased and perverted the Christian message is the result of the same sin and the same darkness.

The vast majority of Christians who have lived in the past nearly two thousand years since the resurrection of Christ and the granting of the Holy Spirit at Pentecost have never participated in a Crusade, an Inquisition, or a pogrom. Countless Christians in many Christian countries have never set up ecclesiastical courts or burned a single heretic. To constantly link all Christians to those who have missed the very essence of Christianity is a violation of the 9th commandment: "You shall not bear false witness against your neighbor." In fact, a blood libel has been attached to the teachings of Christ, often by the very same people who hypocritically object to a blood libel being applied to themselves.

As to the argument that the very idea of Jewish religious leaders plotting to kill Jesus is impossible, some Jews (not all Jews) wanted to kill King David. Some Jews (not all Jews) wanted to kill Joseph and Jeremiah. Isaiah said that there were murderers in Jerusalem. At one point some Jews were about to kill Moses (Exodus 17:4). According to Jewish history, that some Jews (not all Jews) wanted to kill Christ is plausible. Christ's description of those who wanted to solve religious disputes by killing as children of the devil was truthful and accurate, and nothing for Christians to feel embarrassed about, even if unbelievers distort it.

43

The Holocaust and the Old Testament

It would be good if we could stop at this point and go on to the next chapter. Since, however, some have been extremely diligent in their attacks on Christianity, and have left no stone unturned in their attempts to link Christianity and the Bible to Hitler and his crimes, it is necessary to look at the assertion that the atrocities of the Nazis have parallels in the Old Testament.

The most obvious parallel is between Hitler's massacre of the Jews and the Jewish massacres of the Canaanites. Comparisons have also been drawn between the Nuremberg Racial Laws forbidding marriage between Jews and Germans, and Old Testament prohibitions on marriage between Jews and the peoples around them. One of the Nazi war criminals, Julius Streicher, even used this defense during his trial at Nuremberg—the Nazi race laws were no different from what the Jews had done themselves.

Some who try to link Naziism to Christianity will not be pleased to see Naziism linked to Torah as well. Perhaps one of them has written something highlighting the differences between the conquest of Canaan and the Nazi genocide. It is not only the Jews that need to be concerned with this, however. Christians who consider the Old Testament to have been divinely inspired and see it as a vital part of the New Covenant revealed in Christ also have something to say about this.

Most people who make these comparisons are not, unlike the aforementioned Herr Streicher, interested in justifying Nazi crimes. Their motive rather is to attack the Bible. By linking Hitler's ideas and actions to the Bible, they hope to show that the book, and of course the people who believe in it as well, are dangerous, a menace to society; or, they want to discredit the biblical conception of God, and show it to be unworthy of belief.

Usually such people are impervious to argument. Like those anti-Americans who compared the US occupation of Western Europe to the Soviet occupation of Eastern Europe and insisted that NATO was basically the same as the Warsaw Pact, some people who compare certain events and ideas of Torah to the Nazi program of genocide will never be impressed by any amount of arguments. They have an underlying personal motivation which holds reason and logic in captivity.

We need to remember that commandment of Christ's: "Judge not according to the appearance, but judge righteous judgment." Someone may say that the Soviet and the American occupations of Europe were the same—if they refuse to consider or respond intelligently to contrary evidence, what can be done? Someone could argue, "The Germans invaded France in 1940, and the Allies invaded France in 1944," or "the Germans bombed British cities and the Allies bombed German cities" and conclude that the British and the Americans were the same as the Nazis. If people refuse to consider differences of motive and result, they are either incapable of rational discourse on the subject, or else are merely propagandizing, trying to advance their own agenda. Those who argue that the German Christians who supported Hitler's invasion of Poland were just like American Christians who supported their government in the first Gulf War are beyond logic on this point.

The massacres of the Canaanites

Looking first at the massacres of the Canaanites by the Jews, there is one obvious similarity with the Holocaust—lots of people were killed. Thinking only on this level, we could say that a bank robber who shot a teller and a policeman who shot the robber were on the same plane. They both shot someone, so what's the difference? If we explained that the robber shot an innocent victim while the policeman did not, and added that the policeman had a certain authority and right to use his gun that the robber did not have, few people would have difficulty accepting these distinctions.

Of course, the analogy of the bank robber and the policeman is not identical in every respect to the larger question we are examining. If it were identical in every respect it would cease to be an analogy. Yet, while there are differences, the analogy is not totally irrelevant to our subject either. Again, we get back to presuppositions. If the accounts in the Bible are not historically accurate, then they are only a collection of stories and we don't even know if there were any massacres of the Canaanites at all. If there were some massacres they were ordinary historical events, bloody and violent, but no more so than the massacres of the Mongols or the Huns. If, however, the events of the Exodus and the conquest of Canaan are recorded accurately in the Bible, then the entire situation must be viewed in a completely different light.

If God exists as the Bible describes him, he is the giver of life and has complete authority to take it when and as he wills. He could destroy the world by a flood or eliminate Sodom and Gomorrah by fire in a way that no human has the right or the power to do. If in the judgment of God the Jews were to be placed in a certain land so that they might prepare the way for the Messiah, he had the right to give them that land, as the earth is his. If the original inhabitants had to be removed, both as punishment for their wickedness and to ensure that the Jews would be permanently established in the land, God had the right to make that judgment.

This also applies to God destroying the first-born of the Egyptians, which has also been mentioned in this context. God as the giver of life, as the Lord of life and death, has a divine right to take human souls from their bodies whenever he sees fit. Thus against the superficial similarity of many people being killed, we have a difference of agent: on the one hand, the Lord, maker of heaven and earth—on the other hand, a man, Adolf Hitler, who put himself in the place of God.

It is recognized that Hitler was not God, the Lord of life and death, but only a man. That the true God of heaven and earth was acting in the conquest of Canaan and the Israelites were his agents is of course not so incontestably agreed upon, but it is seriously believed by millions, and is at least a legitimate faith proposition in a way that Hitler's divinity is not.

Apart from the difference of agent, there is also a difference of motive. Hitler slaughtered six million Jews according to a completely false ideology of racial superiority that has zero credible adherents today. Moses and the Israelites operated from completely different motives—as genuine agents of a higher power if the Bible is true; according to an ordinary desire for land and territory which has been repeated many times in history if the Bible is not true.

Along with the differences of agent and of motive, there is a third great difference—that of result. Hitler's truth lasted for a very short time, and left only misery and ruin in its wake. He failed to achieve any of his objectives and ended in titanic failure. The belief that God exists, that he worked in the world through the Jewish people, settling them in the land and preparing the way for the Messiah through them, has not died out after a decade or so but has lasted many centuries. It has endured for more than three thousand years after the conquest and has spread throughout the world, giving blessing, hope, and peace to many. The truth of these beliefs is disputed of course, but they are infinitely more credible than the bizarre fantasies of Hitler, fantasies that are universally detested by all decent people.

Yet, the Nazis believed they were in the right. Hitler claimed on numerous occasions to be doing the work of the Lord, and believed that Fate, Destiny, Providence, or whatever was behind him. Is this an example of the dangerous fanaticism that is unleashed when people believe that God is with them? This is called "frightening" by some. They do not consider the atrocities of Lenin, Stalin, and Mao to be equally "frightening" examples of the dangerous fanaticism that is unleashed when man rejects God and relies on human reason alone.

Some people are not really "frightened" at all, though they pretend to be. They are only propagandists in the culture wars, trying to discredit religion because it is a major obstacle to the realization of their secular and anti-religious goals. To this end, any distortion, misinformation, or insinuation will do as long as it makes Christians and Christianity look bad.

People who believe in the Old and New Testaments believe that in Christ we have a new covenant, a better covenant. Jesus Christ is the final and complete revelation of God, and he represents the standard that all sincere Christians aspire to. We recognize that the laws and actions of Moses and the ancient Israelites, while from God, are not his calling for us today. We do not claim to be ancient Israelites, and we recognize that God has never at any other time in the history of the world manifested himself as he did in the events of the Exodus and the conquest of Canaan. The Jews also recognize the uniqueness of Old Testament events and have never tried to emulate them.

Finally, great numbers of people, including civilians, old people, women and children were killed in Allied air raids on Germany and Japan in WWII. Most people accept the great loss of life as necessary and justified. Millions of human babies have also been killed, the vast majority of them solely because the mothers don't want to be bothered with them. This mass killing is perfectly acceptable to opponents of the Bible. They don't object to massive killing that runs into millions if it is done for a suitable cause—and does man have more power than God? Do we have the right to take life and God does not? Some who claim to be so disturbed by the Old Testament conquests are inconsistent, their imagined objectivity notwithstanding.

At this point we can also challenge those who reject the Bible: "Demonstrate that what Hitler did was morally wrong." With no divine laws, no revelation, no higher authority, people who operate strictly according to human reason have no moral basis for condemning Hitler. They may personally feel that what he did was wrong, but in the vast metaphysical darkness and silence of a godless universe, there is no firm and definite "No." If the meaning of life is gratification of self and a pursuit of the will to power, maybe what Hitler did to the Jews was right, and moral whining and hand-wringing is a futile waste of time. Hitler was wrong according to pragmatism only because he lost—if he had handled the Russian and

British campaigns differently, and avoided war with America, he could have won. He made some tactical and strategic mistakes, but there is no proof outside of the Bible that killing Jews was anything other than part of the struggle for survival of the fittest.

The Nuremberg Racial Laws

Diligently pursuing his appointed task of linking the Bible to Naziism, Jim Walker (whose site linking Hitler to Christianity was mentioned in the Introduction) has posted a quote on his website from Julius Streicher, one of the defendants at the Nuremberg war crimes trials. Attempting to justify himself before the tribunal, Herr Streicher said that the Nuremberg Race Laws were modeled on Jewish marriage laws. Here we have what some would call an open and shut case. This will demonstrate to some that the Bible is a bad book, and that the people who believe in it are menaces to society who should be excluded from public life.

It is true that Herr Streicher read the Bible—however, his opinions of the Bible were different from what someone who uncritically accepted Mr. Walker's information might think. The following quotation from *Der Stuermer* sheds more light on what Herr Streicher thought of the Bible, and reveals the folly of taking isolated religious statements by Nazis at face value:

> . . . the history book of the Jews, which is usually called the Holy Scriptures, impresses us as a horrible criminal romance, which makes the 150 penny-dreadfuls of the British Jew, Edgar Wallace, go green with envy. This "holy" book abounds in murder, incest, fraud, theft, and indecency.[27]

Why would someone who hated the Bible and considered it to be a book of lies and murder appeal to it for his defense? It doesn't take any deep philosophical insight to understand that a man on trial for his life might resort to any trick, any evasion, to minimize his guilt. The testimonies of the defendants at Nuremberg do not reveal the courage of honest men prepared to suffer for their convictions. There was a great deal of equivocation, evasion, and dishonesty. The judges at any rate were not convinced by Streicher's argument "We were only following the Bible"—they sentenced him to be hanged.

Jewish marriage laws were related to purity of religious belief, not to purity of race—two vastly different and non-related concepts. The Bible has nothing to do with modern *scientific* racism. The fact that countless Christians in innumerable countries have read the laws of Moses in the Old Testament but never thought of inventing racial laws (let alone enforcing them) shows clearly that this is a modern interpretation, and a German one.

It is interesting to note that a website such as http://www.evilbible.com shares the view of a vicious and brutal Nazi about the Bible as a book of lies, murder, and indecency. That should give some enemies of the Bible cause for reflection, but of course it will not. It is also worthwhile to ask why Walker gave the impression that Herr Streicher believed in the Bible and was following it, when in fact he hated the Bible and saw it as a bunch of lies. It is possible that Walker was not aware of the quote—however, since he has carefully assembled many quotes from Nazi leaders and I found this quote from Streicher in about five minutes in the first links that came up in a search, it is more likely that Walker also came across it but decided not to use it.

Hitler's study notes on the Bible

Continuing his moral crusade against Christianity, Walker has found a single page of Hitler's handwritten notes dated to around 1919.[28] He claims these notes show the Bible's influence on Hitler—a novel theory that has eluded countless historians and students of the Hitler problem. Not surprisingly, a careful (as opposed to a propagandistic) examination of the notes reveals the opposite of what Walker claims.

The first section of the notes, the "Introduction," deals with "the Aryan" and "His Works," and "The Jew" and "His Work." Hitler's starting point is the fundamental division between Jew and Aryan. Those who have some understanding of the Bible know that this is not a biblical teaching. Those who have some knowledge of German intellectual history know that the emphasis on the Jew as the anti-type of the Aryan emerged in Germany in the modern era, and it emerged out of a secular tradition. Such a ridiculous secular doctrine didn't become popular until the modern scientific age.

The second section of the notes is entitled "The Bible—Monumental History of Mankind." Walker makes a great issue of this, exclaiming excitedly that this shows Hitler saw the Bible as a monumental history. However, let's contrast Walker's theory with what Hitler wrote in *Mein Kampf*, in a passage where he states that the Bible is false:

> . . . Since the Jew never possessed a state with definite territorial limits and therefore never called a culture his own . . . he was never a nomad, but only and always a parasite in the body of other peoples . . . The Jew has always been a people with definite racial characteristics and never a religion . . . [vol. I chapt. 11]

Hitler saw the Old Testament as almost completely inaccurate historically, as do all good secularists today. The Jews never had their own country—so much for David, Solomon, and a long line of Hebrew kings. The Jews never wandered as nomads, and didn't even have their own religion. Another passage from this same chapter in *Mein Kampf* states "Since the Jew . . . was never in possession of a culture of his own, the foundations of his intellectual work were always provided by others. His intellect at all times developed through the cultural world surrounding him . . . ." That the Jewish religion was not revealed by God but was derived from surrounding cultures was a basic tenet of both theological and secular liberalism. Hitler was in the mainstream of humanism here.

As to the Bible being a monumental history, it is a history—whether or not that history is true is a different question. Secondly, it is monumental both in its scope—covering the creation of the world and thousands of years of human history—and in its vast influence on Western civilization. Calling something a monumental history is not calling it a true history, however.

That Hitler had a very low view of the Bible is further confirmed (if confirmation were needed) a few lines down in the same section of the notes where he wrote "1st consequence. Purification of the Bible--what of its spirit remains? 2nd consequence. Critical examination of the remainder." After the Bible was "purified," what was left? Not much. A "critical examination of the *remainder*" [my emphasis] reveals a "First people's history (based on) the race law" [parentheses in text].

Forget the creation, the calling of Abraham, the Exodus from Egypt, the history of the Jews in Israel, the teachings of the prophets, the Ten Commandments—all of that was irrelevant. What was *really* important was the race law. The Jews kept their racial integrity by forbidding marriages with other people (most of whom, by the way, were of the same Semitic race as the Jews). This doesn't show Hitler getting his ideas from the Bible—it shows him looking at the Bible with his racist views firmly in place.

Much more could be said about the unbiblical nature of these notes. That truth about Nature is arrived at "via instinct" rather than by revelation shows the influence of German romanticism, which many scholars have linked to Naziism. That "Racial purity is the highest law" and "Miscegenation with inferior types means lowering the level of the whole" show the influence of 19th-century biological racism. The idea that "Privilege through strength (is) the basis of all Nature," that "Victory of the stronger" is the basis of Nature, is social Darwinism. "The eternal course of history" is contrary to Christianity, which teaches that history had a definite beginning and will have a definite end.

The ideas in these notes did not come from the Bible. They came from the secular humanist German philosophies of Hitler's day. There are deep commonalities between these ideas and those presented by, to take one example, Ernst Haeckel, the German social Darwinist and outspoken opponent of Christianity. Haeckel was not an isolated individual either. The ideas expressed in these notes and in *Mein Kampf* were the common property of many German intellectuals, professors, doctors, educators, psychiatrists, and reformers. The popularity in Germany of Darwinian ideas of life as conflict in which progress grew out of the destruction of the weak and the less fit has been amply documented by Richard Weikart in his book *From Darwin to Hitler: Evolutionary Ethics, Eugenics, and Racism in Germany*. The ugliness, inhumanity, and brutality that emerged out of attempts to interpret human life according to a Darwinian ethic are revealed by Weikart in a chilling book that shows the blindness and evil of science and philosophy without higher ethical and moral guidelines.

Walker thinks it "remarkable" that other historians have not referred to these notes—but it is not in the least remarkable, as the notes contain nothing of significance that was not stated openly a few years later in *Mein Kampf*. That Walker could look at these notes and see them as proof of the biblical origins of Hitler's ideas says more about Walker than it does about Hitler. Religious Jews do not have to be concerned that serious students of Hitler's thought will blame his weird racial phobias on his study of Torah.

The Christian way of holiness

It has been asserted here that the biblical definition of a Christian leaves no room for hatred and persecution of Jews. There are many verses in the New Testament about how Christians who have the hope of eternal life are supposed to deal with unbelievers (Jew or Gentile). A few such verses are:

. . . denying ungodliness and worldly lusts, we should live soberly, righteously, and godly in this present world . . . To speak evil of no man, to be no brawlers, but gentle, shewing all meekness unto all men (Titus 2:12, 3:2).

. . . the servant of the Lord must not strive; but be gentle unto all men, apt to teach, patient, in meekness instructing those that oppose themselves; if God peradventure will give them repentance to the acknowledging of the truth . . . (II Timothy 2:24-25).

It is true of course that many with the name of "Christian" have blatantly ignored these and many other commandments. They have cheerfully and willfully engaged in the exact opposite, hating, lying, killing, doing evil, and have been no different from the world around them. In some cases they have even been worse than unbelievers. They will have their judgment, and will answer to the God whom they disobeyed.

It is also true that many have sincerely tried to follow these and other commandments, but have made natural and inevitable human errors. They have however been so far delivered from the power of sin as to be free from cruelty and murder. This is why Crusades, Inquisitions, and pogroms have not been characteristic of the vast majority of Christians.

This is true to such an extent that to say "Christianity has been characterized by bloodshed" is, quite plainly, a falsehood. The entire world has been full of wars and bloodshed since the dawn of history. Christianity does not eliminate that—the Bible even says men will become "worse and worse." Nevertheless, because of the crimes of people who had the name but not the Spirit of Christianity, the teachings of Christ and the apostles are repeatedly linked to Naziism. Therefore, the problem of "Christian" anti-Semitism needs to be further examined.

Therefore all things whatsoever ye would that men should do to you, do ye even so to them: for this is the law and the prophets.
Enter ye in at the strait gate: for wide is the gate, and broad is the way, that leadeth to destruction, and many there be which go in thereat:
Because strait is the gate, and narrow is the way, which leadeth unto life, and few there be that find it.
Beware of false prophets, which come to you in sheep's clothing, but inwardly they are ravening wolves.
Ye shall know them by their fruits. Do men gather grapes of thorns, or figs of thistles?
Even so every good tree bringeth forth good fruit; but a corrupt tree bringeth forth evil fruit.
A good tree cannot bring forth evil fruit, neither can a corrupt tree bring forth good fruit.
Every tree that bringeth not forth good fruit is hewn down, and cast into the fire.
Wherefore by their fruits shall ye know them.
Not every one that saith unto me Lord, Lord, shall enter into the kingdom of heaven; but he that doeth the will of my father which is in heaven.

Many will say unto me in that day, Lord, Lord, have we not prophesied in thy name? and in thy name cast out devils? and in thy name done many wonderful works?
And then I will profess unto them, I never knew you: depart from me, ye that work iniquity. (Matthew)

---

[1] "The Hep! Hep! Riots," *Gates to Jewish Heritage*; http://www.jewishgates.com/file.asp?File_ID=80; accessed March 2006. The meaning and origin of the word "hep" is not clear.

[2] Friedrich Reck-Malleczewen, *Diary of a Man in Despair* (London 1995), p. 34.

[3] Paul Rose, *German Question / Jewish Question: Revolutionary Antisemitism from Kant to Wagner* (Princeton 1990), p. 55. It is permitted to question his definition of the word "Christian" in this context. By "revolutionary antisemitisms" he means the various forms of secular anti-Semitism that emerged in 19th-century Germany.

[4] Ibid., p. xvi.

[5] Daniel Jonah Goldhagen, *Hitler's Willing Executioners: Ordinary Germans and the Holocaust* (New York 1996), pp. 11-12.

[6] Christopher Browning's book *Ordinary Men* (New York 1998) documents the psychology of Nazi killers who were reluctant at first but later learned to relish their task, while others found it increasingly difficult to do so and tried to avoid assignments where they would be required to kill. A few even refused at the outset, showing the power of human conscience even in such extreme circumstances. Browning also carefully exposes serious problems with Goldhagen's concept of the Germans as a nation of killers.

[7] Victor Klemperer, *I Will Bear Witness: A Diary of the Nazi Years 1942-1945*, trans. Martin Chalmers (New York 2001), p. 306. This entry was made in 1944, when it was obvious that the war was lost. Some Nazis did support Hitler to the bitter end, but there were many Germans who realized that their earlier support of Hitler was a terrible mistake and deeply regretted it.

[8] Martin Gilbert, *The Holocaust: A History of the Jews of Europe During the Second World War* (New York 1985), p. 826.

[9] Richard Steigmann-Gall, *The Holy Reich: Nazi Conceptions of Christianity, 1919-1945* (Cambridge 2004), p. 23.

[10] Neal Bascomb's *Hunting Eichmann* (see bibliography) adds some interesting details to this obvious point. He relates that a Protestant pastor (William Hull) met with Eichmann after the death sentence had been passed In Israel and tried to persuade him to repent and believe in Christ. Eichmann insisted that there was no hell, and anyway he had not done anything wrong by following orders and serving his country. He also expressed a belief in pantheism, and stated Nietzsche and Kant had helped him to reject organized religion. Hull did get Eichmann to do some bible study, but only the New Testament—Eichmann wanted nothing to do with the "Jewish fables" of the Old Testament.

[11] Peter Viereck, *Meta-politics: The Roots of the Nazi Mind* (New York 1965), p. 289.

[12] William Tyndale, *The Obedience of a Christian Man* (London 2000), p. 130.

[13] Steigmann-Gall, p. 6.

[14] Ibid., pp. 1-2.

[15] Steven A. Katz, *The Holocaust in Historical Context (Vol. 1)* (New York/Oxford 1994), p. 234-235.

[16] Ibid., p. 226.

[17] Ibid., p. 241.

[18] Ibid., pp. 237, 239-240. In this context, Katz calls Paul's teaching "poisonous." I wonder how many Christians know that unbelievers do not merely reject the Gospel, but consider it to be venomous and harmful as well.

[19] Ibid., p. 248.

[20] Ibid., p. 243.

[21] See chapter 9 of this essay.

[22] Katz, p. 243 (footnote # 47).

[23] Matthew Henry, *Commentary on the Whole Bible*; http://www.ccel.org/h/henry/mhc2/MHC00000.HTM; accessed January 2008.

[24] Katz, p. 172.

[25] Ibid., p. 246.

[26] George Whitefield, *George Whitefield's Journals* (Edinburgh 1998), p. 351)

[27] Stuart Stein, "Individual Responsibility of Defendants: Julius Streicher," *Nuremberg Judgment*; http://www.ess.uwe.ac.uk/genocide/Streicher.htm; accessed January 2008.

[28] Werner Maser, *Hitler's Letters and Notes*, trans. Arnold Pomerans (New York 1974), p. 283.

Chapter 2. Medieval Christian anti-Semitism

Introduction

In spite of what some might dismiss as the empty theologizing of the previous chapter, the fact remains that Jews were badly treated in the Middle Ages when Christianity was dominant. They were tortured, murdered, discriminated against, sometimes even in the name of Christ. Some will therefore refuse to accept my (to them) excessively narrow definition of a Christian. They will assert (contrary to all biblical teaching) that Christians are all who designate themselves as such, irrespective of their personal beliefs and degree of seriousness about living by the teachings of Christ.

Those with this point of view will not only assert that medieval Christian anti-Semitism proves the inherently anti-Jewish nature of the New Testament; they will also argue that centuries of Christian demonization of the Jew played an indispensable part in laying the foundations for the Holocaust. The exact nature of the relationship between Christian and Nazi anti-Semitism may be debated, but the fact of some kind of relationship will be assumed as an incontrovertible fact. This common assumption is strengthened by frequent references to angry diatribes made by Christians against Jews, most notably by Chrysostom and Luther.

Outward similarities between medieval and Nazi persecutions of Jews reinforce this conclusion. In both medieval and Nazi Europe, Jews were singled out, isolated, restricted, persecuted, and killed—case closed. That there were profound differences in motive and in result is often overlooked. To analyze the differences between medieval and modern anti-Semitism, it will be necessary to look at them in some depth. For the present, it might be helpful to observe that it is possible to dislike the same thing for widely divergent and disconnected reasons.

Someone on the anti-religious left might dislike Bush because they feel he faked evidence to lead America into the Iraq war; because he doesn't care about the poor; because he doesn't care about the environment. Someone on the religious right might also dislike President Bush for a number of other reasons: failure to close America's border with Mexico; failure to stand for traditional values in spite of his talk about religion; failure to limit government spending, and so on.

It may be objected that Christian anti-Semitism preceded modern anti-Semitism for centuries and hence was foundational. At this point my analogy breaks down, as every analogy does at some point. If, however, early modern thinkers, relying on reason alone, felt that not the Jewish rejection of Christ but the very Jewish concept of God itself as expressed in the Old Testament was ugly and repulsive to reason; if 19th-century German thinkers saw the Jews as threats to racial purity or saw Christian influence on European culture as negative Jewish influence—were these only variations of a pre-existing anti-Semitism, or were they in fact something new and different? I argue that they were in fact something new and different. It is not reasonable to blame Christianity and the Bible for the excesses and abuses of those who either rejected Christianity or modified it beyond recognition.

For the present, we need to be aware of a crucial difference between medieval and modern anti-Semitism. It is striking that at no time, in many centuries of Christian dominance, was there any attempt to exterminate the entire Jewish people. This is due to far-reaching and inherent differences between the Christian and the Nazi world views. Christianity has within it numerous and deep moral restraints that were completely absent from Nazi ideology and practice. These will be examined in this chapter. This will involve not only philosophizing—a historical examination of the Jewish situation in medieval Europe will show that these restraints were operative. As a result, the Jewish experience even in the depths of the Middle Ages was not one prolonged pogrom, a protracted nightmare of unending Inquisitions, Crusades, and hatred.

For this chapter I have relied heavily on parts of Prof. Samuel Katz's *The Holocaust in Historical Context (Vol.1)*.[1] While I strongly disagree with his presuppositions and conclusions concerning the falsehood of Christianity and the inherent anti-Jewish bias of the New Testament, his overview of the medieval period contains a lot of significant information. In refuting the errors of those who claim that Naziism was the direct result of Christianity and that the Nazis were only carrying out the policies of the church, Prof. Katz shows beyond any possibility of reasonable doubt that medieval Europe was significantly different from such misconceptions of it.

After concluding the discussion of the medieval period with some comments on John Chrysostom's well-known attacks on the Jews, we can examine Martin Luther. A study of his thought and influence will demonstrate that he was very far from being the founder of modern German anti-Semitism, as some like to assert. Matthew Henry's comments on Paul's teachings on the Jews in Romans will be used to demonstrate that a traditional Protestant view of the Jews is not inherently anti-Semitic.

An analogy

If people in a refugee camp are afflicted by various diseases, these diseases could have at the same time both common and different causalities. The common causality would be the unhealthy conditions of the camp. Lack of proper nutrition and hygiene, contaminated water, bad living conditions, these could combine to create an environment in which different diseases could flourish. The differing causality would be the differing means by which diseases are transmitted—from water, from mosquitoes, from bad food, or whatever.

Nazi anti-Semitism and medieval anti-Semitism can be compared in this way. These spiritual and moral diseases derived from sin and evil in the human soul—a lack of spiritual hygiene, one might say. Conceit, arrogance, ignorance, fear, misery provide a fertile breeding ground for these and many other illnesses of the spirit. There were similarities between "Christian" and Nazi anti-Semitism, due to the fact that they derived from a common source—human sin. It is human sin that causes people to blindly serve Satan, giving rise to the long list of evils mentioned by Paul in the first chapter of Romans: wickedness, covetousness, maliciousness, envy, murder, debate, deceit, malignity. Sin makes people to be backbiters, haters of God, despiteful, proud, boasters, inventors of evil things, covenant breakers, without natural affection, implacable, unmerciful.

However, while the varieties of Jew-hatred may have a common origin in this sense, they also have their differing characteristics. Some diseases are more deadly than others, and the Nazi disease was far more deadly than anything that preceded it. They were also transmitted differently—one through grotesque distortions of biblical teachings, the other through secular philosophies. The same evil appears in different degrees in both religious and secular guises.

The Jewish experience in the Middle Ages

I consider myself exceedingly fortunate to have access to Katz's work, even though his overall purpose is very different from mine. He wants to show that medieval anti-Semitism was (a) derived from biblical teaching and (b) instrumental in laying the foundations for the Holocaust. While I disagree with both of those points, I find it exceedingly helpful that Katz gives a picture of the Jewish experience that often conflicts with prevailing stereotypes. He does not minimize Jewish suffering, but in the interests of historical accuracy and a true understanding of Naziism points out major differences between medieval and Nazi anti-Semitism.

Recognizing the obvious fact that well over a thousand years of Christian cultural domination of Europe saw no attempt to exterminate the Jews as a nation, Katz attributes this to certain restraints inherent in the Christian belief system. He elaborates on these limitations at length, and gives numerous examples to show that Jews (when they were not expelled or slaughtered) were allowed to exist, and were even protected. One source, Salo W. Baron, is quoted to show that much of the time the Jews were not treated that badly overall; that often they were better treated than the peasants; that, when tolerated, "much as it suffered from disabilities and contempt, [Jewry] still was a privileged minority in every country where it was tolerated at all." Katz expresses qualified agreement with this, saying that Baron's comments are "salient, as is his reminder that medieval Jewry did have a life other than that expressed in pogroms and despoliations." [2]

The Jews were treated badly in the Middle Ages—so were a lot of other people. Some Jews at any rate had at times better lives and more freedom than many serfs and peasants. Jews were massacred on occasion—so were others. Persecutions of the Jews are attributed to biblical teachings—to what shall we attribute the persecutions of the Albigensians and the Waldensians, or the ravages of the Vikings and the Mongols, not to mention the countless wars in which the Europeans slaughtered each other with gusto when they were all supposedly united spiritually under the Church of Rome? It is not as if the Jews alone suffered while the rest of the Europeans enjoyed lives of comfort and liberty.

Demonstrating a striking degree of scholarly objectivity for someone who rejects the Christian message as false and believes that Christianity did contribute significantly toward the Holocaust, Katz provides other information that conflicts with popular misconceptions. In an earlier chapter he states that approximately 2% of the Jewish population in Europe perished during the Crusades.[3] He refers in the same place to the very small number of Jews killed during the Inquisition, and further admits that Jewish communities in Europe flourished during certain periods.[4] That the Jews during parts of the Middle Ages achieved a level of prosperity and cultural achievement will surprise some who think that Christians did nothing but slaughter Jews throughout the whole period.

Katz's purpose here is not to defend Christianity, and there are details in his book of massacres, tortures, and forced conversions. His purpose is to avoid comparisons of the Holocaust with other events which were significantly different. That the majority of Jews living in "Christian" Europe were allowed to live is attributed to moral restraints in Christianity.[5] Certain aspects of Christian teaching precluded the establishment of an Auschwitz in medieval Europe.

Christian limitations

The Nazi death camps were characterized by complete lawlessness, by a total lack of moral restraint. More than this, not only were restraints abandoned, but moral values were totally reversed. Brutality, cruelty, and indifference to suffering were counted virtues, while kindness and mercy were considered vices. This re-evaluation of values was considered to be simply living according to nature—as Hitler wrote in *Mein Kampf*, Nature looks on "calmly" and "with satisfaction" as "the weak and sickly" succumb in the struggle for survival [vol. I chapt. 11].

That these and other ideas essential to the death camps could not and did not arise during the Middle Ages is due to numerous aspects of Christian teaching. Apart from the beliefs that man was not in nature and at one with the animals as the Nazis claimed, but was above nature and apart from the animals; and that the creation, being merely God's handiwork, was subordinate to higher spiritual values rather than being the source of values, we can identify several important areas of Christian doctrine, all of them referred to by Katz, that radically separate medieval "Christian" anti-Semitism from Nazi anti-Semitism. They are: (a) concepts of the Jews; (b) concepts of government; and (c) moral doctrines.

Concepts of the Jews

In discussions of this topic we are constantly treated to quotes from Chrysostom showing how much Christians hated Jews. We are almost never given quotations from Augustine to provide a more complete and accurate picture. Katz, unlike some, has studied Augustine's writings, and finds four important ideas about the Jews that (he recognizes) were much more normative for the medieval church than the angry and hostile denunciations of Chrysostom.[6]

These ideas of Augustine's are: (i) the future restoration to God's favor of the Jews as a nation; (ii) their continuing existence in exile under God's displeasure a proof of Christian doctrine; (iii) their fall from grace mysteriously a spiritual benefit to the Gentiles; and (iv) having received a mark like the mark of Cain from God as punishment for their murder of Christ, the Jews are, also like Cain, not to be killed (Genesis 4:15). A fifth point not related to Augustine but mentioned by Bernard of Clairvaux has to do with respect for Jews as the people of the prophets and the Messiah.

The first of these, the future restoration of the Jews, is I believe a sound biblical principle—but even if I am mistaken and it is not, it still prohibits any thought of exterminating all of Jewry if sincerely believed. If the Jews will be restored to God's favor in the future, killing them is not desirable—it is in fact a sinful and wicked goal designed to frustrate God's redemptive plan. Incidentally, the belief that the New Testament teaches the future salvation of the Jews as a nation, and that God is reserving them for a further purpose, is one reason why the speculation that Christians are bewildered by the continued existence of the Jews is totally groundless. Many Christians, including myself, consider the survival of the Jewish people to be not a problem for or an affront to the Christian faith, but the direct result of God's higher and hidden purpose.

The second point, that the suffering of the Jews under God's displeasure is a proof of scripture, partly relates to a prophecy of Moses. He wrote that if the Jews angered God sufficiently he would expel them from the land and deliver them into the hands of their enemies (Deuteronomy 28:63-68). Jewish history subsequent to the destruction of Israel by the Romans could understandably be interpreted by Christians as a fulfillment of Moses' prophecy. As to the Jews confirming the reality of Christianity by their exile and suffering (these being signs of God's disfavor), that seems to be an argument of questionable value.

The third point is from Paul's teaching in Romans which we have already looked at briefly: "through their fall salvation is come unto the Gentiles" (11:11). One possible explanation is this: if the Jews as a nation had turned to Christ, they would have followed Christ's teaching of non-resistance to the Romans. There would have been no rebellions, and hence no destruction and expulsion. The Jews would have remained in the land, and they would have remained as believers.

Human nature being what it is, it would have been impossible for the Jews to avoid looking upon themselves, and for the Gentiles to avoid looking on them, as some kind of a spiritual elite. The Gentiles and the Jews could never have become truly one in Christ. By falling away, the Jews made it possible for the Gentiles to enter completely into the fullness of Christ's spiritual blessings, and when the Jews as a nation return to Christ, their centuries of unbelief will make it easier for them (and for us) to recognize that salvation is solely due to God's election and grace.

The fourth point, about the mark of Cain, seems more speculative. Repentance and forgiveness were not offered to Cain, as they were to the Jews; also, it isn't recorded that all of Cain's descendants were permanently marked, so Augustine's reasoning may be weak here. Yet, as Katz concedes in discussing this point, Augustine didn't advocate killing Jews.[7] The fifth point is that the Jews are to be given respect as the nation through whom God shed his light into the world through Moses, the prophets, and finally the Messiah.

As disagreeable as such beliefs are to many Jews, they helped to make it possible for the Jews as a nation to survive.[8] I strongly disagree with Katz's belief that these teachings represent Christian hatred, and that Augustine must be included in the list of patristic Jew-haters. This presupposes that the Bible is false. As to medieval concepts of the Jews as uniquely evil, or in a special relationship with the devil, they are vastly different from modern racial anti-Semitic arguments about Jews as a threat to racial purity. Even if some tie can be made between them—for example, by saying that modern racial anti-Semitism was a mutation of the traditional religious form, and derived its existence from the pre-existing religious form—that still does not reflect adversely on the New Testament which presents a totally different concept of evil and of human sin.

We have already seen in chapter one that biblical concepts of sin and evil do not include medieval fantasies, and are in fact far removed from them. Katz, who feels that the identification of the Jew with the devil comes from the New Testament, admits that this did not become widespread until late in the Middle Ages, even as late as the sixteenth century.[9] He also says that anti-Jewish uprisings increased considerably in the year 1000,[10] and that the first recorded instance of the charge of desecration of the host did not appear until 1234.[11] That something supposedly inherent in the New Testament took a thousand years and more to become fully developed should say a great deal.

Christian doctrinal criticisms of Judaism

If the Torah is true, God cast the Jews out of the land and scattered them abroad, delivering them into the hands of their enemies because of his anger. Does this indicate hatred of Jews, to take Moses literally? Also, if someone specifically says that Jews should not be harmed, that Christians should not have Jewish blood on their hands because God still has a purpose for them, that to me is not hatred. False and wicked people with the name but not the spirit of Christians may think they should execute God's wrath on the Jews, but it is a mistake to link any and every doctrinal disagreement between Christianity and Judaism to the Holocaust. Christians and Christianity are frequently criticized, and this is only to be expected. Many people do not believe in its teachings and find fault with them, and Christians do not object to this. If a Jew says "Jesus was not the Messiah, he did not die on the cross for the sins of mankind or rise from the dead," this is not "hatred." Similarly, if someone disagrees with Jewish doctrines for faith reasons, this is not evidence of "hatred."

If, on the other hand, the Torah is not true and there was no real covenant between God and the Jews at all, then the expulsion from the land had nothing to do with God's anger, and Moses' words have no meaning at all. What does that do to Judaism? "The Torah is a fiction, a collection of myths and folk-tales, Moses never said those things, or, if he did, he was mistaken"—isn't this the deepest possible nullification of Judaism? Isn't that far more contemptuous of Judaism than saying "The Jews have angered God by their unbelief so that he has cast them out of the land, but he is mindful of his covenant with Abraham and will restore them to his favor in the end through faith in Christ"? Christians who hope for the conversion of the Jews are accused of wanting to destroy Judaism, even of wanting to eliminate the Jews by means of a spiritual "Final Solution"—but what of those who say "God did not appear to Moses on Sinai"? Are not they the ones who destroy Judaism?

Concepts of government

Apart from Christian teachings about the Jews (which by the way presupposed their full humanity), a second limitation on the virulence of medieval anti-Semitism wholly lacking in the Nazi period had to do with concepts of government. That the law should be totally centered in the person of the Fuhrer who alone decided what was right is something that never could have happened and never did happen in the many centuries before the modern period. The beliefs that governments themselves were subject to a higher law, and that they were ordained by God for the purpose of restraining evil rather than for the purpose of doing evil—these were of course never fully realized during the Middle Ages. They were, however, recognized and often acted upon, even striven for. That the power of the government was in fact used to restrain evil against the Jews rather than to encourage it will be demonstrated shortly. We have already referred to the Hep riots, which show the beneficent results of more traditional views of government at work in Germany early in the 19th century. That was before the full onslaught of modernism in Germany had totally destroyed traditional ideas of government and replaced them with new theories.

The biblical view of government is poles apart from that of the notorious German "philosopher" Hegel, who is not only well-known for his contribution to the rise of Marxism, but has also been identified by some as one of the progenitors of modern fascism. He felt that the state was an instrument used by the World Spirit to guide mankind to higher levels of freedom and progress. Hence, true freedom was found in obedience to the state. In Hegel's words:

> All the worth which the human being possesses, all spiritual reality, he possesses only through the State . . . the Universal is to be found in the State, in its laws, its universal and rational arrangements. The State is the Divine Idea as it exists on earth.[12]

> . . . the genuine, absolute, final end (is) the sovereignty of the state . . . the means to this end is the sacrifice of personal actuality . . . a self sacrifice which yet is the real existence of one's freedom; the maximum self-subsistence of individuality, yet only as a cog playing its part in the mechanism of an external organization; absolute obedience, renunciation of personal opinions and reasonings, in fact complete absence of mind . . .[13]

Biblical freedom is individual, personal, and in matters of faith beyond the power of the state. In the words of Alcide de Gasperi, who formed Italy's first post-war government in 1945 and had an intimate knowledge of fascism, "The theoretical and practical principles of fascism are the antithesis of the Christian concept of the State, which lays down that the natural rights of personality, family, and society exist before the State."[14]

Moral doctrines

Traditional Christianity not only presented a concept of the state that was antithetical to modern totalitarianism. It also had a deep and profound moral code. This did not eliminate evil from the world, but it did provide a significant check that was abandoned by modern secularists and free-thinkers. Katz writes in the conclusion to the first volume of his work that medieval Christianity did have a moral code that prevented the emergence of Nazi-like philosophy.[15]

Katz makes the common mistake of confusing "Christian" civilization, composed of many people who never received the Spirit of Christ and never made a real effort to follow Christ's teachings, with Christianity itself, as expressed in the New Testament. Writing in unbelief, he claims that much evil has derived from biblical teachings themselves—but many people who do believe in the Bible and sincerely try to live by it think very differently.

Nevertheless, in spite of his bitterness against Christianity and his common failure to distinguish between those who seriously try to live by Christ's teachings on the one hand and those on the other hand who ignore those teachings and trample them underfoot, Katz does recognize that Christian moral teachings about right conduct mitigated the plight of Jews in the Middle Ages. He refers to Christian prohibitions against murder, and to teachings that Christians should show love and forgiveness even to Jews.[16] He might also have mentioned the fear of God and the day of judgment. One of the foundational truths of biblical (as opposed to cultural) Christianity is that the soul lives after death and will appear before God to give an account on the day of judgment. We will be judged not merely for our actions and our words, but even for the secret thoughts of our hearts (Romans 2:16).

Those of us who take this seriously can make many mistakes, even serious ones, but we can not torture, murder, and kill in frenzies of hate. Countless Christians have sincerely if fallibly followed New Testament teachings about kindness, love, and forgiveness toward others. Countless Christians have never harmed a Jew or anyone else. They also should be included in evaluations of Christianity. Those who do torture and kill in the name of Christ will receive a heavier judgment and a severer penalty than ordinary unbelievers.

These and the above mentioned concepts were not merely theories in medieval society but constituted real limits that many Christians seriously sought to follow.[17] To substantiate this assertion Katz gives numerous examples—again, not to defend Christianity (which he has a grudge against), but to avoid obscuring a real understanding of the Holocaust by misleading comparisons.

The restraints in practice

When Christians ignore the Bible and directly violate its teachings, they are held up as examples of how bad Christianity is. When Christians do live by the Bible, even if imperfectly, and live quiet lives harming no one, they are ignored. So many Christians in the Middle Ages never went on a Crusade, never were involved with the Inquisition, never killed anyone—and their names are lost to history. Christianity's historical record can be made to look very sordid indeed if the most attention is given to those that persistently flout its foundational concepts.

There are some historical records that shed a more positive light on medieval Christianity and, unlike some scholars, Katz had the integrity to look at them. Looking first at the political rulers of medieval Europe, we find that chapter 7 of Katz's book contains too many examples of justice and fair dealing accorded to Jews to repeat fully. There were so many such examples that Katz was led to the conclusion that violent attacks on the Jews (in the Crusader period at least) came from below, from the grass roots, and were not planned from above by church or political authorities.[18]

The vicious and devilish brutality of the Inquisition was of course directed from above, but it not only persecuted Moslems and Protestants as well as Jews—it also never had the aim of simply massacring Jews.[19] It was the result of a false concept of the church that was entirely divorced from the New Testament and had nothing to do with biblical Christianity.

Government protection of Jews

A lengthy historical analysis is beyond the scope of this essay. Some examples of attempts by government to control the frenzy of mobs—composed no doubt of large numbers of people who couldn't even read, and if they did had no understanding of Romans or I Corinthians—is necessary, however.

The Emperor Henry IV was angered at attacks on the Jews and gave them royal protection, commanding that they not be harmed, and even that they be helped and given refuge.[20] King Stephen of England (1135-1154) protected the Jews, and one Count Otto of Burgundy, brother of Holy Roman Emperor Henry VI, punished the city of Speyer for anti-Jewish acts. The city was besieged and partly destroyed. A large sum of money was taken from the culprits and turned over to the Jews for the rebuilding of their homes and synagogues.[21]

Louis IX of France placed limits on the Jews, yet also placed them under royal protection. Richard I of England responded severely to an attack on the Jews of York that took place while he was in France. His chancellor, William de Longchamp, was sent to punish the criminals. He dismissed the sheriff and other officials for failing to prevent the attack and fined a number of citizens—the mob leaders fled to Scotland. Louis VII of France rejected false accusations against the Jews, and the Emperor Frederic I stated that whoever harmed a Jew should have his hand cut off, and further decreed that "Anyone who kills a Jew shall be killed."[22] This same emperor (Barbarossa) also outlawed all anti-Jewish sermons. Some German Jews were able to find shelter in the castles of German noblemen during the Crusades, and Katz gives a list of emperors and kings who officially exonerated Jews of false accusations against them.[23]

This brief overview omits many other facts and matters of interpretation. The point is made by Katz that financial self-interest may have influenced certain kings and nobles; it is also pointed out that good intentions and proclamations were not sufficient to prevent many acts of violence that did occur. The few examples given above, however, do indicate that while some completely ignored Christian principles and trampled them underfoot, others did not. The latter should be held up as examples of Christianity, not the former.

The Crusades

At this point, before looking at the policies and practices of the church, a few comments about the Crusades might be in order. The attempts to recapture the "holy" land from the infidels had no basis in the Bible. In Christ's own time the land was controlled by infidels, and Christ taught complete cooperation with them. This explains why in the last five centuries or so of Christianity no one has said "Oh! The Holy Land is controlled by infidel Turks or unbelieving Israelis. Let's conquer it." The fact that the church has considerably less power also has something to do with that, which is fine, as the New Testament never envisioned a powerful state church launching armies of plunder and conquest.

When the Pope said that the Crusades were God's will he was mistaken. The fact that the 4th Crusade never even reached the Holy Land but degenerated into the criminal plundering of Constantinople says a lot about the spiritual quality of the Crusades. It has also been speculated that the Pope encouraged the Crusades as a means of extending papal power into the region, which may or may not be the case.

One point worth mentioning was made by Katz in response to the idea that the Crusaders could be compared to the Nazi extermination squads, the *Einsatzgruppen*. He pointed out that the massacre of Jews in Jerusalem during the First Crusade was not a matter of consistent policy, and noted that such acts were not perpetrated in other areas that the Crusaders passed through on their way to Jerusalem.[24]

The Church of Rome and the Jews

The subject of the church's policy toward the Jews is also a vast one. As a Protestant, I have no personal need to defend the Church of Rome and don't find it difficult to say that this or that church teaching or practice was misguided or contrary to scripture. However, when it comes to equating Christianity with Naziism, I was glad to find that there is more than ample historical documentation to support the contention that medieval anti-Semitism was significantly different from Nazi anti-Semitism. At no time did the church attempt to carry out a policy aimed at exterminating all of the Jews. The official policy of the church was toleration, or expulsion, or conversion—not extermination. Quoting Joshua Trachtenberg, Katz states that the church's policy was for Jews to be "tolerated on humanitarian grounds, and indeed preserved on theological grounds."[25]

As is the case with instances of just behaviour and even virtue on the part of medieval rulers, Katz's analysis of the church contains too many examples for me to cite more than a small percentage of them. Some examples of the church's attempts to show charity to the Jews are as follows. Innocent III, referring to a massacre of Jews, wrote to King Louis IX condemning the crime and demanding that the murderers be punished.[26] He stated that it was forbidden for Christians to murder Jews, and used two of the reasons given earlier: that the Jews will be redeemed in the end, and that the Jews were the people of the prophets who prepared the way for Christ.

One papal bull, known as the *Sicut judaeis*, stated that Christian morality obligated the church to protect the Jews. This proclamation was issued 22 times over some hundreds of years.[27] Its frequent reissuing was, I suppose, occasioned by the fact that it was often ignored. The church was not a modern state and its power, while great, was limited.

Benedict XII strongly condemned the practice of forced baptism (which was never official church policy) and also condemned the killing or injuring of Jews, as well as stealing from them.[28] Innocent IV rejected the charge of ritual murder and other fables, and condemned violations of the Jewish right to trial and fair judgment. He also sent a bull to the archbishop of Vienna, protesting cruelties and injustices done to the Jews, and saying that the Jews should be given compensation for the wrongs done to them and allowed to live unhampered.[29]

Other examples of official statements could be given, but this is more than a matter of declarations. There were also individuals who did what they could to help Jews. They show not the violence and cruelty but the sense of justice and mercy that is inherent in all truly biblical Christianity. Bishop Jean of Speyer protected Jews, as did the archbishops of Mainz and Cologne. Various counts, bishops, and archbishops sought to protect Jews, even risking their lives to do so. The archbishop of Cologne and the bishop of Trier had to flee for their lives when their attempts to protect Jews incurred the wrath of the mob.[30]

Bernard of Clairvaux wrote during the Second Crusade that Jews should not be persecuted or killed, referring to Paul's teaching of the future redemption of the Jews. He also referred to the Jews as the people of Christ and the first Christians. Moreover, he did not merely issue statements but actively worked to help and protect Jews. A contemporary Hebrew chronicle quoted at length by Katz cites Rabbi Ephraim of Bonn to show how Bernard's personal intervention helped to save the lives of Jews. That the Jews on this occasion also handed over a large sum of money is illustrative of the fact that financial considerations were at times involved, not merely spiritual ones.[31]

Katz comes to the conclusion that the great majority of Jews in Medieval Europe were able to survive because—unlike the Nazis—the European religious and political leadership did not have a policy of slaughtering Jews.[32] Statements that the Nazis were just following the polices of the church are the result not only of bias against Christianity, but also of ignorance of history

John Chrysostom

Ordinary and decent medieval Christians who sought to lead "a quiet and peaceable life in all godliness and honesty" (I Timothy 2:2) are forgotten, but someone like John Chrysostom (347?-407) whose attacks on the Jews can be used to blacken the reputation of Christianity is famous throughout the world. His name and quotations from him constantly appear wherever Jewish-Christian relations are discussed, and his angry, bitter, hostile attacks on the Jews have gained him a lot of notoriety.

Since his words have been so widely used to demonstrate the inherent hostility of Christianity toward Judaism, it is necessary to examine them briefly. His *Eight Orations Against the Jews* are a gold mine for those eager to discredit Christianity—and, if they were in fact the result of biblical teaching, they prove conclusively that Christianity is an ugly religion of hatred and bigotry. Of course, if they do not reflect biblical teaching but are in fact a direct denial of many plain teachings and of the examples of the apostles—but let us examine some of his comments first.

To paraphrase, he has been quoted as saying that the synagogue was a curse, worse than a whorehouse, a den of criminals, a fortress of the devil, and a pit of destruction; that the Jews sacrificed their children to the devil and were worse than beasts, lower than animals, knowing nothing except to get drunk, fight, and kill each other; that they were the assassins of Christ; that he hated the Jews and that it was the duty of all Christians to hate the Jews. These are some of the statements that are frequently bandied about.

One Gregory of Nyssa has also been similarly quoted. It seems he saw the Jews as the murderers of Christ and of the prophets, enemies of God, vipers. A certain Hippolytus, whoever he was, asserted that the Jews were in everlasting darkness, with no hope—if the quote is accurate—of future redemption.

Attempts to find some reasonable defense or explanation for Chrysostom's comments were unsuccessful. It appears that we will have to let his comments stand as they are, though I would welcome more information that might mitigate or qualify these statements—statements that would be very embarrassing and troublesome to me as a Christian and would effectively serve to link Christianity to anti-Semitism and hence to National Socialism, were it not for the fact that they are totally contrary to biblical Christianity. They are not scriptural, but rather are a deviation from the message of Christ and the apostles. They are contrary to plain biblical teaching and reveal an unChristlike spirit.

To demonstrate this, it will be necessary first to look at the lives and the teachings of the apostles. Chrysostom's tone and attitude were not theirs. Secondly, we can look at Christ's denunciations of the Pharisees—it will be easy to point out fundamental differences between those and the attacks of Chrysostom. Then it will be possible to speculate on the motives of those who felt led to attack the Jews so bitterly in complete defiance of principles of Christian love. By the way, the significance of Chrysostom has been vastly overestimated. If he had not provided such excellent ammunition for those who want to attack Christianity, few outside of the Orthodox tradition (except for scholars of church history or theologians) would have heard of him. He was not an influential figure in the development of Western Christianity.

The apostles' attitudes toward the Jews

When Peter in the first sermon at Pentecost spoke to those who had been directly involved in the death of Christ, he did not bring a railing and angry accusation against them. He told them of their sin and guilt in no uncertain terms—but in one single sentence, and that very plainly, without rhetorical flourishes (Acts 2:23). After that, he spoke of the resurrection of Christ, and the hope of salvation. He then offered them repentance and eternal life. Salvation, gladness, hope, joy, the promise of the Holy Spirit—this was the substance of his message, not "vipers, demons, snakes, devils, pigs."

When the apostles were first brought before the high priest, the elders, and the scribes, Peter plainly said that they had killed Christ, this in less than one sentence, but then spoke of the resurrection of Christ and salvation through his name. When the apostles were called before the council a second time, once again they say to the priest and the council that they had killed Jesus, again in less than one sentence. Then they move on instantly to God's exaltation of Christ, repentance, and forgiveness of sins.

After this, the apostles are beaten and they depart from the council—and what does the Bible say? That they departed muttering angrily about the wicked Jews, murderers of Christ? No, it says "they departed from the presence of the council, rejoicing that they were counted worthy to suffer shame for his name" (Acts 5:41).

That was a response of men who knew about forgiveness and eternal life. Later in Acts, Paul was attacked by a Jewish mob that tried to kill him. After being rescued by Roman soldiers he still tried to communicate with the mob, and shared with them his experience of Christ. When he was rejected by one synagogue he went to another. He repeatedly went to synagogues, which would have earned him the wrath of Chrysostom I suppose.

Paul did make negative comments about Jews in I Thessalonians 2:14-16 that have already been referred to. As was said before, he says to the Thessalonians that as the Jewish Christians have suffered from the Jews, they also have suffered the same from their own countrymen. This highlights the basic teaching that Jews and Gentiles are all under sin.

Stephen at his trial also made no hostile diatribes. He did say three negative verses about his accusers and soon-to-be executioners, but saying that someone is "stiffnecked and uncircumcised," along with his other comments, is a pretty mild and restrained response to a crowd that is about to subject a man to a cruel death for his religious beliefs. He did say that they were the murderers of Christ—he was speaking to people who had been directly involved.

Further study reveals that in dealing with the problems of the church, the apostles found other things more important than "the Jews." Hebrews speaks of those who "crucify to themselves the Son of God afresh, and put him to an open shame" (6:6). To whom is this referring? To the wicked and evil Jews? No, it refers to people who have experienced the truth of Christianity and then turned away and rejected it. Paul speaks of people who are "guilty of the body and blood of the Lord" (I Corinthians 11:27). To whom is he referring? To the Jews? No, to those who partake of communion unworthily.

In I Corinthians Paul also warns Christians not to keep company with certain types of people. Again, to whom is he referring? To the Jews? He specifically says we are allowed to keep company with unbelievers, but should avoid those who have the name of Christian but are evildoers (5:11). Peter and John also in their letters are more concerned with people who corrupt the church by introducing false teachings than they are with the Jews. I John says "He that committeth sin is of the devil" (3:8), not "Jews are of the devil."

Concerning Christ's highly negative comments about the Pharisees, it is highly significant that the apostles never emulated them. Christ had a unique authority, and a power no other man has ever possessed. When someone can walk on water or heal the eyes of a man blind from birth, then perhaps they might be qualified to emulate Christ in this respect—and, again, it is plain that Jesus was for the most part speaking directly to the Pharisees, not to the entire Jewish nation. I say "for the most part" because prophecies about the coming destruction of Israel have a broader application. Also, Christ's denunciations of the Pharisees could be applied to many leaders in the Christian church today.

Chrysostom's motive

While it is difficult to speculate over so many centuries, I suspect that in his denunciations Chrysostom probably thought that he was emulating Christ and also the Old Testament prophets—but the Old Testament prophets did not have the resurrection of Christ, the forgiveness of sins, and the gift of eternal life to offer. They were called for a different purpose. Christians, if they point out sins at all, should do so to the world equally, in a spiritual way, and at the same time offering the hope of forgiveness. Christ also rebuked the world for sin. We are to be as much like him as we can, but love and grace indicate to us the limits that the apostles never crossed, and we should not cross either.

Concerning the denunciations of Israel by the prophets, many of them are quite severe. When something like them is found in Chrysostom, it is instantly linked to the Nazis and the Holocaust. For example, Ezekiel said that the Jews polluted God's holy name with their idols and that Israel was the sister of Sodom. Reference is made to their whoredom and their filthiness, to their sacrificing their children to idols and to their being worse than the nations around them. They are spiritual whores who have abandoned the Lord and stumble over their iniquities. Their prophets are vain and foolish and speak lies. They desecrate the Lord's temple and God will pour his anger and fury upon them.

Jeremiah said that the prophets and priests were profane, and that the land was defiled with the blood of innocents. The Jews were stiffnecked, their houses were full of deceit, they had betrayed the Lord. Israel was a harlot, a whore, an adulteress. The Jews killed the prophets and could be compared to beasts like the camel and the donkey. In Lamentations Jeremiah said that God had rejected the Jews and exalted her enemies, that Israel was naked and filthy. Isaiah calls the Jews a seed of evildoers, a sinful nation that is full of putrefying sores. God hates their feasts and is tired of them, their offerings are vain and their meetings are iniquity.

Of course, Isaiah and the other prophets did not only denounce the Jews. They also offered many beautiful words of hope and encouragement, and promises of forgiveness. In the prophets, wrath is tempered with mercy—but Christians are not called to be Old Testament prophets, thundering denunciations which (unlike

65

those of the prophets) proceed from human anger rather than from God. Christians are entrusted with the gospel of reconciliation, and we have already seen how the apostles were more concerned with forgiveness and eternal life than they were with angry denunciations, even when talking directly to the people that had been personally involved in the death of Christ.

It is for this reason that Paul writes: ". . . the servant of the Lord must not strive; but be gentle unto all men, apt to teach, patient, In meekness instructing those that oppose themselves; if God peradventure will give them repentance to the acknowledging of the truth." Moreover, Paul also says that Christians should not boast against the Jews and be high and mighty in dealing with them. We are warned that if God broke the Jews off of the olive tree and grafted us in, we also can be broken off, and will be broken off, if we do not continue in God's goodness. To say that we should hate the Jews is, biblically speaking, a lie and a false teaching.

It should be pointed out that Chrysostom's denunciations of Christians who visited Jewish homes and synagogues and even took part in the Passover with Jews show that several centuries after Christ some Christians at any rate did maintain good relations with Jews—odd, if hatred of Jews is the important biblical teaching that some claim. Also, do proud and angry attacks devoid of love and Christian understanding have anything to do with the emergence of the state church? A powerful state church was something not taught by Christ or the apostles, and changed the church from the community of believers it was meant to be into an attractive career for prideful and ambitious men, or for men docile and subservient to the powers that be.

At any rate, it will suffice I hope to conclude with the words of a man more genuinely spiritual than Chrysostom:

> Though I speak with the tongues of men and of angels, and have not charity, I am become as sounding brass, or a tinkling cymbal.
> And though I have the gift of prophecy, and understand all mysteries, and all knowledge; and though I have all faith, so that I could remove mountains, and have not charity, I am nothing. (I Corinthians)

Martin Luther

It is the fashion nowadays to speak of the Renaissance and the so-called Enlightenment as the bases of modern Western civilization. This neglect of the Reformation is a bad mistake, and reveals not only anti-religious bias, but also a profound misconception of history. There were many factors that contributed to the breakup of Medieval Europe—one of the most significant was the extraordinary impact of Martin Luther. His bold and heroic defiance of the papacy; his statements that the Roman Church did not deserve blind obedience; his emphasis on liberty of conscience and individual interpretation of scripture—these were revolutionary, and contributed much more to the emergence of modern civilization than did the witticisms of Voltaire or the paintings of Raphael. In France, the "Enlightenment" quickly led to social collapse, massacres, tyranny, and war. In Germany it led to new and unhealthy concepts of the state, the nation, and the Jews unknown in previous centuries. The Reformation, on the other hand, contributed greatly (along with other factors) to the slow and steady growth of prosperity and democracy throughout much of Europe.

Luther also did a great deal to rescue the church from the medieval corruptions of Rome. His insights into scripture were and are profound, and contributed greatly to the revival of the church. Martin Luther is a man for whom I and many other Christians have deep affection and respect, even as we recognize and deplore his various faults and errors. People who are oblivious to the positive aspects of the Reformation and do not understand Luther's dramatic contribution to the spiritual and (indirectly) to the political liberty which characterized the countries under Reformation influence will never be able to evaluate him objectively.

Yet, Luther had his flaws. One of these was the conventional religious anti-Semitism that he lapsed into towards the end of his life. In his old age, he forgot Christian charity and lashed out against the Jews in bitterness that has reflected badly on the spiritual values he had championed in better days. It would have been good if he could have remembered a few Bible verses, such as " . . . the wrath of man works not the righteousness of God" (James 1:20), or:

> But the tongue can no man tame; it is an unruly evil, full of deadly poison.
> Therewith bless we God, even the Father; and therewith curse we men, which are made after the similitude of God.
> Out of the same mouth proceedeth blessing and cursing. My brethren, these things ought not so to be.
> Doth a fountain send forth at the same place sweet water and bitter? (James 3:8-11).[33]

Luther is vastly more significant for this discussion than Chrysostom. Not only was he a German, praised by Hitler and the Nazis as a hero, but he was also the founder of Protestantism. As such he is still considered by many, including this writer, to have been a deeply spiritual man. His attacks on the Jews written toward the end of his life hence serve as a powerful argument to show that (a) Christianity is inherently and inevitably anti-Semitic and (b) Naziism was derived from or at least influenced by Christianity.

Luther's most important Reformation works, such as *The 95 Theses*, *Address to the Christian Nobility*, *The Babylonian Captivity of the Church*, *Preface to Romans*, *Bondage of the Will*, and others, do not show an excessive preoccupation with Jews. He was much more concerned with preaching basic biblical doctrines and reforming medieval abuses of the church than he was with the Jews, and the idea that he was obsessed with the Jews all of his life is a falsehood. Parenthetically, commenting on Paul's Letter to the Romans and discussing the concepts of Jews contained in that book does not constitute evidence of an "obsession."

Anti-Semitism had nothing to do with Luther's main goals, and his most widely quoted statements about Jews did not come until the end of his life. Moreover, it is necessary to point out—though it shouldn't be—what Luther did not believe about the Jews. He did not believe that they were plotting to control the world, or that they were a threat to the purity of the Aryan master race. Luther was not a modern nationalist, and believed that any genuine French, Italian, Polish or Jewish Christian was spiritually one with the body of Christ apart from racial considerations—the emphasis on race being a modern invention. Hitler's main concerns were totally foreign to Luther.

In support of claims that Luther had a life-long hostility to Jews, earlier comments of his are pointed to that sound bad when misleadingly applied only to Jews, but in fact are general biblical teachings that apply equally to the entire human race. The Jews are under God's condemnation for sin? So is mankind in general (Romans 3:9-12,19). The Jews resist God's grace by rejecting Christ? So did (in Luther's view) the Turks, the Papists, and the radical Protestant sects. Jewish denials of Christ are lies? If the New Testament is true, all denials of its fundamental teachings are false, no matter where they come from or how sincerely they might be believed. God will not hear the prayers of Jews who try to justify themselves by keeping the rules? Neither will he hear the prayers of others, including Christians, who feel that their goodness entitles them to God's favor, or that their Christianity entitles them to ignore Christ's teachings.

If Luther had stopped writing a few years earlier his name would not figure so prominently in these discussions. He wrote a couple of tracts against the Jews, but only one is routinely quoted—*On the Jews and Their Lies*.[34] This unfortunate work contains an often quoted passage saying that the Jews should be persecuted. He advocated burning their synagogues and forcing them to do manual labor, as well as other repressive measures. There is another passage from the same section of the tract (Section 12) which I have never seen quoted anywhere else. It says:

> But what will happen even if we do burn down the Jews' synagogues and forbid them publicly to praise God, to pray, to teach, to utter God's name? They will still keep doing it in secret. If we know that they are doing this in secret, it is the same as if they were doing it publicly. For our knowledge of their secret doings and our toleration of them implies that they are not secret after all, and thus our conscience is encumbered with it before God. So let us beware. In my opinion the problem must be resolved thus: If we wish to wash our hands of the Jews' blasphemy and not share in their guilt, we have to part company with them. They must be driven from our country. Let them think of their fatherland; then they need no longer wail and lie before God against us that we are holding them captive, nor need we then any longer complain that they are burdening us with their blasphemy and their usury. This is the most natural and the best course of action, which will safe guard the interest of both parties.

Luther said, in effect, "The Jews should be persecuted . . . No, that wouldn't accomplish anything. They should be expelled." Why is it that we are incessantly treated to the first part but not the second?

That Luther advocated expulsion is clear from other comments in the tract:

> . . . In addition, no one is holding them here now. The country and the roads are open for them to proceed to their land whenever they wish. If they did so, we would be glad to present

gifts to them on the occasion; it would be good riddance . . . But if the authorities are reluctant to use force and restrain the Jews' devilish wantonness, the latter should, as we said, be expelled from the country and be told to return to their land and their possessions in Jerusalem . . .

This was unChristian and wrong, but it is not nearly as bad as what Luther is accused of. Moreover, it would have prevented the Holocaust. It is not a call for the destruction of Judaism.

Comments elsewhere in the tract that make it sound as if Luther advocated killing Jews need to be understood in this context. Luther's deepest desire for the Jews was their conversion, not their extermination. This is why he says at the end of his tract, "May Christ, our dear Lord, convert them mercifully and preserve us steadfastly and immovably in the knowledge of him, which is eternal life." In the first paragraph of the tract Luther states that the conversion of the Jews is an impossibility, but he later contradicts himself completely:

> Whenever a Jew is sincerely converted, he should be handed one hundred, two hundred, or three hundred florins, as personal circumstances may suggest. With this he could set himself up in some occupation for the support of his poor wife and children . .
> .
>
> . . . Burgensis, who was one of their very learned rabbis, and who through the grace of God became a Christian a very rare happening is much agitated by the fact that they curse us Christians so vilely in their synagogues . . .

Such blatant inconsistencies are not representative of Luther in his prime, and are indications of a mind that was losing its grip.

It is too easy to read these tracts looking backward from the Holocaust. The horrors of the modern scientific age were unimaginable in Luther's time, and the Nazis operated from a mindset vastly different from Luther's—though they found some of his quotes useful for propaganda purposes. In understanding the Nazis, the worst possible construction can and should be put on their statements; but when Luther says that usurers should be hanged, and Jews are usurers, syllogistic reasoning—ergo, the Jews should be hanged—can read a bloodthirsty intentionality into Luther's words that was never manifested by bloody acts in the entire course of his life. He was writing emotionally, not syllogistically. If Luther had really wanted to say "Kill the Jews" he could have done so many times over the years, but did not.

Katz, who criticizes Luther severely, even harshly, also shows evidence that Luther did not view the Jews as the Nazis viewed them. He quotes one passage from Luther saying that Jews should not be harmed. In another, Luther states that money gained by the Jews from usury should be taken from them and used to maintain old and sick Jews, as well as Jews who have converted to Christianity.[35] He quotes Luther yet again stating that Christians should have compassion on the Jews and try to save them, but not take vengeance against them.

Another passage from *On the Jews and Their Lies* might seem like an incitement to killing, yet can be read another way:

I wish and I ask that our rulers who have Jewish subjects exercise a sharp mercy toward these wretched people, as suggested above, to see whether this might not help (though it is doubtful). They must act like a good physician who, when gangrene has set proceeds without mercy to cut, saw, and burn flesh, veins, bone, and marrow. Such a procedure must also be followed in this instance. Burn down their synagogues, forbid all that I enumerated earlier, force them to work, and deal harshly with them, as Moses did in the wilderness, slaying three thousand lest the whole people perish.

Removal of gangrene can mean expulsion, which is what Luther finally advocated. The reference to slaying by Moses refers to the fact that extreme measures had even been used by Moses and that the rulers should also take severe measures—not that they had to copy Moses exactly. Christians often use the Old Testament for examples without imagining that we have the authority and power of Moses, and realizing at the same time that we are in the period of Christ's revelation, not in Old Testament Israel.

Yet, Luther did say:

So we are even at fault in not avenging all this innocent blood of our Lord and of the Christians which they shed for three hundred years after the destruction of Jerusalem, and the blood of the children which they have shed since then (which still shines forth from their eyes and from their skin). We are at fault in not slaying them. Rather we allow them to live freely in our midst . . .

Here Luther sadly deviated from scripture. It is not our duty to avenge Christ's blood, for which we are all responsible, Jews and Gentiles. It is not our calling to be agents of wrath when we know we are worthy of God's wrath ourselves. All that can be said in Luther's defense at this point is that he never acted on these words, that they were sarcastic responses to Jewish complaints and insults and never meant to be acted upon. In his many years of public life and ministry, when he wielded an extraordinary amount of influence, he never did anything to harm the Jews. If it were not for later historical developments with which Luther had nothing to do, no one would be paying attention to this obscure tract. Certainly many serious Christians who have deep respect for Luther and who have (like myself) benefited from his Reformation teachings on scripture, have never seen this tract as anything but a blunder of Luther's.

To understand this question more clearly it is helpful to look at the reasons for Luther's anger. These are almost never discussed. The first paragraph of *On the Jews and Their Lies* mentions a Christian converting to Judaism, but this is not elaborated on—and it says in I John that those who abandon Christianity were never really Christians to begin with: "They went out from us, but they were not of us; for if they had been of us, they would no doubt have continued with us: but they went out, that they might be made manifest that they were not all of us" (2:19). Anyway, the bulk of Luther's tract shows that he was blowing a gasket over different issues entirely (though he referred negatively to conversions to Judaism in his *Table Talk*).

One of the main problems for Luther was not that the Jews threatened his theological vision by their unbelief. That is a theory pleasing to those unfamiliar with Christianity and with the depth and power of Luther's faith. One of his main concerns in this tract was Jewish insults to Jesus and Mary; another concern was Jewish insults to Christians, to Goyim. Citing Burgensis, Anthony Margaritha, and others, Luther believed that the Jews were making the following sorts of comments:

~ that Jesus was a sorcerer and tool of the devil who worked his miracles by magical spells
~ that Jesus was born illegitimately and his mother was a whore
~ that Jesus was conceived while Mary was menstruating and hence was mentally defective
~ that Mary was not *Maria* but *haria*, a dungheap
~ that Jews would say of Jesus "May God exterminate his name," or "May all the devils take him" and spit on the ground or curse when they said the name of Jesus

Luther referred to several sources for these allegations, two of whom—Margaritha and Burgensis—were converted Jews. That at least some of Luther's sources were to an extent reliable is confirmed by Katz in his discussion of Jewish life in the Middle Ages. He quotes one *Chronicle of Solomon bar Simson* in which Jesus, Mary, and Christians are referred to in precisely the manner that Luther claimed.[36] I say this to explain Luther's anger, not to justify it.

Other insults to Christianity of the sort that angered Luther are found in an obscure medieval work called the *Toledoth Yeshu*.[37] This parody of the life of Christ states that he was born illegitimately after Mary was raped. It says that when older, Yeshu showed "shameful disrespect" to the rabbis. Concerning the *Toledoth Yeshu*, one historian gives the following explanation. Given the persecutions endured by medieval Jewry, it was

> . . . impossible for Jews to regard the Prophet of Nazareth as other than the scourge of God, a fiend unmentionable. It was natural for legends to grow up about him, libeling his name and perverting his messages. In the *Toldos Yeshu*, a collection of hideous tales purporting to be his life story, read eagerly during the Middle Ages by an embittered people, one finds the response to centuries of persecution in the name of Jesus.[38]

Various comments Luther made in his tract have to do with this work. His angry response was unChristian and wrong, and has done some damage to the reputation of Christianity—but insofar as Luther was dealing with the *Toledoth Yeshu* and related subjects, his writing does fall within the range of ordinary human reaction to insults and is hence more easily comprehensible. This has nothing to do with believing that the Jews are in a secret conspiracy to rule the world or are a threat to the purity of the Aryan race. It is regrettable that Luther's attacks are gone over and over, while the insults that (in part) provoked his response are ignored. However, even if all of the above insults were made, Luther had no cause for hostility. Jesus personally endured insults and responded calmly, and Luther should have returned good for evil. He should have understood the reasons for such hostility and tried to remedy the problem rather than lashing out in anger.

His anger was intensified by the fact that he had previously tried to help Jews and act decently toward them. Here is another passage from the tract:

> I once experienced this myself. Three learned Jews came to me, hoping to discover a new Jew in me because we were beginning to read Hebrew here in Wittenberg, and remarking that matters would soon improve since we Christians were starting to read their books. When I debated with them, they gave me their glosses, as they usually do. But when I forced them back to the text, they soon fled from it, saying that they were obliged to believe their rabbis as we do the pope and the doctors, etc. I took pity on them and gave them a letter of recommendation to the authorities, asking that for Christ's sake they let them freely go their way. But later, I found out that they called Christ a *tola*, that is, a hanged highwayman. Therefore I do not wish to have anything more to do with any Jew.

Thus if Luther later refused to meet with a Jew who came to seek his assistance, this can be attributed to normal human anger—it is not indicative of a deep seated and bizarre racial hatred. This is not meant to justify Luther's anger. We have already seen a biblical passage saying that "The servant of God must not strive, but be gentle to all." Jesus was struck in the face and didn't respond angrily. Paul was rescued from a mob that tried to kill him yet he continued speaking to them and even complimented them on their zeal for righteousness. This is the ideal, and Luther fell short of it. Nevertheless, this is ordinary and easily comprehensible human anger. It is not like grabbing a baby by the feet, smashing its head against a wall, and then handing the bloody corpse back to the mother with a smile.

If I lived in a conservative Jewish area of Israel and made it known that I thought Moses' mother was a whore and he was the mentally defective leader of a bandit gang who robbed the Egyptians in ordinary human fashion and then invented Torah as a means of manipulating the people, I would not be well received. Not just disagreeing with but ridiculing and scorning the religion of a country that you live in as a foreigner is not a bright idea.

Luther was also angry that Jews would curse Christians in their synagogues, and call them "devils" in conversation. He believed that Jews also called Christians "Edom" and "Haman," and hoped that their Messiah would exterminate the Gentiles when he came. He believed Jews wished misfortune on the Gentiles and cursed the Gentiles in their synagogues and in their homes. He also believed that

> . . . their Talmud and their rabbis record that it is no sin for a Jew to kill a Gentile, but it is only a sin for him to kill a brother Israelite. Nor is it a sin for a Jew to break his oath to a Gentile.

Likewise, they say that it is rendering God a service to steal or rob from a Goy, as they in fact do through their usury.

When Luther made comments like "It serves them right that . . . instead of the beautiful face of the divine word, they have to look into the devil's black, dark, lying behind, and worship his stench," or "You are not worthy of looking at the outside of the Bible, much less of reading it. You should read only the bible that is found under the sow's tail, and eat and drink the letters that drop from there," his defective and unChristlike but obvious human reasoning was this: "The Jews say that Mary was a whore and Jesus was mentally defective—well, they can shove their face up a pig's butt and eat pig feces too."

This might explain the sculpture of the Jewish sow on the back of Luther's church in Wittenberg that was so embarrassing to a visiting Protestant pastor. Such a thing is not a common feature of Protestant churches. There is, I am sure, not a single Protestant church in the entire United States or in many other countries that has a Jewish sow as part of its architectural adornment. This could very well have been added as an unChristian response to Jewish insults; it isn't a genuine expression of Protestantism or of Christianity. Such things are the result of disobedience to Christianity. We have seen a number of verses to this effect. Incidentally, Luther did not, as has been mistakenly claimed, compare the Old Testament to pig feces. He considered it to be the word of God, translated it, and appealed to it often in his Reformation debates.

Yet another cause for Luther's anger was the belief of the Jews that they were morally superior to the Gentiles because of their physical descent from Abraham. The Old Testament says enough about the sinfulness of the Jews to show that mere descent from Abraham was no guarantee of righteousness. Luther was particularly incensed that the Jews should continue to imagine their superiority after their country had been destroyed and they had been scattered throughout the world. This was according to their own scriptures a sign of God's anger upon them—yet they continued to boast of God's favor and claimed to be in a special relationship with him. Luther refers to that here:

> Therefore they boast of being the noblest, yes, the only noble people on earth. So if the Jews boast in their prayer before God and glory in the fact that they are the patriarchs' noble blood, lineage, and children, and that he should regard them and be gracious to them in view of this, while they condemn the Gentiles as ignoble and not of their blood, my dear man, what do you suppose such a prayer will achieve?

Also vexing were Jewish complaints. Luther says "they lament before God that we are holding them captive in exile, and they implore him ardently to deliver his holy people and dear children from our power and the imprisonment in which we hold them." Luther's anger included the attitude that no one had asked the Jews to come there, and if they disliked it and the Goyim so much they should leave.

Luther referred to some traditional superstitions about the Jews—that they poisoned wells, kidnapped children, assassinated people, and so on. He expressed doubt about some of these accusations, but believed them to be plausible and

73

referred to "the judgment of Christ which declares that they are venomous, bitter, vindictive, tricky serpents, assassins, and children of the devil who sting and work harm stealthily wherever they cannot do it openly." This does not confirm that Jesus did in fact condemn the entire Jewish people, instead of the leadership only. Rather it confirms that Luther was sometimes mistaken in his interpretations of scripture (in this area and in others). These hostile, angry, and bitter comments are not representative either of Luther at his best, or of the Reformation as a whole.

Luther's last sermon, which is commonly referred to as another example of his anti-Semitism, is (in the portion having to do with the Jews that I have been able to access overseas) basically a repetition of the ideas already discussed. He does not call for the extermination of the Jews, and states that his main desire is for their conversion. If they will not over time convert, they should be expelled. There is no call for pogroms. Parenthetically, the poster of this information states that some parts may have taken from Luther's tract and added to the sermon posthumously.[39]

The online edition of Luther's *Table Talk* has an entire section devoted to the Jews. Nowhere (in this version at any rate) does Luther say anything about killing the Jews. They are compared to the Turks and to the papists in their sin and unbelief. Many of Luther's comments about the Jews here are reasonable and legitimate. If, for example, the Jews were the people of God merely by reason of being physically descended from Abraham, why did God destroy their beautiful temple and scatter them throughout the world?

When Luther says something about Jews "lying on the ground" this does not mean killing. For example, in one passage in *Table Talk* Luther says, speaking rhetorically to a Jewish audience, "You have been, above fifteen hundred years, a race rejected of God, without government, without laws, without prophets, without temple. This argument ye cannot solve; it strikes you to the ground like a thunderclap; ye can show no other reason for your condition than your sins."[40] Over-eagerness to find fault and lack of understanding do not facilitate these discussions.

Some misconceptions about Luther

Luther has been described as a rabid hater of Jews, but here is yet another passage from his much quoted but little read tract against the Jews:

> God truly honored them highly by circumcision, speaking to them above all other nations on earth and entrusting his word to them. And in order to preserve this word among them, he gave them a special country; he performed great wonders through them, ordained kings and government, and lavished prophets upon them who not only apprised them of the best things pertaining to the present but also promised them the future Messiah, the Savior of the world. It was for his sake that God accorded them all of this, bidding them look for his coming, to expect him confidently and without delay. For God did all of this solely for his sake: for his sake Abraham was called, circumcision was instituted, and the people were thus exalted so that all the world might know from which people, from which country, at which time, yes, from which tribe, family, city, and

person, he would come, lest he be reproached by devils and by men for coming from dark corner [*sic*] or from unknown ancestors. No, his ancestors had to be great patriarchs, excellent kings, and outstanding prophets, who bear witness to him.

Try to imagine Hitler reading this passage and taking it seriously. Luther was angered by Jewish insults but he did not consider Jews to be the enemy of the human race. He also stressed the Jewish origins of the New Testament and of Christianity in his *Table Talk*. How dramatically different this is from Nietzsche's *Antichrist*, where the Old Testament is described as lies cooked up by priests to enslave the people, and where Christianity is exposed as a Jewish plot to make people weak with a false philosophy and hence easier for the Jews to dominate.

Far from considering the Jews to be the ultimate symbol of evil, Luther specifically said that their sin of unbelief was the same as that of Turks, radical Protestants, and papists:

The Turks follow the same pattern with their worship, as do all fanatics. Jews, Turks, papists, radicals abound everywhere. All of them claim to be the church and God's people in accord with their conceit and boast, regardless of the one true faith and the obedience to God's commandments through which alone people become and remain God's children. Even if they do not all pursue the same course, but one chooses this way, another that way, resulting in a variety of forms, they nonetheless all have the same intent and ultimate goal, namely, by means of their own deeds they want to manage to become God's people. And thus they boast and brag that they are the ones whom God will esteem

. . .

. . . If I had not had the experience with my papists, it would have seemed incredible to me that the earth should harbor such base people who knowingly fly in the face of open and manifest truth, that is, of God himself. For I never expected to encounter such hardened minds in any human breast, but only in that of the devil. However, I am no longer amazed by either the Turks' or the Jews' blindness, obduracy, and malice, since I have to witness the same thing in the most holy fathers of the church, in pope, cardinals, and bishops.

It is also a mistake to dismiss Luther as a coarse, brutal, and vulgar man. A university professor who lectured on Aristotle and was a scholar in Greek, Latin, and Hebrew, he had a depth of theological and philosophical sophistication far superior to that of most of his detractors. His urging the nobles to crush the peasant rebellion has often been given as an example of his bloodthirsty and hateful character. There was excessive rhetoric in Luther's comments, but the underlying principle is sound. Governments do have the right to suppress rebellions that often lead to worse abuses than those that sparked the rebellion in the first place. A more strict application of Lutheran views of government would have led to Hitler's execution after the Beer Hall Putsch. Sometimes initial severity can prevent a lot of subsequent misery. How much of what seems to us to be Luther's harshness is really only modern moral spinelessness? Would that someone had crushed Lenin's rebellion in 1917 and put Lenin and all of the leading Bolsheviks including Stalin to death.

Another charge is that Luther was the source, or one of the most important sources, of modern German anti-Semitism. This is based not on any real understanding of 19th-century German cultural history but on the following simplistic logic: "Luther was a greatly influential German and an anti-Semite; therefore, later German anti-Semites derive from Luther." A careful study of Germany in the 19th century reveals the development of new strains of thought and of anti-Semitism entirely unknown in the 16th century.

Particularly ludicrous is the charge that Germans submitted to Hitler because Luther taught obedience to the state (in agreement with Paul's teaching in Romans), that they were just blindly following Luther's influence. This is refuted by even a brief consideration of German history. When the French occupied Germany in the Napoleonic era, fiery nationalists like Fichte and Jahn, as well as the multitudes of Germans who followed them, did not say "We should submit to Napoleon as Christ submitted to the Romans. That's what Luther taught." Doubtless there were Germans who did believe that. They recognized there were more important things than national independence, and may even have perceived Napoleon's reforms as beneficial—but they were not in the vanguard of German cultural development, and would have been roundly abused by the nationalists if they had had the temerity to express the opinion that Napoleon's victory was God's judgment and should not be resisted.

Similarly, in the revolutions of 1848 there were plenty of Germans who resisted the governments of Germany and did not feel in the least constrained by Luther's hypnotic influence that supposedly lingered in the hearts of all Germans for centuries after his death. Germans also didn't hesitate to abuse, criticize, despise, and seek to overthrow the Weimar government—there is no evidence in any histories of the period that I have seen to show that large numbers of Germans were openly saying "God has ordained the Weimar government, and to resist it is to go against God's will. That's what Luther said." If enough Germans had had this very sound and biblical attitude of Luther's, Hitler would never have come to power.

It denies human responsibility, intellect, and will to say that the Germans were just following Luther in submitting to Hitler 400 years later. It is much more reasonable to say that the Germans supported Hitler for one of two reasons: (a) they genuinely liked and approved of Hitler, or (b) they were just going along to stay out of a concentration camp. In the last free election in the spring of 1933, after Hitler had become Chancellor but before he was able to completely consolidate his power, more than half of the electorate did not vote for the Nazi Party. A majority of voters did not approve of Hitler or his party, but once he got his grip firmly on the police and other key elements of power, resistance to Hitler meant a terrible fate.

Moreover, Luther's concept of obedience to governments did not extend to the spiritual realm. Christians are required to obey the government until it interferes with spiritual truth. According to Luther's (and Paul's) concepts of government, the Christians in Nazi Germany had every right to say that the meaning of life was to prepare for eternity by living for Christ. It was not to purify the German race or glorify the German nation. Germans were submissive to Hitler on matters of truth and faith where neither the Bible nor Luther advocated submission.

Lutheran church historian Lowell Green states that the politicization of the German church was greatly increased in 1817, the year in which King Frederick William III of Prussia forcibly unified the Lutheran and the Reformed (Calvinist) Churches into what became known as the Prussian Union. "Old Lutherans" who resisted had their churches taken from them by force. Thousands of them emigrated, especially to America, in order to avoid persecution, or forced union with those whose ideas were different from theirs. They lived with the Calvinists peaceably, but did not want the government to tell them who they must worship with and how.

Green goes on to state that this made the church much more of a bureaucratic arm of the state, and as a result "church life declined alarmingly in the Prussian Union." The damaging process of forcibly subjecting believers to government control spread as Prussia gained control of other territories. Green sees these events as establishing a precedent for Hitler's later attempt to forcibly unite the Protestant churches. He also quotes a German theologian (Hermann Sasse) to the effect that the emphasis on ecclesiastical subservience to the state was more pronounced from this time on. Favorable comments about government by Luther were emphasized, while his more negative comments on government were kept "well-hidden in a drawer."[41]

Misinterpretations of Luther abound. William L. Shirer, who had no understanding of the spiritual principles of the Reformation, was mistaken when he blamed Luther in his *Rise and Fall of the Third Reich* for the close relationship between church and state that characterized much of subsequent German ecclesiastical history. Did the Spanish, the Russians, and the Byzantines have extremely close relationships between church and state because of Luther's influence? Henry VIII rejected Luther's Reformation and defended the papacy, but then set up his own state church—not because of Luther's influence. Shirer's argument is a classic example of the *post hoc ergo propter hoc* fallacy. Fortunately, in dealing with much simpler aspects of straightforward historical narrative, Shirer was much more perceptive. Like many journalists, he had little understanding of spiritual things.

What did Luther have to do with the unification of Germany, World War I, the Weimar Republic, inflation, the specter of the Soviet Union and a German Bolshevik revolution? To imagine that he single-handedly molded the German people and led them to submit to dictatorship does not explain how Lenin, Stalin, and Mao also ruled a nation by fear and terror, crushing all dissent and elevating themselves to the status of demi-gods without the benefit of a Lutheran tradition to teach the people to unthinkingly submit. Richard Evans is justified in referring to the "remote religious cultures and hierarchical politics of the Reformation" as being not directly related to the Third Reich.[42]

Luther's concept of government, which was derived from Romans, was that of the authorities as ordained by God to keep the peace and punish evil so that ordinary people might live decent lives. The idea of the government going on a power-crazed militaristic binge that ultimately brings ruin on the entire country is something else again. It was also a concept of rulers as being themselves subject to a higher law—not a law unto themselves. Hegel's exalted concept of the state and of the individual as subordinate to the state, while certainly not identical to

Hitlerian fascism, is much closer to modern fascism than anything Luther ever said—but it isn't so fashionable or emotionally satisfying to attack Hegel. That during the early 1800's the Jews were protected by German governments as we have seen shows the mollifying influence of traditional, biblical concepts of government—these concepts do not and cannot eliminate evil in the world, but they do restrain it.

Many modern German thinkers too often get lightly passed over while Luther gets relentlessly attacked. The answer is not far to seek. That man is free to reject God's rules and live according to his own desires is the essence of the religion of modern secularism, and its apostles and leading lights must not be called into question. That God does exist, that he has laws, and we find our real happiness within those laws, are anathema to the modern mind—hence biblical Christianity must be discredited by any and every means, fair or foul. Some criticisms of Luther are legitimate—he is certainly not above criticism—but some attacks on Luther are misguided at best, and openly deceitful at worst.

Some objections to Luther are the result of misreading. For example, one passage in *On the Jews and Their Lies* has been said to describe the Jewish synagogue as "a defiled bride, yes, an incorrigible whore and an evil slut with whom God ever had to wrangle, scuffle, and fight." That is certainly a bad thing to say about Jewish houses of worship, but the passage in Part 3 of the tract is in fact not referring to the synagogue at all. Luther is talking about biblical Israel, the Israel of Moses and the prophets. Here is the passage:

> No prophet has ever been able to raise his voice in protest or stand up against them, not even Moses. For in Numbers 16, Korah arose and asserted that they were all holy people of God, and asked why Moses alone should rule and teach. Since that time, the majority of them have been genuine Korahites; there have been very few true Israelites. For just as Korah persecuted Moses, they have never subsequently left a prophet alive or unpersecuted, much less have they obeyed him.
>
> So it became apparent that they were a defiled bride, yes, an incorrigible whore and an evil slut with whom God ever had to wrangle, scuffle, and fight. If he chastised and struck them with his word through the prophets, they contradicted him, killed his prophets, or, like a mad dog, bit the stick with which they were struck. Thus Psalm 95:10 declares: "Forty years long was I grieved with this generation, and said, It is a people that do err in their heart, and they have not known my ways." And Moses himself says in Deuteronomy 31:27: "For I know thy rebellion and thy stiff neck: behold, while I am yet alive with you this day, ye have been rebellious against the Lord; and how much more after my death?" And Isaiah 48:4: "Because I knew that thou art obstinate, and thy neck is an iron sinew, and thy brow brass . . ." And so on; anyone who is interested may read more of this. The Jews are well aware that the prophets upbraided the children of Israel from beginning to end as a disobedient, evil people and as the vilest whore, although they boasted so much of the law of Moses, or circumcision, and of their ancestry.

Here is a good example of one of Luther's main faults, expressing with excessive vehemence principles that were often (though not of course always) sound. Saying "the vilest whore" for example is extreme, but the main point is supported by scripture—does not God say to the prophet Hosea "the land hath committed great whoredom, departing from the Lord"? Moses and the prophets themselves referred to the Jews as stubborn, stiff-necked, rebellious. At one point even Torah says God wanted to wipe them out and start over with Moses (Exodus 32:10). The prophets were speaking by the inspiration of God and Luther was speaking by the inspiration of anger so he was off base, but his main idea was based on scripture. Second, this is often done with Luther—a gory quote is pulled out and made much of, but the circumstances behind it are misunderstood. This happens so often that I am skeptical of any Luther quotes I haven't seen in context myself.

Luther and the Nazis

Much has been made of the professed Nazi admiration for Luther, but the Nazis admired Luther chiefly because he was a German. Calvin was very close to Luther spiritually, but the Nazis had no regard for him—he was French. Luther's sinful outburst against the Jews was a propaganda bonus for them, but that they had no regard for the principles of the Reformation is evident. Luther was for many later Germans only a Nordic hero who helped to emancipate the Germans from a degenerate Italian-Mediterranean influence—not a spiritual leader.

In describing the Nazi government-sponsored celebrations in 1933 of the 450th anniversary of Luther's birthday (*Der Deutsche Luthertag*), Steigmann-Gall's book clearly reveals the unChristian nature of Nazi admiration for Luther. Referring to none of the basic principles of the Reformation—salvation by grace alone through faith, reliance on the Bible alone, and the deity, sacrifice, and resurrection of Christ—the speakers quoted by Steigmann-Gall were concerned with the destiny of the German people; with Germany's awakening; with Luther's sinful anti-Semitic comments. German cultural values (meaning Nazi cultural values) were praised.

A comment is also quoted stating that Luther and Hitler were the same, "of the same stamp."[43] The idea that Hitler the Nazi dictator, mass murderer, and world conqueror was like Luther, or that Luther's German translation of the Bible enabled the Germans not to learn the truths of God that lead to eternal life, but to understand themselves as Germans[44]—these do not, contrary to Steigmann-Gall's assertion, reflect Protestantism. They show no appreciation for the religious principles of the Reformation. They show a patriotic admiration for Luther as a national hero that no one with a serious commitment to the principle of salvation by faith in Christ alone according to the Bible alone would make. Steigmann-Gall misinterprets a clever propaganda show put on by the Nazis at a time when Hitler had not been long in power and was still consolidating his grip.

Since Steigmann-Gall takes every reference to Luther as proof of Protestant belief, it is reasonable to ask if he even knows what Protestantism's basic principles are. I am a committed Protestant myself. Believing that the Old and New Testaments are the inspired and inerrant word of God, and trying to base my life upon them as best I can, I see that the way to forgiveness of my many sins and eternal life is through faith in Christ—and faith includes a desire to serve and obey him out of love. I am deeply thankful for Luther's separation from Rome, and see a lot of sound biblical wisdom in his best writings.

Protestantism in its original sense, as articulated by Luther and by the other reformers, is based on the belief that our understanding of what Christ taught, what Christianity is and how it should be lived, must come from the Bible—not from additional church rules and doctrines added centuries after Christ, many of them directly contrary to the Bible. This magnificent spiritual independence from blind obedience to the papacy—or any other ecclesiastical authority—is central to Protestantism. It has nothing to do with later theories of race derived entirely from secular thinkers.

Steigmann-Gall finds some Protestant pastors and theologians who articulated some proto-Nazi ideas (such as extreme nationalism) and reasons that National Socialism came out of Protestantism. His lack of familiarity with biblical teaching prevents him from seeing that "Protestants" who uttered such sentiments were in fact forsaking their religious heritage and following after false philosophies and doctrines of the world. They reflect the capitulation of the church before the forces of secularism, not the Christian origin of ideas that have nothing whatever to do with the New Testament and with Protestantism in its original sense.

It is significant that in *The Crisis of German Ideology*, George Mosse's highly detailed study of the German Folkish philosophy (which that historian considered to be the real foundation of Naziism), Luther is mentioned only five times: once in passing (with reference to Ulrich von Hutten) and once negatively (he relied too much on the Bible). Other references had to do with Luther as a prophet of a Nordic religion. His revolution against Rome was considered to be only the first step in an ongoing emancipation of Christianity from un-Germanic influences, allowing the emergence of a new and uniquely German faith that was in the end only human philosophy re-expressed in religious language. Thus, the "German Christians" (*Deutsche Christen*) could sincerely speak of purging Christianity of Jewish influences and bringing it into complete conformity with National Socialism as continuing Luther's Reformation.

The driving force of the Reformation eventually degenerated into a dead orthodoxy primarily concerned with theology or with intellectual assent to doctrines. The Pietists sought to bring a greater degree of spiritual vitality back into the church in the 17th and 18th centuries, but when the "Enlightenment" reached Germany much of the Lutheran church abandoned the basic doctrines and sought to make Christianity acceptable by conforming it to the times. "Lutheran" and "Protestant" thus came to mean a flexible Christianity that had long since abandoned its historic roots and retained only the outward appearance of "Protestantism," and often not even that.

Karl Marx, by the way, expressed appreciation for Luther's role in the introduction of the modern age. Does this show the Protestant origins of Marxism? Many people with no Christian faith at all have agreed with Luther's emphasis on individual belief instead of forced adherence to an ecclesiastical power structure. It is poor scholarship to take every expression of appreciation for Luther as proof of Protestant influence, just as it is poor scholarship to jump from Luther to the twentieth century as if powerful secular forces and ideas that Luther never dreamed of had not been at work in the 19th century—a period that also witnessed the dramatic decline of the church in Germany.

If in the sixteenth century someone had tried to assert that the blond blue-eyed Germans were the master race and it was their destiny to rule the world, he would have been dismissed as a nut. If he had agitated for the overthrow of the various German kingdoms so that Germany might be unified under one national government he would certainly have been imprisoned and probably executed. Modern nationalism itself is an unbiblical concept, unknown—along with racism and fascism—until more than a thousand years after Christ. Christian scholar John Montgomery goes further and makes the reasonable assertion that Lutheranism led to an aversion to imperialism. Certainly the Germans of Luther's day and for long thereafter were content with and even flourished in their divided country. It was not until the emergence of modern secularism in the "Enlightenment" that the nation began to assume quasi-religious importance.[45]

Modern ideas could not have been and were not conceived of in Luther's time. It took the triumph of modern secularism and the loss of traditional biblical beliefs to clear the way for new beliefs of an entirely different sort. It is noteworthy in this connection that Hitler referred to Luther only once in *Mein Kampf*, and then not in connection with the Jews. Where Hitler explains his ideas of racial purity at length and in depth he does not appeal to Luther. He appeals to pseudo-science, to human reason unaided or unrestrained by divine revelation, to the logic of Kant, Gobineau, Schopenhauer, Wagner, and Chamberlain.

Hitler's real attitude toward Luther can best be illustrated by some of his comments from *Hitler's Table Talk*. Hitler objected to the German translation of the Bible as "deplorable," and thought it would have been better if the Germans had never been exposed to its "Jewish mumbojumbo."[46] It is commonly said that Hitler quoted Luther—it is seldom said that Hitler quoted Torah as well, and used "an eye for an eye" to justify his invasion of Poland.

At this point I would like to insert another passage from *On the Jews and Their Lies*:

> Oh, what do we poor muck-worms, maggots, stench, and filth presume to boast of before him who is the God and Creator of heaven and earth, who made us out of dirt and out of nothing! And as far as our nature, birth, and essence are concerned, we are but dirt and nothing in his eyes; all that we are and have comes from his grace and his rich mercy.

This is what Luther said of himself, of Christians, of Germans. Someone who believed this sound biblical teaching to be basically true in essence, even without Luther's dramatic rhetoric and penchant for exaggeration, could not possibly be intoxicated with the fantastic and ignorant modern lie of racial superiority. To say that Luther was concerned with exalting Germany is to misrepresent him greatly. He did speak of Germany's oppression by the papacy, but he was mainly concerned with biblical teaching for all, not only for Germans. Whatever natural concern he might have expressed for his country, such as any Englishman or Frenchman might share for their own countries, should not be seen as sinister or unnatural in the light of events centuries later.

Luther has been too often discussed by people with little or no understanding of his beliefs, and by people who are hostile to his beliefs. Even Christians who support Israel and have never harmed a Jew in their life or wanted to are considered to be under the baleful influence of Luther's hate if they repeat biblical statements about the need for all, including Jews, to find forgiveness of sin in Christ.

It seems no stone has been left unturned in the search for ways to discredit Luther. He commissioned some woodcuts by Cranach that are offensive to dainty and fastidious people who, if they go to the movies or watch TV, routinely guzzle sewage that would have seemed horrible and revolting to people of Luther's day. Luther has been accused of tossing around words for excrement with great abandon, which is untrue considering his major works. Paul also referred to dung in Philippians—"I have suffered the loss of all things, and do count them but dung, that I may win Christ"—as did the prophet Zephaniah—"their blood shall be poured out as dust, and their flesh as the dung." There are other references to this unpleasant aspect of reality in the Bible—David makes a "scatological" reference: "they became as dung for the earth." Christ also made reference to a dunghill: "It is neither fit for the land, nor yet for the dunghill."

Luther in perspective

Luther's attacks on the Jews can be compared to David's sin with Bathsheba. David committed adultery and murder, and the biblical record plainly shows that he was guilty of flagrant sin, with no extenuating circumstances to mitigate his guilt (contrary to the assertions of some). The prophet Nathan said plainly that David murdered a man and took his wife. David's response was not to come up with a lot of clever excuses—he said, "I have sinned against the Lord" (II Samuel 12:9-13). Nevertheless, Christians and Jews recognize David as a great man of God, and also recognize that his sin was not characteristic—and what would we think of someone who criticized David and dismissed him solely on the basis if this one sin, with no knowledge, understanding, or appreciation of David's deep spirituality? What would we think of someone who knew nothing of the Psalms, and could see nothing but David's sin?

It is possible that along with human sin, Luther's health was also a factor. It can't be proven, but it is very possible that years of ill health contributed to the emotional and intellectual decline that we see in this unfortunate tract. He refers in his tract on the Jews to a gallstone, a bloody tumor, and other unspecified ailments—not in a self-pitying way but in passing, as part of an analogy. This could have combined with bitterness at a perceived failure of his hoped for Reformation of the church, with even the Protestant groups going off in many directions disagreeable to Luther, and led to the sad spiritual and intellectual decline evidenced in his attacks on Jews.

There is an analogy that can be drawn between Luther and an Old Testament figure, one much greater than Luther but who also got angry at the Jews for their unbelief and disobedience. God commanded Moses to speak to the rock so that water might come forth from it, but Moses was provoked by the unbelief of the Jews and struck the rock angrily instead of speaking to it. As a result, he was rebuked and even punished by God.

Luther also got angry with the Jews, and he lashed out when he should have spoken softly and reasonably. His attacks have been of great service to those who wish to discredit Christianity, but a serious and objective study of the origins of National Socialism reveals that Luther was nothing like the fountainhead of German anti-Semitism that some claim. It is too bad that so many think the

Protestant Reformation in the 16th century is more important for an understanding of National Socialism than the German secular and sometimes overtly anti-religious philosophical tradition of the 19th century.

Jews were not badly treated in Protestant countries before the modern era. Luther's attacks on the Jews were not echoed by any other Reformation leader, nor were they enthusiastically received in his day. One will search in vain for virulent anti-Semitic diatribes in the works of such major Protestant writers as Wesley, Whitefield, Bunyan, Jonathan Edwards, Knox, Melanchthon, Calvin, Spurgeon, and others. Moreover, nowhere in World War II were the Jews more assisted than in countries with a strong Protestant tradition like Holland, Norway and Denmark. Even in Italy, which according to some theories should have been a hotbed of Nazi anti-Semitism and indeed the origin of it, there was little enthusiasm for the Nazis' genocidal program. Mussolini refused to deport Jews and the first Jews were not sent from Italy to the gas chambers until after his fall.[47]

That Jews in Rome were helped by the Vatican after the fall of Mussolini is significant. Pope Pius XII personally opened the Vatican City to non-Aryans seeking refuge and hundreds of Jews were given shelter there.[48] More will have to be said later about the complexities of Hitler's Concordat with the Vatican and other related subjects, but at this point it is sufficient to point out that if the Nazis had really been continuing the policies of the Roman Church as has been claimed, the papal response would have been radically different. It is unfortunate that Poland is so often pointed to as an example of Christian cruelty and support for the Nazis, while the vastly different situation in other countries is mentioned as a matter of record in the history books, but is seldom if ever used to indicate that Lutheranism and Christianity are not inherently anti-Semitic.

It is unfortunate that chapter one of Martin Gilbert's *The Holocaust: A History of the Jews of Europe During the Second World War* begins with Christian anti-Semitism in the first sentence and immediately proceeds to quote Martin Luther. The 19th century in Western Europe is referred to positively (in exactly two sentences) as an age of emancipation and integration for the Jews, and then the violent anti-Semitism of eastern Europe is discussed in great detail. Then we move to World War I, more instances of anti-Semitism in Poland, Lithuania, and the Ukraine, and then to the emergence of Hitler and the Nazi Party. The amount of attention paid to Eastern Europe is curious—the Holocaust did not originate there, it originated in Germany.

More significantly, it is as if the modern secular and racial anti-Semitism of the 19th century had not occurred; as if the nineteenth century were pre-eminently reasonable, and did not contain the seeds of what was to follow. The now widely accepted and automatic assumption that secularism is rational whereas religion is irrational commonly leads to misinterpretation of the evidence—as if the 16th century (or in some cases even the 1st century) had more to do with the Holocaust than the 19th century.

A secular evaluation of Luther

Harvard Professor Steven Ozment's *A Mighty Fortress: A New History of the German People (110 B.C. to the 21st Century)* contains some comments about Luther that are surprising, coming from a secular author. Ozment makes what should be the obvious point that blood and race were not important to Luther. He explains that Luther saw the Jews much as he saw the Catholics and Anabaptists, and makes the telling observation that 16th-century German imperial law was more hostile to Anabaptists than it was to Jews.

Also, many people refer to Luther's exhortations to the German princes to mercilessly crush the peasant rebellion—this is given as proof of what a hateful and bloodthirsty man Luther was. Being more of a historian than a propagandist, Ozment refers to those comments, but also quotes Luther's *Admonition to Peace*, in which (before the rebellion began) he appealed to both the peasants and the princes not to resort to violence.[49] Luther recognized that the peasants had legitimate grievances but, once the fighting began, said the rebellion should be swiftly and mercilessly crushed. He was especially vehement about it so as to make it very clear that the Reformation was not a revolutionary political movement, but he was by no means the cartoon character his uncomprehending and sometimes dishonest critics have represented him as being.

Luther's goal

What was Luther aiming it in his revolutionary critique of Roman Catholicism? His first intent was to reform blatant, long standing, and widely recognized abuses. Initially, he actually expected the sympathy and support of the pope.[50] Thus, Luther's *95 Theses* were not an "attack" on the Church of Rome, but an attempt to reform it, and contain what Luther later came to feel was excessive deference to the pope. Only over time did he come to realize that the Roman hierarchy was resolutely opposed to reform. Luther then set about the task of exposing Roman errors; breaking the power of the Roman Church by debate, preaching, and writing only; and presenting people with basic biblical teachings, according to which much of Roman doctrine and practice was at best superfluous, at worst harmful and deceptive.

It was not Luther's lifelong mission to destroy Judaism. He longed for the conversion of as many people as possible to Christianity, including Jews, but his main Reformation writings show little or no concern with Jews. Neither was it Luther's mission to save Germany. He was not a nationalist, and did not see the Germans as a new Chosen People. Statements that Luther's legitimate concern about the Catholic practice of selling indulgences to raise money were in any way connected with fantasies about Jewish bogeymen only reveal a complete ignorance of Luther's honest and upright indignation over this atrocious and wicked swindle.

The statement that Luther was somehow to blame for secular anti-Jewish philosophical and racial fantasies that emerged centuries later in a totally different context is, in my view, a falsehood. The statement that Luther, like Hitler, was a revolutionary obsessed with "Germanness" and "Jewishness," to my mind at least, falls far outside of the boundaries of serious and legitimate academic discourse. If Luther and Hitler were both "characteristically German figures,"[51] so were Martin Luther King and Elvis Presley both characteristically American. Both King and Elvis were charismatic figures who had intensely devoted followings and both had revolutionary impacts in their respective fields. George Bush, Richard Nixon and Abraham Lincoln were all "characteristically American" as well. That the fruits produced by Hitler and the fruits produced by the Reformation in 400 years of influence in Northern Europe were vastly different is difficult to grasp for those whose analyses are motivated more by hostility and bias than by rational consideration of obvious facts. A dictator like Hitler could not have arisen and in fact did not arise outside of a modern context.

Matthew Henry and Romans 11

Traditional Christian views of Jews being under the wrath of God do not inevitably lead to persecution. A good example of this is found in the writings of Matthew Henry. Though he lived in the 17th and 18th centuries, his commentaries are still studied today. He represents the Evangelical Protestant point of view that allowed Jews to live in many countries for centuries subsequent to the Reformation without fear of pogroms or massacres.

Writing on the events described in Matthew, Henry first states that the destruction of Israel by the Romans was the result of their "turbulent tumultuous temper."[52] Their defeat was a natural consequence of their own sinful actions. He then goes on to add that the words "His blood be on us, and on our children," brought the curse of God upon them. He makes a number of other comments to the effect that God's curse on the Jews was evident in their oppressed and wretched state (it will be recalled this was in the 18th century).

Some will automatically link this to Hitler and the Holocaust, and it is true some have reasoned that punishing the Jews is good—or, at least nothing to be concerned about. Since it is God's will for them to suffer, they are only getting what they deserve. Such ordinary human logic reveals a profound lack of familiarity with the Christian message. The Jews are guilty of sin, but so are we all, and our calling as Christians is to be agents of reconciliation, not of wrath.

A much more genuinely biblical approach, one that is informed not only by theological speculations but also by the grace of God and a consciousness of our own sinfulness, is exemplified by Matthew Henry in his comments on Romans 11. There Henry shows himself to be far removed from bad feeling, let alone hatred, cruelty, and murder. He states the familiar teaching that God still has some sort of a future purpose for the Jews:

> Another thing that qualified this doctrine of the Jews' rejection is that, though for the present they are cast off, yet the rejection is not final; but, when the fulness of time is come, they will be taken in again. They are not cast off for ever, but mercy is remembered in the midst of wrath.
>
> This restoration will be a blessing to the church, as Paul said: Now if the fall of them be the riches of the world, and the diminishing of them the riches of the Gentiles; how much more their fulness? . . . For if the casting away of them be the reconciling of the world, what shall the receiving of them be, but life from the dead? (11:12,15)

On this point Henry says, "It would be as life from the dead; and therefore they must not insult and triumph over those poor Jews, but rather pity them, and desire their welfare, and long for the receiving of them in again." Obviously, if God has a future purpose for the Jews, extermination is not desirable.

Henry adds another point—that the Jews are to be loved for the sake of their ancestors, saying, "The Jews are in a sense a holy nation (Exod. xix. 6), being descended from holy parents. This relates to teachings about the Jews in Romans

3:2 ('unto them were committed the oracles of God') and Romans 11:28 ('they are beloved for the fathers' sakes')." All Christians who revere the Old Testament as the inspired word of God, who feel the Holy Spirit in its pages and are uplifted, inspired, challenged, humbled, or rebuked by its amazing and wonderful profundities have an innate sense of respect and regard for God's mysterious work with the Jewish people. This spirit was totally lacking in 19th-century German theological liberals who felt the Old Testament was only an ordinary human book, full of mistakes, myths, and legends.

A third point is, that those who have experienced God's mercy and forgiveness themselves desire it for others:

> Those that have themselves experienced the grace of God, preventing, distinguishing grace, may thence take encouragement to hope well concerning others . . . This is a suggestion very proper to check the insolence of those Gentile Christians that looked with disdain and triumph upon the condition of the rejected Jews, and trampled upon them; as if he had said, "Their condition, bad as it is, is not so bad as yours was before your conversion; and therefore why may it not be made as good as yours is?" This is his argument (v. 30, 31) . . . It is good for those that have found mercy with God to be often thinking what they were in time past, and how they obtained that mercy. This would help to soften our censures of those that still continue in unbelief, and quicken our prayers for them . . . Those that have found mercy themselves should endeavour that through their mercy others also may obtain mercy.

This is an irresistible argument that must register with all who have personally experienced God's mercy and grace. The good that we have found, we desire for others. It forbids persecution of Jews—and this has been a common understanding among many Christians, as is witnessed by the tolerance many Jews have experienced. Part of the problem with medieval Catholicism was that so few people had access to and understanding of the Bible. Another part of the problem is that Christianity is judged according to the actions of those who refuse to follow its teachings!

One last point was made by Henry in discussing Paul's analogy of the olive tree. This passage of Romans 11 refers to the Gentiles as branches of a wild olive tree that have been grafted on to a good olive tree. The Jews are referred to as branches of the olive tree that were broken off so that the wild branches might be grafted in. Henry considers the olive tree to represent "the visible church," which prior to Christ was the Jewish nation with its temple and worship. It might also be described as "the covenantal relationship with God." Its roots are Abraham, Moses, and the prophets.

In discussing this, Paul warns the Gentile Christians:

> . . . if some of the branches be broken off, and thou, being a wild olive tree, wert graffed in among them, and with them partakest of the root and fatness of the olive tree;

Boast not against the branches. But if thou boast, thou bearest not the root, but the root thee.

Thou wilt say then, The branches were broken off, that I might be graffed in.

Well; because of unbelief they were broken off, and thou standest by faith. Be not highminded, but fear:

For if God spared not the natural branches, take heed lest he also spare not thee.

Behold therefore the goodness and severity of God: on them which fell, severity; but toward thee, goodness, if thou continue in his goodness: otherwise thou also shalt be cut off.

With this warning in mind, Henry writes that Christians should "take heed to themselves, lest they should stumble and fall, as they Jews had done" and adds:

Secondly, A caution not to abuse these privileges. 1. "Be not proud (v. 18): Boast not against the branches. Do not therefore trample upon the Jews as a reprobate people, nor insult over those that are broken off, much less over those that do continue." Grace is given, not to make us proud, but to make us thankful. The law of faith excludes all boasting either of ourselves or against others.

"Be not high-minded, but fear. Be not too confident of your own strength and standing." A holy fear is an excellent preservative against high-mindedness: happy is the man that thus feareth always. We need not fear but God will be true to his word; all the danger is lest we be false to ours. Let us therefore fear, Heb. iv. 1.

The Jews were removed so that the Gentiles might be grafted in. Christians who are too haughty can also be removed. Our ingrafting is an occasion not for pride, hatred, and cruelty, but for humility before God and mercy toward others.

In his attack on Luther, Paul Rose asserts that traditional "Christian" anti-Semites were "perplexed," "infuriated," and "worried"[53] by the refusal of Jews to accept the truths of Christianity. Now, there may be somewhere some obscure writer who presents such ridiculous attitudes, but this has nothing whatever to do with the mainstream of Evangelical Protestantism that emerged out of the Reformation. We are not perplexed by Jewish unbelief, nor are we infuriated, nor are we worried. The Bible teaches that unbelief is the natural state of humanity; that we too were once in the same unbelief; that we have the duty to help those who are as we once were.

Neither are Christians concerned with another drastic mischaracterization of Rose's—that Jewish unbelief is holding Christianity hostage, since Christ cannot return until the Jews are converted.[54] This has nothing to do with biblical Christianity. We believe Christ will return in his time. This will be determined by God's will, not by man's. If there is a prior conversion of the Jews, as many believe there will be, it will be accomplished by God, and the Jews will receive it willingly and gladly. No reputable author in the entire history of Protestant

Christendom since the Reformation has ever said "Those stubborn Jews are keeping Jesus from coming back. I'm so worried, frustrated, and upset."

The return of Christ cannot be advanced or delayed by human activity by so much as a day, an hour, or a second. Mistaken ideas in this area may come from a Jewish belief that the coming of the Messiah is linked to human righteousness and the fulfillment of the law, but this is not a Christian teaching. As is the case with so many others, Rose is criticizing Christianity without understanding it and hence does not represent it fairly or objectively.

Yet, in spite of his bias and lack of historical detachment when it comes to the enlightening and ennobling Protestant Reformation, Rose recognizes that a new element of anti-Semitism was introduced long after Luther. Rose refers to the "new, secularized form of Jew-hatred" that emerged with Kant, and recognizes that the 18th-century "shift from a Christian to a secular morality had produced new possibilities for Jew-hatred." Rose even goes so far as to say that the anti-Semitism of Kant and other secular thinkers was "far more insidiously destructive of Judaism" than the Christian dream of conversion. Rose also recognizes that this new Jew-hatred involved an explicit rejection of religiously motivated anti-Judaism.[55] As we shall see in our study of Kant and other thinkers, the reasoning of traditional religious anti-Judaism was of no use to people who did not even believe in the Bible at all.

A glimpse ahead

Is it necessary to point out that Germany in 1517 was vastly different from Germany in 1917? The centuries that followed the Reformation saw many dramatic changes in all aspects of life—including anti-Semitism. Luther and Henry—to say nothing of the New Testament authors and Christ himself—were in a totally different world spiritually than were the secular racial anti-Semites who did so much to lay the groundwork for the Third Reich. "The Jews are plotting to take over the world! The German race must remain biologically pure to prevail in the struggle for survival of the fittest! Intermarriage with Jews is corrupting our sacred racial inheritance! The Jews have through Christianity introduced false Mediterranean and Semitic values that weaken the German nation!" Those who have an interest in the origin of this bizarre way of looking at life need to study nineteenth-century German thinkers, not Luther. Hitler wrote at length on the Jews in *Mein Kampf*—his reasoning was the result of 19th- and 20th-century values and ideas.

Conclusion

That a great deal of evil has been done in the name of Christ is undeniable. It is evident, however, or should be evident to anyone who considers the Bible impartially, that hating, persecuting, and murdering others are contrary to many plain scriptures. If we really want to understand Christianity, both in itself and in its relationship to Hitler and to the crimes of the Nazis, we need to consider Christianity as it presents itself in the life and teachings of Christ and of the apostles. We also need to consider those who have made a sincere effort to live by those teachings, not those who willfully disregard them.

But, Hitler claimed to be a Christian once or twice. He also professed support for the churches on numerous occasions, and said that Christianity was needed to build a morally strong Germany and assist him in the fight against godless Bolshevism. Not only that, but there are people today who have faith in Hitler's honesty (or pretend to) and claim that he was an upright and truthful man who expressed his religious views with candor and sincerity. These people say "We know Hitler was a Christian because he said so himself!" Therefore, it will be necessary to examine his statements and ideas in another chapter.

> *But the tongue can no man tame; it is an unruly evil, full of deadly poison.*
> *Therewith bless we God, even the Father; and therewith curse we men, which are made after the similitude of God.*
> *Out of the same mouth proceedeth blessing and cursing. My brethren, these things ought not so to be.*
> *Doth a fountain send forth at the same place sweet water and bitter?*
> *Can the fig tree, my brethren, bear olive berries? either a vine, figs? so can no fountain both yield salt water and fresh.*
> *Who is a wise man and endued with knowledge among you? let him shew out of a good conversation his works with meekness of wisdom.*
> *But if ye have bitter envying and strife in your hearts, glory not, and lie not against the truth. (James)*

---

[1] (New York / Oxford 1994). This essay will refer extensively to chapters 6 and 7 ("Medieval Antisemitism: The Process of Mythification" and "Medieval Antisemitism: The Positive Paradox"). Katz's work is meticulously researched, and more than amply documented. Noteworthy is his desire to avoid obscuring the real meaning of the Holocaust by making simplistic and misleading comparisons.

[2] Katz, *Holocaust in Historical Context,* pp. 307-308.

[3] Ibid., p. 82.

[4] Ibid., p. 345.

[5] Ibid., p. 317.

[6] Ibid., p. 260.

[7] Ibid., p. 263.

[8] Ibid., p. 262.

[9] Ibid., p. 270 (footnote #123).

[10] Ibid., (footnote #122).

[11] Ibid., p. 272.

[12] Paul Harrison, "Hegel: Philosophy and history as theology. A history of pantheism"; http://members.aol.com/pantheism0/hegel.htm; accessed January 2008. The words are Hegel's, but the source is unclearly indicated on the website. It is either from Hegel, *The Philosophy of History*, trans. J. Sibree (New York 1956) or from Hegel, *Lectures on the Philosophy of Religion*, ed. Peter Hodgson (Berkeley 1984).

[13] G.W. Hegel, *The Philosophy of Right*, trans. T.M. Knox (Great Books of the Western World, Encyclopedia Britannica 1952), p. 108.

[14] Paul Johnson, *Modern Times: The World from the Twenties to the Nineties* (New York 1991), p. 579.

[15] Katz, p. 579.

[16] Ibid., p. 269.

[17] Ibid., p. 268.

[18] Ibid., p. 330.

[19] Ibid., p. 542.

[20] Ibid., p. 323.

[21] Ibid., p. 358.

[22] Ibid., p. 356.

[23] Ibid., p. 340.

[24] Ibid., pp. 335-336.

[25] Ibid., p. 231.

[26] Ibid., p. 348.

[27] Ibid., pp. 346, 348.

[28] Ibid., p. 350.

[29] Ibid., pp. 338-339.

[30] Ibid., pp. 322, 326.

[31] Ibid., pp. 331- 332.

[32] Ibid., p. 345.

[33] It is ironic that Luther spoke dismissively of the book of James, yet his failure to follow its teachings here led to what many consider Luther's biggest mistake—his uncharacteristic attacks on the Jews.

[34] Martin Luther, "On the Jews and their Lies," *Humanitas International*; http://www.humanitas-international.org/showcase/chronography/documents/luther-jews.htm; accessed January 2008. All quotes from Luther in this section are taken from this source.

[35] Katz, p. 391.

[36] Ibid., p. 364.

[37] "Toledoth Yeshu," *Ancient Jewish Accounts of Jesus*, [Text from Goldstein, *Jesus in the Jewish Tradition*, pp. 148-154]; http://ccat.sas.upenn.edu/humm/Topics/JewishJesus/toledoth.html; accessed January 2008.

[38] Abram Leon Sachar, *A History of the Jews* (New York 1964), p. 125.

[39] James Swan, "Martin Luther's Attitude Toward the Jews," *New Testament Research Ministries*; http://www.ntrmin.org/Luther%20and%20the%20Jews%20(Web).htm#a1; accessed June 2009.

[40] Martin Luther, *The Table Talk of Martin Luther*. Translated by William Hazlitt. *Center for Reformed Theology and Apologetics*; http://www.reformed.org/master /index.html?mainframe=/documents/Table_Talk/table_talk.html; accessed June 2009. This source is consistent with the full version of *Table Talk* included in the complete edition of Luther's works and cited in the bibliography.

[41] Lowell C. Green, *Lutherans Against Hitler: The Untold Story* (St. Louis 2007), pp. 26-28, 38.

[42] Richard J. Evans, *The Coming of the Third Reich* (New York / London 2005), p. 2.

[43] Richard Steigmann-Gall, *The Holy Reich: Nazi Conceptions of Christianity, 1919-1945* (Cambridge 2004), p. 137.

[44] Ibid., p. 136.

[45] John Warwick Montgomery, *In Defense of Martin Luther* (Milwaukee, WI 1970), p. 147.

[46] Adolf Hitler, *Hitler's Table Talk* (London 1953), quoted in "Kevin's Articles on Religion," *Kevin Davidson's Homepage*; http://www.davnet.org/kevin/articles/table.html; accessed June 2008.

[47] Martin Gilbert, *The Holocaust: A History of the Jews of Europe During the Second World War* (New York 1985), pp. 543, 467.

[48] Ibid., p. 623.

[49] Steven Ozment, *A Mighty Fortress: A New History of the German People (100 B.C. to the 21st Century)* (London 2004), p. 104.

[50] Martin Luther, *Martin Luther: Selections from his Writings,* ed. John Dillenberger (New York 1962), p. 5.

[51] Paul Lawrence Rose, *German Question / Jewish Question: Revolutionary Antisemitism from Kant to Wagner* (Princeton 1990), p. 8.

[52] Matthew Henry, *Commentary on the Whole Bible*; http://www.ccel.org/h/henry/mhc2/MHC00000.HTM; accessed January 2008.

[53] Rose, p. 4.

[54] Ibid.

[55] Ibid., pp. 94, 91, 95.

Chapter 3. Hitler's secular and ungodly ideas

Hitler in the light of scripture

All arguments showing irreconcilable differences between Christianity and National Socialism are null and void if it can be shown that Hitler was influenced by or derived his ideas from Christianity. Therefore it will be necessary to look more closely at the Fuhrer himself, and see if it is possible to arrive at a genuine understanding of his statements about the churches, God, and religion.

Hitler had clearly discernible intellectual antecedents. The National Socialist ideology that at first appearance seems so bizarre and inexplicable had predecessors, and many or all of Hitler's ideas had been expressed by others long before. In the words of historian George Mosse, Hitler fulfilled "a concept of life which had permeated much of the nation before he ever entered the scene."[1] An in-depth analysis of that concept of life requires some knowledge of German cultural history and lies outside the scope of this chapter.

Even without such academic knowledge, however, it is possible to come to a spiritual understanding of Hitler's relationship to Christianity. This can be done by comparing what is openly known about Hitler with the teachings of the Bible. The word of God is, as Peter said, a light that shines in a dark place. When with the light of eternal truth we peer into the great darkness of the Third Reich, we can see the real ugliness of Hitler's cruel pseudo-philosophy. We can also see the dangers of the intolerant secularist fanaticism that, rejecting God's truth and God's laws, attempts to reconstruct human society according to human wisdom alone.

This chapter will comment on Hitler's lack of Christian doctrines; his open statements of principles completely contrary to the Bible and even hostile to Christianity; two dubious professions of Christianity; some statements about "Christ," "God," "the Almighty," or "Fate"; his occasional references to the Bible; his statements of support for the churches; and his actual policies toward the churches. Having considered those points, we can then examine the faulty logic, historical inaccuracies, and distorted concepts of Christian doctrines that underlie attempts to argue that Hitler was a Christian.

Before doing so, it is necessary to see what the Bible says about men like Hitler. This was discussed in chapter 1, but a brief review is in order. Here are some nouns and adjectives from Romans that describe Hitler and the Nazis well:

> . . . vain in their imaginations . . . their foolish heart was darkened. Professing themselves to be wise, they became fools . . . filled with all unrighteousness . . . wickedness, covetousness, maliciousness . . . murder . . . deceit . . . proud, boasters, inventors of evil things . . . Without understanding, covenantbreakers, without natural affection, implacable, unmerciful . . . worthy of death . . .

Has anyone ever written a more concise description of the Nazis than this? More apt nouns and adjectives from other books of the New Testament are:

... uncleanness ... hatred ... wrath ... murders ... desirous of vainglory ... having the understanding darkened ... blinded hearts ... corrupt communications ... bitterness ... wrath ... anger ... malice ... spoiled by philosophy and vain deceit ... ungodly ... unholy ... manslayers ... menstealers ... liars ... men of corrupt minds destitute of the truth ...

A passage from II Timothy is particularly appropriate:

... in the last days perilous times shall come.
  For men shall be lovers of their own selves, covetous, boasters, proud, blasphemers, disobedient to parents, unthankful, unholy,
  Without natural affection, truce breakers, false accusers, incontinent, fierce, despisers of those that are good,
  Traitors, heady, highminded, lovers of pleasures more than lovers of God;
  Having a form of godliness, but denying the power thereof: from such turn away ... they shall proceed no further: for their folly shall be manifest unto all men ...

No one was more boastful and proud than Hitler. He coveted more and more territory, more and more power; he broke countless agreements; he was fierce, lacking in natural affection, a false accuser—and he had a form of godliness. He used god-words on occasion and claimed to be sent by God—this rhetoric (whether he actually believed it or not) was useful to him politically. But, lacking the real power of godliness as manifested in a genuinely spiritual life, he was a false prophet. Finally, his folly was manifest unto all, so that today no sensible person believes his ridiculous and contemptible philosophy. Even his own followers were persuaded of Hitler's folly and forced to abandon their evil dreams by the debating tactics of the armed forces of England, America, and Russia.

A blatant absence of Christian doctrines

One highly significant point is that Hitler's assembled religious quotations and statements omit essential Christian doctrines. In all of the references made by Hitler that have any religious content, assembled after diligent search by those who want to link him to Christianity, the following doctrines are conspicuously absent:

~ that God is three in one: Father, Son, and Holy Spirit
~ that Christ now sits at the right hand of God, whence he will return as God to judge the world
~ that he died on the cross *as a sacrifice for the sins of the world*. This last part is put in italics because Hitler did mention the crucifixion once or twice, but merely mentioning the crucifixion (once in comparison to himself) does not constitute Christianity.
~ that Jesus Christ rose from the dead and ascended into heaven
~ that Jesus existed as God before the creation of the world, and entered through a virgin's body, God manifest in the flesh

~ that we are all guilty of sin, and forgiveness of sins comes through faith in Christ and his sacrifice on the cross

~ that there will be a resurrection from the dead, and a day of judgment, on which the chosen of God will be ushered into paradise, while the lost will be sent to punishment in the lake of fire

~ that the Bible is the word of God, directly inspired and infallible and inerrant

~ that if we love Christ and believe in him, we are supposed to follow his teachings

The above mentioned doctrines are at the very center of Christianity. The adult Hitler as far as is known never mentioned any of them. Occasional brief comments about Christ as an Aryan who died in the fight against Judaism or who cleansed the temple; promises to support the church that were later broken; failure to officially withdraw from the Catholic Church or stop paying the church tax; vague statements about God—these are not proofs of Christian belief or influence.

The basic doctrines that Hitler stressed, elaborated on, and consistently practiced derived from 19th-century secular philosophies. Survival of the fittest; subordination of the individual to the state; Aryan supremacy; racial and philosophical anti-Semitism (contamination of the blood by breeding and of the spirit by false ideals); German unification; race as the key to history; glorification of war; contempt for traditional moral values—these ideas did not come from the Bible. Opposition to abortion (by healthy German women), birth control, and homosexuality were based not on divine law or concern for the immortal human soul, but on a desire to strengthen the German race.[2]

Hitler's unbiblical principles (i)

Hitler not merely avoided all reference to uniquely Christian doctrines—he also advocated ideas that were directly contrary to the Bible. It would take too long to wade through *Mein Kampf* and list all of the ideas that contradict Christianity—fortunately, that will not be necessary. Even a few chapters yield many examples of Hitler's paganism.

In volume I chapter 11 ("Nation and Race") we read that the foundational principles of our existence ("the principles to which he himself owes his existence as a man") are not the will of God, but rather cold and pitiless struggle in which the strong survive and the weak die. Moreover, man has not risen because he was created in the image of God, or because he has received divine revelation, but "has only risen on the basis of his knowledge of various laws and secrets of Nature to be lord over those other living creatures." According to Hitler, it is scientific knowledge that exalts us, not divine knowledge. This is pure and undiluted secularism.

Much of Hitler's rhetoric in this same chapter reveals blatant social Darwinism, the belief that the Darwinian struggle between organisms worked on the human level as well.

We find such phrases as:

> . . . it [the offspring of a lower parent] will later succumb in the struggle against the higher level . . .

> . . . the will of Nature for a higher breeding of all life . . .

Only the born weakling can view this as cruel, but he after all is only a weak and limited man; for if this law did not prevail, any conceivable higher development of organic living beings would be unthinkable.

In the struggle for daily bread all those who are weak and sickly or less determined succumb, while the struggle of the males for the female grants the right or opportunity to propagate only to the healthiest. And struggle is always a means for improving a species' health and power of resistance and, therefore, a cause of its higher development.

. . . since the inferior always predominates numerically over the best, if both had the same possibility of preserving life and propagating, the inferior would multiply so much more rapidly that in the end the best would inevitably be driven into the background, unless a correction of this state of affairs were undertaken. Nature does just this by subjecting the weaker part to such severe living conditions that by them alone the number is limited, and by not permitting the remainder to increase promiscuously, but making a new and ruthless choice according to strength and health.

. . . exact scientific truth . . . cold logic . . .

. . . the rigid law of necessity and the right to victory of the best and stronger in this world.
Those who want to live, let them fight, and those who do not want to fight in this world of eternal struggle do not deserve to live.
Even if this were hard-that is how it is! Assuredly, however by far the harder fate is that which strikes the man who thinks he can overcome Nature, but in the last analysis only mocks her. Distress, misfortune, and diseases are her answer.

The extent to which such ideas are consistent with Darwinism is debatable. Those who believe in Darwinism have a number of arguments to detach that theory from National Socialism. Those who do not believe in Darwinism find it much easier to see a connection. What is not debatable is that these ideas do not derive from Christianity.

Hitler also asserted in this same chapter that there is no higher independent truth, that all non-scientific truth is merely the invention of man:

. . . an idea cannot overcome the preconditions for the development and being of humanity, since the idea itself depends only on man. Without human beings there is no human idea in this world, therefore the idea as such is always conditioned by the presence of human beings and hence of all the laws which created the precondition for their existence . . . This applies most of all to those ideas whose content originates, not in an exact scientific truth, but in the world of emotion, or, as it is so beautifully and clearly expressed today, reflects an 'inner experience.' All these ideas, which have nothing to do with cold logic as such, but represent only pure expressions of feeling, ethical conceptions, etc., are chained to the existence of men, to whose intellectual imagination and creative power they owe their existence.

Ideas do not transcend the conditions out of which they arose—there are no eternal truths. Religions and philosophies owe their existence only to the human mind—or so Hitler said. Ethical conceptions do not reflect "exact scientific truth"—how can any materialist refute this? Another statement is:

> . . . this planet once moved through the ether for millions of years without human beings and it can do so again some day if men forget that they owe their higher existence, not to the ideas of a few crazy ideologists, but to the knowledge and ruthless application of Nature's stern and rigid laws.

According to Hitler, we owe our higher existence to the knowledge and application of Nature's laws, not to divine creation. What good secular humanist can disagree with this? And who are those "crazy ideologists"? People who believe in eternal truths that do not "depend only on man"?

Some of Hitler's statements about Jews in this chapter reveal his rejection of the Old Testament. In Hitler's words: "Since the Jew . . . was never in possession of a culture of his own, the foundations of his intellectual work were always provided by others. His intellect at all times developed through the cultural world surrounding him . . . ." He saw the Old Testament as historically inaccurate, like secularists and theological liberals in 19th-century Germany. Jewish religious beliefs were derived from surrounding cultures, not from God. The Old Testament was merely a product of human culture. The foundations of Jewish culture, including concepts of God and religious practices, were borrowed from others, not divinely handed down.

99% of the Old Testament historical record was dismissed by Hitler as inaccurate: ". . . Since the Jew never possessed a state with definite territorial limits and therefore never called a culture his own . . . he was never a nomad, but only and always a parasite in the body of other peoples . . . The Jew has always been a people with definite racial characteristics and never a religion . . . ." So much for Moses, Abraham, David, the Psalms, and Torah.

Hitler also claimed "The Jewish religious doctrine consists primarily in prescriptions for keeping the blood of Jewry pure and for regulating the relation of Jews among themselves, but even more with the rest of the world; in other words, with non-Jews." The essence of Jewish religious law is keeping the blood pure? Jewish marriage laws consist of, I don't know, maybe 0.005% of the whole Old Testament. All of the most essential religious teachings of Judaism meant nothing to Hitler (he did quote "an eye for an eye" once). His numerous references to God were to the god of German philosophy and pseudo-science, not to the God of Abraham, Isaac, and Jacob.

The Jews never had their own culture but only borrowed from other people; they never wandered as nomads and they never had their own state; they never had a real religion—and what religion they did have was borrowed from other people. The real essence of their religion was marriage laws to ensure racial purity. And some maintain that Hitler got his ideas from the Bible. Maybe the Beatles were agents of the Kremlin too, sent to facilitate a Communist takeover by debilitating American youth. Didn't they record a song, "Back in the USSR"? That clearly shows a belief in Communism—doesn't it?

Concerning Hitler's overall view of the Jews, it did not derive from biblical considerations. One of his main objections was the Jewish threat to German racial purity through interbreeding—a subject of no interest to Christians for 1800 years after Christ, and one having no biblical basis. The book of Acts teaches the racial oneness of all mankind, stating that God "hath made of one blood all nations of men for to dwell on all the face of the earth . . .".

Hitler did refer to the Jews killing Christ, but never made the argument that by killing Christ the Jews had brought God's wrath upon them and could only be redeemed by conversion to Christianity. On the contrary, he felt that conversion to Christianity would leave the Jew still a Jew, since the problem was racial, not religious. In his criticisms of the pre-WWI Austrian Christian Social Party, Hitler objected to religious anti-Semitism:

> . . . in the struggle against the Jews on a religious basis they thought they had discovered a slogan transcending all of old Austria's national differences.
>
> It is obvious that combating Jewry on such a basis could provide the Jews with small cause for concern. If the worst came to the worst, a splash of baptismal water could always save the business and the Jew at the same time. With such a superficial motivation, a serious scientific treatment of the whole problem was never achieved, and as a result far too many people, to whom this type of anti-Semitism was bound to be incomprehensible, were repelled. [vol. I chapt. 3, "General Political Considerations Based on My Vienna Period"]

Hitler's use of the word "scientific" in this context is especially significant. It derives from the "scientific fact" of life as a struggle for survival in which racial purity leads to victory, and racial decay leads to decline. The importance of racial purity was fully developed (though outside of a Darwinian context) by the influential 19th-century racist Arthur de Gobineau. Such a belief seems ridiculous to us, but seemed reasonable to many educated people in the Germany of Hitler's childhood. This was combined with a philosophical tradition that presented the Aryan as the ideal and the Jew as the antithesis of that ideal.

Hitler expressed many other unbiblical principles in this chapter of *Mein Kampf*. He believed that happiness did not come from forgiveness of sins and eternal life in heaven, or from an experience of the love of God—it came from understanding of racial laws: "The man who misjudges and disregards the racial laws actually forfeits the happiness that seems destined to be his." Survival of the fittest is loudly proclaimed, with not a word about forgiveness of sins, or eternity in paradise or in hell; this one chapter of *Mein Kampf* alone is sufficient to demonstrate the secular quality of Hitler's thought—and it is necessary to stress that these were not just theories.

These ideas were, unlike Hitler's religious words, confirmed by his actions. Shirer's *Rise and Fall of the Third Reich* (which in spite of some limitations such as superficial comments about "godfearing" evildoers is a good starting point for understanding Hitler), gives a clear example. Using records taken by high-ranking officers present at the meeting as well as a memorandum found in files captured by American troops, Shirer describes a military conference that took place on August 22, 1939, shortly before the invasion of Poland. He quotes Hitler as saying that "The stronger man is right," because the meaning of "this world order . . . lies in the success of the best by the means of force."[3]

In a meeting with his generals less than two weeks before the invasion of Poland, what does Hitler discuss? The teachings of Jesus, the apostles, and the Bible? Martin Luther? He demonstrates a serious commitment to the philosophy which he spelled out at length in *Mein Kampf*. But, there are some who care nothing for this. They "strain at gnats and swallow camels," as Jesus said, hunting for every scrap or clue that might justify their obsession with attacking Christianity, and ignoring clear and obvious statements of secular values that were confirmed by actions.

Shirer's sources reveal a Hitler who was acting consistently with his stated philosophy of life as a struggle in which the weak are eliminated—the philosophy of exact scientific truth to which we supposedly owe our very existence. Ethics are only human inventions. Logic reveals that the strong survive, and the weak die. This is the law of life and the meaning of our existence—and it is impossible to see how any Darwinist could disagree with this statement. That is, according to Darwin, how we got here. Why then should we not base our lives and our actions upon this fundamental truth—if, in fact, it is a truth, which growing numbers of people believe it is not?

This is not to blame National Socialism on Darwin. There were important aspects of Naziism such as slaughtering the Jews and blind obedience to Hitler which Darwin never dreamed of and would have condemned unhesitatingly. Hitler's thought, including his understanding of evolution, was uniquely German. Nevertheless, the idea of survival of the fittest as being the source of all progress (without reference to a divinely given system of ethics and morality) is integral to Hitler's thought.

Hitler's unbiblical principles (ii)

This brief discussion has by no means exhausted the pagan elements in *Mein Kampf*. There is much more. Another chapter, "Personality and the Conception of the Volkish State" [vol. II chapt. 4] not only completely ignores the Bible's limited concept of the state as the instrument of God to punish and restrain evil (as taught in Romans chapt. 13 and I Peter chapt. 2). It advances many thoroughly pagan and secular theories that derive, as is plainly stated in the title, from the German Folkish philosophy, which Hitler described as basic to his concept of the state.

This Folkish philosophy (which we will examine in chapter 5) was a mixture of 19th-century ideas that included Aryan supremacy and anti-Semitism. Its roots were in various secular trends that emerged after the turning away from traditional religion that was one of the most essential characteristics of the so-called

Enlightenment. It has been consistently ignored by some who want to link Hitler to Christianity but do not care for whatever reason to study these matters in depth.

Hitler's chapter on the Folkish state reveals that he saw the purpose of the state as being to further the development of the race, "to educate and promote the existence of those who are the material out of which the State is formed . . . educate them and finally train them." This is necessary because race is "the fundamental element on which all life is based." This reflects the teachings not of Jesus, but of Gobineau. That elements "which show the best racial qualities ought to be encouraged more than the others and especially they should be encouraged to increase and multiply" is a modern idea, not an ancient one.

These and other comments—which were not merely political rhetoric but which agree with Hitler's actions—have nothing to do with the Bible. There are other concepts of Hitler's in this chapter [vol. II chapt. 4] which would meet with the wholehearted approval of any genuine secularist if quoted without reference to the source. For example, Hitler ascribes man's rise above the animal world not to a divine creation, to God breathing the breath of life into Adam, creating Adam and Eve in his image. He ascribes it to wholly secular causes:

> The first step which visibly brought mankind away from the animal world was that which led to the first invention. The invention itself owes its origin to the ruses and stratagems which man employed to assist him in the struggle with other creatures for his existence and often to provide him with the only means he could adopt to achieve success in the struggle . . . everyone who believes in the higher evolution of living organisms must admit that every manifestation of the vital urge and struggle to live must have had a definite beginning in time and that one subject alone must have manifested it for the first time . . . This is more easily understood and more easy to believe in the case of man. His first skilled tactics in the struggle with the rest of the animals undoubtedly originated in his management of creatures which possessed special capabilities   . . . all these inventions help man to raise himself higher and higher above the animal world and to separate himself from that world in an absolutely definite way. Hence they serve to elevate the human species and continually to promote its progress . . .

Man raised himself up above the animal level by his own creative power, and the blessings of mankind come not from God but from human intelligence, with no need of revelation or divine guidance. This is humanism—and the attempt to explain the evolutionary origins of human society was not some weird idea Hitler cooked up by himself. It was a common theme of 19th-century Darwinists who sought to re-interpret all of life in the light of their new theory. Notice also the emphasis on continual progress, a doctrine not of the Bible but of 19th-century thinkers such as Hegel (along with many others) who imagined that the progress of mankind would continue indefinitely.

This chapter contains more social Darwinism—the process of selection and survival of the fittest applied to human society and elevated from a theory of man's origins into a guide to conduct and a source of ethics (or of non-ethics, I should say). Life is a "hard struggle for existence itself. In this struggle there are many who break down and collapse . . . In the realm of thought and of artistic creation, and even in the economic field, this same process of selection takes place . . . This same principle of selection rules . . ." This was, moreover, not merely rhetoric like a few of Hitler's promises to support the churches, but the rule that Hitler lived by and tried to apply consistently to every area of life.

Much more could be said about the unChristian and anti-Christian elements that provide the foundation of Hitler's thought, but the above will be sufficient for some—ten thousand books would not be sufficient for others. It might be useful to conclude this section by looking at some of Martin Bormann's comments about Christianity. He claimed that people should live "naturally," according to the "laws of nature and of life," according to "natural law," not according to the rules of the "naive Christians." Bormann advocated a life "based on scientific foundations," not on Christian dogmas "which were set up almost 2,000 years ago and have petrified into dogmas incompatible with reality." Bormann, like left-wing anti-religious humanists today, believed his views were based on "the latest knowledge of scientific research."[4]

Some have tried to distance Hitler from Bormann by claiming that Bormann was more extreme in his anti-religious views than was Hitler, the Catholic. They do not stop to ask what Catholic would choose an extreme anti-Catholic to be his right hand man—as if a left-wing secular humanist would choose a right-wing Christian fundamentalist to be his closest assistant and advisor. They do not consider that Hitler did not appoint independent-minded people whose ideas clashed with his own to high positions. Bormann attained his high position in the Reich and kept it until the very end by his faithful and loyal devotion to the Fuhrer. If Hitler had to reign in Bormann's excessive zeal on occasion, this was a matter of tactics, not of fundamental disagreement.

Hostility to Christianity in *Mein Kampf*

Hitler not only expressed much philosophy completely contrary to the Bible—he also expressed overt hostility to Christianity. For example, he stated that missionary activity in Africa turned "healthy, though primitive and inferior, human beings into a rotten brood of bastards" [vol. II chapt. 2].[5] Does the idea of people being turned into rotten bastards by converting to Christianity need to be elaborated on? He stated in this context that eugenics and racial health were more important than missions, and complained that the churches were not concerned with racial purity.

Elsewhere he wrote that the greatness of Christianity lay not in its truths but in its "inexorable fanaticism"—hardly a ringing endorsement of belief [vol. I chapt. 12].[6] He also stated that on the Jewish question both denominations were suitable "neither to the requirements of the nation nor to the real needs of religion" [vol. I chapt. 3].[7] Protestantism was more suitable for Germany than Catholicism "in its genesis [German] and later tradition [accommodation to secular philosophy]," but there is still a problem with Protestantism in that "it combats with the greatest hostility any attempt to rescue the nation from the embrace of its most mortal enemy, since its attitude toward the Jews just happens to be more or less dogmatically established."[8] Writing in the 1920s when public disagreement with his ideas was still possible, Hitler interpreted rejection of his racial theories as "the greatest hostility." It must have infuriated Hitler to think that people disagreed with him.

Hitler makes other statements in *Mein Kampf*, so clear in their antagonism that it is surprising they have been overlooked. Referring to the well-known and indisputable Jewish origins of Christianity, Hitler refers to Christianity's "fanatical intolerance" and says the intolerance of Christianity is typically Jewish [vol. II chapt. 5, "Philosophy and Organization"]. Some study of the thought of H.S. Chamberlain, a man whose ideas were very close to and even identical to Hitler's on key points, helps to an understanding of this strange argument. Basically, Chamberlain felt that the original true Aryan religion was based on feeling—it was narrow-minded Jewish dogmatism that introduced the idea of there being one truth and one way. This had infected Christianity, and through Christianity introduced harmful and alien Semitic concepts to European culture. Nietzsche also saw Christianity as the result of negative Jewish influence, and elaborated on this at great length in *The Antichrist*.

Hitler saw the enormous influence of Christianity on European culture as Jewish influence. He referred with "loathing" to the Jewish fanaticism inherent in Christianity, stating:

> The individual may establish with pain today that with the appearance of Christianity the first spiritual terror entered into the far freer ancient world; but he will not be able to contest the fact that since then the world has been afflicted and dominated by this coercion, and that coercion is only broken by coercion, and terror only by terror. Only then can a new state of affairs be constructively created.[9]

Continuing in this vein, Hitler states that Christianity's intolerance arises "for the most part from specifically Jewish modes of thought . . . this type of intolerance and fanaticism positively embodies the Jewish nature."[10] This "philosophy filled with infernal intolerance [Christianity] will only be broken by a new idea."[11]

The vast majority of Christians failed to read *Mein Kampf* or take it seriously during the years when Hitler was on the extreme fringe. By the time he had become a major political force public opposition was already dangerous, and the few who understood Hitler's comments here did not want problems with SA thugs. For the rest who did not know about the book, a few reassuring public statements from Hitler were sufficient. As in other areas, Hitler's stated views were ignored or explained away by people who could not conceive of someone actually meaning such things.

Hitler's main objection to Christianity here was its "intolerance"—the same objection raised by the anti-religious left in America today. How these secularists hate to be told that their way is wrong. Their guilty consciences fill them with rage against bearers of the unpleasant truth that they are wrong. This is why their fake "tolerance" extends to many sorts of evildoers, but not to people who challenge their presuppositions too strongly.

An honest liar

In spite of the blatant secularism and obvious hostility to Christianity in his book, Hitler not only expressed his support for the churches in Germany and promised to protect them; he also quoted the Bible on a few occasions (few relative to the torrent of words he poured out over the years). Moreover, he referred to God, the Lord, Providence, and even on a couple of widely-quoted occasions claimed to be a Christian. Before continuing, however, we need to make one important qualification. Now we know what Hitler was, but the situation was very different in the 1920s and early 1930s. Someone like Hitler had never appeared before, and it was impossible then to imagine the cruelties and horrors that are now automatically associated with his name. Many people, even experienced diplomats and foreign observers, were fooled by Hitler and believed what later proved to be nothing but calculated lies.

Trying to determine when Hitler was lying and when he was telling the truth was difficult for many people at that time, and Hitler was extraordinarily successful at deceiving people. With the advantage of hindsight and historical knowledge, however, we can compare Hitler's statements with his actions. As we do this, a pattern emerges. In the statement of his main goals, Hitler was truthful and did exactly what he said he would do: tear up the Versailles Treaty, rearm Germany, expand to the east, destroy the Weimar democracy, eliminate Jewish influence.

On other occasions, Hitler was a devious and treacherous liar who said one thing and did the exact opposite. He routinely lied and told people whatever would help him to reach his ends. To understand Hitler, it is necessary to compare Hitler's words with his actions and see not merely what he said, but also what he did. People with even an elementary knowledge of this subject don't need any examples, but since so many have tried to discuss Hitler's views as if all of his religious statements can be taken at face value, a few examples might be useful.

Hitler assured Chamberlain at Munich that the Sudetenland would be his last territorial demand, and promised to respect the borders of Czechoslovakia after his demands were met. The worth of these statements is well known. He assured European leaders that Germany wanted peace, while he rearmed Germany at top speed and had his generals prepare for war. When appointed Chancellor by President Hindenburg, he promised to govern legally—a promise which didn't last long.

One could go on and on, but one example from Shirer's history is illuminating. In January of 1934, Hitler sent Ernst Roehm a friendly letter. Hitler thanked Roehm for his contribution to the cause, assured Roehm of his gratitude, and said he was grateful to be able to call Roehm a friend and a comrade.[12] In June of that same year, Hitler had Roehm murdered in the infamous Blood Purge. How much, then, were Hitler's statements of respect for the churches worth? They were shown by his actions to have been totally false.[13]

Hitler the Catholic?

The waters have been muddied by the fact that Hitler on two occasions claimed to be a Christian—at least, there are two quotes that are continually brought up in these discussions. One of the statements is: "I am now as before a Catholic and will always remain so."[14] This is definitive—for those who trust

Hitler and think he was an honest man. But, was this a sincere statement of belief? An informed and objective review of Hitler's life gives the answer—assuming the quote to be genuine, which we will do for the sake of discussion (though evangelists for the "Hitler was a Christian" school of thought explain away and refuse to accept statements by Hitler showing hatred and contempt for Christianity).

Hitler the Catholic. He committed suicide, a mortal sin in the Catholic Church. He did not call for a priest in his last hours, make confession, or seek absolution or ask for last rites. He never went to confession once the entire time he was Chancellor, and numerous laws restricting Catholics and seeking to remove them from every sphere of public life were a notable feature of his regime. He never went to mass once during the entire war, but did attend a Requiem for Marshal Pilsudski of Poland in 1935 (a good photo-op, useful for deceiving people). He never said one single reverential word about the Virgin Mary. Can any serious person imagine Hitler counting rosary beads and going to a priest to confess his sins?

Moreover, in March of 1937 a papal encyclical (*Mit Brennender Sorge*) was read in Catholic churches throughout Germany. It objected to the Nazi cult of race, and called for resistance to perversions of Christian doctrine and morality. The primary loyalty of German Catholics to Rome was reaffirmed—and what was Hitler's response? Did he say "The Holy Father has spoken" or "The Pope has the power of the keys from Peter and as a Catholic I call on all Germans to submit to the claims of Rome"?

Professor John Conway's useful book *The Nazi Persecution of the Churches 1933-1945* relates Hitler's response—it was not that of a devout Catholic.[15] Copies of the encyclical were seized whenever possible, and those caught distributing it were to be arrested. Publication by German church newspapers was forbidden. The Nazi Minister of Church Affairs accused the Roman Church of "treachery," and Hitler refused to pay a courtesy call on the Vatican when he visited Rome in 1938.

What about Hitler's Concordat with the Vatican, the agreement signed in 1933 that promised rights and security to German Catholics in exchange for a Catholic agreement not to interfere in German politics? Does this prove that Hitler was a Catholic? If so, signing an agreement with England proves that Hitler was an Englishman, and the non-aggression pact with the Soviet Union proves that Hitler was a Russian.

The Concordat was extremely advantageous for Hitler. In 1933 he had only recently assumed power, and the process of consolidating his grip over every aspect of German society was still underway. The promise by the Catholics to offer no political opposition was of great assistance to him, and recognition by the Vatican of a regime that was deeply suspect in the eyes of many foreign diplomats and observers was a propaganda prize.

The Concordat would also have been very advantageous for the Vatican—if Hitler had kept its provisions. The Church was promised rights and given a legal status that looked very good—on paper. Hitler, however, began to violate it immediately. The Concordat with the Vatican was repeatedly broken right from the start, and Conway gives more than ample documentation. Pages 278-279 alone contain the following: confiscation of two Jesuit monasteries in Munster... of monasteries, an abbey, the House of the Mission Sisters of the Immaculate

Conception, and other church properties. "The Papal Nuncio himself made representations to the Foreign Ministry about the confiscations of monasteries in Aachen, Dresden, and Vienna." Bernt Engelmann, a German who experienced the Third Reich, relates that immediately after the Concordat was signed in 1933,

> . . . the Nazis launched their program of "bringing into line" the Catholic youth organizations. Their next step was to ban countless Catholic publications. Then they shut down monastery schools and Catholic hospitals, and arrested thousands of priests, monks, and laymen in leading Church positions. The Nazi newspapers, especially the anti-Semitic and anticlerical Stuermer and the official SS newspaper, *Der Schwarze Korps,* specialized in lurid portrayals of the unbridled decadence of the Catholic clergy.[16]

Why didn't the Vatican object? People really should read at least one book on the subject before asking uninformed questions. A short passage from Prof. Conway is useful here:

> In November (1933), Cardinal Pacelli, deeply shocked by the many cases of persecution reported to Rome, threatened to issue an official protest from the Vatican . . . In a note dispatched to the German Foreign Ministry, Pacelli complained bitterly of 'difficulties and persecutions, carried to a virtually intolerable degree, which the Catholic Church in Germany is now enduring in open violation of the Concordat'. An official from the Ministry of the Interior was hastily sent to Rome to smooth the matter over. . .[17]

Conway doesn't say whether this "smoothing over" was accomplished with promises that things would improve, or veiled threats that protests would make things worse, or by assertions that actions by the German government were justified by the failure of the German Catholics to keep completely silent on all political issues.

Why, then, didn't the Vatican excommunicate Hitler and place *Mein Kampf* on the index of forbidden books? Such a question shows a lack of familiarity both with the Roman Church and with realities of life in the Third Reich. If the Pope had excommunicated Hitler and banned his book, this would have placed German Catholics in an anguishing dilemma. They would either have had to openly reject and repudiate Hitler, in which case they would have suffered the severest persecution with devastating damage to the institution of the Church in Germany, or they would have had to break with the Pope and ignore his excommunication. In either case the Roman Church in Germany would have suffered greatly. The Pope, rightly or wrongly, felt that his only course was to continue to lodge numerous but completely ineffectual protests through official channels.

Hitler also was anxious to avoid such a confrontation. A repetition of Bismarck's battles with the Catholic Church would have hindered his political program and later the war effort unnecessarily. He was therefore content to allow persecution of the Church to continue sufficiently to render the Church impotent and to keep it from opposing him politically. Hitler even restrained on occasion some of his more zealous subordinates, such as Bormann and Himmler, from acting out a hostility that Hitler shared but restrained due to a greater awareness of political realities.

This is not to defend the Roman Church. It is only to state that failure to excommunicate Hitler does not prove he was a Catholic "in good standing" as some have claimed. It is true, he never left the church officially, but Jesus said nothing about church membership as a means for cruel and evil people to gain favor with God. Moreover, it is too often forgotten that Hitler was not merely a maniacal dictator. He was also, especially before the war, a very canny politician. What benefit would there have been for him to arbitrarily and unnecessarily alienate himself from a sizable portion of the German electorate?

Returning to Hitler's alleged assertion of his Catholicism, what motive would he have had for telling a lie about religion? The answer is not far to seek. If as has been claimed he made that comment about being a Catholic to one of his generals in 1941, the following scenario is plausible. A general who was not at heart a rabid Nazi (and there were some) may have been troubled by the extreme persecution of the Catholic Church in Poland. Hitler was not hampered by domestic political considerations there, and there was an overt attempt to crush the Polish Catholic Church. If a general, perhaps with a Catholic upbringing, had tried to discuss this with the Fuhrer, Hitler may have tried to reassure him with false words as he had done so often in the past: "I know there are problems. This is regrettably unavoidable in time of war. I give you my solemn word of honor that things will be straightened out as soon as the war is won and the situation is stabilized. I myself am a Catholic and I appreciate your concern. Do your job and things will get better, I assure you. Have I ever told a lie in my life?"

Too many people have tried to discuss Hitler's beliefs without understanding the extent to which he was an inspired and gifted liar, with a real talent for telling people what they wanted to hear. More will be said in chapter 4 about Hitler's actions in dealing with the churches, as opposed to his words, but to conclude this discussion of Hitler's Catholicism an incident from Shirer's history is useful.[18]

In the Blood Purge of 1934, when hundreds of opponents (real or imagined) of the Nazi regime were murdered, one of the victims was Erich Klausener, head of a group called Catholic Action. That this was not an accident is clear from the fact that Klausener's office staff were sent to a concentration camp. A former Chancellor, Franz von Papen (also a Catholic), protested this action to Goering. Goering had him placed under arrest. Later Klausener's widow sued the state for damages—the lawyers representing her were placed in a concentration camp until they agreed to withdraw the suit.

When Hitler said "Poland attacked Germany first," or, "I wanted peace but the Jews forced England and America to war against me," it is not necessary to prove that he was lying. When he said (if he said) "I am a Catholic and will always remain so," it is necessary to show that he was lying. This is not difficult—though there are of course some who will remain unshaken by any evidence or reasoning. Perhaps it meets some deep inner emotional need to attack Christianity, a need that is impervious to facts, logic, and reason.

Honest Adolf strikes again

There was one occasion, during a speech given in 1922, where Hitler not only claimed to be a Christian—he elaborated on it. This reveals something of Hitler's thinking, and has some significant statements—though not in the way that some people think. He stated "My feeling as a Christian points me to my Lord and Savior as a fighter." He referred to Jesus' fight against the Jews and claimed that Jesus "was greatest not as a sufferer but as a fighter." He said that with "boundless love as a Christian and as a man" he read about how Jesus drove the "the brood of vipers and adders" out of the temple. A statement about Christ's "fight against the Jewish poison" is followed by the claim "it was for this that He had to shed his blood upon the Cross." Hitler then spoke of his duty as a Christian "to be a fighter for truth and justice . . . ."[19]

Hitler called Jesus "Lord"—did he make a serious attempt to follow the teachings of Jesus? Those who truly look upon Jesus as their Lord want to obey him. Jesus said, "Not every one that saith unto me Lord, Lord, shall enter into the kingdom of heaven . . ."

As to the passage itself, it is notable for two things: first, its absence of basic teachings about Christ, as has already been pointed out; there is nothing about the most important Christian beliefs concerning Christ. Secondly, it contains a number of elements that have nothing to do with Christianity, and are contrary to Christianity. For example:

~ Hitler relied not on doctrine but on "feeling," his "feeling as a Christian." This is not surprising as Christian doctrine nullifies Hitler's entire philosophy. Christianity based solely on feeling is nothing but humanism in a religious disguise.

~ Jesus "was greatest not as a sufferer but as a fighter." That driving the moneychangers out of the temple was more important than Christ's sacrificial death on the cross is a ludicrous perversion of Christianity. It also ignores Jesus' refusal to fight and his passive submission when arrested and executed.

~ Hitler speaks of "boundless love"—and what is the Bible's definition of love? I Corinthians 13 says that love is patient, kind, not puffed up or self-glorifying, and does not rejoice in sin but rejoices in truth. This is the exact opposite of Hitler. His concept of love (for the German people, for the fatherland, and of course for himself) did not come from scripture.

~ Jesus came to fight "against the Jewish poison" and summoned men to fight against the Jews? This novel interpretation requires a complete rejection of the Sermon on the Mount, as well as of Jesus' many other teachings about the reality of the world to come and eternal life in heaven.

~ This speech shows no understanding of or belief in the sacrificial death of Christ as an atonement for the sins of the world. According to Hitler, Jesus died on the cross not as a sacrifice for the sins of the world but to fight against the Jewish poison.

Hitler said that he had a duty to fight for truth and justice. Did Hitler fight for truth and justice? Christians should stand for those noble qualities—Hitler stood for the exact opposite. This speech does not show Hitler to be a Christian. It shows Hitler using Christian rhetoric for some reason. To understand what that reason might be, some background knowledge is useful.

In 1922, Hitler was still a minor figure, trying to broaden his base and appeal to as wide a section of the electorate as possible. A few Christian words here and there were useful politically, and cost nothing. The significance of this is thrown into sharper relief if we consider the political fate of General Ludendorff. This hero of the First World War shared many of Hitler's basic ideas and cooperated with Hitler in the attempt to overthrow the Bavarian government in 1923. Yet, Hitler rose to prominence while Ludendorff fell into obscurity. An explanation is found in the fact that Ludendorff was an outspoken opponent of Christianity. This alienated many people and led straight into the political wilderness. Richard Evans writes that Ludendorff's attacks on the Catholic Church were "a certain recipe for electoral disaster in Bavaria."[20]

Hitler was a much cannier politician, and he understood that many potential supporters were either Catholics, Christians, or at least respectful of Christianity, even if for no other reason than fond childhood memories. On a personal note let me say that I went to church regularly all through my youth and adolescence. Later, when in college and after, I made no effort to live as a Christian and did not consider myself to be one, but I was nevertheless uncomfortable when people openly rejected Christianity or were too disrespectful of it. I had some fond memories of Christmas Eve services, church activities, singing hymns and felt some respect for Christianity in spite of unbelief.

Hitler wanted votes—and what ordinary politician is going to attack Christianity openly and unnecessarily? This would alienate voters and gain nothing. American politicians can also make a few religious noises on occasion. It sounds good and reassures people. Hitler was smart enough to use a few Christian words once in a while, and give promises to support and protect the church. This is not indicative of a sincere belief in the deity of Christ, with an accompanying desire to serve and obey Christ.

Parenthetically, it is worth noting that Steigmann-Gall's aforementioned *The Holy Reich* translates this speech differently. Where Norman Baynes' Oxford University Press edition reads "who, God's truth! was greatest not as a sufferer but as a fighter," Steigmann-Gall's book reads "who, as the true God, was not only the greatest as a sufferer but also the greatest as a warrior."[21] In the footnote Steigmann-Gall cites the German source directly (*Voelkischer Beobachter*)— apparently he translated it himself.

Not having access to the original, and not having enough confidence in my high-school German to attempt my own translation even if I did, I am compelled to compare these conflicting translations according to external criteria. One question that comes to mind, if Steigmann-Gall's translation is correct, is why did Hitler only state this doctrine in 1922? Secondly, what effort did Hitler make to follow the teachings of Christ? Those who consider Christ to be the true God, God in the flesh, God come to earth in human form, have some regard for his teachings and try to follow them. They will not succeed to perfection—we all fall short— but there will be, on balance, some evidence of concern for Christ's commandments. Reducing Christ to someone who drove the moneychangers out of the temple and died on the cross but did not rise and will not return is not indicative of a sincere belief in his divinity.

There were two commonly cited instances in which Hitler specifically claimed to be a Christian. One of these was from 1922, the other from 1941. Since we can be sure that any other such references would not have been missed by those grasping at every straw that might link Hitler to Christianity, it appears that for nearly twenty years Hitler never claimed to be a Christian (again, assuming that the second statement, which was reported second hand as far as I know, is even genuine).

In 1922, Hitler was (as has been said already) the obscure leader of a minor fringe group. After he began to rise and attract national attention, it must have become obvious that posing as a Christian would have required church attendance and more biblical statements. It might also have led to awkward questions about his doctrines and views on church matters. It was much easier to drop the unnecessary pretense of being a Christian, since it was sufficient for political purposes to make a few statements about God or the Bible once in a while, and assure the churches of his support and respect.

Christ in *Mein Kampf*

Hitler made other references to Christ at odd intervals, one of them being in vol. I chapt. 11 of his book. Since someone might say "Hitler mentioned Jesus! That proves he was a devout, Bible believing Christian who got his views from the New Testament!" we should look at this briefly. The passage is as follows. Speaking of "the Jew," it starts with an idea expressed long before by the "Enlightenment" philosopher Immanuel Kant—"His life is only of this world," and goes on to state that:

> . . . his [the Jew's] spirit is inwardly as alien to true Christianity as his nature two thousand years previous was to the great founder of the new doctrine. Of course, the latter made no secret of his attitude toward the Jewish people, and when necessary he even took to the whip to drive from the temple of the Lord this adversary of all humanity, who then as always saw in religion nothing but an instrument for his business existence.

Far from showing any concern for Christianity, this shows only Hitler's twisted logic. For one thing, Jesus drove out some dishonest traders, not "the Jews." Some dishonest Jewish merchants no more represent "the Jews" than some dishonest German merchants represent the Germans or some dishonest Japanese businessmen represent the Japanese. Jesus did not regard Peter, James, John, Mary Magdalene, or many other Jews as "the adversary of humanity." Also, anyone who thinks Hitler believed the temple in Jerusalem was the house of God is invited to identify themselves. Jesus did many other things during his ministry on earth, but Hitler had no interest in them. Finally, he calls Jesus "the great founder of the new doctrine." This is an evasive way of trying to say something nice about Jesus without really saying anything, just to make the gullible and simple-minded Christians happy. No one who believed Jesus was the son of God come to earth in human form would refer to him as "the founder of the new doctrine."

Hitler described the Jewish spirit as being alien to true Christianity. He also referred to the Jews as plotting to take over the world, being merciless and cruel, as inciting wars and being enemies of humanity. All of his criticisms of the Jews describe his own evils exactly. He accused them of doing the very things he was doing himself. In the same way, he accused them of being alien to true Christianity when it was he himself who was alien to true Christianity.

Another reference to Christ—or at least to Christianity—is in volume I chapter 8 ("The Beginning of my Political Activity"). Here Hitler gives his assessment of Christianity, stating that "In its workings, even the religion of love is only the weak reflection of the will of its exalted founder; its significance, however, lies in the direction which it attempted to give to a universal human development of culture, ethics, and morality."

The "religion of love" does not reflect eternal and divine truths—it reflects only the will of a man, of a man whose deity, resurrection, and return are never mentioned. Also, the significance of this religion lies not in the happiness it brings, in eternal life in heaven or forgiveness of sins—no, its significance lies in "culture, ethics, and morality." This is the same idea of Christianity held by Hegel and by liberal German "Protestant" "theologians." They dispensed with miracles, the supernatural, heaven, and hell, and believed in a Jesus who was a great moral teacher, nothing more. Hitler's idea of Christianity here at least was in the mainstream of 19th-century secularism and theological liberalism. As a politician, he was prudent enough to avoid stating that, in his view, the ethics of the "religion of love" were contrary to nature's law of victory of the stronger and hence were totally false.

Hitler's last will and testament

If a speech made when Hitler was an obscure and aspiring politician carries a lot of weight, surely his last will and testament, written shortly before his death, should carry much more. Confronted with the final reality of death, then if at any time someone's thoughts should turn to religion—if, that is, they are sincerely interested in religion and think it important. When, however, we look at Hitler's last words, what do we find?

There is nothing about God, Jesus, heaven, or the Bible. There are no religious words whatsoever. Moreover, those who were present during Hitler's last days do not record that he called for a priest, or had any interest in religious matters. There are however some statements in Hitler's last words that shed light on his real belief. He said, "In these three decades I have been actuated solely by love and loyalty to my people in all my thoughts, acts, and life. They gave me the strength to make the most difficult decisions which have ever confronted mortal man."[22] The German people gave him his strength, all of his thoughts and acts were devoted to them—this shows Hitler's idolatry of Germany and the German race; it is not Christianity.

Why is it that some will look through every book and speech for any scrap or clue that might remotely link Hitler to Christianity or the Bible in even the most tangential and far-fetched way, and then ignore his last words? John Wesley's dying words were not "I have received my strength from the English people and have been motivated solely by loyalty and love to them." Hitler's exaltation of nation and race to a religious level has deep roots in 19th century German philosophy—not in the teachings of Christ or the apostles.

Hitler's references to God

It would be unwise to state that Hitler was an atheist. He opposed "godless Communism" and frequently stated his belief in some kind of a higher power. Collections of religious statements by Hitler show the use of such words as "God . . . God's will . . . the Lord . . . the Almighty Creator . . . the Lawgiver . . . Providence." Hitler asked for God's blessing, asserted God's creation of the world, claimed to be doing God's will, and gave God credit for his successes—yet German thinkers frequently spoke of some kind of higher power outside of a biblical concept and even called it "God." Such statements do not demonstrate Christian belief. Also, if they prove the evil of all religion, then Stalin and Mao prove the evil of all atheism.

Some atheists are dishonest enough (or complacent enough) to think they can make sweeping, simplistic, blanket condemnations of theism, and then engage in the most subtle and nuanced analysis of the crimes of atheists. Their so-called detached objectivity is nothing but a bad joke.

What were Hitler's views exactly? It might be assumed that, in the context of that time and culture, any reference to God could only be Christian—it certainly wasn't Moslem or Jewish. This is convincing to those with little or no knowledge of common trends in German religion and philosophy. Hitler's concept of God was in some ways similar to Hegel's World Spirit—a nebulous force that worked through certain national groups (the Greeks, the Romans, the French under Napoleon, and, finally, the Germans) to further the development of humanity. Hegel's imaginary World Spirit used great heroes, Men of Destiny, as its agents. These Heroes were not obligated to obey ordinary rules of morality binding on the mere mortals far beneath them. They were justified—according to Hegel—in trampling the common people beneath their bloodstained feet as they led mankind to ever greater heights of glory.

There is another concept of God—Martin Bormann's:

> When we National Socialists speak of a belief in God, we do not understand by God, like naive Christians . . . a human-type being, who sits around somewhere in space . . . The force of natural law, with which all these innumerable planets move in the universe, we call the Almighty or God. The claim that this world force is concerned about the fate of every single being, of every smallest earth bacillus, or can be influenced by so-called prayers or other astonishing things, is based on a proper dose of naivety or alternatively on a commercial shamelessness . . . The more accurately we recognize and observe the laws of nature and of life, the more we adhere to them, so much the more do we conform to the will of the Almighty.[23]

This makes it clear that Bormann was a secular humanist of an exceedingly fanatical and intolerant type.

One scholar who has made a serious effort to understand the intellectual background to Hitler's thought, Daniel Gasman, provides another example of how the word "God" was used in a non-Christian context. Writing about Ernst Haeckel, the German biologist and pre-eminent popularizer of Darwinism and scientific secularism, Prof. Gasman quotes Haeckel as saying that God was present in all things, "God is everywhere." Consistently with a marked trend toward pantheism in 19th-century German philosophy, Haeckel imagined that the universe was a "colossal organism" animated by a divine force that is not apart from and above nature, like the Christian God, but rather at one with nature: "God is almighty; He is the single Creator, the single Cause of all things . . . God is absolute perfection . . . God is the sum of all energy and matter."[24] Other comments reveal a belief that the Cosmos itself was God, a "pantheistic religion" that allowed for "the revival of many symbols of ancient German pagan religion and mythology."[25]

Haeckel was deeply hostile to Christianity, which he repeatedly condemned in the severest terms. The gospels were unreliable, Christianity was outdated and unscientific, Catholicism was bankrupt and Protestantism was "a religious lie of the worst character"[26]—yet, he used the word "God" according to his own understanding of it. He was by no means the only German to use religious language in a thoroughly non-Christian context. Someone who argues "Hitler used the words 'God, Providence, etc.'—this proves he was a Christian"—reveals a twofold ignorance: ignorance of Christian teaching, and ignorance of the whole course of German cultural history since the "Enlightenment." Perhaps my use of the word "ignorance" will seem excessively polemical to some, but I really can think of no other word.

Hitler's comments about God reveal a concept of God very different from scripture. Hitler's God was concerned primarily with blessing Germany, helping the Germans, exalting the Germans, while the non-Aryan peoples of the world were omitted—a peculiar sort of Providence. This "Providence" was an impersonal force that cared nothing about sin, forgiveness for sin, or righteousness on an individual basis, but presided over a vast process of struggle in which the weak perished and the strong survived.

Hitler's God was an abstract concept derived from German philosophy—and all of Hitler's appeals to whatever sort of "God" were nothing but violations of the third Commandment: "Thou shalt not take the name of the Lord thy God in vain." Hitler used God's name either to advance his own agenda or to express a philosophy far removed from the teachings of Christ. He used God's name to exalt himself and the German people, or to create an appearance of piety that was very useful in deceiving foolish and gullible Christians—but more of that in another place.

Finally, it is worth pointing out that Hitler also wrote of gods and goddesses—proving, if all of his religious utterances are taken at face value, that he was a polytheist. "The gods" are referred to in *Mein Kampf*—"the manifestations of decay showed only that the gods had willed Austria's destruction" [vol. I chapt. 3]—and there are references to goddesses as well: to the Goddess of Suffering [vol. I chapt. 2] and the Goddess of Destiny [vol. I chapt.5]. There is even a "goddess of eternal justice and inexorable retribution" which Hitler believed "caused Archduke Francis Ferdinand, the most mortal enemy of Austrian-Germanism, to fall by the bullets which he himself had helped to mold" [vol I chapt.1].

There is also a Goddess of Peace and a God of War. More significantly, there are numerous references to Fate. For those unfamiliar with religion and philosophy, "Fate" is a non-Christian term referring not to the personal God of the

Bible but to an impersonal force of unknown character. This should not have to be explained.

Hitler's references to the Bible

"But, Hitler quoted the Bible! Of course he was a Christian!" A simple answer should be sufficient for this simple-minded argument: Jesus did not say "Blessed are cruel and evil liars and murderers who quote the Bible once in a while." Those with a real understanding of the Bible know this perfectly well, but since some without this understanding have gone on and on about Hitler's Bible quotes we should examine this issue.

The exact nature of Abraham Lincoln's religious beliefs has been widely debated. On the one hand, he did give real evidence of some sort of belief, or at least of respect for the Bible and Christianity. On the other hand, he never publicly spoke of a personal conversion or encounter with Christ, and never referred to many essential biblical doctrines. Much has been written about this—and if someone said "Lincoln quoted the Bible when he said 'A house divided cannot stand!' This proves he was a Christian!" it would be instantly recognized that this person had no real knowledge of the subject.

For a politician to make use of a Bible verse on occasion proves nothing at all—especially, as is the case with Hitler, if those verses have nothing to do with repentance, forgiveness of sins, eternal life, or Christ's divine blood shed on the cross. If Hitler took a biblical concept, such as "a camel passing through the eye of a needle" or "no one can serve two masters," and used it to illustrate a secular idea, this is only a rhetorical device. On the day of judgment Hitler will be held accountable for everything that he said, did, and believed. Being a Christian is not a matter of quoting the Bible once in a while.

Hitler's expressions of support for Christianity and the German churches

Hitler did make some positive comments about Christianity. In a speech of February 1, 1933, he stressed the importance of the churches in German life. A speech from March 23 of the same year states that Hitler regarded the Catholic and Protestant Churches as valuable for "the maintenance of our nationality . . . ." and would not infringe their rights. He called for "honest cooperation between Church and State" and said that his struggle "for a real national community" would benefit the churches.[27] These and other such comments are clear proof of Hitler's Christian beliefs and values—if, that is, you consider Hitler to have been a sincere and honest man. By the way, for a Christian, "maintenance of nationality" is not the purpose of the church.

It is difficult to know how to respond to people who put their faith in Hitler's sincerity. Perhaps the best way is by showing a few other statements from Hitler's speeches. To give a few examples, he said in 1933 that "Germany desires nothing except an equal right to live and equal freedom . . . The German nation wishes to live in peace with the rest of the world . . . National Socialism does not harbour the slightest aggressive intent towards any European nation."[28]

Hitler the Christian, the man of peace and good will, deceived many people in his own day—he is still deceiving people today. For example, a speech given by Hitler in the Reichstag in January 1939 has been cited to prove Hitler's support for the church. It painted a rosy picture of the church in Germany and asserted that

German Christians had religious freedom, that the government did not interfere with the church—however, the same speech also stated that Germany wanted nothing but peace, and that rumors of German attacks were lies.

Why is it necessary to demonstrate that Hitler was a liar? Speaking in the same impartial forum of truth and detached analysis, the Nazi Reichstag, Hitler made some comments about the Polish crisis on September first of that same year, 1939. There he claimed that he had sought a peaceful solution to the problem, but was thwarted by Polish hostility and aggression.

Who would be dense enough to base their understanding of the outbreak of WWII on speeches in the Reichstag? Hitler's political lies are instantly recognizable. His religious lies are equally recognizable to those who have some knowledge of the experience of the German church under Hitler—but many who talk about Hitler and religion have no such understanding. We would pay no attention to someone who claimed "We know that Poland started the war by attacking Germany because Hitler said so," or, "Hitler lied about the invasion of Poland? Where is the proof? Where is the evidence? What motive would he have had for lying?"

But someone stated that Hitler had no reason to lie in expressing his support for the churches. A politician has no reasons to make false promises to win people's support? Some parts of Hitler's program were attractive politically to people who did not share all of his views—making a few positive statements about the church on occasion made his movement more appealing to a broader section of the population. Negotiations with the Catholic Centre Party were necessary for Hitler to gain sufficient control of the Reichstag. Would the Catholics have cooperated with Hitler if he had been known as an open enemy of the church? General Ludendorff was outspoken in his hostility to Christianity—he only succeeded in marginalizing himself, and faded into oblivion.

It is unfortunate that some people discuss Hitler's religious statements with so little understanding. If Hitler had said at Munich, "My goal is to dominate Europe and after I get the Sudetenland I will go for all of Czechoslovakia and then Poland," would he have had his bloodless conquest? If the Nazis had said to the Jews, "We are sending you to extermination camps where you will be put into gas chambers disguised as showers," the Final Solution would have been complicated immensely. If Hitler had said to the Russians, "I will make an agreement with you for my temporary benefit but will attack you as soon as it seems proper," would the Soviets have signed the non-aggression pact? If Hitler had said "I despise Christianity as an outdated and unscientific religion for weaklings, nothing but a Jewish trick, and if I ever get to power I will totally subordinate the churches to the state and do everything I can to eliminate the church's influence from public life" he would never have achieved such a large degree of support, and Hindenburg would never have been pressured to appoint him Chancellor.

It should not be necessary to point out that deceit was an integral part of Hitler's successes. People who ask "Why would Hitler lie about religion?" might just as well ask "Why would he lie at Munich?" or "Why would he lie about his massive rearmament program when allaying French and British suspicions of his intentions?" Many Germans who enthusiastically supported Hitler's political goals would have been considerably less enthusiastic if Hitler had not successfully projected a false appearance of moderation and respect for traditional values and institutions. This is forgotten by people who forget Hitler the cunning politician and think only of Hitler as the maniacal dictator. Those who say that Hitler's promises to support the churches reflect his Christianity are uninformed about historical realities.

The example of the trade unions

A brief discussion of the trade-unions in Nazi Germany might seem to be somewhat off-topic, but there is a striking parallel between Hitler's dealings with the trade unions and his dealings with the churches. It shows so clearly the real nature of Hitler's rhetoric about supporting the churches, and illustrates so clearly Hitler's methods, that it is worth examining.

Prior to Hitler's coming to power, the trade unions were an important factor in German politics (their firm opposition to the right-wing Kapp Putsch in 1920 contributed to its failure). Because of the influence of the unions, the Nazis dealt with them in the same way as they dealt with the churches—first promising support, and then putting them in chains. One difference is that the labor unions were considerably easier to deal with. Having no higher spiritual values, they collapsed immediately, while some of the churches struggled feebly in an effort to preserve some independence, and on rare occasions even spoke out directly.

Shirer records that the Nazis at first adopted a tone of friendship toward labor, and proclaimed May Day, 1933, a national holiday. Hitler spoke to a mass rally of workers and promised them his regime would honor and respect them. On the next day, the labor unions were dissolved, and their leaders were arrested.[29] Needless to say there were no protests from the churches. Was this because of centuries of anti-Semitism?

Robert Ley, appointed by Hitler to lead the German Labor Front, promised to protect and even increase the rights of the workers. This was followed by an action that directly contradicted those nice words—a law outlawing strikes, and decreeing that government appointed trustees would resolve disputes between labor and management. The same Ley who had promised to protect and even increase the rights of the workers now openly stated that employers were to be masters over the workers. German workers became modern serfs, with no unions and no right to bargain or strike.[30]

Is it necessary to point out the significance of this for the larger topic we are discussing? This shows in miniature Hitler's consistent *modus operandi*. Disarm your opponents by telling them what they want to hear, then, when the time is right, strike. Many decent people who try to talk about Hitler and his dealing with the churches do not understand the cunning and deceit of the man. They do not understand it even when the historical record is right before them—and how much harder was it to understand before the facts were known?

"Workers! Your institutions are sacred! Christians, we respect the church! I am the son of a peasant! I am a Christian! I know the importance of religious belief! We will respect the worker! We will respect the churches! That's a promise! You can count on us!" One needs a certain self-transcendence to grasp the full depth and height of Hitler's blatant lies. People who do not understand Hitler's deceitful nature have nothing significant to say about Hitler's beliefs. Who would say "We know Hitler supported labor because we have it in his own words, he said so himself"?

The Nazi party platform supported "positive" Christianity

Some have made a great issue of the fact that Point 24 of the Nazi party platform supported Christianity. It reads:

> We demand freedom for all religious faiths in the state, insofar as they do not endanger its existence or offend the moral and ethical sense of the Germanic race.
>
> The party as such represents the point of view of a positive Christianity without binding itself to any one particular confession. It fights against the Jewish materialist spirit within and without, and is convinced that a lasting recovery of our folk can only come about from within on the principle: COMMON GOOD BEFORE INDIVIDUAL GOOD[31]

Clearly, the Nazis must have thought that National Socialism and Christianity were compatible—if, that is, you take the party platform at face value as an honest document. Some even stress the fact that Hitler declared the platform "inalterable"—a brief study of the platform, however, raises questions about Hitler's honesty. Point 2 stresses the equality of Germans with other nations, and we all know how sincerely Hitler was committed to that principle; Point 6 affirms the Nazi belief in democracy ("The right to choose the government and determine the laws of the State shall belong only to citizens")—it also objects to giving people posts on the basis of party affiliation. Someone who based their understanding of Hitler and the Third Reich on these points of the platform would have some very confused ideas about National Socialism.

Some points reflecting the socialist emphasis of National Socialism were abandoned when Hitler decided to seek the support of wealthy industrialists. For example, Point 11 demands the abolition of unearned income; Points 12 and 13 calls for the abolition of war profits and the nationalization of trusts. These would have been bad news for the Krupps and other industrialists, if they had ever been sincerely applied, which they weren't.

Point 22 demands the abolition of the regular army. Hitler did the opposite. Point 23 demonstrates Hitler's love of honesty and journalistic integrity—it forbids political lies in the press. How would we respond to someone who said "Hitler was honest—it says so right here in the party platform!"? Point 25 calls for "the unconditional authority by the political central parliament of the whole State and all its organizations."

Anyone who has a real understanding of the Third Reich, not to mention politics in general, understands that this party platform was meant to appeal to the electorate and did not fully express Hitler's deepest inner thoughts. When this was drawn up, Hitler was still a minor figure trying to appeal to as many people as possible, and he put together a pleasant mixture of lies, truths, and half truths to deceive the gullible electorate. Some of Shirer's insights are appropriate here. Admittedly, Shirer was a journalist rather than a scholar, but that was an asset in this case as he sought only to record what actually occurred—unlike some scholars who first adopt a prejudiced outlook and then seek justification for it while ignoring contrary evidence. Shirer says of the party platform, "Hitler had not the slightest intention of honoring a single economic plank in the party program,"[32] and then gives specific examples of official actions directly contradictory to points in the platform. Shirer the journalist was more of a scholar than someone such as Steigmann-Gall, who uses the party platform to try and prove that the Nazis were Christians. Presenting point 24 as if it could be taken at face value is scholarship in a vacuum without regard to historical realities. Someone who took a modern American Republican or Democratic political platform as a disingenuous statement of simple truth would be considered politically simple-minded.

Shirer's claim in this context that the socialist parts of the platform had initially been added for no other reason than to get votes is an oversimplification. There was a real socialist element to Hitler's thought—but it took a back seat to his pragmatism. When Hitler realized that he needed the backing of wealthy industrialists to finance his drive to power through the voting booth, he was adaptable enough to readjust his rhetoric and his policies. This caused a conflict with many of his followers who were more ardently socialist—the problem was not resolved until the Roehm purge in 1934.

As to point 24, it calls for "freedom for all religious faiths in the state, insofar as they do not endanger its existence or offend the moral and ethical sense of the Germanic race." This meant freedom for all religions that did not contradict Naziism. The following reference to "positive Christianity" meant, as anyone with any knowledge of the subject is aware, Christianity purged of its "Jewish elements" and totally submissive to Naziism on all key points. This "Germanic Christianity" will be discussed in chapters 4 and 5.

"Positive" Christianity was compatible with National Socialism, but the platform's demand for freedom did not extend to those who contradicted Hitler. Someone who gave the following sermon after Hitler came to power would have suffered swift retribution for his Negative Christianity:

> Germany's defeat in World War I was God's judgment and we should accept his will. The Versailles Treaty is unquestionably unjust, but hatred and revenge will only make a bad situation worse. What is most important is, where will you spend eternity? What will it profit you if Germany is a great and mighty nation, but you die and stand before God only to be rejected and sent to hell? What will it harm you if Germany loses territory, but you die and stand before God and are accepted into paradise, where all of the trials and sufferings of the world will seem like nothing? We have all sinned, and are guilty of sin before a righteous and holy God, but in Jesus Christ God has revealed to us the sure and only way to find forgiveness and eternal life. In fact, we can rejoice in Germany's defeat and humiliation if, stripped of our vain and evil pride, we are left with nothing, and forced to realize the worthlessness of human power and glory, and left with nowhere to turn but Christ. Also, there are some who are asserting that the Germans are a superior race. This is not what the Bible teaches. It says in the book of Acts that God "has made of one blood all nations of men for to dwell on all the face of the earth." Jew and Gentile, we are all under the same condemnation for sin . . .

It should be possible to stop here, but since Steigmann-Gall makes such an involved and clever attempt to link the Nazis to Christianity, his analysis of Point 24 is worth looking at more closely. To begin with, he asserts that since the platform was drawn up before Hitler decided to seek power legally, that therefore it was a "frank expression of the movement's ideology," and not toned down for the sake of public relations.[33]

In response to this, a couple of things can be said. First, even those who seize power by force would like to have more people behind them than fewer. Lenin had a strong emphasis on a revolutionary elite, yet made general statements about "peace" and "land" to broaden his appeal—and Hitler at this time was diligently working to build up a following. Secondly, some parts of the platform (such as the equality of Germany with other nations and opposition to lies in the press) are so patently false as to call the whole document into question. If someone lies on points A, B, and C, why should we trust him on point D? That Hitler wanted to take power by force in no sense precludes the very common political practice of presenting a party platform that is designed to attract followers without presenting the whole truth and nothing but the truth.

Steigmann-Gall's point that the expression of support for "positive Christianity" was more than just a tactical measure is a valid one. "Positive" "Christianity" was a genuine concept with roots in German secular philosophy and Protestant theological liberalism—not just a political tactic. Whether or not this form of "Christianity" had anything to do with the teachings of Christ and the apostles is a question that Steigmann-Gall does not address. He also does not address the fact that even though the Nazis did not invent this peculiar doctrine, they could still appeal to its adherents insincerely, for political advantage. A positive reference to "Christianity" of any sort would have been reassuring to those who shared some of Hitler's main goals (such as opposition to the Treaty of Versailles) yet were doubtful about his personality and methods. There were such people, and Steigmann-Gall gives some indications of this in his book—though just in passing, without giving this point the consideration it deserves.

He claims some links between Christianity and Naziism can be found in the wording of Point 24: "the spiritual struggle against the Jews, the promulgation of a social ethic, and a new syncretism that would bridge Germany's confessional divide."[34] His analysis of these three points reveals a lack of familiarity with both German philosophical history and with biblical teachings.

For example, the fight against "the spirit of Jewish materialism" reflects the values of Kant and of German idealistic philosophy in general, not of the Bible. Nowhere in the New Testament are the Jews condemned for "materialism." In fact, the idea that the Jewish people with their emphasis on the holiness of the one true God could be considered "materialistic" seems strange and even absurd—until we consider the anti-Semitism of Kant. Such considerations are beyond the reach of Steigmann-Gall's scholarship. He neglects the entire tradition of German secular anti-Semitism, and the index to his book shows no references to Kant, Fichte, Schopenhauer, or other related thinkers whose secular proto-Nazisim plainly contradicts his main emphasis.

The second fragile link, the "social ethic" of National Socialism, had literally nothing to do with New Testament Christianity. Does anyone think the New Testament teaches Aryan supremacy and survival of the fittest? The third point, about a syncretism that would bridge the divide between Protestants and

Catholics, refers to a syncretism that was based on the complete abandonment of all Christian doctrines and church rules. Uniting the German people on the basis of their race in obedience to the Fuhrer without regard for the deepest questions of salvation, church authority, and doctrine, reflects something other than Christianity. It meant in practice nothing more than the totalitarian submission of the individual to the state.

In order to link Point 24 to Christianity it is necessary to do three things: ignore all of the basic teachings of the New Testament; ignore the entire secular German philosophical tradition; and take every reference to Christianity as a proof of Christian influence, no matter how insincere, or how sincere but far-fetched, the reference might be. Steigmann-Gall constantly makes all three of these errors. For example Walter Buch, a high ranking official in the Nazi Party, is quoted as saying "Public need before private greed . . . So important and meaningful is this phrase that Jesus Christ placed it in the center of his religious teaching."[35] How Christ placed something at the center of his religious teaching without even mentioning it or anything like it is a mystery that is cleared up when we understand that Buch was stating a total falsehood—either from sincere misconception or from deliberate distortion. The fact that some "theologians" who had abandoned scripture and were following the world may have expressed similar sentiments does not make them biblical.

That the Nazis rejected traditional Christianity and saw themselves as presenting something new is shown by Steigmann-Gall, who on occasion provides evidence that directly contradicts his own thesis. For example, he includes a passage from Joseph Goebbels' novel *Michael* stating that "The various churches have failed. Completely." The churches have failed to meet the demands of the times. A new idea is needed, and millions of people are waiting for it.[36]

The Catholics and Protestants have failed totally. What is needed is something new. This "something new" was provided by National Socialism. It made use of religious language, and appealed to religious instincts. It will, however, seem Christian only to those with no understanding of Christian teaching.

Hitler's policy toward the churches—words contradicted by deeds

Even a brief overview of the historical record reveals that Hitler's church policy was not one of respect, sympathy, and mutual belief. Hitler demanded total obedience, and those who deviated too far from the party line were swiftly punished.

The Nazi policy toward the churches was one of rigorous repression rather than sympathy and support. Here are some of the repressive measures employed by the government in its struggle for the soul of the German people:

~ arrests of clergy and incarceration in concentration camps
~ murders of religious opponents of the regime
~ physical assaults on clergymen ignored by the police
~ academic, social, youth, labor, professional, women's and athletic religious organizations and associations banned
~ seizure of church property, including orphanages, hospitals, monasteries and schools (with religious insignias removed and teachers fired)
~ Catholic civil servants dismissed
~ church publications censored or forbidden

~ religious meetings broken up by SA attacks
~ dissolution of religious political parties
~ attacks on church and Christianity in the press
~ attempts to force German churches into one state controlled church
~ restriction of religious activities to church buildings only
~ surveillance of worship services and church leaders
~ public attacks on the church by Nazi leaders, including Goebbels and Goering
~ criticisms of National Socialism or the government forbidden
~ the establishment of new religious groups forbidden
~ civil servants required to withdraw their children from religious youth organizations with loss of job the penalty for refusing to comply
~ total submission of the church to the state in every respect
~ "separation of church and state" meant the churches were allowed to have no say whatever in political questions
~ high school teachers forbidden to be active in religious youth groups
~ clergymen, including monks and nuns, arrested and tried on trumped up charges
~ prayers forbidden at school assemblies
~ numerous independent religious groups banned completely
~ the complete abolition of all denominational schools (by 1939)

One individual argued that these repressive measures were inherently Christian, that Christians always did such things. Such monumental ignorance of history defies refutation, if it is in fact ignorance, and not rather willful deception.

A blueprint for the future

It is well-known that Hitler stated some of his future objectives in *Mein Kampf*. It is not so well-known that he stated his future policy toward the churches there as well. Long before he had any visible chance of coming to power, Hitler was not only planning conquests in the east—he was also planning the replacement of traditional beliefs with his new philosophy. This can be seen in vol. I chapt. 5 of *Mein Kampf* ("The World War"). It is so significant for our understanding of Hitler's attitude and policies toward the churches that it requires some investigation.

> Hitler first states that an idea, a doctrine, any philosophy "whether of a religious or political nature," cannot be exterminated by brute force. This is such an important point that he elaborates on it at some length: "The application of force alone, without the impetus of a basic spiritual idea as a starting point, can never lead to the destruction of an idea and its dissemination, except in the form of a complete extermination of even the very last exponent of the idea and the destruction of the last tradition."

This would do so much damage as to mean "the disappearance of such a state from the sphere of political importance, often for an indefinite time and some-times forever; for experience shows that such a blood sacrifice strikes the best part of the people . . ." The elimination "of the new doctrine can be carried out only through a process of extermination so great and constantly increasing that in the end all the truly valuable blood is drawn out of the people or state in question."

The "new doctrine" might refer to Marxism, except Hitler did eliminate it abruptly and forcefully, without doing great damage to the nation in the process. About Christianity being the "new doctrine" in question, Hitler refers to Christianity in just those words in vol. I chapt. 11 ("Nation and Race"), where Jesus is referred to as "the great founder of the new doctrine." It was commonly asserted among Germanic opponents of Christianity that it was a new and alien Mediterranean doctrine introduced by the Jews to the detriment of the healthy older German paganism. Also, Hitler is discussing his own plans for a future Germany—and what major body of belief needed to be replaced so that National Socialism might reign uncontested? What other belief was so deeply rooted in the German nation that its extermination by brute force would have damaged the state beyond repair?

How, then, can an opposing philosophy be eliminated? The best way is to get the children: "the first period of childhood is most readily susceptible to the possibility of extermination, while with the mounting years the power of resistance increases . . . " While the children are being raised up in the new way of thinking, force needs at the same time to be applied to the opposing doctrine: "only the continuous and steady application of the methods for repressing a doctrine, etc., makes it possible for a plan to succeed . . . Only in the steady and constant application of force lies the very first prerequisite for success."

This is precisely the policy that was followed toward the churches in the Third Reich, a policy that will be elaborated on in chapter 4 of this study. The children are indoctrinated and brought up in the new philosophy, while constant pressure is maintained against the churches, so as to prevent their spreading and to detach weaker members. Force is applied when necessary, yet overt mass persecution is avoided so as not to create martyrs and feelings of sympathy for the persecuted sects.

Hitler was far too shrewd to use the words "church" or "Christianity" here. He recognized and elaborated on at length that Georg von Schonerer, the pre-war leader of the Austrian Pan-Germans, had alienated the masses and hurt himself with his "Away from Rome" campaign.[37] Hitler had learned from personal observation the futility of trying to oppose differing religious views by brute force alone. He recognized the need to utilize existing social institutions to reach his ends, and was far more subtle and cunning in his dealings than are some scholars who write about Christianity and National Socialism.

In vol. I chapt. 3 of his book ("General Political Considerations Based on my Vienna Period"), Hitler commended Karl Lueger, the mayor of Vienna, for the "infinite shrewdness" of his policy toward the Catholic Church. Lueger manipulated the church to gain his ends, and had a good sense of what was possible and what was not. To eliminate the Catholic Church would have been impossible for Lueger—therefore he manipulated it and used it. This was Hitler's policy exactly—toward both the Catholics and the Protestants.

These same ideas were expressed by Rudolf Hess, one of Hitler's highest ranking aides. In a speech made to a meeting of Nazi *Gauleiters* in 1938, Hess stated that Christianity could not "be destroyed or overcome by external measures" and warned that this would drive people into opposition to National Socialism. He suggested that the solution was to leave the churches alone with their rites and ceremonies, and "Men will be drawn more and more to National Socialism. They will . . . turn away from the Churches out of internal conviction more and more. . ."[38] These comments agree in every detail with those of Hitler, only some of which were printed above. Needless to say, Hess did not arrive at his high position by thinking independently.

Nazi church policies in Austria

Within Germany itself, political realities led to a persecution of the church that was relentless, yet restrained. Outside of Germany, less caution was necessary, and the real attitude of the government toward the churches was more openly revealed.

For example, when the Nazis invaded Austria in 1938, they were welcomed by many Austrians, and Conway gives a quote from the Archbishop of Vienna, Cardinal Innitzer, stating his support for the new Nazi government in Austria. The Cardinal spoke about the danger of Bolshevism, the duty of Christians to be good Germans, and so on.[39]

Perhaps Cardinal Innitzer believed propaganda statements about the support of the Nazi government for the churches; perhaps he thought that professions of loyalty would ensure good relations between the churches and the state; perhaps he sincerely believed in National Socialism and thought God had sent Hitler to save Germany from the Communists. The Austrian Catholics soon found out, however, that Hitler was not the supporter and defender of the church he claimed to be.

Conway describes in detail the situation of the Catholic Church in Austria after the union with Germany.[40] First, the church was deprived of all legal status, with the excuse that the Concordat between Germany and the Church of Rome applied to Germany, not Austria. Three theological faculties (in Salzburg, Graz, and Innsbruck) were closed. Private and church schools were closed or converted to government schools. Kindergartens and orphanages were closed, youth activities were limited, and pastoral access to hospitals was restricted. "Catholic organizations, such as the large *Volksbund der Katholiken Oesterreichs*, were dissolved and their property was confiscated. The Catholic publishing houses were closed."[41]

This was by no means all. The Church was attacked in the press, and in lectures. Conway gives an example of anti-church propaganda including the following points:

> Christianity is a religion for slaves and idiots . . . The New Testament is a Jewish fraud . . . Before Christianity German culture was at a high level which was destroyed by Christianity . . . Christianity is a substitute Judaism; the Jews contrived it; its centre is in Rome . . . The Ten Commandments are the depository of the lowest human instincts . . . a pure race has no need of a redeemer . . . Nero did right in his persecution . . . Christianity is simply the mask of Judaism . . . Christianity has always hindered the development of science, medicine, etc. . . . . Ignatius Loyola was of Hebrew origin . . . The new eternal centre of the world is Nuernberg. Rome is waning . . . the inactivity of

eternal life is foolishness . . . Predestination, rites of the Church, the divine Trinity, original sin, etc.—what bosh![42]

There was also a comment about Jesus "whimpering on the cross," in contrast to the brave death of a Nazi hero. This is confirmed, as if confirmation were needed, by an account narrated by a German who was later executed by the Nazis. He saw a member of the Hitler Youth grab a crucifix off the wall of a classroom and toss it through a window into the street, shouting "Lie there, you dirty Jew!"[43]

Conway goes on to describe the confiscation of church properties, and an anti-Catholic riot which led to the aforementioned Cardinal Innitzer's palace being looted and burned. All of this led to—public professions of support for Hitler by leading church officials! The reasons for this are not far to seek—desire to stay out of a concentration camp; a hope that demonstrations of loyalty would lead to better treatment; and genuine support for some of Hitler's other goals and achievements. Perhaps some Catholics did object, and were among those arrested—sixty Austrian Catholic priests were arrested in May 1938 alone, according to Conway.[44]

He also cites a Nuremberg document that is appropriate here, even though it's about Czechoslovakia:

> At the outbreak of war, 487 Catholic priests were among the thousands of Czech patriots arrested and sent to concentration camps as hostages. Venerable high ecclesiastical dignitaries were dragged to concentration camps in Germany. It was a common sight on the roads near the concentration camps to see a priest dressed in rags, exhausted, pulling a cart, and behind him a youth in SA uniform, whip in hand.[45]

Finally, an appendix to Conway's book cites a "Protest of the Austrian Bishops to the Minister of the Interior."[46] Taken from German government files, it is dated July 1, 1941, and contains the following grievances:

~ confiscation by the Gestapo of the property of "a great number of monasteries and nunneries in Austria," and the forced eviction of their inhabitants. Names of specific institutions are given, as well as the official justification for the seizures: "police measures against opponents of the state."
~ closure of a training college and a seminary with "no judicial inquiry, nor any judicial proceedings."
~ expulsion of Catholic clerics from Austria with no proof of hostile political statements or acts and no judicial procedure.
~ public celebrations of Catholic holidays forbidden, all activities being restricted to church buildings

Those are only a few highlights of a five page document in which the Catholic bishops risked arrest and imprisonment by officially protesting government abuses. They concluded by stating their belief that these and other actions by the government reflected not a concern for the public welfare but rather a deliberate and systematic assault on the church itself.

122

Nazi church policies in the Warthegau

The Nazi persecution of the churches in Poland was much more severe than that of the churches in Austria and Germany. Here there were no political constraints whatever, and the Nazis were able to pursue their goals with complete freedom. Conway's research in this area is invaluable. All quotations in this section come from his book. He gives close attention to a specific region of Poland—the Warthegau.

Wartheland was a region of Poland that had belonged to Germany before 1919. Given to Poland after the war, it was officially restored to Germany by a decree of Hitler in October 1939. Officially designated *Reichsgau* Wartheland, it was referred to as the Warthegau. An SS *Obergruppenfuhrer* named Arthur Greiser was given the task of re-Germanizing the territory. In the words of Conway, "Greiser's ambition was to make the Wartheland a model Nazi *Gau* . . . The Warthegau was to become 'the training ground for the Nazi ideology' and the 'model for the whole party.'"[47] Part of a speech by Greiser marking his second year in office is cited verbatim:

> Here in the virgin territory of the German East, we are all offered the chance of the new reconstruction of the State, which will reflect the principles of National Socialism in all aspects of public life, or at least will come nearest to it. As a result we have the exhilarating feeling that the work of reconstruction which has been laid on our shoulders is today providing the start of a reform for the whole Reich that will be implemented later.[48]

Since Hitler said in a speech in 1922 that he was a Christian, and because he used such words as "providence" or "god" on occasion, and because he had promised to support the church in Germany and work with it, someone might assume that the church in the Warthegau came under the special protection of the Nazi party, and was given all sorts of advantages. This was not the case. Most of the Polish Catholic clergy were ordered to be exterminated or expelled by Himmler. Bormann decreed that the Concordat with the Vatican did not apply. Greiser reported directly to Himmler or Bormann, and his policies were not the result of personal whim:

> The initiative for church policy in the new *Gaus* henceforward came directly from the Nazi party chancellery in Munich . . . for the first time the separation of Church and State was proclaimed as official Nazi policy, in accordance with Bormann's plans first expressed to the Supreme Command of the Armed Forces and later repeated in his circular of June 1941.[49]

Conway cites documents from Bormann asserting that Hitler personally approved government policies toward the churches in the region. These policies were aimed at eliminating or drastically restricting the influence of the church. The Catholic Church was harshly dealt with. Contacts with the Vatican were forbidden; church properties were confiscated; confirmation classes were regulated and limited; all religious instruction was banned in the schools, and all religious activities were confined to church buildings. Church membership was forbidden for people under the age of 21; school teachers were forbidden to be church members; Nazi party members were forbidden to be church members. Church services on Good Friday were forbidden "on the grounds that 'the Party also has its Good Friday—9 November 1923; it also has its martyrs—those who died for the Movement; it also possesses its altar—the *Feldherrnhalle* in Munich.'"[50] This prohibition was defied: "on this matter the churchmen refused to be coerced. So many gathered outside their locked churches on Good Friday morning that the Gestapo was obliged to withdraw its prohibition, and in the following years the services were allowed to proceed without intervention."[51] One will search the history books in vain for instances of liberals, secular humanists, socialists, agnostics, Darwinists, or atheists publicly defying orders of the Nazi government.

In October 1941 the few remaining parish priests were arrested by the Gestapo and hundreds were sent to Dachau, Sachsenhausen, and other camps:

> According to figures recorded in a German Foreign Ministry document, of the 681 regular and 147 monastic priests in the diocese of Posen, no less than 451 were imprisoned or sent to concentration camps, 120 were expelled to the territory of the Government-General in central Poland, 74 were shot or died in concentration camps, 32 were refused permission to carry out their ministry, 24 fled abroad, and 12 were missing.[52]

These were not wartime abuses only, but matters of policy:

> Hitler's decision to allow the *Gauleiters* a free hand in the ideological 're-education' of their territories, placed the territories wholly in the hands of the Nazi extremists without possibility of appeal. In August 1943 the German Catholic bishops in their annual pastoral letter stigmatized the increasing persecution of the church as intolerable and the conditions in the Warthegau as approximating to 'an almost complete suppression of Christian religion'. With growing apprehension they expressed fear that conditions there were, as many Party representatives had exultantly proclaimed, the 'prelude for the future status of the Church in Germany itself.'[53]

An official protest of twenty-eight pages by the Papal Secretary of State (Cardinal Maglione) was sent to the German government. It detailed the many abuses in the Warthegau, including the forcing of hundreds of nuns to do manual labor; the closing of all Catholic schools; the imposition of petty and harassing restrictions (the Gestapo set limited church hours in which services could be held, and people were allowed to attend church in their parish only). Of course, it was ignored, as were many other protests by the Vatican.

This brief overview of Conway's detailed study omits many harassments, persecutions, and evils. More comments not about the Warthegau only, but about Poland, are instructive:

Immediately after the military victory of September 1939, Himmler, in his capacity as Reich Commissar for the Strengthening of the German People's Community (*Reichskommisar fur die Festigung deutscher Volkstums*) laid claim to the new 'fief' of Poland and promptly instigated measures to consolidate the power of the SS within it. By the forcible suppression of all national institutions, by the 'Germanization' (*Germanisierung*) of cultural associations, and by the reduction of the population to the status of slave labor for the German Reich, any sort of resistance would be rendered impossible . . . systematic executions of members of the Polish intelligentsia and ruling classes were carried out . . .

From the first the Catholic Church was one of the main targets of this policy of annihilation. The SS was given a free hand in a reign of terror against both clergy and laity . . . In West Prussia, out of 690 parish priests, at least two-thirds were arrested, and the remainder escaped only by fleeing from their parishes . . . by the end of 1940 only twenty priests were left in their parishes— about three per cent of the number of parish priests in the pre-war period.

The much smaller Evangelical Churches in Poland were treated with equal ferocity.[54]

Karol Kulisz, the director of an Evangelical charity organization died in Buchenwald. A professor of the University of Warsaw's Evangelical Faculty of Theology, Edmund Bursche, died in Mauthausen. ". . . virtually the whole of the Evangelical clergy in the Teschen (Cieszyn) area of Silesia were consigned to the concentration camps of Mauthausen, Buchenwald, Dachau and Oranienburg, their places being taken by Germans who conducted their services in German only."[55]

A final quote from Conway is in order:

In the Warthegau, the model Nazi region that had been carved out of conquered Polish territory, the apotheosis of Nazi Church policy can be seen. The draconian measures introduced there can leave little doubt of what would have happened elsewhere had Hitler been able to carry out his frequently repeated threat 'after the war, to deal decisively with the churches.'[56]

Hitler linked to Christianity

There is no danger that a reasonable, fair, and sincere person with a knowledge of history will think that Hitler was a Christian—however, the world being what it is, there are numbers of people who are not reasonable, fair, or sincere. Some of them have devoted a lot of time and effort to arguing that Hitler was a Christian.

One of the most enthusiastic advocates of the "Hitler-was-a-Christian" school is a certain Mr. Jim Walker. He has put together a very professional-looking website devoted to the subject.[57] With nice layout, photos, and different colored letters, he asserts that Hitler was a Christian. More than that, he claims that Hitler had a strong belief in Jesus and the Bible, and that Hitler acted according to the Bible.

It will be worthwhile to go over this site at some length. The larger purpose is not to refute Mr. Walker, though of course some refutation will be attempted—the larger purpose is to come to a clearer understanding of Hitler's beliefs and actions. Hopefully a closer examination of Walker's assertions will help toward that end. Since requests for permission to quote were left unanswered, I am not able to quote directly from the site as much as I would have liked. Although the site's homepage advertises itself as being for freethinkers, it seems (in my case at any rate) that their "free thinking" allows for one-way criticisms but not for responses.

Perhaps the best way to understand this website is to look at Walker's attempts to show that Jesus was like Hitler. His points are:

~ Jesus said we should not be troubled by wars and rumors of wars (Mark 13:7-8); Hitler was not troubled by war either.

~ Jesus used a whip to drive the money-changers out of the temple; Hitler sometimes carried a whip, and Dietrich Eckart heard Hitler say that he wanted to clean the corruption out of Berlin the way Christ cleared out the temple.

~ Jesus came to bring not peace but a sword (Matthew 10:34) and Hitler also brought war.

~ Jesus brought division (Luke 12:51) and so did Hitler.

~ Jesus said that his enemies should be killed ("But those mine enemies which would not that I should reign over them, bring hither, and slay them before me," Luke 19:27) and Hitler killed or imprisoned his enemies.

~ Jesus was betrayed, and Hitler was also betrayed by his generals.

~ Jesus will reign for 1,000 years (Revelation 20:6), and Hitler wanted his Reich to last for 1,000 years.

~ Hitler on his way to prison compared himself to Christ.

~ Walker finds one more point of similarity, which I confess I don't understand. First, part of John 18:36 is cited. I give the whole verse, but underline the part cited by Walker. Perhaps he left out the first part because it emphasized a major difference between Hitler and Jesus. The verse is: "Jesus answered, My kingdom is not of this world: if my kingdom were of this world, then would my servants fight, that I should not be delivered to the Jews: but now is my kingdom not from hence." Comparing this to Hitler, Walker states (and I repeat his short comment verbatim and in its entirety), "Of course Hitler lived in this world and, indeed, his followers fought for him against the Jews."

Before looking at his arguments, I would like to list differences between Jesus and Hitler that any objective study would have taken into consideration.

~ Jesus never attained or tried to attain political power. Hitler did.

~ Jesus practiced non-violence. He told his followers not to fight for him and passively allowed himself to be killed. Hitler did not advocate or practice non-violence.

~ Jesus is deeply loved, respected, and believed in by countless millions of people throughout the world. Hitler is universally regarded with disgust by all decent people.

~ Jesus' teachings spread throughout the world and have lasted nearly two thousand years. Hitler's false ideology collapsed in an extremely short time and is now believed in by almost no one.

~ Christianity spread in the first crucial centuries of its existence by faith and persuasion alone, in spite of persecution. National Socialism was spread and supported by force and violence.

~ Jesus emphasized forgiveness and love for others. Hitler advocated pitiless cruelty.

~ Jesus taught that there is a world to come after this one, an eternity in heaven or in hell. Hitler never showed any concern for such things.

~ Jesus said, "My kingdom is not of this world." Hitler's kingdom was of this world.

These are simple facts. Two other differences are matters of faith:

~ Hitler died and remains dead, while Jesus died and rose again.

~ Hitler was only a man, and a sinful one, while Jesus is the divine and sinless Son of God.

What, though, can be said about the alleged similarities? First, it is true that Christians should not be troubled by wars and rumors of wars. This is because we know that our lives are in God's hands. He will keep us safe as long as he sees fit, and, when we do depart, we go to be with Christ. "To die is gain," as the Bible says, and we should not fear those that can only destroy the body but after that have nothing they can do to us. Hitler's reasons for not fearing war were considerably different. Like Hegel, he viewed war as good. Like Haeckel and many other thinkers of his day, Hitler saw struggle and conflict as the very foundation of our existence, and thought that war would exalt and purify the strong, and crush the weak. He also saw it as a legitimate means to achieve the end of German domination. Jesus said "Blessed are the peacemakers." To not be troubled by war is vastly different from being enthusiastic about it, and deliberately starting it. Someone who can't see this is in deep trouble intellectually.

Secondly, Jesus once used a whip and Hitler carried a whip. Hitler also spoke of being like Jesus in this respect (we will accept the Eckart quote for the sake of discussion, though Walker goes to great lengths to explain away statements of Hitler's expressing his hatred of Christianity). This gets back to the previously mentioned analogy of the policeman and the bank robber. They both carry a gun—are they the same? One has an authority and a right that the other does not, and one uses the gun for necessary and useful purposes while the other does not. Moreover, if the New Testament account is true, as I believe it is, Jesus as the Son had the right to clear out his own Father's house. I shouldn't need to point out that no one was killed in that incident.

In another section of his site, Walker provides a photo of Hitler with a whip, "acting like Jesus." He gives a source for the photo—it comes from a book of Nazi propaganda called *The Hitler No One Knows: 100 Pictures of the Life of the Fuhrer*, by Heinrich Hoffmann.[58] Written to glorify the Fuhrer, the book has a caption with the photo explaining why Hitler carried a whip: "The 'whip.' Enemy papers excitedly write that Hitler always carries a riding whip. In reality, it is a dog whip that the Fuhrer carries today as a reminder of the time when he could carry no weapon at all. Then the whip was his only defense . . . ." Jesus did not carry a whip around for self defense, or to remind himself of the time when he couldn't carry a weapon. When Walker says Hitler is acting like Jesus here he will convince some who only judge by outward appearances and don't think critically or independently—but he will have to give account for his false words on the day of judgment. "You shall not bear false witness against your neighbor"—this is one of the Ten Commandments. What shall we say against someone who bears false witness not against his neighbor, but against Jesus, the Son of God?

Looking at the third accusation of similarity, the sword that Jesus spoke of was the sword of truth that proceeds from his mouth (Revelation 19:15). It was not a political or military sword like Hitler's Wehrmacht, which is proven by the life of Jesus and by the history of the early church.

Fourthly, and this is related to the previous point, Jesus and Hitler brought division—but leftists who assert their positions bring division also. Everyone who asserts some position brings division between those who agree and disagree. Are those who bring division by asserting that "Criticism of Darwin should not be allowed in school" or "Homosexuality is normal" behaving like Hitler? Anyway, the division that Jesus brought was a division of belief, with freedom for those who disagreed to go their own way. Perhaps Walker imagines he is uniting humanity with his attacks on religion and leading the way toward universal brotherhood—if he could just get rid of those narrow-minded and intolerant fanatics who disagree with him. They are a menace! And so intransigent too.

Fifthly, as far as Jesus killing his enemies, neither he nor his apostles killed anyone. They allowed themselves to be killed. Jesus' statement in Luke is part of a parable. It refers to his return as God to judge the world. That will be a divine judgment. God has the power to take life because it is he who gave it in the first place. A better comparison would be between Hitler and Churchill. Churchill caused a lot of people to be killed by fighting Germany, and some people were imprisoned while he was in power—so, Churchill was like Hitler; and NATO was like the Warsaw Pact; and a judge sentencing a duly convicted criminal to death is like a Mafia boss giving orders to a hit man.

Sixthly, Jesus and Hitler were both betrayed. This means that Matthew, Mark, Luke, and John were like Guderian, Rommel, and Goering—but Jesus' followers returned afterward, except for Judas, and became devoted and faithful followers. Hitler's followers were permanently defeated. Such obvious differences do not escape an impartial, fair, and honest observer.

But Jesus will reign for a thousand years, and Hitler wanted his Reich to last for that same period of time! This doesn't show that Hitler was following Jesus—it shows that he wanted to equal Jesus. He failed. Jesus will not fail—and his kingdom will be one of peace and righteousness that will be a blessing to the world. Hitler's attempt not to serve, follow, and obey Jesus, but to replace him, is illustrated by a painting reproduced in one section of Walker's site. It shows Hitler preaching to a small group of poor, suffering, and oppressed Germans, and has as a title part of a verse from John. This equates Hitler with Jesus, and shows him as the bringer of a new gospel—not the faithful follower of an old one.

This relates to the next point—Hitler on his way to prison comparing himself to Jesus. Hitler did think he was more than an ordinary mortal, and liked to build himself up as much as possible. Comparisons of himself to Christ were great for his ego, and also useful politically as a means of increasing awe and devotion among his followers. This only demonstrates Hitler's folly and conceit. It does not demonstrate that any real spiritual similarity actually existed, any more than his assertions of Aryan supremacy prove the truth of that ludicrous doctrine. Since when does Hitler's assertion of something prove it to be true? Moreover, looking at some differences, Hitler was guilty and Christ was innocent. Hitler got a mild sentence and was released and Christ was executed. Hitler was arrested for political reasons and Christ was not.

Come to think of it, Martin Luther King was also arrested and put in jail—just like Hitler. In fact, King and Hitler had a lot of similarities: both were eloquent speakers; both had a devoted following; both were committed to improving the lot of their peoples; both were very successful. Hitler had a lot in common with Ghandi too—both widely revered, firmly committed to a cause, extremely effective in mobilizing popular support, symbols of national pride, both in opposition to England—of course, there were some differences.

Finally, Walker notes one more point of similarity. Jesus said that if his kingdom were of this world his servants would fight for him, but his kingdom was not of this world. Walker states in the quote given above that Hitler and Jesus both lived in this world, and Hitler's followers defended him from the Jews. It's true Jesus and Hitler both lived in the world—Hitler also had this in common with Walt Disney and numerous other people. That Jesus' kingdom is not of this world and that his followers did not fight for him is a difference, not a similarity between Jesus and Hitler. I don't know what Walker is saying here and I don't think he does either.

The Nazi propagandist Julius Streicher had a different idea about the question of similarities between Jesus and Hitler. He is quoted as having said "It is only on one or two exceptional points that Christ and Hitler stand comparison, for Hitler is far too big a man to be compared with one so petty."[59]

How could someone study Hitler and Christ and find any elements in common? What is the mindset of such a man? I detect five elements in Walker's website that answer this question. The first of these is (a) hostility; a deep hostility toward Christianity is an essential ingredient of Walker's website. A second element is (b) a lack of historical information. A great deal of attention is devoted to Hitler's words—little or nothing is said about what actually happened to the churches in the Third Reich, or about the intellectual background of National Socialism. A third element is (c) a profound illogic, that stresses the most tenuous and vague similarities and ignores stark black and white contrasts. A fourth element is (d) inaccuracy—there are frequent misstatements of fact. Fifthly, there is (e) a vast ignorance of biblical Christianity.

Before examining these elements, I think it necessary to emphasize, as was said in the introduction, that Walker's arguments are significant and merit some attention and discussion. They are becoming increasingly popular. A major news website recently headlined extremely hostile and bitter comments about Christianity by a well-known scientist. The title and subtitle say it all:

FAITH UNDER FIRE
Dawkins: Religion equals 'child abuse'
Scientist compares Moses to Hitler, calls
New Testament 'sado-masochistic doctrine'[60]

These bizarre views are becoming increasingly common, and if enough people who hold them ever get enough political power, it will be the end of religious freedom and the establishment of a secular left-wing dictatorship. Serious persecution of the hated Christians will be a significant aspect of left-wing open mindedness and tolerance. The church has been asleep for a long time. Maybe it will only wake up when it is too late. Such things seem remote now—they also seemed remote to German Christians in 1928. Unexpected developments can plunge even America, the world's only superpower, the hyperpower, into a maelstrom of uncontrollable events with exceedingly unpleasant consequences.

A. Hatred and fear of Christianity

Walker claims that his analysis is free from bias, that his conclusions come only from the facts. However, in the same section he makes a number of comments indicative not of a lack of bias, but of the exact opposite.

For one thing, he compares Christians to heroin addicts. The Marxists also compared belief in God to a drug, and their vicious attempts to exterminate it require no documentation. Obviously, if something like drugs or religion is harmful to society, it is reasonable for the authorities to take all possible measures to eliminate or at least minimize this threat to the public well-being. That Walker's comparison of Christians and heroin addicts is not just a passing analogy is clear from further comments. He writes of the dangers of Christianity and says that Christians will protect themselves at all costs, even to the extent of slaughtering innocent people. He warns that religious believers are fanatics who want to gain political control. The facts that it is unbelievers who are currently slaughtering millions of innocent people (unborn children), that it is unbelievers who are using political control to cram their beliefs down people's throats with opposing views stifled as much as possible, escape him.

Continuing in this vein, Walker says the Bible is a violent book that can be dangerous. He warns against the dangers of the religious right and says that right-wing conservatives are like Hitler. The now defunct Moral Majority is compared to the Nazis. Hitler's condemnations of immorality are compared to those of Christians who oppose pornography and immorality today. He equates religious people with racists and neo-Nazis.

He gives as an example Hitler's educational policy of state control which, he says, is like attempts by the religious right to get control of the educational system. Of course, it is the Left Wing Anti-Christians who have been highly successful at taking control of the schools. The Left Wing Anti-Christians prevent students from being taught about problems with Darwinism, about lifestyles based on traditional morality instead of a bankrupt amorality that embraces perversion of every kind. The Left claims to be open minded, compassionate, and tolerant, even as it seeks to eliminate every vestige of opposition and tolerates no disagreement, while the Christians are like Hitler—at least in the fog of Walker's twilight world.

Walker sees Christians as embryonic Hitlers, trying to seize power so that they can establish a brutal right-wing dictatorship. That he does not objectively examine Stalin and compare him to dangerous secular tendencies and fanaticism on the anti-religious left shows him to be an extremely one-sided individual (though Communism is mentioned briefly, in passing, allowing for a pretense of objectivity if necessary). The threat from the anti-religious left, with its hostility toward religion; intolerance of people with opposing views; use of government power to arbitrarily impose elitist views; and contempt for human life (as proven by the brutal slaughter of millions of unborn babies, classified as "subhuman" or "life-not-worthy-of-living" to use a Nazi phrase and tossed in the garbage without a twinge of conscience)—this threat is ignored by Walker.

Concerning Stalin, here are a few quotes, showing that a brutal tyrant believed in materialism. Does this mean that all atheists and all opponents of organized religion are potential Stalins? If statements about God by evildoers supposedly prove the evil of Christianity and of religious belief in general, do the following quotes from Stalin prove with equal validity that people who reject religion and believe in atheism are evil monsters, scheming to seize power and set up a left-wing anti-religious dictatorship? Of course not. Such logic is only valid for one side, not for both.

> Dialectical materialism is the world outlook of the Marxist-Leninist party. It is called dialectical materialism because its approach to the phenomena of nature, its method of studying and apprehending them, is dialectical, while its interpretation of the phenomena of nature, its conception of these phenomena, its theory, is materialistic . . .
>
> As a matter of fact, Marx and Engels took from Feuerbach's materialism its "inner kernel," developed it into a scientific-philosophical theory of materialism and cast aside its idealistic and religious-ethical encumbrances . . .
>
> (quoting Marx):
>
> "The material, sensuously perceptible world to which we ourselves belong is the only reality . . . Our consciousness and thinking, however supra-sensuous they may seem, are the product of a material, bodily organ, the brain. Matter is not a product of mind, but mind itself is merely the highest product of matter..." (Joseph Stalin, *Dialectical and Historical Materialism*).[61]

Cast aside your idealistic and religious-ethical *encumbrances*. Just follow *reason*, *science* and *logic*. There is no need of a God or divine rules. The material world to which we ourselves belong is the only reality. Mind is merely the highest product of matter.

A cruel, evil, fanatical, intolerant, and intransigent dictator rejected religion. Therefore, can I say that atheists and secular humanists are dangerous, narrow-minded, intolerant fanatics, scheming to seize the levers of power so they can eliminate religion, morality, and private property, and use the power of the state to force their views on people? Of course there will be appropriate punishments for backward, reactionary, and anti-social elements that need to be told what to believe for their own good. Shall we say "Those secular humanists are a menace, cleverly disguising themselves as moderates while they stealthily consolidate their grip on the government and the mass media, plotting to seize control of the schools and forbid all disagreement"?

Someone said that Weimar Germany was a powder keg of right-wing fundamentalists waiting to explode. If I said that Czarist Russia was a powder keg of atheists, Darwinists, humanists, and socialists waiting to explode, knowledgeable people would think I was ignorant of Russian history.

A bias revealed

One of the best ways to illustrate Walker's extreme bias and lack of objectivity when it comes to Christianity is to look at his study of Thomas Jefferson's religion. In an online essay about Thomas Jefferson's religion,[62] Walker approaches the question of Jefferson's beliefs much differently than he approaches the question of Hitler's. With Hitler, every reference to God is given as proof that Hitler was a devout, Bible-believing Christian who tried to be like Jesus. When, however, Walker studies comments by Jefferson using religious language, he is very cautious, and recognizes that the mere use of the word "God" is no proof of Christianity. This is very true of Thomas Jefferson. It is also true of Hitler. Walker posts many quotes from Jefferson showing his hostility to Christianity, but gives us none from Hitler. He cites Jefferson as rejecting the authority of scripture—and Hitler also openly rejected the history of the Old Testament.

The purpose of this is not to compare Hitler and Jefferson. It is to compare Walker's analyses of Hitler and Jefferson. Incidentally, Thomas Jefferson also made a profession of Christianity. Walker did not provide this, so I cite it here. In a letter to Dr. Benjamin Rush, Jefferson wrote that he was opposed to "the corruptions of Christianity," but not to the teachings of Christ himself. Jefferson elaborated, "I am a Christian, in the only sense in which he wished anyone to be: sincerely attached to his doctrines in preference to all others, ascribing to himself every human excellence, and believing he never claimed any other."[63]

In this statement, Jefferson plainly states that he is a Christian—but his Jesus is a merely human Jesus. Jefferson also reveals in other statements that Christianity to him is a system of ethics, not doctrines. We rightly accept that this means Jefferson was not a Christian in the biblical sense of the word. Similarly, when Hitler claimed to be a Christian, it is evident (if not so overtly stated) that he referred to a merely human Jesus—not the Son of God who died on the cross as a sacrifice for the sins of the world, rose from the dead, and will return as God to judge the world.

Both Jefferson and Hitler stated they were Christians. Both used the words "God" or "Supreme Being" or some such terms. Both spoke highly of Jesus and never criticized Jesus. Both objected to abuses of Christian doctrine by the churches—yet in Jefferson's case all of the negative evidence against his being a Christian is brought out, and one conclusion is arrived at. In Hitler's case, none of the negative evidence is brought out—except accidentally—and a totally different conclusion is arrived at.

The reason for this is not far to seek. Walker is an elite commando in the culture wars. His goal is to weaken and hopefully someday eliminate the Christian influence from American society. To achieve this end, Jefferson is detached from Christianity—it supposedly helps to weaken Christian claims on government and society. Conversely, Hitler is attached to Christianity—this makes Christianity look like an evil menace that must be eliminated or at least contained.

B. A lack of information

A second element of Walker's website, in addition to lack of objectivity, is a lack of historical information. Hitler is judged solely by his words—what actually occurred is omitted or distorted. Someone who based their understanding of the outbreak of World War II solely on Hitler's words, with no reference to what actually occurred, would be mistaken. Sometimes Hitler lied, sometimes he told the truth—his actions are the proof of his honesty or dishonesty, and Hitler's actions, and the extreme persecution of Christians under the Nazi regime, are glossed over or ignored by Walker.

An understanding of the situation of the church in Nazi Germany is nowhere in evidence in Walker's arguments. The persecution of Christians is referred to, but is dismissed as persecution of Hitler's political opponents only. It is asserted that Hitler only persecuted religious people who disagreed with him politically. Unfortunately for this argument, anyone who understands the nature of modern totalitarianism and the nature of Hitler's government understands that any and all disagreement with the official line is "political" opposition.

A good example of this is found in Martin Gilbert's *The Holocaust: A History of the Jews of Europe During the Second World War*. This book, by the way, is not an obscure scholarly monograph that can only be found by diligent research. It is one of the many basic and easily accessible books providing necessary information for the consideration of these topics. It tells of a pastor, Julius von Jan, who preached a sermon against the Nazi regime shortly after the Kristallnacht ("night of broken glass") in November of 1938.[64] Conway also gives a more substantive account from which I quote below.

Pastor von Jan objected to the crime of the mass persecution of Jews. He condemned the burning of synagogues, and protested against the persecution of people because of their race. He said this injustice would bring God's punishment on Germany and quoted a Bible verse: "whatsoever a man soweth, that shall he also reap."[65] He warned that the seed of hatred would bring a terrible harvest, and called for repentance—shortly afterward he was attacked by a mob, savagely beaten, and then thrown in prison.

This is the sort of "political" opposition which Hitler or Mao or Stalin could not tolerate—and there were many other instances of Nazi oppression, most of which are lost to history. Conway tells of one pastor who was sent to a concentration camp because he disagreed with a local Nazi leader who claimed "that faith arises out of blood."[66] One can only claim that Hitler did not persecute the church if, like Walker, he ignores the historical record or skips lightly over it with a clever evasion, and takes Hitler's words at face value—as if Hitler were a sincere and honest man, a sort of German Abraham Lincoln. Earlier we referred to the closure of Austrian monasteries and nunneries. Those treacherous monks and nuns must have been a great threat to the power of the Third Reich.

Another aspect of historical knowledge that is totally lacking from this site is the entire course of German cultural, intellectual, and philosophical development during the century and more preceding Hitler's rise to power. Those who have studied that period have found that Hitler did not appear out of nowhere. To say that Naziism came from the Bible, as if the entire preceding century or two of German history had nothing to do with it; as if Hitler's mind was a *tabula rasa* until he started reading the Bible and then got the idea that the Germans were the master race; as if the Bible had anything to do with Germany's defeat in World War I, the depression, the threat of communism, the weaknesses of the Weimar government; to ignore 19th-century German thinkers who expressly rejected the myth of the son of God dying on the cross and rising from the dead, and at the same time proclaimed many of the most fundamental ingredients of National

Socialism—all of this is something considerably less than an informed approach to the question of Hitler's spiritual and philosophical origins.

Also lacking is an awareness of the political realities of the Third Reich. Walker asks why Hitler did not try to destroy the church. Some historical knowledge sheds some light on this. When Hitler first came to power in 1933, he was not the uncontested ruler of Germany. It took some time for him to consolidate his power. In this transitional period, excessive conflict with the church was not to his advantage, and would have considerably complicated the domestic political situation.

Walker refers to claims that Hitler was lying in his statements of support for religion and asserts that he had no reason to lie. This is a common error, to assume that Hitler was always the Fuhrer with total power—forgetting that at one time he was only a politician, even a minor politician, in need of votes; also forgetting that when he was first appointed Chancellor he had to be mindful of real limits and work within them. And why did Hitler need to lie about the reasons for the invasion of Poland? He had the power, he did not have to get anyone's permission—but still he took great pains to present an appearance of legality, even inventing Polish atrocities to justify the invasion.

After getting a firm grip on all of the levers of power, Hitler's next goal was rearmament, to prepare as quickly as possible for the coming war. Here also, excessive conflicts with the churches would have served no useful purpose. When the war began, Hitler needed the complete support of the nation, including loyal military service from people of all sorts—an all-out war with the churches would have been a distraction from the war effort.

Hitler thus had no desire for a head-on conflict which would bring no benefit and cause unnecessary problems. He did realize that religious beliefs were a threat to his unquestioned and total power, and his regime included a consistent and unwavering effort to marginalize the church, strip it of its influence, and exclude it from the public sphere.

A great deal of speculation is not necessary here. An objective study of what actually happened to the churches in the Third Reich will reveal the government's restrictions on and persecution of the churches. Why, then, Walker asks, did Hitler want to unify the Protestant churches into one state church if he was not trying to support and help the church? For the same reason that Chairman Mao wanted to unify all of the Chinese churches in one state controlled organization—to control them more easily. By the way, the beliefs that all differences of doctrine, church organization and worship were trivial and insignificant; that Germans could all be herded by the government into one church against their will on the basis of race; that church organization is a government affair; these show complete hostility and contempt for the churches and for Christian teaching. Hitler failed here because the church alone out of all German organizations, inadequate as its overall record of submission to Hitler undoubtedly was, refused to tamely submit to Hitler's demands. These and other things are known to those who have made a real effort to understand the church in the Third Reich. They are unknown to Walker. His site reflects zero understanding of historical and political reality.

Walker's lack of familiarity with the historical background is also revealed in his attempts to prove Hitler's Christianity by reproducing some of his paintings. Hitler painted a church, and a mountain view with a roadside crucifix. Clearly only a devout, Bible believing Christian would paint a church or a landscape with a crucifix in it—at least according to Walker. Walter S. Frank's in-depth and well-documented analysis of Hitler reveals, however, that Hitler painted a number of other subjects, including Munich's famous beer hall, the Hofbrauhaus. He also did commercial artwork, such as posters and advertisements, and painted on commission—so some of his subjects were chosen by others.[67]

Walker's arguments will seem convincing to those with little or no knowledge of the subject. This applies to his reproduction in the "Nazi artifacts" section of Nazi badges and mementos that combine the cross and the swastika in various ways. A little research will reveal that in 1938 the use of the swastika alongside the cross was forbidden.[68] The so-called "German Christians" who reveled in such displays of devotion to the state had become a political liability and needed to be put in their place. Conway relates that one of the German Christians became so outspoken in his objections to the pagan elements in the Nazi Party that he was sent to a concentration camp.[69]

C. Illogical arguments

A third element is a profound illogic that stresses the most tenuous similarities between Hitler's thought and Christian teaching while ignoring the most blatant differences. It would take a book to deal with all of the examples of this in Walker's site. I would like to mention some examples, however—not for refutation, though some refutation will be presented, but to illustrate a propagandistic mindset that is motivated more by hostility than by a desire to arrive at real understanding. It will also shed some light on the mind of Hitler, to contrast his views with eternal biblical truths—so this analysis might not be as tedious as I had at first feared.

To choose one point out of many, Walker claims that Hitler believed in the God of the Bible. Now, does any serious person think that Hitler believed the Old Testament was the word of God? That God appeared to Abraham and made a special covenant with him by which all the peoples of the earth would be blessed? That those who blessed Abraham and his descendants, the Jews, would be blessed, and those that cursed them would be cursed? That God delivered the Jews from captivity in Egypt, appeared to Moses, gave him divine rules and commandments, led the children of Israel to the promised land, and established them there?

Does any serious person think that Hitler believed God came to earth in human form in the person of Jesus Christ, who died on the cross as a sacrifice for the sins of the world and rose from the dead, so that those who believe in him can be cleansed by his blood and receive forgiveness of sins and eternal life in heaven?

Walker claims that Hitler believed in the God of the Bible, and then attempts to substantiate it with words from Hitler's speeches and from *Mein Kampf* that show Hitler to have had many ideas directly contrary to the Bible's teachings. That is a peculiar sort of logic, to strongly assert a point, and then offer evidence to the contrary.

Looking briefly at this section, which has a few quotes from speeches but many quotes from *Mein Kampf*, we find—as has been said before—that there are no distinctly Christian or biblical doctrines in any of Hitler's words. That God exists, or that he created the world, and influences it providentially, are not distinctly Christian. Jews and Moslems can believe the same, as did many German secular philosophers of the 19th century who rejected Christianity but still felt that there was something up there, guiding the world to a higher development through the use of great men and nations.

There are no quotes from *Mein Kampf* containing essential Christian doctrines. There are some paraphrases of or references to Bible verses (not used to advance any Christian teaching) and some comments about "Providence" and "Fate"—but this has been discussed before. Let us look at some of the unbiblical doctrines revealed in this section, cited by Walker to prove Hitler's Christianity but in fact achieving the opposite:

~ lowering the level of race is a sin against God.

~ the Jewish nation is a racial, not a religious entity (this is proof that Hitler believed in the God of the Bible?).

~ the Jew is the symbol of all evil (Paul said, "I also am an Israelite, of the seed of Abraham, of the tribe of Benjamin").

~ the greatness of Christianity lay not in truth but in fanaticism and intolerance [vol. II chapt. 5].

~ religious education should not be abolished without providing an equivalent (history shows what that equivalent was—a new religion of race and faith in the Fuhrer).

~ the state is a living organism that leads the nation to freedom (not, as the Bible says, an instrument of God to punish evildoers and keep the peace). The state as an organism is an idea from the secular German Folkish philosophy.

~ opposition to Christian missions to Africa, and the statement that it is better to teach parents to adopt an orphan than to preach the gospel of salvation through faith in Jesus Christ (all good humanists will be in solid agreement with Hitler here).

~ a reference to humans as created by God is used to prove that Hitler was a Creationist. But, if all who believe in Creationism are linked in this way to Hitler, then all atheists are linked in the same way to Stalin. We have already seen Hitler's evolutionary concept of human origins in *Mein Kampf*. We have also referred to Martin Bormann's use of the word "God" to mean "the force of natural law."70 Chapter 8 will assert that Hitler was a theistical evolutionist.

~ Hitler believed Catholicism was unscientific, and asserted that the teachings of the Catholic Church were contrary to science [vol. II chapt. 5]. Once again, all humanists must nod in agreement with Hitler's secular wisdom here. Why would Walker even use this quote?

~ Protestants and Catholics can unite in National Socialism; never mind about the Pope, the mass, the Virgin, purgatory, prayers to the saints, doctrines of salvation or justification, church organization, forms of worship. None of that is important—just believe in the Aryans as the master race and the Fuhrer as the Messiah sent by God, and there will be real unity. This shows complete indifference to the Church. "Forget all of those differences, just be a good German and follow me."

~ the purpose of life is struggle and the blood men shed fighting for their homeland is sacred.

These unbiblical doctrines are used to prove Hitler's Christianity. There are many other such comments by Hitler that Walker presents to his own disadvantage. One shows Hitler's hostility to Protestantism. Is Walker aware of

Protestant objections to the Aryan paragraph that forbade converted Jews from serving as pastors? Of traditional Protestantism's defense of the Jewish Old Testament as the word of God?

There are quotes objecting to anti-Semitism that is religious but not racial. Another states that the secret of success is power. Hitler refers to God's grace smiling on the German armies in the First World War—not a biblical concept. Hitler's claim that Christianity's significance lay in the area of ethics and morality was pure secularism and theological liberalism, which dismissed doctrines about Christ, sin, eternal life, and focused only on ethics. To prove Hitler's Christianity Walker gives a quote showing that Hitler had a purely secular and humanist concept of it.

Other quotes prove nothing. Hostility to immorality and degrading entertainments are supposedly similar to those of the Religious Right (unlike the Anti-religious Left which accepts pornography as normal). I worked as an English teacher in China and saw extremely strong official statements about the degrading effects of pornography from the Chinese Communist government. There is a quote about artists having God's grace—but God's grace has to do with faith in Christ, not artistic talent. This is sheer paganism, using some religious language that deceived many gullible Germans and is still deceiving people today.

There is a condemnation of those who misuse religion for political ends. This sounds pretty good, except Hitler often accused people of the very things he was doing himself. The Jews were cruel, devious, cunning, plotting to take over the world; the Poles were attacking Germany; the Czechs were making life miserable for Germans—Hitler did the very things he objected to in others, and his talk about the misuse of religion here sounds very pious—to those who take Hitler's words at face value.

A striking example of Walker's method is found in the "Nazi artifacts" section of his site. He includes a painting supposedly by Hitler of Mary with the baby Jesus. It is a picture of a woman holding a baby that, Walker says, shows Hitler's Christianity. Strangely, however, this picture of a woman with child is found on close inspection to be totally void of any religious symbolism whatever. There is not a single halo, no manger, no wise men, not even a fat naked baby with wings.

How a picture of a woman with a child that has no religious symbolism could only be painted by a Christian needs to be clarified. Probably the picture isn't even genuine anyway. Hitler's clumsiness in drawing human figures has been noticed by more than one person, but these figures are tolerably well drawn. They are unlike any other of Hitler's paintings that I have seen. More important painters than Hitler have had paintings falsely attributed to them—it is a good way to increase the value of an otherwise worthless painting. If anything, the painting with its exaggerated sun's rays beaming down on a fruitful field shows the doctrine of sun-worship, popular in some circles in that period (as we shall see in chapter 5).

I don't know what the technical term is for a logical error of this sort. There must be a name for it. It is a good thing the word "Poland" isn't mentioned in the Bible—it might be used to prove that Hitler got his idea for the invasion of Poland "Right out of the Holy Bible!"

Walker's website teems, swarms, abounds, with many examples of such contorted logic. Christian support for the Gulf Wars is compared to German Christian support for Hitler's wars—as if the Bushes thought the Americans were the master race. Christian condoning of legal war is condemned—does this mean Walker is a committed pacifist, who feels that Hitler should have been allowed to take over the world without resistance, and that slaves should still be sold on the auction blocks of the south today?

Did Hitler act on his beliefs, just like believers today? Feminists and gay rights activists also act on their beliefs—just like Hitler. But Hitler was *intransigent*, and his intransigence is supposedly like that of right-wingers today. And left-wing liberals are "transigent"? Are they willing to have objections to Darwin taught in the classroom? Are they willing to concede that maybe there should be legal restrictions on abortion after all, that people who think homosexuality is disgusting and perverted might just have a point? No, they are fanatical and intolerant and try to stifle all opposing views—we could say "just like Hitler," but that sort of argument only works one way.

D. Misstatements of fact

Another flaw that runs throughout the entire site is inaccurate statements. Some of them are (in paraphrase):

Many Christians are and have been like Hitler.

Perhaps Walker would like to inform us which other Christians advocated Aryan supremacy; the extermination of the Jews; racial purity as the secret of happiness; defilement of racial purity as the greatest sin. He can also tell us which American Christians have seized power, established a dictatorship, put opponents in concentration camps, and embarked on mad campaigns of world conquest.

Christians use inquisitions and wars to exterminate heretics and members of other faiths.

The Baptists, Methodists, Lutherans, Quakers, Pentecostals, and other groups have supported inquisitions and exterminations and persecuted others? Walker equates the medieval Catholic church with all churches. It is true, Christians have supported wars, but so have many non-Christians. The Bible does sanction just wars. It is because of war that we are not all speaking German or Japanese.

The party platform supported "positive Christianity" and Hitler declared the platform inalterable.

Is that why Hitler abolished the army and replaced it with the SA? Insisted on the equality of Germany with other countries? Forbade political lies in the press? Appointed people on the basis of merit rather than party affiliation? Did not allow industrialists to profit from the war?

Germany was a Christian country.

More will be said about that in the following chapter. For the present, it is sufficient to ask: if the entire German nation was so devout, why was the Communist Party (directly affiliated with Moscow) the third largest party in the Reichstag in 1932? Why did the Communist presidential candidate, Ernst Thaelmann, gain 13.2% of the votes in the March 1932 election? Bill Foster, the Communist candidate for the American presidential election in that same year received 0.3% of the vote. Who were all those devout German Christians that voted for an atheist?

Walker is also oblivious to the popularity of Darwinism in Germany (not to mention Freudianism, empiricism, positivism, "Enlightenment" rationalism, and other secular trends). Ernst Haeckel, Germany's leading Darwinist, openly attacked religion as outdated superstition while at the same time arguing for racism, German imperialism, anti-Semitism and political authoritarianism. That an enthusiastic advocate of Darwinism should be so close and even identical to Hitler on some key points is a fact that Walker dare not address.

Hitler's Concordat with the Vatican established the Catholic Church's rights and freedoms in Germany.

The Church was required to withdraw from politics and not interfere with Hitler in any way. Catholics had freedom—on paper—to exist huddled in their sanctuaries, as long as they were totally obedient to the government in every respect. The Catholic Centre Party was dissolved. This is freedom and power? Also, the Concordat was repeatedly broken by Hitler and the Vatican protested against violations numerous times. That is why Catholic orphanages, kindergartens, seminaries, publishing houses, monasteries, and nunneries were closed—because they conflicted with the overall aims of the government.

Incidentally, the Anti-religious Left—like Hitler—wants the Christians to be confined to the churches and separated from politics. That is not a sarcastic, ironic, or rhetorical statement. It is a literal statement of fact. The Nazis and the Communists and the left-wing secular humanists (who dishonestly disguise themselves as moderates) felt and feel that Christians should be excluded from the political process—if not totally, then as much as possible. That way the anti-Christian forces can rule and impose their will on society without the trouble of anyone disagreeing with them. There is nothing that such people hate more than truthful disagreement.

Hitler wanted the Evangelical church to cooperate closely with the government.

Hitler wanted everyone to cooperate (!) closely with the government. To omit the fact that after he came to power he aimed not for close cooperation but for total subordination of the church to the state, and to take his rhetoric at face value, is a significant distortion.

Hitler's anti-Semitism originated from Christianity.

This is followed by a quote from *Mein Kampf* referring to Dr. Karl Lueger's Christian Social Party (Karl Lueger was the mayor of Vienna during Hitler's youth). In the quote, Hitler states only that he became "acquainted" with Karl Lueger and the Christian Social Party—it does not say that Hitler got his ideas from Lueger at all. It doesn't even say what Hitler thought, only that he became acquainted.

As in so many other places, Walker's lack of historical knowledge is a handicap. The following quote from an online biography of Hitler shows how Lueger's anti-Semitism was different from Hitler's.

> Lueger's fairness, however, is hard to dispute. Even the eminent Austrian Jewish writer, Stefan Zweig, who was growing up in Vienna at the time, declared that Lueger's administration

"was perfectly just . . . The Jews who trembled at [his] triumph . . . continued to live with the same rights and esteem as always."[71]

Hitler spoke well of Lueger and his Christian Social Party in some respects, but criticized their deficient concept of anti-Semitism. These statements come from vol. I chapt. 3 of *Mein Kampf*:

> The Christian Social movement . . . erred in its struggle against the Jews . . .
> . . . If, in addition to its enlightened knowledge of the broad masses, the Christian Social Party had had a correct idea of the importance of the racial question . . . there would have resulted a movement which even then in my opinion might have successfully intervened in German destiny . . .
> . . . It is obvious that combating Jewry on such a basis could provide the Jews with small cause for concern. If the worst came to the worst, a splash of baptismal water could always save the business and the Jew at the same time. With such a superficial motivation, a serious scientific treatment of the whole problem was never achieved . . . Lacking was the conviction that this was a vital question for all humanity, with the fate of all non-Jewish peoples depending on its solution.
> Through this halfheartedness the anti-Semitic line of the Christian Social Party lost its value.

> It was a sham anti-Semitism which was almost worse than none at all; for it lulled people into security; they thought they had the foe by the ears, while in reality they themselves were being led by the nose.

Moreover, the Christian community as the Bible describes it is not a political party that consists of people running for office and advocating various social and economic reforms—though Christians may do that of course. The biblical concept of a community of faith has to do with a common salvation and a common hope through the spirit of Christ and the power of his blood to save from sin—subjects with which Karl Lueger and the "Christian" Social Party were not excessively preoccupied.

Hitler kept his Concordat with the Vatican.
The historical record presents numerous cases in which the Concordat was broken, from the very start. Conway reports numerous protests by the Vatican through official channels, all of which were ignored. Finally, in 1936, "after repeated protests by Cardinal Bertram to the Reich Chancellery had all been ignored, an appeal was made for more forceful assistance from Rome."[72] This led to the papal encyclical referred to earlier, that was secretly distributed and read in every Catholic Church in Germany in March, 1937. This encyclical referred directly to the persecution of the Catholic Church in Germany and to violations of the Concordat.

This could have led to an open break between the Vatican and the Nazi government, but both sides pulled back for obvious reasons. Hitler was urgently preparing for war, and a repetition of Bismarck's long and troublesome conflict with the Catholic Church would have been of no benefit, and even a serious detriment. The Catholic Church would also have suffered from a major clash with Hitler, including the devastation of the Church's properties and the possible loss of great numbers of Catholics who, if asked to choose between Hitler and the Pope, might have chosen the former (if only to avoid persecution).

The Catholics had three alternatives: to blindly submit to National Socialism in every respect; to openly defy Hitler; or to endure. Some chose the first and a very few the second. The Vatican opted for the third. This would explain (if not justify) the continuance of routine diplomatic courtesies, and attempts to avoid open hostility (such as continued birthday greetings to Hitler). It wasn't until after the end of the war that the Pope finally denounced Hitler. Speaking to the College of Cardinals in June 1945, Pius XII referred to the suppression of Catholic organizations and public and private Catholic schools; pressures put on Catholic civil servants; propaganda against the Church; the closing and confiscation of church institutions; the total elimination of Catholic publishing and press.

The Pope also referred to the "satanic spectre" of National Socialism and called it "arrogant apostasy from Jesus Christ, the denial of His doctrine and of his work of redemption, the cult of violence, the idolatry of race and blood . . ."[73] I myself am not a Catholic, and think this denunciation of Naziism would have been much more impressive if it had been issued long before. Nevertheless, it does show the official Catholic position on Hitler and National Socialism. It could not contradict more strongly Walker's statement that Hitler never broke the Concordat. I don't know why Walker made that statement, and cannot say if he was willfully misrepresenting the facts, or if he just believed what he had heard elsewhere and did not verify it.

Hitler's Table Talk

Before examining the last of what I take to be five flaws that run through Walker's entire site—an ignorance of Christianity—it might be helpful to look at some other assertions made on this site.

Much is said about a book called *Hitler's Table Talk*, so some background information is in order. For some time during the war, Hitler allowed a couple of stenographers to record his casual conversations. The transcripts were edited by Martin Bormann and survived the war. The book shows Hitler as being extremely hostile to Christianity. In it Hitler refers to Christianity as a lie; a disease; an invention (along with Bolshevism) of the Jew; and as a religion that violates the natural law of struggle by preserving human failures. He predicts that Christianity will die, says it is senseless and unhealthy, and claims (among other things) that Paul falsified the teachings of Jesus.

Reputable historians accept the book, and even Walker accepts some of it as genuine. He asserts, though, that the anti-Christian statements do not reflect Hitler's beliefs, but reflect instead the bias of Bormann, who edited them. To me, this topic is of secondary importance. I have not needed to use *Table Talk* so far (though I believe it is genuine), and think that Hitler's public statements and actions, taken together, reveal what sort of a man Hitler was. Nevertheless, I would like to comment on Walker's attempts to discredit a potentially useful source of insight into Hitler's mind.

First, to repeat a point made earlier in this chapter, is it reasonable to assume that a genuine, serious Christian (such as Walker claims Hitler to have been) would allow someone very hostile to Christianity (as Walker admits Bormann was) to become his trusted secretary? Would a left-wing anti-Christian like Walker choose a right-wing Christian fundamentalist to become his right-hand man and allow him to administer his important affairs? And, if he did, what fundamentalist would want to work with him?

Secondly, there was a real possibility that Hitler would ask to see the result. He would not have been pleased to find that his statements had been so completely falsified as to present the opposite of what he intended. This would not have been beneficial to Bormann's career. If Walker's imaginary Christian fundamentalist assistant had falsified Walker's conversations so as to make him appear to be a devout, Bible-believing Christian, what would Walker's reaction be?

It is asserted that the persecution of the churches was Bormann's project. Odd, that Hitler the Catholic chose a man who openly hated his the church for a close advisor. And why didn't church leaders come to Hitler and inform him that Bormann was making trouble for them? Then Hitler could have fired Bormann and protected the churches and safeguarded their rights, as he had promised he would.

But, Walker asks why Hitler's other private conversations didn't show hostility to Christianity. He then cites two private interviews from 1931 which Hitler had been assured would be kept secret, and hence represent his real views. In these interviews Hitler does not denounce religion and mentions a reconciliation with Catholicism, supposedly showing his interest in religion and the well-being of the church. There is even another conversation quoted in which Hitler states that all men are brothers and should love each other.

We have already looked at reasons why public denunciations of Christianity by Hitler would have interfered with his plans and created unnecessary political obstacles for him. As to the statement about love, I leave it for intelligent people to judge for themselves if Hitler meant those words and practiced them or not—if, that is, he ever really said them. Walker accepts as genuine words by Hitler reported second hand that completely contradict everything that is known about him. Perhaps those statements were falsified to present Hitler in a more favorable light, or maybe Hitler was pulling the wool over someone's eyes, as he did so often and so well. Supposedly confidential statements could still have been made guardedly—would Hitler, who broke his own word so often, trust other people to keep theirs?

Walker goes on to refer to Hitler's high opinion of Christ in the *Table Talk* (why didn't Bormann edit that out as well?). This admiration consists of saying that Jesus' object was to free Palestine. So, Jesus was a national liberator, a Palestinian Simon Bolivar, who was executed by the Jews with no mention made of a resurrection. How does this prove Hitler's Christianity?

But, Walker goes on to ask why Hitler didn't speak negatively of Jesus. Hitler saw Jesus as an Aryan who died fighting the Jews. Why would he condemn an Aryan who died fighting Jewry, whose teachings were later falsified by the apostle Paul? Anyway, there is considerably more to being a Christian than "not condemning Jesus."

A few other statements merit comment—such as the assertion that Hitler's Christianity was only questioned in Germany after WWII. We have already referred to Pastor Julius von Jan. Moreover, Conway relates that in 1936 the governing body of the Prussian Union of the Confessing Church issued a statement denouncing the Nazi "worship of blood and race" and the exaltation of "eternal Germany." It was stated that Naziism was a new religion, "nothing less than Antichrist."[74] The Nazi reaction was predictable. Clergy were prohibited from reading the statement, but many of them ignored the ban and read the statement from their pulpits. This led to the arrests of hundreds of pastors (seven hundred according to Conway). When Walker says that Hitler's Christianity was never questioned until years after 1945, he is mistaken.

Another question raised on this website is, why did Hitler not allow Goering and Goebbels to formally renounce their church membership? So, they wanted to leave the church, but remained in it because Hitler ordered them to? That doesn't sound very devout to me. As to Hitler's reasoning, the answer is simple—public relations.

Then we are given some statements from Speer, who stated that Hitler was strongly opposed to anti-church measures and did not want to replace the church by party ideology. What were those anti-church measures? Walker's own source admits there was a campaign against the church—and who believes Hitler sharply condemned a practice by the Nazi government but did nothing to prevent it? And if Hitler did not want the church to be replaced by party ideology, then why was party ideology taught in the public schools and not traditional church doctrines?

When discussing Speer's memoirs, Walker includes a quote from *Hitler's Table Talk* stating that superstition should be protected, but should not be allowed to compete with the party. This quote is accepted as genuine by Walker because it does not conflict with his purpose. According to his subjective criteria it is genuine, so he presents it as evidence of Hitler's not having wanted to destroy the churches. However, it doesn't say what he thinks it does.

To begin with, Hitler refers here to religion as "superstition." Secondly, Hitler really did not care if someone was a Catholic or Protestant, and Germans of those persuasions were free to go to their respective churches—as long as they believed that the Germans were the master race and obeyed the Fuhrer in every respect. Similarly, abortionists and gay-rights activists don't care if those who go along with them are Protestant or Catholic. Thirdly, the party was sheltered from competition with religion by the simple expedient of excluding the churches from public life, confining them to their sanctuaries, and throwing opponents of the regime into jail.

The rights of the mainline superstitions—Lutheranism and Catholicism—to be muzzled and locked up in their churches were to be protected. Less influential groups had no such rights. Conway provides a Gestapo document listing the lesser groups and sects that were weak enough to be summarily banned over the period of 1933-1938. Some of them, and by no means all, were: Seventh Day Adventists; Bible Faith Fellowship; Free Pentecostalists of Berlin; German People's Church; The Church of the Apostle John; Bible Community; Gathering of Mankind's Friends; Union of Free Religious Communities in Germany; God's Social Parish; Anabaptist Sect; Mission for Awakening in Germany; Christian Gathering; New

Salem Company; Shepherd and Flock; Association for a Common Life; Bahais; Jehovah's Witnesses.[75] But Walker quotes Hitler's 1939 speech to the Reichstag to the effect that there was religious freedom in Germany. Who would accept as truthful Hitler's comments on the origins of WWII? But the facts about the invasion of Poland are well known—the facts about the Bible Faith Fellowship, the Anabaptist Sect, and the Mission for Awakening in Germany are not.

We are then presented with a statement to the effect that Christian churches in Nazi Germany were strong until Hitler's death. Anyone who thinks the German church was strong in 1944 has a peculiar understanding of the Third Reich. Shirer mentions the following incident that shows the strength and freedom of the German church under Hitler. Martin Niemoller, a Lutheran pastor, had been arrested. He was brought before a court for his "underhanded" criticisms of the state (a good example of Nazi freedom of religion). Niemoller was acquitted of the main charge, found guilty of a lesser offense, and released since the time he had spent in prison awaiting trial exceeded the sentence imposed. He was however immediately re-arrested, and kept under "protective custody." He remained in confinement, in prison and in concentration camps (Dachau and Sachsenhausen) until the end of the war.[76]

Of equal value is a quote from Hitler about Luther. Referring to pictures of Frederick the Great, Luther, and Bismarck, Hitler supposedly praised Luther for uniting the Germans by his German translation of the Bible. Why did Hitler admire Luther? Because of Luther's doctrines? His emphasis on the teaching of salvation by faith? His attempted purification of the church? No, because Luther made it possible to unify the German people. This shows Hitler's indifference to theological doctrines—and, by the way, why would a Catholic admire Martin Luther and have his picture on the wall instead of the Pope, the Virgin, or a crucifix? Then there is the quotation from *Table Talk* cited in chapter 2, where Hitler regretted Luther's translation of Jewish "mumbojumbo" into German.

Still in the same section about *Table Talk*, we read a touching story about how Hitler pulled a used New Testament out of his pocket and impressed some visiting deaconesses with it. That was a nice little trick from a man who boasted that he was the finest actor in Europe. I wonder where they found a used Bible for him— maybe from one of his housekeepers: if, that is, the incident really happened.

There are also some quotes from contemporaries praising Hitler's Christianity. Some people (like French and British diplomats, and reporters and editors for England's most prestigious newspapers) were easily fooled and took Hitler's rhetoric at face value. Others were just making propaganda. Historian Paul Johnson has some interesting examples by the way of people praising Stalin in a similar vein. His secular admirers in the West saw him as gentle, wise, and good-natured.[77] H.G. Wells met Stalin in 1934, and described him as "candid, fair, and honest," adding "no one is afraid of him and everyone trusts him."[78] There was also a lot of praise for Chairman Mao by left-wing secularists who projected their hopes and dreams onto him but were totally deceived as to the real nature of the man and of his regime. The blind folly of some religious people who did not see the reality of Hitler is matched by similar qualities on the part of non-religious people who saw Mao as a Chinese Thomas Jefferson whose benign devotion to his subjects and commitment to social justice provided an example for the west to emulate. Simple-mindedness and gullibility are human failings, not secular or religious ones.

Finally, there is a long speech by Hitler praising Jesus as a socialist, this one too from a second hand source—Otto Wagener's *Memoirs of a Confidant*. Steigmann-Gall also quotes this source. According to Wagener, who was chief of staff of the SA and a member of Hitler's inner circle for a few years, Hitler said this about Christ's teachings:

> *We are the first to exhume these teachings! Through us* alone, and not until now, do these teachings celebrate their resurrection. Mary and Magdalene stood at the empty tomb. For they were seeking the dead man. But we intend to raise the treasures of the living Christ![79] [emphasis in the original]

In nearly two thousand years of Christian history, the real teachings of Christ were unknown until Adolf Hitler came along. In this quote, Hitler dismissed traditional Christianity—and what sort of a source was Wagener? An online review of *Memoirs of a Confidant* states that Wagener presents a Hitler that "is so opposed to conflict that he is reluctant to arm his storm troops (SA) against their domestic opponents and agrees with Wagener that the time for large-scale international conflict is definitely past."[80] The time for large-scale international conflict is definitely past, and Hitler really doesn't know if his SA should be armed? All that street brawling must have been deeply troubling to his tender conscience.

These conversations were held, according to the review, over the period from 1929 to 1933. In this period Hitler—while making plenty of bloodthirsty remarks to his followers—consistently presented an image of peace and moderation to the world. Some may take these comments at face value—people with more knowledge of Hitler will not. They also will not accept the image presented by Wagener of a Hitler who was unwittingly controlled by Goering, Goebbels, and Himmler, and unable to prevent them from carrying out their criminal schemes in opposition to his own plans.

Yet, Hitler did mix truth with his lies—one thing that makes it so difficult to determine what he actually meant if one only looks at his words and ignores the historical record. These conversations—reconstructed by Wagener from memory years after the event, while in captivity after the war—are accepted as valid by those who are eager to find any link between Hitler and Christianity, no matter how dubious. If Wagener did reconstruct them accurately, he may have accurately remembered propaganda statements of the sort Hitler was commonly making at that time, presenting himself as a reasonable man of peace. Wagener may also have been deliberately distorting the facts so as to minimize his own guilt by making his association with Hitler seem less reprehensible.

Wagener gives us some other religious statements by Hitler. After some vague and confusing comments about how the Christian communities betrayed and killed Jesus' teachings on socialism at the same time that the Jews killed Christ, Walker provides a quote from Wagener that seems to state the church killed Jesus' socialism; then the Christians claimed Christ had been resurrected so that they might replace his teachings with their own—but the passage is sufficiently muddled to make it possibly genuine. Walker accepts it as valid because it suits him but, as is always the case with Hitler, it contains no essential doctrines. Instead, in the passage cited by Walker as proving Hitler's Christianity, we find attacks on Catholicism because of its Inquisition, witch burnings, and persecution. There is also contempt for organized religion as well—it is dismissed as hypocritical, selfish, greedy, and Pharisaical. Secular humanists can applaud Hitler's wisdom here. Walker can argue, as he does elsewhere on his site, that hostility toward established religion is consistent with some Christian reformers who objected to ecclesiastical abuses, but the specific reference to the Inquisition shows a hostility to the Roman Church on the part of the supposedly Catholic Hitler. Moreover, if these are taken as attacks on the organized church in general, they radically conflict with Hitler's publicly stated views about the importance of the organized churches, and show the hollowness of his promises to cooperate with and support them.

Quotes from Hitler's followers

A selection of quotes from Hitler's top leaders as well as other lesser figures contains little of interest. As before, there are numerous references to God, but nothing of essential doctrines. There is a lot about "positive" or "German" Christianity.

There are also the usual lies one expects in Nazi rhetoric—Goering even claimed at the Nuremberg trials to be a Protestant, and the statement is repeated by Walker as a truthful one. As evidence Goering adduced that he had had marriage, christening, and burial carried out by the church in his house. Nowhere are those ceremonies mentioned as being part of Christianity in the entire New Testament. Moreover, Conway relates an interesting fact about Goering's "Protestantism"—he didn't allow chaplains of any sort in the Air Force.[81] This is why Walker shows us an Army and a Navy chaplain's cap, but not an Air Force one.

Frankly, anyone who takes the testimony of Nazi war criminals at Nuremberg at face value, as if they were upright men of integrity boldly standing for the truth rather than cowards and liars, is deceived. There is also a lie from Baldur von Schirach about religious freedom for members of the Hitler Youth, presented with the attitude that it must be true if Baldur von Schirach said so.

Many of the comments assembled by Walker contain a number of statements that completely contradict biblical doctrines. Some of them state that Germany is God's house; the church should serve the state; doctrines are not important to Christianity; God is found in blood and race; service to Germany is service to God; Hitler is holy.

These and other statements are given as evidence that the Nazis were Christian! We are also told that Christ preached struggle, not forgiveness of sins and eternal life. He died fighting the Jews (nothing about a resurrection). A Nazi slogan about serving the community was claimed to be central to Christ's teaching. Struggle as the basic law of life; elimination of human vermin being obedience to natural law—anyone who thinks this is Christianity should first learn what Christianity is before discussing it.

There are also some distortions in this section. For example, we are informed of death camp commandant Rudolf Hoess' Catholic upbringing. Nothing is said about the fact that he explicitly rejected and turned away from Catholicism. Hoess himself wrote of his rejection of Catholicism. He stated how a priest went to his father and reported a sin he had confessed. This violation of confessional secrecy "destroyed" his faith in the "sacred priesthood" "and doubts began to arise in my mind for the first time . . . I no longer regarded the priesthood as worthy of my trust . . . the deep, genuine faith of a child had been shattered."[82]

Hoess was also deeply offended by the lucrative trade in fraudulent holy relics he observed while serving in Palestine during WWI. He wrote, "I was disgusted by the cynical manner in which this trade in allegedly holy relics was carried on by the representatives of the many churches established there."[83] His description of himself in this context as still being a "devout" Catholic totally contradicts his earlier comments (his memoirs are manifestly full of lies)—but it is unreasonable to link him to Catholicism when he explicitly rejected his family's plans for him to enter the priesthood and formally left the church in 1922.

Getting back to Walker's site, the Nazi emphasis on religious education is referred to—it is not explained that Nazi religion was not of the Christian variety, but was a religion of blood, race, soil, and obedience to the Fuhrer. There is one quote in the entire section that is useful, although not in the way intended. An SA publication (*Der S.A. Mann*) is quoted as saying that the Cross (capitalized in the original) did not represent the Lamb of God dying as a sacrifice for the sins of the world—rather, it represented struggle, Christ's struggle to the death against Judaism. Thus, when people see pictures of crosses used by the Nazis, on graves or monuments for example, most mistakenly think of them as Christian symbols, but actually the Christian symbol of the cross was borrowed and given a new meaning. To Nazis, a Cross represented struggle to the death, as Jesus, the bold Aryan warrior, struggled against Judaism unto death.

Finally, Walker contradicts himself and argues against his whole thesis by including a quote about the necessity of freeing German schools from the chains of Hitler's Concordat with the Vatican. It reflects the Nazi attitude toward the Concordat.

Nazi photos

In this section Walker presents many photos to show that Hitler was supported by Christians. Many of the photos only illustrate the well-known historical fact that the German churches, both Protestant and Catholic, supported Hitler. This can be interpreted to mean that Hitler was a Christian, or that his beliefs were compatible with Christianity. It can also be interpreted to mean that some Christians were gullible and deceived, while others had abandoned traditional Christianity and replaced it with a new faith. It should also be pointed out that others just went along because they were living in a totalitarian dictatorship where support for the dictator was obligatory.

A comment next to a photo of Ludwig Mueller is significant. Walker claims that Hitler's desire to unify the German Church shows his Christianity. Hitler's desire to unite the churches—like Chairman Mao's—has been discussed. The Nazis did derive some support from believers in "Germanic" or "positive" Christianity—a Christianity in which Christ was not the son of God, part of the Trinity, but rather a mere human, a patriot who fought to liberate mankind from the Jews, who died but did not rise again. His death was a symbol only of struggle to the bitter end. This "Christianity" taught that the Germans were the master race, a chosen people destined by Fate / Providence / Heaven / the Almighty / God / the Supreme Being to lead a select portion of mankind to new heights under the leadership of Adolf Hitler, the new Messiah.

This "positive" or "German" Christianity was, however, merely useful as a transitional means of eliminating the old Christianity, as a preparation for the new revelation brought by Hitler and his apostles. We are given an idea of what this new revelation would be by one of Heinrich Himmler's confidants, Felix Kersten. Writing after the war, he related the following comments by Himmler, made after Kersten had remarked on some religious books in Himmler's library:

> I am to prepare a new Nazi religion. I am to draft the new Bible, the Bible of the faith . . . The Fuhrer has decided that, after the victory of the Third Reich, he will abolish Christianity throughout Great Germany, and establish the faith on its ruins. The latter will preserve the idea of God, but it will be very vague and indistinct. The Fuhrer will replace Christ as the savior of humanity. Thus, millions and millions of people will say only Hitler's name in their prayers, and a hundred years from now nothing will be known but the new religion, which will endure for centuries.[84]

Walker would no doubt dismiss this source as hearsay, but since he accepts Wagener's description of Hitler as a peaceful man troubled by SA violence and talking about the love of Christ, it is obvious that his criteria for deciding the authenticity of quotes are purely emotional.

Returning to the photos, there is one of a military chaplain with a group of soldiers. The accompanying comments reveal the hostility to religion that permeates the entire website and clouds Walker's judgment. He claims religion is used to justify wars, and that Christianity encourages soldiers to slaughter other people by promising them forgiveness.

The Bible does say that God has given the governments the power of the sword to keep the peace. If there were no police, society would be in chaos. The criminals would rule and civilization would be impossible. If there were no armed forces we would have to submit to everyone that sought to impose their views by force. Thus, some wars can be justified on religious grounds. But did Hitler justify his wars on religious grounds? Didn't he justify his wars on the basic law of nature, that force is the only determining factor, that life is a struggle—which views he derived not from the Bible but from the *objective* and *scientific* study of nature?

Moreover, soldiers for thousands of years of recorded history in many different regions of the world have been capable of killing without the religious encouragements cited by Walker. The Japanese in WWII, the Vikings, the Mongols, the Huns, the atheistic and secular humanistic Russians, the ancient Mayans, all of these and many other peoples have had wars and slaughters without the Christian assurance of forgiveness of sins and eternal life. To blame the sins and evils of the world on Christianity, or on religion, and to assert that Christians are free to commit all the crimes they like and then go to heaven is an inaccurate representation of Christianity. It is even more inaccurate to present secularists or unbelievers as calm, tolerant, peaceful, rational beings who would never go to war, fight, or kill.

People don't need religious excuses to justify their evil. Someone who does not believe in religion might say:

There is no God, no judgment, no afterlife. You die and that's all. You will not have to give any account for your actions and can commit all the crimes that you like. Furthermore, there is nothing at all wrong with killing people. Man is nothing more than matter, and killing people to benefit society is no different from removing material obstacles to make a place suitable for habitation. You can kill a million, five million people for the good of society, and it is justified.

The countless millions that have been killed according to this logic do not appear on Walker's radar screen. The social Darwinist Ernst Haeckel used some of this reasoning to encourage German soldiers to fight in WWI. There was no after-life to be concerned about, death was a purely natural phenomenon, so soldiers could go into battle and fight for the fatherland without fear.[85]

Walker shows a photo of Goering's "Christian" wedding—but of course we don't know what words were said in the ceremony. Nowhere does the New Testament say anything about church wedding ceremonies, but it does say a lot about a system of ethics and behaviour unknown to Goering. Jesus didn't say "Blessed are vicious and brutal evildoers who have a wedding performed in the church." Incidentally, there are in America non-Christians who have a church wedding strictly for sentimental reasons. Some pastors will perform such a ceremony—it is part of their job. Others will not.

There is a photo of Hitler's mother's grave—this says nothing about Hitler's philosophy and actions. Then there are some propaganda photos of Hitler praying, Hitler leaving a church, Hitler in front of a church or with a church in the background. That Hitler deliberately presented an image as a reasonable and decent man in the years before he came to power is known to those who have studied his rise to power. These photo-ops are illustrative of Nazi propaganda designed to broaden Hitler's base and smooth his path to power, and to facilitate his consolidation to power after he became Chancellor. Why are there no photos of Hitler in front of a church or coming out of a church from the period of 1939-45, or even earlier? Odd, how the church photos stopped being released when they were no longer needed.

Concerning the photo of Hitler leaving the church, we have already referred to the source for it—*The Hitler No One Knows: 100 Pictures of the Life of the Fuhrer*, by Heinrich Hoffmann. Written, it will be recalled, as Nazi propaganda to glorify the Fuhrer, the book has this comment about Hitler leaving the church: "A photograph accidentally becomes a symbol. Adolf Hitler, the supposed 'heretic,' leaves the Marine Church in Wilhelmshaven."[86]

A number of observations can be made about this caption. For one thing, a photograph that just happened to have a strangely bright cross directly over Hitler's head was somehow made by accident. Secondly, here is proof that Hitler was not a heretic—he walked out of a church! How could anyone possibly suspect Hitler of heresy when he was actually photographed walking out of a church? "Here is a photo of me leaving a church once" would not be a strong defense in a real heresy trial—and who were those people who supposed Hitler was a heretic? Could it have been people who thought that race defilement being the original sin had nothing to do with the Bible?

Concerning the photo of Hitler praying, the Bible says "Man looks on the outward appearance, but God looks on the heart." No doubt some people saw the Fuhrer praying, and thought "What a devout and pious man he is." Some of Hitler's associates may have thought "I can't believe how gullible these Christians are." Hitler himself may have been thinking "I've got half an hour to get to the airport." God knows what is in our hearts when we pray, and Jesus spoke of prayers that were acceptable to God, and prayers that were not acceptable.

There is a photo of Hitler with a Catholic official—the words "SMOKING GUN!" are triumphantly added. There are no photos of Hitler with Chamberlain or with a Soviet representative showing English and Russian cooperation with Hitler. This photo shows what is well known—that the Catholic Church cooperated with Hitler. It does not show the deceit with which Hitler disarmed potentially significant opposition from the church, and then when in power did everything he could to eliminate Roman influence. There is an accompanying quote from Cardinal Bertram of Berlin, showing the support of the churches for Hitler. Whether or not this policy of supporting Hitler was a biblical one is an entirely different question. Serious Christians have no trouble recognizing the fact that ecclesiastical power structures nowhere mentioned in the New Testament, whether Protestant or Catholic, often have gone against the teachings and the Spirit of Christ.

Perhaps someday I will make a website responding to Walker. I could include a photo section with the following items:

~ various pictures of Hitler orating, shouting and gesticulating, with accompanying Bible verses: "Blessed are the peacemakers . . . blessed are the meek . . . blessed are the pure in heart . . . blessed are the merciful."

~ a picture of Hitler leaning over a map with the verse "You shall not covet."

~ a picture of some starving concentration camp inmates with the words "Do unto others as you would have them do unto you."

~ a picture of anti-Semitic propaganda with the verse "You shall not bear false witness against your neighbor."

~ a picture of massed formations of German military power with the verse "For all flesh is as grass, and all the glory of man as the flower of grass."

~ a cover of *Mein Kampf* with the words "The Lord knows the thoughts of man, that they are vanity," or "for this cause God shall send them strong delusion, that they should believe a lie."

~ a photograph of a German city destroyed by air raids with the words " . . . he (God) shall bring upon them their own iniquity, and shall cut them off in their own wickedness."

~ a photo of the invasion of Russia and the words "He made a pit, and digged it, and is fallen into the ditch which he made. His mischief shall return upon his own head."

~ a photo of a gas chamber with the words "inventors of evil things . . . they which commit such things are worthy of death."

~ a photo of Hitler "praying" or coming out of a church, with the words "Satan himself is transformed into an angel of light."

~ a photograph of a pile of emaciated corpses with the words "By their fruits ye shall know them."

~ a photograph of Germany's ruined cities with the words "Be not deceived; God is not mocked: for whatsoever a man soweth, that shall he also reap."

I could go on and on, but will content myself with one more example: a photo of German Christians giving the Hitler salute with the words "Ye adulterers and adulteresses, know ye not that the friendship of the world is enmity with God? Whosoever therefore will be a friend of the world is the enemy of God."

Nazi artifacts

Some items exhibited in this section have already been referred to. The rest can be skipped, or referred to briefly. One, a German Army belt buckle that says "God with us" in German, illustrates a violation of one of the Ten Commandments—"You shall not take God's name in vain." Another is a picture of the church Hitler attended as a boy. It proves nothing. Surely if he had attended it once after he came to power, there would have been many photographs of it that the triumphant enemies of Christianity would have pounced on with great rejoicing. Why is it that mandatory boyhood church attendance means a great deal and voluntary non-attendance during adulthood means nothing? And why did Chancellor Hitler never once go back to his boyhood church?

We are shown a cross on the grounds of Hitler's mountain retreat, the Eagle's Nest. Walker asks why Hitler would allow a cross on his property—one can think of a couple of reasons. Perhaps it reminded him of the powerful fighting Aryan Jesus who died in the struggle against Jewish capitalism. Perhaps it was given to him as gift by the locals, and he thought it would be bad public relations to reject it—and even Hitler was mindful of public relations.

Also presented are pictures of a Lutheran church building in Berlin that was decorated under the influence of Germanic Christianity. There is a baptismal font with a carving of Hitler on it, a pulpit carving of Jesus standing next to a German soldier, and stone carvings of helmeted German soldiers along with a crown of thorns and an Alpha and an Omega. Walker also states that there was formerly a swastika on the altar that was removed. All of these do not show the Christian nature of National Socialism. They show German Christians conforming their religion to a false philosophy of the world.

Then we are presented with photos of cards with Christian themes to commemorate deceased soldiers. This presents another reason why Hitler would leave a cross on the grounds of his estate, and why he would make hostile comments about the church privately but not publicly. Many Germans with various degrees of Christian background or belief were fighting for him, who knows how many of them sincerely brainwashed into believing that they were fighting to defend their fatherland against Bolshevism? Would they have fought so well if they had thought that Hitler was the Antichrist? Would they have been inclined to surrender more quickly, or go over to the other side, if they thought that their Fuhrer hated Christianity, if their friends or relatives back home were being persecuted? We now think of Hitler as the Supreme Warlord or the raving maniac in his bunker giving orders to non-existent armies. It is too often forgotten that earlier in his career Hitler had skillfully developed an image of himself as a decent man, at least among Germans who had little access to outside information. This is why the worst Nazi crimes were cloaked in as much secrecy as possible, and why even Hitler found the need to invent plausible justifications for his invasions of Poland and other countries.

A front page of the anti-Semitic publication *Der Stuermer* is reproduced. That the editor, Julius Streicher, hated the Bible and considered it to be a bunch of lies (as was documented in chapter one of this essay) is not mentioned by Walker.

Finally, a piece of anti-Jewish propaganda is presented—a crucifix with a reminder that the Jews killed Christ. Then a Bible verse is added by Walker—the passage in I Thessalonians we have already discussed which says that the Jews killed Christ and the prophets, do not please God, and are contrary to all men. He neglects to state that the same passage places the Gentiles under condemnation as well. He neglects many significant aspects we have discussed earlier—but propaganda does not need such superfluous things as truth or honest representation. A negative association is enough, and the end is achieved. Also omitted are Hitler's statements that religious anti-Semitism was inadequate, because it did not deal with the racial aspect.

E. Ignorance of Christianity

To conclude the analysis of this website, it is necessary to emphasize the lack of understanding of Christian teachings that is one of its most distinguishing characteristics. For example, Walker claims that people just believe in Christianity because of their neurology.

Walker has no evidence for this non-falsifiable and empirically unverifiable faith statement. Moreover, his foundationless faith in materialism eliminates human will and responsibility. People believe in God because of their neurological makeup, atheists reject God because of their neurological makeup, and Hitler wanted to exterminate the Jews because of his neurological makeup. This also eliminates ethics. We cannot say that what Hitler did was wrong, if he was just following his physical makeup—anyway, we are just following ours in condemning him. Whatever is, is, and it is the result of materialistic factors over which we have no control.

Perhaps Walker believes that his opinions are the result of logic and reason, and it is only people who differ too much from him that are the victims of defective neurological systems. This would truly make him a superior sort of being—if it were true, that is. Maybe on the other hand he would admit that his beliefs too were materialistically determined, and hence no more valid or invalid than those of the most primitive backwoods fundamentalist.

Given his materialistic presuppositions, it is inevitable that Walker should have no understanding of or sympathy for the most fundamental aspects of biblical Christianity. Christian teachings are totally incomprehensible to Walker, and he looks on them with hatred, fear, and contempt. This is not the result of Walker's neurology. It is the result of a fallen human will that has been corrupted by sin.

Before looking at some of Walker's specific statements about Christianity, it might be helpful to state some things that Christianity is not.

~ It is not a belief that might makes right, that the basic law of life is struggle.
~ Preservation of racial purity is not the highest law, and race defilement is not the original sin.
~ The blood that a man sheds fighting for his land is not the holiest sacrifice.

~ The Germans are not the chosen people of Providence (or Fate, Destiny, the Almighty, the Supreme Watchamacallit, God, or whatever).

~ It is not the belief that one race is superior to all others.

~ The purpose of government is not to preserve the racial purity of the nation—it is to restrain and punish evildoers.

~ Happiness and meaning in life are not found through unswerving allegiance to someone besides Jesus.

~ Higher ethical ideals and religious or philosophical concepts are not mere inventions of the human mind.

~ Man did not raise himself up above the animals by his own efforts.

~ The good things that we enjoy in life are not the result of our intelligence and efforts alone.

~ God is not an abstract force indifferent to individual love, holiness, sin, and suffering.

Much more could be said along these lines, but the point has been made. What, though, are some of Walker's specific doctrinal confusions that lead him to present such a false picture of Christianity? First, he claims that Hitler's statement of belief in Christianity and his attempts to act like the God of the Bible show him to have been a Christian. Belief in Jesus is all that is required, and Hitler had that belief.

Also, Hitler never criticized Jesus. He honored Jesus and believed in Jesus, Walker asserts—so he was a Christian. The claim is also made that all Christians are sinners, so the fact that Hitler was evil cannot be used to exclude him from the ranks of the believers. Belief alone matters, not actions.

It is added that Hitler was accepted as a Christian by his contemporaries. This is supported by a quote from one Cardinal Faulhaber of Munich, praising Hitler as someone who had real faith in God—but these statements do not prove Hitler was a Christian. They prove that Cardinal Faulhaber didn't know what he was talking about. Can a Cardinal of the Catholic Church be wrong? Cardinal Faulhaber shows that this is possible.

Walker goes on to ask a very profound question: how can we know if someone really is a Christian or not? This gets close to the heart of the matter. How can we know if Hitler was a Christian or not? How can we even be sure that we are Christians? Jesus himself said that there will be those who have done great works in his name that will be turned away on the day of judgment. How do we know we truly are in Christ, that our faith is real?

The authority that we can turn to is the word of God. Admittedly, some parts of it are obscure. Admittedly, Christians disagree on some points. Nevertheless, in discussing not theological obscurities such as predestination or end-times prophecies, but rather the question of Hitler's beliefs and actions, the Bible gives us a clear answer.

Jesus said " . . . the hour is coming, in the which all that are in the graves shall hear his voice, And shall come forth; they that have done good, unto the resurrection of life; and they that have done evil, unto the resurrection of damnation" (John 5:28-29). When the dead are called up out of the grave to stand before the throne of God and be judged, the fact that Hitler spoke positively of Jesus on a few occasions, or at least didn't criticize him, will not save him. Belief in Christianity involves much more than such nebulous and meaningless criteria.

By such absurdly reductive standards, Hindus, Buddhists, Jews, Moslems, and agnostics could also be called "Christians." Ghandi also said "something positive" about Jesus and as far as I know never criticized him. That Hitler had a Catholic education as a boy, or that he claimed to be a Christian once or twice in his adult life, or that he insincerely promised to support the German church—these will not earn him eternal life or forgiveness of sins.

For those with a clear understanding of biblical doctrines, it is not hard to determine the nature of Hitler and his new gospel of blood, soil, and race. Hitler's occasional use of religious language was confusing to many, and it still confuses people today—but we have already seen the teaching that murderers will not inherit the kingdom of God (Galatians 5:21 and Revelation 21:8). This alone is sufficient to burn through the fog of Hitler's rhetoric and to answer the question of Hitler's faith once and for all. If that is not enough, there is also the teaching in I Corinthians that faith without love is worthless.

We have also examined some passages that exclude Hitler from Christianity as the Bible defines it. The wisdom that is from above is "peaceable, gentle . . . full of mercy and good fruits," while earthly wisdom is "devilish," bringing "strife . . . and every evil work" (James). The works of the flesh, of the natural man without the spirit of Christ, include hatred, wrath, strife, and murder, while the fruits of the Spirit of Christ include love, joy, peace, gentleness, and goodness (Galatians). There is no doubt among reasonable people where Hitler fits here.

Walker, however, thinks like many people that saving faith is just a matter of some words about Jesus and some notions in the head that have nothing to do with how we live. The biblical description of faith, however, includes love for God ("faith which works by love") and a desire to please him—not to earn salvation, but as a natural result of having been saved. Faith according to the biblical definition is more than just assent to doctrine.

Where did Hitler ever evidence the slightest desire to follow the teachings of Jesus? To do unto others as he would have others do to him? To love God with all of his heart and soul and mind and his neighbor as himself? To be a peacemaker, to be pure in heart, to be righteous and holy? When Walker asserts that Hitler took Jesus to heart and honored Jesus, we can only conclude that he has either never read the Sermon on the Mount, or that he has read it with no comprehension whatever, or that he has read it with some comprehension but is only making propaganda. No matter if what you say is true or not, as long as people are convinced that Christianity is evil and dangerous you have achieved your goal.

Faith in Christ is faith in Christ as the Son of God who died for us and rose again. It is not faith in a figment of the human imagination whose blood cannot cleanse from sin and whose spirit can't give life. Hitler never referred to or professed faith in the Christ of scripture. His Christ was a Christ of human philosophy, a Christ that did not bring righteousness and forgiveness of sin. In short, Hitler's few and rare statements about Christ refer to a merely human Christ.

In addition to not understanding salvation by faith, Walker also makes the mistake of thinking that in the Christian system, sin is sin, we all sin, so therefore one sin is just as bad as any other. Does this mean that someone who steals a box of pencils from the company supply room is as bad as someone who murders six million people? The Bible clearly lays down standards, stating that wicked people who claim to be Christians should be put out of the church. Other sins are referred to that do not require expulsion—a distinction is drawn between greater and lesser sins.

If someone claims to be a Christian but is a fornicator, a drunkard, an extortioner, or a railer other Christians should not keep company with him, or even eat with him. As it says, ". . . put away from among yourselves that wicked person" (I Corinthians 5:13). The idea of a Christian being a mass murderer is not even considered here. A railer is someone who merely attacks people verbally in an evil and hostile way. Jesus even said that someone who got angry with his brother for no reason or said to him "You fool" was in danger of hell fire (Matthew 5:22).

Hitler was not only a murderer and a liar, he was also a fornicator, living with a woman outside of marriage. Nowhere does the Bible say or imply that someone who says a few words about Jesus once in a while is guaranteed of a place in heaven no matter what. Even if Hitler had plainly expressed a doctrinally sound faith in Christ—which he never did—God judges by the heart. He desires a true confession, not a false one. He desires faith and love in the heart, not just some words that are not even sincere. Any teacher can tell the difference between a student that is trying sincerely and makes ordinary mistakes, and someone who isn't trying and has no interest. Then there is a third kind of student, that physically assaults the teacher and tries to burn the school down.

Paul's letter to the Galatians

A brief look at some teachings of the Bible when compared and contrasted to the life of Hitler might clarify things. Some verses with brief commentary will reveal the errors of the assumptions that faith in Christ is no more than saying some words, any words, about Jesus, and that salvation has nothing to do with one's manner of life.

. . . our Lord Jesus Christ, Who gave himself for our sins, that he might deliver us from this present evil world . . .

That we are to be delivered from this present evil world is a great part of our salvation. Hitler had no concern for this. He perpetuated evil, and was thoroughly enslaved to evil, not delivered from it.

If any man preach any other gospel unto you than that ye have received, let him be accursed.

This shows the Bible's curse on Hitler. He brought a new gospel of salvation for the German people only, through faith in and obedience to him—a new gospel which made no mention of repentance, cleansing of sin, obedience to God, and eternal life in heaven.

. . . the gospel which was preached of me is not after man. For I neither received it of man, neither was I taught it, but by the revelation of Jesus Christ.

Hitler's revelation was from men. It did not come from Christ but came from human philosophy and human wisdom, the wisdom of this world. Haeckel, Hegel, Darwin, Nietzsche, Wagner, Fichte—those and many other men contributed to the culture that led to the Third Reich.

. . . I saw that they walked not uprightly according to the truth of the gospel . . .

Christians are frequently exhorted, charged, encouraged, challenged, to walk according to the truths of God. There is a straight and narrow way of Christ, and those who are in Christ can and do err, but those who persistently show a willful disregard for and even contempt for the teachings of Christ will have to give account on the day of judgment.

. . . the life which I now live in the flesh I live by the faith of the Son of God, who loved me, and gave himself for me.

Faith in Christ includes life—"The just shall live by faith." Faith is not merely some words or ideas that we can then ignore as we go off and commit all of the sins and evils that we like.

. . . that we might receive the promise of the Spirit through faith.

Faith in Christ brings with it the Holy Spirit, which lives in, works in, and guides the believer. Those who do not have this Spirit are not of Christ. Those who do have this Spirit will show some of its fruits, and more of its fruits as they mature. This is not the product of human virtue, but of the Spirit working in them.

Even so we, when we were children, were in bondage under the elements of the world . . .

Hitler remained in bondage to the elements of the world all of his life. False philosophies and corrupt desires such as wrath, hatred, vanity, delusion, held him and his followers in chains of darkness.

And because ye are sons, God hath sent forth the Spirit of his Son into your hearts, crying, Abba, Father.

Saving faith includes receiving the Spirit of God in the heart. As Jesus said, "Except a man be born again, he cannot see the kingdom of God."

For in Christ Jesus neither circumcision availeth anything, nor uncircumcision; but faith which worketh by love.

The only thing that avails us anything in Christ is faith that works by love. Faith is not merely a theory or some words on the lips. As it says in I John, "He that loves not knows not God; for God is love."

For all the law is fulfilled in one word, even in this; Thou shall love thy neighbor as thyself.

This is the law of God. Of course, we cannot fulfill it unless we know God's love, and we cannot know this unless the guilt of our sins has been removed by the blood of Christ.

Walk in the Spirit, and ye shall not fulfil the lust of the flesh . . . But if ye are led of the Spirit, ye are not under the law.

Those who fulfil the lusts of the flesh, the natural man, which are described in this passage as including hatred, wrath, murders, and heresies (including Christ as a warrior whose greatest work was cleansing the temple)—such are not led of the Spirit and still remain under God's condemnation.

. . . they which do such things shall not inherit the kingdom of God.

There is no automatic guarantee of salvation for thieves, liars, drunkards, murderers, sexually immoral people, and teachers of false doctrines, if only they will say some words about Christ or have an outward appearance of religion.

. . . they that are Christ's have crucified the flesh with the affections and lusts.

And they that have not crucified the flesh and its excessive and sinful desires are not Christ's. This crucifixion does not exclude all possibility of error or sin. Christians can and do err—but God knows our hearts, and he knows if we have died to self through faith in Christ, but then make ordinary human errors. Paul recognized the Corinthian Christians as being in Christ, but pointed out their errors. They were divided into factions; one of them was committing serious immorality and this was tolerated; Christians were taking each other to court; they were celebrating communion improperly. These were their sins and errors—not viciousness, brutality, false teachings about the person and work of Christ, and mass murders.

. . . if a man think himself to be something, when he is nothing, he deceiveth himself.

Hitler deceived himself.

. . . let every man prove his own work . . . Be not deceived; God is not mocked: for whatsoever a man soweth, that shall he also reap. For he that soweth to his flesh shall of the flesh reap corruption; but he that soweth to the Spirit shall of the Spirit reap life everlasting.

I can talk about God all day, go to church, have an appearance of godliness—but what am I doing? Am I living for God, loving God, obeying God? Hitler sowed to his flesh and he reaped corruption, as did all of those who followed him—no matter if they went to church ten times a day or not.

God forbid that I should glory, save in the cross of our Lord Jesus Christ, by whom the world is crucified unto me, and I unto the world.

No one who believed this and understood this could possibly have the slightest concern for Hitler's vain glorification of the German nation and the German race. In the light of the cross of Jesus Christ, all such vanity is less than rubbish.

For in Christ Jesus neither circumcision availeth anything, nor uncircumcision, but a new creature. And as many as walk according to this rule, peace be on them, and mercy, and upon the Israel of God.

Infant baptism, church membership, words about Christ, who knows what kind of ideas about Christ, good deeds—nothing avails in Christ but being a new creature. This requires the receiving of the Holy Spirit—without the Spirit we are not of Christ, and are still in our sins. The peace of God is upon those who walk according to this rule, not upon those who, like Hitler, despised it, rejected it, and trampled it underfoot.

What was Hitler?

How can we finally evaluate Hitler? It says in I John that "many false prophets are gone out into the world." Since Hitler did not confess Jesus Christ as God come in the flesh, he was according to the rule of scripture a false prophet who represented the spirit of antichrist. As a false prophet, he brought the curse of God upon himself.

Hitler claimed to have been sent by God, and he was lying as usual. He claimed that belief in him and obedience to him would bring happiness and blessing. He never once mentioned repentance for sin and preparation for eternity in the kingdom of God through cleansing by the blood of Christ, though he did have some philosophical concept of eternity involved with the eternity of the German nation (one of Fichte's ideas).

Similarities between Hitler and Christ or Hitler and God only show Hitler trying to make himself like God, to be equal with God—while sincere Christians want to love and obey and serve God, not replace him. Hitler the skillful deceiver and spiritual counterfeiter copied some aspects of religion. This accounts for an occasional appearance of religiosity, a few words about the Bible here and there, some references to God, a few comments about Christ at rare intervals—but never any serious comments about the basics of Christian belief.

A vague appearance of religiosity, some appeals for Christian support—these lies are transparent to anyone with a serious understanding of Christianity. Why, then, did so many German Christians follow Hitler? This will be discussed in the next chapter. For the present, I would like to ask my Christian brothers and sisters: what will we do if another deceiver appears in our life-time? If America is in shambles, and a deliverer arises who offers us peace, hope, and security, along with many unChristian and unbiblical teachings, including sinful and wicked teachings, will we forget the Saviour? Will this world be more real, more important to us, than the next one? And if the next false prophet—and there will be more—turns with hostility on the church for refusing to obey him, will we obey the *commandment* of Jesus, not to fear those who can only destroy the body, and after that have nothing they can do? Or will we cling to our poor and miserable bodies so desperately, not really believing that to die is gain? Hitler fought bravely in WWI and was not afraid to die. Are pagans braver than Christians? Unfortunately, the answer is too often "Yes."

What is our standard? How can we know that we are in Christ? Are we dying to self and taking up the cross? Walking in the straight and narrow way? Showing the fruits of the Spirit in our lives? Is our doctrine sound, and do we have the Christ of scripture, God manifest in the flesh, in our hearts? Or do we have misguided and unbiblical concepts of Christ in our minds while the world and the flesh reign in our hearts? Do we have the witness of the Spirit, assuring us that we are born of God, or do we have only theories and doctrines? Do we embrace and befriend false teachers who destroy the gospel, as if leading people astray spiritually is something of no consequence to us? Are our churches social clubs where people go to feel good about themselves? And if we are not standing for Christ now, will we stand later? This might relate to the parable of the fig tree that was made to wither because it bore no fruit, even though the time of fruit was not yet. What if this is saying to us that now is the time to bear fruit for Christ, or any time, not only the times that seem agreeable to normal human logic? What if we are planning to live for Christ or do something for Christ later, when we feel the time is right, but we are called to account before then?

But all of these questions, as well as others that have to do with faith which works by love, were irrelevant to the Nazi dictator. He was far too great and powerful to be concerned with such trivia. He never spoke of higher spiritual truths, he didn't even mention them. In many pages of talk and hours of speechifying he showed a concern for other things. His wisdom, his power, his brief moment of dark and sinister glory—it was all of this world, and only of this world. It has passed away. There will be another world, a world of revelation of the righteousness and holiness of God. Cruel and miserable evildoers whose sins have not been cleansed by the blood of Christ will have no part in it. When Hitler stands before the judgment seat of Christ and receives a just reward for his deeds there will be a final end to debates about the real nature of Hitler.

> *I marvel that ye are so soon removed from him that called you into the grace of Christ unto another gospel:*
> *Which is not another; but there be some that trouble you, and would pervert the gospel of Christ.*
> *But though we, or an angel from heaven, preach any other gospel unto you than that which we have preached unto you, let him be accursed. (Galatians)*

[1] George Mosse, *The Crisis of German Ideology: Intellectual Origins of the Third Reich* (New York 1971), p. 301.

[2] More will be said about this in chapter eight. Richard Weikart deals with this in depth in his book *Hitler's Ethic: The Nazi Pursuit of Evolutionary Progress* (New York 2009).

[3] William L. Shirer, *The Rise and Fall of the Third Reich* (New York 1960), p. 532.

[4] John Conway, *The Nazi Persecution of the Churches 1933-1945* (Vancouver 1968), p. 383.

[5] Adolf Hitler, *Mein Kampf*, trans. Ralph Manheim (Boston 1999), p. 403.

[6] Ibid., p. 351.

[7] Ibid., p. 111.

[8] Ibid., pp. 112-113.

[9] Ibid., pp. 454-455.

[10] Ibid., p. 454.

[11] Ibid.

[12] Shirer, p. 208.

[13] Given recent talk about Nazi persecution of homosexuals, it is worth pointing out that Roehm's homosexuality was blatant and well-known. This never bothered Hitler or prevented him from working with Roehm before he felt that Roehm had become too much of a threat.

[14] "Was Hitler an Atheist?" *Critical Thought and Religious Liberty*; http://www.stephenjaygould.org/ctrl/quotes_hitler.html; accessed January 2008.

[15] Conway, p. 166.

[16] Bernt Engelmann, *In Hitler's Germany: Everyday Life in the Third Reich*, trans. Krishna Winston (New York 1986), pp. 34-35.

[17] Conway, p. 64.

[18] Shirer, pp. 223, 269-270.

[19] "Was Hitler an Atheist?" (Gould website, see note 14), citing an Oxford University Press edition of Hitler's speeches [*The Speeches of Adolf Hitler: April 1922-August 1939*, Vol. 1, ed. Norman H. Baynes (New York 1942)], pp. 19-20.

[20] Richard Evans, *The Coming of the Third Reich* (New York 2005), p. 201.

[21] Richard Steigmann-Gall, *The Holy Reich: Nazi Conceptions of Christianity, 1919-1945* (Cambridge 2003), p. 27 (hardback).

[22] "The Private and Political Testaments of Hitler, April 29, 1945"; http://www.ibiblio.org/pha/policy/1945/450429a.html; accessed May 2007.

[23] Conway, p. 384.

[24] Daniel Gasman, *The Scientific Origins of National Socialism* (London 2004), p. 65.

[25] Ibid., p. 67.

[26] Ibid., p. 62.

[27] Adolf Hitler, *Speeches and Quotes* (London 2008), p. 90 (all three quotes).

[28] Ibid., pp. 12, 16.

[29] Shirer, 202-203.

[30] Ibid., pp. 202-203, 263.

[31] "The 25 Points of Hitler's Nazi Party," Scrapbookpages.com; http://www.scrapbookpages.com/DachauScrapbook/25Points.html; accessed January 2008.

[32] Shirer, p. 261.

[33] Richard Steigmann-Gall, *The Holy Reich: Nazi Conceptions of Christianity, 1919-1945* (Cambridge 2004), p. 14 (paperback).

[34] Ibid.

[35] Ibid., p. 44.

[36] Ibid., p. 21.

[37] Georg von Schonerer was the leader of the Austrian Pan-Germans, a racist and anti-Semitic organization that has been identified as an immediate ancestor of the Nazi party. A little more will be said about him in chapter 5.

[38] Conway, p. 167.

[39] Ibid., p. 220.

[40] Ibid., pp. 224-228.

[41] Ibid., p. 225.

[42] Ibid., pp. 226-227.

[43] Friedrich Reck-Malleczewen, *Diary of a Man in Despair,* trans. Paul Rubens (London 1995), p. 33.

[44] Conway, p. 225.

[45] Ibid., p. 297.

[46] Ibid., pp. 393-397.

[47] Ibid., pp. 311-312.

[48] Ibid., p. 311.

[49] Ibid., pp. 314.

[50] Ibid., pp. 321-322.

[51] Ibid., p. 322.

[52] Ibid., p. 324.

[53] Ibid., pp. 324-325.

[54] Ibid., pp. 295-296.

[55] Ibid., pp. 296-297.

[56] Ibid., p. 292.

[57] Jim Walker, "Hitler's Christianity," *NoBeliefs.com*; http://www.nobeliefs.com/Hitler1.htm; accessed January 2008.

[58] "The Hitler No One Knows," *German Propaganda Archive*, Calvin College; http://www.bytwerk.com/gpa/hitler2.htm; accessed January 2008.

[59] Lawrence Rees, *The Nazis: A Warning from History* (New York 1997), p. 14.

[60] "Dawkins: Religion equals 'child abuse' "; *Faith Under Fire: WorldNetDaily*; http://www.worldnetdaily.com/news/article.asp?ARTICLE_ID=48252; accessed May 2007.

[61] Joseph Stalin, "Dialectical and Historical Materialism," *The Art Bin*; http://art-bin.com/art/ostalineng.html; accessed January 2008.

[62] Jim Walker, "Thomas Jefferson on Christianity and Religion," *NoBeliefs.com*; http://www.nobeliefs.com/jefferson.htm; accessed January 2008.

[63] Thomas Jefferson, "Syllabus of an Estimate of the Merit of the Doctrines of Jesus, Compared with Those of Others"; http://www.angelfire.com/co/JeffersonBible/jeffbsyl.html; accessed January 2008.

[64] Martin Gilbert, *The Holocaust: A History of the Jews of Europe During the Second World War* (New York 1985), p. 73.

[65] Conway, pp. 375-376.

[66] Ibid., p. 75.

[67] Walter S. Frank, "Adolf Hitler: The Making of a Fuhrer (Who was Responsible?)," *smoter .com*; http://www.smoter.com/theartis.htm; accessed January 2008. Shirer mentions this also.

[68] Conway, p. 59.

[69] Ibid., p. 60.

[70] See note 4 above.

[71] Frank (see note 67), http://www.smoter.com/lueger.htm.

[72] Conway, p. 165.

[73] Ibid., p. 326.

[74] Ibid., p. 122.

[75] Ibid., pp. 370-374.

[76] Shirer, p. 239.

[77] Paul Johnson, *Modern Times: The World From the Twenties to the Nineties* (New York 1991), p. 276.

[78] Martin Amis, *Koba the Dread* (London 2003), p. 21. Amis here cites Martin Malia's *The Soviet Tragedy: A History of Socialism in Russia, 1917-1991*.

[79] Steigmann-Gall, pp. 27-28.

[80] Gordon A. Craig, "Enshrining the Fuhrer," *The New York Times* August 25, 1985; http://query.nytimes.com/gst/fullpage.html?res=9A07E4D7163BF936A1575BC0A963948260; accessed January 2008.

[81] Conway, p. 238.

[82] Rudolf Hoess, *Commandant of Auschwitz*, trans. Constantine Fitzgibbon (London 2000), pp. 34-35.

[83] Ibid., p. 39. An interesting overview of this subject is found in John Jay Hughes, "A Mass Murderer Repents," *Institute for Christian Spirituality*; http://theology.shu.edu/lectures/massmurder.htm; accessed January 2008.

[84] Alexander Kimel, "Holocaust and Christianity," *Holocaust Educational Digest*; http://www.kimel.net/christi.html; accessedJanuary 2008.

[85] Gasman, p. 131. More will be said about this in chapter 8.

[86] See note 58.

Chapter 4. The Christians in Nazi Germany

Judging by outward appearances

The first three chapters of this essay should be enough to demonstrate the vast gulf that separates the teachings of Christ from the teachings of Hitler. Nevertheless, those who want to link Hitler to Christianity in some way, any way, consistently point to the support of German Christians for Hitler. Surely, they say, if Hitler had really been so opposed to Christianity he would not have been publicly supported by bishops, pastors, cardinals, scholars, and theologians. If anyone knows who or who is not a Christian it should surely be such ecclesiastical authorities.

Another argument is that the churches were to an extent responsible for Hitler's coming to power, as they either endorsed Hitler or at least failed to oppose him. This is related to the argument that Germany was a Christian country—that a Christian country gave birth to Hitler is of course an indictment of Christianity. This line of thought is strengthened by the "Germanic Christians" (*Deutsche Christen*) who rejected traditional Christianity, thought the Germans were God's chosen people and wanted to eliminate Jewish influences from Christianity—National Socialism was perfectly compatible with their understanding of Christianity. That their "Christianity" had nothing to do with the teachings of Christ is irrelevant to many.

Such logic has been highly effective. A picture is worth a thousand words, as the saying goes, and photographs of uniformed SA men in church, of ecclesiastical dignitaries giving the Hitler salute or shaking hands with Hitler, of a cross-wearing chaplain in a German military unit—these have an influence on those who know little or nothing of the teachings of Christ. This is especially true in this TV age, where for so many people image is reality—though if a photograph of a renowned scientist like Max Planck giving the Hitler salute could be produced, it would not cast doubt on the validity of the scientific enterprise. Richard Evans states that Planck opened his addresses to the Kaiser Wilhelm Society with the Hitler salute, and adds that Nobel prize-winning physicist Werner Heisenberg also cooperated with the Hitler regime. Does this reflect negatively on science?[1]

Before responding to such accusations, some background information is necessary. Germany was not a Christian country; many Germans never voted for or wanted Hitler; Hitler was never elected by a majority but was appointed to his position. Hitler knew that there were many Germans who did not believe in him and, once appointed, he relied to a great extent on fear and oppression to stay in power. An understanding of these basic facts is necessary before we can examine Hitler's church policies and the responses of the Christians to those policies.

It will also be necessary to look at the silence of the churches while the Jews were so cruelly persecuted. Those who were not silent and who did speak out, or who at least tried to help, should not be forgotten. They are not remembered often enough. As to those who kept silent, their reasoning should not be misrepresented. Those who supported Nazi cruelties or were indifferent to them should not be lumped together with those who disapproved but only kept silent out of fear.

Finally, we will have to consider what the duty and the responsibility of the German churches was. Was it just to preach the gospel? But what is the gospel—abstract doctrines that have nothing to do with human suffering? Acquiescing in false philosophies that lead people astray? Thinking what the government tells us to think? Jesus said we should render to Caesar what was due to Caesar—but what is due to Caesar? To what extent were the actions of the Christians in Germany consistent with the teachings of Christ and representative of Christianity as a whole?

Modern Germany—a Christian nation?

People with little or no knowledge either of Christianity or of German history and culture like to imagine that Germany was a Christian nation—a strongly Christian nation, a deeply Christian nation. Yet, when we look at the lifeblood of German culture in the 19th and early 20th centuries and consider the poets, philosophers, novelists, scientists, and painters that made German culture renowned throughout the world, do we find that even one of them was a serious Bible-believing Christian? Beethoven, Schiller, Goethe, Schopenhauer—Christians? Goethe laughed at Christianity. Schiller's "Ode to Joy" is nothing but pagan romanticism devoid of any Christian content. Hegel considered himself a "Protestant" yet had no regard for the fundamentals of the faith. He felt they were a distraction and a hindrance from Christ's real teaching, which was only ethics. And what shall we say of Stefan George, Bert Brecht, Fritz Lang, Lotte Lenya, George Grosz and Marlene Dietrich—Christians? Then of course there are Thomas Mann, Oswald Spengler, the German expressionist painters and poets, Wagner, Nietzsche, Haeckel, physicists like Heisenberg and Planck—Christians? Is there one major figure in the 130-odd years of German cultural history from 1800 to 1933 that was a dedicated biblical Christian?

Looking at any general secular history of Weimar Germany, we do not get the impression of a deeply Christian culture. No one who has studied the German labor movement will argue that its leaders were concerned about salvation from sin and eternal life in paradise through faith in Christ. Such teachings were scorned as escapist bourgeois fantasies used to oppress the people. Popular German culture of the 1920s was certainly not preoccupied with biblical themes. Large numbers of people were not speaking out from a biblical perspective against Darwinism, Freudianism, positivism, or other forms of secularism that were rampant in Germany.

Peter Gay's book *Weimar Culture* has more to say about Freud, psychoanalysis, and the Psychoanalytical Institute in Berlin than it does about the churches (Luther is briefly mentioned in passing). Significantly, Gay says: "By the turn of the century and the time of the First World War it was clear that, although Germany professed, in theory, to be a Christian state, secularization had spread to wide sections of the population . . . ."[2] The Frankfurt School of Marxist anthropologists and theoreticians is one example of many that could be given to illustrate this trend.

Historian Paul Johnson elaborates on the secular nature of the culture out of which Hitler emerged. He refers to Freud's well-known influence, and states in the same context, "Stage and night-club shows in Berlin were the least inhibited of any major capital. Plays, novels, and even paintings touched on such themes as homosexuality, sado-masochism, transvestism and incest."[3] Much more could be written about the vice and depravity that flourished in Weimar Germany.

Students of the period know that Germany, in the brief period between the wars, was a world-centre of modern culture, that German art, cinema, and theater were on the cutting edge of the avant-garde. Johnson gives useful information about this. After referring to Klee, Kandinsky, Mies van der Rohe, Walter Gropius and the integration of modern art with the latest architectural techniques at the famed Bauhaus he writes "Weimar was less hostile to modernism than any other society or political system."[4] That there were contrary forces on the extreme right which eventually triumphed does not alter the fact that calling Germany a strongly Christian country shows a lack of familiarity with Germany, or with Christianity, or with both.

Germany in 1933 was in fact a darkly pagan country in which Christian influence had been steadily declining for well over a century. The forces of secularism easily triumphed over the church in every significant field of cultural and intellectual endeavour. Traditional ecclesiastics like Ernst Wilhelm Hengstenberg (1802-1869) who fought in vain to stem the tide are now only a minor footnote, mentioned in passing if at all. Darwinism, "Enlightenment" and scientific rationalism, Marxism, racism, militarism, imperialism, the Folkish movement (that considered the Germans a new Chosen People destined to lead mankind), theological liberalism that considered the Bible to be full of mistakes, myths, and folk tales—these were the dominant forces in modern Germany, not biblical Christianity. That such modernist trends contributed to the hunger for certainty, meaning, and purpose which made National Socialism seem more compelling is a common observation. Richard Evans, for example, writes of the "fear and disorientation" engendered by social and cultural (as well as by political and economic) change.[5]

Yet, one source uses a 1939 census to show that 95% of all Germans in the Nazi era were loyal to their Catholic or Protestant churches. Was this in fact the case? I doubt that this census asked if the participants believed that Jesus Christ was God come to earth in human form to die on the cross as a sacrifice for the sins of the world; that he rose from the dead; that only those who believe in him can be saved from sin; that the Bible is the divinely inspired word of God.

There is another factor to be considered in the statement that 95% of the people in Hitler's Germany retained their affiliation with the Catholic or Protestant churches they had been assigned to in infancy. If people were asked to state their religious affiliation in an official census, stating "None" would have been a dangerous thing to do. If one could not point to membership in the Nazi Party, stating "none" might have led to certain *questions*, such as: "Were you ever affiliated with the Communist Party?" We have already seen that in the presidential election of 1932 Ernst Thaelmann, the Communist candidate, received 13% of the vote. The Communist Party was the third largest party in the Reichstag in 1932. No doubt every single one of the Germans who voted for Thaelmann or the Communist Party later declared themselves "Lutherans" or "Catholics" when asked by government pollsters. Members of the smaller independent churches that as we saw in chapter three were banned by the government would also have been prudent to state "Lutheran" or "Catholic." This would not have been to earn favor with the government, as someone has suggested. It would have been to avoid attracting attention to oneself. Since most had had some childhood experience with those churches, they could easily answer further questions if necessary.

Jesus taught that the way to eternal life is a straight and narrow way and few find it. The number of people sincerely dedicated to following the teachings of Christ has never been a majority in any country. The world lies in wickedness, as it says in I John, and will continue to lie in wickedness until Christ returns. People who say "Germany was a Christian country" need to consider not only the teachings of Christ, but also the profound influence of Darwinism, Freudianism, positivism, Marxism, and other secular philosophies that flourished in Germany. They also should consider that these and other secular currents entered the churches. Hegelian, Kantian, and other rationalistic philosophies were presented in religious language, and basic biblical truths were abandoned, leading to rhetoric that sounds very Christian to the unbeliever today but in fact was something very different from historic Christianity.

How did Hitler deceive an entire nation? He didn't.

Along with the idea that Germany was a Christian nation, another misconception that needs to be dispelled is the commonly held belief that the Germans voted Hitler into power. Hitler never received a majority in a free election. In the dramatic election of 1930, economic hardship caused by the depression led to a literally astonishing Nazi victory in the parliamentary elections. They increased their representation from 12 seats to 107, making them the second largest party overnight. In the presidential election of March 1932, however, the Nazis did not come even close to obtaining a majority vote. Hitler ran against Hindenburg (the incumbent), Thaelmann (the Communist candidate) and Duesterberg (who represented the Nationalists). Hitler received 30.1% of the vote, less than a third. Hindenburg received 49.6%, Thaelmann 13.2%, and Duesterberg 6.8%.

Since no one had gained an absolute majority, a second election was held in April. This time Hitler obtained 36.8% of the vote, while Hindenburg got 53% and Thaelmann 10.2%. Well over half the electorate rejected the extremes of right and left, and stated their preference for a continuation of the Weimar Republic. In an election in the state of Lippe in January 1933, the same month that Hitler came to power, the Nazis received 39% of the vote.

That so many Germans did vote for the Nazis shows the deep spiritual illness that afflicted Germany. Hitler generated intense enthusiasm and that is a strong indictment of the German nation, but millions of Germans, nearly two thirds of the electorate, voted against Hitler. Even though he skillfully projected an image of moderation and toned down his radical statements in order to win more moderate voters, many Germans did not accept his ideas or his program.

Hitler became Chancellor in January 1933 by presidential appointment. This was done according to the Weimar constitution, which empowered President Hindenburg to give the office of Chancellor to someone capable of forming a majority coalition in the Reichstag. After Kurt von Schleicher, the last Chancellor before Hitler, submitted his resignation Hindenburg gave the position to Hitler. Hindenburg had previously rejected the idea of appointing Hitler—according to Shirer, as recently as two or three days before.[6] He was, however, in his eighties, his powers were failing, and in the political instability of Weimar Germany it seemed that no one else but Hitler was capable of forming a parliamentary majority and restoring desperately needed order to a failing system.

Those who know about these events will excuse this extremely brief repetition of well-known historical facts. It was occasioned by comments from those who like to discuss Christianity and Hitler without having grasped some elementary aspects of the situation. Incidentally, Shirer records the interesting fact that on Sunday, January 29, the day before Hitler was appointed, there was a demonstration of a hundred thousand workers in the center of Berlin, expressing their opposition to the appointment of Hitler as Chancellor.[7] No doubt many of them were among the first to suffer when the Nazis cracked down on labor and left-wing groups. Evans relates in his history of the Third Reich that there were other Communist-inspired demonstrations protesting Hitler's appointment as Chancellor. He mentions Munich, Worms, Altona, and other places.[8]

Hitler's appointment did not instantly confer dictatorial power on him. Not only were his powers limited by the Weimar constitution, which was of course still in effect. He also had to govern in coalition with other parties, and out of eleven cabinet positions, only three were held by Nazis (including the chancellorship). There was also a significant amount of general opposition to Hitler, of which the mass demonstration by labor was one indication. A previous attempt to set up a right-wing government had been defeated by a general strike in 1920, and Hitler's future was by no means certain. Some were even confident that he had been tamed, and that the realities of political power would force him to moderate his extremist principles. The power of the forces that Hitler unleashed was undreamed of, however, and it was not suspected by those who arranged a delicate power-sharing scheme that Hitler would be able to outsmart them all and seize complete power within a remarkably short time.

Hoping to gain an absolute majority in the Reichstag so that he could govern without the cumbrances of a coalition, Hitler persuaded the President to call for new elections. These were held on March 5th, 1933. In the last democratic election of the Third Reich, the Nazis gained 44% of the vote. Again, a majority of Germans rejected Hitler.

The process by which Hitler proceeded to eliminate democracy in Germany is too complex to be recounted at length here. The use of physical violence and even murder to intimidate and remove opponents; the removal of officials, who were replaced by Nazis; Hindenburg's signing of a constitutional and legal emergency decree (after the Reichstag fire) suspending civil liberties; mass arrests of political opponents; parliamentary conferral of full dictatorial power on Hitler—all of these and other events were beyond the control of millions of Germans who never voted for Hitler. They soon found themselves in a police state not of their making, one in which any criticism, however slight, could lead to loss of job, beating, torture, and even death.

A quotation from Hitler biographer Ian Kershaw is apt here: "The mass of the German people had no part in, or knowledge of, the intrigues of high politics in the second half of 1932. They were by now largely powerless to affect the political dramas which would determine their future." He adds later, the events that led to Hitler's obtaining the chancellorship "amounted to an extraordinary political drama. It was a drama that unfolded largely out of sight of the German people."[9]

The extent to which the German people came to genuinely accept the dictatorship is unclear. How much of the adulation for Hitler—like that given to Stalin and to Mao—was voluntary and how much of it was the result of fear and coercion? Undoubtedly, Hitler's elimination of unemployment and the instability of the Weimar Republic, his withdrawal from the League of Nations, his repudiation of the Versailles Treaty, and other aspects of Hitler's early years in power made Hitler a hero, even a demi-god, to many Germans. Nevertheless, there was far from universal enthusiasm for Hitler's militaristic adventures. Shirer, who was living in Germany at the time, described the marked lack of enthusiasm of the German people when war broke out in 1939.[10] Friedrich Reck-Malleczewen wrote in his diary of the gladness with which many Germans welcomed the Allied invasion of North Africa in 1943 and looked forward to the defeat of their own country. He also gave a concrete pre-war example of how the plebiscites expressing near total support for Hitler's actions were crudely falsified.[11]

It is a mistake to judge solely by photographs. It does not take 100% of a city's population to line the streets with cheering crowds. Moreover, as was the case in Stalin's Russia and Mao's China, attendance could have been and almost certainly was mandatory for government employees, factory workers, schoolchildren—and woe to the individuals that drew attention to themselves by a suspicious lack of enthusiasm. After all, if the leader represents the people, then someone who does not like the leader is "against the people." A study of common elements in modern totalitarian dictatorships of both the right and the left would lead to a greater understanding of the Third Reich than Hitler's vague comments about some sort of a Supreme Being that seemed strangely concerned with only the German people. There are clear, direct, obvious, and extended parallels between Hitler, Lenin, Stalin, and Mao.

Hitler's supposed magic over the German people is not so great as has been imagined. After gaining national fame as the leader of the Munich putsch, Hitler and his party remained in the political wilderness for years. In the election of 1928, after about seven years of Hitler's leadership of the party, the Nazis received less than 3% of the vote. It is generally agreed that without the Depression the Weimar government could have survived. Hitler's dark and mysterious power was exceedingly great, but it was only effective in certain circumstances. The fear of a Communist revolution in particular should not be dismissed too lightly by those who are unaware of the size and power of the Russian-backed German Communist Party. The German Communists attempted to seize power on more than one occasion, most notably in Munich and in Berlin. In the economic and political turmoil of the last years of the Weimar Republic, the prospect of Germany going the way of Russia was more than just a paranoid fantasy. Because of this fear some Germans supported Hitler with reservations, feeling there was no other alternative. It will never be known how many Germans supported Hitler but didn't realize their mistake until it was too late and there was nothing they could do about it.

A master of deceit

It also needs to be pointed out that much of the support Hitler gained, as well as some of the weakness of the opposition to him, was due to deceit. The fact that Hitler was in his rise a highly effective, even brilliant politician, is too often obscured by what he later became. It is also too little realized by people who assert Hitler's Christianity that after the failure of the Beer Hall Putsch, Hitler came to realize that the path to power lay through the democratic process. Accordingly, he moderated his image and skillfully portrayed himself as being more modest, sober, and responsible than he really was.

Once he decided he needed votes, Hitler was remarkably successful at presenting himself differently to different groups. To labor, he was a friend of labor. To business, he was a friend of business. To the army, he was a friend of the army. To the churches, he was a friend of the churches, and would protect them, even strengthen their influence. When questioned by skeptical people on seeming contradictions, he easily persuaded them that his words to them were his real intention, and statements to others were just politics.

Hitler did the same thing on the international level. He would assure the diplomatic community that his sole intention was peace. When asked about his military buildup, he could explain that it was a cure for unemployment, or necessary for defense against the Russians. When asked about bellicose statements by his followers, he could with great sincerity deplore their excesses and state that he had difficulty controlling them. When asked about his own belligerent statements, he could explain them away as political rhetoric, but assert with great candor that his real views and intention were nothing other than what he was sharing at that moment.

All of the people who so lightly took Hitler at his word were deceived, except for those who wanted Germany to rule the world—and in the end they were deceived as well. Many Germans—workers, farmers, businessmen, Christians, military leaders—thought Hitler would benefit them. In the end they were totally enslaved to a gigantic totalitarian bureaucracy and to the whims of a cruel dictator. This does not in any way excuse or justify those Christians who supported Hitler or were willing to tolerate him. There was enough in Hitler's statements and record to show that he was a treacherous, cruel, and violent man with an ungodly philosophy. To rely on him to support and protect the church was exceedingly foolish and completely at odds with the New Testament concept of the church.

Hitler's deception of the churches was only possible because too many churchgoers were more mindful of earthly things than of heavenly ones. We have to face the fact that too many people with the name of Christians were more concerned with recovery of territory lost in WWI, a solution to economic problems, political stability, government protection to prop up their worldly establishments, or the Communist threat than they were with spiritual realities.

It is easy to be wise after the fact, but someone like Hitler had never been seen before. Such brazen deception was literally inconceivable to decent people—and how many Americans would be so wise and far-sighted? Not as many as we would like to think. It was literally impossible for anyone to imagine the horror that Hitler would inflict on Germany and on the world. How many expressions of support for Hitler were made in 1933 or early in his rule, when it was sincerely believed that Hitler would solve Germany's problems? Of course if the Germans could have foreseen clearly what Hitler would do and what his policies would result in they would never have supported him. A significant amount of Hitler's initial support was generated by disillusionment with the Weimar government, rather than by enthusiastic agreement with all of Hitler's ideas. How often is it that in trying to make things better, we only make them worse? Sometimes patiently enduring a bad situation is better than rushing around advocating quick schemes for reform.

Much of the often pointed to support of Christians for Hitler shows only political naïveté, even blindness on the part of average German voters, not any real spiritual connection. A good example of this is the Lutheran pastor, Martin Niemoller. This WWI hero and prominent Lutheran churchman initially supported Hitler. In his autobiography he condemned the by then extinct Weimar Republic, and welcomed the Nazi revolution. He even hoped that the Nazis would bring about a revival of the nation. Such folly greatly diminishes the respect one might otherwise have had for Niemoller—he more than paid for his errors, however, in his years of imprisonment. Leo Stein, a Jew who was with Niemoller in Moabit prison and in Sachsenhausen recalled his conversations with Niemoller and later published them in a magazine article. This article sheds a lot of light on the problem of doctrinally orthodox Christians who supported Hitler.[12]

Stein recorded that Niemoller stressed the Jewishness of Christianity, affirmed that Jesus was a Jew; and stated that without the Old Testament there could be no Christianity. In this context, he made the comment already quoted in chapter three: "Whoever is an anti-Semite and persecutes the Jews can never be a real Christian. Hitler is the true anti-Christ."

Given these sentiments, Stein wondered how Niemoller could have been a member of the Nazi party, and asked him about this. Niemoller responded:

> "I find myself wondering about that too," he answered. "I wonder about it as much as I regret it. Still, it is true that Hitler betrayed me. I had an audience with him, as a representative of the Protestant Church, shortly before he became Chancellor, in 1932. Hitler promised me on his word of honor, to protect the Church, and not to issue any anti-Church laws. He also agreed not to allow pogroms against the Jews, assuring me as follows: 'There will be restrictions against the Jews, but there will be no ghettos, no pogroms, in Germany' . . . Hitler's assurance satisfied me at the time. On the other hand, I hated the growing atheistic movement, which was fostered and promoted by the Social Democrats and the Communists. Their hostility toward the Church made me pin my hopes on Hitler for a while."

Niemoller then stated that he was paying for his mistake—and he paid for it dearly. The leaders of the Catholic Centre Party were also deceived or intimidated. They agreed to support the Enabling Bill of 1933 that gave Hitler dictatorial power. Would they have done so if they could have foreseen the result?

A promise from Hitler not to harm the Jews may seem like a self-justifying invention of Niemoller's, but Hitler told others the same thing. For example, in 1930 he told prominent businessman and rumored presidential candidate Wilhelm Cuno that, in Kershaw's words, "there would be no violent persecution of Jews under Nazi rule." Hitler understood that many shared some of his aims but were by no means enthusiastic about his extreme anti-Semitism.[13] In a speech delivered to hundreds of businessmen in 1932, Hitler blamed Marxism for Germany's problems but didn't even mention the Jews. Evans' comment is apt here:

"Antisemitism, so prominent in Nazi propaganda in the 1920s, took a back seat, and had little influence in winning the Nazis support in the elections of the early 1930s."[14]

The churches' responsibility for Hitler's rise

To what extent, then, did the churches contribute to Hitler's accession to power? Certainly, by either supporting him actively or by failing to speak out against false Nazi doctrines, the churches helped Hitler directly and indirectly. The army also supported Hitler, dazzled by his glittering promises of rearmament and conquest. Big business supported Hitler, and gave him crucial funding during his rise—they were eager for the profits to be derived from rearmament, and were taken in by his promise of economic and political stability. Labor also supported Hitler, to an extent, hoping for a solution to unemployment. One might argue that those people were all Christians, since they lived in Germany, but military power, conquest, job security and big profits are not biblical priorities. The early Christians weren't concerned about them. Does it need to be said that Jesus had no interest in such things?

The churches did not stand for biblical truth as they should have. They did not, with very rare exceptions, expose National Socialism as a false philosophy contrary to biblical teaching. They did not forcefully present the biblical view that a quiet and peaceful life with eternity in paradise to follow was better than war, conquest, and revenge followed by an eternity in hell. The great majority of Christians did not present the truth in such a way as to contradict reigning falsehoods. They either kept silent, or spoke in theological abstractions that had little or nothing to do with the burning issues of the day. The Nazi government did not mind if the Christians said "We should love our neighbors as we love ourselves"—they could easily dismiss that as a useless fantasy. If Christians had said, "We should love our neighbors as we love ourselves, and that includes Jews. Persecuting Jews is wrong, and Hitler's racial ideas are false," they would have experienced the most fiery persecution.

It should not be overlooked, by the way, that the atheistic Communists also greatly helped Hitler in his rise. On orders from Moscow, the German Communist Party resolutely opposed a broad union of all anti-fascist forces against Hitler. It was thought that if Hitler came to power this would hasten the fall of the Weimar Republic, which would then hasten the accession of the Communists to power. A stable democracy was against the revolutionary aspirations of the Communists, and they helped to sabotage it. The Reds and the Nazis at times even worked together to bring down the Weimar government (for example, in disrupting sessions of the Reichstag and in the Berlin transport strike of 1932). Thus, the Supreme Genius Stalin, the Granite Bolshevik, led to the destruction of the German Communist Party by his blind policies. Ignorant of the political realities of Germany, Stalin (and the actions of the German Communist Party) show the dangers of mixing atheism and politics. They prove that atheists should not be allowed to interfere in government—at least according to the foolish logic of those who say that Hitler's rise shows the dangers of mixing religion and politics.

Intimidation, violence, repression, and fear

Hitler knew that a significant number of Germans were not enamored of him and his policies, and he initiated a drastic policy of extreme brutality to eliminate all opposition, including potential opposition. Even before Hitler came to power the SA, the storm troopers, were active throughout Germany, and those who were too outspoken in their opposition to Hitler were in real danger. Attacks, beatings, murders by Hitler's supporters were ignored by the police or leniently treated by the courts. After Hitler became Chancellor, concentration camps were established where people were liable to be incarcerated for any reason, with no judicial process. Even a negative remark made in private could lead to denunciation and arrest.

Bernt Engelmann, a German who (as was said in chapter 3) lived through that period wrote of the "wave of terror" that swept over Germany. Communists and Social Democrats, labor leaders, intellectuals—Engelmann estimates that over 100,000 people were arrested, beaten, tortured, and often killed. In his words,

> The main thing was that each individual knew or at least suspected how brutally and ruthlessly the regime dealt with anyone who refused to be "brought into line" or disobeyed any of the thousands of regulations and prohibitions. That's how a small minority succeeded in holding the great majority in check.[15]

Writing of the S.D., or *Sicherheitsdienst*, the Security Service headed by Reinhard Heydrich, Shirer effectively describes how Heydrich's nationwide network of informers was used to control and intimidate the German people. Any anti-Nazi comment—even to a friend, a relative, or a secretary—might be reported. More direct means were also employed to silence anyone who might be less than enthusiastic about the new Germany. Gangs of brownshirts had complete freedom to beat up or even torture and kill anyone they pleased, while the police did nothing.[16]

How many people don't take this into account when they speak so lightly about the failure of the German churches to oppose Hitler? The great majority of people who criticize the German Christians so cheerfully would behave no differently in a similar situation. If America ever collapses and suffers extreme political turmoil and economic chaos; if Americans are ever hungry enough, and desperate enough, they too will enthusiastically hail a savior who can offer them peace and security. Some who are so proud of their liberalism and tolerance now would be hailing the new messiah as loudly as anyone else—and if we knew that criticism of the government would lead to our arrest and imprisonment, even execution, how few brave and noble martyrs there would be among us. Admittedly, such a scenario seems unlikely today—but it seemed unlikely in Germany in 1913 also. At that time, Germany was an exceedingly powerful nation—strong, stable, and prosperous. It took only a few years to bring disastrous and unexpected changes

One final incident recorded by Shirer in his history is illustrative. A certain Frau Solf, whose husband had been a Colonial Minister under Wilhelm II, hosted a social gathering in 1943. Some representatives of the high society of the old pre-Nazi order attended, including a granddaughter of Bismarck and a nephew of

Germany's WWI ambassador to the US. Strong anti-Nazi sentiments were expressed at the gathering—they were reported to the Gestapo by a "Swiss doctor" who was also a government spy. Within a few months, time being needed for investigation and further observation, the participants were all arrested. Most of them were executed.[17]

It is difficult for those of us who live in freedom and comfort to imagine the fear of those who were liable to be arrested and executed even for negative remarks made in private—and this incident was not an isolated one, as everyone knows who has read about day-to-day life in Nazi Germany. It is true, Christians should not fear death, and very few had that kind of faith. There were, however, some exceptions.

A question of human nature

Historians Robert Wistrich and Saul Friedländer both make the point that American Jews did not make any real effort to put public pressure on the American government to accept more Jewish refugees. Their reason for not making more waves was, according to both authors, fear of stirring up latent American anti-Semitism.

It is quite remarkable that German Christians were supposed to speak out for the Jews in the face of death, torture, or concentration camps, while American Jews did not speak out only because they were afraid people might not like it! A more aggressive public relations campaign in conjunction with Christian relief groups already trying to help European Jews might have met with more public support than anticipated. Thousands of lives could conceivably have been saved—but the Jewish community in America had a comfortable situation and (allowing as always for exceptions) did not want to rock the boat.

More significantly, Friedländer documents that the leaders of French Jewry "pointedly continued to ignore the fate of the foreign Jews and to plead for the French Israelites only." In dealing with the Vichy authorities, "Time and again some of the most prestigious names of French Jewry confirmed that, in their view, the fate of the foreign Jews was none of their concern."[18]

The Jews in Germany too manifested this tendency. Friedländer also shows that "In late 1939 and early 1940, in order to keep all emigration openings for German Jews only, German Jewish leadership attempted to bar endangered Polish Jews from emigrating from the Reich to Palestine."[19] Come to think of it, there must have been some Jews living in the American south in the days of Jim Crow and lynching. Did they speak out for persecuted blacks? Did they risk their lives and their positions to speak out for strangers? If not, why not? Because of Torah, or some defect inherent in Judaism? Or because they were ordinary people behaving as ordinary people usually do?

A few rare exceptions

Before considering Hitler's church policies it is necessary to understand that he was confronting potential opposition. The few Christians who did speak out and who did object represented a much larger number who agreed with them but did not dare to show it. Hitler had to deal with the churches carefully lest overt and violent persecution drive many more people into open opposition.

That the churches posed a potentially serious obstacle to Hitler's plans for the total spiritual enslavement of the German people is not difficult to demonstrate. One example is a man not yet totally lost to history, one Pastor Kloetzel. In his gripping narrative of life in Nazi Germany, Bernt Engelmann relates that Pastor Kloetzel spoke out in his sermons against "despotism" and "racial insanity."[20] He was arrested in 1935 and a few weeks later died in a concentration camp. At his memorial service, the church was packed, with hundreds standing outside. Engelmann relates that even some Catholics attended the service, including his own father, "who had not been to church in years."[21]

Engelmann estimates that by 1937 about 1600 Protestant pastors were in concentration camps. There were of course many other Germans who were in sympathy with them but did not care to share their fate. Pastor Kloetzel had hundreds of admirers and mourners, even from those of a different church. The 1600 Engelmann mentions also had many sympathizers. This was a potential problem for Hitler and he was well aware of it.

There was more opposition to Hitler than is often recognized. In 1935 a group of Lutheran Churches known as the Confessing Church issued a bold statement in response to attacks on Christianity in a book written by Alfred Rosenberg, a high-ranking Nazi official. They rejected Nazi ideology as a new religion that violated the first of the Ten Commandments by putting blood, race, and the German nation in the place of God. The statement further rejected Rosenberg's ideology as the ideology of the anti-Christ. Even though there was no direct attack on Hitler himself and Hitler had supposedly disavowed Rosenberg's book, the Nazi reaction was severe. An official ban was placed on the statement and clergymen were forbidden to read it. Literally hundreds of pastors were arrested for ignoring the ban, and protests against these repressive measures led to further arrests.[22]

We need to remember those hundreds of pastors who defied the government's command not to write, distribute, and read statements critical of Nazi ideology. They did not know that, if arrested, they would be shortly released, as nearly all of them were. There was a real possibility of something much worse, and they accepted it. Some of them no doubt suffered again—surely their names were recorded by the Gestapo for future reference. A month or so in a concentration camp seems like a light thing compared to the horrors of the death camps, but it was not a light thing at that time, and their courage needs to be remembered. There were no such protests from Darwinists—why should there be? Beasts know only survival, and in Nazi Germany survival meant either keeping your mouth shut or else agreeing with the government.

One man whose commitment to eternal and divinely revealed truth led him to disagree with the state was the Lutheran pastor briefly mentioned in chapter 3, Pastor von Jan of Oberlenningen in Wuerttemberg. Shortly after the infamous Crystal Night pogrom of 1938 in which Jews all over Germany were savagely attacked, Pastor von Jan preached directly on the pogrom. He stated that it was a crime, "many crimes," and said it was the result of "the great apostasy from God and Christ, arising out of organized anti-Christianity." He condemned the burning of synagogues, and the arrest of loyal citizens solely because of their race. He then mentioned the fear that gripped the nation, saying "No one dares to speak."

Not content with condemning the crimes against the Jews as if this were a matter of human justice alone, he spoke of God's justice and warned that:

. . . this injustice condemns our people in the sight of God, and must bring his justified punishment upon Germany. Since it is written: "Be not deceived; God is not mocked: for whatsoever a man soweth, that shall he also reap." . . . What a terrible harvest will ensue, if God does not grant to us and our people his grace through genuine contrition.[23]

This is the most direct and outspoken public condemnation of Naziism delivered by any Christian figure that I have run across. The response was predictable. Some days later, a mob of hundreds of people came looking for the pastor. He was brought back to the vicarage from a Bible study in a nearby village. On getting out of the car he was attacked by the mob, which "descended on him like wild animals." He was severely beaten, and displayed half conscious from the roof of a woodshed so that he could be seen by the mob. He was then taken to the town hall for interrogation, while the mob outside seethed "with bloodthirsty talk and shouting and swearing, denouncing Jan as a traitor to the people, and a slave of Judaism." The pastor was taken to prison. I have been unable to find out if he survived the war.

At this point, one feels tempted to be angry at those who talk about Hitler's Christianity and the Christian foundations of National Socialism. One could reproach them with ignorance, but that will not deter them. Their purpose is not to reasonably discuss the matter—it is to attack Christianity, and when refuted with facts they will ignore you and continue unfazed. So, we have no recourse but to say what we can, and leave them with God.

To me, Pastor von Jan represents the ideal of Christian conduct in the Third Reich. He did not confine himself to sufficiently vague generalities, protesting a little on a theoretical theological plane, enough to salve his conscience, while at the same time being careful not to cross the line and provoke the wrath of the authorities. He used only one weapon, truth, and though he accomplished nothing in the world's eyes he won a tremendous spiritual victory.

I do not know of course all of his doctrines, his manner of life, or his salvation experience. Though I am a Protestant, I am not a Lutheran. Only God knows the secrets of that man's heart—but to me he behaved as a Christian ought to behave, loving truth more than life, and not fearing those who could only destroy his body but could not touch his soul. He must have endured many compromises of conscience in the preceding years. Perhaps, after years of enduring Hitler salutes during the worship service, singing Nazi propaganda songs like the Horst Wessel Song along with hymns, having to preach with swastika banners adorning the sanctuary, perhaps after years of wanting to speak out but fearing to do so for his family's sake if not for his own—perhaps, after all of that, the Spirit of God came upon him, and he forgot earthly considerations. He may have had a profound supernatural conviction that to die really was gain, as the Bible says, and desired nothing more than eternal life in paradise with Christ. I believe it was by the power of the Holy Spirit that he uttered words of prophetic truth about God's wrath on Germany—words which seemed impossible then but came to pass in a very short time.

No doubt Pastor Jan's broken and bleeding body was a source of satisfaction to his persecutors. It would have taken great faith and spiritual insight to see then that he was the winner and they were the losers. Not only did he bring honor to the name of Christ, but if he suffered for Christ, and spoke for Christ, as I have no reason to doubt that he did, he will attain to a more glorious resurrection. Perhaps, as in Christ's parable of the rich man and Lazarus, his tormentors will see that righteous and holy man of God in heaven from their places of suffering in hell.

More could be said about other pastors. Johann Gerhard Behrens, a Lutheran pastor in Stade, was mocked as being "a bondsman of the Jews," accused of describing the anti-Semitic magazine *Der Stürmer* as a "filthy tabloid," and of preaching against Nazi doctrines. Not long after he was attacked on the street and paraded through Stade by storm troopers "under a hail of ridicule and abuse." He was taken to the police station, but later released. In 1942, Pastor Karl Friedrich Stellbrink stated from the pulpit that the near total destruction of Lübeck by the RAF was the result of God's judgment. He was arrested, tried, condemned to death, and beheaded, along with three Roman Catholics who were also charged with treason.[24]

Christian opposition to the euthanasia program

The Nazis developed a euthanasia program to eliminate senile people, lunatics, and the incurably ill. Such people, considered to be not worthy of living, were transferred to state institutions where they were killed by gas or injections. This was a secret program. Relatives were notified that the patient had died due to natural causes, and those involved in the program were required to keep it hidden.

In spite of attempts to maintain secrecy, the thousands of deaths—perhaps 100,000 in all—inevitably attracted attention. Rumors spread to such an extent that not only patients but also relatives and inhabitants of areas around the state killing institutions began to be aware of the program. The most outspoken opposition from the churches in the history of the Third Reich came in reaction. Once again, only a small minority spoke out, and the great majority of Christians kept silent—yet those who did speak out demonstrated a larger amount of potential opposition that Hitler had to deal with carefully.

The boldest opponent of this evil and sinister practice was the Catholic Bishop Galen of Muenster. In August, 1941, he preached a sermon publicly denouncing the government's program. Elaborating on it in detail and not just confining himself to safe and suitably vague theological obfuscations, he was very direct in his denunciations. His words had a great impact, and copies of the sermon were distributed throughout Germany, and even reached soldiers in the front lines.

This direct challenge to the government could not be ignored. Bormann called for Galen's execution, and other Nazis called for his hanging or imprisonment. Copies of the sermon were confiscated by the Gestapo, and Hitler ordered an investigation.[25] There was still doubt at the highest level as to how to proceed. Goebbels felt that persecution of the popular bishop would do more harm than good to the party, and advocated delay. Others also felt that making a martyr of the bishop would cause even greater problems. A note from Bormann dated August 13th (ten days after the sermon was preached) indicated that the Fuhrer was still undecided, but after a month the Church Ministry was officially informed that Hitler would not, for the time being, take action against Galen.[26]

There were other opponents of the program, well-known to scholars but unknown to the general public. In 1940, an Evangelical bishop, Theophil Wurm, and a Catholic Cardinal, Adolf Bertram, protested directly to the authorities, knowing that they risked their lives or at least their liberty in doing so. It should be pointed out that Bishop Wurm's protest was carefully phrased to avoid giving offense, and even appealed to the Fuhrer's previously stated position in support of "Positive Christianity." Opposition to Christianity was attributed only to "certain circles" in the party, and it was hoped that Hitler's support of "Positive Christianity" would include support for Christian belief in "the merciful and humane handling of suffering fellow men."[27]

Other bishops also protested, and called for an end to the killing of helpless lunatics and invalids. Bishop Preysing of Berlin publicly condemned it in a sermon in 1941, and an Evangelical pastor named Braune presented evidence to four different government ministries in Berlin before he was arrested and imprisoned—fortunately only for ten weeks. Another pastor, Ernst Wilm, gave a lecture on the subject and was sent to Dachau—he remained there until the war was over.

All of this was not without effect. Rumors spread so widely throughout the country that reports reached Berlin of front line soldiers fearing that they would be exterminated if too severely wounded.[28] Even the authorities—including Himmler—were beginning to have doubts at this point, though not about the morality of the program of course. Hitler halted the operation, but this was only temporary. Killing centers were moved to more remote locations and the practice of notifying relatives was stopped, but the operations were resumed. In 1943 they were expanded to include orphaned German children.[29]

It is worth pointing out that opponents of abortion in America, who can use all of the means available in a free society to halt a practice that they consider to be morally wrong, have not been able to stop the practice. What then could the Germans do in a totalitarian society?

Hitler's policy toward the churches

The purposes of mentioning a few outstanding cases of opposition to Hitler is not to give a false impression of the churches united in a bold stand against falsehood. The great majority of "Christians" either supported Hitler or remained silent. The purpose is to indicate that Hitler recognized the churches as a possible source of opposition, and subjected them to a carefully calculated policy of repression.

Hitler's anti-church policies were mentioned briefly in chapter 3 in order to show the hollowness of his statements in support of the churches. This chapter requires a more careful analysis. Before we discuss the response of the Christians and the duty of the churches in depth, we need to know what it was they were up against.

There are four distinct periods we need to consider: Hitler's attempts to gain power prior to 1933; the brief initial period of his dictatorship when he consolidated his power; the years of rearmament in preparation for war; and the war years. In the first period, prior to 1933, Hitler was seeking as many votes as possible. He deliberately refrained from extreme anti-Christian public statements in his speeches, and distanced himself from such overtly anti-Christian party leaders as Alfred Rosenberg. Before looking at the next three periods—initial consolidation of power after 1933, rearmament, and the war years—it will be helpful to look at Rosenberg more carefully. This will demonstrate Hitler's duplicity and the overt Nazi hostility to Christianity that Hitler pretended to reject for political reasons but in fact tolerated and even encouraged.

Alfred Rosenberg

This Nazi "thinker," a member of Hitler's inner circle, expressed the idea that Christianity was founded on Judaism by the Jewish villain Paul. He saw Christianity as a mask of the Jews and denounced the Lutheran Churches as racial traitors. He called for the abolition of the Old Testament and accused the Protestants and Catholics of betraying Germany. He advocated a new faith— National Socialism—with a new prophet—Adolf Hitler—and a new gospel— Aryan supremacy. The Holy Land, for Rosenberg, was no longer Palestine—it was the sacred soil of Germany, sanctified by the blood of her defenders.

Not surprisingly, Christians were concerned about such statements and would not have been overly enthusiastic about a party that officially stated such views. If Hitler had said such things publicly he would not only have lost many votes. He also would not have had the cooperation of the Catholic Centre Party after coming to power in 1933, and President Hindenburg would have been under much less pressure to appoint Hitler. With his keen grasp of political realities, Hitler therefore rejected a book by Rosenberg containing such ideas and said it was not an official party statement. The fact that Hitler did not fire Rosenberg but conferred with him frequently and appointed him the official director of party ideology should have led to further questioning.

Hitler frequently distanced himself from the extremism of his supporters even while he did nothing to stop them. This is such an elementary trick that it should not need to be pointed out. Hitler did not accept or need to accept all of Rosenberg's ramblings about the wickedness of the ancient Etruscans or the origins of the Aryan race in the lost continent of Atlantis. He could and did dismiss that as superfluous—but can anyone seriously assert that Rosenberg would have been admitted to Hitler's inner circle and given a high official position if he contradicted Hitler on essential points? Joachim Fest shrewdly remarks that in spite of his criticisms, "Hitler was far closer to the party's philosopher [Rosenberg] than such comments would suggest." [30]

That Hitler's disavowal of Rosenberg's writings was insincere is evidenced by historical fact. Viereck relates that a Protestant clergyman named Kuenneth wrote a refutation of Rosenberg's ideas. His rebuttal was banned, showing that the government officially supported Rosenberg's views. [31] Conway also relates that a Catholic university chaplain who criticized Rosenberg's book (*The Myth of the Twentieth Century*) was reported by some students and sentenced to prison for eighteen months. [32] This same source also relates that criticism by the churches of Nazi ideology—including that of Rosenberg—was eventually forbidden altogether. Conway includes a futile plea to the government from a pastor, who said:

> It is not the attacks on Rosenberg's ideas which make confusion and disquiet, but rather the spreading of those ideas themselves. They are spread abroad despite the fact that the state rests on a basis of positive Christianity, and despite *the repeated declarations of the Fuhrer* that the national government sees in the two Christian denominations the most important factors for the maintenance of our national way of life . . . Catholics and Protestants alike wish to express their support of the State and devote their energy to its service, but they need freedom to do so

from the side of the State. They can't understand why the authorities should seek to prevent by force the teaching and defense of true Christian doctrines while the enemies of Christianity who are the enemies of the State since this is after all a Christian country, are allowed to work undisturbed.[33]

I don't know if this individual was expressing himself in the most diplomatic possible way so as to avoid being sent to a concentration camp, or if he sincerely did not understand why Rosenberg's attacks on Christianity were widely circulated and opposing views were forbidden. Perhaps he truly believed the repeated declarations of the Fuhrer, and thought that the state rested on a basis of positive Christianity. Perhaps over time he came to understand that "positive Christianity" meant "keep your mouth shut and do as you're told."

A frank and candid Hitler would have said, "Rosenberg's book does not represent party doctrine. It is a private statement only, and I reject it—but I will appoint the author to a high position in government, confer with him frequently, the teachings of the book will be widely disseminated, and criticism of the book will be punished." As is always the case, subsequent developments are the test which shows the validity of Hitler's statements—or the contrary.

Much of this is not a great mystery but is only ordinary politics. There are many American congressman, governors, mayors, local elected officials, who are not serious Christians and do not believe in the Bible—but they are not going to come out and say "I don't believe in the Bible and I don't believe Jesus was the Son of God." This would not benefit them in any way politically and would surely cost them some votes—so they avoid the subject. They are, however, honest enough (most of them) to refrain from outright lies on the subject—unlike Hitler, and unlike Hillary Clinton, talking about "the scriptures" or posing on a Billy Graham platform.

Consolidation, rearmament, and war

Once Hitler achieved power, his immediate goal was to eliminate all opposition and establish himself as the uncontested ruler of Germany. This was accomplished with remarkable speed—yet, the churches remained something of a problem. Even though they yielded to Hitler's conquest with no significant opposition, they remained sources of influence and even rivalry. As such, they needed to be controlled.

Hitler, like Lenin, Stalin, and Mao, could tolerate no opposition. The whole society had to be brought into conformity to the state. This meant that the churches, like every other aspect of society, had to be subordinated to the state and to the Nazi ideology. They could not, however, be eliminated outright.

We referred in chapter 3 to von Schonerer, the pre-WWI leader of the Austrian Pan-Germans who strongly denounced Catholicism. Von Schonerer had an "Away from Rome" policy, and Hitler's comments on this shed light on his own policy toward the churches. Hitler stated that von Schonerer's policy served only to alienate large numbers of people and cost him much valuable political support. It was much better, Hitler stated, to focus on a single enemy and thus draw supporters from different camps. Moreover, von Schonerer's attacks on Rome did not harm the church in the least but only intensified the devotion of its followers.

The relevance of this to Hitler's policy of trying to limit the churches without attacking them head on does not need to be elaborated on.

Hitler knew that an open attack on the churches would cause a great deal of problems and yield no benefit. During the first year or so he needed to consolidate his power. This was accomplished with great skill and as the churches provided no strong opposition there was no urgent need to deal with them directly. It was at this time that Hitler made some of his most quotable comments flattering the churches about their importance to the national well-being and stressing his respect for them. He was also talking a lot about his love of international peace and harmony at the same time.

During the period of rearmament, Hitler again would have gained nothing but unnecessary problems by attacking the churches. His top priorities lay elsewhere. Similarly, during the war years intensifying the church conflict would have complicated the domestic situation immeasurably while providing no benefit. The churches were with rare exceptions docile and obedient, and some of them, led by the "Germanic Christians," even supported Hitler openly.

Nevertheless, Hitler's final aim, or one of them, was the total and unthinking obedience of the entire German nation. The knowledge that some people had different values independent of the state was a matter of concern. So, while the churches could not be attacked head-on, they could not be given a free reign to divert people's loyalties either. For this reason Hitler pursued the policy described in *Mein Kampf* and referred to in chapter 3: "a steady and constant application of force" to limit the churches' influence, combined with complete control of education so as to bring up the next generation in complete agreement with Nazi teachings.

Three lines of attack

The Nazis, like the Communists and unbelievers in general, did not emphasize or care much about doctrinal differences between Protestants and Catholics, or between liberals and conservatives. People who asserted belief in God, Jesus, and the Bible in some way were considered "Christians," and the underlying approach of the Nazi government to both Protestants and Catholics was the same. There was more hostility toward Catholicism because of its connection to Rome, and because of its doctrinal rigidity (in contrast to Protestant liberalism, which was much more accommodating doctrinally). Nevertheless, the basic policy was to crush what little direct opposition there was, and eliminate as much of the churches' influence on society as possible. This was to be accomplished by censorship, elimination of political and educational activities, and by intimidation or even outright but controlled and regulated repression and persecution when lesser means failed.

Conway, who researched this question in depth and made ample use of Nazi government archives to obtain memos and official policy statements, saw that there were three main lines of attack: (a) administrative control, (b) ideological challenge, and (c) outright persecution. He traces Nazi policies along these lines in great detail, with more than ample documentation.

Before going into essential details, it is worth emphasizing an important but little known aspect of Nazi church policy: that is, that the top Nazi leaders themselves were divided on how to deal with the churches. Some, such as Rudolf Hess, argued that a more effective method of eliminating the churches' influence was to avoid unnecessary disputes with the churches, and allow them to fade away gradually—keeping them of course on a tight leash in the meantime. Hess gave a speech to Nazi *Gauleiters* in 1938 and elaborated on this point:

> A religion which has influenced, indeed dominated, the life of a people for two thousand years cannot be destroyed or overcome by external measures—and certainly not through superficial ridicule, or agitation or attacks on God. Such ineptitude and lack of taste could only too easily drive men who would otherwise have supported the new Reich into opposition even in the political field. This cannot be said often enough . . .
>
> The more we National Socialists avoid religious disputes and stay away from church ceremonies, and rather earn the loyalty of the people through fulfilling our duties, so men will be drawn more and more to National Socialism. They will recognize that Providence is with us and our work, as a divinely ordained institution, and therefore turn away from the Churches out of internal conviction more and more . . .[34]

Recalling that Rudolf Hess was Hitler's private secretary and deputy leader of the party (later replaced by Bormann) and also the next in line to succeed Hitler after Goering, we can see that these comments have more than ordinary significance. They reveal two integral aspects of the Nazi policy toward the churches: the view of the churches as rivals for the allegiance of the German people; and the belief that National Socialism would eventually replace Christianity.

Others, such as Himmler, Bormann, and Heydrich were more openly hostile to the churches and advocated breaking them as swiftly as possible by direct persecution. Conway's description of Heydrich is significant:

> Heydrich's hatred of the churches, especially of the Catholic Church, bordered on the pathological. He was obsessed with the idea that the churches, led by the Vatican, were conspiring to destroy Germany. Blinded by an apostate's hatred, his evaluation of the church situation was always so biased and his suggestions so radical, that even Hitler, perhaps for tactical reasons, was obliged to restrain his subordinate.[35]

In the same passage Conway goes on to give an example of the differing attitudes that characterized Nazi government at the highest levels: "His [Heydrich's] successor, Kaltenbrunner . . . believed that the Gestapo could be employed more profitably than by persecuting the churches—a view in which, however, he was strongly opposed by Martin Bormann."[36]

Himmler was also hostile to the church, and officially left it in 1936 (he should have been expelled long before). The weekly SS newspaper, "The Black Corps," frequently attacked the churches. Himmler even devised Nazi baptismal and marriage ceremonies to replace those of the church. The baptismal ceremony included an altar with Hitler's picture on it, and a copy of *Mein Kampf*.

Himmler was directly involved in the attempt to destroy the Polish Catholic Church. After all, members of an inferior race who existed only to serve Germany had no need of a church. He was also instrumental in the struggle against the churches in Germany, where political realities demanded a more restrained approach. A section of the Gestapo, IV B, was set up to collect information and devise appropriate actions against "Political Churches, Sects, and Jews."[37] Part of this section, IV B 4, was led by Adolf Eichmann, and implemented the Final Solution. It is revealing that the churches and the Jews were placed administratively in the same section [Catholics (B1); Protestants (B2); Freemasons (B3); Jews (B4)]—the idea of Christianity as essentially Jewish was common among the Nazis. After all, as Nietzsche pointed out, and is only common knowledge, Christianity derived to a great extent from Judaism. "Political Churches," by the way, were churches that were not 100% docile and obedient.

Bormann's hostility to Christianity and the churches was so overt that even those who try to claim that Hitler was a Christian don't deny it. He argued that National Socialism and Christianity were completely irreconcilable. He also felt that one of the goals of National Socialism was to liberate the German soul from Christianity's baneful influence. Conway cites a circular from Bormann to Nazi officials stating "Never again must influence in the leadership of the people be yielded to the Churches. This (influence) must be broken completely and finally."[38] That people who want to eliminate the political influence of Christianity in America today share the views of Martin Bormann says something about them.

Hitler's two personal secretaries, Hess and Bormann, both felt National Socialism was incompatible with Christianity. The inference is obvious. Neither of those men reached their positions by independence of thought and outspoken disagreements with the Fuhrer on fundamental questions. Behind those men was Hitler, who had the final say. It is a generally recognized feature of his government that Hitler allowed subordinates with competing views to vie with each other, and he tolerated or even encouraged different outlooks—but only in questions of specific policies, not in fundamentals of Nazi doctrine.

In matters of church policy, Hitler was more flexible, and shifted his emphasis from time to time according to circumstances. Several examples can be given out of many. Just as anti-Jewish signs were removed from public places for the Olympics, anti-church propaganda was toned down before the Saar plebiscite of 1935. It was felt that too much negative publicity would not encourage citizens of the strongly Catholic Saarland as they considered returning to German control.

More significantly, Bormann's above mentioned circular to the *Gauleiters* calling openly for the elimination of the church led to disagreements at the highest levels of government. As long as the churches were submissive to Hitler, and they were, and loyally supported the war effort (this was in 1941), what benefit was there in stirring up internal conflicts unnecessarily? Others felt that National Socialism was compatible with a positive Christianity that was purged of Jewish elements and that preached blind obedience to Hitler as the agent of Providence. They resented Bormann's hot-headed radicalism and possibly also his by then exalted position.

Hitler himself decided the issue on the basis of expediency. Bormann's circular was issued on June 9, 1941. The invasion of the Soviet Union was less than two weeks away, and Hitler felt that overt attacks on the churches would lead to an unnecessary weakening of national unity.[39] The circular was therefore withdrawn a few days after it was issued—for political reasons.

Even without such needless provocations, the Catholics were beginning to show a lack of enthusiasm for the war effort. A pastoral letter resulting from a meeting of German Catholic bishops at the end of the same month (June 1941) failed to express support for the invasion of Russia, but dealt instead "with the limitations and restrictions placed on the church's activities."[40] The response of the executive of the German Evangelical Churches was much more suitable. It thanked Hitler for his challenge to fight on behalf of western civilization, and criticized England for aligning itself with Bolshevism and seeking the annihilation of Germany

Another example of Hitler's desire to avoid open warfare with the churches is the response of the government to the sermons of the aforementioned Catholic Bishop Galen. Bishop Galen had initially advocated cooperation with Hitler's new government, but fairly soon he was trying to oppose Rosenberg's propagandizing. In 1941 he protested seizures of church property by the Gestapo in two sermons. In this same period other Catholic bishops, as well as the Papal Nuncio, were protesting seizures of monasteries and other facilities by the government. Hitler called a halt to arbitrary seizures of church property, feeling that national unity was essential to the war effort. Another circular from Bormann is cited by Conway in this context, stating that harassment of the churches must stop. Particularly interesting is a passage from Goebbels' diary dated March 1942: "The Church question should, if possible, remain untouched during the war, however much these parsons prove to be recalcitrant in this or that area. After the war we shall have plenty of possibilities of bringing them to see sense."[41]

1. Administrative control

The brief examples given above do not even begin to represent the oppressive measures taken by the state in its attempts to completely subordinate the church. They only serve to indicate that there was a significant amount of expediency in government policies. The final goal was the complete and unquestioned dominance of National Socialism, including the slavish and unthinking obedience of the entire nation to Hitler. That goal was striven for in various ways.

It was said earlier that the Nazi government sought to totally enslave the churches by three means: administrative control; ideological challenge; and outright persecution. It is now necessary to examine these at some length—not exhaustively, but at least enough to give some idea of the problems that Christians faced. Concerning administrative control, there was at first an ambitious attempt to forcibly unify all of the Protestant churches into one National Evangelical Church. This does not indicate Hitler's religious belief, as has been claimed. It indicates a totalitarian desire to ensure that no aspect of life is outside of the government's control.

The Nazi-designated Reich Bishop, Ludwig Mueller, tried to force a national administration on the churches with the help of the Gestapo. This led to such strong opposition and internal turmoil that the project was abandoned. This opposition on the part of the churches was not opposition to National Socialism. The vast majority of Protestants gave their allegiance and support to Hitler (whether willingly or out of fear)—hence their attempts to maintain at least some sort of theoretical doctrinal and administrative independence from the state could easily be tolerated. Given loyalty to the Fuhrer, administrative squabbles over church organization seemed not worth pursuing.

It was also felt that these conflicts were damaging to Germany's image abroad. In 1934 Reich Bishop Mueller's assistant August Jaeger (backed by the Gestapo) decreed that the Protestant churches of Bavaria were to be arbitrarily placed under his authority. He placed an uncooperative bishop under house arrest and commanded that all disobedience to government control of the church must cease. This was done in spite of earlier promises from the government that force would not be used.

Jaeger's actions caused such hostility that public demonstrations in which ten thousand participated occurred in Bavaria and in Wuerttemberg, where another bishop, Theophil Wurm, had been similarly deposed. These and other church disturbances were getting so much unfavorable publicity overseas and contrasted so dramatically with Nazi propaganda about a Germany unified in its support for the new government that the Nazi Foreign Minister personally informed Reich Bishop Mueller that "if he could not unite the Evangelical Church by peaceful means . . . he would no longer receive the support of the Reich Chancellor."[42] Even the Pope expressed his concern over the treatment of the Evangelicals, realizing that the Catholics might get the same treatment. Conway relates that the Archbishop of Canterbury also protested to the German ambassador, and states:

> So many similar reports flowed into the Foreign Ministry that on 16 October Neurath insisted on a personal interview with Hitler to draw his attention to the need for an early settlement . . . Hitler was left in no doubt that Jaeger's activities were proving to be a liability, and that the Church question was increasingly becoming a question of the political prestige of the Reich itself.[43]

This led to a reversal of policy. Jaeger was compelled to resign, and the two bishops he had deposed for disobedience were reinstated. This was treated as a victory for the Evangelical Church both in Germany and abroad—it was, however, merely a change of tactics on Hitler's part. There was no need, after all, to excessively control church administration as long as the churches obeyed the government in all essential respects—which they did.

The Nazis now had to find a consistent way of dealing with the churches. There were expressions of confidence that the churches would eventually die out, but for the present there were different options that needed to be considered. In general, there was a policy of attempting to eliminate church influence from public life—that will be discussed under the next subheading—"The ideological challenge." Administratively, the government sought to avoid unnecessary conflicts, and the press was also forbidden to discuss church problems. This helped toward an appearance of unity, though underlying problems were far from solved.

The Evangelical churches were now deeply divided between the Germanic Christians on the one hand, who enthusiastically cooperated with the government and felt that their own version of Aryan Christianity was in harmony with Naziism, and those on the other hand who did not publicly challenge the basic tenets of National Socialism (with very rare exceptions) but still tried to maintain a certain level of independence on the administrative level (the Confessing Church, or *Bekennende Kirche*). The Confessing Church leaders also wanted to maintain some independence in the area of doctrine and theology while avoiding disloyalty to Hitler. But, though they did not question Hitler's leadership and were in no sense an immediate threat, even this lack of unanimity was troubling to a totalitarian government.

As a result, yet another attempt was made to bring a government-imposed unity to the divided churches. This was the establishment of a Ministry of Church Affairs in 1935. The head of this ministry was one Hans Kerrl, Reich and Prussian Minister for Ecclesiastical Affairs. His tasks were to ensure that the Catholics followed the Concordat (that is, were submissive to the government); bring the divided Protestant groups into unity and into conformity with the demands of the state; and to oversee all administrative and legal problems pertaining to the churches.

Kerrl personally believed in "Positive Christianity." He felt that a Christianity purged of its Jewish elements (meaning the Old Testament) and the corruptions of Paul (who was after all also a Jew) was not only compatible with National Socialism, but necessary to it. He believed that God was leading and guiding the German people to greatness through his messenger Adolf Hitler, and hoped that a unified German church in agreement with his doctrines and loyal to the government would be an important aspect of the Third Reich.

Kerrl also believed that Hitler, National Socialism, and the Third Reich were part of the divine order of things, and felt that belief in his version of God was essential to National Socialist ideology. He presented Jesus as nothing more than a fighter against Judaism, ascribed wholly to Nazi doctrines of race and world domination, and called Hitler "the herald of a new revelation." He asserted that "National Socialism is the fulfillment of the will of God which is demonstrated to us in our blood . . . Christianity is not dependent upon the Apostles' Creed . . . The true Christianity is represented in the Party."[44]

Trying to start out on a positive note, Kerrl amnestied pastors who had been convicted or in some way disciplined for opposition to administrative measures attempting to subjugate the churches. He also established some commissions to try and straighten out the by then extremely confused legal situation in the Protestant churches.

Kerrl faced opposition from the outset. High-ranking Nazis such as Rosenberg, Himmler, and Bormann opposed Kerrl's efforts. They felt that the desired end was not the unification of the church but its replacement. It was also possible that a unified and stable church might in the end emerge as a rival to the party, and until such time as they could be done away with the churches were best left in a disorganized and divided state. They continued to harass, restrict, and limit the churches, and their activities totally contradicted Kerrl's assurances of government support for the churches.

Christians who had not gone completely over to German or Positive Christianity were not receptive to Kerrl's plans or ideas either. Members of the Confessing Church refused to accept Kerrl's program. Their leader, Martin Niemoller, eventually became too outspoken and was arrested, as has been said in chapter 3. One bishop, Otto Dibelius, wrote an open letter to Kerrl, stating that (in Conway's words):

The Christian faith . . . was based on the historical personality of Jesus Christ, the crucified and resurrected. It was not subject to new revelations or interpretations according to political expediency. Any attempt to make it so constituted an invasion of the church's autonomy by the state.[45]

Hanging Nazi flags in sanctuaries, giving the Hitler salute, singing Nazi songs like the Horst Wessel song along with hymns, never publicly contradicting the basic tenets of Naziism, and repeatedly expressing loyalty to the Fuhrer were not enough. What was required was mindless obedience to the government, and even safely theoretical theological disagreement was viewed as a threat. Some Christians even went so far as to contest the Nazi plan of forbidding non-Aryans (meaning Jews) from serving as pastors. Saying nothing while Jews were taken away, even supporting the removal of Jews from German life were also not enough—the idea that a Jew who converted to Christianity could serve as a pastor in a church, as if faith and religious belief were more important than race, was a direct contradiction to Nazi doctrines.

Kerrl had told Hitler that he could bring the churches into line within two years, yet troublesome dissension continued with no end in sight. This dissension was in no sense a threat to the government, but still there remained a disquieting lack of the total unanimity demanded by the Fuhrer. There was so much opposition to Kerrl's attempts to force the churches into line (both administratively and doctrinally) that Kerrl eventually abandoned persuasion and resorted to force.

In 1937 Bishop Dibelius was put on trial for his open letter—it violated a law against "conspiracy." Obviously, anyone who criticized the government was conspiring against it. A church council meeting in Berlin was broken up by the Gestapo and some of the members were arrested. Other dissenting church leaders were also arrested, including Pastor Niemoller—the most visible opponent of total state domination of the church. Hundreds of pastors were arrested. One, Paul Schneider, refused a Gestapo order to leave his parish and was sent to Buchenwald, where he died.[46] Other repressive measures included: forbidding certain pastors to preach; expulsion of pastors from their parishes; cancellation of salaries (the Lutheran Church was a state church); banning of private seminaries; seizing an Evangelical publishing house; destroying a large church in Berlin on the pretext of urban renewal.

Bishop Dibelius was acquitted, and Kerrl's attempt to have him sent to a concentration camp was rejected by the Ministry of Justice—possibly at the instigation of Kerrl's rivals who wanted Kerrl's policy of pacification and unification to fail. Niemoller was also acquitted, but was immediately re-arrested and sent to the Sachsenhausen concentration camp. He remained in confinement until the end of the war. Niemoller was more harshly dealt with as he had earned Hitler's personal animosity. Niemoller biographer James Bentley states that "whenever anyone mentioned Niemoller, Hitler invariably flew into a rage." Bentley attributes this information to the British ambassador Sir Nevile Henderson. He also states that captured state papers show that Goebbels wanted to have Niemoller killed, but Rosenberg prevented this due to concern for international opinion.[47]

Not only did Kerrl fail to bring about the desired harmony of the churches; he also was unable to keep all handling of church affairs in his control. Attacks on the churches from Himmler and others who were vastly more influential than he was, and much closer to the Fuhrer, continued. In fact, Kerrl's position was hopeless. He could not restrain the radical anti-church elements of the party, nor could he reduce the Confessing Church to docile and unthinking obedience.

It became evident that his Ministry was failing, and Kerrl's influence quickly waned. In the end, he was not even able to get a personal audience with the Fuhrer, and he died in 1941, "an exhausted and embittered man," as Conway relates.[48] This same source also quotes some comments of Hitler's about Kerrl, taken from *Table Talk*: "Kerrl, with the noblest of intentions, wanted to attempt a synthesis between National Socialism and Christianity. I do not believe this is possible, and I see the obstacle in Christianity itself. . . ."[49]

Parenthetically, since Conway describes Kerrl's attempted synthesis between National Socialism and Christianity at length and in depth, Steigmann-Gall's comment that Conway failed to consider this aspect of the debate shows that he did not come to grips with the one book that most convincingly refutes his thesis.[50]

2. The ideological challenge

While Kerrl sought to unify and pacify the churches, the anti-Christian ideological campaign waged by the government continued unabated. This campaign had a short-term goal—to eliminate the churches' influence from public life—and a long-term goal—to hasten the demise of the churches.

We have already seen one aspect of this policy—the extremely anti-Christian official ideology of Rosenberg was disseminated freely, while rebuttals to it were forbidden and critics were silenced (either by jail or by fear of jail). The aforementioned Bishop Galen tried in 1935 to protest a Nazi rally in his bishopric where Rosenberg was scheduled to speak. The Nazis responded by staging a mass rally directly in front of his palace. The bishop was publicly denounced, and Rosenberg asked in his speech how anyone could claim that Naziism was intolerant when the bishop was allowed to write such letters without being thrown in jail.[51]

State control of the press meant that the teachings of National Socialism were incessantly broadcast, while church publications and publishing houses were strictly censored and even banned. Any attempt whatever to publicly disagree with Nazi doctrines was deemed "political" and hence an offense against the state. Churches were criticized in the press by high officials, even Goebbels and Goering, but were not allowed to respond.

This ideological campaign was of course not confined to the press. Religious organizations that might compete for the allegiance of the people were limited and finally banned. The churches were to be strictly limited to their sanctuaries, and any means of outreach or public service—orphanages, rest homes, youth groups, professional associations—were either banned, seized, or forcibly amalgamated with Nazi organizations.

A vital sector of this campaign was of course the schools. Although Hitler had promised to support and protect the churches, a systematic campaign was begun to eliminate religious education. Hitler repeatedly stressed the importance of educating the youth in the spirit of National Socialism, and Christian education was an obstacle to this goal. The purpose was not to eliminate religious education. It was felt that children needed a religious education, and instruction in moral values—the values of Aryan supremacy, anti-Semitism, German domination, and blind obedience to the Fuhrer.

The process by which church influence on education was eliminated, not overnight but slowly and by degrees, could be described at great length. Church schools were harassed and restricted, if not seized outright. Parents were subjected to extreme pressures, including the threat of loss of employment, if they continued to send their children to religious schools. Uncooperative people were considered enemies or potential enemies of the state. Any attempt by the churches to defend their schools was forbidden. Rigged elections in which 97% of the voters called for public schools rather than religious ones were used to justify the authorities' arbitrary measures. Clerics who called for the continuance of church schools were denounced for their "political" interference.

So effective was this campaign that all church schools had been completely abolished by 1939. Religious schools were either closed or converted to public schools. Public schools were of course quickly and easily brought into harmony with National Socialist practices. Religious classes in those schools were either canceled or made to conform to National Socialism. Jesus was presented as a Nordic fighter against Jewry; Christmas was transformed to a secular holiday; students were discouraged from saying grace. Religious pictures of Christ or saints were removed, openly Christian teachers who did not conform to Nazi doctrines were deemed unsuitable, and students were taught about Adolf Hitler during the religious period.

The Nazification of the educational system was not confined to the lower levels. Opponents of Naziism were dismissed from institutions of higher learning and theological schools were subjected to government pressures of various sorts. Some were closed, others had their staffs reduced, and vacancies were left unfilled. Nazis or people sympathetic to Naziism were appointed to key positions, and excessive criticisms of the regime were not tolerated. One example is striking.

In 1933 Wolf Meyer-Erlach, a pro-Nazi pastor who gave anti-Semitic and anti-Communist radio broadcasts was appointed a Professor of Theology at the University of Jena—in spite of the fact that he had no academic qualifications. The next year he became Dean of the Theological Faculty, and the year after that, in 1935, he was a candidate for the presidency of the University. He received only 8 votes out of 116, but was appointed to the post nevertheless. He then began giving professorships to Nazis.[52]

This brief overview does not begin to do justice to the subject. It does illustrate a general trend, but numerous aspects of this ideological campaign have yet to be mentioned. That membership in the Hitler Youth might be a job requirement for high school graduates; that Hitler Youth were taught that Christianity and Judaism (along with Masonry) were enemies of Germany; that Hitler Youth activities were timed to coincide with church activities so as to keep young people away from the churches; that prayers were forbidden at school assemblies—these are more aspects of the ideological campaign against the churches.

From the actions of the Nazi government, from official documents, from public statements in the press by Nazi officials, the Nazi vision for the future of the churches was plain: they should be isolated from the public arena and totally subordinated to the state. They should remain silent while their rights, properties, and organizations were systematically limited or eliminated—until such time as they would die out and be replaced by a new faith, a new religion.

One highly effective policy toward this end was strictly limiting church activities to within church buildings. Group outings, sports events, parades, political parties, publications, kindergartens, schools, professional organizations, public lectures, were all restricted or forbidden. Christians were supposed to do nothing more than sit in their church buildings and discuss theology, or maybe collect contributions for charity.

3. Persecution

It has already been said that in Poland the policy of the government toward the churches was one of open persecution. Thousands of priests were sent to concentration camps or executed for any reason, even trivial ones. They were assigned to the harshest and most degrading work in the camps, along with the Jews. Other Catholics were sent to Germany as forced laborers, and many church buildings were closed or destroyed.

In Germany itself, such a policy of outright destruction was not adopted. Many Catholics and Protestants were serving in Hitler's armies, some of them in the sincere belief that they were fighting to defend their country from Bolshevism. If their priests, pastors, or relatives back home were being thrown into jail their devotion to the Fuhrer would have been diminished, and the internal situation in Germany would have been greatly complicated.

The government allowed the churches in Germany to remain open and to function. At the same time, the free expression of ideas not in harmony with National Socialism could not be tolerated either; hence, the Nazi government pursued a carefully calculated policy of doing everything possible to limit the influence of the church, and to forbid any significant challenge to governmental authority. Christians were free to believe in God and Jesus, as long as they gave total obedience to Hitler. He understood that actions were more important than theological rhetoric, however lofty the latter might be. Direct dissent was swiftly dealt with—except in very rare circumstances, as we have seen in the case of Bishop Galen.

Before looking at specific examples, it is necessary to stress again the climate of fear, the constant pressure from knowing that the churches were spied on, watched, observed. Any criticism of the government or even disagreement with fundamental Nazi doctrines was considered dangerous. Any offense, real or imagined, could lead to being taken away at any time, with no legal recourse. Those who were taken away either never returned, or returned radically changed after even a short time in a concentration camp.

The danger of being arrested was very real. Conway relates that in May of 1935, the President of the Confessing Church Synod asked member churches to pray for sixteen pastors who had been sent to concentration camps or to prison, or had been expelled from their parishes. He also requested prayer for their congregations.[53] With a diligent desire for information unknown to some who enjoy talking about Hitler's imagined Christianity, Conway quotes in this context a bulletin from the Bavarian Political Police. Taken from government archives, it reads:

The Reich Minister for Church Affairs has decided not to take action against the holding of such services of intercession. However the personal details of such priests who conduct these services are to be sent in. Any attempt to publicize the prayers of intercession in the press, in leaflets or in parish magazines, is to be prevented, but no action should be taken against the official church gazettes.[54]

People look at photographs of church dignitaries shaking hands with Hitler or giving the Hitler salute. There are no photographs of those sixteen pastors being taken away from their families, or doing heavy labor in a concentration camp. There isn't a photo of a pastor being dragged out of bed in the middle of the night and beaten by a gang of thugs. Photographs of Paul Schneider, the previously mentioned pastor who died in Buchenwald after disobeying an order from the Gestapo to leave his parish, are not prominently displayed by enemies of Christianity. Shirer's *Berlin Diary* has an entry dated June 15, 1937, that speaks volumes: "Five more Protestant pastors arrested yesterday, including Jacobi from the big Gedaechtniskirche. Hardly keep up with the church war anymore since they arrested my informant, a young pastor; have no wish to endanger the life of another one."[55]

It is true that the great majority of pastors and priests never went to prison or a concentration camp. Some of them sincerely supported National Socialism, or embraced it. Others kept their anti-Nazi sentiments to themselves. The few that did speak out, and did suffer, however, are given far too little attention.

Needless to say, the situation of the churches deteriorated as the war progressed. Blatant nationwide persecution was avoided, but every pretext was used to continue harassment and limitation of the churches. Monasteries, hospitals, convents, and other institutions—so many of them were seized that one church official, Cardinal Bertram, wrote of "a systematic campaign for the destruction of all that was Christian."[56] The Vatican sent an official protest to the German Embassy in January 1942 stating that due to the "suppression of abbeys, monasteries, convents, and religious houses in such great numbers, one is led to infer a deliberate intention of rendering impossible the very existence of the Orders and Congregations in Germany."[57] Prior to this the papal Nuncio had sent frequent protests—all of them to no avail.

There was not only the confiscation of buildings. There was a consistent policy of repression in every area of life. It is difficult for us to imagine a situation in which failure to obey the government in even the slightest matter could lead to loss of a job, denial of promotion, beating, or arrest. In considering the responses of the Christians it is necessary to remember the ever-present reality of prisons and concentration camps. Someone who has read even one account of life in those camps can understand the fear that they inspired. Originally set up not to exterminate but to punish and "re-educate," they had extremely cruel regimes of labor, abuse, beating, torture, murder. The extent to which Hitler ruled by violence and fear is not sufficiently understood. Too often people with no real feeling for the situation say or imply that the entire nation of Germans (all of them devout, Bible-believing Christians, naturally) were joyfully following Hitler and exterminating Jews. Others mention Hitler's policy of repression as an obvious fact, but don't seem to grasp the implications or sense the human dimension.

Murder was also an option. During the Blood Purge of 1934, not only SA leaders but other opponents, real or imagined, were gunned down. Fritz Gerlach, editor of a Catholic weekly critical of the Nazis; Adalbert Probst, Director of the Catholic Youth Sports Association; and Erich Klausner, General Secretary of Catholic Action (that attempted to coordinate the activities of Catholic organizations) were all murdered. The Catholic Bishop of Berlin, Bishop Bares, wrote to Hitler personally about Klausner's death. Rejecting the official statement that Klausner had committed suicide, Bishop Bares sought some explanation, but was careful to stress that his death was not the result of deliberate policy, but "only the result of an unfortunate chain of unforeseen events."[58]

In his book *Metapolitics: The Roots of the Nazi Mind*, Peter Viereck quotes the following Nazi propaganda song, stating that students at the University of Munich were forced to write down and learn the song at compulsory lectures.

> The old Jewish shame is at last swept away;
> The black band of rascals [Catholic priests—*Viereck's note*] rages on.
> German men, German women, beat the black band to a jelly.
> Hang them on the gallows. . . . Ravens have been waiting.
>
> Plunge the knives into the parson's body.
> We'll be ready for any massacre.
> Hoist the Hohenzollerns high on the lamp-post!
> Hurl the hand-grenades into the churches.[59]

In the same vein, a Nazi propaganda poster from the 1932 Reichstag election shows a black Catholic priest bound to a red Marxist, both of them being smashed by the power of National Socialism.[60] The persecution that German Christians experienced was the direct result of the incompatibility between Christianity and Naziism. Some can imagine that hostile acts were carried out against the wishes or without the knowledge of a Fuhrer who admired the churches and respected them, but how much their imaginations have to do with historical realities is another question. Hitler stated that "the pious Catholic Christian Center [Party] always had the Jewish-atheist Marxists as beloved allies."[61]

The response of the churches

Apart from rare instances of outspoken opposition, some but by no means all examples of which were given above, what were the responses of the Christians in Germany to the government's attempts to break and to silence them? The response of many was silence—and it must be said that the main motive seems to have been one of fear, of the desire to survive. This fear was the result of sinful human nature, not of Christianity. It was manifested in Stalin's Russia and in Mao's China, and indicts not Christianity but human failure to follow the teachings of Christianity.

The one group that most consistently opposed Naziism, boldly refusing to compromise or cooperate with it in any way, was the Jehovah's Witnesses. It is sad that those who deny the deity of Christ, one of the most fundamental teachings of Christianity, should have been braver and more committed to their faith than many outwardly orthodox Christians. This can be attributed to a couple of factors. One is, that mere theology is not enough. We can talk about Jesus all day and say all kinds of orthodox things in Sunday school conversations—but when it comes to die, are we really confident that our lives are in God's hands? That because he has created us and decides when we will leave this world, that we can go like sheep to the slaughter? That is what Christ, our example, did. Perhaps we will never be put to such a test. If we are, we will not pass it if we have a dead faith, rather than a living one.

A second factor is that human will power is itself capable of martyrdom and self sacrifice. Since ancient history is now so much neglected many do not know the story of Regulus, the Roman who was cruelly tortured to death after he voluntarily returned to Carthaginian captivity solely to keep his word. Even Nazis and Russian Communists were very brave, and fought and died fearlessly for their beliefs. Hitler himself faced death countless times in WWI—it is not hard to see why he would despise people who claimed to know the truth about life but had far less courage than he did.

Jesus said that we should not fear those who can only destroy the body but after that have nothing more that they can do. If more Germans had had this kind of faith, the history of the church in Nazi Germany would have been considerably brighter. There would have been many people boldly and continuously speaking out against the lies of National Socialist ideology.

The Confessing Church

The leaders of what came to be known as the Confessing Church tried to maintain some doctrinal independence from the government. They sought to resist the take-over of the churches and showed a certain independence totally lacking among the secularists. Nevertheless, it must be said again that they were almost always careful not to cross the line and openly denounce the Fuhrer or the teachings of National Socialism. Their opposition to government control was almost always so tempered by caution as to prevent them from coming into open conflicts with the government.

When Hitler sought to unify the Protestant Churches under the authority of Ludwig Mueller, his personal appointee to the position of Reich Bishop, the Germanic Christians supported the new "Bishop" wholeheartedly. When the Reich Bishop began to impose Germanic doctrines on the church and arbitrarily gave administrative and ecclesiastical positions to his supporters, a significant number of churchmen rebelled. They objected to the scrapping of the Old Testament, the appointments of unqualified individuals in violation of church procedure, and the belief that the church should merely be an instrument of the state. They also objected to the "Aryan paragraph," that would have required all non-Aryans—meaning Jews—to be dismissed from church positions.

Martin Niemoller, pastor of a church in Berlin, organized a "Pastor's Emergency League" in response. This league, which later became the Confessing Church, sought to hold the church to the historic doctrines of scripture and the principles of the Protestant Reformation—without at the same time being openly disloyal to Hitler. Its members (publicly at least) took Hitler's earlier promises to protect the rights of the churches at face value, and acted as if the abuses of the Germanic Christians were contrary to official government policy. Somehow, they refused to notice that Mueller was Hitler's personal choice.

Thousands of pastors joined the league (over 7,000 out of 18,000 pastors by 1934),[62] and it became clear that the total Nazification of the church would not proceed smoothly. In fact, the church was the only organized body in all of Nazi Germany that publicly attempted to resist total domination by the government. Bishop Mueller resorted to authoritarian tactics, but only succeeded in stirring up so much internal opposition and hostility that Hitler's propaganda about an entire nation united behind him was being seriously damaged abroad. The Nazi government, therefore, which had previously backed the Germanic Christians (even to the extent of influencing church elections by confiscating opposition election materials and forcibly dissolving meetings) stepped back and proclaimed official neutrality in the struggle between the two factions.

Some photographs of SA men in church come from this period, when SA, Hitler Youth, and Labor Corps members were required by their superiors to attend church so as to support the Germanic Christians and intimidate their opponents.[63] This is partially confirmed by Steigmann-Gall who gives the following quote from a party circular issued by a Nazi *Gauleiter*: "Participation in the church vote is mandatory for every party member."[64] It is not difficult to imagine the feeling of a pastor thinking of resisting government control when he stood in the pulpit before a congregation full of SA men.

Apart from public image abroad, there were other reasons that made the government back away from the church struggle. For one thing, Hindenburg was still alive. His authority was still a significant factor, and he had received numerous protests over state violations of church autonomy (violating promises Hitler had made not even a month before). More importantly, the Confessing Church posed no direct threat to Hitler's authority. Almost all of the Confessing churchmen were careful to show their loyalty to the state, and they refrained from fundamental criticisms of Hitler. They wanted to cling to their historic doctrines, and not have state appointed administrators and bishops arbitrarily crammed down their throats. They didn't want to be required to fire the exceedingly rare Jewish converts on church staffs either, but in general they were willing to cooperate with the government. They remained loyal subjects of Hitler. Their quarrels were largely over matters of church administration and doctrines, and they did not pose a direct threat to Hitler's power.

Accordingly, the government ceased supporting the Germanic Christians so overtly. The Germanic Christians were even kept at arms length, and they found their activities restricted. Reich Bishop Mueller was forbidden to speak at secular gatherings, and the Germanic Christian symbol of a cross together with a swastika was banned.[65] The Germanic Christians had proven to be a political liability by causing useless conflicts that did not serve the interests of the state, and so they were put in their rightful place of dutiful obedience.

This does not mean that the Confessing Church was left unmolested. Even the feeble resistance to the government of some pastors loyal to Hitler was troubling in a totalitarian state—hence, some of the repressive measures we have already referred to were applied. Pastors who were too outspoken were forbidden to preach, deprived of their salaries, expelled from their parishes, and even imprisoned on occasion. Private seminaries, where Confessing Church members might prepare for the ministry outside the control of the state, were also banned.

To further distance the party from any form of Christianity, steps were taken to separate the party from any religious affiliation. In 1933, Rudolf Hess banned even the discussion of religious problems at party meetings, and forbade the singing of hymns.[66] Party leaders were not allowed to hold any church office, and party members in uniform were not allowed to participate in church services or to appear even with non-Christian religious groups like the German Faith Movement (a group that openly rejected Christianity and advocated a new Germanic faith). Priests and pastors were required to leave the SS in 1934; later, priests were not allowed to become members of the party, nor were theological students. As of 1938, clergymen were allowed to hold no party office.[67]

Parenthetically, the idea that some Nazis were singing hymns at party meetings gives ammunition to those who call the Nazis "Christians"—but Germanic Christians who saw National Socialism as merely the latest stage in a progressively unfolding revelation, and who saw Hitler's revolution as the continuation of the Protestant Reformation, could easily have sung Luther's famous hymn "A mighty fortress is our God" thinking that Germany, their god, had become a mighty fortress thanks to Hitler's rearmament program.

The Barmen Declaration

In May of 1934, leaders of the Confessing Church issued a statement that sought to clarify their concept of the church's relationship to the state. It rejected the false doctrines of the Germanic Christians, and also denied that the church should be nothing more than an arm of the state. It was, however, an abstract document—clear enough to delineate a small corner of administrative and theological independence without crossing the line and provoking the authorities.[68]

We must not forget the terrible conditions that those men labored under as they struggled to retain some spiritual independence from Nazi tyranny. To speak out too boldly would have meant swift action by the government and a terrible fate, and few people would say as much as they did—most would say even less, or nothing at all. Nevertheless, it must be said that the underlying spirit of the Barmen Declaration was one of caution. The lordship of Christ over every area of life was proclaimed in theory—but how much meaning did this have, coming from men who openly asserted their loyalty to Hitler?

If John the Baptist had been a theologian instead of a plain preacher of truth, he could have given a speech about marriage in such a way as to be doctrinally correct but without giving offense to Herod by mentioning Herod's unlawful marriage. Jesus could have uttered abstract doctrines which, though true in themselves, never spoke directly to the abuses of the Pharisees. The Barmen Declaration correctly pointed out that Christ's teachings extended to all of life—nice words, but that Christ's teaching "Do unto others as you would have them do unto you" might apply to Jews was carefully avoided. That Christ's teachings meant Aryan supremacy was not the meaning of life, that it would profit Germans nothing if they gained the world but lost their souls, were also prudently omitted, as were many other New Testament teachings.

Various reasons have been advanced for the caution of the authors of the Barmen Declaration. They were, it has been said, concerned with "the Gospel," not with politics—but if they were so concerned about "the Gospel," why were they not warning Germans of the coming day of judgment and helping them to find forgiveness through the blood of Christ, informing them that racial purity and Aryan supremacy would not bring them eternal life? That liars, murderers, and evil doers were headed for an eternity of punishment? That is part of the gospel too.

It has been said that there was not enough support for open resistance to Hitler, that a bolder approach would have had no followers—but the church is not supposed to carefully calculate the odds before it presents biblical truth. If the first Christians had calculated the odds and decided to remain silent, where would the church have been?

But, it has been said, they had a Lutheran respect for political power. This respect was mysteriously absent during the Weimar era—the Weimar government too was ordained of God. It was also absent from Luther. He did not only plainly show his belief that the secular authorities have no power over biblical truth—he also literally laid his life on the line. He was not afraid to die for his beliefs, and did not carefully present safely abstract doctrinal generalities.

To an extent, the Barmen Declaration had only to do with a struggle between two factions in the church. Would the Germanic Christians be allowed, using the power of the state, to cram their doctrines, pastors, and bishops down people's throats by force? Or would those who were loyal to Hitler but wanted to cling to their biblical doctrines and Old Testament stories be allowed a limited measure of independence to manage their churches? That is, would the Confessing Church's chain be long enough to give it a little freedom of movement in the dungeon of National Socialism, or would the Confessing Church be fastened hand and foot to the wall?

Yet, the Declaration was also more than that. In asserting even in theory the independence of religious belief from state control, it opened the door to a real threat. The Nazi government's desired monopoly on faith and truth could endure no rival, not even a potential one. Cautious as the Declaration was, it was still unsettling to the authorities. Copies of the Declaration were seized by the Gestapo, and even possession of a copy carried with it the threat of a concentration camp. More severe measures were not necessary since, as has been stated, many of the Confessing churchmen were loyal subjects.

Not surprisingly, the Confessing Church did not develop into a strong center of resistance to Hitler. The dangers were too great, and only a very small number were prepared to risk their all. This small number seems like only a drop in the bucket when compared to the millions and millions of slain—but their lives are recorded in the heavenly books and will not be forgotten before God. If their works were for Christ and in Christ, they will receive an imperishable reward.

Jesus did say, "Give not that which is holy unto the dogs, neither cast ye your pearls before swine, lest they trample them under their feet, and turn again and rend you." It was not obligatory upon the Christians to walk up to any Nazi at random and start preaching Christ. There is a time and a place to be silent—Jesus himself was silent for years until he began his public ministry. But, when Christians are required to give assent to false doctrines, then the necessity of taking a stand has been thrust upon them.

The main purpose of this essay is not to criticize the Christians of Germany. The purpose is to illustrate the nature of the relationship between Christianity and National Socialism. To this end, it is necessary to point out that support for National Socialism and failure to speak out against its many falsehoods derived not from the Bible but, as has already been said, from disobedience to the Bible.

Significantly, the Confessing Christians were a minority in the Evangelical church. The majority supported Hitler or at least kept quiet and went along. In this their behaviour was no different from that of the world—and what shall we say of Christians whose behaviour is no different from that of the world? The same phenomenon is evident in America today—vast numbers of nominal Christians whose everyday behaviour is no different from the world's. At least the Christians in Germany had the excuse of fear—though this too was a sin. Yet, in spite of their obvious weaknesses and failures, the churches, Catholic and Protestant, were the only organized bodies that put up any sustained resistance to Hitler at all. The labor unions, the universities, big business, the army, and all professional societies were effortlessly coordinated by the Nazi regime and completely silenced. In Kershaw's words, "The Christian churches were exceptions to the process."[69] They made many compromises, too many compromises, but only there was there enough spiritual life to prevent the total submission that elsewhere prevailed.

An ineffectual protest

A clear illustration of the problem faced by the Confessing Churchmen who wanted to speak out yet remain loyal at the same time is found in an incident that occurred in 1935. In that year, leaders of the Confessing Church wrote a personal protest to Hitler. They asked if hostile actions against the churches by the state were the result of official policy, contrary to Hitler's earlier promises to support the churches and maintain their status and privileges. The Church leaders also rejected the Nazi concept of "Positive Christianity" (Christianity with all teachings contrary to Naziism removed) and protested against police measures taken against the churches. The state's policy of closing church schools and limiting church activities in the fields of press and radio was criticized, and anti-Semitism was rejected. The statement about the Jews was striking: "If Christians are pressed to adopt an anti-Semitic attitude as part of the National Socialist ideology, which will incite them to hate the Jews, then this is against the Christian commandment to love one's neighbor."[70]

The churchmen went on to condemn the concentration camps and the lawlessness of the Gestapo, as well as the elevation of the nation to the place of God. More astonishingly, they even objected to the glorification of Hitler, who was allowing himself to be presented and adulated as much more than a merely human political leader (the idea of a devout secularist, atheist, or Darwinist making such a protest is absurd).

The message was sent to Hitler directly through his Presidential Secretary, and appears at first glance to have been a very courageous act. Conway suggests, however, that the memorandum was an expression not of courage but of naivety. These churchmen wanted to be loyal to Hitler, and it seems that they believed that calling his attention to these abuses would in some way help the situation. Subsequent developments support this view, although it is also possible that this was on the part of some a statement for conscience' sake from which no real results were expected.

Sending the memorandum to Hitler privately instead of publicly disseminating it allowed the churchmen to avoid a head-on confrontation with the government. It also allowed Hitler to ignore the message, which he did. A copy was sent to Switzerland, however, where it was published, and discussed in the foreign press.

This led to accusations of "treachery" and "conspiracy" against the Confessing Church leaders. Instead of standing behind the statement and distributing copies to their congregations, which would have created a political firestorm, the churchmen backed down. Wanting (sincerely or fearfully) to be loyal supporters of the state yet unable to deny the document, they sought a way out by issuing "a very much watered down version of their protest."[71]

The revised version omitted objections to the concentration camps, to anti-Semitism, and to the excessive elevation of Hitler and the nation. Instead, it "limited its protests to the attacks against the Evangelical Church and to the irreconcilability of Rosenberg's ideology with Christian doctrine."[72] Even this was too daring for some of the bishops, however—they thought such an approach would damage church-state relations. A few months later this same group of bishops offered a much more helpful statement, expressing their total support for the Fuhrer in his struggle against Bolshevism.

The government's reaction was restrained. A Dr. Weissler who was responsible for publishing the document in Switzerland was arrested and sent to Sachsenhausen. He died there within a few months.[73] No direct action was taken against the churches, however. Conway suggests that this was possibly due to a desire to avoid negative publicity during the Olympic Games—the image of national unity would have been tarnished. Another possibility is that the capitulation of the churchmen meant that this was not a direct threat to Hitler's power and so required no significant response.

The Germanic Christians

Using the term "Christian" very loosely, in a common worldly sense rather than in a biblical sense, it must be said that a significant number of German Christians supported Hitler sincerely. These, the "Germanic Christians," thought that Christianity was compatible with National Socialism, and even believed that National Socialism was the latest manifestation of a continually developing and changing Christian faith.

One group, the Federation for a German Church, sought a uniquely German gospel for the German people. Members of this group blamed the Jews for Germany's defeat in WWI, and sought to eliminate the Jewish background of Christianity. They rejected democracy and thought that authoritarianism was an essential part of national spiritual renewal. They also saw Germany as a unique creation of God and a source of divine revelation.

Another such group was the Thuringian German Christians. The Thuringian Christians wanted to scrap all of the doctrines and institutions of the Lutheran Church. They thought the Bible was unscientific, and found Hitler's revelation to be much more suitable to the modern age. Orthodoxy was less important than activism, and rescuing the German nation from its plight was more important than biblical teachings. Someone who saved Germany was doing the will of God, and Hitler's renewal of Germany was considered to be Christianity in action.

A third group was the Christian German Movement. This group sought to involve the church in right-wing politics, and provided chaplains for Hitler's SA. They were opposed by more orthodox church authorities, but combined with the two aforementioned groups and formed the Faith Movement of German Christians. They issued a statement of their principles in June, 1932.[74] Even before Hitler came to power they were advocating anti-Semitism and racial purity, and stressing the importance of race and nation. All of this was presented as "faith in Christ" and the "Kingdom of Heaven." They contrasted the unquestionable dynamism of National Socialism with the deadness of the churches, and thought that this new spiritual force could be used for national renewal.

Doctrinally, the German Christians totally abandoned Scripture. They rejected original sin as an insult to the Aryan man. The human race was not fallen but was ascending. The Germans were destined by their own efforts to become a "higher, nobler, superman type. We must ourselves become Christ."[75] Blood, soil, race, and Volk were divine creations and Hitler was doing the will of God in defending them. Paul's theology was the result of an inferiority complex, and the cross was redefined as a symbol of the German Volk's sacrifice for National Socialism.

These Germanic Christians were of course useful to Hitler and, like any ordinary politician, he was careful not to alienate them. His political strategy required appealing to as broad a base of the electorate as possible, and his avoidance of outright attacks on Christianity paid rich dividends. The violence of the SA was explained away as unfortunate, inevitable in times of turmoil but in no way part of official Nazi policy. Rosenberg's hostile attacks on Christianity were disavowed, and the need for Germans to unite was stressed instead. Hitler emphasized the value of the churches and promised to protect and even increase their influence. References to God, Providence, occasional photos of Hitler in front of a church, occasional biblical references or a few odd comments about Christ (none of them showing any spiritual depth)—these elementary techniques were used to convey the image of Hitler as a respectable, moderate, decent, even pious man. They were quite effective in appealing to people like the Germanic Christians who were already in agreement with much of Hitler's philosophy anyway.

Parenthetically, atheists, agnostics, and skeptics should not look with derision on these groups as evidence of the folly of religious belief. The various Communist groups, committed to diagnosing and solving mankind's problems by reason alone, were also groping in a dark world of false theories and false solutions. Many of them saw the Soviet Union as the beacon of humanity, and considered Stalin to be in the vanguard of human progress. Christians who reject the authority of scripture and invent their own philosophies to suit the times are spiritually akin to atheists who do the same—the only difference is that one group disguises its unbelief with religious language while the other does not.

Easily deceived by Hitler, the Germanic Christians hoped that the spiritual energy Hitler unleashed could be used to revive the churches and even bring about a spiritual renaissance in Germany. They emphasized the "holiness" of family, race, and state, advocated racial purity, opposed Communism, warned of the dangers of Jewish pollution, and felt that Hitler was doing the will of God by rescuing Germany and leading it to glory. They saw their main task as being Germans—that is, faithful and loyal supporters of Hitler—and sought to bring the church into complete harmony with the state.

This meant the removal of all "un-German" elements from Christianity, including not only the Old Testament but also the teachings of Paul. Paul, of course, was only a Jew who had corrupted the teachings of the fighting Aryan Jesus. Peter, James, and John were too trivial to mention. Luther was viewed not as a church reformer but as a Nordic hero who emancipated Germany from corrupt Mediterranean influences, and the alignment of the church with National

Socialism was considered to be a continuation of the Protestant Reformation. The anti-Semitism of the Germanic Christians had more to do with modern theories of race and nation than with the crucifixion of Christ—who was, after all, only a man anyway.

This is what invariably happens when basic doctrines are abandoned and people are free to follow their own feelings. Christ is fashioned to fit the times—thus we get the Aryan Christ of the Germanic Christians; the revolutionary, anti-capitalist Christ of left-wing liberation "theology"; the feminist Christ, the "Child of Humanity," of the women's liberationists; the compassionate Christ of the social activists; the wise moral teacher of the Deists—anything but the Son of God, who died, and rose again, and will return as God manifest to judge the world.

The Germanic Christians provided a lot of ammunition to those who want to prove that National Socialism was derived from Christianity. If Dr. Dietrich, the Evangelical Bishop of Nassau, congratulated Hitler after the Blood Purge of 1934, and said that "Hitler has been sent to us by God,"[76] is there any need to inquire further? The fact that this "bishop" might have rejected all of the basic teachings of Christianity and be dishonestly presenting a new gospel under the name of the old is seldom if ever considered.

The culmination of apostasy

This new form of Christianity was not just a clever political device cooked up by the Nazis. Its roots went far back into German culture, even as far as Kant. Preached notably by Houston Stewart Chamberlain and Paul de Lagarde among others, Germanic Christianity was in essence only secular national philosophies dressed up in religious language.

Following the so-called Enlightenment, countless Protestant churches abandoned the miraculous and the divine as "contrary to reason." Subordinating scripture to the human mind rather than subordinating the mind to scripture, they gradually abandoned all of the essential doctrines of Christianity. The Bible was considered to be an unscientific book full of myths; Jesus' miracles either never occurred at all, or had natural explanations; sin, the day of judgment, heaven, hell, the Trinity, were dismissed, and emphasis was focused on Jesus as a wise moral teacher. Friedrich Schleiermacher, F.C. Bauer, Albrecht Ritschl, Julius Wellhausen, and Adolf von Harnack - these and other theologians diligently undermined the Bible and the historic Christian faith and had a great responsibility for the Protestant churches' collapse before National Socialism.

Apostles of new doctrines asserted that the real essence of Christ's teaching was ethical ("Love your neighbor as you love yourself"), while many traditional teachings were ignored as superfluous, or reinterpreted to be compatible with the demands of secular reason. Schleiermacher (1768-1834), one of Germany's leading "Protestant" "pastors" and "theologians" of the day, was so eager to accommodate the despisers of Christianity and groveled so abjectly before them that he even asserted Jesus did not die on the cross but only swooned, and was mistakenly placed in the tomb. Jesus then managed to revive and emerge from the tomb, subsequent to which stories about his death and resurrection were invented—this started a new religion which swept through the Roman empire.

Since Schleiermacher is so representative of the liberal "Protestantism" that contributed to the destruction of Protestantism in Germany and also contributed greatly to the spiritual emptiness of Germany that (along with other factors) left the Germans thirsting for a Fuhrer, a brief examination of his teachings is in order. This will also help to explain many of the "Christians" who supported Hitler, "Christians" who had long since abandoned the basic tenets of Christianity.

Expressing the belief which dominates liberal Protestantism to this very day—that true religion consists primarily in feeling rather than doctrine—Schleiermacher had a vague concept of the "eternal" and the "infinite" that he equated with Christianity. Romanticism was thus given a religious facade. He dreamed of personal communion between man and God without repentance for sin, and without salvation by faith in Christ, which he considered to be at best secondary accretions to true religion. This communion with God required no death or resurrection of Christ, only "sincerity." Aware that Christianity was being increasingly rejected by educated people, he sought to make it more respectable by eliminating its objectionable elements. Thus, Christianity was reduced to whatever the world would tolerate after everything offensive or disturbing had been removed.

This represented a dominant response on the part of the church to the secular challenge: total surrender. It also represented a major shift in the understanding of both Christianity and Protestantism. The importance of this for an understanding of Christian support for Hitler cannot be overestimated. Christians who emphasized race, nation, Fuhrer and state without regard to biblical teachings were the end result of a century and more of theological liberalism mixed with German philosophy, and not the end result of the teachings of Christ and the apostles. This is an essential point missed by too many who do not understand the extent to which the seminaries and churches had been filled with a secular fog in the century preceding Hitler.

Man's deepest spiritual needs are not met by a mixture of Kant, Spinoza, Plato, and a Jesus who was nothing more than a wise spiritual teacher. It is much more sensible to just abandon Christianity altogether, if its central teachings are not true. This of course is precisely what many Germans had already done and would continue to do with greater vehemence as the century progressed.

Wellhausen and Bultmann

Since so much has been written blaming Christianity for the Holocaust, asserting that the Nazis were Christians or the sons of Christians; since people like to point at "seminary" professors, "pastors," "scholars," and "theologians" who supported Hitler, thus greatly hindering efforts to expose the true roots of National Socialism, some brief comments about other German theological philosophers are in order.

One of these was Julius Wellhausen. A biblical "scholar" and professor of Oriental languages, he sought to study the Old Testament "scientifically"—not that he had any empirically verifiable results. He imagined that his conclusions were scholarly, but in fact they were nothing more than his own opinions. A leading advocate of the so-called higher criticism of the Bible, he asserted that the events described in Torah were written centuries after the fact, and had never occurred. Needless to say, for Wellhausen not only the Old Testament (Moses did not receive a revelation from God on Sinai) but also the New Testament were human inventions, written long after the facts they purport to describe, full of mistakes and myths. Anti-biblical opinions were automatically invested with the sanctity of science, and were questioned only by those who were "unscientific." But, of course, this was not science at all.

People who object to the church's failure to withstand Hitler, or who point to the church's acceptance and even approval of Hitler, do not understand the extent to which German Protestantism was in many cases dead, and in many other cases dying. As difficult as it might be for a non-Christian to believe that a Protestant seminary would be deeply hostile to the Christian faith, it is true nonetheless. What did those so-called theologians who supported Hitler think of the inerrancy of scripture? The virgin birth of Christ? The elementary biblical truth that being a blonde-haired blue-eyed Aryan would count for nothing on the day of judgment? That it profited a man nothing if his country gained *Lebensraum* in the east but he himself lost his immortal soul? That Hitler needed to repent of his sins and be cleansed by the blood of Christ or he would be cast into the lake of fire to suffer eternal torment?

The Protestant church had reached such a state by 1933 that one of its leading "theologians," Rudolf Bultmann (1884-1976), dispensed with Christianity altogether and advocated nothing more than secular existentialism dressed up in religious language. He rejected original sin, any supernatural influence of God's Holy Spirit, the divinity, atoning death, resurrection, and return of Christ. He found the Bible to be full of mythology and sought to "de-mythologize it" by removing all supernatural elements or explaining them in merely human terms.

One website, which I have been unable to independently verify but which seems reasonable enough, stated that Bultmann's attempt to "demythologize" the New Testament "originated in a 1941 lecture, subsequently duplicated, which was designed to be a help in pastoralia to former pupils serving as chaplains in Hitler's army."[77] If this was in fact the case, and I see no reason to doubt it, this explains something about the "chaplains" in the Nazi armies.

Another source refers to a "sermon" "preached" by Bultmann in 1938, a month after the Crystal Night pogrom.[78] Actually, it was a speech and not a sermon. In his speech he asserted that the Jewish messianic hope was not "essentially foreign to our own way of life." This sounds like a defense of Judaism—except for the fact that "this messianic hope 'is by no means confined to Israel,' as witness the beliefs of the 'north Germanic tribes,' 'the Aryan Persians,' or the German poet Karl Immermann." The Jewish messianic hope is relevant to us today—but so is the messianic hope of the German tribes, the Persians, an obscure German poet, and who knows who else—just about anyone I would guess. Needless to say that kind of talk didn't get Bultmann in trouble with the authorities.

This was the depth of unbelief to which much of the so-called Protestant church had sunk. How could an institution where men like Bultmann were allowed to remain possibly mount any serious opposition to Hitler? It has been said that Bultmann was a member of the Confessing Church and opposed Hitler. It is difficult to understand what his "confession" consisted of. It is certain that his opposition to Hitler did not end his teaching career. No angry mobs ever attacked him for his bold statements of truth. Someone wrote that Bultmann was watched by the Gestapo—so were many other people, and most of them made sure to stay out of trouble.

One brilliant scholar, Gerhard Kittel of Tubingen University, enthusiastically embraced National Socialism. He thought it derived from Christian morality and would bring spiritual renewal to the German nation. He defended anti-Jewish legislation, saw the Jews as a threat to Germany, and felt that Hitler was sent by God to save the German people. Is it possible that his scholarship was worthless, a complete waste of time? What does it profit a man if he writes a fat theological dictionary but is deceived by Hitler? And what shall we say of the German churchman who wrote that the evil in *Mein Kampf* was cleverly concealed and difficult to recognize? Theologian Helmut Thielicke wrote that "one had to look very closely and read his terrible book *Mein Kampf* very carefully to see the cloven hoof beneath the angel's luminous robes." [79]This is a remarkable statement, given the blatant paganism and racial nonsense of Hitler's book.

Influenced by Kant, Hegel, Darwin, and Fichte, by the wisdom of the world that passes away rather than by the Holy Spirit, German "theologians" led the way in establishing an entirely new religion which consisted primarily of vague feelings about God without regard for doctrinal truths. Operating under the unwarranted assumption that 19th-century science was superior to biblical revelation, they served only to undermine Christianity. Far from the simplicity of Christ, they asserted that the Bible had poetical and moral truth, but not historical truth. Nevertheless, it was for them still the "words of God" because on occasion you could get a glimmer of God consciousness from somewhere while reading it.

This is what scripture calls "the sleight of men, and cunning craftiness, whereby they lie in wait to deceive." Such "trees whose fruit withereth, without fruit, twice dead," "turned aside unto vain jangling," "doting about questions and strifes of words"—they had indeed a lot to do with the spiritual emptiness that preceded Hitler and was one of the essential pre-conditions for his success.

"Protestantism" in the end came to be a form of Christianity that adapted itself, chameleon-like, to the times. Feeling and intuition came to be regarded as more reliable than outmoded doctrines. This view was often presented with a great show of scholarship and theological or philosophical erudition, and personal opinion and preference were disguised as "scientific" or "scholarly," but all of this was in essence only the reigning philosophy of the world dressed up in religious language. Hence, too many nominal Protestants were like sheep without a shepherd. Hungry, lost, confused, they were easily deceived by Hitler's glittering promises of a bright new dawn for Germany—a new day in which the rights of the churches would be respected, protected, and even increased.

Too many Christians were as a result like the foolish man described by Christ in the Sermon on the Mount. They built their house not on the rock of Christ's words, but on the sand of human wisdom and philosophy: "And the rain descended, and the floods came, and the winds blew, and beat upon that house; and it fell: and great was the fall of it." Many of the "pastors" and "theologians" and "Christians" who embraced Hitler belonged to churches that had long since abandoned the historic Christian faith and were nothing more than empty shells. Their imposing edifices concealed a deep spiritual emptiness that left the churches for the most part powerless to resist the driving power of new ideologies. Having thrown away the word of God, the sword of the Spirit, the helmet of salvation, the breastplate of righteousness—all of the spiritual armor of the Christian—they went forth to combat Goliath armed only with human intelligence and human courage. Inevitably, they failed. Many didn't even confront Goliath at all—they tamely submitted, or ran over and joined his side.

If David had had the spirit of 19th-century theological liberals or their descendents, the Germanic Christians, he would have seen Goliath challenging the armies of Israel and reasoned thus:

> Those stories in Torah are a bunch of myths and legends. There is some kind of a God up there, but this Goliath has a lot of good ideas. We should have a constructive dialogue, that will resolve this conflict—especially if the result of this dialogue is that we give in to Goliath completely. That will spare us a lot of grief and help us to become more liked and respected by the Philistines.

Many Christians will have no difficulty agreeing with Francis Schaeffer's statement that "the higher critical methods of the study of the Bible . . . destroyed the authority of the Bible for the Protestant church in Germany." He also notes that "there was a span of approximately eighty years from the time when the higher critical methods originated and became widely accepted in Germany to the disintegration of German culture and the rise of totalitarianism under Hitler."[80]

The Catholics

The situation of the Catholics under Hitler was in many ways identical to that of the Protestants. There were more outright condemnations of Hitler from the Catholic side before 1933. In some parts of Germany membership in the Nazi Party was forbidden to Catholics. One bishop, the Bishop of Mainz, even went so far as to refuse to administer the sacraments to party members. Conway relates that in 1931, Cardinal Bertram warned in a sermon against extreme nationalism, racism and despising of God's commandments. He condemned "Aryan-heathen teaching" as the "foolish imaginings of false prophets."[81]

Such men were exceptions, and their attitudes were not a matter of official policy consistently applied in Catholic churches throughout Germany. After Hitler came to power, such outspoken opposition almost completely ceased. Partly this was due to fear. Catholics, like anyone else, don't want to be beaten, tortured, or killed. Yet, there was also Catholic support for Hitler. Like the Protestants, a significant number of Catholics felt the appeal of National Socialism, and were in harmony with some of Hitler's political goals. Some were attracted to Naziism's authoritarian and anti-modernistic tendencies and it was believed by some that Hitler would benefit the Catholic Church. Thus, Cardinal Faulhaber of Munich was able to praise Hitler, referring in July 1933 to his "statesmanlike far-sightedness" and expressing the hope that the Concordat would benefit the German people spiritually.[82] In this context Conway gives numerous examples of early Catholic enthusiasm for Hitler, including not only such outward trappings of Naziism such as flags, songs, and the Nazi salute, but also voluntary dissolution of many Catholic organizations, and expressions of loyalty to the state and to Hitler.

Anchored as they were in Rome, the Catholics were much less vulnerable to the theological drift that led so many Protestant churches to their final shipwreck in the Third Reich, but the Catholics were not immune to the appeal of an authoritarian government that would end the slide to modernism, govern on a more hierarchical basis, and protect the rights of the church. There were German

Catholics who went to church and even served in high positions but were vulnerable to the charms of Naziism. American Catholics today are similarly attracted to secular movements like feminism, abortion rights, homosexuality, and left-wing political activism. Here again Hitler's policy of avoiding outright attacks on the churches minimized a lot of potential opposition and greatly eased his path to power.

The Concordat

The situation of the Catholics was also complicated by the Concordat. Since the Pope had committed the Catholics to not opposing Hitler politically, and since Hitler considered any disagreement or contradiction whatever to be political, Catholics were obligated to keep silent or—like the Protestants—face persecution.

Concerning the Concordat, a basic point has been missed in many of the discussions about it. After the end of the war the Pope condemned National Socialism in the strongest possible terms, as was mentioned before in this essay. "Satanic . . . arrogant apostasy from Jesus Christ . . . idolatry of race and blood."[83] I concur with the Pope's assessment here, but have to wonder—was it prudent for the Vatican to sign an agreement with arrogant and satanic apostates, asking them to protect the rights of the church and promising in exchange to avoid opposing said apostates?

It seems inarguable that in 1933 the Pope failed to discern the true nature of National Socialism. He believed that an agreement with Hitler had some validity, and thought it would strengthen and protect the status of the Catholic Church in Germany. He did not expect that the Nazis would so consistently violate the agreement as to render it worthless.

In my view, the Pope made a major blunder in signing the Concordat. The Pope was deceived by Hitler. Hitler gained a propaganda prize, and the cessation of all Catholic political opposition to a government officially legitimized by the Vatican. The Catholics gained nothing in return but a piece of paper—and frequent protests by the Vatican through official channels pointing out violations of the Concordat accomplished nothing.

Of course, no one could have guessed in 1933 what Hitler would become. Many experienced diplomats were deceived by Hitler. Many took Hitler's promises at face value—but the Pope should have had more acumen and spiritual insight than an ordinary statesman. He didn't. Moreover, there were plenty of pagan elements clearly evident in *Mein Kampf*. These should have served, and could have served, as a clear warning to anyone with real spiritual discernment.

The Pope did issue an encyclical, *Mit Brennender Sorge*, already referred to in chapter 3. This encyclical denouncing violations of the Concordat and rejecting the false doctrines of race and Folk was a direct defiance of the government and asserted that the Catholics should follow Rome, not Hitler. The government's response was mixed. The vast majority of German Catholics were causing no trouble for the government, and it was thought that an excessively harsh reaction would lead to further complications. It was in this context that Rudolf Hess made the comments quoted earlier to the effect that the churches should be left to wither away gradually (strictly controlled in the meantime of course). Yet, while a head on clash with the church would not have been politically advantageous, giving religious people too much freedom to influence others would also hinder the progress of National Socialism. Thus, there was a policy of limiting and restricting the church, of trying to confine its influence to the sanctuary—there people could talk about Jesus as much as they liked, safely isolated from society as a whole.

To this end, lesser measures were taken to combat the encyclical. Its publication and distribution were forbidden, and other restrictions and harassments were to continue, but a direct clash with the church was avoided. This was helped by the fact that the Vatican and the German Catholic churches, after this brief outburst, remained prudently silent. The Vatican also wanted to avoid a conflict. This is why the Nazi theoretician Alfred Rosenberg's book *The Myth of the Twentieth Century* was placed on the index of forbidden books but Hitler's *Mein Kampf* was not. Attacking Rosenberg was considerably safer, although eventually refutations of Rosenberg or any other Nazi propaganda were forbidden as well.

At this point I feel obligated to comment that when Martin Luther pointed out serious problems with Catholic doctrine and practice he was loudly condemned by the Pope. He was excommunicated and anathematized in the severest terms. When, however, Hitler not only preached many doctrines openly contradictory to Christianity but also subjected Polish Catholics to terrible persecution and did everything within the realm of political possibility to eliminate Catholic influence in Germany, the Vatican said very little. I can only attribute this to fear of persecution. The Pope was afraid to take a bold and uncompromising stand for truth and did not openly condemn Hitler until it was safe to do so. It may of course be argued that he was motivated for concern for the safety of German Catholics, and for the preservation of the church in Germany.

Pope Pius did make an effort to help the Jews. Martin Gilbert relates that:

> Pope Pius XII had personally ordered the Vatican clergy to open the sanctuaries of Vatican City to all 'non-Aryans' in need of refuge. By the morning of October 16th, [this was after Mussolini's fall and the occupation of Italy by the Germans] a total of 477 Jews had been given shelter in the Vatican and its enclaves, while another 4,238 had been given sanctuary in the many monasteries and convents in Rome.[84]

Though some have studied the question in more depth than I have, it seems that the failure of the Pope to speak out more boldly on behalf of the Jews was due more to caution than to anything else. Protests from him would have not saved anyone, and would have subjected German Catholics to even greater pressures than those they were already facing.

The failure of the churches to speak out for the Jews

It is undeniable that the churches said very little about the persecution of the Jews—those few individuals who did speak out were extraordinary exceptions. It is possible to show that many others kept silent not because of approval, but because of fear. The churches were silent when the Communist Party was crushed; when thousands of Germans were imprisoned or murdered; when small independent religious groups were banned. Prior to the outcry against euthanasia (in which very few Christians participated), the churches did not speak up for other Germans either—was this due to anti-Semitism?

Why don't people consider that the Russians also kept silent during Stalin's purges and mass arrests? Their friends, co-workers, relatives, closest family members were taken away—and the Russians kept silent. Not only did they not protest, they continued to praise and glorify Stalin. Why? Because Martin Luther had preached obedience to the authorities centuries ago and the Russians were somehow under his magic spell and unable to think for themselves? Because centuries of Greek Orthodox Christianity had conditioned them to feel nothing for their husbands, wives, colleagues, children, and friends? Or was it because they were in the grip of fear? Was it because their first goal was survival, and they desperately wanted to live, to stay out of the Gulag—and because they knew that speaking out would accomplish nothing but their own destruction? Similarly, in Mao's China, the Chinese too kept silent. Knowing that even a wrong word can lead to arrest, beating, torture, cruel imprisonment and death does have an inhibiting effect on most people. I doubt that anyone will attribute the fearful passivity of the Chinese to centuries of Christian influence.

Examples can be given to show that there were Germans who disapproved of what the Nazis did, but did not speak out because so doing would have led to their own persecution. Martin Gilbert, writing about the state-organized criminal barbarism of the Crystal Night pogrom in 1938, relates in his history of the Holocaust that some Germans wept while watching Jews being persecuted.[85] This is confirmed by Shirer, who was living in Germany at the time. He stated from his own experience that not only foreigners but also "many Germans were as horrified by the November 9 inferno as were Americans and Englishmen and other foreigners."[86]

Pastor von Jan, one of the few who did speak out, mentioned that "No one dares to speak." It is very easy to criticize others, but keeping silent is ordinary human nature, not the result of Christianity. In fact, it is disobedience to Christ, who said ". . . fear not them which kill the body, but are not able to kill the soul: but rather fear him which is able to destroy both body and soul in hell." That some were mindful of this explains why this extraordinary public objection to Nazi practices was made by a Christian, not by a secularist with no higher or enduring moral values. Why should people who think of themselves as being essentially and fundamentally nothing more than animals stick their necks out? Attempts to fabricate an ethical system based on survival of the fittest are like pulling a rabbit out of a magician's hat. Both are only tricks—with the difference that the rabbit at least is real.

Other examples can be given—not, unfortunately, nearly as many as there should have been, but more than many people are aware of. After the Crystal Night pogrom a Catholic priest, Provost Bernhard Lichtenberg, publicly expressed concern for the Jews. He was later arrested and died in captivity. A Protestant pastor named Grueber set up an office to help Christian Jews. He and his assistant, one Dr. Sylten, were both arrested—the latter died in Dachau.[87] One Elisabeth Schmitz, a high school teacher and a member of the Confessing Church, wrote a letter to the pastor of a prominent Lutheran church in Berlin, calling on the church to speak out on behalf of the Jews and to assist them as well. She also resigned her teaching position because she was unable to teach Nazi doctrines.[88]

When the deportation of Jews from Germany began later during the war, this was clearly something more than merely restricting the Jews within German society and there were some faint stirrings of protest. Nevertheless, silence reigned with rare exceptions. One individual who stood out was Theophil Wurm, the Evangelical bishop of Wuerttemberg referred to earlier.

Bishop Wurm had originally cherished the delusion that the Nazi movement would be morally beneficial to Germany and eliminate unhealthy secular influences. He had a prejudice against "Jews and foreigners"[89] and accepted the need for racial laws, but had also opposed the Jewish boycott of 1933 and had even gone so far as to try and rally church leaders against the boycott.[90]

Wurm soon discovered his error in supporting Hitler, and found himself in the center of the Confessing Church's struggle to prevent being totally enslaved by the state. Wurm suffered house arrest and temporary removal from his post (as referred to earlier in this chapter), but was reinstated. By 1941, he had begun to write letters to government officials, including Goebbels and Hitler. It was in this year that "a near-fatal illness galvanized his determination to devote all his remaining energies to the pursuit of church unity and national renewal."[91]

Gilbert records in his history of the Holocaust that the bishop wrote to the German government in 1943, protesting the persecution of "men and women under German rule," and stating "There must be an end to putting to death members of other nations and races who are not even accorded a trial by either civil or military courts. A day will come when we shall have to pay for this."[92]

Wurm also wrote, in a letter to Hans Lammers, the State Secretary of the Reich Chancellery: "We Christians consider the policy of exterminating the Jews as a grave injustice and of fatal consequences for the German people. Our people see the suffering imposed on us by the air raids as an act of punishment for what was done to the Jews."[93]

The phrase "our people" indicates that there were Christians in Germany whose beliefs did not include the extermination of Jews as subhumans. Confirmation of this assertion is provided by the diary of Victor Klemperer. In his entry of January 29, 1944, he wrote: "Today Frau Stuehler for the first time heard someone say out loud in a queue of women that the Jews really had been treated too badly, they were 'human beings, too' after all, and the attacks on Berlin and the destruction of Leipzig were retribution."[94]

On July 16, 1943, Bishop Wurm even wrote a letter to Hitler, stating that the "persecution and extermination" of non-Aryans were crimes that "stand in sharpest contradiction to the law of God and violate the foundation of all Western thought and life—the elemental God-given right to human existence and human dignity."[95] Possibly (or probably) Hitler never received the letter. It could have been received by a sympathetic official and covered up—but it could easily have led to imprisonment and death, and the bishop was genuinely heroic in writing it. Why didn't some German Darwinists write a letter of protest saying "We feel that the persecution of Jews interferes with natural selection and survival of the fittest and should be stopped because it is against the laws of science"? But no Darwinist could ever write such a letter because Darwinism has zero ethical basis, and in fact destroys ethics.

The bishop wrote to the Church Ministry (again in 1943) stating:

> The measures taken against the Jews . . . so far as they do not take place in the scope of the laws at present in force, have for a long time been depressing many circles in our nation, particularly the Christian ones. In the present difficult

206

circumstances, the question automatically arises whether our nation has not made itself guilty of bereaving men of their homes, their occupations and their lives without the sentence of a civil or military court.[96]

This quote reminds us again that the bishop was speaking for a larger number of people. It also shows that someone might accept the Nuremberg laws or anti-Jewish boycotts but still recoil at the thought of extermination. Someone may advocate the expulsion of illegal aliens from America without having any thought of sending them to extermination camps.

The same statement of Bishop Wurm's to the Church Ministry declared that, "in view of a possible political exploitation of a public protest by the enemy countries, the Christian Churches have exercised great restraint in this respect." Even in his protest he sought to reassure the government of the church's loyalty— but the bishop went on to state that Christians "cannot, however, possibly be silent when lately even Jews living in mixed marriage with Christian Germans, some even being themselves members of Christian Churches, have been torn from their homes and occupations to be transported to the East."[97]

Now, it is not the Bible's teaching that Christians should only be concerned about their own, and the rest of the world can perish in misery. Paul wrote to the members of the church in Galatia, "As we have therefore opportunity, let us do good unto all men, especially unto them who are of the household of faith." We should reject the concept of the church saying nothing while innocent non-Christians are persecuted, and only speaking out when the flood tide begins to reach the church doors. Nevertheless, the bishop's limited and ineffectual protest was much better than nothing, and a brave act worthy of respect.

Bishop Wurm wrote other letters to government officials. These were circulated secretly among the churches, and expressed the sentiments of those who still saw Jews as human beings. Ultimately, correspondence between Bishop Wurm and the Reich Chancellery was officially banned. Hans Lammers, the chief of the Reich Chancellery, forbade him to write further. In the words of Diephouse's study,

> Wurm himself interpreted his silencing as a pre-emptive move by Lammers and other moderates in the Fuhrer's circle designed to protect him from possible detention and trial, sanctions that Hitler may indeed have considered and elected to defer out of concern for their effect on wartime morale.[98]

Friedländer suggests in his book *The Years of Extermination: Nazi Germany and the Jews 1939-1945* that Wurm was silenced too easily.[99] This is a difficult criticism to evaluate. If I rebuke a man for his wrongdoing and he responds with hostility, even threatening my life, am I obligated to keep chasing after him? Certainly, the churches could have and should have said far more than they did, yet I think Wurm deserves more credit for literally risking his life.

Wurm's early support for Hitler, as well as negative statements made about Jews even after the war, greatly detract from his stature. Nevertheless, his willingness to protest government policies shows the power of biblical truth to help us transcend (however imperfectly) our environment and our biases. It is unfortunate that Wurm was such a rare exception, in no sense representative of German Christians as a whole. It is also worth pointing out that he respectfully framed his protests so as to avoid crossing a certain line. If, for example, he had openly proclaimed that National Socialism was a false philosophy, that the Germans were not the master race, and that Hitler was a disaster for Germany, he would surely have been swiftly silenced without regard for possible political fallout.

The Catholic leaders also made some effort to express themselves. In 1941, the Catholic bishops protested against the violation done to the sanctity of marriage by the deportation of Jews married to Catholics, but the Nazis could easily afford to ignore such protests. Like those of Bishop Wurm, they had no significant impact. One of the protests by the Catholic bishops contained a qualification by one of the signers, Cardinal Bertram. He explained that his protest was not the result of "lack of love for the German nationality, or of feeling for national dignity, or of underestimation of the harmful Jewish influences upon German culture and national interests."[100] Even in their protests people were careful not to alienate the government.

Some vague spiritual platitudes about love for one's fellow man, for all mankind, were uttered in pulpits but were ignored by the Nazis—another example of safely abstract theologizing accomplishing nothing. Yet, there were two other attempts to speak out that require mention. In 1943 the Prussian Synod of the Confessing Church sent a pastoral letter to the Confessing Churches. Dealing with the biblical commandment, "Thou shalt not kill," it stated that the state's power to take life was limited to criminals or to war-time enemies (so much for blind and unthinking obedience to the state as a Lutheran doctrine). The letter further stated that Nazi terms such as "eradication," "liquidation," and "unfit to live," were not part of God's law. Finally, it asserted that "The murdering of men solely because they are members of a foreign race, or because they are old, or mentally ill, or the relatives of a criminal, cannot be considered as carrying out the authority entrusted to the state by God."[101]

Again, the government's response is not recorded. No doubt the Nazi government had long since learned that occasional objections by the churches were insignificant, led to no further action, and did not demand immediate response—though if the doctrines had become widespread enough to be perceived as a threat, the government would not have tolerated such heresies. Moreover, the sons and husbands of church members were fighting an increasingly desperate battle—their willingness to fight would unquestionably have been diminished if their relatives, wives, friends, and parents, were being thrown into jail. The government therefore sought to an extent to avoid creating martyrs, but enough people were arrested to serve as examples, and there was danger in any kind of deviation from the required ideological norm.

One last highly revealing event took place, also in 1943. Perhaps the feeling that the war was being lost was beginning to have an influence. At any rate, the Evangelical bishop of Bavaria was approached by a group of laymen who had written a bold statement condemning the persecution of the Jews. It said that the church should "ardently withstand" the state's attempts to "destroy the Jews." It asserted that the duty of the church was to present the truths of Christ to the Jews—but the "Church can only make this belief credible to Israel if she simultaneously accepts those Jews who have 'fallen amongst murderers.'"[102]

More strikingly, the statement referred to Paul's warning that the Gentiles should not be proud against the Jews but should fear God (Romans 11:20), and said that the church should resist the use of God's curse over Israel as an excuse for passivity in the face of evil. It even asserted the indissoluble bond between the church and the Jews, and stated that the church "can no longer attempt to save herself by avoiding the attacks made on the Jews. She must rather witness to the fact that along with Israel it is the Church and her Master Jesus Christ who are being assaulted."[103]

This bold statement is quite impressive—however, when the bishop asked for at least two people to put their names to the document, no one volunteered. This is a clear case of people who were silent not because of anti-Semitism, but because of fear. It is consistently said that the Christians were silent about the Jews because of biblical teaching—but here were some who clearly understood that biblical teaching did not mean National Socialist racial anti-Semitism, yet still kept silent.

It should not need to be pointed out that there is a huge difference between keeping silent out of agreement, and keeping silent out of a desire to save one's life. This latter motive is almost invariably passed over by those who do not understand biblical teachings about the Jews, misrepresent the Bible, and do not understand Christianity in general. They are for some reason overly eager to attach only the worst motives to ordinary people in extremely dangerous and difficult circumstances.

The point has been made that the churches did speak out against the euthanasia program, and even had some impact—proving that they could have done something to help the Jews if they had really wanted to. This seemingly reasonable argument omits some important considerations. For one thing, most Christians did not speak out on that either. They kept silent, and it was only a few rare individuals who objected. This was surely not due to anti-Semitism. Moreover, euthanasia was never as central to Hitler's ideology. It was a peripheral issue and objections to it could be seen as less than objections to Naziism itself. Finally, the protests did have some effect, but the program was continued regardless.

The Germanic Christians should not be forgotten. They of course had no difficulty with the persecution of the Jews. A statement issued by Germanic Christian leaders in 1941 blamed the Jews for the war and stated that government measures against the Jews were "indispensable for the safeguarding of German life."[104] Reference was also made in the statement to the crucifixion of Christ (nothing about his resurrection or return, needless to say), and to Luther's demand for the expulsion of the Jews. Here again, the question is "To what extent were they displaying faithfulness to and obedience to the teachings of Christ?" When Christ said we should love our neighbor as we love ourselves, and that we should treat others like we want them to treat us, he did not say "except the Jews."

Yet, there were others outwardly more orthodox who did refer to God's anger at the Jews. Some may have been only trying to justify their own inactivity. Others who meant this sincerely should have known that Christians are called to share God's love and mercy with the whole world, not to be agents of wrath, or to take pleasure in wrath.

Martin Niemoller

A more doctrinally orthodox Christian who expressed traditional anti-Semitic sentiment yet still fell very far short of advocating the extermination of the Jews was Martin Niemoller. He initially supported Hitler, yet never imagined that the Jews would be subjected to a Final Solution. This was inconceivable to ordinary people in 1933.

People too often fail to distinguish between kinds and degrees of anti-Semitism. Leo Stein, whose description of Niemoller has already been referred to in this chapter, also testified that while Niemoller was in the prison camp he went out of his way to help Jews, sharing rations with them and asserting that Nazi persecutions were contrary to Christianity. It was perfectly possible for people to feel traditional anti-Semitism of a religious sort yet still see Jews as human beings who should not be exterminated. I don't like millions of illegal aliens coming into America. I see the aliens as causing a lot of problems—but this does not mean I want the government to slaughter them.

Some of Niemoller's anti-Jewish comments that are bandied about need to be interpreted with this in mind. He is reported to have said that the Jews had done great harm to Germany, and that he even disliked converted Jews. One quote has him saying that God's anger was upon the Jews due to the crucifixion, and they deserved the bad things that happened to them. It has also been argued that Niemoller would not have supported the Nazis, as he initially did, if he had not shared their racial attitudes.

It is a fact that some Germans supported Hitler's political aims, but did not share the Nazis' extremist racial ideology. They supported Hitler with some hesitation, and he was careful not to alienate them. Hitler even toned down his anti-Semitism in order to attract votes. It is also a fact that people prior to the Holocaust could have a certain dislike for Jews yet not see them as vermin or subhumans. Before the Holocaust made anti-Semitism thoroughly odious, there were Americans who looked down on Jews as peculiar people and disliked them in a vague sort of way, but never instituted a pogrom or harmed Jews.

Niemoller could very well have had a conventional, pre-Holocaust anti-Semitism which was unloving and unbiblical, yet still far removed from the gas chambers and the ovens. And which of his anti-Jewish remarks were made before a Nazi court when he was on trial for his life? Many criticisms of Niemoller have been made by those who are predisposed to be hostile, and are hence less than fair.

A sermon by Niemoller

As to Niemoller's anti-Jewish attitudes (some of which have been exaggerated), I have been fortunate to obtain portions of one of Niemoller's sermons from 1935. They were sent to me by a Holocaust scholar, Prof. Robert Michael, when I was unable to access the source he gave me for reference. I assume what I was sent as an e-mail attachment was from that source, or similar to it, though no bibliographical information was included with the attachment. I have since been unable to get hold of Michael for further clarification on this source, which is included in the bibliography.[105] I welcome correction or further information.

The sermon supposedly shows the depths of Niemoller's anti-Semitism, but when looked at from the point of view of belief in the Bible, it says something quite different. Referring to the "dark and sinister" nature of Jewish history—does "sinister" refer to the actions of the Jews, or the cruelties inflicted upon them?—the sermon attributes this to God's anger, and states that Jewish suffering will not end until the Jews convert to Christianity. Until then they are guilty before God of the blood of God's messengers whom they have murdered. These are ideas that never produced a death camp in 1800 years and never will. Hitler did not appeal to such logic in his lengthy analyses of the Jewish question in *Mein Kampf*.

Then Pastor Niemoller goes on to, of all things, compare the Jews to the Nazis! Both Jews and Nazis, he asserted, denied "faith, salvation, and forgiveness through Christ." Both Hitler and the Jews claimed to be upright, even pious. Both Hitler and the Jews rejected Christ, and both Nazis and Jews were without the forgiveness of sins made available through Christ. Finally, Niemoller saw both the German and the Jewish nations as being "proud," "pure-blooded," and "race conscious" nations that saw no need for Christ. There was also an exhortation that Christians should not hate the Jews, as "the Jews were already hated and cursed by God" [Michael's paraphrase].

Now, while it may seem singularly obtuse to link the victims so closely with their tormentors—as if there were no difference between an unbelieving murderer and his unbelieving victim—this does not set the Jews up "as the standard by which" the Nazis should be judged. For one thing, it is a very strong indictment of National Socialism from a Christian point of view, stating clearly that the Nazis had rejected Christ, and did not have the forgiveness of sins that was found in Christ. This was a clear statement, made publicly, that National Socialism was contrary to Christianity. Would that there had been more of this prior to 1933.

Moreover, one can imagine the Nazis' reaction to being told "You think the Jews are bad? In God's eyes you are bad also!" Failing to draw more of a distinction between the persecutors and their victims may seem insensitive and obtuse to us, but Niemoller was walking very close to the edge of a precipice already. He was probably trying to go as far as he could, but no farther. But to state that Niemoller's comments show that the Jew represents the standard of evil for Christians is inaccurate. The Bible states that Jews and Gentiles are both equally under sin. Niemoller also stated in a sermon that Christians were called to love their enemies, "with no room for exceptions," and taught that Christians were not supposed to be agents of God's anger.[106]

Niemoller was the most well-known and outspoken ecclesiastical opponent of Hitler, and even personally disagreed with Hitler at a meeting of church leaders with the Fuhrer in 1934. The Gestapo searched his house that same night, and a bomb was set off in the hallway of his home a few days later. Niemoller's early support of Hitler and his excessive negativism about Jews greatly diminish his stature, but surely it is an error to say, as someone did, that the only difference between Niemoller's conventional anti-Semitism and Nazi racial anti-Semitism was that in Niemoller's view the Jews could be changed by conversion and baptism. This little difference entirely nullifies the Nazi concept of race. It also presupposes the full humanity of Jews.

Niemoller's views have been held by others who did not advocate fascism, militarism, imperialism, world domination, and genocide. To say that Niemoller's dislike for Jews was the same as Hitler's bizarre hatred of Jews is erroneous. To go farther and say that Niemoller's attitudes were the foundation of Hitler's is to ignore the entire course of 19th-century German philosophical and cultural development.

Dietrich Bonhoeffer

Although Martin Niemoller was initially the most well-known public symbol of Christian opposition to Hitler, the more popular writings of Dietrich Bonhoeffer (such as *The Cost of Discipleship*) and his involvement in the plot to assassinate Hitler have led in the decades following World War II to a great increase in interest. It is safe to say that Bonhoeffer is now one of the most revered (or at least highly respected) figures in modern church history.

An examination of his theology would go too far beyond the confines of this study.[107] For our purpose it is sufficient to discuss three aspects of his life and witness: a few biographical facts; his involvement in the plot to kill Hitler; and his alleged anti-Semitism. Concerning Bonhoeffer's biography, much has been written about it elsewhere. His early recognition of the Nazi threat and his strenuous efforts to keep the German Lutheran Church from surrendering completely to Hitler deserve more recognition by secular historians. His imprisonment and execution are too well known to require repetition here, but I would like to mention that his decision to voluntarily return to Germany when he could have remained safely abroad was genuinely heroic (Niemoller and the German-Jewish spiritual leader Leo Baeck were encouraged to leave Germany but also chose to remain).

As to the plot to kill Hitler, Bonhoeffer's reasoning is easy to understand—but is it biblical? We can agree with the belief that Christians should not simply talk about Jesus, theology, and church politics while they remain indifferent to the evil and suffering around them—but does it follow that individual Christians are called by God, or allowed by God, to engage in political assassination? While governments have the right and the duty to keep the peace (as we shall see shortly in our discussion of Romans 13), I do not believe that is the right or the calling of individual Christians. One may respond that, given the evil of Hitler, something had to be done, but it is arguable that Bonhoeffer's efforts could have caused more suffering rather than less, and protracted the war rather than shortened it.

By Shirer's account, the conspirators in Berlin were poorly organized and bungled the attempt to seize power in the critical period between the explosion in the Fuhrer's bunker and the later confirmation of his survival. If, then, the attempt to kill Hitler had succeeded but the attempt to seize power in Berlin had failed, the reins of government would have remained in the hands of Goering, Himmler, Bormann, and Goebbels. If those men, fanatically devoted to the Nazi ideology but lacking Hitler's faith in his infallible military genius, had given more freedom to the generals to make decisions, the German army could have fallen back, regrouped, and adopted more defensible positions. This could have delayed the end of the war by a few months or even longer. If the war had ended not in the spring of 1945 but in the fall, and if the process of exterminating Jews had been urgently pursued all the while, how many more people would have died? Thus, killing Hitler might have had the reverse of the intended effect.

About Bonhoeffer's anti-Semitic views, he did assert some of the traditional religious ideas linked by many to anti-Semitism. That Christianity has replaced Judaism as a more complete revelation; that the church should present Christian

212

teachings to the Jews (and to everyone else) and welcome conversions; that the Jews were under God's anger because of their rejection of Christ—these ideas can be found in Bonhoeffer's writings. Whether or not Bonhoeffer changed these views over time is debated by serious students of Bonhoeffer.[108] What is not debatable is that Bonhhoeffer saw the Jews as human beings, not as vermin; completely rejected the ideology of Aryan racial superiority; had no desire to see the Jews exterminated; and wanted the German church to take a stronger stand on behalf of the Jews.

What should have been done?

Given the realities of life in the Third Reich, what should the churches have done? An answer to this requires some understanding of the role and purpose of the church in the world, and also of God's biblical plan for human government. These topics are debated among Christians, but it is possible to make a few observations that should be generally agreed upon by those who believe in the Bible.

Defining the one true spiritual church as the body of Christ, composed of those who love Christ and have his Spirit (which brings with it a sincere desire to live for Christ), we can say according to scripture that the church has two functions in this lost and sinful world. One is to provide fellowship for believers; the other is to show the love of Christ and the truths of Christ to the world.

Concerning the first of these, Christians come together to worship, to pray, to be taught, exhorted, encouraged, comforted, and corrected if necessary by other believers. The second purpose is more public, and more complex. Part of it includes showing God's love through practical ministries. Such obvious good works as helping the poor, the sick, the aged, the oppressed, orphans—churches have done a lot of work in these areas over the centuries.

Showing God's love to the world involves much more than such charitable activity however. It also involves spreading the truths of Christ, the teachings of Christ. This involves not only the presentation of such vital doctrines as the Trinity, the virgin birth, and the death, resurrection, and the return of Christ. It also involves opposition to false doctrines and teachings that oppose biblical truth.

Paul did not only preach basic truths, though he did that with great spiritual power. He also opposed false doctrines that led people away from the truth. This is referred to as "the pulling down of strongholds; Casting down imaginations, and every high thing that exalts itself against the knowledge of God," as it says in II Corinthians. Thus, Paul spoke against the teaching that there was no resurrection from the dead; that Christians needed to keep Jewish ceremonial laws; that the resurrection had occurred already.

Paul would have been a pitiful evangelist if he had kept silent in the face of the teaching "There is no resurrection from the dead." Jesus also did not merely present safely general truths—he opposed those who obscured the truth, who led people astray with false teachings. John the Baptist and the Old Testament prophets did the same.

The German churches fell short in all areas. There was little or no love shown toward the world (which includes the Jews) and there was little or no public declaration of basic biblical truths to the lost. True, the government wouldn't have allowed it, but even during the much freer Weimar era general histories have not recorded any strong proclamations of Christian teaching. If there were any, and there must have been some, even if only a few, the majority of Germans (like most Americans) wanted nothing to do with gospel truths. The message that we are guilty of sin and headed for an eternity separated from God without the forgiveness found through Christ was anathema not only to the Nazi government, but to unbelievers as well—and even to many nominal or liberal Christians.

The false teachings that were leading the Germans astray were also insufficiently opposed. If Christians in Germany had stood more boldly for the truth, which with rare exceptions they did not, they would have informed the German people of the resurrection from the dead; of the day of judgment; of an eternity in heaven or hell after this life; of our guilt before God; of our need for the forgiveness of sins available through Christ. They would have stressed that the Bible, in the Old and New Testaments, was the inspired and inerrant word of God. They would have denied that the Old Testament was nothing but Jewish stories and affirmed that Hitler was mistaken when he said in *Mein Kampf* that the Jews never had their own country, and only borrowed their religious ideas from surrounding peoples.

Christians applying God's truth to the world around them would have pointed out long before 1933 that racial purity and Aryan supremacy were unbiblical concepts; that the entire human race, Jew and Gentile, was all under sin; that Gentiles were inherently no different from and no better than Jews; that it would profit a German nothing if his fatherland gained national power and glory on earth, while he himself was cast into hell. It would have been pointed out that National Socialism had nothing to do with the real meaning of life; that it was National Socialism, and not Christianity, that thoroughly falsified life and was in fact anti-humanity.

Christians genuinely concerned with the Gospel of Christ, the Good News of Christ, would have pointed out that loving your neighbor as yourself, and doing unto others as you would have them do unto you, applied to Jews also. They would have explained that there was no such thing as a "master race"; that those who practiced hatred, cruelty, evil and lies would inevitably receive the just condemnation of an angry God for their evil unless they repented, and turned from their evil ways; that Hitler himself was in danger of judgment and in need of both repentance and acts demonstrative of repentance, that he might find salvation in Christ.

Such preaching, relying on the power of truth alone, would have seriously hindered Hitler's rise to power if there had been enough of it. If enough Germans had believed those doctrines, Hitler would have been permanently confined to the lunatic fringe—possibly even locked up for a very long time or even executed after his attempt to seize power in 1923. But, this sort of biblical preaching was not present in Germany to any significant extent. A detailed study of this issue, Lowell Green's *Lutherans Against Hitler*, shows many leading churchmen engaging in intricate theological debates but not directly condemning the evil staring them in the face. It was not Green's intent to be negative, but I found obscure and abstract debates among theologians while the fires were raging around them to be insufferably tedious.

Speculating on the reasons for this silence, we can find a number of causes: loss of basic doctrines and scriptural authority; dependence on the state; allowing people who were joined to the church in infancy to remain church members for life with no concern for their doctrines or manner of life; concern more for this world than the one that is to come; naked fear—but the point here is not to condemn. The Christians in Germany behaved as ordinary people would, and we would do the same unless God gave us grace. The point is not to criticize but to clarify the relationship between Naziism and the churches.

The real problem was that the Spirit of Christ was insufficiently present. Many of the churches were very weak—others were dead, totally lifeless behind their great ecclesiastical edifices. That a church can have pastors, seminaries, buildings, choirs, congregations, all of the outward appearances of a church, yet still be dead, is a biblical truth. Revelation describes such a church, the church of Sardis. It had the name of a church, but was in fact dead. Many churches in America today are dead, and others are dying.

It is possible for two people to have a dead marriage. They are legally married, live together, have the outward appearance before the world of a marriage, but care nothing for each other, dislike each other, cheat on each other freely, and have no real husband and wife relationship. Someone can also have the outward appearance of health, yet have a rapidly growing brain tumor that will unexpectedly manifest itself and bring a quick death.

What we see in the support of Christians for Hitler or in their silence, then, is not evidence of a connection between Naziism and Christianity. On the contrary, what we see is Christians failing for whatever reason to stand for Christ, to proclaim biblical truths, and to show God's love to all, including Jews, in a very cruel world.

Romans 13—the authority of government and the sovereignty of God

This leads to a complex question. Romans chapter 13 teaches that God ordains the authorities: "Let every soul be subject unto the higher powers. For there is no power but of God: the powers that be are ordained of God." Didn't this Christian teaching encourage, even require the German Christians to submit to Hitler? Some theoretically orthodox German Christians used that excuse—but were they justified in so doing?

The purpose of government as ordained by God and described in Romans is to regulate society, to maintain order by punishing and controlling evil. This is evident from another part of the same passage which says that the authorities have the power of the sword from God to punish evil. This plan is distorted and corrupted in this fallen world (like so many other things), but it remains the real purpose of government—and it is easy to see that without this controlling function of government, society would be in chaos and civilization would be impossible. Governments have however been granted no authority over spiritual matters or religious beliefs. Christians are never supposed to submit their consciences and their beliefs to the dictates of government—in fact, they are specifically commanded not to do so. "We must obey God rather than man," as Peter said.

When a government requires Christians to violate the commands of Christ it has exceeded its boundaries and we have no obligation to submit. This is not a justification for revolution, as we see Christ, the apostles, and the early Christians patiently enduring government persecution. Christians in Germany who were sincere in their love of Christ and in their desire to please him did not have the slightest obligation to give assent to doctrines they knew to be false. They had the right to stand for biblical teaching—but this would have brought fiery persecution. Those who suffered for Christ would have obtained a more glorious resurrection.

They also would have helped to eliminate much of the subsequent confusion about the relationship of Christianity to National Socialism. That the vast majority of German Christians did not take this course is testimony either to spiritual weakness and cowardice, or to total unbelief. Many Germans who liked for whatever reason to hang around in churches did not believe in or understand these teachings.

Also, the idea of being obedient to the authorities is not one we can apply subjectively. It is not only those governments we happen to like that have been ordained by God. If the German Christians had really believed that the authorities were ordained by God and should for that reason be obeyed, they would have supported the Weimar government. More of this attitude would have prevented Hitler from coming to power in the first place. German "Christians" who were hostile to the Weimar government and worked or hoped for its overthrow, and then said "We should obey Hitler as the authorities are ordained by God" were guilty of a blatant inconsistency.

Some other concepts in this passage on government also have great relevance for an understanding of the situation of the Christians under Hitler. For example, it says:

> For rulers are not a terror to good works, but to the evil. Will you then not be afraid of the power? Do that which is good, and you shall have praise of the same:
>
> For he is the minister of God to you for good. But if you do that which is evil, be afraid; for he bears not the sword in vain: for he is the minister of God, a revenger to execute wrath upon him that does evil.

How could Christians who did good receive praise of the authorities in Nazi Germany? How could the Nazi government be a minister of God to Christians for good? Wasn't Hitler a terror to good works, to good people? It seems impossible to apply this passage to Christians in the Third Reich, but it is necessary to note that Paul was not writing to the world at large. He was writing, as it says in the opening sentences of the first chapter of the letter, to the saints of God; to people who had experienced the power of God to salvation; who knew that the world lies in wickedness, but believed and knew they had been chosen and called of God; who understood that to die was gain; who believed that the hairs of their heads were numbered by God.

They had faith that their times were in God's hands and believed they would not die until it was God's time for them to go to a better world. They did not fear those that could only destroy the body, but after that had nothing more that they could do. They knew what the Bible meant when it said "Fear none of those things which you will suffer," and could endure torture, "not accepting deliverance; that they might obtain a better resurrection," as it says in Hebrews. The believers to whom Paul was writing understood the words in Philippians, ". . . in nothing terrified by your adversaries: which is to them an evident token of perdition . . . ."

Not only did they not fear death and suffering. They were able to rejoice (with God's help) if they were made partakers of Christ's sufferings, and glorify God when they suffered for his sake, as God speaking through Peter said: "if any man suffer as a Christian, let him not be ashamed; but let him glorify God on this behalf." He also says:

> Beloved, think it not strange concerning the fiery trial which is to try you, as though some strange thing happened unto you:
> But rejoice, inasmuch as you are partakers of Christ's sufferings; that, when his glory shall be revealed, ye may be glad also with exceeding joy.

As to having the praise of the authorities when we do well, this is part of God's purpose for government. Since, however, God gives people latitude to obey him or not, the true purpose of government is often lost, distorted, or totally perverted. This was the case in Nazi Germany where evil was rewarded and good was punished. Thus we see in Nazi Germany a perversion of all of life, including government. Hitler's wickedness does not, however, invalidate scripture, since even the hatred and persecution of evil men works to the glory and praise of God, and of the righteous who suffer for Christ. Peter wrote in the passage just cited above that we can rejoice when we suffer for Christ. The persecution and hatred of the wicked is also to the praise and honor of Christ.

Peter and Paul were writing to a small group of devoted followers of Christ who had a peace that the world could not give or take away. Jesus even said that those who are persecuted for his sake are blessed and supremely happy, though this is folly and stupidity to the world. Unbelievers at that time might have contrasted Herod in his glory with John the Baptist in a dungeon and imagined that the former was better off, but they had no understanding of the world to come. With this in mind we can understand that Hitler or other worldly powers of evil are "not a terror to good works."

What about Hitler as an authority ordained by God, though? If God ordained Hitler, how can he escape the charge of being evil and doing evil? It says in the book of Daniel that God "changes the times and the seasons: he removes kings, and sets up kings." It also says that "the most High rules in the kingdom of men, and gives it to whomsoever he will, and sets up over it the basest of men." Was that true just for Bible times but not today? Many Christians do have that attitude, even if they don't like to state it openly. "That was true then," they think, "but this is the real world we are talking about here." Also, wasn't God in the Old Testament dealing with the nation of Israel in a special way that does not necessarily have to extend to the whole world?

God did deal with Old Testament Israel in a special way, but does it follow that he does not govern the rest of the world at all? That major historical occurrences are the products only of human will or blind chance? Many Christians today do have a God who does only good things, like save people from sin and receive them into heaven, or help them with a problem, a job, or an illness. The God of the Bible who rules over the world has been lost, however. Many Christians who flatter themselves on their orthodoxy do have a very feeble and shallow idea of God.

Couldn't God have caused Hitler to be killed in World War I? Hitler was in the thick of some of the most destructive battles in the history of the world, yet he survived while people all around him were slaughtered. Couldn't God have caused Hitler to drop dead of a heart attack after the war? God could easily have removed

Hitler at any time but decided not to. Was it because God was helpless, powerless to intervene, or because God was subject to human free will and unable to override it, that Hitler was allowed to survive, and flourish, and magnify himself to such an astonishing height of evil? Or was it because Hitler was in some way part of the grand scheme of things? Hitler was not allowed to win, but what if he was allowed to act for a time, and the limits were precisely set, to the day and to the hour?

Hebrews teaches that God sustains "all things by the word of his power." Does he sustain them without knowing, without seeing, without a plan or a purpose? At the same time, we have to assert the biblical principle of God's holiness. He cannot do evil or even be tempted with evil. But, if God wanted to send his wrath on a corrupt and decadent Europe, all he needed to do was to remove his restraining hand and allow Satan to work. World Wars I and II can then be seen as the work of the devil himself—and God can allow evil for a time, setting its boundaries and limits, before he finally destroys it at the end of the world.

Within the biblical system, we can recognize evil as being truly evil, and attribute it to Satan and to human sin. We can at the same time however recognize God's higher authority over it, and see that nothing happens apart from God's larger purposes. We should also not forget the final day of judgment. There will come a time when those who did evil on earth and got away with it will stand before a higher court. There will be no tricky attorneys, legal loopholes, or incompetent judges. A perfect and final rendering will be given to all evildoers who have not received God's mercy and forgiveness, and the strictest requirements of justice will be fully satisfied. God will be vindicated, and sin and evil will be forever destroyed.

These and other concepts may not be agreeable to us, but they are consistent with scripture. Moreover, we can thank the goodness and mercy of God that Hitler was not allowed to win the war and rule the world. Those who have faith can see the finger of God in the mighty alliance of powers that combined to bring Hitler down—while those who do not have the eyes of faith will of course see all of this as merely human activity.

Along with God's actual and present-day sovereignty (as opposed to his theoretical Sunday-school-chat sovereignty), another concept that has been lost is the God of wrath. For those who are outside of Christ (I am referring to the world as a whole), the Old Testament God is still very much on the throne. He is a God who gives life, and has a right to take it. Here are some verses from the prophets pertaining to God's wrath:

> I will gather them out of all countries, whither I have driven them in mine anger, and in my fury, and in my great wrath . . .

> Therefore is the anger of the Lord kindled against his people, and he has stretched forth his hand against them, and has smitten them: and the hills did tremble, and their carcasses were torn in the midst of the streets. For all this his anger is not turned away, but his hand is stretched out still.

Therefore thus says the Lord, Behold, I will bring evil upon them, which they shall not be able to escape; and though they shall cry unto me, I will not hearken to them.

And I will pour out mine indignation upon you, I will blow against you in the fire of my wrath, and deliver you into the hand of brutish men, and skilful to destroy.
You shall be fuel for the fire; your blood shall be in the midst of the land; you shall be no more remembered: for I the Lord have spoken it.

Why do you cry for your affliction? your sorrow is incurable for the multitude of your iniquity: because your sins were increased, I have done these things unto you.

If God wanted to bring wrath on complacent, conceited, and ignorant Europe, and Hitler was his instrument to do so, he remains God whether we disapprove or not. We conform ourselves to him, he does not conform himself to us. In Ezekiel God also says that he will leave a few survivors "from the sword, from the famine, and from the pestilence." The same book says that God directly sends these things and they will not cease until God's fury is accomplished—and were not disease, hunger, and violence (using "sword" metaphorically) the main causes of death in Europe's devastating wars? "Brutish men, and skilful to destroy"— weren't the Nazi brutes exceedingly skilful at destruction? It has already been said that God does not do evil—but if he removes his protecting hand and allows Satan to work, that is biblical.

It may be objected that Ezekiel was a prophet for Old Testament times, while in Christ we have a higher revelation of God. But, if the Old Testament is not the true word of God, the entire New Testament falls to the ground like a house of cards. If the Old Testament is the word of God, as sincere followers of Christ believe it to be, did God have the power to do those things then, but not now? Since Christ rose from the dead, has God lost his authority over those who reject Christ and are outside of Christ?

Also, where was God during these titanic events of the 20th century? Was he absent? Indifferent? Helpless? Out of control? Did Hitler, Stalin, Roosevelt, and Churchill shape the destinies of mankind while God sat on the sidelines? Those of us who believe in the Bible would instantly reject someone who said "God does not do good in the world." Such an inactive God is worthless—we might just as well be atheists. But, does God only do what we call good? Is he only allowed to act in areas and in ways that we approve of, as if our understandings were the measure to which God must conform himself? Or, is God allowed to give us freedom to act within certain limits, so that our good might be truly good, and our evil might be truly evil?

It says in Zephaniah that God will punish people who say "The Lord will not do good, neither will he do evil." Such people have devised a God of their own imagination, a weak, paltry God that is not the God of scripture. God himself cannot be tainted with the most minute particle of evil, but since evil has come into the world God does in some way that we do not know have the power to regulate it and set its limits. A detailed discussion of this is beyond the scope of

219

this essay. Briefly, we can say that God could have easily prevented Hitler from coming to power if he had chosen to, but did not.

God's plan includes giving Satan some authority on earth. The devil is able to act for a time, but always within strict limits. Thus Hitler, although he was magnified by Satan for a short time, was not allowed to win the war and conquer the world. The evil that he did do will be exposed and properly dealt with on the day of judgment. There will be a final vindication of God's justice.

In the meantime, Christians are under no obligation according to the Bible to submit to the state on spiritual matters. On the contrary, they are obligated to do the opposite. If they fail to do so, it is the result of their choice and their sin, not of biblical teaching—and it should be repeated that the purpose here is not to condemn. It is to clarify. We are told in the Bible not to judge, but we are also commanded to discern. We can discern without judging, and recognize that Romans 13 in no way requires us to lie about our beliefs, keep them hidden, or violate the commandments of Christ. As to those who failed to stand as they should have, here we must recognize that their actions were the result of ordinary human nature, not of the New Testament.

A Christmas in Nazi Germany

In December of 1939 William Russell, an official at the American Embassy in Berlin, went for a short vacation in Germany's Harz Mountains. He stayed with "the friend of a friend" in a house in the countryside, and had a peaceful, idyllic holiday.

On Christmas morning he skied down to the village with his host and went to the local church. As he related in his book *Berlin Embassy,*

> A crowd of villagers stood outside the door, talking in the brilliant sunshine. In Berlin, Sunday finds no such crowds of people around the church doors. The Party trains the children to look down on the church and on religion. Every Sunday the Nazis carefully plan a program of morning activity for the Hitler Youths and the Hitler Girls and those infants too young to belong to either organization.[109]

Russell went on to briefly describe the service. He mentioned the white candles, the stained glass, and said the little stone chapel "had a feeling of peace within its aged walls, and this peace seeped into our bodies and our hearts." About the sermon, Russell wrote: ". . . the theme of his talk was that the present war is the punishment of God for our falling away from Christ."[110]

Russell's book contains many other points of interest—for example, one of Goebbels' rules for filmmaking was "No films which glorify or mention the church." He mentions one film in which even the word "church" was removed from the dialogue by the censor.[111] Elsewhere he says that Hans Kerrl, the Reich Minister of Religion, was "frequently seen in Berlin dives until the wee hours of the morning." He relates that another worker at the embassy had seen "this leader of all German churches" very drunk and flirting with a waitress at 4 a.m.[112]

There are those who enjoy linking Christianity to Hitler, but when Christ appears in glory with his holy angels to bring judgment upon the world, then it will be clearly seen who was a Christian and who was not, what Christianity was and what it was not.

Christians in other lands

In Nazi occupied Europe, where there was more possibility of action, there are more examples of Christians whose obedience to the teachings of Christ led not to persecution but to the reverse. These examples, though too few and too rare, show how biblical Christianity can help people to transcend the forces of evil.

One famous example is that of Pastor Andre Trocme. He and his wife Magda, and many others in the small French village of Le Chambon, helped to save many Jews, providing them with food, lodging, and false documents. They felt it was their Christian duty to help anyone, Jewish or not. A moving account of this spiritual heroism is found in Philip Hallie's book *Lest Innocent Blood Be Shed: The Story of the Village of Le Chambon and How Goodness Happened There.*

One winter night a cold and hungry Jewish woman came to the pastor's door asking for help, literally risking her life to knock at a stranger's door. She was given food and shelter. Can anyone imagine her seeking out the home of a university professor of biology and asking him for help? "Please, sir, I understand you have written some books about Darwinism, and I need your help, I am a Jew, with nowhere to go"? And can one imagine the professor saying "The teaching of survival-of-the-fittest tells me I must help my fellow-man"? Survival-of-the-fittest tells me to look out for number one.

Sources record the attempts to help Jewish refugees made by Christian groups such as the YMCA, the American Friends Service Committee, and others. I have not yet found reference to groups of Darwinists in America or England saying that their philosophy compelled them to be concerned about suffering and starving people in other parts of the world. What a joke. Darwinism is fundamentally, necessarily, and essentially inhumane. If people starve to death or perish from illness or violence, that's just the way life is. We are only animals after all, with no immortal souls, no spark of the divine, and nothing in essence to distinguish us from the beasts. We don't get excited if other animals are dying—why the *unscientific* species bias in favor of people?

This is not to say that only Christians took risks to help others. That would be an absurd oversimplification. There were Christians who did nothing, and non-Christians who helped at great risk to themselves—but the non-Christians followed a basic human impulse that was inarticulate, without foundation. The Christians were acting out of obedience to Christ.

There are other instances too many to record here. Stephen of Sofia, the Greek Orthodox Metropolitan of Bulgaria, publicly declared it was wrong to torture and persecute Jews, and Boris III, king of Bulgaria, had wide popular support in his resistance to German demands that the Jews be deported.[113] The Dutch were also more outspoken than is widely known in publicly objecting to Nazi persecutions. Friedländer refers to a student strike in Holland in 1940 as well as to public and official protests from some (not all) Protestant and Catholic churches.

In this context, Friedländer states "Historically puzzling is the fact that almost *none* of this [public protest] occurred in France."[114] It is less puzzling if we consider the expulsion of the French Huguenots and the reliance on political power to prop up a state church by brute force, in complete defiance of all of the most essential teachings of biblical Christianity.

221

Actions like those few just mentioned would have been impossible in Nazi Germany. An entire village conspiring to hide Jews, or organized and public protests, would have met with drastic retribution in Germany. This raises the question as to why such virulent evil should have arisen in Germany. Denmark, Sweden, Norway, Finland, and Holland also had Lutheran traditions, yet their lack of enthusiasm for demented Nazi racial phobias is well known. Surely, if Naziism's bizarre ideas came out of Christianity, then other nations should have been similarly affected.

Answering this will require the more lengthy examination attempted in the following chapters. Here, though, it is appropriate to state that one of the main factors was Germany's vastly greater power and wealth. This inflamed the Germans with pride and the lust for dominion to which smaller countries were immune. This lust for power led to the catastrophe of the First World War, and inflamed yet more passions of revenge and hatred unknown to countries with less turbulent histories. This confirms the Christian teaching that it is better to live a quiet life of peacefulness and simplicity than to have great wealth and power with all sorts of turmoil and evil passions.

A final point is the drastic differences between the western countries and eastern countries such as Poland, Lithuania, and the Ukraine. There was much more enthusiastic cooperation with the Germans in the Final Solution in the east than in the west—why? It seems reasonable to speculate that the more oppressive and violent recent histories of the eastern countries infected the people with hatred and bitterness, and the churches too succumbed, following the world rather than resisting it.

> *Therefore whosoever heareth these sayings of mine, and doeth them, I will liken him unto a wise man, which built his house upon a rock;*
> *And the rain descended, and the floods came, and the winds blew, and beat upon that house; and it fell not: for it was founded upon a rock.*
> *And everyone that heareth these sayings of mine, and doeth them not, shall be likened unto a foolish man, which built his house upon the sand:*
> *And the rain descended, and the floods came, and the winds blew, and beat upon that house; and it fell: and great was the fall of it. (Matthew)*

---

[1] Richard Evans, *The Coming of the Third Reich* (New York 2005), p. 424.

[2] Peter Gay, *Weimar Culture: The Outsider as Insider* (New York 1968), p. 242.

[3] Paul Johnson, *Modern Times: The World from the Twenties to the Nineties* (New York 1991), p. 114.

[4] Ibid., p. 114.

[5] Evans, p. 445.

[6] William L. Shirer, *The Rise and Fall of the Third Reich* (New York 1960), p. 4.

[7] Ibid., p. 3.

[8] Evans, p. 314.

[9] Ian Kershaw, *Hitler, 1889-1936: Hubris* (New York 2000), pp. 404, 413.

[10] Shirer, pp. 399, 597-598.

[11] Friedrich Reck-Malleczewen, *Diary of a Man in Despair*, trans. Paul Rubens (London 1995), p. 179. This is not to deny the fact of Hitler's popularity, it is to qualify it.

[12] Leo Stein, "Niemoller Speaks," The National Jewish Monthly May 1941. *Homepage of Harold Marcuse*; http://www.history.ucsb.edu/faculty/marcuse/projects /niem/njm415/NatJewMonthly415.htm; accessed May 2007. In his biography *Martin Niemöller*, James Bentley asserts that Stein's narrative was fraudulent. Had he conclusively refuted it, I would have deleted references to it.

[13] Kershaw, pp. 357, 410.

[14] Evans, pp. 448-449. The speech to the businessmen is referred to on p. 245.

[15] Bernt Engelmann, *In Hitler's Germany: Everyday Life in the Third Reich*, trans. Krishna Winston (New York 1986), pp. 52, 44.

[16] Shirer, pp. 273, 203.

[17] Ibid., p. 1025.

[18] Saul Friedländer, *The Years of Extermination: Nazi Germany and the Jews 1939-1945* (London 2007), pp. 177-178.

[19] Ibid., p. 192.

[20] Engelmann, p. 59.

[21] Ibid., p. 61.

[22] John Conway, *The Nazi Persecution of the Churches 139-1945* (Vancouver 1968), p. 122.

[23] Ibid. p. 375.

[24] Lowell C. Green, *Lutherans Against Hitler* (St. Louis 2007), pp. 145-146, 285-186. Green gives no further details about the Catholics.

[25] Conway, pp. 278-283.

[26] Ibid., p. 282.

[27] Ibid., p. 270.

[28] Ibid., p. 269.

[29] Ibid., p. 272.

[30] Joachim Fest, *Hitler*, trans. Richard and Clara Winston (New York 1974), p. 532.

[31] Peter Viereck, *Meta-politics: The Roots of the Nazi Mind* (New York 1965), p. 284.

[32] Conway, p. 112.

[33] Ibid., p. 421.

[34] Ibid., p. 167.

[35] Ibid., p. 287.

[36] Ibid.

[37] Ibid., p. 169

[38] Ibid., p. 260.

[39] Ibid.

[40] Ibid., p. 277.

[41] Ibid., p. 285.

[42] Ibid., p. 100.

[43] Ibid.

[44] Ibid., p. 205.

[45] Ibid., p. 208.

[46] Ibid., p. 209. Reports of Paul Schneider's refusal to conform even under the tortures that killed him can be read in Claude R. Foster's *Paul Schneider: The Buchenwald Apostle* (West Chester University Press), and Don Stephens' *War and Grace: Short Biographies from the World Wars* (Evangelical Press). A newly released book about Paul Schneider is Rudolf Wentorf's *Witness of Buchenwald*, trans. Daniel Bloesch, (Vancouver 2008).

[47] James Bentley, *Martin Niemöller* (London 1984), p. 145.

[48] Conway, p. 253.

[49] Ibid.

[50] Richard Steigmann-Gall, *The Holy Reich: Nazi Conceptions of Christianity, 1919-1945* (Cambridge 2004), p. 5.

[51] Conway, p. 127.

[52] Ibid., p. 58.

[53] Ibid., p. 113.

[54] Ibid., p. 422.

[55] William L. Shirer, *Berlin Diary* (New York 1941), p. 76.

[56] Conway, p. 258.

[57] Ibid., p. 257.

[58] Ibid., p. 94.

[59] Viereck, p. 259. Lutheran ministers also wore black robes.

[60] "Pre-1933 Nazi Posters, *German Propaganda Archive*, Calvin College; http://www.calvin.edu/academic/cas/gpa/posters1.htm; accessed January 2008.

[61] Adolf Hitler, *Hitler's Second Book: The Unpublished Sequel to Mein Kampf*, trans. Krista Smith (New York 2006), p. 60.

[62] Bentley, p. 70.

[63] Conway, p. 99.

[64] Steigmann-Gall, p. 74.

[65] Conway, pp. 58-59.

[66] Ibid., p. 75.

[67] Ibid., pp. 75, 160.

[68] The Swiss-German theologian Karl Barth played a critical role in the formulation of the Barmen Declaration. For a brief but interesting examination of his theological liberalism and his tendency to use religious language while denying the historicity of the Bible, see Barry Hankins' *Francis Schaeffer and the Shaping of Evangelical America* (Grand Rapids, MI 2008), pp. 38-41.

[69] Kershaw, p. 435.

[70] Conway, p. 162.

[71] Ibid., p. 164.

[72] Ibid.

73 Ibid.

74 Ibid., p. 340.

75 Green, p. 45, quoting *Kirchliche Zeitschrift*.

76 Conway, p. 94.

77 David L. Edwards, "Rudolf Bultmann: Scholar of Faith," *Religion Online: Christian Century*, September 1-8, 1976, pp. 728-730; http://www.religion-online.org/showarticle.asp?title=1827; accessed May 2007.

78 James Kay, review of Christian Faith in Dark Times: Theological Conflicts in the Shadow of Hitler by Jack Forstman, *Theology Today* 50, no. 4 (1993); http://theologytoday.ptsem.edu/jan1994/v50-4-bookreview6.htm; accessed May 2007.

79 Bentley, p. 43.

80 Francis Schaeffer, *The Great Evangelical Disaster* (Westchester, IL 1984), pp. 37, 35.

81 Conway, p. 7.

82 Ibid., p. 61.

83 Ibid., p. 326.

84 Martin Gilbert, *The Holocaust: A History of the Jews of Europe During the Second World War* (New York 1985) p. 623.

85 Ibid., p. 70.

86 Shirer, *Rise and Fall*, p. 435.

87 Conway, p. 262.

88 John Conway, review of *Elisabeth Schmitz und ihre Denkschrift gegen die Judenverfolgung. Konturen einer vergessenen Biographie* (1893-1977), ed. Manfred Gailus, Association of Contemporary Church Historians (Arbeitsgemeinschaft kirchlicher Zeitgeschichtler) Newsletter Vol.XIV, no 11 (November 2008); http://www.calvin.edu/academic/cas/akz/; accessed November 2008.

89 Conway, *Nazi Persecution of the Churches*, p. 262.

90 David J. Diephouse, "Antisemitism as Moral Discourse: Theophil Wurm and Protestant Opposition to the Holocaust," paper presented to the 30th Annual Scholar's Conference on the Holocaust and the Churches, Philadelphia, March 2000, p.4 [page numbers are from document sent by Prof. Diephouse as an e-mail attachment].

91 Ibid., p. 9.

92 Gilbert, p. 591.

93 Ibid.

94 Victor Klemperer, *I Will Bear Witness: A Diary of the Nazi Years 1942-1945* (New York 2001), p. 294.

95 Diephouse, p. 6. Diephouse cites the *Landeskirchliches Archiv Stuttgart* and also *Landesbischof Wurm*, ed. Gerhard Schaefer. Some of the comments quoted from Gilbert were from this same letter of July 16th, but he uses in two paragraphs letters from different dates without precisely indicating which was which.

96 Conway, pp. 264-265.

97 Ibid., p. 265.

98 Diephouse, p. 6.

99 Friedländer, p. 517.

[100] Conway, p. 266.

[101] Ibid., pp. 266-267.

[102] Ibid., p. 264.

[103] Ibid.

[104] Ibid., p. 263.

[105] Robert Michael, "Theological Myth, German Antisemitism, and the Holocaust: The Case of Martin Niemoeller," *Holocaust and Genocide Studies: An International Journal* 2, no. 1 (1987): 105-22.

[106] Bentley, p. 67. This seems to be the same sermon as the one just referred to, but neither source gives specific information.

[107] In early writings such as *Creation and Fall*, or *Christ the Center*, Bonhoeffer shows that he was in the mainstream of theological liberalism when it came to the inerrancy of scripture.

[108] Matthew Hockenos, Review of The Reluctant Revolutionary: Dietrich Bonhoeffer's Collision with Prusso-German History, by John A. Moses; *Association of Contemporary Church Historians (Arbeitsgemeinschaft kirchlicher Zeitgeschichtler) Newsletter* vol. XV, no. 7 (July 2009); http://www.calvin.edu/academic/cas/akz/akz2907.htm; accessed July 2009.

[109] William Russell, *Berlin Embassy* (New York 2005), p. 144.

[110] Ibid.

[111] Ibid., p. 190.

[112] Ibid., p. 187.

[113] Robert S. Wistrich, *Hitler and the Holocaust: How and Why the Holocaust Happened* (London 2002), pp. 169-170. See also Friedländer, pp. 484-485.

[114] Friedländer, p. 125.

PART II: The Origins of National Socialism

Chapter 5. The philosophical background

The mystery of Hitler

In his book *Explaining Hitler*, journalist Ron Rosenbaum comes to the conclusion that there is as yet no real explanation to the mystery of how Hitler became such a towering figure of evil. After interviewing renowned scholars and historians, experts in the fields of Hitler and Holocaust studies, Rosenbaum concludes that the missing explanation is "locked up tight in the inaccessible, indecipherable mind of God."[1]

In the course of the book, Rosenbaum and the people he interviews raise many questions. Did Hitler have free will, or was he merely the inevitable product of larger social forces? Would the same things have happened if Hitler had never lived? Did he sincerely believe in his ideology, or was he only cynically manipulating the masses? Hitler was evil—but what is evil? Nazi death camp commandant Rudolf Hoess stated at the end of his prison memoirs that he was not an evil person. He tried to portray himself as a conscientious official who was only doing his duty.[2]

This is far from an exhaustive list of the many questions raised by Hitler. Should we stress such modern aspects of National Socialism as its masterful application of technology and bureaucracy, or should we describe it as a rebellion against modernism? Many have assumed there is no point in even trying to understand Hitler's bizarre ideas at all. It is thought that the Nazi ideology is so far removed from ordinary thought patterns and from Western culture as a whole as to defy real understanding. It would be much simpler to dismiss Hitler as a crackpot and leave it at that—but how does a crackpot become the leader of a modern Western state and persuade millions to do his will?

The need for a world view

It should be obvious that if we want to understand Hitler we need to have some kind of general understanding of life itself, a world view. How can we grapple with significant questions of right and wrong, good and evil, or human motivation and psychology if we do not have any understanding of life as a whole?

At this point we run into a seemingly insurmountable obstacle. If we try to understand Hitler and his ideas from the vantage point of a world view or belief about the meaning of life, who is to say that our belief or vantage point is the right one? There is no universal agreement on which view is right—hence, any interpretation of Hitler according to a specific viewpoint will not be convincing or acceptable to all.

If, of course, a deeper understanding of life is not possible; if we cannot ever know the real meaning of life; if life's meaning is either non-existent, or permanently concealed from us—then we must give up any attempt to understand Hitler on the deepest level. We can get some ideas and collect some information, but a final understanding is beyond us. All we can do is record the facts of what occurred and do our best to make sure it doesn't happen again.

As a Christian, I reject this misguided approach, this spiritual and philosophical defeatism. I believe that a higher and deeper understanding of the nature and purpose of life has been revealed to us by God in the Bible, that the Bible presents a clear and accurate picture of human life, its nature and its purpose. With this understanding, we can try to interpret the whole of life, not merely Hitler and the Holocaust. I don't mean that we can understand life exhaustively, in every detail—our minds are too small for that. I don't mean that we can be infallibly right either. General principles of God's revelation, though eternally true, leave a lot of room for variety (and for error) as we try to apply them to the riddles of life. Nevertheless, I believe it is in the light of the eternal truths of scripture that we need to consider the false philosophy of Hitler and his abominable crimes.

Many Holocaust scholars, experts, professors, theologians, historians, will automatically dismiss any attempt to study Hitler and National Socialism in this way. They want nothing to do with scriptural Christianity and accept it as a given that biblical teachings are irrelevant. They will continue going around in endless circles, futilely trying to discuss evil, sin, free will, psychology, ethics, morality, without any firmly defined understanding of spiritual realities.

One scholar was disturbed by the fact that the Holocaust had not yet found a fixed place in the consciousness of Western society—but how can it, when the reigning philosophy is "Do your own thing"? People who believe that life has no higher purpose, that we are essentially nothing more than animals who emerged by accident in a silent universe, cannot possibly integrate whatever lessons there might be learned from all of this into a higher system of values, because they have no real system. Ian Kershaw is right in asserting that "Only the application of constructs, concepts, and even theories which reside outside the sphere of historical experience can provide order to make sense of experience in a historical analysis."[3] That scriptural Christianity might provide such constructs and concepts is a possibility few are willing to consider in our misguided age.

Those who do not merely reject Christianity, but also refuse to admit the reality of any higher spiritual world, have no empirically verifiable data or laboratory experiments to substantiate their non-falsifiable faith opinions. They imagine that they are objective, but they are not. Others who do not dismiss the spiritual dimension altogether feel that it is beyond the boundaries of scholarly discourse. It is so subjective, so impossible to prove, and leads so quickly into interminable discussions that have no end or benefit, that it is best discussed privately, if at all. It certainly has no place in a scholarly work, they will argue, the purpose of scholarship being to assemble facts and draw conclusions from those facts—conclusions which, if not certain, are at least plausible, clearly related to facts and evidence at hand. According to this view, any effective analysis must be, as Kershaw claims, "confined to strictly scholarly parameters of analysis."[4]

To my mind, this approach to an understanding of Hitler and National Socialism precludes higher understanding from the outset. Surely such extraordinary results must be related to extraordinary causes, causes that are forever beyond the reach of those who fondly imagine we are nothing more than products of our environment, who leave insufficient place in their scholarly theories for human will, emotions, and understanding. Are those who argue that the Fuhrer was a "weak" dictator, solely the product of social forces, presenting the result of a very blinkered view of life rather than the result of objective historical study?

I believe that biblical teaching provides the most complete explanation for all of the various aspects of Hitler's ideology, and of the acts resulting from that ideology. Kershaw states, "Arguably, indeed, an *adequate* explanation of Naziism is an intellectual impossibility."[5] The point is indeed arguable, and it would be unwise to be too dogmatic in affirming or denying an explanation. How successful my own attempt might be is of course open to question. Nevertheless, I believe that if we transcend the arbitrary limitations of a narrow-minded secularism, we can attain to a higher degree of understanding than is commonly assumed. Incidentally, it doesn't follow that our ideas are wrong merely because people reject them. It also doesn't follow that what are today considered the proper scholarly parameters are eternal and inviolable parameters outside of which nothing worthwhile can be written. Solzhenitsyn defied scholarly convention by writing history with a deeply moral and personal dimension—that is one of the reasons his work *The Gulag Archipelago* was vastly more influential than a scholarly and boring work of mere historical fact could ever have been.

An analogy

We are familiar with the analogy of the blind men who tried to understand an elephant by touching it. Feeling different parts of the elephant, they came to different conceptions of what an elephant might be. This is significant for our study of Hitler. Many have tried to come to an understanding of Naziism by only looking at the parts—though many others it must be said have not blindly but rather deliberately concentrated on one area while recognizing the importance of others. Some are eager to link Hitler to Darwin, and notice the significant parallels between Hitler's ideology and Darwin's theory of the survival of the fittest.

Others have more of an interest in 19th-century German philosophy and find striking similarities between Hitler's ideas on government and national destiny and those of Hegel and Fichte. The Folkish movement (from the German word *Volk*, related to the English word "folk"), a loose collection of advocates of militarism, imperialism, racism, authoritarianism, and anti-Semitism also had much in common with National Socialism—some have sought for an explanation of Hitler there. The relationship between Hitler's ideas and Nietzsche's has been emphasized, as has the Hitler-Wagner connection. After all, Wagner was not only a composer but a prolific anti-Semitic political writer who expressed many of the ideas of National Socialism. The anti-Semitism of Kant has also been pointed to as a source of Hitler's ideas. Some have even completely ignored all of the essential teachings of Christ and the gospels, and then tried to link Hitler to Christianity.

Many seek more secular economic, political, or psychological explanations. They want to confine themselves to what they imagine is certain and sure knowledge as opposed to endless speculation. The Marxists attempted this sort of an explanation, blaming Naziism and fascism on capitalism. Wilhelm Reich saw fascism as a collective psychological response to "the oppressions of capitalism and sexual repression."[6]

This essay argues that National Socialism, however bizarre its conclusions, was based on an intellectually comprehensible foundation and followed a discernible logic. It agrees in general with the thesis presented by Prof. Mosse in his book *The Crisis of German Ideology*. Prof. Mosse demonstrates that essential elements of Naziism were evident in respectable circles in Germany long before 1933. It is necessary to look at German history and thought in order to discern more clearly the roots of National Socialism.

The attempts to subjugate Europe and exterminate the Jews were the results of a clearly thought out and well articulated ideology. Spiritually, we can assign this ideology to Satan and to human sin—yet these were at work in the peculiar philosophical, spiritual, political and historical circumstances of Germany. How was Hitler's philosophy worked out and developed over the course of more than a century? What we need is the genealogy of an ideology.

The complexity of such a genealogy is readily apparent. Racism, nationalism, militarism, imperialism, fascism, anti-Semitism; the works of a number of thinkers who did not cause National Socialism but who helped to create a cultural climate conducive to it; historical, economic, and political factors; the decline of traditional religion in the 19th century and the resultant search for substitutes—all of these need to be taken into account.   It should be stressed that these will need to be considered in the context of German culture and history. Since National Socialism flourished in no other country, it was undeniably German. Failure to take this point into account has led to numerous oversimplifications about the relationship of National Socialism to Christianity. As to those who feel that there is no point in even trying to understand Hitler's tortured thought processes, they give up too easily. Hitler did not, after all, come out of nowhere. There are definite links between his thoughts and actions and the philosophies of those who came before him. Hitler was a man of his time, and his ideas had deep roots in German culture. In the words of economist F. A. Hayek,   "It is a common mistake to regard National Socialism as a mere revolt against reason, an irrational movement without intellectual background . . . The doctrines of National Socialism are the culmination of a long evolution of thought, a process in which thinkers who have had great influence far beyond the confines of Germany have taken part."[7]

The role of technology

What might be called "the wandering star of imperial dominion" came to rest over Germany in the 19th and 20th centuries. The Germans rose from being a small and weak collection of states to greater and greater heights of power, finally establishing a mighty empire. Something similar has been seen many times in history—yet there were a couple of dark and terrible differences that separated Germany from other great conquering nations of the past: those two differences were technology and ideology.

It would be foolish to blame the Holocaust or the rise of Naziism on technology. After all, many countries have experienced complete modernization without turning into fascist nightmare states. At the same time, it would be foolish to deny the fact that it was technology that gave the Nazi regime its terrible power. If the Nazis had not had railroads, they could not have transported Jews to designated killing points from all over Europe. The existence of the means contributed to the conception of the idea. If the means of transportation had not existed, the idea could not have been conceived. Moreover, if the Germans had had to rely on bows, arrows, swords, and spears, their ability to destroy would have been vastly diminished. It was technology which exponentially increased the destructive power of evil men.

I can be forgiven for making such elementary observations as it seems that reasonable implications are not always drawn from these facts. The modern industrial and scientific revolution empowered the perpetrators of the Holocaust to conceive and to commit previously unimaginable crimes. This is ignored by some who automatically (and unthinkingly) exempt modernism from fundamental criticism. Superficial criticisms of modernism are acceptable, but nothing that cuts too deep.

National Socialism was not only uniquely German, it was also uniquely modern. Without the rise of the nation state; without the power of airplanes, railroads, radio, barbed wire, machine guns, tanks, and gas chambers; without the modern ideologies that fed upon the hunger left by the abandonment of traditional religion—without all of these the Third Reich could never have occurred. It was the misfortune of the Germans, and of the peoples around them, that the Germans in their hour of greatness had military power undreamed of by any other previous conquering nations in history.

Can it be said that the Germans went to greater extremes of cruelty partly at least because they had the means to do so? If the Mongols (who made pyramids of human skulls) or the Vikings (who enjoyed warfare and considered it a normal part of life) had had access to the blessings of modern technology, who knows what they might have been capable of?

Of course, the Germans did not only have technology. They also had an ideology. It was this ideology that guided them to heights of cruelty and spiritual delusion equaled and even surpassed in some ways by the Soviets, but unknown before the modern era. There have been deluded and violent men throughout history, but they did not have the vast power of a modern nation state at their disposal. They also did not have the beliefs that pitiless cruelty was a virtue, that slaughtering millions of people was for the good of mankind. Can we describe the Nazis as nothing more than Vikings or Mongols, their lust for cruelty, conquest and war sanctified by a warped ideology and exponentially augmented by the power of modern technology?

The Holocaust, as unique as it was, as terrible as it was, can still be placed within the traditional Christian framework. The age-old sins of hatred, lies, cruelty, callousness, cowardice, inhumanity, fear, devotion to a false ideal, theft, murder—all of these manifested themselves for the nth time in the Holocaust and were, in fact, nothing new. These basic sins were, however, magnified to an extent previously unknown because of the enabling power of technology. Science, supposedly the hope of mankind and guide to a better future, turned out, in this case, to be the exact opposite. Education and emancipated human wisdom, by eliminating concepts of sin, judgment, and the fear of God, allowed human passions to become inflamed to a previously unknown degree. Thus, one of the deepest and darkest lessons of Hitler and his crimes, and one of the most difficult to grasp, is that the entire modernist project of improving humanity by eliminating religion and relying on science and reason alone is a foolish mistake of gigantic proportions. It is also an ongoing mistake that has continued to manifest itself in the corruption of civilization in new ways since 1945.

Some Russian history

There are more specific historical precedents that illustrate the ordinary evil passions that lay behind much of Hitler's achievement. They show that Hitler was to some extent only a vastly more powerful example of a certain type previously known to history. For example, in his book *Russian Rebels: 1600-1800*, Paul Avrich makes a number of comments about the origins, leaders, and events of pre-revolutionary Russian peasant rebellions. The bloody histories of Ivan Bolotnikov, Stenka Razin, Kondrati Bulavin, and Emelian Pugachev are pertinent to the rise and fall of Hitler.

All four men emerged out of great hardship and social disruption. Defeat in war; famine; loss of traditional ways of life; the collapse of governmental authority; hatred borne of injustice and oppression—these conditions allowed ample opportunity for talented demagogues to play on the passions of the mobs. Razin, Pugachev, Bolotnikov and Bulavin were gifted leaders with a charismatic ability to inspire and lead the masses. Their military leadership brought them initial victories that gave them an air of invincibility, and they were looked on as saviors of the people.

Nikolai Kostomarov, a 19th-century Russian historian, described Stenka Razin in these words: "There was something fascinating in his speech . . . The crowd sensed some supernatural strength in him, against which it was useless to struggle. They called him a sorcerer; and in fact there was in his soul some dreadful and mysterious darkness."[8]

There were many differences between Hitler and Razin of course, but the passage is suggestive. Consider some more comments about Pugachev, the 18th-century rebel leader whose movement was (like the others) finally crushed. Avrich describes him as a "messianic ruler," and quotes a couple of other writers thus:

> . . . 'the rural population went in crowds to meet Pugachev and greeted him as their saviour' [Frederick the Great on Pugachev] .
> . . 'In their blind ignorance,' wrote General Golitsyn, 'the common people everywhere greet this infernal monster with exclamations of joy' . . .[9]

There are other close parallels between Hitler's Third Reich and these more primitive peasant rebellions. One is extreme violence and brutality. In Pugachev's rebellion hatred for the landlords led to an attempt to exterminate them completely. Avrich writes of a "cyclonic fury" of slaughter. The rebels strangled, burned alive, beat to death, tortured—an eyewitness spoke of countless decapitated, hanged, and mutilated bodies.[10]

Of course, since the rebels of the 17th and 18th centuries didn't have the benefits of modern technology to assist them, they were unable to perpetrate truly advanced and scientific atrocities. This is one of the differences, but still the parallels are evident. Especially noteworthy is the manner in which the misery of the people made them look for someone to blame. They blamed the boyars, the nobles, whom they considered to be the origin of their misfortunes:

> . . . Biblical myth was mingled with a pagan demonology in which the nobility formed an alien breed of parasites sucking the

232

blood of the people . . . the boyars were wicked usurpers, demons in human form who throve on the people's enslavement. To eliminate them—to 'cleanse' or 'remove' them from the land, as rebel propaganda put it—was their devout wish . . . eliminate the traitors and the bloodsuckers . . .[11]

Writing of Bolotnikov's revolt, Avrich states that "The boyars, in their eyes, had ceased to be human beings and had become the incarnation of evil, monsters endowed with infernal powers, onto whom the downtrodden projected all that they feared and hated . . ." [12]

A rabble-rousing firebrand with charismatic gifts of leadership articulates the fury of people who have suffered not only defeat in war and great economic hardship, but also the loss of their traditional customs and way of life. He sets off on a violent campaign of conquest and revenge before he is finally brought down by superior forces and the rebellion ends, having accomplished nothing but misery and destruction. Hitler had some instructive precedents.

Germany, Russia, China, Italy, and Japan

We don't need to go back centuries to find other historical examples showing that the meaning of Hitler is more than just a German problem. In the 20th century Germany, Russia, and China all experienced the collapse of an imperial dynasty: Germany's in 1918, Russia's in 1917, and China's in 1911-12. In all three countries, attempts at democratic government failed. Power was seized by a strongman, one-party dictatorships led by infallible leaders were established, and incredible devastation and suffering followed as a result of imposing misguided ideologies.

The German democratic experiment lasted a little longer as the Germans had had some prior experience of democracy, were more advanced economically, and had a more stable political situation. Nevertheless, it too collapsed. There are of course many other differences—but the similarities are important.

It will not do to neglect the Japanese. The Japanese especially were fiercely militaristic and authoritarian; obsessed with the need for more *Lebensraum* (living space); cruel in their military occupations and contemptuous of life, carrying out senseless and brutal massacres as well as horrible medical experiments; achieving initial stupendous successes followed by a blind and foolish attack on a much larger nation ending in crushing defeat.

There are more similarities between Germany and Japan. Both countries were modernized in the second half of the 19th century and swiftly became great powers. Both saw the emergence in the 1920s of ultra-nationalistic extremists whose murders and acts of violence were treated leniently by the courts. Constitutional government broke down in both countries in the 20s and 30s, to be replaced by repressive and adventuristic authoritarianism.

It won't do to overlook Mussolini either. The Italians happily lacked the German passion for violence, and differences between the military performances of the two countries are well-known, but Mussolini did have a significant influence on the up-and-coming Fuhrer. Hitler studied and learned from Mussolini's pioneering experiments, and had great respect for the Duce—at least in the beginning. Such considerations show that in discussing National Socialism we need to understand larger principles of life, not German history and culture alone. Other countries such as Poland, Portugal, Turkey, Hungary, and Bulgaria could also be referred to for evidence of similar social forces at work.

There has been much speculation about Germany's *Sonderweg*, it's unique historical development—destiny, if you will. There are many factors to this that are indisputably German; there are deeper factors that are not German, but human. Similarities between Germany and other countries underscore the futility of trying to explain National Socialism without having a coherent philosophy of human nature as well.

The roots of an ideology

Brutal, revengeful, ambitious, proud, cruel, destructive, charismatic, strikingly successful at first yet crushed by superior forces in the end, the Russian rebels did not have, as has been said before, the power of modern science and technology at their disposal. Moreover, they were not (unlike the Soviets, the Germans, and the Communist Chinese) motivated by a compelling ideology, but only by base passions and a crude vision. Hence, lacking the sophistication of modern man, their destructive power was vastly circumscribed.

Solzhenitsyn said in *The Gulag Archipelago* (as I recall) that it takes a false ideology to truly unleash the evil in man. By the power of an ideology one does more than merely delight in such primitive emotions as hatred and love of violence. No, with the help of an ideology one can perpetrate the most horrible mass atrocities on Jews, kulaks, or unborn infants in the sincere belief that one is benefiting mankind. Joachim Fest makes the profound observation that believing Nazis were "crowned by the idea of a special mission . . . of obeying a 'higher law,' of being the agent of an ideal."[13]

It is to the Nazi ideology itself that we now turn. Having discussed elsewhere its origins in Satan and in human sin, we will examine its intellectual origins in the secularism of the so-called Enlightenment, and then trace its development through over a century of German intellectual and cultural history. It will be seen that it was the rejection of biblical beliefs throughout the course of the entire 19th century and before that opened the door to horrors never seen before in the entire history of the human race.

Many will be dissatisfied with such an analysis. They will reject its underlying presuppositions and many of its conclusions. They are invited to attempt a better explanation of National Socialism. If they succeed, I hope I will be among the first to congratulate them and benefit from their work, and to recognize and correct any errors I have made.

As to those who argue that Hitler didn't have a coherent world view but was concerned solely with gaining power, they neglect to consider that even if their thesis is true, Hitler still needed to adapt himself to the needs of his time. If I were seeking nothing but power for myself in 21st-century America, I would get nowhere by telling the Americans that we were the master race and should invade Canada and Mexico for the sake of *Lebensraum*.

Hitler's world view

In his academic study of Hitler's thought, German historian Eberhard Jaeckel defines "world view" initially only as "the way in which somebody viewed or views the world." After making the obvious but important point that Hitler did view the world in a certain way, Jaeckel then proceeds to explore what Hitler's world view actually was. Even with Jaeckel's more specific definition of "world view"—that individual parts or ideas must be self-consistent and related to each other, even if not fully defined or worked out in all details according to formal academic requirements—it can still be said that Hitler did have a system of thought.[14]

This system of thought was directly related to discernible currents in modern German philosophy and culture. Hence Hitler biographer Joachim Fest writes, "It cannot be too strongly emphasized that Hitler's rise was made possible only by the unique conjunction of individual with general prerequisites, by the barely decipherable correspondence that the man entered into with the age and the age with the man." Fest then comments on the weakness of theories that present Hitler "as a fundamental antithesis to the age and its people," and adds "He was not so much the great contradiction of the age as its mirror image."[15] The correspondence that he refers to as "barely decipherable" is, I believe, decipherable. I don't mean totally—we can't even decipher ourselves totally—but enough to see a pattern of which Hitler was a logical (though not inevitable) result.

Hitler had an evil genius that allowed him to assemble ideas developed by others and hammer them into an effective political movement. Others had said it all before—Hitler only did what others talked about. As Joachim Fest said of Hitler, "what distinguished him from all his ilk was his capacity for political action. He was the exception, the intellectual with a practical understanding of power."[16] Hitler was in fact what he claimed to be—a rare instance of "the programmatic thinker and the politician become one." He did in fact have a world view, a *Weltanschauung*, and this world view was as he said "the granite foundation of my present actions." Hitler was, as he often did, stating his real conviction when he said in *Mein Kampf* that "Every power which does not grow out of a firm intellectual base will remain wavering and insecure. It lacks the stability which can only rest on a fanatical *Weltanschauung*." Hitler's ideas were broadly self-consistent and coherent (given his false and ugly premises), and meet Jaeckel's more specific requirements for a legitimate world view.[17]

A well-behaved young man

Before delving into the intellectual roots of National Socialism, it is worth noting evidence showing Hitler to have been in many respects a decent enough if eccentric youth. This shifts the attention away from his childhood to his later ideas. Many people have had childhoods much worse than Hitler's and did not turn out so bad.

Some information about Hitler's early life is found in Walter S. Frank's well-documented and insightful online biography of Hitler, *Adolf Hitler: The Making of a Fuhrer (Who was Responsible?)*. I appreciate his permission to quote his work at length. Asterisks are Frank's footnotes—those interested in documentation are invited to go to the site (http://www.smoter.com/hitler.htm). Much of this comes from an account by August Kubizek, *The Young Hitler I Knew*. That Kubizek was Hitler's friend in Linz and shared lodgings with him in Vienna are accepted facts, and his published narrative describing his friendship with the youthful Hitler is considered basically genuine by legitimate historians (though not of course infallible in every detail). In Frank's words:

> Kubizek was particularly amazed by Adolf's refined speech which made him very persuasive, even with grown-ups. Kubizek was always astonished at how, when they were alone, Hitler could rant on about a particular subject and get himself worked up; yet, when dealing with others he kept calm and had an air of reasonableness. Hitler was normally polite to people, was not vain, and could be very sensitive if he felt someone was unhappy or sick. Kubizek also wrote that Adolf helped him through difficult times and always had time for people he liked.* Hitler was well-liked and respected by almost everyone he met.*
>
> Kubizek was also awed by the seriousness and wide range of knowledge Hitler showed for one as young as he was . . . Hitler's interests were boundless. He was interested in agriculture, city planning, mythology, history, politics, and world events, including air travel. The Wright bothers had flown their heavier-than-air plane at Kitty Hawk a few years before and Hitler was very impressed. He was interested in everything, Kubizek noted, and wasn't indifferent about anything.*
>
> Kubizek would come to write a book about his experiences with the young Hitler. If the portents in retrospect and the occasional melodramatic moments are overlooked, he describes Hitler as a fairly normal teenager with an inquiring mind. Since many historians like to portray the young Hitler as unbalanced, ignorant, lazy, and stupid, a few have attempted to discredit Kubizek anytime he portrays the young Hitler in a decent light. Paula Hitler, however (who was about the only acquaintance who never tried to capitalize on her brother's name), stated that as a teenager Adolf had opinions about everything and constantly read. She also stated that he often used to give persuasive lectures on themes concerning history and politics to her and her mother.*
>
> Around this time the Hitler family began seeing a new doctor named Eduard Bloch. He described "Adolf" as a "well mannered," "neat," "obedient boy" who would "bow.... courteously" whenever they met. He found Adolf to be "neither robust nor sickly" but "frail looking" with "large, melancholy and thoughtful....gray-blue eyes....inherited from his mother." Dr. Bloch, like Kubizek, also described Adolf as a "quiet," and a "well-bred boy of fourteen or fifteen" who was "old for his age."* [Part I "The Boy," Sect. 3 "Friends and Lovers"]

Hitler's letters and postcards to Kubizek were polite, friendly, and even showed some humor. On April 20, 1908 (his nineteenth birthday), Hitler wrote his friend, joked about the weather, then added

I am very pleased that you are bringing a viola. On Tuesday I shall buy myself two crowns' worth of cotton wool and twenty kreuzers worth of paste, for my ears naturally. That—on top of this—you are going blind affects me deeply: you will play more wrong notes than ever. Then you will become blind and I gradually mad. Oh dear! But meanwhile I wish you and your esteemed parents at least a happy Easter and send them my hearty greetings as well as to you.[18]

What Hitler wrote on this and on other occasions was no different from what any ordinary person might have written in a similar situation.

The secret of Hitler does not lie in his childhood. Spiritually, it lies in mysteries of sin and evil. Humanly speaking, it lies in the ideas he came to believe and put into practice. These ideas did not come out of nowhere. Yet, while there was some normality to Hitler and he was not just a freak, there was another side to his personality as well. Kubizek speaks of his friend as sometimes showing "boundless anger, shaken to his very depths." When he first revealed his rejection by the Art Academy it was in an explosion of rage. "His face was livid . . . the eyes glittered. There was something sinister about them, as if all the hate of which he was capable lay in those glowing eyes." There were numerous other occasions on which a polite and friendly adolescent Hitler would burst out "in a ferment of rage, hard and intractable."[19] Some may patronizingly dismiss Kubizek's account as exaggerations written from hindsight—but do any of them want to argue that Hitler was only a normal, healthy, well-adjusted adolescent? What if Kubizek accurately stated the facts here?

Such personal aspects to the Hitler riddle are largely inaccessible to us—yet, it is plausible to think of a gifted young Hitler who was in some ways normal, in other ways deeply disturbed. Certainly, adolescent unhappiness, anger, even rage and hatred of society combined perfectly with the ideas he came to believe and practice. Such ideas did not come out of nowhere, and are (unlike Hitler's adolescent psychiatry) subject to our sustained investigation.

Descartes and the "Enlightenment"

Not many people would trace the roots of National Socialism back to the 17th-century French philosopher Descartes (1596-1650), but it was Descartes who based his thought on the idea that divine revelation was not necessary to understand the meaning of life. He sought wisdom within himself, using his own reason and logic. For this reason he has been called the first modern philosopher, the father of modern philosophy, although that dubious honor has also been claimed for Immanuel Kant, whom we will examine later in this study.

From this vantage point of human reason alone without divine revelation, a thousand paths diverge. They go in different directions, some of them intersecting, some combining and separating again, some of them broad and well-traveled, some of them obscure and known to few—but all of them go downward and away from God, and deeper into the darkness of the world. One of those paths led to the horrors whose intellectual origins we are now discussing.

Descartes did not openly despise God. He even felt the need of some sort of a theoretical and inactive God to give his airy cogitations some coherence and stability—but he did reject the revelation of God in scripture. He considered it beneath his lofty and profound intelligence. From there, because of sin's law of moral gravity that continually pulls the natural man away from God, it was a short step to the urbane and genteel mockery and witticisms of Voltaire, the so-called *philosophe*—and from thence to the open hostility toward Christianity that was manifested in the French Revolution. The law of moral gravity is just as real as the corresponding natural law and it pulls us down more deeply into sin and folly if we do not hold fast to higher truth. We see this in America today. First Christianity is politely rejected, then hated and despised.

Descartes did not cause the trend away from Christianity, though he contributed to it in a significant way. It is safer to say that he represented the trend, that he articulated a belief that was very attractive to the natural mind and became more so as time went by—man set free from religion, man able to understand and arrange his life on his own, without reference to any higher power. The illusion of freedom this brings is intoxicating to those who become drunk with it, and the 18th and 19th centuries—for many reasons too complex to try and analyze here—saw a general decline in the hold of religious ideas over an increasing segment of society as a whole. Lesslie Newbigin was correct in referring to "the new Cartesian starting point, which has been so foundational for all that has followed . . . ."[20]

This rejection of God and the elevation of human reason brought with it a new concept of the Jews, one that can be seen in the writings of Voltaire and Thomas Jefferson. These men were not concerned about the crucifixion of Christ. They were not concerned about God's wrath on the Jews, or see their existence as a threat to Christianity—after all, they didn't even believe in Christianity themselves. Voltaire and Jefferson objected to Judaism because it was *unreasonable*. Judaism embodied a concept of life that was abhorrent to them for secular reasons, and their vehement attacks on it are different in tone and in substance from what had been seen in the preceding centuries. For example, Jefferson, writing in his "Syllabus of an Estimate of the Merit of the Doctrines of Jesus, Compared with Those of Others," observed:

> II. Jews.
> 1. Their system was Deism; that is, the belief in one only God. But their ideas of him and of his attributes were degrading and injurious.
> 2. Their Ethics were not only imperfect, but often irreconcilable with the sound dictates of reason and morality, as they respect intercourse with those around us; and repulsive and anti-social, as respecting other nations.[21]

Jefferson found Jews repulsive because he found the Old Testament God repulsive. This is not the view of a Christian, and Jefferson's estrangement from biblical Christianity is revealed in the same "Syllabus." He asserted there that Jesus was only a moralist, said he did not even want to discuss Christ's participation in the Godhead, and stated that the Bible was not reliable, that its authors were "unlettered and ignorant men, who wrote, too, from memory, and not till long after the transactions had passed." As a result, we don't know exactly what Jesus taught: ". . . the doctrines he really delivered were defective as a whole, and fragments only of what he did deliver have come to us mutilated, misstated, and often unintelligible."[22] Jefferson in a letter referring to the syllabus (on the same website) explicitly called himself a Christian, but explained that he accepted Jesus' moral system while rejecting the many other (to him) useless and unnecessary doctrines that are in fact at the very heart of Christianity.

Jefferson had a horror of religious intolerance, and would never have persecuted Jews or anyone else for their religion, but his idea of Judaism is a good example of a new kind of anti-Semitism that arose not from Christianity, but from the rejection of Christianity. Traditional "Christian" anti-Semitism saw the truths of God in the Old Testament, but operated from a misguided understanding of the Jewish rejection of Christ. Jefferson and his ilk saw Judaism as being offensive from the very start. Not the rejection of Christ but the laws of Torah and the God of Abraham, Isaac, and Jacob with his holiness, wrath and divine judgments earned the contempt of Jefferson.

Voltaire also had an intense dislike of Jews (though he may have moderated it later in life). In his *Dictionnaire philosophique*, Voltaire wrote that the Jews "are a totally ignorant nation who for many years have combined contemptible miserliness and the most revolting superstition with a violent hatred of all those nations which have tolerated them."[23]

It will be objected that Luther also made hostile comments—the only major Protestant writer ever to have done so, showing this is not endemic to Protestantism—but Jefferson and Voltaire are as was just said examples of a different kind of anti-Semitism. It is this modern secular anti-Semitism that concerns us here, and while Jefferson and Voltaire had been very much influenced by traditional values and hence were very far removed from the disasters of the age of secular science and progress, their new approach to the Jews—based not on Christian principles but on human philosophy and logic that rejected Christian principles—is of great significance. It flourished—with a different tone and emphasis—in the 19th century German philosophers, the children of the "Enlightenment." We shall see a direct connection between it and the emergence in Germany of the Folkish movement that reasoned from secular philosophy to virulent anti-Semitism.

Historian Paul Johnson wrote of this influence. Referring not only to Voltaire but also to other anti-Semitic Frenchmen such as Diderot and Baron d'Holbach, he observes that "these French writers, above all Voltaire, were widely read throughout Europe—and imitated. It was not long before the first German idealists, like Fichte, were taking up the same theme."[24]

An interesting contrast to Voltaire and Jefferson is found in America's second president, John Adams. It shows that respect for the Bible mitigates against modern secular and pseudo-scientific bigotry (which is not to say that Adams was a Christian, but his respect for Christianity clearly defined his attitude toward Jews):

> Most "enlightened" American Christians such as Adams saw Jews as an ancient people who, by enunciating monotheism, laid the groundwork for Christianity. He also saw them as individuals who deserved rights and protection under the law. Like many of his peers, Adams venerated ancient Jews and thought contemporary Jews worthy of respect, but found Judaism, the

religion of the Jewish people, an anachronism and the Jewish people candidates for conversion to Christianity.[25]

In an 1808 letter criticizing the depiction of Jews by the French Enlightenment philosopher Voltaire, Adams expressed his respect for ancient Jewry. Adams wrote of Voltaire,

> How is it possible [that he] should represent the Hebrews in such a contemptible light? They are the most glorious nation that ever inhabited this Earth. The Romans and their Empire were but a Bauble in comparison of the Jews. They have given religion to three quarters of the Globe and have influenced the affairs of Mankind more, and more happily, than any other Nation ancient or modern.[26]

Some will object to a distinct separation between religious and secular-philosophical anti-Semitisms. Paul Rose, for example, claims that although Voltaire was hostile to Christianity, "his critique of Judaism was still constructed around a Christian framework, albeit an updated, secularized one."[27] As was said in chapter 1, there is a continuity between secular and religious anti-Semitisms: a continuity of sin and evil. Yet, that same power of sin expresses itself in different ways with different results. Many centuries of "Christian" anti-Semitism did not produce an Auschwitz or a Hitler. The unique combinations of philosophy and, later, pseudo-science were new and different—radically and fundamentally so.

A few words about the French Revolution & Napoleon
The principles of the "Enlightenment" spread with great speed throughout the ranks of the German intelligentsia, but before looking into that it is worth commenting on the fact that some people will look for every hint, scrap, or clue, no matter how faint, that might connect Hitler to Christianity, while they ignore the remarkable events that occurred in a neighboring country less than a hundred and fifty years before Hitler came to power and less than a century before he was born.

Leaving aside the many differences between France and Germany, between Hitler and Napoleon or the revolutionaries who preceded Napoleon, in both countries there was an attempt to impose a new vision of man and society. This vision led to the shedding of rivers of blood—for the benefit of humanity of course. Like the Nazis, the French revolutionaries relied on external symbols, using flags, caps, songs, and new holidays and rituals to intensify devotion to the new faith. They gloried in replacing the old society with a new one, and used force, violence, repression, even mass murder to ensure the success of their experiment.

This is more than a matter of outward appearances. The ideas of Rousseau had a significant impact on German thinkers, including Kant, Fichte, and Hegel, three major figures in our study. Rousseau's strong repudiation of "culture" and "civilization"; his emphasis on feeling and passion as opposed to reason; his belief in a "general will" of the people, to which the individual must sacrifice his personal inclinations, involving in Rousseau's words individual submission to "the supreme direction of society's leaders";[28] his belief in the right of the state to put people to death not for specific crimes but only for the sake of the general welfare as the leaders saw it—these ideals were enthusiastically embraced by the most violent practitioners of French revolutionary terror. Have those people who constantly point to the "Enlightenment" as the foundation of modern Western civilization ever heard of Marat, Robespierre, Saint-Just, the guillotine, and the Reign of Terror? Societies that emerged out of the Protestant Reformation, though flawed, were vastly more stable and democratic.

Concerning the relationship between Hitler and Napoleon, Alistair Horne's brief biography of Napoleon has some useful information. Horne distances Napoleon from Hitler, and rightly points out that Napoleon was a civilized man in comparison to Hitler—but was Napoleon's ability to commit evil limited only by his lack of means (primitive technology) and by his lack of modern ideology? Napoleon did not have the modern belief—derived from secularism—that he could remake mankind. He also did not have the belief—again derived from secularism—that elimination of undesirables was both beneficial to the human race, and in agreement with the latest scientific theories.

Napoleon was motivated solely by an old-fashioned love of power and glory that has manifested itself countless times in human history—hence the power of sin in him had a more limited scope. Nevertheless there are significant parallels between the two men. For one thing, Napoleon systematically looted vast art treasures from conquered countries. For another, he relied on plebiscites to give an aura of legitimacy to his authoritarian rule (not surprisingly, he was always endorsed by a majority vote). He had grandiose plans for the rebuilding of Paris that were never realized.

More significantly, Napoleon was not a religious believer, yet he felt a common religious tradition (in this case Catholicism) was necessary to the social cohesion of the state. On his death bed he refused to admit the priests who had come to administer last rites, yet he presented himself as a champion of the Church, signed a Concordat with the Vatican, and relied on the Church to give his regime more legitimacy in the eyes of the common people.[29]

Horne referred to Napoleon's "intuitive sense," his "indomitable will to power," his "firmness of aim."[30] It is no wonder that Hitler publicly venerated Napoleon by visiting his tomb. The two men had much in common, and it is not reasonable to use the real differences between them to obscure the equally real parallels. There are great differences between England and America or between the Wright brothers' rickety little biplane and a modern jumbo jet. Does it therefore follow that there are no connections at all?

That similarities between the two conquerors are omitted by some who write at length on Christianity and National Socialism says a great deal about their motives and their methodology. That a man who was never accused of being a devout, Bible believing Christian; who subordinated the church to the state; who led his nation to dizzying heights of conquest, only to fall before a powerful coalition raised against him; who became so intoxicated with his own genius and brilliance that he made disastrous miscalculations which led to his downfall; who was honored by Hitler—that he would be ignored by some anti-Christian propagandists is only to be expected. A study of Napoleon would not after all contribute toward the desired end of blackening Christianity.

If Hitler had visited Martin Luther's tomb the way he visited Napoleon's, it would be triumphantly gloated over by enemies of Christianity. That people such as the French revolutionaries and Napoleon, who were not even remotely Christian, should be so strikingly similar to Hitler in some ways (if not in all) should say a great deal about the unChristian and unbiblical nature of Hitler's philosophy and actions.

Referring to Himmler's early rise in the Nazi bureaucracy, one of his biographers (Peter Padfield) states, "According to Otto Strasser, Himmler's models at this time were Napoleon's chief of police, Fouché, and the head of Stalin's secret police, Dzerzhinsky."[31] Horne also described Napoleon's Chief of Police Fouché as "the forerunner of twentieth-century police chiefs like Himmler and Beria."[32] For some reason Himmler wasn't getting his ideas from the Protestant Reformation or from the four gospels.

The French so-called *philosophes* thought they could reject Christianity and divine revelation yet still maintain some kind of humanist ethic. They did not realize that without a biblical foundation, their ethical values were like cut flowers in a vase—nice to look at, but deprived of their root and soon to wither. Not surprisingly, the attempt to establish a new society on the basis of reason alone quickly exploded in uncontrollable violence and ended in tyranny.

The "Enlightenment" in Germany

That the "Enlightenment's" central principle of autonomous reason quickly became accepted in Germany attests to the spiritual weakness of the churches. Established religion in Germany had by the end of the 18th century degenerated into a sterile orthodoxy, a theological system without the driving spiritual power of before. This is not to say that there were no people in Germany seriously dedicated to following the teachings of Christ—nor is it to say that Christian tradition did not still have a deep hold on the nation as a whole. Yet, it was increasingly a matter of culture and of custom rather than vital faith. This problem was acknowledged within the church. It was recognized by some that official Christianity had degenerated into a lifeless system of doctrines, and spiritual revival was sought by various means. The Pietists, of whom the most well-known today are Count Zinzendorf and the Moravian Brethren, sought a more authentic experience of biblical Christianity. Nevertheless, in spite of their efforts, the influence of Christianity in Germany had already begun to wane. The new doctrines from France were widely accepted by the intelligentsia with little or no resistance.

Man set free from bondage to tradition! Independent human reason as the highest source of moral law! Man, liberated from superstition and able to think freely at last! This was intoxicating wine, and those who became drunk with it had no need of a Son of God dying on the cross and rising from the dead. The day of judgment, eternity in heaven for those who believed in God, eternity in hell for evil-doers, divine laws and commandments—all of these were lightly dispensed with as outdated superstitions, obstacles to spiritual and moral progress. There were many significant differences in tone and emphasis between the German and the French "Enlightenments," but this underlying belief in the supremacy of human thought was the foundation of both.

Having said this by way of introduction, it is now necessary to look at some German philosophers and see how they unknowingly contributed to the emergence of National Socialism. The decades after their deaths saw such dramatic historical developments as industrialization and national unification.

These new developments, along with the rise of modern science and the disaster of WWI, introduced pressures and intellectual currents that philosophers in the more civilized pre-modern age could never have imagined. It is reasonable to assume that they would have been horrified with and disgusted by Hitler. Nevertheless, just as the Wright brothers set in motion a chain of developments of which they did not have the slightest inkling, so the early German philosophers contributed to events far beyond their ability to foresee.

The philosophical opinions of Kant, Hegel, Fichte, Schopenhauer and others are therefore of more than merely academic interest. At first confined to very limited intellectual circles, they grew in popularity in the ensuing decades. More than one scholar has noted three distinct stages in this march of ideas: from a few intellectuals in the first part of the century, to the professional and upper middle classes by the last half of the 19th century and the first part of the 20th, to the masses after 1918. Of course, the ideas were significantly modified along the way—new concepts were added, irrelevant concepts were abandoned. In spite of these changes, some central aspects of what came to be known as the Folkish philosophy, a belief in Germany superiority that many have rightly identified as the direct predecessor of National Socialism, can be clearly seen in the ideas of the secular philosophers.

A brief overview

An intriguing short article by Dieter Just on German philosophy called "I think—therefore I am not" (*Ich denke—also bin ich nicht*) aptly summarizes some of the main points of this part of our study.[33] Just maintains that "an intellectual revolution against God" occurred in western Europe in the 18th and 19th centuries. This was of course against the God of the Old and the New Testaments, a creator of the world and "supreme moral legislator" whose laws we were supposed to obey. The revolution included Anglo-Saxon philosophy, "but nowhere was it as radical as it was in Germany" (he is referring here to the general course of the 19th century, and not the short-lived excesses of the French revolution).

He goes on to assert that this philosophical revolution provided the foundation "from which the German political right developed a national ideology or *Weltanschauung* during the 19th century." He states in this context his belief that modern German anti-Semitism developed from this, not from the Christian religion. He elaborates on the process by which the German right ignored concepts of German philosophy that did not suit its agenda, and focused on those concepts agreeable to its nationalistic will to power. Just also believes that a new anti-Semitism emerged that derived its ideas from philosophical doctrines rather than from the Bible. Adding my own comment, we can understand German imperialism as the basic lust for power that has appeared so many times in history, but this time strengthened and deepened by philosophy in a way unknown in previous times. What if the Mongols had had university educations and had studied philosophy? They could have reasoned that they were part of a historical process, the actualization or immanence of the Absolute Idea in history or some such thing, and used philosophy to justify what was really only the most primitive love of violence, power and glory.

Just also points out the fundamentally egotistical nature of this philosophy— autonomous man is the only source of moral law—and makes the important but

243

often overlooked point that the extremely conservative and officially Christian German governments that reigned in the times of Kant, Fichte, and Hegel required those writers to conceal anti-Christian sentiments and to describe their philosophies as either Christian or as compatible with Christianity.

I would add to this that the philosophical reinterpretation and secularization of the terms "Protestant" and "Christian" also allowed many ideas that had nothing to do with, and were directly contrary to, the Bible to be described as "Christian." By expanding those terms to allow for the abandonment of traditional doctrines and their replacement with new ones, secular thinkers could deny such things as the inspiration of the Bible, the deity of Christ, his resurrection from the dead, and his return to judge the world, yet still call themselves "Christian" and "Protestant." This, along with an ignorance of biblical teaching, is behind much of the confusion that hinders objective discussion of the relationship between Christianity and secular philosophies. So many people reason, "It has the name 'Christian,' therefore it is Christian."

In the words of Alister McGrath, "As clerical power began to decline in the eighteenth century, Western society began to look to others for moral vision and intellectual inspiration. It found such leaders in the growing community of intellectuals."[34] Too many people talk about "Christian Europe" and "Christian Germany" as if the great movement toward secularism that began in the eighteenth century and became increasingly dominant in the 19th century had never occurred. McGrath continues,

> At some point, perhaps one that can never be determined with historical accuracy, Western society came to believe that it should look elsewhere than to its clergy for guidance. Instead, they turned to the intellectuals, who were able to portray their clerical opponents as lazy fools who could do no more than unthinkingly repeat the slogans and nostrums of an increasingly distant past. A new future lay ahead, and society needed brave new thinkers to lead them to its lush Promethean pastures.[35]

These "brave new thinkers" were, in Germany around the beginning of the 19th century, philosophers. Their impact will be discussed in the following pages. That "cultural phenomena tend to eventually reflect philosophical movements,"[36] that there are philosophical understandings behind social movements; that the ideas of philosophers can, over time, enter the cultural life of a nation and influence politics and economics—these ideas will seem irrelevant to those whose blinkered materialism forces them to focus only on the more obvious and readily apparent historical forces. Yet, the following pages will seek to demonstrate the contrary—that there is a direct (if lengthy and at times convoluted) connection between the follies of abstract academic philosophers and the terrors of the Third Reich. In the words of J. Gresham Machen, "What is today a matter of academic speculation begins tomorrow to move armies and pull down empires."[37]

Kant

Many people have ignored the obvious similarities and commonalities between Hitler's ideas and those of 19th-century German "philosophers" (misosophers). This is partly because many students of Hitler have no interest in philosophy themselves. They don't know about it, and hence can't see it in Hitler's writings. Others who do have some knowledge of German philosophy assume from the outset that it had nothing to do with Hitler and refuse to explore the possibility. They either think Hitler was too crazy and/or stupid to read, or else they like German philosophy, believe it has validity and merit, and take it for granted that Hitler's ideas came from elsewhere.

Such views are simplistic. Things are not always what they seem, and a few have studied Hitler's intellectual roots with surprising results. For example, in a book called *German Idealism and the Jew: The Inner Anti-Semitism of Philosophy and German Jewish Responses*, Professor Michael Mack of the Hebrew University in Jerusalem examined Immanuel Kant's anti-Semitism and its subsequent influence on later German philosophers. One review of the book stated that Prof. Mack identified Kant as "the intellectual father of the Holocaust."[38]

Mack himself did not put it so bluntly. His book is a sophisticated analysis of certain aspects of German philosophy, and does not directly assert that "Kant's ideas led to the Holocaust." What Mack does do is show how Kant's secular philosophical anti-Semitism initiated a new way of looking at the Jews that was taken up and elaborated on by Fichte, Hegel, Feuerbach, Schopenhauer, Wagner, and even H.S. Chamberlain. Since the last two are often directly linked to Hitler and had much in common with him, this does connect Kant's ideas to the Holocaust. Mack also demonstrates how the later biological racism that emerged in the second half of the nineteenth century both reinforced and was reinforced by the pre-existing philosophical anti-Semitism.[39]

At first glance there would seem to be no connection between Immanuel Kant and Adolf Hitler. Called by some the greatest philosopher of the "Enlightenment," Kant (1724-1804) was certainly far removed from Hitler, to judge by outward appearances. A quiet man who occupied himself with books and ideas rather than with political power and military conquests, much of his philosophy had nothing to do with National Socialism. Jews were peripheral to his thinking, and weird phobias about Jewish domination were not concerns of his. Nevertheless, he had a concept of the Jews that was echoed by others after him, became foundational to 19th-century secular anti-Semitism, and was identical to comments about Jews made by Hitler in *Mein Kampf*.

It was inevitable that someone committed to the principles of the so-called Enlightenment should have had a philosophical hostility toward Judaism. A God such as that described in the Old Testament was thoroughly objectionable to those who relied on human reason rather than on divine revelation. A God of laws and rules who punished those who disobeyed him and blessed those who obeyed him; who demanded unconditional obedience; who sent fire and slaughter on his enemies; who was particularly concerned with one people out of all the peoples of the earth; who commanded death for immorality or even for working on the Sabbath—this sort of God was wholly repugnant, "repulsive," as Jefferson said above, and "often irreconcilable with the sound dictates of reason and morality."

This explains the common attitudes toward Jews that run through German idealistic philosophy. Kant articulated them, but even if he had never lived at all the attitude toward the Jews would have inevitably been the same. Thus, if Kant's views are in some ways identical to those of later thinkers, it is because Kant articulated a common approach, or expressed what others felt themselves—not that he single-handedly caused it. Anti-Semitism became deeply rooted in German "philosophy" because of the conflict between divine revelation and autonomous human reason in the German cultural context, not because of a single individual. Nevertheless, it was because Kant represented a deep underlying current that his impact was so great. He introduced academic and intellectual anti-Semitism to Germany. In the words of historian Paul Lawrence Rose, "Kant's basic ideas were elaborated into a historical and philosophical critique of Judaism that until very recently commanded virtually unquestioning support in German culture."[40]

Kant's objections to Jews were philosophical, not racial. Secular Jews such as Spinoza who rejected outdated biblical superstitions could be accepted into the brotherhood of man. Those who clung to their superstitions did not have to be shoved into gas chambers—Kant could never have conceived of such a thing— but he did see Judaism as an obstacle to progress, contrary to truth and to reason. This is why Kant said "The euthanasia of Judaism is pure moral religion."[41] If people understood God according to Kant's enlightened, progressive, and humanistic view of him, then Judaism would die a peaceful death—not through extermination squads or death camps, but by the light of reason. Parenthetically, it has been suggested that some enlightened advocates of Jewish emancipation expected that allowing the Jews to enter the mainstream of society would lead to their disappearance through assimilation. Is this too simple a solution to the problem of how some could strongly object to the Jews and see them as having a negative influence, yet still advocate their civil emancipation?

Kant had yet more to say about the Jews. In his work *Religion Within the Limits of Reason Alone* Kant wrote, "Judaism is really not a religion at all, but merely a union of a number of people who formed themselves into a commonwealth under purely political laws, and not into a church." In the same vein, he said "since no religion can be conceived of which involves no belief in a future life, Judaism, which, when taken in its purity is seen to lack this belief, is not a religious faith at all."[42]

A couple of points need to be made about this. First, the Jews "formed themselves"—they were not chosen and led by God. Kant did not of course accept the Old Testament as the historically accurate word of God. They had "purely political laws"—the idea of a divine manifestation and divine laws is dismissed by Kant. Secondly, his assertion that the Jews had no concept of an afterlife reveals his ignorance of the subject. True, the Old Testament does not stress the resurrection from the dead and eternity in heaven or in hell the way the New Testament does, but it plainly shows an awareness of them. A few examples of this are:

> And many of them that sleep in the dust of the earth shall awake, some to everlasting life, and some to shame and everlasting contempt. And they that be wise shall shine as the brightness of the firmament; and they that turn many to righteousness as the stars for ever and ever. (Daniel 12:2-3)

> I will dwell in the house of the Lord forever. (Psalm 23:6)

For I know that my redeemer lives, and that he shall stand at the latter day upon the earth: And though after my skin worms destroy this body, yet in my flesh shall I see God. (Job 19:26)

The wicked shall be turned into hell, and all the nations that forget God. (Psalm 9:17)

You will show me the path of life: in your presence is fullness of joy; at your right hand there are pleasures for evermore. (Psalm 16:11)

For, behold, I create new heavens and a new earth: and the former shall not be remembered, nor come into mind. But be ye glad and rejoice forever in that which I create . . . (Isaiah 65:17-18)

So, Kant was ignorant of scripture. Blinded by his philosophy, he stumbled on to another criticism of Judaism—his dismissal of the Jews as "materialistic." An internet search of "Jewish materialism Nazis" will quickly yield references to this standard Nazi attack on Judaism. This seems rather puzzling at first. Of course Marxism and left-wing socialism could falsely be ascribed to Judaism, but how could Judaism itself, with its concept of a divine creative power and its vision of world peace so wonderfully expressed by Isaiah possibly be considered materialistic? The answer can be found in Kant.

Jeet Heer, another reviewer of Prof. Mack's book, puts it this way: "For Kant, motives could only be good if they were not aimed at any material benefit. He saw Judaism as an inherently materialist religion, based upon a quid pro quo between God and His chosen people."[43] A quote from Prof. Mack follows, stating that Kant "posited Judaism as an abstract principle that does nothing else but, paradoxically, desire the consumption of material goods."

Torah states that if the Jews obey God, he will bless them and they will prosper. If they disobey him they will be punished, and disaster will come upon them if they persist in disobedience long enough. To Kant's mind this was a very low and materialistic concept of God. The selfish, mean-spirited, and ignoble Jews obeyed God only for the sake of material benefits, and were incapable of higher ideals (such as those of Kant). Of course, this omits the spiritual dimension of Judaism, including the statement repeated by Jesus that the highest law of Judaism is to love God and to love one's neighbor. The obedience required by God included external observances, but was primarily a matter of the heart and the spirit. Those who obeyed external rules not from the heart but only for the sake of gain were already in violation of the essence of Judaism. It has been objected that Shakespeare also had a stereotype of miserly Jews, as did many others—but Kant elevated it to the level of a philosophical principle.

Dietrich Eckart, known by historians to have had a significant influence on Hitler, wrote "The Jew has no sense of the experience of what is eternal or of the need of immortality. Ergo: he has no soul, and is therefore the opposite pole of the Germans, who are always striving for something higher. They are as light is to darkness."[44] How different this is from Luther, who wrote that Jewish rejection of truth was identical to Turkish or Papist rejection of truth.

Another aspect to the criticism of Judaism as materialistic had to do with the supposedly static and fixed nature of Judaism. The German philosophers saw the discovery of truth as an ongoing process, with man reaching ever greater heights of spiritual freedom and consciousness as he progressed farther along the paths of philosophy. Orthodox Judaism was the very antithesis of that. Permanently fossilized in what were perceived as dead and lifeless rules, with a fixed rather than a developing concept of God, Judaism came to represent everything that life was not. The Jews were seen as being enslaved to dead dogmas, unlike the philosophical free spirits who were able to discover new worlds (never mind that their philosophical constructs were wholly or largely false and soon to be abandoned, while Judaism remains a vital force).

German philosophy and anti-Semitism in *Mein Kampf*

Some of Kant's logic is found in *Mein Kampf*. Looking again at a central chapter—"Nation and Race" [vol. I chapt. 11]—we find a number of relevant statements. One of them is, "Due to his own original special nature, the Jew cannot possess a religious institution, if for no other reason because he lacks idealism in any form, and hence belief in a hereafter is absolutely foreign to him." Another quote is, "The Jewish religious doctrine consists primarily in prescriptions for keeping the blood of Jewry pure and for regulating the relation of Jews among themselves, but even more with the rest of the world; in other words, with non-Jews."

Both Kant and Hitler believed that "the Jew" lacked any concept of the afterlife, and that their commonwealth, their social arrangement, was merely a social or political one. Elsewhere in this same chapter Hitler says of the Jew that "His life is only of this world." That "the Jew" was concerned only with material things is expressed thus: " . . . this adversary of all humanity . . . then as always saw in religion nothing but an instrument for his business existence." Hitler here expresses his belief that the Jewish religion was only materialistic—Jews obeyed God only for the sake of material benefit. The supposedly Jewish invention of Marxism would confirm this impression of Jews as materialists.

That Hitler used Kant's reasoning here doesn't mean that Hitler read Kant, though he may have, even if only in a second-hand summary of Kant's ideas on the Jews (Hitler's reading habits will be examined later in this section). It also doesn't mean that Kant caused Hitler. It does mean that Hitler's anti-Semitism is in this respect radically different from traditional religious anti-Semitism but identical to Kant's (though not in other respects, racial anti-Semitism being a later scientific development).

These ideas were not mentioned by Hitler just in passing. They were foundational to his anti-Semitism and formed one of his most persistent anti-Jewish themes: that selfish Jewish egotism undermined civilization. This began with Kant but was elaborated on and magnified by others, notably Fichte, Schopenhauer, Wagner and H.S. Chamberlain. Hitler reasoned from Jewish selfishness and egotism, lack of all higher principles, and short-sighted desire only for material gain to present Judaism as a force that undermined culture and in the end would destroy civilization. In so doing, he was following a pattern of logic not contrary to the German "Enlightenment" but directly related to it.

Writing in the context of a decades-long tradition with many precedents, Hitler explained the corrosive influence of selfish Jewish egotism on society. He defined idealism as the subordination of the self to the group, the willingness of the individual to sacrifice himself for a higher purpose. He saw this "idealism" as being essential to society, to civilization, and to culture. Since the Jews lacked this instinct, their influence ultimately led to the disintegration of society. The connection of Jews with the disintegrating forces of modern society will be discussed in more detail later—it was a favorite theme of Richard Wagner's. Speaking of "the Jew" in this context, Hitler wrote:

> . . . he lacks completely the most essential requirement for a cultured people, the idealistic attitude. In the Jewish people the will to self-sacrifice does not go beyond the individual's naked instinct of self-preservation . . .

> . . . Here again the Jew is led by nothing but the naked egoism of the individual.

> . . . No, the Jew possesses no culture-creating force of any sort, since the idealism, without which there is no true higher development of man, is not present in him and never was present. Hence his intellect will never have a constructive effect, but will be destructive, and in very rare cases perhaps will at most be stimulating, but then as the prototype of the 'force which always wants evil and nevertheless creates good.' Not through him does any progress of mankind occur, but in spite of him.

Hitler failed to recognize here that a selfish concern for nothing other than one's own benefit is a human trait, not a Jewish one. Like Kant, he based his understanding of Judaism on a total misperception of the religion. It was a misrepresentation derived from modern secularism, not from traditional anti-Semitism, much less from biblical Christianity.

I have been unable to find a purported quote from Hitler critical of Kant in *Mein Kampf*. Hitler was under no more of an obligation than anyone else to accept 100% of any philosopher. Like the rest of us, he would find some things to agree with or disagree with in any writer. There was a complimentary reference to Kant in the *Table Talk*:

> In our part of the world, the Jews would have immediately eliminated Schopenhauer, Nietzsche, and Kant. If the Bolsheviks had dominion over us for two hundred years, what works of our past would be handed on to posterity? Our great men would fall into oblivion, or else they'd be presented to future generations as criminals and bandits.[45]

One source which I was unable to verify said that the plans for the great library Hitler planned to build in Linz included three statues of philosophers in the inner hall—Kant, Nietzsche, and Schopenhauer.

Kant's racism

As a further point of similarity with Hitler, the brilliant philosopher Kant was also a white supremacist. "'Humanity is at its greatest perfection in the race of the whites,' Kant wrote in his book *Physical Geography*. 'The yellow Indians do have a meagre talent. The Negroes are far below them, and at the lowest point are a part of the American people.'"[46] Kant also "fought in his lectures against the intermarriage of nations which 'gradually extinguishes the characters, and is, despite any pretended philanthropy, not beneficial to mankind.'"[47] In his concern for racial purity, Kant was far ahead of later racial pseudobiology.

Kant's idea of "race" had to do with national, cultural, religious, and psychological elements which—in the case of the Jews—included a special "Jewish essence." "In this way, Kant developed a notion of racial immutability without reference to pseudobiology."[48] This immutability he related to the Jewish religion, to their concept of God, a concept that—in his view—alienated them from humanity on a profound level. The pseudobiology that came later, deeply influenced by Gobineau and by German variations on evolutionary theory, was thus not completely divorced from earlier views of the Jews. Mack elaborates on the manner in which Kant's anti-Semitic pseudophilosophy (which he calls "pseudotheology") and later pseudobiology were related. This is not just a matter of scholarly curiosity either. To quote Donald Levine, Kant "gave expression to thought ways so deeply embedded in German culture that his ideas were embraced and reworked by hundreds of German philosophers and poets."[49] George Mosse writes in *The Crisis of German Ideology* (a detailed study of 19th-century German thought that members of the Hitler-was-a-Christian school should be careful to avoid) that racial theorists and Volkish authors were influenced (at least in part) by Kant.[50] He is careful to point out that certain characteristics of modern racism were unknown to Kant and would be supplied by more recent "scientific" advances.

Mosse also asserts that the later German supremacist Houston Stewart Chamberlain made use of Kant's philosophy of racial values. The tiny group of Kant's admirers today can say he was taken out of context, that his philosophy was distorted. Nevertheless, he provides an interesting example of the folly of human reason without revelation. He also provides us with sources of a new way of thinking much more relevant to Hitler than the Reformation or Roman Palestine.

Kant also made other negative comments about Jews:

> In presenting his case for the prosecution, Mack observes that Kant consistently equated Jewish identity with a host of undesirable traits, including superstition, dishonesty, worldliness and even cowardliness.

> "Every coward is a liar; Jews for example, not only in business, but also in common life," Kant noted in a lecture on practical philosophy.[51]

To what extent were Kant's ideas derived from medieval stereotypes? One should not have to point out the difference between those who felt that the Jews were under God's wrath due to their rejection of Christ, and those who cared little or nothing about the death of Christ but objected to the very concept of the Old Testament God himself.

It was the great European-wide rejection of traditional concepts of divine revelation that set the stage for modern secular anti-Semitism. In his attitude toward the Jews and the inferiority of non-white peoples, Kant was merely a mouthpiece for general trends, and those general trends would have gone in the same direction had he never lived. Ephesians teaches that there is a "spirit that now works in the children of disobedience" (2:2). It moves them in the same direction, and accounts for general currents of thought that are contrary to God and, like the philosophy of Kant, in rebellion against God. Kant imagined that he was discovering new truths, when in fact he was being manipulated by lying powers of spiritual deception.

If someone who lived 400 years before Hitler and wrote in the Protestant Reformation could have a great influence, or if someone who lived many centuries before in Roman Palestine could have an influence, could someone who died less than a century before Hitler was born also have an influence? Luther made negative comments about Jews—so did Kant. Hitler used the latter's reasoning, not the former's.

Why is it then that Luther's objections to Jews are constantly repeated, while Kant's are so consistently overlooked? One reason is that Luther was a popular national hero and the Nazis found his name and a few cut-and-paste quotes useful. Another reason is that many people are misled by the perception of Hitler as nothing more than a maniac. It is assumed as a given that his ideas have no rational basis, and hence the rational basis is seldom looked for. Hitler's connection with the ideas of Kant—whether derived from first-, second-, or third-hand sources—is ignored.

A third answer is that those who believe in the Bible get raked over the coals while those like Kant who reject the Bible and are supposedly reasonable get a free pass. Yet, if we look at some of Kant's statements we will find that they are very significant for our study. Kant articulated deep spiritual and intellectual trends that persisted and gained in intensity throughout the 19th century. Those trends were expressed by other thinkers as well, and contributed greatly to the concept of Jews as being fundamentally contrary to life in a secular, non-religious sense.

Concluding thoughts on Kant

Mack is careful to state that he is aware of the danger of reading backward from the Holocaust—yet, he points out that the Holocaust was not an abstract event that materialized out of nowhere. He convincingly traces Kant's influence on a century of modern secular philosophical (and, later, racial) German anti-Semitism. In so doing he raises disturbing questions about the so-called Enlightenment itself.

If Mack's understanding is correct, as I believe it is, the Nazis did not represent an overt repudiation of the "Enlightenment." There were (in Mack's words) "disturbing aspects of Enlightenment thought"[52] and a profound irrationality at the very heart of Kant's ambitious program for the emancipation of humanity. Moreover, Kant's anti-Semitism was not an aberration, a curiosity extrinsic to his thought, but was (as Mack demonstrates) directly related to Kant's philosophy on the deepest levels of metaphysics and epistemology.

More could be said about Kant's new secularized version of Christianity. Kant sought to remove Christianity from its Jewish foundations,[53] and thus was one of the first (if not the first) to introduce new ideas that would blossom into the Germanic or Aryan Christianity we will study later in this chapter. He used some Christian concepts and terminology—but to express his own ideas. For Kant, Christ was merely a revolutionary who introduced a new idea of freedom, and the cross was a symbol not a divine sacrifice for sin, but of Kant's personal understanding of freedom through dying to false values.[54]

Other people have noticed ominous parallels between Kant's thought and the horrors later to come. For example, Kant's famous attempt to arrive at ethical standards by reason alone—his loftily named categorical imperative—could easily justify killing Jews: "Jews are a menace to humanity. If everyone did as I am doing and killed Jews, mankind as a whole would benefit. Therefore, killing Jews is ethical."

It has also been suggested that Kant's high degree of intellectual abstraction, his indifference to the external world, and his disregard for the significance of merely physical phenomena, could in much different circumstances encourage a philosophical indifference to the triviality of human suffering. His concept of subjection to the state is particularly ominous.[55] Philosophical historian Stephen R.C. Hicks discusses in some detail not only these points, but also Kant's emphasis on the positive effects of conflict and war on human development— making war not an evil or a regrettable necessity, but something natural, necessary, and desirable. Also significant in this context is Kant's indifference to the sufferings of individuals in the grand process that leads to the higher intellectual development of the human species. [56] Kant thought that "*democracy*, in the truest sense of the word, is necessarily a *despotism*"; "So long as human culture remains at its present stage, war is therefore an indispensable means of advancing it further"; "For man in turn is a mere trifle in relation to the omnipotence of nature, or rather to its inaccessible highest cause"; the significance of these erroneous ideas does not need to be pointed out.[57]

The source that cited the passage from *Table Talk* given above states, ". . . Kant was a particular favorite among academic philosophers of the Third Reich!"[58] This seems rather improbable, yet at his trial Adolf Eichmann made some comments about Kant that indicate how this might have been possible. Discussing Kant's ethics, Eichmann said "for someone like myself it is not possible to understand all of the subject of Kant completely; instead, I only took from these writings what I could understand, and what my imagination could somehow grasp."[59]

The failure to understand that the Nazis would not consistently study an entire philosophy but would only take parts that seemed useful or comprehensible and ignore the rest has confused some scholars. They find an aspect of some philosophy—Hegel's, Darwin's, Haeckel's or Nietzsche's for example—that does not agree with National Socialism or contradicts it and blithely reason that therefore there can be no connection at all. Also, it should be pointed out that anthologies were published that highlighted the thoughts of various thinkers on the Jewish question. Such books—one of them was Treitschke's *Handbuch des Judentums*—made it easy for people to familiarize themselves with others' ideas on the Jews without having to come to grips with more complex ideas. Georges van Vrekham says that several such anthologies were published, that they were very popular, and that they were reprinted throughout the Hitler years.[60]

Historian Richard Evans wrote that "the history of modern anti-Semitism in Germany began with the court preacher Adolf Stöcker."[61] Since Stöcker was active in the latter part of the 19th century, Evans is, in the light of Mack's and others' analyses of German anti-Semitism, missing some important information about a subject that should have been central to his history. Mack not only sheds light on the roots of modern German anti-Semitism—he also calls into question some of the deepest presuppositions of "Enlightenment" thought, and shows that Kant was, in an important sense, deeply irrational.

Kant did not understand the origin, purpose, or benefits of Jewish law, or its relationship to Christianity. He had a false idea of freedom, and a false idea of rationality. In the words of Christian apologist John Montgomery, "Kant separated ethics from theology, morals from God: this he believed to be one of his greatest contributions; in fact, it was one of his greatest mistakes."[62] Dismissing faith as "laziness and cowardice"; calling for "resolution and courage" to dismiss divine guidance; exhorting people to "walk unaided" and live dangerously without the "leading strings" of religion[63]—in these things Kant erred deeply, and set forth on a dark path that was to end in catastrophe and unimaginable suffering.

Hitler and Fichte

In 1945, American soldiers discovered several thousand books from Hitler's personal library packed in crates and stashed in a salt mine near the Berghof, his mountain retreat. They were sent to the Library of Congress, where duplicates or books showing no sign of Hitler's ownership were weeded out. Books with Hitler's bookplate or bearing inscriptions to Hitler were kept—about 1200 books in all. Named the Third Reich collection, they are available for scholarly research, though little attention has been paid to them. Many of them were unread, and a few marginal notations by Hitler seemed insignificant.

Recently Timothy Ryback—a historian, journalist, and former Harvard lecturer—made a careful study of the books.[64] He also examined a much smaller collection of 80 Hitler books in Brown University's rare book collection. Moreover, he researched the subjects of Hitler's library and reading habits in depth, and estimated the total size of Hitler's library to have been about 10,000 volumes. Many of them were presentation copies from publishers or authors, or gifts from associates and acquaintances.

Most of the books have disappeared. Ryback records that Hitler's library at the Berghof was looted by locals and by allied soldiers. He even relates that some visiting US congressmen were filmed emerging from the ruins carrying books. Other books from Hitler's library in Berlin were destroyed or taken by Russians, and thousands disappeared into the Soviet Union. The approximately 10% of the books that remain in the Library of Congress collection (by Ryback's estimate) yield some interesting clues.

Hitler received many gift books, including one from Heinrich Himmler entitled *Death and Immortality in the World View of Indo-Germanic Thinkers*. It was given on *Julfest* 1938, Julfest being the term the Nazis invented as a substitute for "Christmas." For some odd reason the "Christian" Nazis didn't want to celebrate Jesus' birthday (exactly like modern secularists today).

More interesting for our analysis is a first edition of the works of Johann Gottlieb Fichte (1762-1814). Given to Hitler as a gift by the filmmaker Leni Riefenstahl, these volumes are significant in that Hitler read part of them, and made many notations. Ryback records that a hundred pages of Fichte's philosophical and theological speculations are heavily marked—underlined, with exclamation points and question marks. Ryback took the trouble to authenticate these markings by comparing them with those found on Hitler's handwritten speeches in the Federal German Archives. He found that the markings were identical.

Part of this material contained an attempt to explain the Christian doctrine of the Trinity according to human reason: the Holy Spirit was taken to represent human reason, and the Son represented the material or physical expression of some sort of a nebulous force of nature, which was God. This shows how someone can use religious language outside of a Christian context, to express very unChristian ideas. The adaptation of Christian terminology to express concepts derived from secular philosophy was a common practice. Mack's previously cited study pointedly notes the secularization of Christianity.

There are a couple of other significant inferences to be drawn from this seemingly minor discovery. First, since no one would voluntarily read a hundred pages of ponderous German philosophy without having an intellectual bent, it confirms numerous contemporary recollections of Hitler as having been a heavy reader (Ryback gives a number of such testimonies). Secondly, it shows some interest in German philosophy. Is it likely that Hitler read Fichte, but was ignorant of Kant and Hegel? This makes exact parallels between Hitler's ideas and those of the philosophers more significant.

Fichte had other ideas that were much more directly related to National Socialism. Fortunately, a lengthy analysis will not be necessary. Much of what Fichte wrote was extraneous to Hitler's program, and is of interest only to students of dusty and obscure 19th-century philosophies. This means we will not have to waste too much time discussing Fichte's philosophy, but can leave much of it lying in a well-merited oblivion. More relevant ideas can be summarized— and at this point it should be emphasized that though Hitler was a reader, he was not concerned with comprehensive understanding.

Ryback quotes a passage from chapter 2 of *Mein Kampf* illustrating Hitler's selective reading habits. He would concentrate on what he agreed with or found useful, and ignore the rest. This is confirmed by the following quote directly from *Mein Kampf*: "The art of reading as of learning is this: to retain the essential, to forget the non-essential" [*Mein Kampf*, vol. I chapt. 1].

These are not the comments of a scholar—Hitler read looking for confirmation of his own opinions. They are not the comments of a stupid, crazy, or ignorant person either. Someone who read this quote without knowing who the author was would think it had been written by a serious man. Those who dismiss Hitler as having no intelligence will never understand him.

In reading Fichte or other authors, Hitler would focus on what agreed with his purposes or his world view. There was much for Hitler to agree with in Fichte's philosophizing. As with Kant, whether Hitler got ideas identical to Fichte's directly from that author or not is immaterial. The point is not that Fichte was identical to Hitler or that he caused Hitler. The point is that Fichte represented an increasingly accepted set of values and a way of thinking that helped to prepare the way for Hitler.

Hitler the intellectual?

Before continuing, it is worth saying a little more about Hitler's reading and interest in books. The idea that Hitler was a reader and was familiar with various thinkers whose works are distinctly echoed in *Mein Kampf* is an important part of this essay. Ryback's analysis shows further confirmation of this contention, apart from what has been mentioned already.

After giving first person evidence from people that knew him showing that the young Hitler did read books, Ryback notes that half of the value of Hitler's fire insurance policy of 1934 covered his art holdings. The other half covered his books. Hitler's interest in and seriousness about art is well known. That he had a serious interest in books is less well-known. Hitler was widely if superficially read in areas of interest to him.

Ryback's instructive article goes on to elaborate that Hitler had three libraries: one in Munich, one at the Berghof, his mountain retreat, and one at his official residence in Berlin. Photographs of the library at the Berghof show bookcases with glass doors, oriental carpets, globes—Hitler went to some expense to provide a proper setting for his books. One correspondent who met with Hitler and personally surveyed Hitler's library thought it had over 15,000 books. Many of them were books of military history, especially the campaigns of Napoleon and the Prussian kings. Also included were books on the sculpture, painting, architecture, and the theater. There was a lot of popular fiction, as well as books on other subjects, including religion and, as we know from the Fichte volumes, philosophy.

The vast majority of these books have, as was said, been lost. It would be quite interesting to see which other books had been read carefully and marked. Ryback refers to several other spiritual books that were marked by Hitler, but unfortunately doesn't give their names. Perhaps an examination of Hitler's intact library would confirm the assertion that Wagner's political and anti-Semitic writings were his favorite reading material. One book, *Worte Christi* (*Words of Christ*), was given to Hitler as a gift in 1935. Ryback records that it had been much handled, but was unmarked except for a short penciled line by one passage: "You should love God, your Lord, with all your heart, with all your soul, with all your spirit: this is the foremost and greatest commandment. Another is equally important: Love your neighbor as you would love yourself." If Hitler had believed those words and taken them to heart, the entire history of Europe would have been vastly different.

Part of the riddle of Hitler is that he was more of a reader than most people realize. That he read and studied deeply and put together a coherent philosophy consistent with a long-standing secular philosophical tradition in Germany will seem incredible to many, but then many other things Hitler said and did were also incredible. They were real nonetheless. Inability to comprehend something does not constitute a refutation. The refusal to credit Hitler with any intellectual ability whatever is a common error.

The brilliance of Hitler as a politician and a statesman, rising from nothing to the pinnacle of power, shows extraordinary ability. It is not reasonable to dismiss Hitler as a maniac, evil though he was, mad though he was in the end. It is not reasonable to assume that a man who arose from obscurity to leadership of one of the world's great powers through brilliant political and oratorical skills was void of intelligence. Schwerin von Krosigk, the Finance Minister in Hitler's first cabinet, described the new chancellor as "polite and calm" well prepared to conduct government business, with a good memory and the ability to "grasp the essentials of a problem."[65]

Given the stubborn persistence of stereotypes about Hitler, it might be helpful to give a little more information. The fact that Hitler was a heavy reader is pertinent here. Some comments about Hitler's reading habits are found in Walter S. Frank's online essay.[66]

Describing Hitler's lifestyle in Munich before 1914, Frank refers to the Popps, the couple from whom Hitler rented a room. Citing another historian (Werner Maser) he writes:

> There were times when he would just stay in his room for days painting or "with his nose buried in heavy books" he obtained from the Bavarian State Library which was a fifteen minute walk from his room. Mrs. Popp noted that he often "read and studied from morning to night." She noticed that the books covered a wide variety of subjects including politics, and once asked Hitler what he expected to gain by all that reading. Hitler, she said, smiled and took her by the arm and while walking beside her said: "Dear Frau Popp, does anyone know what is, or what isn't, likely to be of use to him in the future?" [Part II "The Young Man," Sect.7 "A Real German"]

Frank gives other information on Hitler's reading, as a boy, as a young man in Vienna, and as a soldier:

> During this period Adolf also acquired the habit of reading since his father had a small library. Adolf's mind was fired by the exploits of the Norwegian Arctic explorer and oceanographer, Fridtjof Nansen (1922 Nobel Peace Prize winner), and also the Swedish explorer, Sven Hedin, who had recently traversed the ancient silk routes from Russia, through Tibet to Peking.

"One Christmas," Hitler would later state, "I was given a beautiful illustrated edition [of Defoe's Robinson Crusoe]." He found it unmatched in "desert-island stories." He also read Don Quixote, Uncle Tom's Cabin, and Gulliver's Travels, all of which he later hailed as "universal works." His favorite stories, however, were still tales of the American west and he read all he came across. [Part. I "The Boy," Sect. 2 "High School Days"]

Referring to Hitler's time in Vienna and in the army, Frank writes:

> The Hofburg, containing among other things, one of the most extensive (and beautiful) libraries in the world, was only a mile away from their room and Hitler visited there regularly. He continued to read on architecture and art, but also mythology,

religion, history and biography. [Part II "The Young Man," Sect. 4 "Teenage Dreams"]

Hitler read during his military service also. During quiet times in his sector, Hitler, one of his comrades noted, "always had a book spread out in front of him," which he carried in his back pack. He still refused to read popular novels or short stories, since he considered them frivolous, and he had nothing but contempt for seedy works. "I hated nothing more than trash literature," Hitler would later tell an acquaintance. As in all wars, young men who had never seriously thought about God, and even those who had claimed earlier to be atheists, turned to God for comfort. Hitler was no exception. In an early letter to Mr. Popp, Hitler ask him to "please save the newspaper" that noted his Iron Cross award because he wanted to "have it as a keepsake if the Lord should spare my life." He also turned to the Bible for comfort and read the "Gospels." Finding little comfort ("turning of both cheeks is not a very good recipe for the front" he would later write), he abandoned the Bible and because as he said, "war forces one to think deeply about human nature," turned to philosophy. [Part III "The Soldier," Sect.9 "A Born Soldier"].

Ryback's previously mentioned article "Hitler's Forgotten Library" also gives other evidence of the young Hitler's tendency to read widely. It quotes Hitler's boyhood friend Kubizek stating that Hitler was a heavy reader, and was registered with three libraries in his hometown. Hitler's world was in books, according to Kubizek as quoted by Ryback and Hitler later based his life on an abstract philosophy void of the human dimension. Conceding that Kubizek's memory is not the last word on the subject, Ryback presents corroboration from other sources, one of them being a cousin who related that Hitler was constantly reading.

Finally, skimming a chapter of *Mein Kampf* reveals more of Hitler's own references to reading.

Every book I acquired aroused his [hunger's] interest; a visit to the Opera prompted his attentions for days at a time; my life was a continuous struggle with this pitiless friend. And yet during this time I studied as never before. Aside from my architecture and my rare visits to the Opera, paid-for in hunger, I had but one pleasure: my books.

At that time I read enormously and thoroughly. All the free time my work left me was employed in my studies. In this way I forged in a few years' time the foundations of a knowledge from which I still draw nourishment today.

I painted to make a living and studied for pleasure.

Thus I was able to supplement my visual instruction in the social problem by theoretical study. I studied more or less all of the books I was able to obtain regarding this whole field, and for the rest immersed myself in my own thoughts.

I could read and draw until late into the night, and never grow tired. In addition, I had the greatest interest in everything connected with politics, but this did not seem to me very significant. On the contrary: in my eyes this was the self-evident duty of every thinking man. Anyone who failed to understand this lost the right to any criticism or complaint.

[vol. I chapt. 2: "Years of Study and Suffering in Vienna"]

Richard Steigmann-Gall in *The Holy Reich*, a book that tries to link Hitler to Christianity, dismisses in a single sentence the idea that Hitler might have been an intellectual.[67] Since the index to his book shows no references at all to important writers in the secular tradition who are frequently linked to Hitler, it is reasonable to ask if his abrupt dismissal is the result of pre-conceived ideas rather than substantive analysis.

Ian Kershaw agrees that Hitler read widely during his years in Vienna, but unsystematically, and only to confirm existing opinions. Hitler's opinions did have to begin at some point, however, so reading could just as well have introduced Hitler to new ideas he later adapted to his own world view. In the introduction to his biography Kershaw warns about "the trap . . . of grossly underestimating his [Hitler's] abilities." He was speaking of the mature Hitler, but that warning could apply to the adolescent Hitler just as well.[68]

Kershaw is skeptical of the claim of Hitler's friend Kubizek that Hitler in his youth read some well-known classical authors such as Goethe, Dante, and Schiller, but elsewhere he accepts much of Kubizek's narrative as genuine. There is no reason a brilliant but confused adolescent could not have haphazardly read a wide number of books, including some classics.

Mein Kampf contains classical references to Hecuba, Ephialtes, Homer's *Odyssey* (the isle of the Phaeacians), Prometheus, the Hellenic Ideal, the Persian wars and the Age of Pericles, the Punic wars and the rise of Rome. Hitler's unpublished *Second Book* refers to the subjugation of the Helots by the Spartans, and shows some real knowledge of military history. In his study of Hitler's worldview, Jaeckel states that Hitler "argued historically again and again, and he had a considerable if idiosyncratic knowledge of history."[69] This does not mean Hitler was a scholar. He made passing references of the sort that a self-taught reader might be capable of.

There are also distinct traces of Hegel, Kant, Fichte, Schopenhauer, Gobineau, and Darwin in Hitler's two books. There are ideas identical with some of those of Richard Wagner, H.S. Chamberlain, Haeckel, and Nietzsche. People dismiss the idea of an intellectual Hitler too easily. His ideas did have intellectual roots— some of those roots were in another German philosopher whom we need to examine.

Fichte and National Socialism

Once you reject the Bible and the concept of divine revelation, you are free from dogma, liberated, emancipated—but where do you go from there? The German misosophers were not atheists. They recognized that there was some sort of a higher spiritual reality, and were much more religious than the French "*philosophes*." This has been attributed to Leibniz (1646-1716) and the German Pietists. A deeper reason might be that the German governments (Germany was not unified at that time) were far more benevolent and less oppressive than the French monarchy had been. Hence the church-state alliance that existed all over Europe would have seemed considerably less offensive in Germany. Moreover, the Protestant part of Germany had long since shed what the so-called *philosophes* regarded as the useless medieval superstitions of Catholicism, so Christianity in Germany was perceived as less contrary to reason, more open to development and change. Having left Rome, German Protestantism became over time more flexible and open to accommodation with philosophy.

Whatever the reasons, German secular philosophy in the first part of the 19th century had a deep sense of a higher spiritual power at work in human destiny. But, rejecting the biblical concept of God, German thinkers invented a god according to their own imaginings—one that was agreeable to the dictates of human reason, and nothing more than an invention of human reason. This concept of god was often pantheistic. God was seen as a sort of vital force within the cosmos. Goethe imagined a *Gott-Natur*, a God-Nature. Schelling's work *On the World Soul* (*Von der Weltseele*) (1798) imagined some sort of vital spirit at work within the world, but not transcendently.

Another aspect of German philosophy was the discernment of a definite course of spiritual development in human history. History was seen as moving toward a destined end—and this was agreeable to reason. There was a clear and undeniable progression from the most primitive man to the early civilizations of Mesopotamia to the glories of Greece to the more widespread diffusion of law and culture in the Roman empire to the vast improvements of modern Europe—it was an ascending process. This process was attributed to some higher power at work. It was imagined that the casting off of traditional religious dogmas was the latest stage in this process. Revealed religion was seen as rigid, arbitrary, external—a barrier to the dynamic development of the human race. Moreover, since it was derived from Mediterranean and Semitic sources, it was also foreign, a hindrance to a uniquely German cultural development. That the glorious onward and upward ascent of humanity toward higher and higher levels of development might be abruptly terminated by the return of Christ was not considered worthy of consideration.

All of this may seem remote from Hitler, but there is more—much more. The concept of some sort of philosophical god or natural force or higher spiritual law at work in the development of mankind had remarkable implications when applied by Fichte to the German nation. As the natural universal force, the Absolute, or the Cosmic Whatsis worked to advance humanity, its basic operative agent was the national group. The Greeks, the Romans, and now the Germans—the cosmic force used nations as its instrument. Hence, national groups were manifestations of the Life Force in action. The transcendent, the absolute, manifested itself in the nation. Nations were manifestations of the divine, and as such assumed more than ordinary significance.

Fichte wrote in one of his *Addresses to the German Nation*:

> Spiritual nature was able to present the essence of humanity in
> extremely diverse gradations in individuals and in individuality
> as a whole, in peoples. Only when each people, left to itself,
> develops and forms itself in accordance with its own peculiar
> quality, and only when in every people each individual develops

himself in accordance with that common quality, as well as in accordance with his own peculiar quality—then, and then only, does the manifestation of divinity appear in its true mirror as it ought to be . . . .[70]

The different peoples were supposed to develop freely according to their own various qualities. This is called "that law, which is the highest law in the spiritual world!" and an expression of "the rule of law and divine order."[71] Now, the highest spiritual law is the development of the nation—from which it follows that the greatest sin is that which hinders the development of the nation. We are entering a new concept of spirituality here, one that elevates the national group far above its unimportant place in the New Testament.

The acceptance of various nationalities sounds at first like the beneficent and tolerant nationalism of Johann von Herder (1744-1803). This seems harmless enough—but once begun, the process of exalting the nation beyond its proper place did not stop within reasonable limits. As Jesus said, "A little leaven leavens the whole loaf." Fichte went on to argue that the purest race, the least degenerate, the one closest in spirit to the primeval forces of Nature/Spirit/Absolute was, by coincidence, the same race of which he happened to be a member—the German race. Because—unlike the decadent French and Jews—the Germans were purer, and hence closer to the powers of nature, they were capable of leading mankind to a higher level of cultural awareness. Other national groups would presumably be free to develop their lesser inner qualities as they tagged along behind the lofty and superior Germans.

Given the exalted status of the nation in the grand scheme of things, the fatherland was described by Fichte as the meeting point between heaven and earth. This idea of the nation, the people, the Folk as being the individual's means of participation in higher spiritual reality was elaborated on and amplified by later thinkers such as Paul de Lagarde and Julius Langbehn.

Membership in the Folk was essential not only to finding personal fulfillment and life's deeper meaning—it was also the door to eternity. Germans die, but the fatherland goes on and on. There is eternal life—in the fatherland. A few more quotes from one of Fichte's *Addresses to the German Nation* are appropriate here: "Love that is truly love, and not a mere transitory lust, never clings to what is transient; only in the eternal does it awaken and become kindled, and there alone does it rest."[72]

We need permanence, eternity, membership in something greater than ourselves—all of that is found, according to Fichte, in the nation.

> Life merely as such, the mere continuance of changing existence, has in any case never had any value for him [the individual], he has wished for it only as the source of what is permanent. But this permanence is promised to him only by the continuous and independent existence of his nation. In order to save his nation he must be ready even to die that it may live, and that he may live in it the only life for which he has ever wished.[73]

The identical sentiment was expressed by Hitler in 1943. The stenographic records of Hitler's military conferences show him referring in this way to General

Paulus' failure to commit suicide rather than surrender at Stalingrad: "What is life? Life is the Nation. The individual must die anyway. Beyond the life of the individual is the Nation."[74] Like Fichte, Hitler found the meaning of life and immortality in the nation—though he made "nation" synonymous with "Aryan race" in a way that was foreign to Fichte.

The individual dies, but the nation lives on. The individual is of secondary importance—it is the nation that is valuable, the only source of permanence, and only in the nation do we find real life. The emphasis on the group rather than on the individual became deeper and more widespread later in the century, but by no means did it begin there. As Fichte wrote,

> He who regards his invisible life as eternal, but not his visible life as similarly eternal, may perhaps have a heaven and therein a fatherland, but here below he has no fatherland, for this, too, is regarded only in the image of eternity—eternity visible and made sensuous—and for this reason also he is unable to love his fatherland. If none has been handed down to such a man, he is to be pitied. But he to whom a fatherland has been handed down, and in whose soul heaven and earth, visible and invisible meet and mingle, and thus, and only thus, create a true and enduring heaven—such a man fights to the last drop of his blood to hand on the precious possession unimpaired to his posterity.[75]

This contains a swipe at Christianity. Those who look for their eternity in an invisible world have a fatherland in heaven ("perhaps"), but they have no earthly fatherland. They are unable to love their fatherland and are to be pitied. The real man finds his true and enduring home not in an invisible spiritual eternity, which may or may not be real, but in the fatherland, the "true and enduring heaven." The culture was still too conservative to allow for open attacks on Christianity, but the fundamental antagonism was inevitable. It would become much more open later in the century.

Now the deepest fulfillment and participation in the hidden spiritual meaning of life lie in Germany, where "heaven and earth, visible and invisible meet and mingle." It is the nation that gives life meaning. This completely contradicts Christianity which asserts that the individual's immortal soul is more important than the nation. Christianity also teaches that freedom is an inner spiritual state not dependent on this or that place. A German may be as free or as unfree spiritually as a Frenchman or a Chinaman. Fichte had a different idea of freedom. For him, freedom meant being a German. The foundation of democracy is severely cracked when we accept that the individual is less important than the state or the race.

> Freedom to them [the ancient Germans] meant just this: remaining Germans and continuing to settle their own affairs, independently and in accordance with the original spirit of their race, going on with their development in accordance with the same spirit, and propagating this independence in their posterity.[76]

Fichte would have agreed with Hitler's belief that ". . . this nation can only be happy if it can live its life in accordance with its own nature and in its own way . . . We National Socialists believe that in the long run man can be happy only in his own nation."[77]

This elevation of nationalism to the level of a religion is still far from Auschwitz, but we are getting a little closer—and Fichte had yet more to say. A national group does not exist in the abstract—it needs a government, a state. This state is (in the imagination of Fichte) an instrument of higher destiny. As the state is used by a higher power to lead the nation upward, it must not be confined or restricted by ordinary ethical rules that apply to individuals.

Because of such concepts, it has been said that Fichte's *Addresses to the German Nation* were foundational to much of subsequent German history—yet, haven't many rulers of many nations throughout history followed this ethic (or lack of ethic)? If Fichte emphasized force and cunning as essential to state policy this was nothing new. It is as old as human history. Even stating that Germany was destined to rule and had the right to use every means to fulfill that destiny was only dressing up in philosophical language the same primitive love of power that animated the Romans and the Babylonians.

According to Fichte's misosophy, the Germans were justified in seizing territory for living space (*Lebensraum*) and dominating Europe by force without regard to treaties (scraps of paper) or international morality (sentimental rubbish). Later in life Fichte may have calmed down and expressed more moderate views, but extreme nationalists would select only those ideas that were of interest to them.

Another concept of Fichte's that would have met with Hitler's approval was the idea that the German race had a unity of thought, language, and culture that transcended national boundaries. Such artificial divisions as lines drawn on maps could not separate Germans.

> The first, original, and truly natural boundaries of States are beyond doubt their internal boundaries. Those who speak the same language are joined to each other by a multitude of invisible bonds by nature herself, long before any human art begins . . . From this internal boundary, which is drawn by the spiritual nature of man himself, the marking of the external boundary by dwelling-place results as a consequence; and in the natural view of things it is not because men dwell between certain mountains and rivers that they are a people, but, on the contrary, men dwell together—and, if their luck has so arranged it, are protected by rivers and mountains—because they were a people already by a law of nature which is much higher.
>
> Thus was the German nation placed—sufficiently united within itself by a common language and a common way of thinking, and sharply enough severed from the other peoples—in the middle of Europe, as a wall to divide races not akin . . .[78]

External political boundaries are artificial. A people united by language and by a way of thinking (modern racial *science* not yet having been invented) had a unity that transcended political boundaries. This being so, what could be more natural, more reasonable, than to eliminate artificial boundaries and unite the Folk according to higher spiritual principles of organic unity? In seeking to unify all Germans Hitler was acting out 19th-century concepts, not 16th-century ones. The Christian teachers of the Reformation and long after were not interested in uniting all Germans.

Also relevant to an understanding of National Socialism is Fichte's concept of national purity. It has been claimed this began with Kant, or with Herder—but no matter which individual first articulated it, the fantasy of Germanic purity and superiority was gratifying and readily received by those seeking meaning in life outside of the confines of traditional religion. The elevation of the nation far beyond its proper place was the direct result of the abandonment of Christianity.

In the eighth of his *Addresses to the German Nation*, Fichte wrote that "love of fatherland must itself govern the state and be the supreme, final, and absolute authority."[79] This is not Hitler, but it removes barriers to Hitler. No real Christian would ever have said that our highest goal is the fatherland. In the words of Pascal, "Since [man's] true nature has been lost, anything can become his nature: similarly, true good being lost, anything can become his true good . . . he has fallen from his true place, and cannot find it again. He searches everywhere, anxiously but in vain, in the midst of impenetrable darkness."[80] The Germans increasingly sought meaning in their nation as the old religious beliefs faded and the rationalism of the so-called Enlightenment began to disintegrate. Fichte was one of the pioneers of this change—so much so that he can justifiably be called the "seminal figure of modern German revolutionary nationalism."[81]

Now that the nationalist project has been thoroughly discredited, people are looking for meaning as members of other groups. Ethnicity, gender, class, and sexual or political orientation now form the basis for new identities and new meanings. They will prove and are proving to be equally false and equally destructive, as people ignorant of life's higher purpose seek for meaning and purpose in the wrong places. It is these new allegiances, not old-fashioned nationalism, that are the breeding grounds for new totalitarianisms and new evils. The problem is not with the ordinary and natural affection and concern for one's country, or even devotion to one's country, that are normally called "patriotism." The failure to distinguish between normal patriotism and the philosophical elevation of the nation have led many to mistakenly think that conservative regard for one's country is inherently fascist—but fascism emerges out of the abandonment of traditional religious values and the need for a replacement for God.

Fichte, the Jews, and Christianity

Fichte stated in his Twelfth Address that it was the German race that created modern Europe, and that Germany was "pointing the way to a regeneration of the human race."[82] Now keeping Germany pure (first spiritually and culturally, later also racially) has become essential for the future of humanity. Fichte claimed that the preservation of the Folk was the greatest virtue, and warned that dilution and contamination of the Folk would lead to the separation of the Folk from the higher spiritual powers. This would cause serious damage. In Fichte's words, pure national groups like the Germans cannot "absorb and mingle with itself any other people of different descent and language . . . without itself becoming confused, in the beginning at any rate, and violently disturbing the progress of its culture."[83] Foreign ideas, especially French and Jewish ones, would corrupt the Folk.

In the tradition of Kant, Fichte saw the Jews as fearfully enslaved to religious laws that alienated them from the rest of humanity. Hence they lacked love, reason, spiritual freedom—in short, all of the essential qualities of humanity. In his words, not only was Jewry "founded on a hatred of all humankind." The Jews also were "a people excluded by the strongest human bond of all—by religion" from the joys of normal society and feeling. Such attitudes led to Fichte's oft quoted statement, "As to giving them civil rights, I see no other way than that of some night cutting off their heads and attaching in their place others in which there is not a single Jewish idea. To protect ourselves from them I see no means other than to conquer for them their promised land and to pack them off there." Fichte wrote, "self-seeking is the root of all other corruption,"[84] and the Jews, with their false idea of God that led to greed, selfishness, and materialism, were the epitome of that self-seeking. The Jews represented for Fichte everything that was wrong with society.

Fichte did not advocate the extermination of the Jews, but found them to be an alien body, a state within a state, that contaminated the purity of the Folk by importing false and unGerman values. He objected to giving civil rights to Jews, and felt they could not be citizens. In this context he made comments that explain Hitler's bizarre idea that the victory of the Jewish race would lead to the end of humanity. In the Thirteenth Address he stated that the invisible spiritual qualities of a nation were its essential link to the mystic life force of the cosmos. If those qualities were lost by mixing, the nation would be separated from its spiritual source. This "separation from spiritual nature . . . will cause all men to be fused together in their uniform and collective destruction."[85] In other words, the corruption of Europe's leading and fundamental race would mean the end of humanity's progress. In Fichte's words, "But, as Germany sinks, the rest of Europe is seen to sink with it."[86] And this man imagined he was a philosopher. How much philosophy is a complete waste of time at best, and harmful at worst?

But who would want to so corrupt and eliminate the distinctive features of the most noble race on the planet? Who would want to commit "so monstrous an act of brutality or enmity against the human race" as to undermine the unique features of the finest, best, noblest, and purest race on earth? Who would plot a universal dominion based on ruining the German character? Someone could only do this if they were motivated by "the lust for booty," for material gain. Such miserable greedy schemers would be cold, lacking in normal human feelings, oblivious to higher ideals. "Where is there in modern Europe a nation so lacking in honor" that it could deliberately set out to undermine the Germans? Who would be motivated by the love of material gain? Who would want to suck the life juices out of the German people and drain them dry? "The detestation of the whole human race"[87] would fall upon such miserable corrupters of the German race, humanity's best hope.

In his book *Contribution to the Correct Understanding of the French Revolution* (1793), Fichte openly expressed his opinion of the Jews: "In the bosom of almost all the nations of Europe there spreads a powerful state driven by hostile feelings that is continually at war with all the others, and that in certain states terribly oppresses the citizens. I speak of Jewry [*Judentum*]."[88] These and related ideas in his *Contribution* were his only overt attacks on the Jews. He never repudiated them or elaborated on them. Fichte later consistently avoided mentioning Jews even in writings where references to them would seem necessary, and some have found this avoidance puzzling. My own speculation is that Fichte wanted to keep his own writings *Judenrein*, free of Jews, feeling that even negative references to such contemptible people would stain his Germanic prose. Those in the know would understand exactly who was meant—those who didn't get the point were not worth bothering with. Whatever the case, Rose's assessment seems clear: Fichte "bears a large responsibility for the rise of both revolutionary and nationalist Jew-hatred."[89] If Fichte did later moderate his views, that would have been of no interest to Nazi propagandists who pointed to Fichte as one of their ancestors. Again, they would not seek to understand the totality of Fichte's thought. They would only pull out such phrases or concepts as were useful and disregard the rest.

Fichte also had some interest in Christian doctrines. He came to recognize the importance of religion to ethics and was concerned, as we have seen, with reinterpreting biblical terminology in a manner agreeable to human reason. Fichte even argued that Christianity was part of the social contract, and that adherence to the Christian religion was necessary for full partnership in the state—but what sort of Christianity? Fichte's concept of Christianity was "Enlightenment" secularism dressed up in religious language. Both French and German philosophers of the period made human reason their guide and abandoned divine revelation, but German idealism "sought not merely to expel theology, like the French Enlightenment, but to swallow it."[90]

This is not irrelevant to Hitler, and Fichte's philosophical reinterpretation of religion might shed some light on Hitler's idea of God. At one point in a passage of Fichte's works read and marked by Hitler, Fichte speculated on where Jesus had derived his power from. Hitler underlined the answer: Jesus power came from his total identification with that natural force Fichte called "God."[91] Fichte, incidentally, believed in an Aryan Christ, and sought to rescue Christianity from its Jewish corruptions.

God not as the God of scripture but as some sort of cosmic force was basic to German idealistic philosophy. If Hitler accepted the concept of God as a force in the cosmos that worked to elevate mankind through the superior the German race—a stupid concept, but one advocated by university professors like Fichte, Hegel, and many others, and common in later 19th-century German thought—then his belief in himself as an agent of a higher power, a man of destiny, makes sense. Hitler saw himself as deriving power from his "absolute identification" with a god of human philosophy. More will be said about this shortly.

Many dismiss Hitler's frequent statements about having been sent by Providence, spared by Providence, chosen by Providence as nothing but rhetoric. Hitler did often tell the truth, and was very honest in stating his main goals. If he was honest about wanting to get rid of the Jews, expand to the east, tear up the Versailles Treaty, end the Weimar democracy, rule the world, there is no reason why he could not also have been honest in stating that he believed himself to be the agent of a higher power. There are numerous statements of his to this effect, and none of them were contradicted by his actions, as his numerous lies on a lower plane were contradicted by his actions. Some opponents of religion will be quick to assert that this is an example of how religion gives people crazy ideas and causes a lot of suffering. They will find it easy enough to show, however, that while Hitler's philosophy reflects negatively on all religion, Stalin's atheism does not reflect negatively on all atheism! They are capable of such gymnastics because they lack integrity. They will also exempt philosophy from their critiques, and are afraid to admit or even to consider that independent human reason freed from religion introduced the basic ideas of Hitler's world view.

Returning to the subject of Fichte, this brief overview does not pretend to cover all of his thought, or show how his views changed over time as he faded from an ardent nationalist to a more harmless contemplative fantasizer. It does show that certain essential elements of National Socialism were current more than a century before Hitler came to power, and they did not come from Christianity and the Bible. The fact that liberal Protestants who were attracted by philosophy abandoned biblical truth, adopted secular principles of nationalism, and expressed essentially worldly philosophies in religious language is confusing to some scholars and historians who have no understanding of the Bible. It will not confuse those who have a reasonable degree of understanding of the New Testament. The total absence in the New Testament of teachings on the importance of nationalism and love of one's fatherland is due to the Christian emphasis on the world to come. Those who hope for a heavenly kingdom that abides forever will not become obsessed with worldly power that fades away.

John Bunyan's profoundly spiritual work *Pilgrim's Progress* describes a place called Vanity Fair. Symbolic of the sinful world, it contains a French row, a German row, an English row, and so on. This is typical of the Christian attitude that prevented nationalism from arising in its extreme forms until the decline of religion in the modern era. Those of us who believe we are just passing through this world on the way to a better place can have some natural affection for our country, but will not become obsessed by it. It is no coincidence that the turning away from revealed religion that characterized both the French and the German "Enlightenments" was swiftly followed by extreme, even virulent forms of nationalism. Those who reject God will look for something more—and the nation seemed to human reason like a plausible substitute. Large enough to give a sense of belonging, yet tangible enough to be easily grasped and understood (unlike the mysteries of God), the nation became an object of devotion—and later in the century almost an object of worship.

The elevation of the nation far beyond its rightful place in the great scheme of things was one of the most essential principles of Hitler's thought. If one may speculate on Hitler's childhood a little, it is generally accepted by historians that Hitler's account in *Mein Kampf* of his stormy and negative relationship with his father is accurate. Without a father's love and guidance to help him attain a proper sense of self-worth, and with no particular academic achievement or ability, especially given the nationalistic rivalries of the Austro-Hungarian Empire in Hitler's childhood, Hitler must have derived a profound sense of self-worth just from being a German. No doubt during his days as a down-and-out loser in Vienna and Munich, the thought that he was a German also sustained him and gave him a sense of importance.

If Hitler had profited from Catholic religious instruction in his childhood he would have understood that being a German had nothing to do with his personal self-worth. He would have understood that a sinful and evil German was less to be admired than a virtuous Frenchman, African, Pole, or Jew. He would have understood that our purpose and meaning in life did not come from the nation, but from higher and more enduring spiritual values. His passionate emphasis on the nation and the race is incomprehensible outside of a modern secular context. That some Germans even today are still trying to define their identity in terms of their nation, rather than in terms of timeless truths that far transcend nationality, is a powerful testimony to the dullness of the human spirit. Even the Roman Stoics could see that there was a larger aspect to life and to the human personality that transcended national boundaries.

The danger of philosophy

The German-Jewish poet Heinrich Heine (1797-1856) could clearly see the dangers of these and related ideas. Approximately a century before Hitler came to power Heine recognized the implications of the secular German philosophy that began to emerge immediately after the turning away from traditional religion. In a book-length essay called *On the History of Religion and Philosophy in Germany* Heine wrote:

> Thought goes before deed as lightning before thunder. German thunder is certainly German; it is not very agile and begins to rumble very slowly. But it will come and when you hear crashing, as it has never crashed before in all of world history, you will know, German thunder has finally reached its goal.[92]

This was not a lucky guess on Heine's part, a mere curiosity for students of the Third Reich to puzzle over briefly and then pass by in pursuit of popular and easily comprehensible explanations for Hitler. Heine foresaw that "Kantian criticism, Fichtean transcendental idealism, and even *Naturphilosophie* [nature philosophy],"[93] with their repudiation of traditional ethics and values, were extremely dangerous. "Because of these very doctrines," he elaborated, "revolutionary forces have developed which are simply biding their time to break out and to be able to fill the world with horror and admiration"[94]—and many people did admire Hitler.

Heine predicted that people armed with these new ideas "will mercilessly tear up the soil of our European life in order to destroy the past to its very roots. Armed Fichteans will come onto the scene, who, with fanatic will, will be untamable by self-interest or fear." They will be "inflexible in a social upheaval" and "not moved by any traditional reverence."[95]

Then comes that remarkable and often quoted passage that was based not on poetic feeling or vague intuition, but on an understanding of philosophy far beyond the reach of many who like to talk about Hitler today:

> . . . so the *Naturphilosoph* [the nature philosopher] will enter into terrible association with the original powers of nature. He will be able to conjure up the demonic forces of Old Germanic pantheism, and that lust for battle which we find among the Old Germans will awaken in him, which does not battle to destroy, or to conquer, but solely for the sake of the battle itself. Christianity—and this is its greatest merit—has to some extent tamed that brutal Germanic lust for battle, but could not destroy

it; and if ever that restraining talisman, the cross, breaks, the savagery of the old fighters will rattle forth again, the absurd frenzy of the berserker, of which the old Nordic poets sing and tell so much. That talisman is brittle, and the day will come when it breaks apart miserably. The old stone gods will then emerge from their forgotten ruins and rub the dust of millennia from their eyes. Thor, with the giant hammer, will spring up at last, and destroy the Gothic domes.[96]

Of course, Heine did not foresee World War I and the many other specific circumstances of Hitler's rise. He could not have guessed at later developments, such as the extraordinary power of an industrialized and united Germany, or the emergence of social Darwinism that baptized vicious brutality as "the latest scientific findings." Nevertheless, in predicting that the removal of Christianity's traditional ethic and the emphasis on being at one with nature, living according to nature, would end in catastrophe, Heine showed more understanding than do many of the people who write about the origins of National Socialism today—and he was writing without the advantage of hindsight.

Heine was not the only one to see this new trend. The German-Jewish thinker Saul Ascher (1767-1822) also noticed the waning of traditional religious anti-Semitism and the emergence of a new and more serious form of hostility, especially in the writings of Fichte. Ascher wrote, "There is evolving before our eyes a quite new species of opponents armed with more dreadful weapons than their predecessors . . . A new epic of Jew-hatred begins with Fichte's *Contribution* . . . ."[97]

Friedrich Ludwig Jahn

In May 1933, book burnings were held in various places across Germany, carried out by university students who reveled in violent anti-intellectualism. These incidents were perceived then and are perceived today as perfect symbols of Nazi tyranny.

Shirer was mistaken in saying that this was the first book burning that had occurred since the Middle Ages.[98] In fact, it was the first book burning that had occurred—in Germany at least—since 1817. In that year, representatives of a student youth congress meeting at the famous Wartburg castle publicly burned anti-nationalist and reactionary books in huge bonfires. When Heine made his oft-repeated quote "Where one burns books, one will soon burn people," he had recent events in mind.

The book burning incident has been connected with an early nationalist agitator named Friedrich Ludwig Jahn (1778-1852). Peter Viereck saw Jahn as the main inspiration behind the congress, and asserted that the Nazi book burnings were deliberate imitations of Jahn.[99] Jahn had been instrumental in organizing nationalist student societies and was a leading apostle of nationalism and resistance to the French during the Napoleonic era. Nicknamed "Father Jahn," he represented an early emergence of key elements that were to develop slowly throughout the century and come to fruition in the Third Reich. Praised by Nazi propagandists as a forefather of National Socialism, he merits further study.

Described by a committee of the German Diet as one of the chief spiritual leaders of a new Germany (along with Fichte),[100] Jahn was a popular speaker more than a philosopher, and wrote for the masses. Nevertheless, he derived some basic ideas from German philosophy. His book *German Volkdom* (1810) had a wider appeal than Fichte's difficult philosophy, but had some points in common with it. Statements about the eternity of the Folk, the German People, were in perfect agreement with Fichte, as was Jahn's emphasis on the need for keeping the Folk pure—"The purer a people, the better; the more mixed, the worse . . . Animal hybrids have no genuine power of propagation, and hybrid peoples have just as little posterity."[101]

These words of Jahn's could have been pasted directly into *Mein Kampf* or into the writings of late 19th-century German social Darwinists without alteration. Also significant was Jahn's call for the union of state and Folk in a new Reich. This Reich should include all the Germanic peoples, including the Swiss, the Dutch, and the Danes. He also dreamed of eliminating the traditional borders within Germany and creating one centralized and unified state. Jahn was far ahead of his time. This goes well beyond mere patriotism and the natural desire to see Germany liberated from French rule.

Naturally, this state should be led by a Fuhrer—"The Volk will honor him as saviour."[102] Viereck concedes that Jahn was inconsistent and at times offered different solutions including democracy—but what evils have not been done in the name of democracy? The fact that Jahn used such words as "parliament" or "democracy" does not mean much. Point 25 of the Nazi Party platform refers to a "parliament."

Jahn had modern views of Christianity. He felt that the church should be integrated with the state, and should be Germanic in character. Spreading this German Christianity to the inferior peoples of the east was part of Germany's mission. Christianity was placed at the service of worldly philosophy, and subordinated to human reason. That Jahn was very far from biblical Christianity can be seen in a quote of Jahn's used by the Nazi philosopher Rosenberg in his *Myth of the Twentieth Century*. Stating that the awakening of the masses to an awareness of "the eternity of their own Volkhood [people-ness]" was history's most holy moment[103] shows concepts of holiness and eternity derived from secular human imagination, not from the Bible. Behold, how proud and deluded reason begins to go astray so quickly after liberating itself from the confines of biblical doctrine. Now we see patriotism being elevated to a religious level, with the nation or the race providing meaning, purpose, eternity, and even standards of good and evil. What helps the nation is good, what harms it is bad. When Hitler described the blood shed in defense of the fatherland as a holy sacrifice, he was moved by the same idea that animated Jahn.

One of Jahn's contemporaries, Heinrich Steffens, noticed the increasingly religious quality of the new German nationalism, and found it dangerous.[104] If after all, the Folk is not merely our source of meaning in life, our eternity, but also is the force of history, then it deserves our highest devotion. Jesus, in contrast, was not in the least bit concerned that his "fatherland" was occupied by foreigners. He was more concerned with another world to come after this one and advocated cooperation with the Romans. No doubt there were Christians in Jahn's day who understood that to live under French rule and later go to heaven was better than to live under German rule and later go to hell. Manifestations of extreme nationalism within the German Protestant churches show not the

Christian basis of nationalism, but rather the capitulation of the churches to secular philosophies.

Jahn's concepts not only of history but also of education were echoed by Hitler. The idea of popular education as a means of instilling not facts, education, and knowledge into children but rather German values was one of Jahn's (and Fichte's) ideas. Of course, all education is aimed at instilling something into children—a belief that Darwinism is true and that homosexuality is normal, that religion is bad or irrelevant are the ideas taught by modern America's leftist anti-religious educators. Like Hitler, Jahn advocated using education to instill uniquely German values (as opposed to general Western values). His concept of the Germans as "humanity's holy people" (along with the Greeks),[105] a concept shared (if not in identical terms) with Fichte and Hegel, is not the educational basis for rearing children with a healthy attitude toward life.

There are other parallels. Just as the Nazis concealed training programs for their future air force behind sport flying clubs, so Jahn disguised his nationalistic student organizations as gymnastics clubs. Members of these clubs wore special uniforms, and behaved in a belligerent manner to those out of conformity with their Germanic ideals. Viereck saw them as predecessors of the Storm Troopers, and states that it was watching these groups of Jahn's that gave rise to Steffens' fears cited above.

Particularly significant is Jahn's anti-Semitism. He stated that the Jews were vagabonds, "lifeless" and "frivolous" phantoms because they lacked a national homeland.[106] The significance of this for modern German anti-Semitism should not be underestimated. It was not the brainchild of Jahn only, but was the logical outcome of a certain brand of philosophy, and was a theme repeated with gathering intensity as the century progressed.

That the Jews crucified Christ was not an issue. That their continued survival called Christianity into question was not an issue. What was at issue was that the Jews could not participate in everything that made life meaningful according to new ways of thinking that placed the nation at the center of our earthly existence. Having no state, no nation, no fatherland, no participation in the mystical outworking of the hidden forces of the cosmos in world history, the Jews were nothing but lifeless phantoms. They came to represent everything that life was not—in a secular context, not a Christian one. When we combine this with the idea that selfish and materialistic Jewish values were static, fixed, eternal, totally at odds with the concept of truth unveiling itself as humanity progressed to higher levels of consciousness through philosophy and intellectual freedom, we find new reasons for seeing the Jews as symbols of anti-humanity. Their weddings, books, achievements, hopes, loves, dreams, fears, were all lifeless in the weird light not of Christianity but of secular philosophy emancipated from divine revelation.

That many Jews were not at all concerned about Germany's defeat by Napoleon, and in fact welcomed Napoleon's reforms, would not have been lost on German nationalists. This would have been evidence of selfish Jewish materialism—a concern solely for their own advancement, with no regard for the well-being of the Folk. The Jews who did loyally support the struggle against Napoleon of course could be ignored, or even resented for their attempts to be Germans.[107]

Anti-Semitism was not yet a racial concept. Jews who abandoned their life-denying concepts and assimilated could be accepted into the German family—but even this began to be questioned as the age sank more deeply into the quagmire of modernism, and racial emphases added yet another ingredient to the poisonous new brew of secular anti-Semitism.

Although Jahn was in many ways a minor figure, he is useful for illustrating the existence of embryonic Nazi-like tendencies in Germany long before Hitler. Viereck has been accused of overemphasizing the importance of Jahn, but Jahn was significant enough to have earned the attention of Metternich. This prince of reaction recognized the dangers to his system of Jahn's ardent nationalism, and wrote to General Wintzingerode, "But what will become of the sovereignty of your King if men like Jahn and Arndt are produced in Germany?"[108]

That the Nazis did not fail to recognize the importance of Jahn is illustrated by a couple of quotes from Nazi writers. One K.M. Bungardt praised Jahn as "a new human type." Another Nazi "intellectual," B. Theune, said Jahn had invented the term "folkdom," and hence was "the natural starting-point for every analysis of the concept of Volk."[109] As a man of the early nineteenth century Jahn was obviously different in many ways from Hitler, yet the spiritual currents he articulated were to be magnified and intensified as the century progressed. Jahn's "fierce nationalist Jew-hatred" and his "nationalism inflamed with Germanic romanticism"[110] justified the praise of his Nazi descendants.

Hegel

Much more significant historically and philosophically is the gigantic figure of Hegel. His thought is extremely complex— but some of his concepts are practical, easily understood—and identical to some key concepts of National Socialism. In his *Rise and Fall of the Third Reich*, Shirer mentions several such concepts. Admittedly, Shirer was not a philosopher, and he omits some later writers who served as mediating links between Hegel and the modern era. The straightforward historical narrative that makes Shirer's book such a good introduction is very different from the careful analysis of the academically trained philosopher— however, Hitler was not a trained philosopher either. It is known that he read philosophy. It is absurd to think that he read Fichte but had no concept of Hegel, or at least of some of Hegel's more easily accessible ideas—even if only at second or third hand. I think Hitler read parts of Hegel himself, even if only in summaries or excerpts from the original works. No one will suspect Hitler of having diligently worked through all or most of Hegel's philosophy, and such ideas as "substantive individuality" or "accidentality is the concept of the finite" don't concern us here.

Most of Hegel's ideas were totally irrelevant to the Third Reich—but not all of them. Fichte's successor at the University of Berlin, Georg Wilhelm Friedrich Hegel (1770-1831) saw war as good and necessary—a purifier without which there would be no progress and society would become stagnant. He also had faith in the German people as uniquely destined to lead mankind to greatness. He stressed the importance of "heroes," great men like Napoleon destined by some sort of fate, providence, or "World Spirit" to greatness. Hegel's concept of the state was also thoroughly agreeable to the totalitarians who shortly followed him. Hegel saw the state as being supreme—the duty of the individual was to obey the state.

Militarism; complete subordination of the individual to the state; German superiority; special individuals chosen by destiny—these alone do not make a

Nazi dictatorship. Hegel was far removed from Hitler, but he contributed in no small measure to a cultural climate receptive to Hitler's ideas—particularly as the ideas that were confined at first to academic circles became more widespread in the ensuing decades. Hegel, Kant, and Fichte did not so much cause these trends as articulate them, and bring them into clearer focus. The basic underlying currents were there—invisible spiritual, emotional, and psychological currents. They grew, developed, intensified, and changed with the emergence of many other historical and social factors. Hegel contributed to them significantly.

Someone may say "There is no proof Hitler read Hegel." There is no proof that he didn't. There is proof that he read Hegel's predecessor, Fichte, and good evidence that he read Hegel's successor, Schopenhauer. Even if Hitler did not read Hegel, many people did. His ideas were widely circulated and Hitler picked them up somewhere.

Hegel's philosophy

Let us briefly examine Hegel's "philosophy," and see how the rejection of revelation and the reliance on reason alone led not to a calm, peaceful, progressive society of enlightened individuals, but to the exact opposite. Rejecting the Bible but still aware of some kind of a higher spiritual reality, Hegel invented a "World Spirit" to satisfy his emotional needs and to account for some aspects of human society and history. Hegel detected an undeniable progression in human history, from its most primitive origins to its current apogee in 19th-century Europe in general, and in 19th-century Prussia in particular. This he attributed to the World Spirit, a god of his own invention, agreeable to his personal taste.

This imaginary man-made god was active in the world, guiding mankind in a steady ascent toward higher levels of self consciousness and inner freedom. From the most primitive times through the Greeks, the Romans, the French, and now through the new chosen people, the Germans, the World Spirit was at work. Hitler's references to a guiding force behind history are consistent with this concept, and his statements on the historical progress of the human race reflect the world view articulated by Hegel. Like many others in the period, Hegel saw history as a process, and so did Hitler: "The progress of humanity is like climbing an endless ladder" [*Mein Kampf*, vol. I chapt. 11]. This concept of human history as unendingly progressive is of course not biblical.

The idea of a people favored by God also did not derive from Christianity. The God of the Old Testament had worked with a chosen people, the Jews, but now in the New Testament dispensation sheds his Spirit into the world to individuals through faith in Christ. In the teachings of Christ and the apostles, personal belief and action are infinitely more important than nation and race. Hence, those who equate Hitler's concept of a higher power working through the Germans with Christianity while ignoring Hegel and Fichte are distorting the history of philosophy and betraying a total ignorance of biblical teaching in this area. When, for example, Steigmann-Gall tries to link National Socialism to liberal Christianity by stating that one thing they had in common was the idea that "God worked providentially through history to liberate humanity from materialism in order to realize his moral kingdom on earth,"[111] the failure to point out that this idea was derived not from the Bible but from Fichte, from Hegel, and from a solid chain of Folkish thinkers, is a serious omission.

Hegel also came up with a number of other new ideas. Imagining that by the power of his mind he had penetrated reality to an extent that no one had ever gone before, he observed that the progress of human history was accomplished by human agents. From this he reasoned his way philosophically to the idea of the great man, the World Historical Hero, as an instrument of the higher power. These great men were in a special category, far above the ordinary considerations of mere mortals. Such men were not squeamish or hampered by morality as they followed their destined paths to greatness. Individual suffering was not important as the World Spirit rolled inexorably on its way.

When thinkers later in the century expressed the idea of cultural and social progress being made over the corpses of the vanquished, they were expressing ideas that were perfectly consistent with Hegel's concept of history. When the physician Ludwig Buechner wrote the following words in 1882, he was in harmony with Hegel's concept of history: ". . . history as well as nature mark every step forward, even the smallest, with innumerable piles of corpses."[112] This is inevitable, when the divine concept of creation is lost, and people are reduced to philosophical ciphers, insignificant little naughts in grand and sweeping but false and inhumane historical schemes.

Hegel's lack of basic human feeling is illustrated by his reaction to personally seeing Napoleon:

> . . . After the Battle of Jena in 1806 when Napoleon defeated the Prussians, Hegel saw the emperor riding past.
> The encounter had a profound impact. "I saw the Emperor—this world-spirit—go out from the city to survey his realm," he wrote on October 13, 1806. "It is a truly wonderful experience to see such an individual, on horseback, concentrating on one point, stretching over the world and dominating it" For Hegel, Napoleon embodied the world-historical hero of the age, driving forward the self-realization of God in history.[113]

How wonderful, to dominate the world! Never mind that Napoleon's glorious domination extended over a very small percentage of humanity and lasted but a brief moment. Never mind that Napoleon was a proud, cruel, deceitful, and violent man who would have to die shortly and ultimately give an account to God for the manner in which he had wasted his life. Napoleon accomplished the defeat and occupation of his country, and was responsible for countless deaths and innumerable suffering, all to no purpose—but Hegel was oblivious to such elementary considerations of humanity and morality. He considered the historical process to be above moral and ethical considerations.

Hegel looked at Napoleon as teenage girls looked at the Beatles—to such a low moral state was he brought by his reliance on reason alone. The widows, the orphans, the shattered bodies on bloody battlefields were irrelevant. The brilliant philosopher was a moral and spiritual blind man, groping in darkness as he foamed out torrents of empty words.

The connection between his concept of the World Historical Hero and Hitler is obvious—as a great man, a Man of Destiny, Hitler was far above the petty moral considerations that burden ordinary individuals. That Hitler at times thought in Hegelian terms is illustrated by the following quote:

273

However weak the individual may be when compared with the omnipotence and will of Providence, yet at the moment when he acts as Providence would have him act, he becomes immeasurably strong. Then there streams down upon him that force which has marked all greatness in the world's history.[114]

This is pure and undiluted Hegel.

It has been rightly said that Darwinism led to the devaluation of the human personality, but the trend is already clearly evident in Hegel. His self-invented philosophical historical process was not concerned with individuals. As Stephen Hicks has pointed out, in Hegel's system the "deeper cosmic forces" follow their course "with little or no regard for the individual."[115] This is inevitable once the account of the creation of man in Genesis is lost. Once you remove the divine spark of human souls originating with God, some depersonalization is always the result. Only the first few chapters of Genesis and nothing else account for the unique dignity yet also the terrible fall of man.

This was not unique to Hegel. Kant also thought that nature was concerned only with the advancement of the human species, not with individuals. As he wrote in "Speculative Beginning of Human History," the "path that for the species leads to *progress* from the worse to the better does not do so for the individual."[116] Individual happiness or unhappiness was irrelevant. This by the way is one reason Darwinism caught on so quickly—it was the expression on a biological level of a powerful trend towards depersonalization and abstract, inhuman visions of "progress" based on conflict that was already in place. It has even been asked if Darwinism was not merely the spirit of the age expressed in scientific sounding language.

Hegel also observed that the Great Historical Heroes wielded governmental power, and deduced that governments were agents of his imaginary World Spirit. From this he figured out that the individual should be subordinate to the state. By obeying the state, we live according to the World Spirit, and hence are truly free. Obedience is freedom, subservience is liberty. In Hegel's words:

> All the worth which the human being possesses, all spiritual reality, he possesses only through the State . . . the Universal is to be found in the State, in its laws, its universal and rational arrangements. The State is the Divine Idea as it exists on earth.[117]
>
> . . . the genuine, absolute, final end (is) the sovereignty of the state . . . the means to this end is the sacrifice of personal actuality . . . a self sacrifice which yet is the real existence of one's freedom; the maximum self-subsistence of individuality, yet only as a cog playing its part in the mechanism of an external organization; absolute obedience, renunciation of personal opinions and reasonings, in fact complete *absence* of mind . . . [emphasis in the original].[118]
>
> . . . the duty to maintain this substantive individuality, i.e. the independence and sovereignty of the state, at the risk and

sacrifice of property and life, as well as of opinion and everything else naturally comprised in the compass of life . . .[119]

Anyone who does not see the connection between this and fascism should not, in my opinion, try to discuss the origins of National Socialism. Such repulsive and dehumanizing views were foundational to National Socialism. Particularly noteworthy is the idea that we are truly free only in subservience to the state. This was a common theme of later totalitarian thinkers: democracy, an unrestricted press, a parliament with conflicting parties, electoral contests—these were not signs of freedom, they were signs of chaos and disorder. Real freedom consisted in submission, a harmony of national unity with no one singing off key or walking out of step. When a Nazi lawyer argued in 1933 that full humanity was only realized in subordination to the state, he was not uttering strange new ideas that had just suddenly appeared somehow in miraculous contradiction to the entire Western heritage. Do some people need to be informed that the Western heritage includes not only Locke, Mill, and Voltaire?

Hegel felt that the "history of the world is nothing but the development of the idea of freedom."[120] This sounds very good, but the student of Hegel soon learns that there is a difference between *objective freedom* and *subjective freedom*. True freedom, "objective freedom," is gained by obedience to the historical process as it is worked out by the World Spirit. Since this Spirit works in the world through the agency of the state, true freedom involves submission to the state as well. "Subjective freedom" is a false freedom. People imagine they are free if they can do what they like, but their limited wills are isolated from the World Spirit, hence they are trapped in selfish egotism and alienated from higher spiritual realities. Hegel mimics Christianity here, as Christianity also states that the freedom of self will is not true freedom, and we become truly free only in obedience to God—but this spiritual freedom in God is found through Christ, and is radically different from Hegel's concept of freedom through submission to the state. This is putting the state in the place of God—the essence of modern totalitarianism. Hegel's statement that "One must worship the state as a terrestrial divinity"[121] was truly revolutionary. It is no wonder that he has been linked to both right-wing (Nazi) and left-wing (Communist) collectivism and authoritarianism.

The Bible presents very different concepts of the state and of freedom. The state is appointed by God to keep the peace, and is itself subject to a higher law in the Christian system; hence it has no deep mystical significance. The individual is to find true meaning and purpose elsewhere. Biblical freedom is individual, personal, and in matters of faith beyond the power of the state. Alcide de Gasperi's words cited in chapter 2 bear repeating here: "The theoretical and practical principles of fascism are the antithesis of the Christian concept of the State, which lays down that the natural rights of personality, family, and society exist before the State."[122] It is secularism, not biblical Christianity, that is the greatest threat to individual liberty today.

It is significant that the declining belief in God among early 19th-century German intellectuals was accompanied by an increasing emphasis on the state. The same is observable in America today—a marked decline in the influence of religion since World War I has been accompanied by a huge increase in state power. Not surprisingly, as people lose sight of life's higher meaning they rely more and more on the state, which becomes a substitute for God.

Some may object that Hegel was a Christian—a Christian who thought that such doctrines as the deity, sacrificial death, resurrection and return of Christ were irrelevant distractions from Christ's main message, which was ethics. Hegel contributed greatly to the concept of Christianity and of Protestantism as something fluid, evolving, changing with the times, reaching higher and higher levels of rationality unrestricted by dead and confining dogmas. He saw Christianity as a step forward in the advancement of mankind, but considered this to be merely one stage in an ongoing process of which he himself was on the cutting edge.

This has to do with a point that has caused some confusion. Hegel saw Luther's Reformation as a distinct step forward on the march toward freedom. He recognized the value of breaking free from submission to Roman dogma and stated "This is the essence of the Reformation: man is in his very nature destined to be free."[123] For Hegel, the significance of Protestantism was that it "introduced the principle of *subjectivity*" by emphasizing individual belief.[124] The Reformation (as Hegel understood it) did not end in 1517, however. It continued with greater degrees of freedom from the dead hand of traditional dogmas—not only of papal dogma, but of biblical dogma as well.

For this reason many German secular thinkers—as well as Nazi politicians—found Protestantism vastly more congenial than Catholicism. Not only was there nationalistic vanity to be derived from the fact that Luther was a German (the Nazis weren't interested in people from other countries whose basic ideas were identical to Luther's). More importantly, having broken free from submission to church dogma, Protestantism was much more susceptible to new philosophical trends and developments. When the institutional Protestant church abandoned biblical absolutes and historical doctrines and opened up to the exciting new philosophical influences of the "Enlightenment" and German idealistic philosophy, it came to be seen as "progressive," an ally rather than an obstacle to progress—unlike the doctrinally more stubborn Catholics. Catholic loyalty to the Vatican (a foreign power) was also a source of hostility.

There were of course other thinkers, scholars, and academics moving in the same direction as Hegel—an online essay by Phil Orenstein names some of many.[125] Jakob Fries, professor at the University of Jena; Ernst Moritz Arndt, professor at the University of Bonn; Friedrich Ruhs, Chairman of the History Department at Berlin University—these, along with student activists, writers, agitators, and politicians demonstrate that Hegel and Fichte were not mere ivory tower speculators. Their ideas had much to do with the darkening realities of German politics.

Another one of Hegel's ideas was that the highest state of development in the world had been reached by—you guessed it—the Germans. Incidentally, the purpose here is not to refute Hegel. The purpose is to try and illuminate the real nature of National Socialism. Vain fantasies of German superiority quickly began to emerge within a generation after the casting off of biblical truth in the inaccurately named "Enlightenment." The concept took different forms after Hegel's death—it was expressed before him and modified after him—but he contributed to it in no small measure. In so doing he exemplified the mindset that lent itself so readily to further abuses in the ensuing decades. As Jesus said, "A little leaven leavens the whole loaf."

Hegel also observed that war was a part of the process by which civilization progressed to higher levels—he saw war as good. That Hitler also saw war as good, something to be sought after rather than something to be avoided, was totally incomprehensible to those who tried to negotiate with him at Munich. They should have read some German philosophy. Of course, people long before Hegel also saw war as desirable. If Hegel had never lived at all there would have been more European wars. But, as we consider these questions in their German context, we need to see the very real parallels between Hitler and the generations immediately preceding.

Here are some quotes from Hegel on war:

> War is not to be regarded as an absolute evil and as a purely external accident . . . War has the higher significance that by its agency, as I have remarked elsewhere, "the ethical health of peoples is preserved in their indifference to the stabilization of finite institutions; just as the blowing of the winds preserves the sea from the foulness which would be the result of a prolonged calm, so also corruption in nations would be the product of prolonged, let alone 'perpetual', peace" . . . As a result of war, nations are strengthened, but peoples involved in civil strife also acquire peace at home through making wars abroad.[126]

When Heinrich von Treitschke, a professor at the University of Berlin much later in the century, lectured to his gullible students on war as being good, he was pontificating in the best Hegelian tradition—and these ideas were not merely academic, but were later put into practice. Hitler also stated on more than one occasion that too much peace would not be good for the German people.[127]

Of course, Hegel has his defenders among the tiny number of nearly extinct Hegelians. They assert that Hegel's ideas were taken out of context, and obscure the issue with subtleties—and, much of Hegel's thought was far removed from the metaphysical crudities of National Socialism. Nevertheless, Hegel's statements about war, great men, Germany's superiority, and the superiority of the state are plain enough, and his attitudes were effortlessly combined with social Darwinism later in the century. When General Friedrich von Bernhardi stated that war was a "biological necessity" that prevented decadence, he illustrated the manner in which earlier philosophies were strengthened and intensified by more up-to-date pseudo-science.[128]

Hegel and the Jews

Hegel, to all appearances, was not an overt anti-Semite. He made some early anti-Jewish statements which he deliberately left unpublished in his lifetime. These writings followed the Kantian critique of Judaism as an obstacle to the freedom of spirit and human emancipation offered by German philosophy. The mature Hegel never either restated or repudiated his early comments, yet his negative concept of Judaism was "largely implicit in his later philosophy of religion."[129]

Hegel was more sympathetic towards the Jews than others and did not fall into extremes of Jew-hatred, but he did add another weapon to the arsenal of others more extreme than himself by presenting the Jews as outdated and superfluous. Their concept of God may have been an important step in the progress of civilization, and was a distinct advance from primitive polytheism, but that was a long time ago. Hegel saw the Jews of his day as having outlived their usefulness—there was no further need or purpose for them.

Calling the Jews obsolete and superfluous is a long way from calling them destroyers of racial purity and enemies of the human race. Nevertheless, Hegel's philosophy helped toward the formation of a new concept of the Jew as a negative symbol. If the state led by the mighty hero is the instrument of the Absolute (or World Spirit, whatever) by which nations are elevated to greatness and the human race is advanced, what shall we say of those who have no state, no world historical heroes, and are completely excluded from the process of life? If the meaning of life for the individual is found through participation in the nation, what can be said of those who have no nation? Rose asserts that Hegel's philosophy of history thus "provided revolutionary anti-Semitism with one of its theoretical pillars"—that the Jews were a "fossil nation," a "ghost race," a "parasite race" that contributed nothing but only lived off of the culture of others. This had something to do with Kant's idea of the Jewish subjection to God's laws and rules as separating them from the rest of humanity.[130]

If truth is an ongoing process of development, aren't those who (contrary to reason) cling to static concepts fundamentally estranged from the whole meaning and purpose of life? Their reliance on laws, rules, customs, rituals, ceremonies showed Hegel that the Jews had a concept of truth that was totally at odds with the fundamental reality of the universe. Also, if the nation is an instrument of destiny, what of an alien body that insists on remaining apart and does not share in the full cultural life of the nation? To the Christian, such a question is irrelevant—to the secular German philosopher, it was of great importance. An alien body residing in the nation was an obstacle to progress, representing values at odds with the purpose of the nation in the grand scheme of things. This alien body could easily come to be seen as Hitler saw it—sponging off of the healthy natural body, benefiting from its culture but remaining apart.

Hegel advocated civil rights for Jews, and considered them to be human beings. More likely than not, he thought that opening doors would encourage assimilation and allow the Jews to rejoin the flow of human history by abandoning their outdated and useless religion. This option would be increasingly dismissed by those who noted that many Jews would not assimilate, and who feared that assimilation would lead to racial and cultural impurity.

Schopenhauer

The idea that Hitler may have been deeply indebted to Schopenhauer, that Schopenhauer's thought also played a significant part in the formation of National Socialist ideology, is too little considered. Schopenhauer's emphasis on finding peace of mind through self-nullification, on avoiding the unhappiness of unfulfilled desire by denying desire altogether, seems far removed from Hitler. Nevertheless, there is credible evidence that Hitler read Schopenhauer extensively during a crucial period of his life.

Ryback's previously mentioned article states that Hans Frank, Hitler's lawyer and later Governor General of Poland, recalled after the war that Hitler claimed to have read Schopenhauer's *The World as Will and Representation* during his military service in WWI. Kershaw's biography makes this point as well, referring to Frank's postwar memoirs, and to Hitler's wartime conversations.[131] John Toland's biography of Hitler quotes him as saying to Frank "In the later years of the war I read Schopenhauer and reached for him again and again."[132] Hitler also quoted Schopenhauer in *Mein Kampf*: "The Jew's life as a parasite in the body of other nations and states explains a characteristic which once caused Schopenhauer, as has already been mentioned, to call him the 'great master in lying'" [*Mein Kampf* vol. II chapt. 11]. This is an obvious compliment to Schopenhauer, as Hitler did not usually credit his sources. Schopenhauer is the only philosopher referred to by name in *Hitler's Second Book*.[133]

Those who are determined to deny any intellectual capacity to Hitler, or who want to link National Socialism to other causes, can always discredit second-hand quotations—though what motive could Frank possibly have had for inventing a story about Hitler reading Schopenhauer? Kershaw is skeptical of Hitler's claim to have read Schopenhauer, yet much of Schopenhauer's thought blends perfectly with some key aspects of National Socialist doctrine. The credible evidence that Hitler read Schopenhauer is confirmed by broad areas of congruity between Hitler's thought and Schopenhauer's. The question here, as with Hegel and Fichte, is not merely what Schopenhauer said or actually intended, but how he was perceived later in different historical contexts.

If we accept that Hitler read philosophy and derived ideas from it, some of the mystery surrounding him begins to dissipate. Given Hitler's talent for fastening on concepts he could use and ignoring everything else, he could later specifically condemn Schopenhauer's pessimism and state "Where would I get if I listened to all his transcendental talk? A nice ultimate wisdom that! To reduce oneself to a minimum of desire and will. Once will is gone, all is gone. This life is war"[134] yet still retain other aspects of his thought. The *Table Talk* shows Hitler praising Schopenhauer. This passage was quoted above in connection with Kant: "In our part of the world, the Jews would have immediately eliminated Schopenhauer, Nietzsche, and Kant . . ."[135]

An incident from Hitler's Vienna days in which he tried to lecture on Schopenhauer but was put in his place and compelled to admit he had only read some of Schopenhauer's work is used by Kershaw to show that Hitler had not really read Schopenhauer.[136] Since this was before the war, the time when Hitler claimed to have read Schopenhauer seriously, this incident—assuming it to be true—might only illustrate initial enthusiasm for a new author. It might also illustrate not ignorance of Schopenhauer, but rather inability to deal with intelligent contradiction.

Before proceeding, a little background information on Schopenhauer is necessary. Arthur Schopenhauer (1788-1860) studied at the University of Berlin when Fichte was lecturing there. He falls within the Kantian and Fichtean tradition of German philosophy, as he believed that there was an underlying or governing principle of the universe, and that this principle was discoverable by human philosophical wisdom, not divine revelation (which he rejected as being suitable only for someone "still in his childhood"). In his words:

> Whoever seriously thinks that superhuman beings have ever
> given our race information as to the aim of its existence and that
> of the world, is still in his childhood. There is no other revelation

than the thoughts of the wise, even though these thoughts, liable to error as is the lot of everything human, are often clothed in strange allegories and myths under the name of religion.[137]

Another quotation from Eichmann shows the relevance of Schopenhauer to this discussion. Speaking this time not at his trial but to his interrogator before the trial, Eichmann said that Schopenhauer helped him to break away from his childhood religious influences:

> More and more I came to the conclusion that God can't possibly be as small as in the Bible stories. I thought I had found my own belief. And I read Schopenhauer, who says the way of religious faith is safer and the way of freedom is a dangerous way, which the individual must perpetually work out for himself . . .[138]

What was the underlying principle that Schopenhauer discovered with his human wisdom? He identified the innermost essence of everything as a vague, purposeless, blindly striving impersonal Will. All activity, whether natural or human, was merely a manifestation of this dominant and irresistible Will. Life was a ceaseless struggle of conflicting wills, animated blindly by the unthinking and unfeeling Will that was the foundation of all activity. There was no need for individuals to be concerned about death, as the Will of which we are only the particular manifestations was eternal. Thus we are guaranteed an abstract eternal life, not a personal one.

A passage from *Mein Kampf* is appropriate here: " . . . it [true idealism] corresponds in its innermost depths to the ultimate will of Nature. It alone leads men to voluntary recognition of the privilege of force and strength, and thus makes them into a dust particle of that order which shapes and forms the whole universe" [vol. I chapt. 11]. There is an "ultimate will" that shapes reality, and we are partakers of it. The reference to dust particles is also significant. When Hitler eliminated millions of people, he thought he was only cleaning up unhealthy dust particles. This complete indifference to the value of human life, seen in Hegel and now expressed more openly by Schopenhauer, was one of the deepest and cruelest aspects of Naziism. It follows inevitably from the loss of the divine creation of man in Genesis. If we are not created by God, then we really are nothing special.

Another passage from *Mein Kampf* also illustrates the harmony of Hitler's thought with Schopenhauer's: ". . . the subordination of the inferior and weaker in accordance with the eternal will that dominates this universe . . . the Folkish philosophy of life corresponds to the innermost will of nature . . . ."[139] This will was of course an impersonal will, unconcerned with the dust particles of humanity that were tossed around by it.

Accepting the idea of Schopenhauer's influence on Hitler not only explains Hitler's reference to an "ultimate will" or "innermost will" dominating the universe. It also explains the latter's emphasis on the primacy of will over reason. Schopenhauer argued that Will was dominant, that it made the decisions for which reason only afterward sought the explanation and justification. Moreover, if Hitler believed that he was the representation or personification of the underlying Will that was the basis of reality, this would explain the unshakeable faith in the

280

rightness of his decisions. As the embodiment of the underlying Will, his own will was merely an extension of the profound That-which-is, and hence must inevitably be fulfilled. Hitler's striking rise to power, with his will overcoming countless seemingly insuperable obstacles and being fulfilled in every respect up to the fall of France, no doubt convinced him that whatever he willed must necessarily come to pass—hence his reliance on intuition rather than on objective appraisal of facts.

There are profound differences between Hitler's ideas and Schopenhauer's. The latter claimed that the secret of happiness was the nullification of desire (his indebtedness to Oriental thought was great), whereas Hitler had a totally different conception. Yet, it is possible for two people to agree on something—a problem, a fact, a philosophical truth—yet respond to it in markedly different ways. One could easily agree with Schopenhauer that the underlying reality of life was Will, but then reason that the proper way to achieve happiness was not denial of the will, but rather gratification of the will to the greatest possible extent. Not elimination of self, but rather the fullest amplification of self could then be seen as the desired end. Thus Hitler could have accepted Schopenhauer's premise, but departed from it in a strikingly different direction. Nietzsche was also deeply influenced by Schopenhauer, yet Nietzsche sought not nullification of the will but gratification of the will to the maximum degree.

Another difference between Schopenhauer's thought and Hitler's is that Schopenhauer denied the character of deity to his impersonal force, and rightly so. Something that is blind, purposeless, and impersonal can't properly be called "God" in any traditional sense. Hitler on the other hand often referred to a God or to a Providence that worked to advance the German people. He also spoke of a personified Nature, a "she" acting with purpose to achieve "her" ends. There is some ambiguity here, both on Hitler's part and on Schopenhauer's. Neither of them was entirely consistent. For example, Schopenhauer apparently felt uncomfortable in his impersonal universe and so also personified nature. He wrote:

> . . . it is not the individual that nature cares for, but only the species; and in all seriousness she urges the preservation of the species, since she provides for this so lavishly through the immense surplus of the seed and the great strength of the fructifying impulse. The individual, on the contrary has no value for nature, and can have none, for infinite time, infinite space and the infinite number of possible individuals therein are her kingdom. Therefore nature is always ready to let the individual fall, and the individual is accordingly not only exposed to destruction in a thousand ways from the most insignificant accidents, but is even destined for this and is led towards it by nature herself, from the moment that individual has served the maintenance of the species.[140]

This harmonizes well with a statement of Hitler's:

> Nature looks on calmly, with satisfaction, in fact. In the struggle for daily bread all those who are weak and sickly or less

determined succumb, while the struggle of the males for the female grants the right or opportunity to propagate only to the healthiest. And struggle is always a means for improving a species' health and power of resistance and, therefore, a cause of its higher development [*Mein Kampf*, vol. I chapt. 11].

The individual has no value. We should not be surprised if those who believe in this philosophy act accordingly. We should be surprised if in the end they do not act accordingly. Biblical teaching directly contradicts this false and ugly idea of humanism. It was with this attitude that Nazis could look calmly on sick, starving, and dying people and view it as natural, ordinary, a fact of life.

The profound harmony between Schopenhauer's concept of life here and Darwin's is also evident. The ground was well-cultivated and watered, ready long in advance for the reception of Darwin's ideas. This explains not only why they caught on so quickly, but also why they were taken to further extremes than they were in other countries. As to Hitler's use of the word "God," there are many examples in German philosophy of how the word "God" was used in a non-Christian context to represent not the God of Abraham, Isaac, and Jacob, but rather a philosophical concept dreamed up by human minds.

It is worth noting that Schopenhauer explicitly denied pantheism. He asserted that pantheism would make God a part of the evil in the world. Hence he preferred a blind and purposeless force, irresistible and immanent, but far from divine. This is not consistent with Hitler's idea of a force that exalted the German race, and had sent Hitler as a leader to accomplish that effect. If, however, we can combine a Schopenhauerian will with a Hegelian teleology, giving a vague and impersonal force that worked in nature to effect the advancement of the best, then Schopenhauer's ideas can be seen to fit very well with Hitler's. Peter Viereck says in his study that Richard Wagner made precisely this adaptation, and Wagner's ideas were in many ways close and even identical to Hitler's. This will be discussed in chapter six.

This also fits perfectly with Hitler's ideas and assumptions, if not with all of his rhetoric. Whatever the case, a "God" that agreed perfectly with all of Hitler's inclinations and allowed him, helped him, to do everything that he pleased, was not a God in any real sense of the word. Incidentally, given Himmler's belief in reincarnation and karma, Nietzsche's belief in a caste system, and Schopenhauer's interest in Oriental religion, a study on aspects of Oriental thought and National Socialism might yield some more details.

It is significant that Schopenhauer's concept of Will marks a further stage in the decline of human concepts of God subsequent to the "Enlightenment." The descent from the vast and all-powerful yet personal God of the Judaeo-Christian tradition to the God of the deists, impersonal and remote yet still some kind of a God, was followed by a further descent to Hegel's World Spirit—a nebulous philosophical abstraction even less meaningful than the God of the deists. Schopenhauer then postulated some kind of aimless force without any personality at all. This descending concept of the divine reached its final end in the atheism of Nietzsche—it is intimately related to the emergence of Germany as a substitute for God and National Socialism as a substitute for religion.

Schopenhauer's anti-Semitism

Schopenhauer's concepts of the Jews are extremely important to this study. Not only do they demonstrate how ideas introduced by Kant were added to, modified, and radicalized in the following decades—they also are closely related to even more extreme ideas that emerged later, and reveal those views in adolescent form.

Schopenhauer accepted Kant's understanding of the Jews as materialists, alienated from society, from nature, and from higher truth by their adherence to a false concept of God and his restrictive laws. A greater degree of radicalism begins to be evident in Schopenhauer, however. For one thing, there is more overt hostility to Christianity. Kant, Fichte, and Hegel had been more outwardly respectful of Christianity, though they denied its essential teachings. Schopenhauer, on the other hand, condemned Christianity openly—and he blamed it on the Jews. Hence he wrote in *The World As Will and Idea*, "it is to be regarded generally as a great misfortune that the people whose culture was to be the principal basis for our own were not the Indians or the Greeks, but these very Jews."[141]

The link between Judaism and Christianity is more plainly stated in *Religion*: "Christianity contains, in fact, a great and essential imperfection in limiting its precepts to man, and in refusing rights to the animal world . . . Such are the effects of the first chapter of Genesis, and, in fact, of the whole Jewish conception of nature."[142] Schopenhauer claimed that Jews were cruel to animals because of their concept of animals as beneath them. "The view that animals have no rights and humans no duties to them . . . is revoltingly crude, a barbarism of the west, the source of which is to be found in Judaism."[143] The problem with Europe was Christianity, and the problem with Christianity was that it was too much under the influence of Jewish concepts. That humans were by nature nothing more than animals was an important theme of Wagner's, Haeckel's, Nietzsche's, and Hitler's—and Jewish cruelty to animals was stressed in Nazi propaganda.

"Man is at bottom a dreadful wild animal," Schopenhauer wrote, but is currently in "the tamed state called civilization." In essence, "man is a beast of prey."[144] It doesn't take a great deal of imagination to see how someone might reason from this to conclude that civilization was an artificial constraint that hindered man from living freely according to his real nature as a beast of prey. This introduces a very important but insufficiently recognized element of modern German anti-Semitism—that Christianity had had a bad effect on European civilization, and the Jews were to blame for this. Jewish values working through Christianity had divided the unity of nature and separated man from the animals by its false teaching of the uniqueness of man, and by its stifling and unnatural ethical requirements. We are essentially animals, in Schopenhauer's view: "A man must be bereft of all his sense or completely chloroformed by the *Foetor* [odor] *Judaicus* not to see that in all essential respects the animal is absolutely identical with us."[145] This was followed by a pioneering appeal for animal rights.

Schopenhauer also harped on the theme of Jews as aliens and parasites. They had no culture of their own, but only lived off the vitality of other cultures. Their false view of life (which had become enshrined in Christianity) meant that Jews were an obstacle to the cultural and spiritual liberation of the German people. More specifically, their (and the Christians') mistaken beliefs in human free will, rationalism, and a moral universe created by a rational God led to a misguided emphasis on optimistic values and beliefs contrary to the philosophical truths of Schopenhauer—and his pessimistic ideas about the pointlessness of life were, he firmly believed, necessary for the advancement of mankind. Jewish-Christian error also included the intolerant belief that their way was the right way and the only way, when in fact it was Schopenhauer's view that was the right way and the only way.

As a result, Schopenhauer thought that Judaism should be eliminated for the sake of humanity. "Schopenhauer was adamant that Judaism must be destroyed."[146] He did not call openly for the destruction of Christianity. The destruction of Judaism was to be achieved, however, by assimilation. Hence, Schopenhauer advocated granting civil rights to Jews. They could intermarry with Gentiles, and then, as Schopenhauer put it, "in the course of a century there will be only a very few Jews left and soon the ghost will be exorcized."[147] Schopenhauer of course did not understand biological racism, and the necessity of keeping the blood pure.

Two other points about Schopenhauer merit mention. One was his early advocacy of Aryan Christianity. He felt that Christianity had originated in India but later had been contaminated by the Jews. Thus, he saw some merit in Christianity and felt it could be harmonized with his own philosophy once purged of Jewish influences. Secondly, it may be argued that his hostility to Judaism was the result of hostility to organized religion in general, and not specifically anti-Semitic. To refute this objection, Rose cites a lengthy excerpt from Schopenhauer's essay "On Religion." There Schopenhauer wrote of Moses as a murderer and called the Jews "a sneaking dirty race afflicted with filthy diseases," who "were at all times and by all nations loathed and despised." He relates this to Kant's argument that the Jews "were the only people on earth who did not credit man with any existence beyond this life."[148]

Gobineau

Hegel, Kant, Fichte, Schopenhauer—in all of this we are still a long way from Hitler. We are getting closer, but a number of other missing elements need to be added. Not surprisingly, complex phenomena such as Hitler, National Socialism, and the horrors of WWII can't be reduced to simple explanations. Other German thinkers added yet more vital elements—as did a Frenchman, Arthur de Gobineau.

Gobineau (1816-1882) was a French diplomat, novelist, scholar, and philosopher. A reactionary aristocrat with a hostility toward democracy and popular culture, he studied the problems of life and history and came to the conclusion that the key to understanding it all was the concept of race. A true son of the "Enlightenment," he rejected the superstitions of Christianity and came to a more modern and secular conclusion—that the crucial factor in the rise and fall of civilizations was racial purity. Pure races grew strong and dominated; impure races declined and died out. His book *Essay on the Inequality of the Human Races* (1853-55) had an influence that is difficult to imagine today.

Gobineau's philosophy is expressed in *Mein Kampf*:

> The Germanic inhabitant of the American continent, who has remained racially pure and unmixed, rose to be the master of the

continent; he will remain the master as long as he does not fall a victim to defilement of the blood…

. . . All great cultures of the past perished only because the originally creative race died out from blood poisoning [*Mein Kampf*, vol. I chapt. 11].

Rudolf Hoess, the commandant of Auschwitz, stated "Humanity's strong races must dominate the weaker ones, therefore, and keep themselves racially pure. Admixture of blood with weaker races was fatal."[149] It is possible that Hoess was only repeating the required slogans and was nothing but a criminal who would have said anything to attain a position of power. It is also possible that he truly believed this philosophy and felt he was protecting the German race. Whatever the case, the idea of racial purity being essential to the survival of a people was not invented by Hitler.

The purest race of modern times was, in Gobineau's philosophical and scholarly view, the Aryan race. The Aryans were the aristocrats among nations, and Aryan vitality included a natural and healthy desire for war and conquest—a desire that was hindered by Christian values.[150] Racial purity is a modern secular concept, not a religious one. Some may point to the concept of purity of blood as an issue in the Spanish Inquisition, but this had to do with the fact that Moslem and Jewish converts to Christianity would sometimes continue to practice their former religions in secret. Concern about blood purity was therefore related to sincerity of belief, not to the survival of the race. This is apart from the fact that the Inquisition itself had nothing to do with the teachings of Christ and was an evil concept from start to finish—one which the vast majority of the world's Christians have never tried or wanted to emulate.

Gobineau's "philosophy" was never widely popular in France, and did not become well-known in Germany until later in the century. It is possible that Gobineau's "biological racism had greater resonance in Germany than in France"[151] because France had exhausted its aggressive and militaristic spirit and was lapsing into the passivity of a declining culture, while Germany was on the rise. England was still too much under the influence of traditional Christian values that had been more easily rejected by the German intelligentsia. Whatever the reason, the fact that Gobineau's thought caught on nowhere so well as in Germany emphasizes the uniquely German nature of the racist tendencies Hitler fed upon (Schopenhauer spoke favorably of Gobineau).

Gobineau never became a Nazi saint—not only was he a Frenchman, but his book was not overtly anti-Semitic. (Paul Rose states that Gobineau later became more anti-Semitic due to the influence of Richard Wagner).[152] Gobineau also identified the Aryan race with aristocratic elements in various countries rather than with the Germans alone. Nevertheless, his emphasis on the importance of racial purity for the survival of a people was central to Hitler's thought. Gobineau also believed in white supremacy. He wrote that civilization originated with the white race. This was Hitler's idea as well. Hitler's bizarre beliefs in racial pollution as the original sin; in the preservation of purity of blood as our holiest obligation; in race-mixing and racial decline as sins against "the Creator"—these make sense if you accept Gobineau's ideas.

Someone asserted there is no evidence that Hitler read Gobineau, but Gobineau's main idea is directly stated and elaborated on in *Mein Kampf*—and why couldn't Hitler have read Gobineau? It would be remarkable if he did not, given his interest in the subject—and Gobineau's thought was popular in the Bayreuth circle of Wagner's relatives and admirers that Hitler frequented. It was a member of that circle, one Ludwig Schemann, who founded the Gobineau Society in Germany in 1894 to spread Gobineau's ideas in Germany. He is quoted as having said "only Germany can be the receptacle for Gobineau and his ideas."[153]

Some have sought to link modern racism to the Bible by referring to a 19th-century American argument in favor of chattel slavery. It was argued by some that the blacks were under the "curse of Ham." Ham, one of the three sons of Noah, was cursed for dishonoring his father. The Africans were his descendants, it was claimed, and hence were obligated to endure slavery.

Apart from the fact that the Bible links Ham not only to African but also to Middle Eastern peoples, a number of points need to be mentioned. First, Gobineau and other modern German racists did not (as far as I know) appeal to the story of Ham. We are not discussing all racism everywhere in the world, but modern secular German racism. Second, the idea of blacks being under the curse of Ham was (like South African apartheid) never a central teaching in many of the times and places where Christianity flourished. It occurred in a very limited cultural and historical context only and was obviously related to the love of money which the Bible condemns. Anyway, the curse said that Ham's son Canaan would be a servant to his brothers, not that the curse would last for thousands of years. Also, an ancient near Eastern servant was different from a chattel slave.

Assigning inferior status to a race contradicts plain teachings of the Bible. Jesus said "Do unto others as you would have them do unto you." Paul said in the book of Acts that God "hath made of one blood all nations of men for to dwell on all the face of the earth." Passages in the Old Testament condemn rich landowners for depriving workers of their wages. It says in Jeremiah, "Woe unto him that buildeth his house by unrighteousness, and his chambers by wrong; that useth his neighbor's service without wages, and giveth him not for his work."

Finally, to advocate some form of economically profitable racism is one thing. To see racial purity as essential to the survival of a people as Hitler and Gobineau did is something entirely different. True, some German "pastors" or "theologians" expressed racist sentiments and some Nazis also sought to express their racial concepts in religious terms. Hans Schemm, head of the National Socialist Teachers League, stated ". . . race is willed by God," and, ". . . we want nothing else but to keep the race pure, in order to fulfill God's law."[154] This can be presented as proof of the Christian origins of Nazi racism; however, when you consider that racial purity was important to Gobineau, but not to any New Testament writer; that the New Testament has much to say about fulfilling God's law, all of it entirely different from this; that the whole human race is condemned as being under sin, Jews equally with Gentiles; then we realize that secular ideas are being dressed up in religious language. Those who thought they were fulfilling God's law by keeping the race pure will be in for a very unpleasant surprise when they come before Christ on the day of judgment and find he commanded no such thing.

As absurd as they seem to us today, Gobineau's theories were no more ridiculous than some of Marx's. Everything is based on race or economics? The elite are the Aryans or the workers? The greatest sin was racial impurity or capitalism and profits? Such were the fruits of nineteenth century human wisdom.

One historian, Paul Johnson, sees a common origin of the two theories of history as a process driven by conflict (either racial or economic). Just as Marx modified Hegel's concept of progress to come up with a new system in which class struggle, not the clash of ideas, was seen as the motivating force of history, so Folkish thinkers also modified the concept of progress. They presented the conflict of races as the driving force behind the onward and upward advance of humanity. In Johnson's words: "The notion of obeying 'iron laws' or a 'higher law', rather than the traditional, absolute morality taught in the churches, was a Hegelian one. Marx and Lenin translated it into a class concept; Hitler into a race one."[155] Johnson neglects to point out that this idea of race as the key to history had been articulated before Hitler was born. In Mosse's words, Gobineau "set the stage and supplied the props" for a new ideology emphasizing the centrality of race.[156]

As with any theory, Gobineau's was liable to interpretation and alteration. Exactly who were the Aryans? Was racial decay inevitable (as the pessimistic Gobineau believed), or could it be avoided and if so how? Gobineau's theory was modified in various ways, but he was a pioneer and his influence was substantial. He seems irrelevant to us today, but the man who elevated racism to a "philosophical" level had a significant impact on Germany later in the century. Several important figures whose ideas were close to or even identical to Hitler's in some key areas—Richard Wagner, H.S. Chamberlain, and Ernst Haeckel— explicitly named Gobineau and endorsed some (though not necessarily all) aspects of his thought.

A number of other less-well known thinkers acknowledged Gobineau's influence—Ludwig Moltmann, Ludwig Schemann, Eugen Fischer, Josef Reimer were a few of them.[157] The spread of social Darwinism (the belief that the law of survival-of-the-fittest should be applied to human society) gave added relevance to Gobineau's thought. Elevating the struggle for survival from the level of individual organisms to the level of nations and races made racial purity seem more vital than ever.

The Folkish movement

A vaguely defined higher power working in the world through the instrumentality of nations and peoples; an emphasis on the state and great leaders as instruments of that power; the concept of the German people as the national group best suited by nature to be in harmony with the hidden spiritual force of the cosmos; life as essentially struggle; racial purity as the key to survival; the Jews as a harmful alien influence—as the 19th century progressed, concepts first presented by a few philosophers gained in strength and popularity. Significantly modified by changing social, political, and economic pressures, as well as by the later addition of new concepts such as German interpretations of Darwinism, occult mysticism, and even atheism, these to us foolish ideas came eventually to assume a quasi-religious or even a religious status and were widely believed by many.

This emphasis on the German people (the Folk, German *Volk*, adjective *völkisch*) as a superior people of destiny came to be known as the Folkish movement. It was a very broad movement supported by widening intellectual, academic, and professional circles as the 19th century progressed. A general concept that admitted different emphases, the essential principles of the Folkish movement were in many respects identical to and foundational to Naziism—so much so that in his book *The Crisis of German Ideology*, Prof. George Mosse identifies this movement as the origin of National Socialism. I am thankful to Prof. Mosse for the light he has shed on this aspect of Naziism's origins—though his study omits or minimizes the additional later influences of Darwin, Haeckel and Nietzsche.

The significance of the Folkish movement for our study is indicated by the fact that vol. II chapt. 4 of *Mein Kampf* is entitled "Personality and the Conception of the Folkish State." If Hitler had used the word "Christianity" in a chapter title and devoted many paragraphs to setting forth biblical concepts of government, the enemies of Christianity would be delighted. But, if he refers to something called "Folkish," that is of minor interest. It shouldn't be. The Folkish philosophy was integral to Hitler's thought. Its popularity was a crucial part of Naziism's acceptance by significant portions of Germany's population, and Hitler himself identified the Folkish basis of National Socialism.

In vol. II chapt. 1 of *Mein Kampf* ("Philosophy and Party"), Hitler described Folkism as "a general, philosophical, ideal conception of the highest truth," and stated that the NSDAP was "a party formulation of the folkish concept." He added in this same chapter that the NSDAP formed "a political creed" which made possible "the victorious struggle of this world view."[158] He even went so far as to state that his party had emerged out of all of the other various folkish groups: "From all these the NSDAP had slowly crystallized out as the victor by 1920" [vol. II chapt. 8 "The Strong Man is Mightiest Alone"].[159] Those other groups shared many, most, or all of Hitler's ideas, but their leaders lacked his political brilliance and were unable to form effective parties.

Hitler had no use for mere theorizing that was not translated into action and dismissed people who only talked about folkish values with contempt: "A world view can be right a thousand times, but it will be without significance for the life of the Volk if it does not combine with the goals of a fighting movement, a political party."[160] Hitler actualized a set of values others had only talked about—values that were perfectly consistent with Hitler's actions.

Folkism was a derivative of secular thinking that appealed to the worst instincts of pride and earthly vain-glory. Directly related to the fantasies of Kant, Hegel, Fichte, Jahn, and Schopenhauer, it provided much of the foundation of National Socialist ideology. It is with reason that Robert Wistrich described the NSDAP as "the most militant of the many disparate *völkisch* anti-Semitic sects and groupings that mushroomed in the aftermath of war and defeat."[161]

Paul Lagarde

The best way to bring the Folkish movement into focus is to look at two of its most significant popularizers: Paul Lagarde and Julius Langbehn. Lagarde (1827-1891) was much more broadly influential than excessively academic philosophers, and his contribution was great. Nevertheless, it is useful to remember how much of what Lagarde taught had been said before. In the words of Dieter Just, a modern German scholar:

> Fichte, who put his philosophy at the service of the wars against Napoleon, has laid the foundation for the *volkische*

ideology of the German political Right as early as 1808, in his *Reden an die deutsche Nation* [*Addresses to the German Nation*]—a foundation which was to remain alive through the Alldeutscher Verband up to Hitler.[162]

Like Fichte, and Hegel, Lagarde believed that there was some vital force at work in the cosmos. This life force manifested itself most clearly and most immediately in the German nation. Due to their unique spiritual qualities, the Germans were in Lagarde's opinion the most suited to perceive this force, understand it, and be used by it as an agent in the grand scheme of world history. Lagarde even came to see the Folk, the German people, as the point of contact with this cosmic force, the intermediary between the individual and this higher unseen spiritual reality.[163] Self-fulfillment for the individual was thus found through membership in the Folk.

For the Germans to be most fully harmonized with the transcendental force, the purity of the German nation needed to be preserved. This required the elimination of non-Germanic elements that contaminated the spiritual essence of the nation. Moreover, it was by participation in the Folk that individuals could be most in harmony with the universe, and hence most truly free, most deeply fulfilled. Thus, true freedom meant being a part of the German nation.

Liberalism and democracy were viewed as having a negative, disintegrating effect. Apart from being alien and un-Germanic in themselves—after all, the simple and noble German warriors of ancient times knew nothing of such things—they were viewed as spiritually harmful. They reduced the unity of the Folk to a squabbling mass of selfishly individualistic competing groups, which hindered the spiritual unity necessary to participation in the cosmic life force. This is part of the basic idea Hitler expressed when he expatiated on the negative effects of supposedly Jewish individualism. As absurd as this sounds to us today, it makes sense, if you start from Kant, Hegel and Fichte—and Mosse documents the widening acceptance of these and related views.

All of this presupposed of course the falsehood of traditional Christianity. Lagarde thought that the original dynamism of Jesus had been stifled by the Jewish legalism of Paul, and tried to recover Christianity in its original form in order to revitalize the fatherland.[164] Here is the origin of the so-called Germanic Christianity that the Nazis later appealed to. The rediscovery of an original Aryan Christianity purified of its corrupting Semitic elements was a major theme of H.S. Chamberlain, the last major Folkish prophet before Hitler. Viereck states that Naziism's "positive Christianity" grew out of Lagarde's attempts to purify Christianity of its Jewish elements and come up with a new suitably Germanic religion. He could have mentioned Kant, Fichte, and Schopenhauer as well.

Lagarde's concept of history was deeply Hegelian: "History, for Lagarde, was the expression of a religious spirit, which manifested itself through a continuous revelation."[165] This was of course not the Christian view of Christ and the teachings of the New Testament as the final revelation.

Lagarde did not have a racial emphasis; Mosse explains that racial anti-Semitism did not become more popular until after 1870, and Lagarde's basic concepts had been formed long before. Lagarde was a philosophical, not a racial anti-Semite, but even without the benefit of modern pseudo-science he reasoned his way to a deep hatred of Jews, arguing that (in Mosse's words) Jews should be exterminated "like bacillae."[166] In *Juden und Indogermanen* Lagarde asserted that the Jews were parasites, and wrote "With trichinae and bacilli, one does not negotiate, nor are they subjected to education. They are to be exterminated as quickly and as thoroughly as possible." Lagarde was not an isolated eccentric. Eugen Duhring wrote that the Jews should be killed, and wrote after 1918 that "The world must settle its account with the Hebrew people in a radical manner . . . There is no room on earth for Hebrew existence."[167]

Lagarde's reasoning is not impossible to follow. Like other anti-Semites, he found something positive to say about the early Hebrews. A true people, occupying their land and defending it as warriors, the Israelites could be fit into Lagarde's concept of life. Scattered throughout the world, however, and no longer a fighting people, the Jews had become separated from the transcendental life force. Modern day Jews had nothing to do with the ancient Hebrews and were worthy only of contempt.

The Jews thus were a symbol of everything that life was not. Moreover, the Jewish legalism introduced by Paul had produced the spiritually enervating Christianity that corrupted and debased the purity of the old pre-Christian Germanic society. Thus, it was Jewish values through the medium of Christianity that had spiritually infected the Folk with an alien religion. The theme of Christianity as an alien Semitic import was to become increasingly common as the century progressed.

Also, the modern Jews quite naturally tended to align themselves with the forces of liberalism that promised them greater rights and opportunities—proof to Lagarde (who was hostile to liberalism) that the selfish and materialistic Jews were incapable of appreciating the higher spiritual values of the Folk and sought only their own personal advantage with no regard for higher spiritual ideals.

Lagarde did not merely see Jewish ways of thinking—whether traditional and religious or modern and secular—as incompatible with the spiritual values of the German people. Deeply influenced by the idea of life as conflict, Lagarde went on to imagine a fundamental conflict between Jewish values and German ones. The Jewish character was incompatible with the German character on the deepest level; hence the Jews were not merely an obstacle but even a danger that jeopardized the regeneration of the German people.

A couple of points need to be stressed here. Lagarde's ideas are false and contemptible, but reasonable according to a discernible if peculiar logic. Secondly, in expressing these ideas Lagarde was very much in harmony with the culture of his day, and was widely accepted. Mosse demonstrates at length and in detail that these and other ideas of the Folkish ideology became increasingly popular in German society. Thirdly, Mosse does not attribute the origin of these ideas to the Bible, but to German philosophy. Mosse also linked Kant's racist ideas to the Folkish movement, but not for some reason his anti-Semitic ones.

It is worth pointing out that Hitler read Lagarde. Ryback's previously referred to article on Hitler's library states that Hitler marked more than fifty pages of Lagarde's *German Essays*.[168] This does not prove Hitler got his ideas from Lagarde or was created by Lagarde. It does prove he was aware of those ideas; he certainly found much that was useful to him in Lagarde, even if it only confirmed existing tendencies. Part of the noxious fog surrounding Hitler's ideas begins to dissipate when we consider that those ideas were not new, and in fact were the end result of a distinct tradition.

German romanticism

Elaborating on the Folkish ideology, Mosse states that "The intellectual and ideological character of Volkish thought was a direct product of the romantic movement of nineteenth-century Europe."[169] Since Mosse not only shows National Socialism's origins in the Folkish movement but also linked the Folkish movement to romanticism, a few comments on romanticism might not be too much of a digression.

German romanticism, different from the romanticism of Keats and Wordsworth, was a broad movement large enough to include not only Fichte, Hegel, Schopenhauer, and Wagner, but also a host of poets, painters, journalists, writers, students, professors, and scholars. It rejected the concept of fixed, permanent, and unchanging truth presented by traditional religion, and saw truth rather as evolving, changing, becoming. Such laws of revealed religion as the threat of divine punishment for sin to name only one were considered to be false, artificial, barriers to self-fulfillment. A more authentic experience of life was sought through contact with the higher cosmic reality, a living force often described in pantheistic terms (not all romantics, of course, were identical in every respect, and many combined their romanticism with nationalism, religion, and rationalism in varying degrees).

Through contact with some vague spiritual force, one could be truly fulfilled and find meaning in life, a place in the cosmos. This explains many references to "God" or the "divine" that were totally removed from a traditional Christian context. Such references have misled those like Steigmann-Gall who talk about Christianity in Germany with little or no understanding of Christianity. This is particularly true when it comes to "Protestant" "theologians" who openly abandoned revelation and converted to romanticism and / or idealistic philosophy, but dishonestly expressed their new secular faith in the empty religious terms they found so comforting and meaningful.

This is illustrated by the "theologian" Friedrich Schleiermacher (1768-1834). As a good romantic, he saw religion not as a system of dogmas, laws, and rules but as a sense of the infinite, an intuition, a feeling for God. He proposed the theory that Christ did not actually die on the cross but only swooned, and revived in the tomb. Later "Protestants" with this sort of "faith" easily accommodated their ideas to new racial theories.

The elaborate philosophical edifices of Kant, Hegel, and others were also based on their personal feeling for what was reasonable and true. Seeking to be one with Nature, to live in harmony with it rather than to have dominion over it, the romantics emphasized life and feeling as laws unto themselves. That the Nazis also claimed to be living according to nature is a strong link between Naziism and German romanticism. Dispensing with the false and artificial rules, laws, and dogmas of traditional religion freed the Nazis to live according to nature—and nature for them meant pitiless struggle.

Knowing no higher law but self, having no higher truth other than what their own brains had invented, the German romantics had an emphasis on the mystical and the emotional. This later descended to the irrational and in some circles to the occult. The Nazi emphasis on blood, the instinctive life force, over reason was related to this. Nazi emphasis on feeling and will over intellect was no mere aberration but had roots in over a century of thought. Viereck has been criticized for over-simplifying the connection between Romanticism and Naziism, and much of romanticism had nothing to do with Naziism. Many romantics were anything but Nazis, and the later influence of Haeckel's social Darwinism is too much neglected in Viereck's study—but there are connections nevertheless, and some of Viereck's refutations of his critics were effective.[170]

In confining his study more narrowly to the Folkish movement and the Folkish ideology I think Mosse is much more precise than Viereck, and more prudent. After all, the Folkish movement has many more exact parallels with and is closer in time to National Socialism than was romanticism. Romanticism is a much broader term, and includes many individuals that had little to do with Hitler. It is the linking of romanticism to Hitler that has provoked the strongest criticisms I have seen of Viereck's book. Nevertheless, as was just stated above, Mosse saw a causal relationship between the romantic movement and Naziism. He cites the discrediting of the rational and an emphasis on the emotional, and also mentions a pantheistic view of the universe, allowing for the desire for some kind of contact through the ideas of nation and race with a vague "force."

"Romanticism led to Hitler" or "Romanticism led to the Folkish movement that led to Hitler"—the latter is more precise, but two major studies by recognized authorities in the field point to the secular rather than to the religious basis of National Socialism.

The intensification of Folkish tendencies

A brief summary of romanticism and of one of the Folkish movement's leading theoreticians by no means exhausts the subject. More needs to be said about the addition of racial pseudo-science, as well as militarism, authoritarianism, and imperialism—other vital ingredients of the toxic philosophical brew cooked up by man in his wisdom, once set free from traditional religion.

At this point a digression is necessary. Mosse makes the profoundly insightful assertion that historical, social, and economic factors contributed to the spread and strengthening of Folkish ideas. He sees two aspects to this: political unification and industrialization. I would like to add a third—the love of power.

Concerning the first of these, Mosse demonstrates that the political unification of Germany in 1870 led to a deep disillusionment, after the initial excitement wore off. German nationalists had longed and worked for unification for years. When it came, there was disappointment. Their deepest spiritual hungers remained unfilled. Hence they continued to seek for a deeper and purer spiritual unification of the German people, hoping in this way to find the satisfaction denied them by Bismarck's very unspiritual state.

As to industrialization, the increasing complexity of social and economic problems also led to disillusionment. A united and powerful Germany not only failed to meet deeper spiritual needs, but it introduced serious new problems, including the destruction of traditional culture and all of the other well-known negative side-effects of rapid industrialization. Mosse states that these two factors of political unity and industrialization led to an ideological crisis in the 1870s.[171] Mosse does not neglect the crucial importance of later events, without which National Socialism could never have come to power—nor does he omit, as we have seen, the earlier origins of Folkish ideology. Yet, he sees the latter part of the 19th century as a critical period in the strengthening and consolidation of ideas that were essential to the widespread acceptance of National Socialism.

To this was added one of the greatest sources of evil in human history—the love of power. After easily winning three short and glorious wars with Denmark, Austria, and France, Germany emerged as the most powerful country on the continent. It is not hard to see how those ignorant of spiritual values, who looked to the nation for their self worth and sense of belonging in the universe, should be deeply gratified by the thought of German power. In the latter decades of the century there was an increasing emphasis on German domination and the glories of war, empire, and conquest. This was the result of human pride, vanity, conceit, and sin.

Julius Langbehn

Another central figure in the development of Folkish philosophy was one Julius Langbehn. Like Mosse, Daniel Gasman describes Lagarde and Langbehn as "the chief nineteenth-century prophets of the Folkish movement."[172] Langbehn (1851-1907) seems like an obscure and insignificant figure now, but he had influence in his day. His book, *Rembrandt as Educator* (1890) was read by millions of people and remained popular until 1914.

Langbehn believed that the life spirit of the cosmos interacted with the human race through the unit of the Folk. This was in harmony with spiritualist movements of the 19th century. Lagarde's emphasis on an invisible spiritual reality is connected to the "theosophy" of Madame Blavatski, and the cult of Swedenborg. It also agrees well with the ideas of Hegel and Fichte, but Langbehn had an added emphasis on the Folk as a "necessary intermediary in the vital transfusion of spiritual substances"[173] which was more mystical.

The need for some understanding of spiritual reality beyond that offered by science, yet outside of that offered by traditional Christianity, led to an emphasis on the occult, reincarnation, spiritualism, and peculiar adaptations of oriental religion that were much more widespread than is commonly realized. This combined with German philosophy to give the German Folk an entirely new dimension. Langbehn had such an emphasis on the Folk as the point of contact with hidden spiritual forces that the Folk came to be seen as taking the place of Christ.[174] Not Christ but the German Folk became the intermediary between man and the unseen spiritual world. Through union not with Christ, but with the Folk, one found one's deepest fulfillment and place in the cosmos.

All of this sounds more and more like religion—and what began as philosophical ideas and concepts did begin to assume the qualities of a religion. In the end, the Folkish movement became a counterfeit faith that directly mimicked Christianity. What sort of a religion was it? There was a new Chosen People—not the Old Testament Hebrews or the elect of God in Christ, but the Germans. There was also a new promised land—Germany. This included all of the adjacent territories where Germans lived, unnaturally separated from the Folk by artificial boundaries. There was a new god—the World Spirit, Absolute, cosmic life force, transcendental essence, whatever. When the Germans were in defeat, there would be a new Messiah—a false prophet offering false salvation by the false religion.

There was also a substitute concept of evil. Traditional Christianity presents Satan and original sin in man as the sources of evil in the world. Without those concepts, the valid need for some principle of evil—since evil does exist in the world, and needs some explanation—fell upon the Jews. The concepts of God, meaning, life, and purpose descended from the lofty heights of biblical spirituality to a lower earthly plane, and the concept of evil declined correspondingly. The Folk offered a more easily understandable concept of higher meaning, and the Jew offered a more easily understandable concept of evil, of what life was not.

With this came a substitute sanctification. Just as Christians need to be purified of sin, so the Folk needed to be purified of alien elements so that it could be more in tune with mysterious cosmic forces. Hence, the racial emphasis becomes more noticeable in Langbehn.[175] The German race's unique spiritual qualities were stressed, and racial purity became more important.

Not surprisingly, this emphasis on German racial spirituality included hostility to Jews. Jews who kept to themselves were tolerable, but assimilated Jews polluted the purity of the Folk. "These Jews, identified as the 'pest and cholera,' had to be exterminated."[176] Later Langbehn's anti-Semitism intensified and he expanded his condemnations to all Jews. Representing modernity and materialism, Jews were inevitably the enemies of German culture and values.[177] Some of Viereck's comments on Langbehn are useful. He states that Langbehn's writings were more popular than Lagarde's, and effectively contrasted the upright Aryan with the devious and cunning Jew.

The significance of Lagarde and Langbehn cannot be overstressed. They did not invent a new philosophy out of thin air, but expressed ideas current in the society around them. That these ideas were not confined to a few lonely eccentrics is amply demonstrated by Mosse throughout his meticulously researched book. Youth movements, educational institutions, textbooks and curricula, professors and high school teachers, journals, books (including novels), professional associations, workers' unions, student organizations and fraternities—these became vehicles for the spread of Folkish ideas. Mosse quotes Fritz Stern thus: ". . . a thousand teachers in republican Germany who in their youth had worshipped Lagarde or Langbehn were just as important in the triumph of National Socialism as all the putative millions of marks that Hitler collected from the German tycoons."[178]

The Folkish movement did not reach the masses until after the Great War, as more than one writer has said, but the previous decades of its inception and consolidation were critical. Without Germany's defeat in 1918 subsequent events would never have occurred—but without a century of preparation, the events subsequent to 1918 would not have taken the course that they did.

The Pan-German Association

The ideas of Lagarde and Langbehn found practical applications. As the political, economic, and military power of Germany increased in the late 1800's, there was a corresponding desire among growing segments of German society to not merely talk about Folkish ideas, but to implement them. The best single example of this is the Pan-German Association. Established in 1890, it was a super-patriotic group that advocated territorial expansion in Europe and imperialism overseas. Seeking to unify Germany both culturally and racially, the Pan-Germans were also aristocratic and elitist. They opposed democracy as alien to the German spirit and thought that dictatorship was the most suitable form of government. Opposed to communism, leftism, and leveling democratic mass-socialism (not to be confused with Hitler's authoritarian and elitist socialism), they were anti-Semitic as well.

Their hostility to Jews had a Folkish basis. To them, Jews were materialists, inherently contrary to Germanic spirituality. This was a by now standard philosophical objection to Jews, though the Pan-Germans appealed to people with different views and the religious element could be stressed by individuals to varying degrees.

Heinrich Class, who became president of the Association in 1908 and remained active until his retirement from politics in 1933, wanted to eliminate Jewish cultural influence from German life. He felt that various professions—including banking, teaching, the theater, and literary journalism—should be closed to Jews. Mastheads of newspapers employing Jews should include a star of David. Class supported the "Juden Ordnung" of 1919, a proposal by the Society Against Jewish Domination to exclude Jews from German society.[179] This ominously foreshadowed the Nuremberg Laws.[180] Not surprisingly, Class was a member of the Gobineau Society.

John Toland's biography of Hitler quotes some of Class' comments: "The Jewish race is the source of all dangers. The Jew and the German are like fire and water . . . We await the Fuhrer! Patience, patience, he will come. Persevere, work and unite."[181] Stressing the widening diffusion of these ideas throughout Germany in the late 1800's, Mosse describes the respectable nature of the Pan-Germans—they included merchants, teachers, white collar workers, academics, civil servants, and politicians. Teachers were especially effective in indoctrinating students with Folkish values.

Before WWI the Pan-Germans were the most important of various Folkish groups. After the war the association splintered as the crises of post-war Germany led to disagreements on the proper course to follow. It further declined in the 1920s, and Class was unable to unite the various Folkish groups. He had hopes that he might be the born leader of the nation, the saviour, but he lacked Hitler's oratorical and organizational abilities, and membership dropped drastically in the decade before 1933. Most of the lost members went over to the Nazis. Though Class himself was at first sympathetic to Hitler, he broke with Hitler and condemned him in 1932.

The relevance of the Pan-Germans to National Socialism is confirmed (if confirmation is needed) by some comments Hitler made in *Mein Kampf*. Referring to one Georg von Schonerer (1842-1921), the leader of the Austrian Pan-Germans, Hitler commends him for his correct understanding of the Jewish question, but criticizes him for his inability to connect with the masses and for his lack of effectiveness as a political leader [vol. I chapt. 3, "General Political Considerations Based on my Vienna Period"].

The Folkish movement and Christianity

The Folkish thinkers had no use for traditional Christianity, and the concept of Christ was radically changed to meet the demands of their new human philosophy. Christ became merely a symbol to which any philosophical values could be attached, and Christian rhetoric was used to advance very unbiblical values. A good example of this is one Eugen Diederichs, one of Germany's most well-known publishers around the beginning of the 20th century.

Diederichs is referred to by Mosse as a Christian—but what sort of a Christian? He saw Jesus as a symbol of some vague and intangible cosmic spirit. He thought that the truth of the spirit embodied in Christ had been killed by Paul's dogmatic doctrines, and he rejected the orthodox, historical Christ. Diederichs was strongly opposed to conventional Christianity. He rejected Luther's Reformation because of its emphasis on the Bible, and believed in sun-worship. Rejecting biblical revelation and relying on his own intelligence, he came to the conclusion that the rays of the life-giving sun contained the spirit, the secret life force of the cosmos (*Geist*).[182]

People who read a little about Germany see the words "Christian," "Christianity," "Jesus," but don't have the faintest idea of how those terms were detached from traditional Christianity and given a new content to suit the times. Since much of traditional Christianity could not be adapted, however, there was also increasing hostility to it, even open rejection. One educator, Ludwig Gurlitt, condemned Christianity's harmful effects on German culture. He saw opposition to Christianity as the Folk's healthy reaction to a poison.[183]

It should not be imagined that Gurlitt was an isolated case. Mosse uses individuals to illustrate broader trends, and there were many with Gurlitt's views. Hermann Lietz, another educator, stated that medieval German writings were superior to the Old Testament. Detached from the Old Testament, Christ was then Germanized and transformed into a heroic figure agreeable to modern secular values.[184] Since by Mosse's reckoning there were literally dozens of boarding schools that sought to transmit Germanic ideology to their students according to the program established by Lietz,[185] we can have some inkling of the significance of these ideas.

That the Jews killed Christ was not vitally important to the Folkists—Christ was, after all, only a man to them (though traditional religious views did persist of course, and were combined with Folkish values to varying degrees). That the Jews rejected Christianity was not a factor either, for the Folkists also rejected it in its traditional sense. The Jews came to be a symbol of evil as they represented the antithesis of everything that made life worth living according to the values of a non-Christian philosophy. Having no state, no nation, the Jews were peculiar half creatures who represented false and harmful values. These false and harmful values included Christianity, which had permeated Germany from top to bottom with Jewish concepts. Julius von Jan, the Lutheran pastor who denounced the Crystal Night pogrom from the pulpit, was denounced as a "slave of the Jews."[186] Why? because his non-Aryan concepts of a just and righteous God were Jewish, derived from Jews and elaborated on by Jews.

Beware lest any man spoil you through philosophy and vain deceit, after the tradition of men, after the rudiments of the world, and not after Christ. (Colossians)

---

[1] Ron Rosenbaum, *Explaining Hitler* (New York 1998), p. xlvi.

[2] Rudolf Hoess, *Commandant of Auschwitz*, trans. Constantine Fitzgibbon (London 2000), p. 181.

[3] Ian Kershaw, *The Nazi Dictatorship: Problems and Perspectives of Interpretation* (London 2000), p. 235.

[4] Ibid., p. 259.

[5] Ibid., p. 4.

[6] Robert Thomas, "The Nature of Nazi Ideology," *Libertarian Alliance*; www.libertarian.co.uk/lapubs/histn/histn015.pdf; accessed January 2008.

[7] F. A. Hayek, *The Road to Serfdom* (Chicago 2007), p. 181.

[8] Paul Avrich, *Russian Rebels 1600-1800* (New York/London 1972), p. 69.

[9] Ibid., pp. 250, 228.

[10] Ibid., pp. 233-234.

[11] Ibid., pp. 228, 256, 89.

[12] Ibid., pp. 46.

[13] Joachim C. Fest, *Hitler,* trans. Richard and Clara Winston (New York 1974), p. 377.

[14] Eberhard Jäckel, *Hitler's World View: A Blueprint for Power* (Cambridge, MA 1997), pp. 23-24.

[15] Fest, p. 7.

[16] Ibid., p. 383.

[17] Jäckel, p. 13 (for the three quotes from *Mein Kampf*), and pp.23-24 for a discussion of world view.

[18] August Kubizek, *The Young Hitler I Knew,* trans. Geoffrey Brooks (London 2006), p. 206.

[19] Ibid., pp. 159, 160, 126.

[20] Phillip Johnson, *The Wedge of Truth: Splitting the Foundations of Naturalism* (Downers Grove, IL 2000), p. 188 (quoting Newbigin's *Truth to Tell: The Gospel as Public Truth*, in reference to modernity in general, not to the Third Reich).

[21] Thomas Jefferson, "Syllabus of an Estimate of the Merit of the Doctrines of Jesus, Compared with Those of Others"; http://www.angelfire.com/co/JeffersonBible/jeffbsyl.html; accessed January 2008.

[22] Ibid.

[23] Paul Johnson, *A History of the Jews* (London 1987), p. 309.

[24] Ibid.

[25] Michael Feldberg, "John Adams embraces a Jewish homeland," *Homepage for Lewis Loflin*; http://www.sullivan-county.com/id2/adams_jews.htm; accessed January 2008.

[26] Ibid.

[27] Paul Lawrence Rose, *German Question / Jewish Question: Revolutionary Antisemitism from Kant to Wagner* (Princeton 1990), p. 10.

[28] A brief overview of Rousseau is found in Stephen Hicks' book *Explaining Postmodernism: Skepticism and Socialism from Rousseau to Foucault*, pp. 92-106. The quote from Rousseau comes from p. 99 of this work. Hicks also demonstrates Rousseau's significant impact on German philosophy. More comments confirming Rousseau's authoritarian and anti-democratic views can be found in Jean-Jacques Rousseau, *The Social Contract*, trans. Maurice Cranston (London 2004), pp. 32, 37, 99.

[29] Alistair Horne, *The Age of Napoleon* (New York 2006), pp. 14-19.

[30] Ibid., p. 53

[31] Peter Padfield, *Himmler: Reichsfuhrer-SS* (New York 1990) p. 90.

[32] Horne, p. 58.

[33] Dieter Just, "*Ich denke—also bin ich nicht*," English summary by Herbert Renz-Polster; http://www.d-just.de/text1eng.htm; accessed May 2007.

[34] Alister McGrath, *The Twilight of Atheism: The Rise and Fall of Disbelief in the Modern World* (London 2004), p. 49.

[35] Ibid.

[36] James K. A. Smith, *Who's Afraid of Postmodernism? Taking Derrida, Lyotard, and Foucault to Church* (Grand Rapids 2008), p. 20.

[37] Stanley N. Gundry and Steven B. Cowan, eds. *Five Views on Apologetics* (Grand Rapids MI 2000), p. 289.

[38] Barrett Pashak, review of German Idealism and the Jew: The Inner Anti-Semitism of Philosophy and German Jewish Responses, by Michael Mack. Constantinbrunner.info; http://www.constantinbrunner.info/pages/mack.htm; accessed January 2008.

[39] Michael Mack, *German Idealism and the Jew: The Inner Anti-Semitism of Philosophy and German Jewish Responses* (Chicago 2003).

[40] Paul Lawrence Rose, *Wagner: Race and Revolution* (New Haven 1992), p. 7.

[41] Pashak, citing Mack p. 35.

[42] Spengler, "Islam: Religion or political ideology?"; *Asia Times Online;* http://www.atimes.com/atimes/Front_Page/FH10Aa01.html; accessed May 2007.

[43] Jeet Heer, "Enlightened Kant racist," review of German Idealism and the Jew: The Inner Anti-Semitism of Philosophy and German Jewish Responses, by Michael Mack, *Adelaide Institute*; http://www.adelaideinstitute.org/Germany/kant.htm; accessed January 2008. See Mack, p. 38.

[44] Quoted in Georges van Vrekhem, *Hitler and His God: The Background to the Hitler Phenomenon* (New Delhi 2006), p. 62. Hitler praised Eckart in the closing words of the second volume of *Mein Kampf.*

[45] Jacob Golomb and Robert Wistrich, eds., "Nietzsche, Godfather of Fascism? On the Uses and Abuses of Philosophy," *Princeton University Press website*; http://www.pupress.princeton.edu/chapters/i7403.html; accessed January 2008.

[46] Jeet Heer.

[47] Thomas Teo, "The historical problematization of 'mixed race' in psychological and human-scientific discourses"; http://www.yorku.ca/tteo/teach/Teo2004.htm; accessed January 2008.

[48] Mack, p. 36.

[49] Ibid., p. 210.

[50] George Mosse, *The Crisis of German Ideology: Intellectual Origins of the Third Reich* (New York 1971), pp.88-89.

[51] Heer.

[52] Mack, p. 109.

[53] Ibid., pp. 24, 185.

[54] Ibid., pp. 32, 152, 159.

[55] Ibid., p. 163.

[56] Stephen R.C. Hicks, *Explaining Postmodernism: Skepticism and Socialism from Rousseau to Foucault* (Phoenix, AZ 2004), pp. 106-109. Kant in some places strongly

condemns war, but is not consistent and elsewhere concedes it has benefits. Hicks' study reveals the incipient totalitarianism, militarism, and inhumanity of certain aspects of Kant's philosophy, though Hicks does not state this point so bluntly. Kant's boasted rationality was a fraud.

[57] Immanuel Kant, *An Answer to the Question: "What is Enlightenment?"*, trans. H.B. Nisbet (London 2009), pp. 22, 102-103, 80 (in that order – italics in original).

[58] Heer.

[59] "The Trial of Adolf Eichmann Session 105 (Part 4 of 4)," *The Nizkor Project*; http://www.nizkor.org/hweb/people/e/eichmann-adolf/transcripts/Sessions /Session105-04.html; accessed January 2008.

[60] van Vrekhem, p. 199.

[61] Richard J. Evans, *The Coming of the Third Reich* (New York 2005), p. 27. Evans may have been influenced here by a comment in Howard Sachar's *A History of the Jews in the Modern World* (New York 2006) assigning a significant portion of blame to Stoecker, yet Sachar also mentions other important figures in this regard (such as Karl Lueger and Georg von Schoenerer), and contradicts his own assertion of Stoecker's primacy..

[62] John Warwick Montgomery, *Tractatus Logico-Theologicus* (Bonn 2003), p. 171.

[63] Kant, p. 1.

[64] Timothy W. Ryback, "Hitler's Forgotten Library: The Man, His Books, and His Search For God." *The Atlantic Monthly*. May 2003. http:www.fpp.co.uk/Hitler/library/Atlantic_Monthly.html; accessed May 2007. Ryback modified some of the ideas presented in this article in a book published a few years later, *Hitler's Private Library: The Books that Shaped his Life* (London 2010).

[65] Ian Kershaw, *Hitler, 1889-1936: Hubris* (New York 2000), p. 437.

[66] Walter S. Frank, "Adolf Hitler: The Making of a Fuhrer (Who was Responsible?)," *Smoter .com*; http://www.smoter.com/hitler.htm; accessed January 2008.

[67] Richard Steigmann-Gall, *The Holy Reich: Nazi Conceptions of Christianity, 1919-1945* (Cambridge 2004), p. 10.

[68] Kershaw, *Hitler*, pp. 41, xxv.

[69] Jäckel, p. 87.

[70] Johann Gottlieb Fichte, *Addresses to the German Nation*, trans. R.F. Jones and G.H. Turnbull (Chicago and London 1922), p. 232.

[71] Ibid.

[72] Ibid., p. 136.

[73] Ibid.

[74] William L. Shirer, *The Rise and Fall of the Third Reich* (New York 1960), p. 933.

[75] Fichte, p. 137.

[76] Ibid., p. 144.

[77] Adolf Hitler, *Hitler Speeches and Quotes* (London 2008), p. 30.

[78] Fichte, p. 223.

[79] Ibid., p. 138.

[80] Blaise Pascal, *Pensées,* trans. A.J. Krailsheimer (London 1995), p. 118.

[81] Rose, *Wagner,* p. 6.

[82] Fichte, p. 219.

[83] Ibid., p. 224.

[84] Rose, *Wagner,* p. 9 and Hicks, *Explaining Postmodernism,* p. 115 (quoting *Addresses to the German Nation*).

[85] Fichte, p. 232.

[86] Hicks, p. 118, citing *Addresses to the German Nation.*

[87] Fichte, p. 235.

[88] Rose, *German Question / Jewish Question,* p. 119.

[89] Ibid., pp. 122, 131.

[90] Johann Gottlieb Fichte, *Addresses to the German Nation,* trans. R.F. Jones and G.H. Turnbull, ed. George Armstrong Kelley (New York 1968), p. viii.

[91] Ryback (see note #64).

[92] Heinrich Heine, *On the History of Religion and Philosophy in German* , trans. Howard Milgate (Cambridge 2007), p. 116.

[93] Ibid., p. 115.

[94] Ibid.

[95] Ibid.

[96] Ibid., p. 116.

[97] Rose, *German Question / Jewish Question,* pp. 117-118.

[98] Shirer, p. 241.

[99] Viereck, p. 85. Luther also burned books of church law and papal decrees, but this was not suppression of unpopular opinions. It was defiance of a repressive and authoritarian power structure.

[100] Ibid., p. 68.

[101] Ibid., p. 70.

[102] Ibid., p. 73.

[103] Ibid., p. 228.

[104] Ibid., p. 75.

[105] Ibid., p. 69.

[106] Ibid., p. 70.

[107] Similarly, Jewish involvement in Munich's 1919 Soviet was used to confirm a link between Jews and Communism.

[108] Prince Klemens von Metternich, *Memoirs of Prince Metternich* (1880—Vol 03), "free online text repository"; http://www.literature.at/elib /index.php5?title=Metternich_-_Memoirs_of_Prince_Metternich_-_1880_-_Vol_03; accessed July 2008.

[109] Viereck, p. 63.

[110] Rose, *German Question / Jewish Question,* p. 17.

[111] Steigmann-Gall, p. 15.

[112] Weikart, p. 81.

[113] Paul Harrison, "Hegel: Philosophy and history as theology," *Pantheist History;*

http://members.aol.com/pantheism0/hegel.htm; accessed January 2008.

[114] quoted in John Snell, ed., *The Nazi Revolution: Germany's Guilt or Germany's Fate?* (Lexington, Mass. 1959), p. 7.

[115] Hicks, p. 50.

[116] Ibid., p. 107.

[117] Paul Harrison, see above.

[118] G.W. Hegel, *The Philosophy of Right*, trans. T.M. Knox (Great Books of the Western World, Encyclopedia Britannica 1952), p. 108.

[119] Ibid., p. 107.

[120] G.W. Hegel, *The Philosophy of History*, trans. J. Sibree (Great Books of the Western World, Encyclopedia Britannica 1952), p. 369.

[121] Hicks, p. 122.

[122] Paul Johnson, *Modern Times: The World from the Twenties to the Nineties* (New York 1991), p. 579.

[123] Hegel, *Philosophy of History*, p. 350.

[124] Ibid., p. 360.

[125] Phil Orenstein, "Heil, Professor!", *FrontPageMagazine.com*, July 14, 2006; http://www.frontpagemag.com/Articles/ReadArticle.asp?ID=23293; accessed May 2007.

[126] "Hegel's Philosophy of Right (Third Part: Ethical Life, iii. The State)," *Hegel by HyperText*; http://www.marxists.org/reference/archive/hegel/works/pr/prstate2.htm#PR324; accessed January 2008.

[127] Shirer, p. 532.

[128] Evans, p. 35.

[129] Rose, *German Question / Jewish Question*, p. 109.

[130] Ibid., pp. 109, 112.

[131] Kershaw, *Hitler*, p. 634 (endnote 108).

[132] John Toland, quoted in "The Cosmic Consciousness of a Dynamic Trio: The Hitler Connection." *How the Philosophy of Friedrich Nietzsche Explains the Resurrection and Eternal Return of Jesus Christ;* http://lempisophia.org/Title%20Page.htm; accessed December 2006.

[133] Adolf Hitler, *Hitler's Second Book: The Unpublished Sequel to Mein Kampf,* trans. by Krista Smith (New York 2006), p. 144.

[134] John Toland, *Cosmic Consciousness*.

[135] Jacob Golomb and Robert Wistrich (see note #27).

[136] Kershaw, *Hitler*, p. 616 (endnote 103).

[137] Arthur Schopenhauer, *Religion*, trans. T. Bailey Saunders, eBooks@Adelaide; http://etext.library.adelaide.edu.au/s/schopenhauer/arthur/religion/chapter6.html; accessed May 2007 – or see Arthur Schopenhauer, *The Horrors and Absurdities of Religion* (London 2008), p. 137.

[138] Jochen von Lang, and Claus Sibyll, eds., *Eichmann Interrogated: Transcripts from the Archives of the Israeli Police*, trans. Ralph Manheim (New York 1983), p. 39.

[139] Shirer, p. 88.

[140] "The Cosmic Consciousness of a Dynamic Trio: The Hitler Connection." *How the Philosophy of Friedrich Nietzsche Explains the Resurrection and Eternal Return of Jesus Christ*. http://lempisophia.org/Title%20Page.htm; accessed December 2006. In spite of the eccentric title, this site contained [it is no longer accessible] a very detailed analysis of Schopenhauer's thought, and explained some deep parallels between his ideas and some aspects of National Socialism (not to deny, of course, the fact of very real differences as well).

[141] Arthur Schopenhauer, *The World as Will and Idea*, trans. R.B. Haldane and J. Kemp, *Internet Archive*; http://www.archive.org/stream/theworldaswillan01schouoft/theworldaswillan01schouoft_djvu.txt; accessed September 2009.

[142] Arthur Schopenhauer, *Religion*, accessed September 2009.

[143] Rose, *Wagner*, p. 165 (quoting Schopenhauer's *On the Basis of Morality*).

[144] Arthur Schopenhauer, *The Horrors and Absurdities of Religion* (London 2009), pp. 33, 35.

[145] Rose, *Wagner*, p. 94 (quoting "On Religion" in *Parerga and Paralipomena*).

[146] Ibid., p. 92.

[147] Rose, *German Question / Jewish Question*, p. 36 (citing *Parerga and Paralipomena*).

[148] Rose, *Wagner*, p. 93.

[149] John Jay Hughes, "A Mass Murderer Repents," *Immaculate Conception Seminary School of Theology*; http://theology.shu.edu/lectures/massmurder.htm; accessed January 2008.

[150] Robert Thomas (see note #6).

[151] Jonathan Judaken. "Review of Richard Weikart, *From Darwin to Hitler: Evolutionary Ethics, Eugenics, and Racism in Germany*," *H-Ideas, H-Net Reviews*, June, 2005. URL:http://www.h-net.org/reviews/showrev.cgi?path=80951126890820; accessed May 2007.

[152] Rose, *German Question / Jewish Question*, p. 13.

[153] Mosse, p. 91.

[154] Steigmann-Gall, p. 35.

[155] Johnson, p. 296.

[156] Mosse, p. 90.

[157] See Richard Weikart's *From Darwin to Hitler: Evolutionary Ethics, Eugenics, and Racism in Germany* (New York 2004) for more details.

[158] Adolf Hitler, *Mein Kampf*, trans. Ralph Manheim (Boston, New York 1999) pp. 373-385.

[159] Ibid., p. 514.

[160] Mosse, p. 298.

[161] Robert S. Wistrich, *Hitler and the Holocaust: How and Why the Holocaust Happened* (London 2002), p. 39.

[162] Dieter Just (see note #19).

[163] Mosse, p. 15.

[164] Ibid., pp. 32, 34.

[165] Ibid.

[166] Ibid., p. 39. This is a good example of scientific and medical terminology used to give anti-Semitism more credibility.

[167] Rose, *Wagner*, p. 180 (both quotes).

[168] Ryback (see note #36).

[169] Mosse, pp. 9, 13.

[170] See the appendix to the edition of Viereck's work given in the bibliography. His writing is dated, but should not be dismissed solely on that account.

[171] Mosse, p. 4.

[172] Daniel Gasman, *The Scientific Origins of National Socialism* (New Brunswick USA/London 2004), p. 155.

[173] Mosse, p. 42.

[174] Ibid., p. 43.

[175] Ibid., p. 44.

[176] Ibid.

[177] Ibid., pp. 44-45.

[178] Ibid., p. 152.

[179] Ibid., p. 222.

[180] Ibid.

[181] John Toland, *Adolf Hitler* (Garden City, NY 1976), p. 109.

[182] Mosse, pp. 55, 59.

[183] Ibid., p. 155.

[184] Ibid., p. 163.

[185] Ibid., p. 160.

[186] John Conway, *The Nazi Persecution of the Churches 1933-1945* (Vancouver 1968), pp. 375-376.

Chapter 6. Wagner

A Folkish prophet

Richard Wagner figures largely in many discussions of the emergence of National Socialism. One reason for this is that Hitler is well-known to have been a great admirer of Wagner's music. He knew much of Wagner's work by heart, and is often quoted as having said that understanding Wagner was important to an understanding of National Socialism. It has even been suggested that the elaborately staged Nuremberg party rallies had elements of Wagnerian opera.

More importantly, Wagner was an enthusiastic advocate not only of racism and racial purity, but also of German nationalism, authoritarianism, socialism, and anti-Semitism. Peter Viereck, who studied Wagner's writings in detail, states that Wagner's later writings served as a "stylistic model" for Hitler when he was writing *Mein Kampf*.[1] This is independently corroborated by Ralph Manheim, an English translator of *Mein Kampf*, who refers to Hitler's "flights of Wagnerian terminology."[2]

Viereck also asserts that the 25 points of the Nazi party platform were identical to Wagner's agenda. Further, he states that at one point in *Mein Kampf* Hitler's wording was almost identical to Wagner's. Viereck even went so far as to describe Wagner as the single main source of National Socialism.[3] Paul Lawrence Rose writes that Hitler's "world view was soaked in the revolutionary anti-Semitism of Wagner."[4]

George Mosse, who also studied the 19th-century origins of National Socialism in depth, takes a much different approach. He is more concerned with general trends of thought and ideological presuppositions, and states that these are more important to an understanding of Hitler than such individuals as Wagner or Nietzsche.[5] Yet, in order to illustrate these trends of thought, he studies many individuals and shows how their ideas contributed to the climate out of which National Socialism arose. He examines a publisher, a novelist, an educator—why not a composer as well?

Whatever the relationship between Wagner and Hitler may have been, a detailed analysis of Wagner's thought reveals something of the ideas that helped (along with many other factors) to lay the foundations of the Third Reich. Wagner expressed views held by many, and if we set aside for the moment the question of Wagner's influence on Hitler and concentrate on Wagner's ideas in and of themselves, we will find much that sums up and even magnifies the Folkish trends that we have already examined. Having done that, we can consider the different question of Hitler's relationship to Wagner.

A problem of philosophy

Wagner (1813-1883) was not only a composer; he also had a deep devotion to German philosophy. In pursuit of its wisdom, he arrived at many ideas essential to the emergence of National Socialism. Some of Wagner's concepts were squarely in the philosophical tradition of Kant, Fichte, Hegel, and Schopenhauer. Briefly, Wagner saw a meaning and purpose to life that was found by human reason and intuition, not divine revelation or traditional religious belief. This reliance on human reason alone was of course the fundamental principle of the so-called Enlightenment. It led in Wagner's case (as in so many others') to very unpleasant results.

How can we best approach the complex subject of Wagner's racist, nationalist, anti-Semitic, socialist, revolutionary philosophy? To begin with, after abandoning earlier views of materialism and universal progress, Wagner came to believe in Schopenhauer's concept of Will, a blind and unconscious force. He then (if Viereck is right here, as he seems to be) modified the idea, and combined Schopenhauer's irresistibly striving will with a Hegelian goal or purpose. Thus, Will strives incessantly throughout the world, but not blindly or purposelessly. It has the end of elevating or advancing the human race, with the superior Aryan race as its cutting edge or focal point.[6]

More detailed comments by Rose shed light on Wagner's thought here and tend to confirm what might otherwise be dismissed as mere speculation on the part of Viereck. In *Wagner: Race and Revolution*, Rose refers to Schopenhauer as the "great intellectual passion" in Wagner's life, yet explains that Wagner did not fully accept Schopenhauer's pessimism about the pointlessness of striving and so proceeded to modify it. In Rose's words, Wagner "permitted himself to subvert some of his [Schopenhauer's] doctrines."[7] Given Wagner's previous admiration of Hegel—"I so admired Hegel's powerful mind that he seemed to me the very keystone of all philosophy"[8]—Viereck's suggestion that Wagner combined Schopenhauer and Hegel is very plausible.

So, a Schopenhauerian concept of life emphasizing "struggle" and "will," yet as part of a higher concept of progress, allows this struggle to lead somewhere rather than to nowhere—that "somewhere" being the progress and elevation of the human race. This was, Rose shows, combined with German Darwinism, which added an entirely new scientific and biological dimension to what had been merely philosophy before. Rose elaborates on Wagner's relationship to Darwin. Citing Cosima Wagner's diaries, Rose explains that Wagner began to read Darwin's *Origin of Species* in 1872, and quickly adopted it to his Schopenhauerian philosophy of life as conflict (not a difficult thing to do). In 1877, the reading of Darwin's *The Descent of Man* (again according to Cosima) had a further impact on Wagner. This led Wagner to two important confirmations of his own ideas: that humans and animals are not distinct, but are one (also taught by Schopenhauer); and that through breeding and selection not only animals, but also the human race could be advanced and elevated. Rose notes that Wagner's personal library contained five books by Darwin. It is worth stressing that Rose sees Darwin as confirming or lending more credibility to ideas Wagner had already held.[9]

Yet, there was some ambivalence in Wagner's approach to Darwin. Wagner's formative years were before the advent of Darwinism, and he preferred a more mystical and vaguely defined origin for the Aryan race. Hence he could claim that the yellow races might trace themselves back to the monkeys, while the Germans traced their origins back to "the gods."[10] This combination of "Enlightenment" and scientific rationalism with intuitive and mystical German romanticism allowed him to see life as a Darwinian scenario in which human origins remained a mystery, and a vague philosophical "Godhead" was still conceivable.

In Wagner's words, "Godhead is Nature, the will which seeks salvation and, to quote Darwin, selects the strongest to bring this salvation about."[11] Thus, in

Wagner's vision of reality there is a power at work in the world that uses conflict and elimination of the unfit to improve the human race—a very creative and innovative combination of Hegel, Schopenhauer, and Darwin. Rose mentions two other influences on Wagner's modification of Schopenhauer in addition to Darwin (he omits Hegel). One was the French vegetarian Jean-Antoine Gleizès; the other was Gobineau.

The importance of racial purity

Two significant conclusions followed from these ideas. One was that the Folk needed to be purified. Secondly, the Folk also needed to be unified. Both were necessary so that "the force," or "god," could use the chosen and favored German race more effectively for the advancement of mankind. Concerning the first of these, purification, the German Folk was contaminated by alien influences and needed to be purified so as to be more fully in harmony with the mystic life force. What were those influences? According to Wagner, one was French rationalism which had corrupted the primitive nobility of the Aryan soul.[12] This was part of a consistent reaction in German thought against the excessive rationalism of the "Enlightenment." This greater emphasis on emotion, intuition, mysticism, and passion was part of the general concept of German romanticism.

A second contaminant, along with decadent French rationalism, was Judaism. A third was Christianity. From these flowed the various evils of democracy, a free press, capitalism, pacifism, internationalism, and racial degeneration—all of which had been unknown to the proud and fierce warriors of pre-Christian Germany so glorified in Wagner's operas. Much of his operatic work can be seen as an evangelistic appeal to revive the primitive culture that had been corrupted by French rationalism and by the alien Semitic and Mediterranean import of Christianity.

Essential to all of this was the belief that the Aryan Folk was an elite among the peoples of the world. The essay "Hero-dom and Christendom" states that "we should have no History of Man at all, had there been no movements, creations and achievements of the white men."[13] Naturally, among the white races the Germans were the best. Germans were, to Wagner, more capable of noble qualities such as courage, honor, and pride than other peoples. In order to retain and further develop their innate superiority, the Germans needed to avoid mixing with lower and inferior races.

According to Viereck, who for some reason omits Darwin, it was Wagner's reading of Gobineau which led him to a greater emphasis on the importance of racial purity,[14] and evidence of Gobineau's influence in Wagner's writing is not difficult to find. In his tract "Know Thyself" he wrote that the Germans had lost or were losing their innate virtues due to racial corruption and claimed that "great characters . . . far rather come to light—nay, almost solely—in pure-bred races; where it seems that the still unbroken nature-force of Race at first makes up for every higher human virtue yet unformed . . ." Such primitive virtue (based not on civilization or on culture but on race) "may be met even to-day in the old nobility of German origin, although in unmistakable degeneration; and that degeneration we should have to take seriously into account if we wished to explain the fall of the German Folk, now exposed defenseless to the inroads of the Jews."[15]

An argument that Wagner rejected Gobineau's racial theories is not born out by an examination of works Wagner wrote after having spent time with Gobineau.

His "Introduction to a work of Count Gobineau's" praises Gobineau's aforementioned work on race in history as "great," a "masterpiece."[16] The impurity of the German race is contrasted with the "purity" of the Jews, who have a strong racial instinct and so forbid intermarriage. He also speaks of "the ruin of the white races" due to impurity caused by mingling with lesser races. He goes on to assert the "oneness of the human *species*," in agreement with Gobineau's belief that the lesser races were still human beings in spite of their inferiority. The concept of some people as subhuman took more time to develop.

Wagner also wrote in "Hero-dom and Christendom":

> Upon looking back to these characteristics and the inviolably noble code that flowed therefrom we certainly are justified in seeking the cause of their loss and its decay in a depravation of those races' blood, since we see the fall undoubtedly accompany their hybridising. This fact has been so completely established by the talented and energetic author named above [Gobineau], that we need only refer our friends to his work on the Disparity of the Races of Man, to rest assured that what we now propose to link thereto will not be viewed as superficial guess-work.[17]

Those who assert Wagner quarreled with Gobineau and rejected his work have missed this part of Wagner's essay. It might have been that Gobineau rejected Wagner's peculiar religious views which we shall examine shortly. People who agree on key points can disagree on others, even strongly. Nevertheless, Wagner's own writings make it clear that the problem of racial purity was important to him, even if he may have disagreed with Gobineau on some points. If for example Wagner agreed with Gobineau on the importance of racial purity, but disagreed with him on the solution to the problem of racial decay, or on the true identity of the superior Aryan race, that would explain how Wagner could praise Gobineau's main thesis but part company with him in finding a correct response.

Racial unity and the need for a leader

Wagner not only thought the German Folk should be pure—he also thought it should be politically unified.[18] It is too little realized that Hitler's dream of bringing all Germans into one nation was not a new one. This dream was the result of philosophy, not the vague emotionalism most people today equate with patriotism. It obviously had nothing to do with the Bible. As has been said, Jesus commanded cooperation with the Romans, the foreign invaders. Wagner here is linked not to Christians but to Fichte and to Jahn—in his youth Wagner had been a member of the national student league founded by Jahn.

The Folk needed to be unified not only externally but also internally. Wagner felt that the German people should be a single organic unit, the citizens working together like cells of a body. Democratic traditions, parliaments, conflicting parties, clashes of group or sectional interest that are considered healthy in a democracy were harmful in Wagner's eyes. They represented disease. He felt that true freedom was found when all of the members of the Folk were in harmony, working together as agents of a single will. Freedom to him meant, as it did to Hegel, being part of a smoothly functioning collective (we have already referred to Wagner's admiration for Hegel). When Hitler referred to the state as "the living organism of a nationality" [*Mein Kampf* vol. II chapt. 2][19] he was in perfect agreement with Wagner, and within a pronounced German anti-democratic tradition. Jesus Christ's concept of freedom was totally different.

This led naturally and logically to the Fuhrer principle. Wagner felt the Folk should follow a single individual—and of course this individual could be no ordinary person. The leader Wagner envisioned was the personification of the mysterious life force, the underlying Will working through the agency of the Folk. For a while he considered that the leader might be a king—not a hereditary monarch, but one chosen by the tribe as in olden times, and given complete power not because of his birth but because of his leadership ability. The mere concept of king however was inadequate to convey the special status of the racial hero who was something more than human. Viereck quotes from Wagner's treatise "On State and Religion" here, and goes on to explain that Wagner saw his ideal leader as a demigod, the German people personified.[20]

"Hero-dom and Christendom" contains other comments on the Hero. Wagner uses Hercules as an example of the "arduous labours in which the noblest Aryan stems and races throve to grandeur of demigods." He speaks of heroic ancestors who "like Herakles and Siegfried" "were conscious of divine descent." Their pride, courage, and truthfulness were "root-qualities of the Aryan race." Now, however, there is "decay" due to "deprivation" of the blood, a "fall" caused by their "hybridizing." Therefore now we "must seek the Hero where he turns against the ruin of his race, the downfall of its code of honour . . . the hero become wondrously divine—the *Saint*."

With such a leader, what need is there of parliaments and democracy? The leader represents the people, so what need is there of parties? As was the case in Soviet and Chinese Communism, the leader represented "the people" (or "the proletariat")—hence any disobedience to the leader was contrary to the best interests of "the people." Wagner was not an isolated eccentric on this point. The prevalence of such ideas combined with the shameful birth of the Weimar democracy and its repeated failings to make the concept of a Fuhrer welcome to many (though of course not all) Germans.

The starry-eyed statesmen who sought to arbitrarily impose democracy on Germany by force did not know or care about the many Germans who believed democracy was bad and did not want it. The beliefs that democracy was not really the rule of the people at all, but was only a swindle designed by Frenchmen or Jews to keep the Germans weak and disunited; that only a dictatorship truly represented the people—these derived from a school of thought of which Wagner was merely one well-known representative out of many. Mosse's *The Crisis of German Ideology* describes very effectively how these and related ideas had permeated much of German society in the decades preceding 1914.

Wagner's socialism

Another significant aspect of Wagner's desire to see the German people unified was socialism. A hostility to the very real abuses of industrialism was shared by many on the right and on the left, and Wagner rejected capitalism, private property, and money.[21] He used gold in his operas to represent the curse of capitalism, or of Judaism (according to Wagner the two were intimately related), and asserted that private property was the basic root of many social ills. As a good romantic, he felt that integration with nature was the cure to modern social ailments.[22] A desire to be free of false and artificial restraints and live according to nature was a common theme in Wagner's day.

Some of this is similar if not identical to Marx. Viereck records that the young Wagner wanted to abolish class distinctions, work, property, and money. As a youthful member of Feuerbach's Young Hegelians with their concept of materialistic progress and the coming happiness of mankind, Wagner could easily have moved in the same direction as Marx. He moved toward Schopenhauer instead, and toward the Folkish philosophy. As a result, Wagner (like others of the collectivist, anti-democratic right) found the solution to the problems of capitalism and democracy not in internationalism and the domination of the proletariat, but in nationalism and the domination of an Aryan elite. By the unification of the German Folk and the elimination of alien influences, with all society in harmony under the will of the leader, the evils of exploitation could be abolished.

Part of Wagner's socialism was, like that of Marx, a deep hatred of the bourgeois status quo. He longed for a revolution that would destroy the corruption and decadence of a decaying, artificial civilization, and wrote in 1848, "the lofty goddess Revolution comes rustling on the wings of storm . . . destroying and fulfilling, she fares across the earth. Before her soughs the storm . . . but in her wake opens out a never-dreamt paradise of happiness."[23] Civilization could be built anew, but only after the old order had been destroyed—and Wagner was serious about this destruction. He wrote in a letter of 1850, "With complete soberness of mind and without any delusion I assure you that I do not believe in any other type of revolution than that which starts with the burning down of Paris . . . Are you terrified? . . . Strong nerves will be needed, and only real men will survive, that is, those who have become men only by privation and by supreme terror." He then goes on to speak of the "redeemer" who will destroy all obstacles "with lightning speed" and adds, "the next storm will surpass all the preceding ones."[24]

In the war of 1870 Wagner hoped for the destruction of Paris and worried lest a premature peace might interfere. He later wrote of the "joy" the war had given him. He called himself "an out-and-out revolutionary, a destroyer of the old by the creation of the new" and expressed "the bloodiest hatred for our whole civilization, contempt for all things deriving from it, and a longing for nature."[25] If Wagner made some comments about peace somewhere, so did Lenin, Stalin, Mao, and Hitler.

At this point it is worth clarifying that in Wagner's day the German right and left were not polar opposites. Both were united in their longing for a revolution to destroy the corrupt, commercialized bourgeois status quo, and both were hostile to democracy, political liberalism, capitalism, and traditional religion. The collectivist left, however, saw internationalism and the dominance of the working class as the solution; the collectivist right stressed a unity of nation and of race. Combining nationalism and socialism was not a new contribution of Hitler's (though creating an effective political party and mass movement was). Many on the right thought of themselves as the true socialists.[26]

Wagner's parallels with Marx here are important. Not only did both men hate bourgeois society and yearn for its destruction—they also had some similar ideas about the Jews. In Marx's private correspondence, "there were numerous derogatory references to Jews who symbolized financial power and the capitalist mentality."[27] In his essay "About the Jewish Question," Marx claimed that Judaism was based solely on self interest, and that Judaism was a cult of money. Chapter 9 will explore in some detail the spiritual kinship between modern secular right- and left-wing totalitarianisms.

Wagner and Christianity

Wagner managed to fit Jesus into his revolutionary scenario. In a play of 1849 he represented Jesus as eliminating private property and triumphing over selfish Jewish egotism and materialism. This included the abolition of bourgeois marriage (another dream of Marx and Engels). Jesus was thus a revolutionary and a socialist whose teachings would free us from the curse of money, capitalism, and Judaism. Wagner's Jesus was of course an Aryan, not a Jew.

Essential to an understanding of Wagner's religious beliefs is his concept of traditional Christianity as corrupted by Judaism (Simon Weil's detailed online study "Wagner and the Jews" is very helpful here). Wagner thought that the basis of Christianity came from India. He wrote "The latest scientific inquiries have established beyond dispute [i.e. this is an unsubstantiated assertion—*Weil's note*] that the idea underlying Christianity has its origin in India."[28] The use of the term "scientific" is significant—it is similar to the belief of 19th-century German "theologians" that their attempts to explain Christianity in strictly human terms were scientific. In fact their supposedly scientific inquiries were, as Weil pointedly observes, unsubstantiated assertions. Words such as "nearly certain," "the latest findings," "beyond dispute," were dishonestly used by tricky philosophers and theologians to make imaginary concepts seem more authoritative than they really were.

Wagner's wife Cosima wrote in her diary that "R. [Wagner] deplores the fact that the Jewish religion has been grafted on to Christianity and has completely spoiled it."[29] In Weil's words, "Wagner conceives of a 'Jewish' way of doing things which has somehow infiltrated Christianity, destroying it from within."[30] To take a few more statements from Wagner:

> Christianity is [as it is] because we know it only in the mixture with and distortion by narrow-hearted Judaism . . .[31]

> . . . they [the Jews] had won a share in the development of the Christian religion well fitted to deliver it itself into their hands in time, with all its increment of culture, sovereignty, and civilization.[32]

In "Hero-dom and Christendom" Wagner refers to the "huge perversion of the Semite-Latin Church."[33] This is related in the same passage to "the falsehood of our whole civilization."

The belief that Christianity was fundamentally Jewish clarifies what might otherwise be an incomprehensible comment from Wagner's "Know Thyself"— that "our entire civilization is a barbaro-judaic medley."[34] How could the Western world possibly have been considered to be Judaized? The Jews remained a small and restricted minority in Europe. In no sense could the values of Torah and traditional Judaism be said to dominate Europe—unless we consider the belief that Christianity itself was the result of Jewish values. This is a point that

Nietzsche made and elaborated on at length in *The Antichrist*. Another quote from Cosima's diary is pertinent here: "When the children have gone he [Wagner] discusses the similarity between the present world situation and the fall of the Roman Empire, when national virtues also ceased to flourish, Christianity having torn down the national barriers; now the Jews are completing this work."[35] Wagner was (not surprisingly) hostile to Luther because he translated the Bible into German, and introduced Mediterranean Semitic values into Europe more effectively.[36]

If the Jews had corrupted Christianity, what was pure Christianity? This was a common theme among those who did not just dismiss Christianity altogether. Naturally, various ideas of "pure" Christianity were cooked up to suit individual taste. What Wagner's ideas of Christianity were requires some understanding. They included the above mentioned ideas of racial purity, Aryan supremacy, and authoritarianism. Wagner also added elements of Schopenhauer's philosophy to create what Weil aptly calls "Schopenhauerian Christianity." This is examined at length in chapter 7 of Weil's aforementioned work "Wagner and the Jews."

What was Schopenhauerian Christianity? Christ's death as a sacrifice for the sins of the world, his resurrection and return, the day of judgment, heaven and hell, God's law, sin, repentance—these were all left out. In the writings of Wagner's son-in-law H. S. Chamberlain we shall see such basic doctrines dismissed as evidence of petty and narrow-minded Jewish legalism and materialism, of selfishly trying to serve God within the deadening confines of out-dated dogma for the sake of advantage and personal gain.

To understand Wagner's references to Christ and Christianity in spite of his unbiblical beliefs, in spite of his lack of emphasis on the teachings of Jesus in his operas and in his voluminous writings, we need to do more than cut and paste a few quotes, as some have done who are more concerned with blackening Christianity than with understanding 19th-century German culture. We need to make a serious effort to understand Wagner's religious views.

A more detailed study of Wagner's Christianity demonstrates how a Christianity and a Christ stripped of traditional doctrines were adapted to the needs of pagan philosophy. It sheds a lot of light on the previously described Germanic Christians, whose "Christianity" included obedience to Hitler and the dressing up of Nazi doctrines in rags of borrowed religious god-words. A Jesus who can be equated with Siegfried or with Wotan (a point emphasized by Steigmann-Gall to show Wagner's Christianity)[37] is something different from that of traditional Christianity.

Weil briefly presents key elements of Schopenhauer's thought which Wagner followed and incorporated into his "Christianity" (with numerous quotes from Wagner for corroboration). Some of those elements are:

~ an underlying Will, a Will-to-live, is active in all things; life is essentially a conflict of wills, a constant striving. Wagner writes in a letter, "Will has sought nothing but to live, namely to nourish itself by the extermination of others, and to reproduce itself by propagation."38

~ man is a beast of prey, fighting, conquering, subjugating. Due to the ceaseless clash of innumerable wills, life is primarily violence. A quote from Wagner's "Religion and Art" reads

Attack and defence, want and war, victory and defeat, lordship and thraldom, all sealed with the seal of blood; this from henceforth is the History of Man. The victory of the stronger is followed close on by enervation . . . uprooting of the degenerate by fresh raw forces, of blood-thirst still unslaked . . . the only food for the world-conqueror appears to be human blood and corpses . . .[39]

~ life is also suffering. Hence, suffering is "the point of departure for religion" and Christianity is "the religion of suffering."[40]

Here, as Weil points out, Wagner's Schopenhauerian philosophy blends with his version of Christianity. Christ's suffering on the cross becomes not a divine sacrifice for the sins of the world, but only a symbol of human suffering. Wagner refers to Christ as God, but his Christ is a philosophical concept, "God whom we comprehend in the deepest anguish of fellow suffering."[41] Thus, as the Nazis took Christ's death on the cross and used it as a symbol of "struggle," of fight to the bitter end (as we saw in chapter three), so Wagner used it as a symbol of suffering. Needless to say, Christ's resurrection from the dead is omitted—the Wagnerian deity was not strong enough to overcome death and was a deity only in an abstract philosophical sense.

There is yet more to be said about the meaning of Christ's death for Wagner, but further reference to Schopenhauer's thought is necessary. Schopenhauer saw suffering as the result of our inability to satisfy the insatiable demands of Will. Hence, the only solution was self-negation. Wagner transferred this Buddhist concept to Christ. In Wagner's words, "Redemption is to be found only in the deliberate negation of the will."[42] Christ's death on the cross—again, without a resurrection—was seen not only as a symbol of human suffering but also as the ultimate act of self-negation, of the will's "turning against itself." This was the "source of salvation."[43] As Schopenhauer said in *The World as Will and Representation*, "We should interpret Jesus Christ always in the universal, as the symbol of the personification of the denial of the will-to-live . . ."[44]

This is borrowing Christ to illustrate principles of secular philosophy influenced by Buddhism. As Weil points out, "To define Christianity (or Jesus) in terms of a philosophical concept is to automatically separate it from the mainstream."[45] He then gives more quotes from Wagner to show his thinking here. Wagner wrote, "This act of the 'negation of the will' is the true characteristic of the saint, which finds its last completion in the absolute cessation of personal consciousness . . ."[46] Thus, Jesus is the redeemer only insofar as he shows us how to die to self and find relief from the misery of the world through a Buddhist sort of self-nullification. Wagner wrote, ". . . it was Schopenhauer who revealed Christianity to me."[47] All references by Wagner to Christ need to be understood in this context, and not pointed to with triumph as proof of Christian influence on National Socialism.

Wagner's talk about Christ is at times difficult to understand. In his essay "Hero-dom and Christendom" he wrote that the blood of Christ transcended race—"The blood of the saviour . . . who would impiously ask its race, if white or other?" Wagner here sees Christ as a symbol of all humanity in which even the lower non-white races were included. He went on to call the blood of Christ

"Divine." This sounds very orthodox, except that he explains that this "Divine" blood's "source might dimly be approached in what we termed the human species' bond of union, its aptitude for Conscious Suffering." Not sure how to express himself—hence the tentative "might dimly be approached"—Wagner suggests that the bond which unites humanity is the aptitude for conscious suffering, the ability to be aware of our fate and to experience it truthfully. Christ somehow emerged from this, human in his origin, yet attaining to an abstract and philosophical sort of divinity by becoming a symbolic representative of all humanity.

Wagner goes on to explain that this is "the last step reached by Nature in the ascending series of her fashionings." Christ reached this exalted level through some sort of a natural process. The process is not explained, but Christ's death is "the last step." Nature produces nothing higher than the death of Christ, for here she attains "the annulling of the internecine warfare of the Will . . . in the Saviour's blood we must now recognize the quintessence of free-willed suffering itself."[48] Freely-willed suffering (we should face our fate rather than try to escape from it) finds its rest in the annulment of the will. This is the holiness, righteousness, and peace brought by a sacrifice that has everything to do with German philosophy and nothing to do with the Bible.

Wagner explains in this same essay that this sort of salvation through dying to self is available to the entire human race, that Christ's blood "shed itself on all the human family, for noblest cleansing of man's blood from every stain." Wagner even suggests that this might raise "the very lowest races to the purity of gods. This would have been the antidote to the decline of races through commingling . . ." and would bring about a "universal moral concord," the fruit of Wagnerian Christianity, a mixture of Buddhism and Schopenhauer, salvation through denial of self.

What does all of this mean? Wagner agreed with Gobineau that racial mixing led to racial decline. Apparently Wagner's solution to the problem was dying to self, nullification of self-will. This would solve the problem of race mixing if the members of the lower races would as a result of dying to self not aspire to anything higher. Content with their lot, they would remain in their proper places and not try to mix with higher races or imitate them—but Wagner does not make this point clear.

At this point an objection might be legitimately raised: Wagner, like Schopenhauer, definitely seems to have little in common with Hitler here. His concern for inner peace through renunciation of will does not demonstrate any relationship with National Socialism—but Wagner was double-minded on this point, as was Schopenhauer. Wagner preached self-renunciation, but strove mightily to fulfill his own vision of society. Self-negation was a concept he talked about, but often blatantly contradicted in his struggles for German unity, purity, and cultural domination, and in his calls for a violent revolution to overthrow the corrupt status quo.[49] That Schopenhauer did not live according to his professed principle of self-renunciation either has been commented upon by others.

In spite of all of his talk about Christ, Wagner was deeply hostile to traditional Christianity. He saw it as having had a corrupting influence on German *Kultur*, and wrote that the Christian clergy had crippled the warriors who remained his ideal.[50] He identified it, along with French intellectualism and Jewish values, or lack of values, as an alien influence Germany needed to be rid of. His operas were among other things a conscious attempt to restore the lost pagan virtues of primitive pre-Christian Germany ("primitive" being a word with positive connotations for Wagner). As Steigmann-Gall relates, "Wagner's operas openly celebrated the pagan, tribal gods of a mythical pre-Christian Germany."[51]

It should be evident that someone who advocated so many values that are not found in the Bible, and are contrary to the Bible, and who also glorified pagan gods, should not be considered a Christian. Nevertheless, Steigmann-Gall asserts that even Wagner's celebration of pagan gods "was not a turn against Christianity."[52] He gives as evidence (a) one of Wagner's operas (*Parsifal*); (b) a comment of Wagner's taken from a secondary source and (c) "exchanges with his wife," again from a secondary source, in which Wagner is said to have said something positive about Christianity.

Concerning the first of these, *Parsifal*, Steigmann-Gall cites Nietzsche who claims that in this work Wagner "sank down before the cross"—yet in the same sentence Steigmann-Gall informs us that Thomas Mann saw the play as "a dramatization of proto-Nazi racialist thinking."[53] Why we should accept Nietzsche's opinion over Mann's is not explained—and what is this alleged "collapse before the cross" about? Is it an opera about how people need to repent of their sins and believe in Jesus so that they can go to heaven? On the contrary— based on Arthurian legend, it is something about the Holy Grail and a magic spear. Did Nietzsche have such an intense hatred of Christianity that even mentioning Christ in the context of Arthurian legend was "Christianity"? Whatever the case, Nietzsche's dubious comment is hardly proof of Wagner's Christianity. Rose believes the opera is about the redemption of the Aryan race, about Aryan triumph. One of Hitler's associates stated that Hitler saw *Parsifal* as a "most profound drama" about "the incurable ailment of corrupted blood." Its main theme was (still in Hitler's reported words), "that selection and renewal are possible only amid the continuous tension of a lasting struggle." Following these comments, Hitler then hummed a suitable Wagnerian melody (presumably from *Parsifal*).[54]

Secondly, it is claimed that "Wagner believed paganism's highest God, Wotan, became 'completely identified' with 'Christ himself, the son of God,'" and that pre-Christian faith was easily attached to Christ who became "the stem-God once again."[55] Saying that Christ could be completely identified with Wotan reveals a belief in the Aryan Christ from whom all Semitic influences had been removed—not the Christ whose parents had him circumcised on the eight day according to the law of Moses; not the Christ who rose from the dead, a part of the Trinity who will return as God to judge the world. A Christ who can be easily assimilated with Wotan is a Christ from whom all essential doctrines have been removed. He can then be set up as a symbol to which anything can be attached.

It is a mistake to think that any and every reference to Christ as "divine" or "Son of God" is proof of Christianity. By this logic, Hindus could be called Christians. They accept Christ as divine—he is just one more God out of many. Ghandi said positive things about Jesus and tried to follow some of his teachings. He was 500 times the Christian that Wagner was, yet who would call him a Christian?

Steigmann-Gall's third attempt to link Wagner to Christianity (a lifetime of naked paganism notwithstanding) is based on a few phrases taken from "exchanges" with his wife. Quoting again not from Wagner's works but from some magazine article, we read that Wagner "often stated his belief that 'Jesus was the source of all morality . . . that Christ brought salvation and joy . . . that Jesus was the true redeemer."[56] Viereck also says that Wagner considered himself a Christian—and a Nordic, a Buddhist, and a Hellene as well.[57] That Jesus was a true "redeemer" who did not rise from the dead and who brought "salvation" not through forgiveness of sin but through Buddhist self-nullification; that Christ was a philosophical symbol of suffering humanity and of Aryan racial purity; that Christianity involves much more than any and every reference to Christ in no matter what philosophical context; these concepts are beyond the scope of Steigmann-Gall's exceedingly biased study.

True Aryan Christianity, in Wagner's eyes, consisted of the ideas we have seen above. With this understanding of "Christianity," many could consider themselves Christians even as they scrapped all of the traditional doctrines and invented what was in essence a new religion—secular philosophy and super-patriotic nationalism adorned with a few cheap religious trinkets but void of any Christian teaching.

Wagner and the Jews

Like Hitler, Wagner stressed the racial toughness of the Jews:

> The Jew . . . is the most astounding instance of racial congruence ever offered by world-history. Without a fatherland, a mother-tongue, midst every people's land and tongue he finds himself again, in virtue of his absolute and indelible idiosyncracy; even commixture of blood does not hurt him; let Jew or Jewess intermarry with the most distinct of races, a Jew will always come to birth . . .[58]

This theme of the racial toughness of the Jews was echoed by Nietzsche as well. How else to explain the mysterious survival of the Jews once God is removed from the picture? For Christians and Jews, it is not racial toughness or peculiar qualities of Jewish blood that have preserved the Jewish nation over the centuries, but the will of God.

More significantly, Wagner's concept of "the Jew" contained four ideas fundamental to National Socialism and necessary to an understanding of the Holocaust. One was the concept of the Jew as a threat to racial purity, a biological threat. Another idea was that of the Jew as the source of all of the evils in society. A third was the belief that the Jews were striving for world domination. The fourth concept was the belief that the Jews should be eliminated.

The importance of racial purity has already been elaborated on. Pure races rose and dominated, impure races declined and fell. For the Germans to fulfill their destiny as leaders of the world, they needed to be pure, and the Jews polluted them racially. A second significant element was the idea of the Jew as the source of all evil. How could someone develop the weird belief that the Jews were behind all social ills? Big department stores, the stock exchange, bad music and art, pacifism, democracy, Marxism, the labor movement, international bankers— everything that was contrary to an idealized primitive Germanic simplicity was the fault of the Jews. Wagner even blamed Judaism (and Christianity) for turning people into carnivores with their false teaching of humans as somehow higher or more special than animals. Since this bizarre manner of thinking is so central to National Socialism it is worth trying to examine in some detail. Again, it is not that Wagner invented these ideas, but rather that he expressed them so well.

Significantly, Wagner's reasoning is secular, not religious—though he did make the occasional reference to traditional anti-Semitism. The starting point, again, is the "Enlightenment" hostility of Kant to Judaism. In Feuerbach's words, "Utility is the supreme principle of Judaism . . . the Jew's principle—their God—is the most practical principle, namely egoism, which takes the form of religion."[59] This theme is standard with Wagner and he dedicated "The Artwork of the Future" to Feuerbach.[60] Void of all higher ideals, Jews followed only selfish advantage, profit, material gain. A passage from Weil is appropriate here:

> In the only references to the Jews in "The Artwork of the Future," Wagner follows this line, contrasting enjoyment of the "endless charm" of Nature with "our modern Judaistic Utilism" (p.177). He repeats his idea as "the Judaeo-oriental theory of [Nature's] subservience to human use" (p.179). This suggests that applying Nature for Man's use is archetypally Jewish. It further implies that the Jews utilise Nature rather than intuitively respond to it. That is they make Nature serve their ends rather than themselves follow Nature's ends.[61]

Everything contrary to Nature in modern society was the result of "Judaistic Utilism." Jewish values were behind modern society's alienation from nature. This thought, that Jews manipulate nature and so live unnaturally instead of following nature and living naturally is expressed in *Mein Kampf*. Arguing that we must live according to the natural law of struggle, Hitler rejects the idea that we are not solely bound to nature's law, but are in a sense above nature:

> Here, of course, we encounter the objection of the modern pacifist, as truly Jewish in its effrontery as it is stupid! 'Man's role is to overcome Nature!'
> Millions thoughtlessly parrot this Jewish nonsense and end up by really imagining that they themselves represent a kind of conqueror of Nature . . . [vol. I chapt. 11, Nation and Race].

In Hitler's view and in Wagner's we should follow nature and be at one with it, not try to transcend it or imagine we are above it. In Weil's words,

> Effectively the Jew is cut-off from intuitive contact with the Folk. He is bound to be an outsider. This also suggests that the Jew cannot get in touch with Nature. For this can only be done via one's intuition. This supposition is borne out by Wagner's contrast of Nature with "our modern Judaistic Utilism". Wagner considered that society was decayed as a result of its denial of nature. These ideas suggest that a denial of Nature was archetypically "Jewish."[62]

316

Selfishness, greed, the concern solely for personal advantage without regard for a higher ideal—this was, in the eyes of Wagner and of other Folkish thinkers, the essence of Judaism. The selfish and spiritless materialism of the Jews would have been confirmed by their welcome of Napoleon's reforms during his rule over Germany. Oblivious to the ideals of patriotism and nationhood—than which nothing could be higher according to secular German nationalists—indifferent to the shame of foreign occupation, the Jews saw only their personal advantage, nothing more. Hence, anyone who lacked higher ideals was revealing not human sin and failure such as can be found anywhere—they were betraying Jewish influence!

The importance of this sort of thinking should not be underestimated. Wagner took this so far as to reason that since the selfish and greedy Jews were concerned only with money, anyone who acted according to such considerations was showing the result of Jewish corruption—and since so much of society was directly related to the profit motive, it was possible to see the Jewish influence everywhere. As Wagner wrote, "Judaism is the evil conscience of our modern civilization . . . [the Jew] rules, and will rule, so long as Money remains the power before which all our doings and dealings lose their force . . . ."[63]

Cosima wrote, ". . . the Jews: they comprise our civilization, he [Wagner] says—that is obvious, and that is why it is worth nothing."[64] Whatever is done by profit motive is the result of Jewish influence and thus, logically, is under the control of the Jews. This is why Wagner could assert that almost all of the newspapers and magazines were controlled—indirectly or directly—by Jews.[65] Wagner was correct in seeing that much social and cultural activity was based on financial considerations, and was right in condemning this. He was wrong in blaming this on the Jews. In Wagner's fantasy world, the original Germans were selfless, uncorrupted, and pure. They lived simple lives in an idyllic German paradise of farming, feasting, and warring. Modern corruptions came from, where else, Judaism, first through the medium of Christianity and now through the medium of soulless capitalism and profiteering.

A longing for an imaginary past of primitive German virtue, heroism, and glory was by no means an eccentricity of Wagner's—at least, it was not a personal eccentricity. An idealized past was a standard theme of certain segments of German society. This was part of the romantic fascination with medievalism, and also a reaction against the increasing complexities of the modern age.

The imagined corruption of noble Germanic simplicity by Jewish values supposedly began with the Germanic conquest of the Roman Empire. As Wagner stated in "Hero-dom and Christendom," "The accident of their [the Germans] becoming masters of the great Latino-Semite realm was fatal to them . . . ."[66] It was Jewish influence through Christianity that had corrupted the German Folk—and it was this Jewish-Christian influence that Wagner was seeking to counteract in his writings and in his operas.

Wagner had an ideal of society—everything contrary to that ideal was the result of French rationalism, or of Jewish influence (which included Christianity). The latter was much more insidious—the French after all had their own nation and their own language. Cosima Wagner wrote in her diary "'Fine fellow' R. [Wagner] exclaims, 'losing their own language, when that's what a people preserves longest. It shows they are mainly there to live like parasites in the body of others.'"[67] In order for German culture to flourish in all of its primitive pagan glory, the parasites had to be eliminated. Another entry from Cosima's diary is illustrative: ". . . the picture he [Wagner] keeps before his eyes to characterise the present day world [is]: fine horses, noble, eager, fiery, with a good hard-working capable earnest coachman, and inside the carriage, master of all these creatures, a bloated Jewish banker."[68] Parenthetically, the grouping of the coachman with the horses as "creatures" is indicative of another theme of Wagner's, and of Haeckel's, and of Nietzsche's, and of Hitler's: the conception of man as essentially an animal.

Concerning Wagner's desire for a Germany free of Jewish influence, it is necessary to stress his hatred of Jews. Writing about his essay "Judaism in Music," Wagner said "I felt a long-repressed hatred for this Jewry, and this hatred is as necessary to my nature as gall is to blood." He wrote in a letter of "cursed Jew scum."[69] Hatred of Jews was essential to his being—not surprisingly, since he blamed the Jews for what was wrong with the world. In this same context Weil introduces a quote from 1848 showing traditional anti-Semitism—"we still avenge Christ on the Jews of today"—but the main approach in the pamphlets of Wagner's already cited and in the analyses of Weil, Viereck, and Rose was secular. The image presented was not that of Jews as having rejected the Son of God and therefore under God's wrath—and it should be remembered that Christ was not, for Wagner, the Son of God, God come to earth in human form, and returning as God to judge the world.

With these principles in his mind, Wagner commented on the Synagogue. Quoting Wagner's tract "Judaism in Music," Weil writes:

> Wagner asserts that because the Jewish service has remained unchanged for "thousands of years", the result is decay. The content and form of the service have grown "senseless and distorted", its purity "terribly sullied". The whole has "fall[en] to bits" and is without a "breath of feeling". He finds the service "repugnant".[70]

Wagner goes on to describe the synagogue service by saying "Who has not been seized with a feeling of the greatest revulsion, of horror mingled with the absurd, at hearing that sense-and-sound confounding gurgle, jodel, and cackle, which no intentional caricature can make more repugnant . . . ."[71] How different this is from some comments made by John Wesley in his *Journal*. He wrote in 1770, "I was desired to hear Mr. Leoni sing at the Jewish synagogue. I never before saw a Jewish congregation behave so decently. Indeed, the place itself is so solemn that it might strike an awe upon those who have any thought of God."[72]

There is an implied criticism of Jews here, that in other services they had behaved less decently, but Wesley's *Journal* contains many much more direct criticisms of Christian congregations. It is a stark contrast to Wagner, who even went so far as to compare the Jews to maggots. In the same treatise he asserted that Jews could never thrive in a healthy culture. This is why there were no Jewish composers in the days of Beethoven and Mozart—German musical culture was healthier then. When a culture was dead or dying, however, then the Jews could flourish. "Only when a body's inner death is manifest, do outside elements win the power of lodgement in it . . . In genuine Life alone can we . . . find again the ghost [? = Spirit – *Weil's note*] of Art, and not within its worm-befretted carcass."[73]

Unlike Weil, I don't see the image of Jews as worms in a dead carcass as coming from Christian medieval sources. The logic here is contemporary. In fact, it may be recalled from chapter 2 that Luther also referred to maggots, but in a 16th-century rather than a 19th-century context. In his treatise *On the Jews and Their Lies* Luther wrote:

> Oh, what do we poor muck-worms, maggots, stench, and filth presume to boast of before him who is the God and Creator of heaven and earth, who made us out of dirt and out of nothing! And as far as our nature, birth, and essence are concerned, we are but dirt and nothing in his eyes; all that we are and have comes from his grace and his rich mercy.

Here it is not the Jews who are worms because they embody decay. It is the human race, including the Germans, who are worms and maggots before God because of his holiness and our sinfulness. As David said in the psalms, "I am a worm, and no man . . . ." Such an attitude renders any thoughts of racial superiority impossible—as if one grasshopper should imagine itself superior because it could jump a little farther than another. It was not until the decline of religious values in the modern era that race became an important factor in German thought.

Getting back to the subject of Wagner, another reason for his hostility to Jews was that he thought they were deliberately seeking domination. "The tribal God of a petty nation [The Jews] had promised his people eventual rulership of the whole world and all that lives and moves therein, if only they adhered to laws whose strictest following would keep them barred against all other nations of the earth."[74] Another statement is " . . . his race is certainly ensured dominion over all that lives and lives not" (this according to "certain promises of his god").[75] In Weil's words, "Wagner thinks the Jews have only one interest. They want to rule the world."[76] That this lust for domination is part of the Jewish religion was elaborated on at length by Wagner's son-in-law Houston Stewart Chamberlain. He connected it to Old Testament prophecies about the coming of the Messiah and his world rule.

What, then, was to be done with the Jews? Wagner thought that they needed to be gotten rid of. He wrote to the Jews directly, " . . . take ye part in the regenerative work of deliverance through self-annulment . . . only one thing can redeem you from the burden of your curse: the redemption of Ahasuerus—Going under!"[77] Ahasuerus, incidentally, was a legendary Jew cursed by Christ and condemned to wander eternally until Christ returned—then he would be allowed to die. This medieval fantasy with zero biblical basis was used by Wagner as a literary device, but that the Jews are condemned to suffer due to their rejection of Christ is not relevant to his arguments. Why should people be concerned about such things when they didn't even believe in the historicity of the Gospels to begin with?

It can be argued that by "self-annulment" or "self-immolation" Wagner was referring to assimilation, but there are some problems with this. First, what if the Jews do not want to assimilate? Can such hateful and evil people be tolerated

319

indefinitely to corrupt the noble simplicity of the Aryans? Wagner said "I consider the Jewish race the born enemy of pure humanity and all that is noble in man; there is no doubt that we Germans especially will be destroyed by them."[78]

Weil goes on to give other reasons why he feels that Wagner is not calling for disappearance through assimilation. For one thing, even if the Jews wanted to assimilate, they were incapable of changing. As Cosima wrote in her diary, "Jews can never really become anything else."[79] Wagner states that a Jew who tries to assimilate is "the most heartless of all human beings."[80] He also states that when a Jew tries to assimilate "the instinctive ill-will of the Folk confronts him . . . [he is] thrust back with contumely from any contact with the Folk."[81] In Weil's words, "These considerations lead to the suspicion that Wagner did not sincerely want to see the Jews assimilated. That, in fact, Wagner is merely attempting to deflect attention from his hatred by holding out the possibility of an assimilation he does not believe in. I think he is being disingenuous."[82] If I might disagree with someone who has studied Wagner much more than I have, I think it is more precise to say not that Wagner is deflecting attention from his hatred, which he stated openly, but rather that he is deflecting attention from his ultimate design, which was too far ahead of the complacent and superficial conservatism still widespread in Wilhelmine Germany.

Weil elsewhere states that "Wagner is softening his idea of revolution for public consumption. Accordingly he leaves out all references to murder, burning of cities, and terrible wrath."[83] Wagner concealed his desire for a violent overthrow of the existing order, at least in his public utterances—he could have done the same in discussing his plans for the Jews. It might be said in response, especially by admirers of Wagner's music, that he was only engaging in rhetoric. The same was said of Hitler also. Certainly, fantasizing about eliminating the Jews because they are the source of all evil is not indicative of a healthy mindset.

That Wagner was not above advocating violence against Jews is confirmed by entries in Cosima Wagner's diary. Referring to pogroms that took place in Kiev and Odessa in 1881, she wrote, "An article about anti-Jewish demonstrations makes him remark, 'That is the only way it can be done—by throwing these fellows out and giving them a thrashing' . . . In the newspaper there are again reports of Jew-baiting in Russia, and R. [Wagner] observes that is all that is left, expression of a people's strength."[84] This is not surprising, given his previous statements about the Jews as the "enemy of pure humanity and all that is noble in man."

Wagner considered himself to be the champion of pure humanity, the representative of all that is noble in man, and wrote "I may well be the last German who, as an artist, has known how to hold his ground in the face of a Judaism that is now all-powerful."[85] It is ridiculous to describe the Jews in Germany in the late 1800's as being "all powerful"—unless you accept that capitalism, the profit motive, Christianity, democracy, a free press, and everything else contrary to Wagner's idealized pre-Christian Germanic past were the result of Judaism. When Gregor Strasser and his secretary Heinrich Himmler spoke of eliminating spiritless Jewish materialism and going back to an idealized past,[86] they were revealing the same spirit that animated Wagner and so many other Germans.

We have seen much of this before, especially in Lagarde and Langbehn. Mosse studies in detail novelists, educators, and other intellectuals who shared

Wagner's longing for a lost, primitive ideal. What makes Wagner more significant is not the uniqueness or eccentricity of his ideas, but rather his stature as an artist. Wagner shows the extent to which Folkish ideas had penetrated, reaching even the highest levels of culture.

It has been argued that Wagner was not really much of an anti-Semite. For one thing, he had some Jewish friends. Moreover, he didn't sign a popular anti-Semitic petition. However, as is so often the case, outward appearances can be misleading. Rose documents from Wagner's own words how he was friendly to some Jews who were useful to him (wealthy Jewish supporters, for example), but was manipulative in his dealings with them and spoke badly of them privately. As to not signing the Antisemitic Petition in 1880, Rose concludes (after some quotations from Wagner and Cosima) that he refused to sign it because it was too tame, and not extreme enough.[87]

Wagner and Hitler

That Wagner (not only as an individual but also as a representative of deep and powerful cultural trends) helps to explain the emergence of National Socialism is plain enough, but how much does this have to do with Hitler personally? Was he directly influenced by Wagner's ideas? The exact nature of the relationship between Hitler and Wagner is not central to this study. What is central is the fact that ideas basic to National Socialism developed outside of the Christian tradition. Nevertheless, parallels between Wagner's thought and Hitler's call for comment. Authoritarianism, racial purity, German unification, anti-Semitism, and Aryan supremacy; a vague socialism based on hostility to the abuses of capitalism accompanied by a rejection of Marxism and left-wing socialism—these similarities are more than accidental.

Hitler's teenage friend Kubizek asserts that Hitler not only read Wagner, he "read avidly everything he could get hold of concerning Wagner . . . He was particularly keen on biographical literature about him, read his notes, letters, diaries, his self-appraisal, his confessions. Day by day he penetrated ever deeper into the man's life." Kubizek further states, "His devotion to, and veneration of, Wagner took almost the form of a religion."[88] Now, no one is required to automatically believe everything Kubizek says, but we have already referred to strong evidence of Wagnerian influence on Hitler's writing—and what reason would Kubizek have had to invent such things? Even without Kubizek's statements, it is reasonable that someone who was deeply attracted to a composer as Hitler was would be interested in that composer's ideas.

It would be absurd to argue that a normal, healthy young Hitler stumbled across Wagner's writings and was transformed by them into a monster. If Hitler read Wagner at all, he could merely have found nourishment for already established character traits. Whatever the nature of the influence, it would be strange to insist dogmatically that Hitler was neither aware of nor attracted to Wagner's thought. He visited Wagner's home in Bayreuth numerous times, and was on familiar terms with the "Wagner circle" or the "Bayreuth circle." This group included the aforementioned Cosima Wagner (Richard's widow), his son-in-law Houston Stewart Chamberlain, and his son Siegfried. This circle was dedicated to popularizing Wagner's ideas. Is it reasonable to assume they did not discuss Wagner's ideas? Is it reasonable to assume that the young Hitler, whom we have already seen to have been an avid reader, should take no interest in the ideas and writings of the composer to whom he was so deeply attracted?

Some reflexively react against attempts to overestimate the Hitler-Wagner relationship. To blame it all on Wagner seems too reductive, so people go to the opposite extreme and the entire question of Hitler's relationship to Wagner is dismissed. There is however no good reason to assume that Hitler had no exposure to Wagner's writings. There are some reasons however why those who dismiss the idea of a serious Hitler-Wagner relationship might be less than fully objective. Some people are attracted to Wagner's music and do not want to admit that one of their favorite composers had anything to do with Hitler. They may also prefer to ignore Wagner's writings so as not to have to confront him more directly.

Others have no interest in Wagner at all and are entirely ignorant of his ideas and writings. They see nothing other than Wagner's music and assume Hitler's attraction to Wagner was purely a matter of musical taste. A third reason is that people have their own ideas about what created Hitler. Anything that does not conform to their pre-conceived ideas is immediately excluded. Some scholars are singularly guilty of this, and can in fact be exceedingly narrow-minded and incapable of dealing with new ideas, in spite of their book knowledge.

A part of this third reason is the refusal to accept that the young Hitler might have had some kind of an intellectual life. No attempt is made to understand the basis of his thought as it is assumed no such basis exists. Bizarre ideas of racial superiority and Jews as plague bacillae are considered unworthy of serious consideration or study—that they might have emerged out of a distinct intellectual tradition is not considered.

All of the above arguments ignore the inconvenient fact of the close parallels between the ideas of the two men (of course there were differences). Attempts to detach Hitler from Wagner rely on logic that to me seems quite weak and does not hold up to sustained analysis. For example, it is argued that Hitler rarely mentioned Wagner in public—yet Hitler rarely if ever mentioned other people in public either. Except for the unavoidable autobiographical references in *Mein Kampf*, Hitler rarely if ever mentioned his father in public. He rarely if ever mentioned Roehm after the Blood Purge, or wealthy and influential supporters who helped him in the early days of the movement.

A related argument is that Hitler did not ascribe his ideas to Wagner—yet the fact that he does not discuss influences does not mean that there were none. The Fuhrer was not a man who advertised his influences. This was due to the fact that he deliberately fostered an image of himself as (and believed himself to be) a Man of Destiny, chosen by Providence, more than a mere mortal, the incarnation of the Folk-will. It would have been beneath his dignity and damaging to the image he consciously presented to say "When I was young I was deeply influenced by so and so, and I got a lot of great ideas from such and such." Occasional statements, hints, references were made in private, but the fact that Hitler never said "I got a lot of ideas from Wagner" is not a basis for serious argument. He thought his ideas were self-evidently true, derived from ultimate reality, and above any question of mere influence.

It is argued that there is no evidence Hitler read Wagner. This is not correct, if Viereck's assertions about stylistic similarities are true. It is not sufficient to argue that Viereck is out-of-date, or that he simplistically overemphasized the Hitler-

Wagner connection. Those criticisms do not affect the truth or falsehood of asserted parallels between the writings of the two. Moreover, there would have been no evidence that Hitler had read Fichte and Lagarde if a small portion of his huge library had not survived. Who knows what other books disappeared, possibly well-worn collections of Wagner's writings, heavily underlined with enthusiastic exclamation points and marginal notes? And of course there is no way of determining what Hitler read in the libraries of Vienna and Munich. Perhaps some of the writings by Wagner that he read are still on the shelves there.

It has also been argued that Hitler's private references to Wagner had to do with music, not ideas—but Hitler may have been relaxing, discussing music for pleasure rather than deep philosophical truths, posing as a man of art and culture rather than discussing his influences. And, he did make some private references to Wagner that show more than an interest in Wagner's music alone. Citing two of Goebbels' writings (*Vom Kaiserhof zur Reichskanzlei* and *Muenchner Neueste Nachrichten*), Viereck states that Hitler saw his struggle as mystically linked to Wagner's.[89] Hitler biographer Joachim Fest devotes approximately three pages to exploring personal similarities between Hitler and Wagner. He refers to Wagner as the youthful Hitler's "idol" and presents some quotes from Hermann Rauschning's reminiscences of conversations with Hitler in which Hitler openly states Wagner's importance as a prophet and forerunner of National Socialism.[90] Kubizek states Hitler saw parallels between Wagner's life and his own.

Hermann Rauschning quoted Hitler as having acknowledged Wagner's influence, but Rauschning is widely dismissed as he plagiarized some of his material from Hitler's published speeches or from the writings of Nietzsche. It is also said that Rauschning, a Nazi official who defected before the war, exaggerated the importance of his contacts with Hitler and had the assistance of a journalist in putting together a book (*Hitler Speaks*) which was really only anti-Hitler propaganda. This essay in no way relies on Rauschning to prove a Hitler-Wagner relationship, but it is possible that Rauschning needed more material to make a book and added extra quotations to a core of truth. He may even have allowed his collaborator to add some propaganda or sensationalism to increase marketability.

Some of the objections to Rauschning seem rather trivial. It has been asserted that he only met with Hitler four times, and that Rauschning exaggerated his relationship to Hitler—the last part is plausible enough, but I don't see how anyone can say with confidence who Hitler met every day in the 1930's, what they talked about, and for how long. Arguing that the picture we get from Rauschning is different from that supplied by other contemporaries is irrelevant—someone who defected and was speaking from the safety of England would present a different picture from someone still in Hitler's circle. That Rauschning had a journalist help him with the book is not in and of itself a valid objection either—many people need professional help in preparing a book. Kershaw states that "there is nothing in it [Rauschning's book] which is not consonant with what is otherwise known of Hitler's character and opinions."[91]

To think that Hitler had a passion for Wagner's music but had no interest in the man or in what he believed is implausible. Particularly striking is Kubizek's account of how deeply Hitler was moved by a performance of Wagner's opera *Rienzi*. I quote at length from Walter S. Frank's online biography of Hitler, *Adolf*

Hitler: The Making of a Fuhrer (Who was Responsible?).[92] Asterisks indicating footnotes are Frank's.

> In the Winter of 1906, Hitler and Kubizek attended an opera of Wagner's *Rienzi*. The story is set in fourteenth century Rome and tells the story of a man of the people, trying to free them from the oppression of the upper classes. The privileged make an attempt to kill Rienzi but are overpowered and after violating their oath of submission are exterminated. Rienzi rises to the position of dictator and in one scene the trumpets blare and the people shout: "Heil, Rienzi. Heil the tribune of the people." Hitler was completely enthralled by the music and by the character of the rebel Rienzi who had been goaded to political action after witnessing the death of his younger brother. Rienzi in the end, however, is stoned and burned to death by those who never really wanted the freedom he offered.
>
> The long opera was not over until after midnight and Hitler, quite out of context, showed a side of his personality that Kubizek had never seen. After the performance Hitler talked for over an hour about politics . . . He confided to Kubizek that he believed in fate and that even he could be called upon someday by the people "to lead them out of servitude to heights of freedom." (This at first appears to be one of Kubizek's exaggerations or recollections borrowed from others (including *Mein Kampf*), however, Adolf Hitler would tell more than one person that the "beginning" of his success began the first time he saw the opera *Rienzi*. It would be hard to deny that the first time he saw the opera was with Kubizek.) Years later Hitler would comment to another friend on the story of Rienzi: "Listening to this blessed music as a young man in the theater at Linz, I had the vision that I too must someday succeed in uniting the German Empire and making it great once more."* He believed that he was destined for a "special mission."*

The source for "Listening to this blessed music . . ." is given as Speer's *Spandau, The Secret Diaries*. The note about a "special mission" refers to Kubizek. Viereck [citing a German author, W. Daim] states that Hitler, referring to that performance of *Rienzi*, told Wagner's widow Cosima, "'In that hour it [the Nazi dream—*Viereck's note*] began.'"[93]

One writer finds it suspicious that a version of Kubizek's book published under the Nazis in 1944-45 omitted the *Rienzi* incident, which was included in the post-war version. He suggests that the material was added later by a ghost writer—but what if it was first deleted by a censor? An account of Hitler's youth by someone who knew him would have undergone the closest scrutiny for anything contrary to the Fuhrer image, likely even by Hitler himself. He may very well have thought that such an incident was not suitable to his demi-god status, as if the Man of Destiny should have been influenced too much by youthful enthusiasm. Some historians are far too inclined to confuse their suppositions and hunches with fact. Certainly other aspects of Kubizek's later account, such as

Hitler's elaborate fantasies about winning the lottery or his frequent irrational outbursts of rage, would not have contributed to the glorification of the Leader.

Kershaw dismisses Kubizek's recollection of the *Rienzi* incident as "highly fanciful" and "melodramatically absurd."[94] The judgment of an authority of Kershaw's stature should not be lightly dismissed, but neither should it be automatically considered as the last word on the subject. Kershaw states elsewhere that Kubizek's recollections "have been shown to be a more credible source on Hitler's youth than was once thought," and grants that "they do contain important reflections of the young Hitler's personality."[95] He even considers that some of Kubizek's descriptions of Hitler have "an authentic ring," adding that "the very singularity of the episodes he describes . . . suggests they were beyond his own originality or fantasy."[96] He does not provide any objective criteria by which we can separate the true from the false in Kubizek's narrative.

Since Hitler's life, if it had been written in a fantasy novel in 1910, would have seemed incredible and unbelievable, and since even in the light of historical fact so much of what Hitler did still seems incredible, it is reasonable to believe that there may have been incredible aspects to Hitler's adolescence as well. This is especially true if we accept the reality of a higher and unseen spiritual dimension to life—a dimension that Kershaw specifically avoids. If there are invisible spiritual powers of darkness, there is no reason why they could not have given Hitler some inkling of his calling and higher purpose. Such speculation lies outside of the confines of Kershaw's analysis, however.

Personally, I am inclined to give Kubizek more credit than Kershaw (and others) do. For example, Kershaw also dismisses Kubizek's statement that Hitler (who was not yet 14) wept at his father's funeral. Now, we can all agree that Hitler would not have wept out of love for his dear father to whom he had been so close, but what if Hitler had wept out of years of unhappiness, frustration, loneliness, bitterness, and the misery of never having had a real relationship with his father? Kubizek's account is plausible. If it is unproven, neither is it disproven. I once knew a man whose alcoholic father had abandoned him as a child. Years later he wept at his father's death, a reaction which he said had surprised him and he did not expect. Elsewhere Kershaw demonstrates that a criticism of Kubizek's accuracy is mistaken, and Hitler was in fact present at his mother's funeral as Kubizek had claimed.

People who rightly reject monocausal explanations of Hitler do not need to be concerned that Naziism will be blamed on Hitler's having viewed an opera. Countless young men have had dreams of doing great things for their country, and *Rienzi* no doubt inflamed the patriotic passions of others as well. The point is that Hitler's relationship with Wagner, whatever it was, goes beyond mere music appreciation. Whatever the case, this essay does not stand or fall with Kubizek.

It is worth speculating that, if Hitler was attracted to Wagner's writings as a teenager, he did acquire many of the essential elements of his world view fairly early in life. Extreme anti-Semitism, racism, German supremacy, right wing nationalistic socialism, dictatorship, militarism, a desire to violently sweep away a corrupt civilization and return to living by simple "natural" values—there is no irrefutable reason to insist that the young Hitler was not attracted to these ideas and in fundamental agreement with them. If this is the case, then many of Hitler's ideas were formed sooner that is commonly thought to be the case (though we need to consider the influences of Chamberlain and Haeckel in the following chapters).

Some clarification

It might help at this point to examine Hitler's socialism and anti-Semitism in more detail, as the hypothesis of a strong Wagnerian-Folkish influence makes them more comprehensible. Concerning socialism, it is commonly assumed that this word was only a word used by the Nazis to appeal to the workers. Hitler did not, after all, abolish capitalism, and he relied heavily on big business, which in turn profited greatly. Moreover, the overtly socialist planks of the party platform were never implemented—ergo, Hitler was not really a socialist. Also, socialism is on the left end of the political spectrum, while Hitler was on the right, so what connection could there be?

Hitler's concept of socialism is not well known today, but it was a common feature of that period. It involved a unity not of economic class, but of national community in the short run, and later of race on an international, even global scale. This solidarity of blood required not the abolition of capitalism, but the subordination of capitalism to the service of the nation. The problem of class conflict was recognized, but would be solved not by eliminating classes, but by unifying them psychologically and spiritually on the basis of race.

The extent of Hitler's socialism is too often neglected. The Nazi propaganda film *Triumph of the Will* shows Hitler exhorting massed formations of German laborers, telling them that there should be no class divisions, that all Germans should labor together as one. The fact that Hitler's socialism contained many conservative elements should not blind us to the presence of left-wing elements as well. Hitler's references in his closing speech in *Triumph of the Will* to those who were in the party but did not belong to it could have been repeated verbatim by Stalin and by Mao.

Hitler's speeches were full of references to socialism. He stated in a speech of 1937 that the purpose of the Labour Service was to break down class barriers and teach the dignity of labor. He boasted in the same speech that his government was "the highest form of Socialism," because people were no longer working for themselves, but for the benefit of the nation as a whole. Furthermore, they were not rigidly confined to a class system, but could find their place in society by their merits alone. As he stressed in another speech of 1936, what was important was not "profits for the individual," but "service to the nation." Thus, Germany had solved the problem of class struggle—"Today there is no more class struggle in Germany," only unity.[97]

Like Wagner and Marx, Hitler also had a deep hostility to unrestrained capitalism. The following passage from *Mein Kampf* [vol. I chapt. 11, "Nation and Race"] is illustrative. It could have come from any Marxist writing:

> The tremendous economic development leads to a change in the social stratification of the people. The small craftsman slowly dies out, and as a result the worker's possibility of achieving an independent existence becomes rarer and rarer; in consequence the worker becomes visibly proletarianized. There arises the industrial factory worker whose most essential characteristic is to be sought in the fact that he hardly ever is in a position to found

an existence of his own in later life. He is propertyless in the truest sense of the word. His old age is a torment and can scarcely be designated as living . . .

. . . More and more masses of people, numbering millions, moved from peasant villages to the larger cities to earn their bread as factory workers in the newly established industries. The working and living conditions of the new class were more than dismal . . . The formal transference of the old working hours to the industrial large-scale enterprise was positively catastrophic, for the actual work done before was but little in view of the absence of our present intensive working methods. Thus, though previously the fourteen-or even fifteen-hour working day had been bearable, it certainly ceased to be bearable at a time when every minute was exploited to the fullest. The result of this senseless transference of the old working hours to the new industrial activity was really unfortunate in two respects: the worker's health was undermined and his faith in a higher justice destroyed. To this finally was added the miserable wages on the one hand and the employer's correspondingly and obviously so vastly superior position on the other.

Hitler's solution to the evils of capitalism was the subordination of everything to the state. Businessmen were allowed to make their profits, as long as their activities were directed toward the good of the nation as a whole. As to the plight of the worker, that was ameliorated in theory by state regulation and the provision of welfare benefits. In practice, Hitler's rhetoric was not fulfilled, and workers in the Third Reich were rigorously exploited,

Significantly, Hitler shared the hostility of Wagner and of Marx toward the bourgeoisie. Dull, complacent, boring people, interested in their families, their quiet lives, more traditionally religious, opposed to revolution and to dramatic new schemes for reforming mankind—they represented a significant obstacle to radicalism, whether from the right or from the left. Hitler railed against them in *Mein Kampf*. He stated that "Our present bourgeoisie has become worthless," prophesied that the bourgeois world was "doomed," and condemned its "imbecility, weakness, and cowardice."[98]

Hitler's hatred of bourgeois values and his commitment to a revolutionary ethic influenced by views unknown before the modern era completely nullify vain attempts to link Hitler to traditional religious values—as if people who disapprove of immorality show an attitude of exclusiveness or superiority that might someday explode in another Holocaust.

Because of his hostility, Hitler longed for a revolution to sweep away the corrupt world that stood between mankind and the perfect society. Kubizek writes that Hitler dreamed of an ideal state that would bring sweeping social reform. Before this could come about, however, "a revolutionary arm had first to put an end to the existing political conditions which had become unbearable." His own personal torment "urged him on to radical and total solutions," and he longed for "the storm of the revolution" (words attributed by Kubizek to Hitler) to bring these sweeping changes about. Hitler's own miserable life and personality ("his miserable position" in Kubizek's words) aroused a furious hatred of what he saw as society's injustices.[99]

Hitler's youthful anti-Semitism

If Hitler did indeed begin reading Wagner's hateful and inflammatory anti-Semitic comments at a young age, it answers a lot of questions—but there are still some ambiguities. The first documented statement we have by Hitler himself asserting his anti-Semitism is in a letter of 1919. In it he states that pogroms were the result of an irrational form of anti-Semitism, whereas a "rational anti-Semitism" must have as its goal "the elimination of the Jews altogether." After all, sporadic outbursts of blind violence do not achieve anything. This reflects a developed position on the Jewish "problem," and was not the result of an instantaneous change. For this obvious reason, Jaeckel concludes it is "quite credible" that Hitler had become an anti-Semite during his years in Vienna.[100]

According to Kubizek, Hitler's hatred of Jews began in Linz. This is more than a mere question of having read Wagner. After quoting a statement in which Hitler claims Jews were not an issue for him in Linz (neither at school nor at home), Kubizek states that his own recollections were different. He claims that Hitler's father was definitely anti-Jewish, and a follower of the Austrian anti-Semite von Schonerer. Kubizek also states that teachers at Hitler's school openly expressed their hatred of Jews. He adds that Hitler was anti-Jewish before he left Linz, and recalls a hostile comment Hitler made about a synagogue there.[101]

Hitler, though, claimed he became anti-Semitic at a later date. Possibly, since there were few Jews in Linz, Hitler might have made a few conventional anti-Semitic remarks without having thought much about it. He may not have taken the issue seriously until later in Vienna (Kubizek mentions this possibility). This would explain how Hitler could have given a watercolor to Dr. Bloch, the Jewish doctor who treated his mother as she was dying of cancer. We can agree with Kershaw that "The deep, visceral hatred of his later antisemitism was of a different order altogether. That was certainly not present in his Linz years."[102] More likely than not, Hitler distorted the facts so as to make his anti-Semitism appear to be the result of thought, study, and experience, instead of just an inherited and unscientific prejudice.

Kershaw dismisses Kubizek's claim that Hitler was anti-Semitic in Linz, but I think his reasoning is not convincing. He claims that Kubizek's account of Hitler taking him to a synagogue in Vienna to witness a Jewish wedding has "the appearance of an outright fabrication."[103] If we consider, though, that Wagner himself visited a Jewish synagogue, and later wrote of its "gurgle, jodel, and cackle" (as was mentioned earlier in this chapter), then Kubizek's account becomes much more plausible. His statements that he went with Hitler to observe the Austrian Parliament to study something that Hitler despised; that they went for a walk through an area notorious for prostitution, which Hitler railed against; that they visited the Prater, Vienna's pleasure gardens, where Hitler angrily observed the people drinking wine and enjoying themselves with various amusements—these seem very natural, and I don't think any historian would doubt them or find them out of character.

Kubizek's claim that Hitler joined the Antisemitic League in Vienna in 1908 is also dismissed by Kershaw as no such organization existed then. Kubizek may just have misremembered the name though. He may also have been referring to a new group that subsequently merged with a larger one and left no trace. Someone may even have collected funds from people for his organization and then disappeared. Kershaw's reasoning is far from iron-clad. Stating that "Kubizek was keen to distance himself in his post-war memoirs from the radical views of his friend on the 'Jewish Question'" and so had a motive for claiming Hitler was anti-Semitic before he went to Vienna is curious.[104] If that were Kubizek's motive, he should have claimed that Hitler became an anti-Semite after they went their separate ways, and that while Kubizek knew Hitler he had no such ideas. To claim that Hitler was already an anti-Semite while they were friends does not distance Kubizek from Hitler here, it does the opposite.

Saying Kubizek was "probably incorrect" in referring to Hitler's father's anti-Semitism is not convincing either. "Probably" means there is no definite clear-cut evidence. Kubizek's assertion that Alois Hitler was a follower of von Schonerer's anti-Semitism while being at the same time "unreservedly" loyal to the Austrian state that von Schonerer wanted to unite with Prussia seems contradictory, yet Alois may have disagreed with von Schonerer on Austrian independence, while agreeing with him about the Jews.[105]

Another argument of Kershaw's, that there is no real proof that Hitler was an anti-Semite when he parted with Kubizek in 1908, is not irrefutable either. After all, what proof would there be? We have a few postcards from that period, a brief letter or two (none of them serious or political), and that is all. More significant is the objection that Reinhold Hanisch, Hitler's companion for a short time in Vienna, claims Hitler had friendly relations with Jews. A man named Robinsohn helped Hitler out financially from time to time. Josef Neumann helped Hitler sell his pictures. Jacob Altenberg spoke well of Hitler—along with other Jewish dealers, he bought Hitler's paintings.[106]

This valid argument against Kubizek can be seen in a different light, however, if we consider that Wagner was proper and even friendly in his dealings with Jews who were useful to him, even as he spoke maliciously and spitefully of them in private. Rose elaborates on this in some detail. To give several examples, Wagner was obligated to allow a Jew, Hermann Levi, to conduct one of his operas because King Ludwig of Bavaria insisted on it, and Wagner dared not offend the king. Writing to the king about this, Wagner claimed he was a humane man and even had Jewish friends, but in the same letter described the Jews as "the born enemy of pure humanity and all that is noble."[107]

Then there was the Jewish pianist Karl Taussig. He was a "key fundraiser for Bayreuth" and was very useful to Wagner—so, he was outwardly friendly to Taussig. After Taussig's death, however, Cosima referred to him in her diary as "a poor character . . . conscious of the curse of his Jewishness." Joseph Rubenstein was another wealthy and useful Jew that Wagner was friendly towards outwardly, while privately he looked on him with contempt.[108]

Some Jews were useful, even essential to Hitler at one point in his life, so he smiled and kept his mouth shut. This could have made him hate them even more. This would also explain why Hitler kept his anti-Semitism to himself during the war (if accounts we have of that are correct)—the regimental adjutant, Hugo Gutmann, was Jewish. A letter Hitler wrote during the war referred to purifying the homeland of "foreignism" and "inner internationalism." For Wagner, and for all such anti-Semites, the Jews were the most conspicuous foreign element in Germany and these words would have automatically included them.[109] Kershaw

329

recognizes this aspect of the problem, records several negative comments Hitler made about Jews during the period he was supposedly friendly with them, and makes the point that Hitler's dependence on Jews even as he was reading anti-Semitic literature would have heightened his hostility. He recognizes Hitler manipulated people, and could have used his Jewish relationships to his advantage while keeping his real opinions to himself. He concludes this section of his biography with the reasonable and generally agreed upon observation that the war and later political events radicalized Hitler's anti-Semitism.[110]

Wagner's combination of (a) German philosophical speculation; (b) romantic intuition and feeling; and (c) new scientific theories derived from Darwin, make him an extraordinary symbol of the convergence of powerful trends that helped so much to prepare the way for Hitler. Even if Wagner's powerful yet demented and ugly musical genius had not enthralled Hitler, Wagner in and of himself would be of great significance to our study.

The influence on Hitler is highly important as well. If we consider that Hitler as a young man did in fact venerate Wagner and study him deeply, more of the pieces fall into place. Wagner can be reasonably described as a true spiritual founder of Naziism, and the source of a deep and lasting personal, psychological, intellectual, and spiritual influence on the adolescent Hitler. This is not to say that Wagner explains everything, however. There are three more thinkers we have yet to consider, all of whom made their unique contributions as well. H. S. Chamberlain, Ernst Haeckel, and Friedrich Nietzsche compel our attention.

> . . . *evil men and seducers shall wax worse and worse, deceiving, and being deceived. (II Timothy)*

---

[1] Peter Viereck, *Meta-politics: The Roots of the Nazi Mind* (New York 1965), p. 108.

[2] Adolf Hitler, *Mein Kampf,* trans. Ralph Manheim (Boston, New York, 1999), p. ix.

[3] Viereck, pp. 137, 141, 91, 130.

[4] Paul Lawrence Rose, *Wagner: Race and Revolution* (New Haven 1992), p. 190.

[5] George L. Mosse, *The Crisis of German Ideology: Intellectual Origins of the Third Reich* (New York 1971), p. 6.

[6] Viereck, pp. 104-106.

[7] Rose, pp. 91, 136.

[8] Ibid., p. 29 (citing Wagner's autobiography).

[9] Ibid., pp. 136-137.

[10] Viereck, p. 116. Viereck makes this point by putting together two separate passages from the essay "Hero-dom and Christendom."

[11] Rose, p. 137 (citing Cosima Wagner's diaries).

[12] Viereck, pp. 113, 118.

[13] Richard Wagner, "Hero-dom and Christendom," trans. William Ashton Ellis; http://users.belgacom.net/wagnerlibrary/prose/waghero.htm; accessed October 2007.

[14] Viereck, p. 116.

[15] Wagner, "Know Thyself," trans. William Ashton Ellis; http://users.belgacom.net/wagnerlibrary/prose/wagknow.htm; accessed October 2007.

[16] Wagner, "Introduction to a Work of Count Gobineau's," trans. William Ashton Ellis; http://users.belgacom.net/wagnerlibrary/prose/wlpr0155.htm#d0e393; accessed October 2007.

[17] Wagner, "Hero-dom and Christendom."

[18] Viereck, p. 101.

[19] Hitler, p. 394.

[20] Viereck, pp. 114, 110.

[21] Ibid., p. 120.

[22] Ibid., p. 121.

[23] Rose, p. 51.

[24] Ibid., p. 90 (all quotes).

[25] Rose, *Wagner*, p. 113 (joy of war) and Paul Lawrence Rose, *German Question / Jewish Question: Revolutionary Antisemitism from Kant to Wagner* (Princeton 1990), p. 375 (other quotes).

[26] see Stephen R.C. Hicks, *Explaining Postmodernism: Skepticism and Socialism from Rousseau to Foucault* (Phoenix, AZ 2004) for an insightful overview of this, especially chapter 4, "The Climate of Collectivism." More information can also be found in F.A. Hayek's *The Road to Serfdom* chapter 12, "The Socialist Roots of Naziism" (London 2007).

[27] Dan Cohn-Sherbok, *Fifty Key Jewish Thinkers* (New York 2007), p. 148.

[28] Simon Weil, "Wagner and the Jews"; chapt.10, quoting *Letters to Roeckel VI* July 1855, p. 139; http://members.aol.com/wagnerbuch/intro.htm; accessed January 2008.

[29] Ibid. chapt. 10, quoting *Cosima Wagner's Diaries I* [CWD] 17/3/1870.

[30] Weil, chapt. 10.

[31] Ibid., chapt. 10, quoting *Correspondence between Wagner and Liszt* Vol. II June 1855 p.98.

[32] Wagner, "Religion and Art," William Ashton Ellis Trans.; http://users.belgacom.net/wagnerlibrary/prose/wlpr0126.htm; accessed October 2007.

[33] Wagner, "Hero-dom and Christendom."

[34] Wagner, "Know Thyself."

[35] Weil, chapt. 10, quoting CWD II 5/11/1878.

[36] Rose, *Wagner*, p. 150.

[37] Richard Steigmann-Gall, *The Holy Reich: Nazi Conceptions of Christianity, 1919-1945* (Cambridge 2004), p. 101.

[38] Weil, chapt. 7, quoting *Letters to Rockel* VI Summer 1855, p. 131.

[39] Ibid., quoting Wagner's "Religion and Art" 1880.

[40] Ibid., quoting CWD II 25/3/1881.

[41] Ibid., quoting Wagner's *Selected Letters*, p. 641-2, 14/4/1865.

[42] Ibid., quoting *Letters to Rockel*, p. 133-4.

[43] Ibid., citing "Self and World" in *Schopenhauer's Philosophy*, Janaway p. 284.

[44] Weil, chapt. 7.

[45] Ibid.

[46] Weil, chapt. 7, quoting *Correspondence of Wagner and Liszt* Vol. II p. 99.

[47] Ibid., quoting CWD II 19/2/1879.

[48] Wagner, "Hero-dom and Christendom."

[49] Weil, chapt. 1, "The Most Terrible and Destructive Revolution."

[50] Viereck, p. 295.

[51] Steigmann-Gall, p. 101.

[52] Ibid.

[53] Ibid.

[54] Rose, *German Question / Jewish Question*, p. 335 and Rose, *Wagner*, p. 182. Rose quotes Hermann Rauschning's *Hitler's Gespräche*. In this source Hitler spoke of the opera's "absurd externals." *Parsifal* may therefore have been the only one of Wagner's operas to be banned in the Third Reich because the common people would have focused on those seemingly Christian externals and missed Wagner's Schopenhauerian artistic racial vision. More will be said about Rauschning's reliability shortly.

[55] Steigmann-Gall, p. 101.

[56] Ibid.

[57] Viereck, p. 118.

[58] Weil chapt. 10, quoting Wagner's "Know Thyself."

[59] Weil, chapter 2.

[60] Ibid.

[61] Ibid.

[62] Ibid.

[63] Ibid., quoting Wagner's "Judaism in Music," 1850 PW3, p. 81.

[64] Weil chapt. 10, quoting CWDII 20/5/1882.

[65] Viereck, p. 118.

[66] Wagner, "Hero-dom and Christendom."

[67] Weil chapt. 10, quoting CWDII 30, 11, 1879.

[68] Ibid., quoting CWDII 1/8/1881.

[69] Rose, *Wagner*, p. 37.

[70] Weil, chapt. 2.

[71] Ibid.

[72] John Wesley, *The Journal of John Wesley*, abridged by Christopher Idle (Oxford 2003), p. 196.

[73] Weil, chapt. 2.

[74] Weil chapt. 10, quoting Wagner's "Religion and Art" *Prose Works* [PW]6 1880, p. 232.

[75] Ibid., quoting Wagner's "Know Thyself" PW6 1881, p. 271.

[76] Ibid.

[77] Weil chapt. 2, quoting Wagner's "Judaism in Music."

[78] Ibid., chapt. 10, quoting Wagner's *Selected Letters*, p. 918, 22/11/188.

[79] Ibid., quoting CWD II 25/5/1878.

[80] Ibid. chapt 2, quoting "Judaism in Music."

[81] Weil, chapt. 2 (source not given).

[82] Ibid. (Weil's words).

[83] Ibid. chapt. 10.

[84] Ibid. chapt. 2, quoting CWDII 14/8/1881.

[85] Ibid. chapt. 10 quoting *Selected Letters*, p. 918, 22/11/1881.

[86] Peter Padfield, *Himmler: Reichsführer-SS* (New York 1990), p. 80.

[87] Rose, *Wagner*, p. 129.

[88] August Kubizek, *The Young Hitler I Knew*, trans. Geoffrey Brooks (London 2006), pp. 84, 187.

[89] Viereck, p. 133.

[90] Joachim C. Fest, *Hitler*, trans. Richard and Clara Winston (New York 1974), pp. 48-51.

[91] Ian Kershaw, *The Nazi Dictatorship: Problems and Perspectives of Interpretation* (London 2000), p. 156.

[92] Walter S. Frank, *Adolf Hitler: The Making of a Fuhrer (Who was Responsible?)*; Part I "The Boy," Sect. 3 "Friends and Lovers"; http://www.smoter.com/hitler.htm; accessed January 2008.

[93] Viereck, p. 125.

[94] Ian Kershaw, *Hitler, 1889-1936: Hubris* (New York 2000), p. 610 (footnote #128).

[95] Ibid., p. 21 (both quotes).

[96] Ibid., p.615 (footnote #85, both quotes).

[97] Adolf Hitler, *Hitler Speeches and Quotes* (London 2008), pp. 63, 34, 58-59.

[98] Hitler, *Mein Kampf*, pp. 407, 406, 680.

[99] Kubizek, pp. 172-173, 163-164, ???

[100] Eberhard Jäckel, *Hitler's World View: A Blueprint for Power* (Cambridge 1997), pp. 48-49.

[101] Kubizek, pp. 93-94.

[102] Kershaw, *Hitler*, p. 63.

[103] Ibid., p. 62.

[104] Ibid.

[105] Ibid., p. 62, and Kubizek, pp. 59, 63.

[106] Kershaw, *Hitler*, pp. 63-64.

[107] Rose, *Wagner*, p. 121.

[108] Ibid., pp. 123-124.

[109] Fest, pp. 68-71.

[110] Kershaw, *Hitler*, pp. 65-67. This corresponds with an intensification of anti-Semitism in Germany after 1918—see Richard Evans' *The Coming of the Third Reich* (London 2005), p. 152.

Chapter 7. Chamberlain

A spiritual founder of National Socialism

Wagner's ideas were systematized and elaborated on by his English born son-in-law, Houston Stewart Chamberlain (1855-1927). The Thomas Aquinas of Wilhelmine racism and anti-Semitism, Chamberlain drew on his years of study in the fields of history, literature, philosophy, philology, biblical textual criticism, theology, archaeology, comparative religion, and anthropology to write a massive work called *The Foundations of the Nineteenth Century* (published in 1899). It summarized and systematized the Folkish concepts of German superiority and hatred of Jews that began with Kant and were amplified by Fichte, Lagarde, Langbehn, and Wagner (among of course many others less prominent).

The book is of little interest today, and has lapsed into a well-merited oblivion. The pseudo-philosophical wisdom that made the book a great success in Germany before WWI (and in no other country) seems ridiculous today. Now it takes no little historical empathy to imagine anyone taking such a book seriously. It argues for Aryan supremacy, shows the evil nature of Judaism, and also sets forth in great detail the now totally abandoned Germanic Christianity that has confused so many people who try to discuss the relationship of Christianity to National Socialism with a very superficial knowledge of the historical background.

I had originally intended to pass over Chamberlain's book with a brief summary, as its main ideas seemed so ridiculous as to require little comment—though for those who lacked true spiritual values and so judged by science, technology, and superficial "culture" alone, the Europeans were at that time far ahead of the rest of the world. And who dominated among the Europeans? Not the southern or the eastern Europeans, but the northern Europeans, the superior Germanic peoples.

A glance at Chamberlain's book, however, quickly revealed that a short overview would not do. Ideas that seem nonsensical to us did not seem so to many of Chamberlain's day. Two chapters in particular have a great deal of relevance to the questions of National Socialism's philosophical origins and its relationship to Christianity. Chapter 5, "The Entrance of the Jews into Western History," precisely delineates the Jewish threat to civilization and throws into sharp relief the secular nature of the modern racial anti-Semitism so integral to the Holocaust. It has many parallels and commonalities with Hitler's ideas. An English edition of *Mein Kampf* contains an editor's note stating "Many of Hitler's ideas seem to originate in Chamberlain."[1] Chapter 3, "The Revelation of Christ," sheds light on the thought processes that allowed so many German "Christians" to effortlessly accept Hitler.[2]

Before looking at these two chapters, it might be helpful to give a brief overview of some information about Chamberlain presented by Shirer in his history. Shirer's overview of Chamberlain's ideas is a useful introduction but cursory and incomplete. Most would consider Shirer's statement that Chamberlain was the "spiritual founder" of Hitler's Germany[3] to be a great oversimplification. Nevertheless, the historical facts he presents are pertinent.

For one thing, he gives some information about the great success of Chamberlain's book—it was very well received and sold 100,000 copies by 1914. That such stuff was popular reading material says a great deal about German culture prior to Hitler. Also significant is information about the Nazis' appreciation of Chamberlain. According to Shirer, who lived for years in the Third Reich, Chamberlain was hailed in countless articles and books as a prophet and founder of National Socialism.[4] Steigmann-Gall relates that Artur Dinter, the *Gauleiter* of Thuringia, attributed his "total spiritual rebirth" to *The Foundations of the Nineteenth Century*.[5] Alfred Rosenberg, Nazi ideologue-in-chief and Reich Minister for the Occupied Eastern Territories was also deeply impressed with Chamberlain's book. He considered Chamberlain to be one of National Socialism's grandparents (along with Lagarde, Wagner, and Nietzsche).[6] Chamberlain was part of the Bayreuth Circle, and Hitler met with him at least twice.

When Hitler was in prison in 1924, with no prospect of success and his career seemingly in ruins, Chamberlain wrote an article hailing Hitler as the man chosen by God to save Germany. Chamberlain was an early member of the Nazi party, and on his seventieth birthday in 1925 the official Nazi newspaper, the *Voelkischer Beobachter*, praised his book as the Nazi gospel. Eulogizing him after his death, this same source stated that the weapons he provided had not yet been fully used.[7] Chamberlain's statement that Hitler had restored his faith in the German people has been quoted often. Hitler attended his funeral in 1927.

Chamberlain was of course not identical to Hitler in every respect. Chamberlain accepted the possibility of assimilation for Jews who renounced Judaism, and had more of an emphasis on Germanic Christianity and wrote at length about it, unlike Hitler (who criticized him for this in his *Table Talk*). Nevertheless, the enthusiastic admiration for Hitler by Chamberlain was reciprocated by the Nazis, and an examination of his writings shows that the Nazis admired him with good reason. There is much of the Third Reich in his book that should not be overlooked by those who have an interest in the foundations of National Socialism.

Chamberlain on the Jews—a philosophical and scientific approach

In examining Chamberlain's contribution to Nazi racial anti-Semitism, it is first worth noting what he did not say about the Jews. Concentrating on chapter 5, we see that he did not rely on traditional religious anti-Semitic reasoning, except perhaps for a few comments on negative statements in the Talmud, a traditional theme. He didn't mention well-poisoning, the use of Christian blood for ritual purposes, or God's wrath on the Jews for the crucifixion of Christ. In fact, Chamberlain specifically condemned religious anti-Semitism. He stated that we should judge "the Jew" "from the lofty heights of our superiority, not from the low depths of hatred and superstition, and still less from the swampy shallows of misunderstanding in which our religious teachers have been wading for the last two thousand years."[8] He stated that much anti-Semitism was "merely ignorant blind prejudice"—not the philosophical and scientific wisdom presented by a scholar such as himself.

Himmler was impressed by this approach. As a young man he commented on Chamberlain's pamphlet *Race and Nation* (*Rasse und Nation*), writing "A truth of which one is convinced: it is objective and not hate-filled anti-Semitism.

Therefore it is all the more effective. This atrocious Jewry . . . ."[9] Hitler also condemned anti-Semitism "based on religious ideas rather than racial knowledge" [*Mein Kampf*, vol. I chapt. 3].[10] After all, religious anti-Semitism allowed the Jew to escape merely by the trick of baptism; it also had no concern for the crucial issue of racial purity.

In his analysis of the Jews, whom did Chamberlain quote? He quoted Herder (*Ideen zur Geschichte der Menscheit*)—because of their lack of a nation the Jewish people "never attained to the ripeness of political culture on its own soil, and consequently never to the real feeling of honour and freedom." This of course is related to the unbiblical Folkish concept of nationhood as a fundamental aspect of meaning in life. Chamberlain quoted Goethe—"How should we let the Jews share in our highest culture, when they deny its origin and source?" (*Wilhelm Meister's Wanderjahre*). Another source was Kant. Chamberlain quoted the "great thinker" as saying in his *Anthropologie* that, for a sensible man, nothing is more difficult than "the commands of a bustling do-nothingness (*Nichts-thuerei*), such as those which Judaism established." Schopenhauer was also highly praised as "one of the greatest thinkers that ever lived . . . ."

Luther was referred to a few times in the chapter but only in passing: on the superfluity of Deuteronomy as a repetition of other books; on a question of translation relating to the color of David's skin; and on the morality of a hungry man stealing bread. One other reference to Luther bore indirectly on the Jewish question. It had to do with princes hanging thieves for minor thefts but doing business with others who rob and steal on a much grander scale (*Von Kaufhandlung und Wucher*). Chamberlain added that this was a policy "by which not only the Jews but others also profit." He was anxious to point out that not only Jews but also Gentiles could be swindlers and crooks, thus keeping his anti-Semitism on a *scientific* and *rational* basis, free from ignorant prejudice.

Those who want to link Naziism to Christianity will find little evidence for their thesis in this chapter of Chamberlain's book. Chamberlain was a modern man who preached secular—not religious—anti-Semitism. This chapter does refer to the Jewish inability to accept Christ—but it sees this rejection not as a source of God's anger, but as an example of Jewish materialism, of the inability of the Jews to relate to higher spiritual values. In Chamberlain's words, "the revelation of Christ has no significance for the Jew! I do not here speak of pious orthodoxy at all . . . This clear demonstration . . . is by no means given in order to let religious prejudice with its dangerous bias settle the matter . . . ."

The two most important aspects of Chamberlain's analysis of the Jewish "problem" were racial and philosophical rather than religious. As he wrote in a summary towards the end of the chapter: "My reply to the question, Who is the Jew? has been, in the first place, to point out whence he came, what was his physical foundation, and secondly, to reveal the leading idea of Judaism in its origin and nature . . . The two facts of race and ideal are fundamental." Thus the chapter consists of an historical examination of the racial origins of the Jewish people, as well as an analysis of the Jewish ideal. The first is largely based on Gobineau's racial theories, as well as on the liberal "Protestant" approach to the Bible's historical narratives about the Jews as purely human in origin. The second is based on Kant's concept of the Jews as materialists, lacking all sense of higher ideals, and on Wagner's related concept of the Jews being driven solely by egotism—though Chamberlain added his own ideas into the mix. The analysis of the Jewish ideal contains another theme of Chamberlain's, a theme elaborated on repeatedly and at length—of traditional Christianity as having been corrupted by Judaism, as having infected all of European civilization with unhealthy and artificial Semitic values.

At least one scholar has been led astray by the fact that Chamberlain did say a few positive things about the Jews. For example, he found some good sayings in the Talmud. He cited one about the importance of education and stated "one finds many a fine saying amid the rubbish of the Talmud . . . it must also be mentioned that besides the beautiful moral sayings there are very ugly and abominable ones." He saw a noble purpose in the use of Jewish law—"to keep the thought of God continually alive among the people"—and admitted that "thousands of good souls lived contented and happy in the fulfillment of the law; and yet what happened here was a stroke of violence against nature." He then elaborated in the following sentences:

> It is contrary to nature to hem in every step of a man; contrary to nature to plague a whole people with priestly subtleties, and to forbid all healthy, free, intellectual nourishment; contrary to nature to preach pride, hatred and isolation as the bases of our moral relations to our fellow-men; contrary to nature to transfer all our efforts from the present to the future. To establish Judaism, religion was killed, and then mummified . . . the whole literature of the world has nothing to show that is so dreary, so childishly wearisome, so composed of the desert sand of absolute sterility, as this collection of the wisest discussions which were held among Jews for centuries concerning the Thora [the quoted text consistently uses "Thora" for "Torah"].

In the same vein Chamberlain stated that the Jews "deserve admiration" and had "excellent qualities," including "a really admirable example of loyalty to self, to their own nation and to the faith of their fathers." Chamberlain even referred to "the excellent qualities of the Jewish character."

Chamberlain wanted to make some such statements to demonstrate his scholarly objectivity, to show that he was a real thinker, not just a superstitious and emotional anti-Semite. He also made many other observations of a less positive nature. On the first page of chapter 5 he stated:

> The Indo-European, moved by ideal motives, opened the gates in friendship: the Jew rushed in like an enemy, stormed all positions and planted the flag of his, to us, alien nature . . . Are we for that reason to revile the Jews? That would be as ignoble as it is unworthy and senseless. The Jews deserve admiration, for they have acted with absolute consistency according to the logic and truth of their own individuality . . .

As a result,

> . . . we live to-day in a Jewish age . . . this alien people has become precisely in the course of the nineteenth century a

disproportionately important and in many spheres actually dominant constituent of our life . . . our governments, our law, our science, our commerce, our literature, our art . . . practically all branches of our life have become more or less willing slaves of the Jews.

Chamberlain was not an isolated case. To give only one example out of many, the notorious anti-Semite Wilhelm Marr also wrote, "All our social, commercial, and industrial developments are built on a Jewish world view."[11]

For their singleness of purpose and effectiveness at keeping themselves intact as a nation and subordinating the Europeans to their control the Jews were to be admired. Such positive statements are comparable to an objective military analysis of a deadly enemy: they have good tactics, bravery, are well-equipped and so on. This is only the starting point however. Chamberlain also described Judaism later in the chapter as "a curse to all that is noblest and an everlasting disgrace to Christianity." In fact it was his ideas about the Jews that were a disgrace, though not to Christianity which they had nothing to do with. He claimed that Judaism had "spread like a poison over the whole earth." The Jewish lust for world dominion was "a direct criminal attempt upon all the peoples of the earth," it "poisons the heart of the Jew." Their false and unnatural faith "destroyed in the Jewish heart the purely human legacy which is common to us all."

The following brief passage summarizes Chamberlain's idea of the Jews clearly. After referring to the "insane pride" that isolates them "from all the nations of the earth," to the "senseless, unreasonable, and impossible" law that "lulls them with criminal hopes . . . isolating them from suffering, striving and creating humanity," he described the Jews as " . . . so inevitably the enemy, open or secret, of every other human being, and a danger to every culture, that at all times and places it [Judaism] has inspired the deepest mistrust in the most highly gifted, and horror in the unerring instincts of the common people." A similar statement by Hitler is found in an edition of his papers edited by Werner Maser. Commenting on the Jewish threat, Hitler wrote "What the wise man grasps with his mind the man in the street grasps instinctively."[12]

Before examining the reasoning behind Chamberlain's analysis, it is worth noting how accurately Chamberlain's description of the Jews applies to the Nazis themselves. Naziism was a "curse" to all that is noblest, and the support of German "Christians" for Hitler was a disgrace. Naziism spread like a poison over much of the earth, and Hitler's lust for world domination led to his criminal attempt upon Europe. Genuine human feelings were destroyed within the heart of those who followed Hitler, and the insane pride of the Nazis isolated them completely from the sufferings of people around them. The Nazis had criminal hopes, were the enemies of all other human beings and a danger to surrounding cultures. Their crimes inspire horror in the minds of all decent people everywhere.

It is not a coincidence that the picture of the world Jewish conspiracy in the fraudulent Protocols of the Elders of Zion also fits the Nazis well. The Jews were allegedly devious, cunning, cruel, plotting and scheming to take over the world, when of course it was not the Jews but the Nazis to whom this might be applied. It seems clear and has been commented on by others, that the Nazis—and Chamberlain—projected the evil that was within themselves onto the Jews.

Despite a show of detached objectivity Chamberlain, like his father-in-law, nourished a deep hatred of the Jews. He saw them as enemies of civilization. His hostility was so overt that one can only speculate on the motives of those who try to whitewash it. It might be that an emphasis on Folkish anti-Semitism as expressed by Lagarde, Langbehn, Wagner, and Chamberlain does not fit their pet theories, and hence must be discounted to make way for something more personally gratifying—such, for example, as abusing Martin Luther and discrediting Christianity. Or it may be that someone skimmed through the chapter and picked out a few quotes without having read carefully. Scholars are by no means always objective—they can even be less objective than informed laymen.

Two key presuppositions

There are two aspects of Chamberlain's study of the physical origins of the Jews that need to be elaborated on. One was Gobineau's theory that race was the key to history. Pure races flourished and dominated, impure races declined and fell. Chamberlain disagreed with Gobineau here and there—for example, on the question of whether the Arabs were the result of Caucasians breeding with Negroes. Nevertheless, Gobineau's influence is evident. For example, Chamberlain wrote about the "law of nature, that great peoples result only from the ennoblement of the race and that this can only take place under definite conditions, the neglect of which brings in its train degeneration and sterility." Near the beginning of the chapter Chamberlain warned about the insidious effects of Jewish racial pollution. If the contamination of Indo-Europeans with Jewish blood "were to go on for a few centuries, there would be in Europe only one single people of pure race, that of the Jews, all the rest would be a herd of pseudo-Hebraic mestizos, a people beyond all doubt degenerate physically, mentally, and morally."

The Jews, according to Chamberlain's logic, were able to corrupt the blood of others while maintaining their own racial identity because of their strict laws against intermarriage:

> . . . never for a moment have they [the Jews] allowed themselves to forget the sacredness of physical laws . . . Consider with what mastery they use the law of blood to extend their power . . . Their daughters might marry outside the Israelite people, but not their sons . . . This is the admirable law by which real Judaism was founded.

Hitler also wrote of the Jewish policy of deliberately undermining nations through racial pollution: " . . . the Jew systematically endeavours to lower the racial quality of a people by permanently adulterating the blood of the individuals who make up that people."[13]

Chamberlain did allow as has been said for the assimilation of the Jews—if a Jew "has succeeded in throwing off the fetters of Ezra and Nehemiah, and if the law of Moses has no place in his brain, and contempt of others no place in his heart." He quoted Herder again in this context: " 'What a prospect it would be,' cries Herder, 'to see the Jews purely humanized in their way of thinking!' " Hitler went much farther than Chamberlain here.

In addition to Gobineau's emphasis on the importance of racial purity, Chamberlain also relied on the methodology and the vocabulary of liberal "Protestant" biblical textual criticism to explain the history of the Jews in secular rather than in biblical terms. The critical methods of Julius Wellhausen and the Tubingen school of so-called higher criticism of the Bible were integral to Chamberlain's rewriting of the biblical text to reach a pre-determined end. Operating from the "Enlightenment" assumption that divine revelation was not a credible source of knowledge, Chamberlain and the critics whose methods he used sought to analyze the national history of the Jews as a "perfectly historical human development." Eliminating from the outset any possibility of divine intervention in human affairs, men who interpreted the Bible by the rule of secular philosophy sought to give a scientific, objective account of the purely natural history of the Jews.

Since liberal "Protestantism's" contribution to modern secular anti-Semitism has been so little noticed, and since it was essential to Chamberlain's approach, it is worth some digression. Chamberlain not only used the vocabulary of the textual critics—"jahvistic" and "elohistic" texts, "Deutero-Isaiah," "later interpolations," for example—he also accepted their presuppositions. He saw the Bible as a purely human book, full of mistakes, contradictions, free inventions and reworkings of older oral traditions inserted by later editors. Wellhausen is repeatedly cited and called a "scholar of the first rank" whose conclusions are "scientifically perfected." The Bible was proven "absolutely" to be historically false in many places, the editorial work of "pious" forgers. In Chamberlain's words:

> . . . the historical books of the Old Testament were collected from various sources and put together in the form in which they have come down to us, naturally only after those sources had been revised, expunged and interpolated in order to push the new hierocracy and the new faith in Jehovah . . . but so stupidly edited that it is only with the most unspeakable difficulty that we can find out the intention of the Prophets . . .

Naturally, with such an attitude Chamberlain was free (like the other "scholars") to cut and paste to his heart's content. This passage of the Bible was authentic, and reflected the noble simplicity of the primitive and warlike early Hebrews, this passage was a fiction—everything was interpreted to meet the preconceived goal of the critic. This was essential to Chamberlain's approach to the study of Jewish history.

That one of the immediate ancestors of National Socialism used the methods invented by seminary professors and "scholars" to arrive at his anti-Semitic ends should not be lightly glossed over. Steigmann-Gall notes the liberal "Protestant" influence on Chamberlain, and uses this to argue for a liberal Protestant influence on National Socialism. After all, if the "Protestant" liberals influenced Chamberlain—and they did—and Chamberlain influenced National Socialism—and he did—then the connection is obvious. What this reasoning fails to take into account is the fact that liberal "Protestant" scholars were interpreting the Bible according to secular principles. They abandoned historic Christianity in doing so and in fact were not Protestants at all. Neither were they Christians.

Traditional, historic, orthodox Christianity believes that both the Old and the New Testaments are the divinely inspired and inerrant word of God. Rejecting the Old Testament as a false and unhistorical book full of mistakes and lies undermines the whole Christian edifice—and it is not surprising that those who take this approach to the Old Testament take it toward the New as well. Chamberlain and the liberal "theologians" and "scholars" also found the New Testament to be historically unreliable, full of mistakes, errors, distortions, not divinely inspired, not a sure guide to spiritual things. This will be evident when we examine Chamberlain's views on Christianity and the person of Jesus Christ. The two books stand and fall together, they are true together, or false together—at least from the point of view of orthodox biblical Christianity.

A secular history of the Jewish people

The marriage of liberal "Protestant" "scholarship" with Folkish philosophy had a disastrous effect. Attempting to explain the origins of the Jewish "race" in the light of secular concepts, Chamberlain claimed that the Jewish nation emerged from the purely Semitic Bedouins (who, he pointed out, had long narrow skulls). He saw some truth in the traditions of wandering nomads preserved in Genesis, and stated that "Biblical criticism already gives us full information" about which parts of those early legends may be considered authentic. Wandering Bedouins emigrated to Ur, where they possibly cross-bred with the Sumero-Accadians. They then wandered to Syria where they definitely cross-bred with the non-Semitic Hittites and Armenians. This is where they acquired their round skulls and the ostensibly Jewish nose, which is in fact a Hittite nose. Chamberlain provided the reader with pictures of various types of noses and skulls. These ancestors of the Jews also cross-bred with non-Syrian Amorites (these Amorites were Indo-Europeans—tall, fair, blue-eyed, with long skulls). Parenthetically, the idea that the "so-called Jewish nose" was the result of Syrian blood was a scientific fact: "In the case of this anthropological discovery we have to do with no hypothetical assertions . . . it is the sure result of thorough scientific investigation . . . ." Calling their speculations "scientific" was and is a dishonest trick widely practiced by biblical "scholars."

The crossing of pure Bedouin Semites with Syrian Hittites and Armenians, Indo-European Amorites, and possibly Sumero-Accadians (as a good racial scientist Chamberlain was modestly cautious about the last group) led to the Hebrews—a general term that included the Moabites and Edomites. Thus the Hebrews out of whom the Israelites later sprang were already racial half-castes. Chamberlain asserted that "this historical testimony is confirmed in an irrefutable manner by that of science." The myth of direct descent from Abraham was in Chamberlain's view a later fiction added by biblical editors for their own nefarious purposes.

Some Hebrews then wandered down to Egypt for a short time, from whence they returned to Palestine and conquered some territory. This made them for the first time "Israelites." Chamberlain dismissed the 400 year stay in Egypt as a fiction, and the events of the Exodus were not worth mentioning. Then the Israelites began to breed again with the non-Semitic Hittites dwelling in Canaan. Much of the Jewish religion was borrowed from these Hittites. "The Israelite borrowed from the Canaanite the whole tradition of the Prophets, as also the whole outward cult and the tradition of the sacred places." The "laying out of the

Jewish temple, of the outer and inner court, of the curtain before the Holy of Holies . . . all these (said to have been dictated by God to Moses on Mount Sinai) are exact imitations of the primeval Hittite cult." This borrowing showed the lack of imagination so characteristic of the Semite, as the Jews still retained many aspects of the Semitic character in spite of their mongrel status. Chamberlain hypothesized that there may have been fresh infusions of pure Semitic blood from Arabia.

The tribe of Judah separated from the other tribes. It is from this branch that "the Jew" later emerged (the other tribes died out). Somewhere at this point in the narrative the greatness of David and Solomon is described as possibly being the result of the Indo-European Amorite blood mixture, though Chamberlain admitted that this was speculation. Goliath, incidentally, is portrayed as a "brave" man who "challenges the Israelites to a knightly combat but is killed by the treacherously slung stone . . . The legend which ascribes this cowardly act to David is a late interpretation."

In this part of the "history," prior to the emergence of the real Jew, Chamberlain made a number of noteworthy comments. He stressed that the Israelites were the result of a mixing of human types. Significantly, it was not a mixing of different related types having positive results, such as occurred with the Greeks and later with the English. It was a mixing "between types that morally and physically are absolutely distinct." This had a very bad result. "All historically great races and nations have been produced by mixing; but wherever the difference of type is too great to be bridged over, then we have mongrels." Thus the Israelites were a mongrel race—about 50% Syrian, 5% genuine Semite, 10% Amorite Indo-European, and 35% "indefinable mixed forms."

This mixing was "an incestuous crime against nature." Such a crime "can only be followed by a miserable or a tragical fate." Hence the mere existence of the Jews was sinful—"their existence is a crime against the holy laws of life." "The crossing between Bedouin and the Syrian was—from the anatomical point of view—probably worse than that between Spaniard and South American Indian." It was this crossing of incompatible types that led to the racial monstrosity of the Jewish people. "These are certain results of exact anatomical anthropology and of historical investigation" (one could say that it was the crossing of incompatible philosophies that led to the intellectual monstrosity of Chamberlain's ideas). The harmfulness of race-mixing was fundamental to Chamberlain's thought and to Hitler's.

With the destruction of the northern kingdom, the tribe of Judah stood alone. "It was only now—that is, from the year 721 before Christ—that the true Jew could begin to develop." Judaism really got started however in 702 BC, when Sennacherib's siege of Jerusalem was miraculously lifted. In that day, "the Jew was born, and with him the Jehovah whom we know from the Bible. That day was the turning-point in the history of Judah." In Chamberlain's words,

> The faith in the providence of Jehovah, the confident belief that all prosperity depended upon passive obedience to his commands, that every national calamity came as a trial or punishment, the unshakeable conviction that Judah was the chosen people of God, while other nations stood far below it—in

fact, the whole complex of conceptions which was to form the soul of Judaism—now came into existence.

Shortly after that, a "clever fraud" was perpetrated. The book of Deuteronomy was cooked up and falsely presented as a book written by Moses. It introduced "a rule of the priesthood, such as had never existed in Israel or Judah." It introduced for the first time "the fanatically dogmatic assertion that the Jews alone were the people of God," as well as "the prohibition of mixed marriages, as also the commandment to 'destroy' all 'heathens' wherever Jews dwell…" Thus the Jews were to blame for first introducing religious intolerance into the world.

This was followed by the Babylonian Captivity—a fortunate period for the Jews, since without it:

> . . . the true yet so wonderfully artificial Judaism would never have survived . . . It was in the Captivity that specific Judaism had its foundation, and this was brought about by Ezekiel . . . hence it is that Judaism has from the very beginning borne the stamp of the Captivity. Its faith is not the faith of a healthy, free people that is fighting for its existence in honest rivalry; it breathes impotence and thirst for vengeance, and seeks to blind men to the misery of the moment by forecasting an impossible future.

It was Ezekiel who invented "the Jehovah of Judaism, monotheism in a frightful, distorted form." This Jewish God is cruel and calls for all peoples of the earth to be destroyed except for the Jews: "Whoever wishes to give a clear answer to the question, Who is the Jew? must never forget the one fact, that the Jew, thanks to Ezekiel, is the teacher of all intolerance, of all fanaticism in faith, and of all murder for the sake of religion." Moreover, a religious hierarchy with all of its rules was craftily devised to keep the people in subjugation. It was at this time that various books were combined and edited to produce the Torah.

The destruction of Judah and the Captivity also led to an awakening of the Jewish racial conscience. The Jews for the first time "became conscious of their racial sin," and because of this "deep consciousness of sin" caused by the realization that they were a bastard race of half-breed mongrels, "the whole Jewish history from the beginning had to be falsified, and the Jews represented as a people chosen above all other peoples by God and of stainlessly pure race." Ezekiel instituted "Draconian laws" to prevent further race mixing. This led to the paradox of the Jews as a race that was both racially pure and racially impure at the same time: racially impure in its origins, racially pure in that its post-exilic laws required the Jews to keep themselves apart and intact as a nation down through the centuries. Thus "the Jewish race is in truth a permanent but at the same time a mongrel race which always retains this mongrel character." This is what Hitler meant when he referred to the Jews as "a people who are not entirely uniform in terms of race."[14]

For this reason, as was said earlier, "the Jews deserve admiration." They have not forgotten the "sacredness of physical laws" and "use the law of blood to extend their power"—that is, because "their daughters might marry outside the Israelite people, but not their sons," the Jews are able to "infect the Indo-

343

Europeans with Jewish blood" while keeping their own race intact. "This is the admirable law by which real Judaism is founded." Moreover, since Jewish blood had a peculiar degenerative power, the offspring of a Jewish mother and a Gentile was not elevated by the Gentile blood but rather brought down by the Jewish blood.

From their guilt over the crime of race mixing emerged the Jewish sense of sin. Thus the "ever-threatening conception of sin" was "brought into our bright world" by the Jews. Numerous references to Jewish influences on Christianity elsewhere make it plain that he included Christianity here. It was after all Christianity that introduced the concepts of eternal punishment, fear of God, and the need for forgiveness to previously simple pagans who had no such alien and Semitic notions, who were able to wench and plunder and feast to their hearts' content. This is an aspect of Nazi anti-Semitism that has been too little recognized—hostility toward the Jews for having given birth to Christianity.

This is the "greatness" of the Jew—that out of the misery, shame, and crime of his racial bastardy he invented a system that allowed him to survive, and not only to survive, but to assert superiority and to prevail over other peoples. "To save their nation" was a "noble goal." The hope of "rearing a noble race from the hopelessly mongrel Israelite is nothing if not brilliant." "The men who founded Judaism were not impelled by evil, selfish, motives, but goaded on by a demoniacal power, such as only honest fanatics can possess; for the terrible work which they completed is perfect in every point."

Unfortunately, their work introduced a poison to the detriment of the human race, a poison which has had "a large, and in many ways undoubtedly fatal, influence upon the course of European history since the first century." "The indirect influence of Judaism on Christianity was and still is immense; its direct influence on the 19th century appears for the first time as a new influence in the history of culture: it thus becomes one of the burning subjects of the day."

The last sentence of the chapter is, "We have to deal here with a question affecting not only the present, but also the future of the world." This relates to Hitler's statement:

> Should the Jew, with the aid of his Marxist creed, triumph over the people of this world, his Crown will be the funeral wreath of mankind, and this planet will once again follow its orbit through ether, without any human life on its surface, as it did millions of years ago.[15]

In the minds of Chamberlain and Hitler, the question of the Jew was important for the future of the human race. Thus, Hitler claimed in this same passage to be acting "in accordance with the will of the Almighty creator. In standing guard against the Jew I am defending the handiwork of the Lord."[16] Hitler believed, and Chamberlain would have agreed, that he was defending the existence of the human race by eliminating the Jews—as if the God of heaven and earth had ever asked for that kind of assistance; as if the human race had not survived for thousands of years without Hitler's protection.

The Jewish idea

Further analysis sheds more light on Chamberlain's hostility to Judaism. The real "demoniacal power" of Judaism and the precise nature of its threat to civilization has to be understood not only in terms of the contamination of European blood by mongrel blood, but also in terms of its intellectual and spiritual influence. Chamberlain spent many pages analyzing the Jewish spirit. Attempting to follow his logic reveals something of the dark night from which National Socialism emerged. It reveals the mindset of a man who was enthralled with Hitler upon meeting him, and who enthusiastically proclaimed him as the saviour of Germany. It should also be repeated that Chamberlain was a successful writer whose book struck a deep chord in certain influential segments of German society, including even the Kaiser himself.

Chamberlain's concept of the Jewish ideal as inimical to culture and true civilization had at least three aspects (in addition to the racial aspect just considered). One was the objection to the Jewish dogmatic claim to eternal truth (with which traditional Christianity was infected); another was the Kantian idea of Jews as materialistic, knowing only personal gain and advantage. This was coupled with Wagner's related concept of "the Jew" as dominated only by egotistical will, to the exclusion of deeper thought and feeling. Jews were as a result thought to be alienated from all higher intellectual and spiritual impulses, separated from the common experience of humanity. A third aspect of Chamberlain's analysis was a grotesque distortion of messianic prophecies to mean that the Jews hoped and strove for world domination.

Chamberlain much preferred the mythology of the Greeks and the Hindus to the Bible. He believed the essence of religion was a sense of wonder and awe before the mystery of being. This could be expressed in innumerable ways. To say that there was one true God, one true way, and all others were false; that there were eternal and divine laws to which we were supposed to submit—this was extremely offensive to him. He did not express it so bluntly, but this statement makes it clear: "the living feeling of a great world-secret, the vague realization that the natural is 'supernatural,' is common to all; it unites the Australian negro to a Goethe and a Newton. The Semite alone stands apart." Incidentally, Chamberlain felt that even though the Semitic blood of the Jews had been adulterated, they had nevertheless retained the Semitic concept of God—harsh, unyielding, intolerant. He related this to the barrenness of the desert, which deadened the imagination. The deep, dark, mysterious forests of the Indo-Europeans, on the other hand, stimulated a sense of non-dogmatic mystery and wonder.

Secondly, Chamberlain also used the argument that we have seen in Kant—that the Jews were fundamentally materialistic, serving God for the sake of material benefit. They keep his rules and he blesses them with prosperity—none of the lofty metaphysical speculations of a German philosopher or the beautiful myths of the Greeks, only a clear-cut and easily definable God who says "Do this and you will be blessed." Chamberlain referred to Jacob's bargain with Jehovah in Genesis chapter 28 as an example of Jews serving God for personal gain and asserts "Beyond question the argument—'obey the law, for it will pay you'— forms the chief and fundamental motive in Deuteronomy." How different this is from Kant, "who desires no outward gifts simply because his all-embracing mind possesses the whole world." Even the biblical account of the creation of the world was taken as evidence of Jewish materialism. There was no beautiful mythology, only a dull, flat, pedantic "God did this, then that" without majesty, wonder, or mystery. Moreover, it claimed to be literal truth, meaning that the Jews alone had the true understanding. This mean-spirited arrogance was typical of the Semite.

Jewish materialism and lack of a religious imagination was the reason for Jewish subservience to a dull and dead religion of supposed fact. Chamberlain claimed that "the will is the predominant power in the soul of the Semite." This "egoism of the Semite" means that "selfishness predominates . . . religion degenerates into fanaticism" ("fanaticism" meaning a claim to certain and sure truth). Loftier capacities such as nobility, self-sacrifice, and genuine creativity were absent from the heart of the Jew. For this reason the "most outstanding characteristic" of the Jew was "the absolute lack of every metaphysical emotion, every philosophical capacity!"

Chamberlain quoted other scholars to support his thesis, Renan ("The Semitic people almost totally lack the questioning thirst after knowledge") and Grau ("The Hebrews, like all Semites, are much too subjective to allow the pure impulse of knowledge to become a power in them"). Thus, according to the latest scientific research, Jews were egotistical, selfish, exclusive, dogmatic, and intolerant fanatics who insisted that their way was the only way. Motivated solely by stubborn will, they clung to their outdated and lifeless laws. Even modern and secularist Jews, "Jewish atheists of the most modern type . . . so-called free-thinkers . . . prove themselves to be genuine children of the religion of the Thora and the Talmud." They did this "by their lack of understanding for everything genuinely great outside the narrow limits of their own circle of thought, and by their ridiculous overestimation of every Lilliputian intellectual work which has a Jew for its author."

Jews were not merely materialistic and egotistical. Worse, they had an evil lust for world domination. Chamberlain arrived at this conclusion through a misinterpretation of some prophecies about God's final rule over the world. The Jewish messianic hope was understood to be an "unshakeable confidence in the universal empire of the Jews, which Jehovah promised." The Jews will endure "every sacrifice and every shame, in order at some time, no matter when, to enter into the Messianic empire of supreme power, to the eternal glory of Jehovah." "Jehovah is not the God of the cosmic universe, but the God of the Jews; he has only destroyed the other gods, consumed them, as he will one day consume other nations, with the exception of those who shall serve the Jews as slaves." A lengthier passage sheds more light into the paranoid fantasy world in which National Socialism flourished:

> . . . absolutely forged, from the first to the last word, are such chapters as Isaiah lx., that famous Messianic prophecy, according to which all the kings of the world will lie in the dust before the Jews . . . (the Jew) will put his foot upon the neck of all the nations of the world and be Lord and possessor of the whole earth. This one basis of Jewish religion includes, therefore, a direct criminal attempt upon all the peoples of the earth . . . it is the hope itself which is criminal and which poisons the heart of the Jew.

This idea was also expressed by Hitler. In Maser's aforementioned collection of Hitler's notes, we find Hitler commenting on the Jewish "drive to seize world control . . . Jahwe's prophecy is only an expression of this clear objective."[17]

The real source of the evil character of the Jews, in Chamberlain's eyes, was the Torah. Chamberlain agreed with Herder's theory about the Jewish lack of a national experience, stating the Jew "is not the result of a normal national life." Another facet of the problem was the desert environment in which the Jews originated. The Jewish lack of imagination was "the result of life in the desert for thousands of years, during which the intellect was starved and the feelings confined to a narrow circle." Nevertheless, it was the teachings of Torah which had turned the Jews into a menace to world civilization.

Again, the Jews who wrote the Torah were driven by a "noble goal" as was said above—to save their nation. The falsification of the historical record to present themselves as chosen people of God was "brilliant." Their work was "a true work of art," and was the source of the strength of the Jewish people, of "that vigour which so far has successfully defied every destiny." "What saved the small people of the Jews . . . What kept it together when it was scattered over the world? What made it possible for the new world-principle of Christianity to spring from its midst? This book alone."

The influence of the Torah was great—unfortunately, it was mostly negative. The Jewish law "produces the delusive idea of a particular selectness, of a special pleasantness in the sight of God, of an incomparable future; it isolates them in an insane pride from all the nations of the earth." Not only that, but the Torah is "senseless, unreasonable, and impossible in practice; it nourishes them with lying memories and lulls them with criminal hopes."

These ideas arose out of the belief that there was no direct divine revelation; that human reason alone was an adequate guide to life; that the Bible was a merely human invention, full of mistakes and outright lies. These ideas arose out of the German "Enlightenment." Chamberlain appealed to the wisdom of Herder, Kant, Schopenhauer, Goethe, and of worldly "theologians" who interpreted the Bible according to secular principles. This is a form of anti-Semitism directly related to Hitler, a form of anti-Semitism previously unknown in many centuries of Christian history. From Hitler to Chamberlain and Wagner, and then through Lagarde and Langbehn back to Hegel, Fichte, and Kant—the links are clear, the connections obvious.

The influence of Judaism

Chamberlain's concept of the Jewish influence on Western civilization is striking. He stated that the Jews had "exercised a large, and in many ways undoubtedly fatal, influence upon the course of European history since the first century." This went far beyond the insidious Jewish control of international finance, though this was a problem:

> . . . all the wars of the nineteenth century are so peculiarly connected with Jewish financial operations, from Napoleon's Russian campaign and Nathan Rothschild's role of spectator at the battle of Waterloo to the consulting of the Bleichroeders on the German side and of Alphonse Rothschild on the French side at the peace transactions of the year 1871, and to the

"Commune," which from the beginning was looked upon by all intelligent people as a Jewish-Napoleonic machination.

Much worse were the Jewish spiritual and cultural influences that permeated all of society. To repeat a quote given above:

> . . . we live today in a Jewish age . . . this alien people has become precisely in the course of the nineteenth century a disproportionately important and in many spheres actually dominant constituent of our life . . . our governments, our law, our science, our commerce, our literature, our art . . . practically all branches of our life have become more or less willing slaves of the Jews . . .

He later added, "Is it possible to read the daily papers without becoming acquainted with Jewish ways of thinking, Jewish taste, Jewish morals, Jewish aims?"

Judaism was not merely a race or a religion:

> . . . the term Jew rather denotes a special way of thinking and feeling. A man can very soon become a Jew without being an Israelite; often it needs only to have frequent intercourse with Jews, to read Jewish newspapers, to accustom himself to Jewish philosophy, literature and art.

This Jewish way of thinking was harmful: "If the Jewish influence were to gain the upper hand in Europe, we should have one more example of negative, destructive power." To show that the Jewish problem was not merely a racial one, Chamberlain referred to Paul's statement in Romans 2 that "he is not a Jew, which is one outwardly . . . but he is a Jew, which is one inwardly." Here Chamberlain was referring to Judaism not only as a religion or a race, but as "a special way of thinking and feeling" that non-Jews could be affected by without knowing it. Needless to say, Paul's teachings later in Romans on God's plan and purpose for the Jews were ignored entirely.

It was Christianity that introduced the alien, Semitic element into Europe, thus allowing people to become Jews in spirit if not in blood:

> As Kant rightly says, the preservation of Judaism is primarily the work of Christianity. From its midst—if not from its stem and spirit—Jesus Christ and the earliest members of the Christian church arose. Jewish history, Jewish conceptions, Jewish thought and poetry became important elements in our mental life . . . If we had not ceremoniously adopted the Jew into our family circle, he would no more have found a home.

Thus there had been:

> . . . an infiltration of the Semitic spirit as in our own European history since the beginning of the Christian era . . . the entrance

of the Jews into Western history derived its chief significance from the fact that the Christian church was founded on a Semitic basis . . .

Prior to the coming of Christianity, the Aryans had reasonable concepts of sin (being a coward in battle) or rebirth (making a new start). When Christianity came these were reinterpreted in a Jewish context and introduced into Christianity in a way reflecting only Jewish dogmatism. Thus ". . . the young Christian Church developed a series of ancient Aryan conceptions—of sin, redemption, rebirth, grace, &c. (things till then and afterwards quite unknown to the Jews)—and gave them a clear and visible form, by introducing them into the Jewish historical scheme."

The idea of religion being based on historical facts and doctrines as opposed to cloudy mysticism or personal feeling was considered by Chamberlain to be the result of the materialism and limited imagination typical of the Semite. Even the idea of immortality in a literal heaven, of "happiness in the future world" was "Downright materialism!" This is the "negative influence of Judaism," "infection with fundamental views of a materialist kind." Chamberlain went so far as to state that the Roman Catholic concept of the papacy was the result of Jewish influence: "now there was but one God, one altar, one High priest; the world was richer by the idea (though not yet by the word) Church; the foundation of the present Roman church, with its infallible head, was laid." This was also true of the "Judaic justification by works, which the Roman Catholic Church adopted from the Jews."

It was Jewish insistence on the ideas of one God and one truth that introduced religious intolerance into the world. Because of the Torah and "the fanatically dogmatic assertion that the Jews alone were the people of God . . . the world was richer by the idea of religious intolerance." This led to religious wars, unknown to the primitive Aryans, who weren't dogmatic about religion and didn't fight wars over it (they preferred to fight for plunder or for the sheer joy of it. This was admirable and heroic). Therefore,

> . . . the many millions who were massacred by or for
> Christianity, as well as the many Jews who died for their faith,
> are all victims of the forgeries of Ezra and the great synagogue . .
> . the Jew, thanks to Ezekiel, is the teacher of all intolerance, of
> all fanaticism in faith, and of all murder for the sake of religion.

For these reasons Chamberlain felt obliged to write at length on "the share they [the Jews] had in the rise of Christianity, on account of the peculiar and absolutely un-Aryan spirit which they instilled into it." Chamberlain took this so far as to assert that even the idea of "a personal, directly present God, who is almighty to give and to destroy" was a Jewish concept.

It was because of the intolerant Jewish (and Christian) denial of the vague and general Aryan concept of the supernatural that:

> Olympus and Walhalla became depopulated, because the Jews
> so wished it; Jehovah, who had said to the Israelites, 'Ye are my
> people and I am your God,' now became the God of the Indo-

Europeans; from the Jews we adopted the fatal doctrine of unconditional religious intolerance.

Of course it was through Christianity that the "intolerance" of personal belief in one true way of faith was introduced.

Hitler was in complete agreement with Chamberlain here. As was shown in chapter 3, he saw Judaism as being responsible for the fanatical intolerance of Christianity, which insisted that there was only one true way to God. Christianity's intolerance arises "for the most part from specifically Jewish modes of thought . . . this type of intolerance and fanaticism positively embodies the Jewish nature" [vol. II chapt. 5].[18]

It is significant that one of Chamberlain's (and Hitler's) chief objections to the Jewish concept of God was its "intolerance." This is one of the main objections to traditional Christianity currently being raised by secularists today. To state that there is one true God, whether Jewish or Christian, and that to believe in him and obey him is the only right way of life condemns all other religions and human endeavors. This excites the animosity of those who, like Chamberlain, rely on themselves alone. The humanists (whose views may be expressed in religious language) hate to be told that their views are wrong. Thus they despise the intolerant people who presume to assert that there is only one way. This is because of their guilty consciences, and because of fear that their lives are based on a false foundation. As Jesus said, "The world cannot hate you; but me it hateth, because I testify of it, that the works thereof are evil."

Also significant is the profoundly secular approach that underlies Chamberlain's seemingly religious rhetoric. The reliance on man's reason as the sole guide, without God's eternal law or divine revelation, is the common denominator which underlies the whole modernist experiment. The French *philosophes*, the German romantic thinkers, the Folkish movement, National Socialism, Communism, Darwinism, and secular humanism in its myriad manifestations—they all presume man's independence from God. In fact, they are nothing more than rebellion against God. That a secular world view can be concealed behind religious rhetoric, including even statements about Christ being "divine," "the Son of God," is difficult to credit. Many people, including Christians, have been fooled by god-words used to advance a radically unbiblical agenda. This is especially confusing to non-Christians, who equate Christian-sounding words with Christianity.

The Revelation of Christ?

The third chapter of Chamberlain's book, "The Revelation of Christ," provided (along with other Folkish thinkers) a "theological" foundation for the so-called Germanic Christianity that originated in Germany in the 19th century, but died out in 1945 and has not been heard from since. Chamberlain's doctrines in this area don't pertain directly to Hitler and are seldom studied, but they shed light on an aspect of the Third Reich that has led countless students of the subject astray—the enthusiasm of many German "Christians" for Hitler.

Before looking more closely at Chamberlain's ideas about Christ, let us first consider what he did not say about Jesus. In the entire chapter he never mentioned the Trinity. That Christ was God come to earth in human form, the brightness of God's glory and the express image of his person, the creator of the world who sustains all things by the word of his power—these biblical concepts were not important to Chamberlain. He did not—in an entire chapter about Christ—mention the return of Jesus as God to judge the world, nor did he mention Christ's resurrection from the dead, or the virgin birth. Christ's blood shed on the cross as a divine sacrifice for sin was not mentioned. Christ's teachings about a day of judgment followed by an eternity in heaven or in hell were also omitted.

There are of course many "pastors," "bishops," "theologians," and "Christians" today who will say such things are not essential. They will argue that such doctrines are the outdated relics of a bygone age, that the main thing is to have some kind of belief in some kind of a person named "Jesus" who somehow did something but we're not sure exactly what. What is most important, these people will argue, is to be sincere, to be a good person, and that is all God expects of us—if, that is, there really is a God.

Many Christians understand that without these essential doctrines Christianity is nothing but a delusion and a complete waste of time – but Chamberlain did not mention those essentials because he did not believe in them or care about them. In fact, he specifically condemned orthodox Christianity on the first page of the chapter. He wrote, "To look upon this Figure [Jesus Christ] solely by the light of a church doctrine . . . is voluntarily to put on blinkers and to narrow our view of the eternally Divine."[19] It can be objected that there are church doctrines which do obscure the light of Christ, and that is certainly true—however, a consideration of the chapter leaves no doubt that Chamberlain refers here to the above-mentioned doctrines that are foundational to the Christian faith. It will be said that he here refers to Christ as "Divine"—his peculiar understanding of the term "Divine" will be examined shortly.

Chamberlain also made it clear that he had a humanistic view of scripture. Comparing Christ to Buddha, he stated "We have historical proofs of their having actually existed," but adds "the traditions regarding them, though containing much that is fabulous and uncertain, obscure and contradictory, nevertheless give us a faithful picture of the main features of their real lives." How can the "traditions" of Christ's life and teaching be "fabulous and uncertain, obscure and contradictory," yet at the same time give a "faithful picture" of the main features of the life of Christ? This riddle is explained by a phrase in the following sentence: "the sure result of the scientific investigations of the nineteenth century."

Here Chamberlain revealed that his thought was squarely based on the shifting sands of liberal German theology. Only a liberal theologian could imagine that his attempts to extricate the core of truth from a mass of myths, mistakes, and lies were scientific. German liberal theologians lacked the intellectual integrity and honesty to admit that if the Bible is not accurate, then it has about as much value as the plays of Euripides, possibly even less. Only a liberal theologian could disguise his attacks on the trustworthiness of the Bible behind a facade of reverence for the Bible—as Chamberlain did when he wrote a few pages later about "the unexpected antiquity of the gospels and the extensive authenticity of the manuscripts which we possess."

What this authenticity meant, once the scientists with their white coats, laboratory apparatuses, and minute examination of crumbling old parchments had concluded their research is made clear when Chamberlain on the one hand affirms positively that the Bible gives us a faithful picture of the main features of Christ's life, and on the other hand claims there "is not the slightest foundation for the supposition that Christ's parents were of Jewish descent."

As to Christ's physical antecedents, Chamberlain first said Jesus was "most probably not" a Jew racially, but later said "The probability that Christ was no Jew, that he had not a drop of genuinely Jewish blood in his veins, is so great that it is almost equivalent to a certainty." On the next page he stated ". . . that Jesus Christ did not belong to it [the Jewish race] can be regarded as certain."

This is typical of liberal textual criticism. The wildest purely imaginary hypotheses are first presented as reasonable, then probable, then "almost certain" or "nearly certain," and then "certain." Great chains of inference and deduction are linked to the initial hypothesis, and dishonestly presented as scientific proof. It took Chamberlain's *scientific* modern biblical criticism to reveal the truth that Jesus' circumcision on the 8th day, the lineages of Joseph and of Mary, Mary's purification according to the law of Moses, the sacrifice offered in the temple, and the fulfillments of Old Testament prophecies were all spurious additions, unworthy of consideration by a modern philosopher. Of course, all of this presupposes a human father for Christ. Chamberlain would not have engaged in his hallucinations about non-Jewish settlements in the Galilee if he had believed that Christ was born of a virgin, having no human father because God was his Father.

Unable to deny that Christ did after all grow up in Palestine, Chamberlain admitted that "Christ belonged morally to the Jews." After all, "whoever lived in the Jewish intellectual world was bound to come under the influence of Jewish ideas." There is even a confession that Christ was a Jew in the sense that he showed the "Jewish" emphasis on self-will in his teachings on conversion, "in contrast to the Aryan negation of the will." Nevertheless, Chamberlain went to great lengths to define and eliminate the Jewish elements from the New Testament. He asked "how shall we, above all, be able to sift and separate from the 'bread of life' this specifically Jewish element which is so threateningly perilous to our spirit . . . ?" He tried to form "exact ideas as to what in this figure [Christ] is Jewish and what is not." This was not easy, as the stories of Christ's life and the teachings of the New Testament were a confused jumble of various elements: "Jewish religious idiosyncrasy, Syrian mysticism, Egyptian asceticism, Hellenic metaphysics, soon too Roman traditions of State and Pontifex, as also the superstitions of the barbarians; every form of misunderstanding and stupidity had a share in the work." Fortunately (or the believer in the Bible will say, unfortunately) "many have devoted themselves to the unraveling of this tangle."

After detaching Christ from his Jewish origins, along with continued attacks on the Jews ("the real inner life is almost totally wanting in them," and Isaiah prophesies that one day they will rule the world), he then went on to present Christ's teachings as a complete nullification of Judaism. He did not follow the traditionally Christian line of thinking that the Old Testament was revealed by God, but was completed in the final revelation of Christ. He argued instead that the Old Testament was largely a fraud, and asserted that Christ had completely rejected the Jewish idea of fixed doctrines, presenting rather a much freer approach whereby everyone was free to find their own personal "salvation" without regard to anything but themselves.

Chamberlain based this idea on Christ's teaching "The Kingdom of God is within you." Fixed doctrines, eternal truths, God's creation of the world, the laws of Moses, heaven and hell, righteousness and holiness in the biblical sense—these were all dispensed with as Jewish, fetters that hindered the free spiritual development of the Aryan man. In spite of the Jewish background to the life of Christ, Chamberlain managed to save the day by declaring that in spite of everything "the Saviour departed *in toto* from the doctrines of Judaism," and created an entirely new message of inner spiritual freedom entirely divorced from the law and the prophets (except for a few isolated passages that were authentic because Chamberlain could interpret them to support his theories).

It is with this in mind that we have to consider Chamberlain's idea that in accepting Christianity "we adopted very great and sublime spiritual impulses; we were taught by prophets, who preached such strict and pure morals as could have been found nowhere else save on the distant shores of India . . . ." He went on in this vein to state:

> . . . we became acquainted with such a living and life-molding faith in a higher divine power that it inevitably changed our spirit and gave it a new direction. Though Christ was the master-builder, we got the architecture from the Jews. Isaiah, Jeremiah, the Psalmists became, and still are, living powers in our spiritual life.

This seemingly contradictory compliment to the Jews is clarified when we recall Chamberlain's statement in chapter 5, that one chapter of Isaiah was "absolutely forged, from the first to the last word." Chamberlain found some isolated passages in the Old Testament which he thought were authentic, and reflected primitive true religion—the rest were later additions of the devious rabbis. This was the essence of 19th-century German theological liberalism—only those passages personally agreeable to the critic were genuine.

Christ was the "master-builder" of a new revelation that emerged out of Judaism but totally condemned Judaism and broke away from it. Christ's new revelation of inner freedom was later obscured by traditional dogmatism and the restoration of the Semitic concepts he had tried to eliminate—but his revelation was being recovered thanks to the labors of scholars, philosophers, and textual critics who had discovered the Old and New Testaments to be merely human books, from which agreeable parts could be selected at will. This allowed for creative interpretation of the Bible, for spiritual "freedom," as opposed to the "bondage" of dogmatism and literalism.

Thanks to the "mythological and philosophical development" which had taken place in Germany over the preceding century, removing doctrines and infallible scriptures and allowing the free play of human philosophy, Christianity had been rescued from its Semitic corruptions and made authentically Indo-European again. Thus, while the "direct influence of Judaism on Christianity was and still is immense," if the Semitic influences could be discerned and removed, Christianity was the genuine and true religion (as interpreted by German philosophy and scholarship). This Christianity would of course conform to the demands and personal beliefs of those who created it.

Chamberlain also claimed:

> That which has been transferred from the sacred books of the Hebrews to the Christian religion does not come down from the senility of real Judaism, but partly from the youth of the much wider and more imaginative "Israelite" people, partly from the mature years of the Judean, just after he had separated from Israel and when he had not yet proudly isolated himself from the other nations of the earth.

According to this purely subjective approach, only the parts of the Bible that agree with us and meet our demands are genuine.

Needless to say, the vast majority of New Testament teachings were ignored entirely. Paul was mentioned a few times. He was called "by far the greatest of the Apostles," and he was quoted on the importance of love, and on the power of the cross (though his concept of Christ's death was radically different from Chamberlain's). There were however no in-depth references to any apostolic teachings on holiness, sin, repentance, or the Christian life. There was instead high praise for Paul de Lagarde, "one of the most important theologists of our time"—we have already referred to Lagarde's contributions to Aryan "Christianity."

Chamberlain's attitude toward the New Testament is not difficult to discern. Nowhere did he treat it as the divinely inspired word of God. One passage states that, whether or not the miracles of Christ actually occurred, "people believed that they saw the dead come to life and the sick rise healed from their beds." This testifies not to the miracle working power that Christ received from the Father, but "to the life-giving impression which radiated from this figure." This separation of faith from fact reduces Christianity to empty words of no value and no significance.

Chamberlain's "theology" was dishonest and hypocritical. When Christ was on earth he did not severely criticize the thieves, the murderers, the sexually immoral people, the drunkards, the prostitutes, the homosexuals (though he presented teachings of holiness and righteousness that exclude such activities). His strongest words were for the false teachers who led people astray with corruptions of divine truth—and it was the corrupters of divine truth in the name of Christianity who damaged the German churches by reducing Christianity to a vain philosophy void of doctrine, holiness, repentance, and divine revelation.

What else did Chamberlain say about Christ? We will need first to look at his concept of the person of Christ, then at his understanding of the message of Christ. As to the former, he called Jesus "the one Divine Man," and stated "He was divine," "His personality was so divinely great . . . ." Christ "became the God of the young, vigorous Indo-Europeans," "the centre and source of Christianity." The churches "derive all their power [from] the contemplation of the Son of Man upon the Cross." This sounds very orthodox, but that Chamberlain had something other than simple-minded orthodoxy in mind soon becomes apparent.

Comparing Christ and Buddha, Chamberlain stated that "Both are characterized by their divine earnestness." He recognized profound differences between them, yet both in some sense partook of the divine. Also, "they have both incomparably magnetic personalities . . . What unites them is their sublimity of character." Moreover, Christ left us a compelling example, and the "power of Buddha over the world rests on similar foundations." This is possible because, as he said in the following sentence, "The true source of all religion is, I repeat, in the case of the great majority of living people, not a doctrine but a life."

In another place, Chamberlain said about the person of Christ, "To the believer Jesus is the Son of God, not of a human being; for the unbeliever it will be difficult to find a formula to characterise so briefly and yet so expressively the undeniable fact of this incomparable and inexplicable personality." This sounds orthodox, until it becomes evident that while the explanation "Son of God" may be suitable for the orthodox, the 19th-century scientific philosopher needed something more. Chamberlain stated his desire "to remove from myself all suspicion of being taken in tow by that superficial 'historical' school, which undertakes to explain the inexplicable." I take this to be a reference to the "superficial" school of traditional Christianity which takes the Gospel narratives as historical fact. Elsewhere he referred to the "inherited delusion" of the "strictly orthodox Churchman" who completely misunderstood the relationship of Christ to Judaism.

As to the example Christ left for us with his incomparably sublime character, Chamberlain spoke of Christ's execution and stated "only, by death, was destiny fulfilled and the example given." Christ's death fulfilled his destiny—no wonder his resurrection from the dead and his return as God to judge the world are never mentioned. And what was the example Christ left us? What were his teachings? Chamberlain's analysis presents us with the Christ of German philosophy, of secularism in general, and of "liberal" "Protestant" "theology"—Christ as a moral teacher only. We "have in the revelation of Christ the one foundation of all moral culture." "From the point of view of universal history we have every reason to put the achievement of Christ on a parallel with the achievements of the Hellenes . . . What Greece did for the intellect, Christ did for the moral life."

This is all that remains of Christ after the miracles and the deity are removed. This was the Christ of Thomas Jefferson, of Kant, Hegel, Bultmann, and Tillich—a human Christ. This was also the Christ of Hitler. As was mentioned in chapter 3, he wrote in *Mein Kampf* that the significance of "the religion of love" lay "in the direction which it attempted to give to a universal human development of culture, ethics, and morality" [vol. I chapt. 8, "The Beginning of my Political Activity"].[20]

Yet, Chamberlain sought to invest this human figure with something more—he described Christ as the incarnation of an idea. In his words,

> . . . ideas are immortal . . . and in such figures as Buddha and Christ an idea—that is, a definite conception of human existence—acquires such a living bodily form, becomes so thoroughly an experience of life, is placed so clearly before the eyes of all men, that it can never more disappear from their consciousness.

What were the teachings of Christ, this "embodiment of an idea," this philosophical concept incarnate, not God in the flesh but a philosophical idea in the flesh? Chamberlain referred to a "belief in divine almightiness, in divine Providence and in the freedom of the human will, as well as the almost exclusive emphasizing of the moral nature of men and their equality before God ('the last shall be first')." He stated that these "are essential elements of the personality of Christ"—yet they (along with some other ideas of Christ the sublime moral genius) were mentioned in passing. There are a couple of other teachings of Christ that Chamberlain elaborated on at great length. First, there was Christ's idea that "the kingdom of God is within you"; second, the idea that "Except ye be converted, ye shall not enter into the Kingdom of God . . . Except a man be born again, he cannot see the Kingdom of God."

This again sounds orthodox, a clear emphasis on essential doctrines of biblical Christianity—yet what was Chamberlain's understanding of those concepts? For Chamberlain—and he elaborated on this at length—the idea that the Kingdom of God is within us was understood to mean that we had within ourselves, of ourselves, the power to transform ourselves, to raise ourselves up to a higher level of consciousness. The conversion he emphasized was a human work, wrought by human power unaided. This belief that the answer lies within ourselves had nothing to do with the need for a divine work of grace wrought in the heart by the Holy Spirit. It had everything to do with humanism—and Chamberlain was a humanist, a religious humanist rather than a secular one, but a humanist nonetheless.

Consider some of his statements. Concerning the Kingdom of God being innate within us naturally, he referred early in the chapter to "the Holy of Holies of my own heart." This was not merely a rhetorical phrase, for he stated a few pages later that "Heaven and earth pass away, while the human breast conceals in its depths the only thing that is everlasting." This is not the kingdom of God which we enter through repentance, cleansing by the blood of Christ, and receipt of the Holy Spirit granted by God through faith in Christ. He also referred to "that immeasurable power of life in the heart of man" and stated that Christ revealed to us "a power in the human breast, capable—if it ever should be fully realized—of completely changing humanity." This was the "hidden power in the unfathomed and unfathomable depths of the human heart, a power capable of completely transforming man . . . ." This idea of man having within himself the power to bring about his own transformation was shared by Hitler and Marx. It is believed today by current New Age teachers.

Another teaching of Christ emphasized by Chamberlain was the new birth. Chamberlain saw this as a quickening of the latent power already within us. There needs to be "a 'conversion' of the direction of life," but what sort of conversion, and in what direction? It is not newness of life through the receipt of the Holy Spirit, but rather "an absolute renunciation of much that makes up the life of the greater proportion of mankind . . . this renunciation is the 'conversion' which, we are told, leads to the Kingdom of Heaven . . . ." This is obviously related to the ideas of Wagner and Schopenhauer.

The biblical new birth includes renunciation. There needs to be a renunciation of sin, of the old self that is naturally corrupted by sin, but there is much more to it than mere renunciation. It requires a divine work from above and from without—not only to change the individual, but to enable the individual to persist and grow in that change once it has been effected. Chamberlain's "new birth" was purely an act of human will, inspired by the example of Christ's death only: "the human will, from the beginning of time the seed of all the misfortune and misery that descended upon the human race, was henceforth to minister to the new birth of this race, to the rise of a new human species."

Mankind can regenerate itself—it is insufficiently realized that this was Hitler's dream. He was not merely a destroyer, but envisioned a new species, a new race, purified of outdated concepts, and leading mankind—or at least a certain portion of mankind—on to ever more glorious heights. That Hitler thought he had positive beliefs that would benefit humanity will seem incredible to many, but that doesn't mean it is impossible.

The fundamental dream of some aspects of modern secularism, to make mankind anew, the dream that captivated Marx, Lenin, Stalin, Mao, and Hitler (as well as today's secularists) is presented here in these ideas of Chamberlain's—but they dispensed with Chamberlain's pseudo-theology. The "voluntary masterful conversion of will" that Chamberlain described depended on man alone. And what was the end-result of this secular conversion, this counterfeit of the divine transformation taught by Christ? "Selfishness, superstition, prejudice, envy, hatred," "everything that drives, compels, and constrains the human half-ape"— these were to be replaced by "sublime pride," by "the strongest will, the surest consciousness of self."

That this rejuvenation of mankind, this shedding of common faults and rising to a higher level, was connected not to the brotherhood of man but rather to Aryan supremacy is made evident in other chapters of Chamberlain's book. It was also perfectly compatible with National Socialism. Hitler and Himmler imagined themselves to be free of selfishness (they gave their all for the fatherland), superstition (their beliefs were rational and scientific), and prejudice (their ideas were enlightened, rational, and true). They could even imagine they were free of hatred. Himmler boasted that the SS had been able to remain decent fellows while they carried out their duty to exterminate the Jews—no ignorant prejudice or hatred there, only selfless devotion to the higher cause of making humanity anew.

Chamberlain's idea was that, by an act of will we could repudiate our lower human feelings and awaken the latent power within. This of course was something the Germans were especially good at, being uniquely favored by some sort of vague and ill-defined "God" or "Providence." Chamberlain referred to his ideas as the "new Teuton philosophy." He used the words of Christ and even wrote of the love and forgiveness of Christ, but all in a pagan context. Even "love" was not the love of God for sinners, but the love of self, and the love of "God" for people who deserved his love because of their innate virtue. Thus, forgiving your enemies was described as "sublime pride," an indication of superiority. The words "eternal life" were used but not with regard to life after death in heaven with God—indeed, Chamberlain expressly rejected this Semitic notion. "And this Kingdom of God, what is it? A Nirvana? a Dream-Paradise? a future reward for deeds done here below?" No, "the kingdom of God is within you," and nowhere else. In what sense, then does Christ's death signify "entrance into eternal life"? Chamberlain's ideas here are not spelled out directly.

A clearer idea of Chamberlain's ideas can be derived from a consideration of his understanding of the essence of true religion. For him, true religion derived not from divine revelation but from human feeling. In this he was very close to atheism. Both atheists and Chamberlain agree religion derives from man only— Chamberlain saw this as right and good, a path to truth, while the atheist sees it as a delusion, but their concept of the origin of religion is identical. Self-made religions are thus very close to atheism, since a God that is based solely on our imagination and allows us to do whatever we like is really no God at all.

Returning to the subject of Chamberlain's concept of religion, we find that ". . . the feelings are, as we have said, the fountain head of all genuine religion; this spring which the Jews had well-nigh choked with their formalism and hard-hearted rationalism Christ opened up." He quoted Goethe's lines "*Ist nicht der Kern der Natur / Menschen im Herzen*?" (Is not the core of nature / In the heart of man?), stated "That is religion!" and added, ". . . this instinct, 'to seek the core of nature in the heart,' the Jews lack to a startling degree . . . ." The "real inner life is almost totally wanting in them." This real inner life, the source of all religion, was most highly developed in the Aryans.

Chamberlain went on to explain the primitive Aryan religion that pre-dated Christianity. The "oldest documents (which go far back beyond the Jewish)" revealed the Aryan "following a vague impulse which forces him to investigate in his own heart." This simple Aryan was "joyous, full of animal spirits," drinking, hunting, robbing, fighting, enjoying life to the fullest—"but suddenly he begins to think: the great riddle of existence holds him absolutely spellbound." He was not concerned with a rationalistic approach, or a dogmatic one, but wanted only to "put the world and himself in harmony." To do this he listened and heard "in his own heart the mysterious music of existence," and hearing it, "he utters his own song." Then "nature becomes alive" and the Aryan "sinks in reverence upon his knees," not imaging that he had found a dogmatic explanation of the origin of the world, but having "faint forebodings of a loftier vocation." He "discovers in himself the germ of immeasurable destinies, 'the seed of immortality.' "

From this experience the Aryan "is impelled onward and upward"—and "this glance into the unfathomable depths of his own soul, this longing to soar upwards, this is religion. Religion has primarily nothing to do with superstition [biblical doctrine] or with morals; it is a state of mind." Thus "the religious man" found "direct contact with a world beyond reason" by looking within himself, and following his feelings. His "feeling of the Infinite" was "too lively" for "a hard and fast chronological cosmogony and theogony." As a creator, he heard his own music and sang his own song. In this way "the Indo-Europeans by purely religious ways had attained to conceptions of an individual Divinity that were infinitely more sublime than the painfully stunted idea which the Jews had formed of the Creator of the world."

These sentiments were restated by Alfred Rosenberg in his book *Myth of the Twentieth Century*. He wrote that "Before it could fully blossom, the joyous message of German mysticism was strangled by the anti-European church with all the means in its power."[21] Chamberlain was not identical to Rosenberg and Rosenberg was not identical to Hitler—but underlying their differences there is a broad and deep current of shared beliefs and values.

The supposed Jewish contribution of monotheism was dismissed with disdain: "The Brahman of the Indian philosophers is beyond doubt the greatest religious thought ever conceived"—far superior to "the crassly materialistic sediment of Semitic idolatry in the Jewish ark of the covenant with its Egyptian sphinxes . . ." Significantly, Chamberlain—like Hitler in *Mein Kampf*—rejected Jewish (and Christian) monotheism but personified Nature. "She" was "inexhaustibly inventive," she "shows us a new thing whenever it pleases her." This concept of nature as something purposeful and active was a direct contradiction of the biblical concept. It was a vain and contentless substitute for people who rejected the biblical God but still needed to imagine that there was some sort of higher purpose at work in the world.

This, then, was Chamberlain's religion—not creeds, dogmas, doctrines, rules, but a vague sense of the Infinite, a purely individualistic search within the self to find one's own music and one's own song. Christ showed the way to a higher level of being through dying to our lower self and rising to new heights of self awareness. This is the essence of humanism and of the modern experiment—to look within the self for answers—though of course many modernists had no use even for a de-spiritualized Christ used only as an example.

About Martin Luther, Chamberlain did not mention Luther's tract *On the Jews and Their Lies*—as we have seen, he specifically repudiated religious anti-Semitism. He made a few references to Luther in passing in this chapter—on the oneness of God; as an example (along with Augustine, Voltaire, Kant, and Goethe) of the "Indo-European reaction against the Semitic spirit"; on Christ as an example. In another chapter of this work, however, chapter nine ("From the Year 1200 to the Year 1800") we find the following statements:

> Luther is above all a political hero; we must recognize this in order to judge him fairly and to understand his pre-eminent position in the history of Europe...

> . . . the essentially political and national character of his Reformation is clear to all . . . Luther is the first man who is perfectly conscious of the importance of the struggle between imperialism and nationalism . . .

> . . . Luther, however, while calling upon princes, nobles, citizens and people to prepare for the strife, does not remain satisfied with the merely negative work of revolt from Rome; he also gives the Germans a language common to all and uniting them all, and lays hold of the two points in the purely political organisation which determined the success of nationalism, namely, the Church and the School.

> Nowhere can we feel the warm heart-throb of the Teuton better than when Luther begins to speak of education.

Even a little research should be sufficient to expose the fallacy of assuming that every favorable reference to Luther is proof of Protestantism. That the Bible was the divinely inspired and infallible word of God; that Christians should look to the Bible alone and not to the rules of the church; that Christ's sacrificial work on the cross did not need to be supplemented by church rules—these and other foundational doctrines of the Reformation were of no interest to Chamberlain.

It is a common error to assume that dated 19th-century ideas (and uniquely German ideas at that) are "Christian" merely because they were sometimes expressed in borrowed Christian language. One can point to some proto-Nazi ideas in the thought of leading "Protestant" "theologians" of their day, without considering that they had abandoned essentials of the faith and were expressing in religious language unbiblical ideas that originated in worldly philosophies.

It is also a mistake to assume that one positive reference to Chamberlain in one article in a Confessing Church journal proves that the Confessing Church as a whole endorsed Chamberlain. That is a huge inference to derive from one article in an obscure journal written by who knows who under who knows what circumstances—especially when we consider that any article critical of Chamberlain would not have been allowed.

On a different note, it speaks volumes that in the chapter on the revelation of Christ Chamberlain devoted some space to discussing human skulls. He stated that the form of the head and the structure of the brain influenced the thoughts, and elaborated thus:

> . . . the shape of the skull in particular is one of those characteristics which are inherited with ineradicable persistency, so that races are distinguished by craniological measurements and, in the case of mixed races, the original elements which occur by atavism become still manifest to the investigator! . . . When will men understand that form is not an unimportant accident, a mere chance, but an expression of the innermost being?

Given this manner of looking at things, it is not difficult to understand why someone might want to have a collection of human skulls from people of different races. There is nothing wrong with collecting skulls of different kinds of apes and monkeys, is there? As Paul said so well in Romans, those who refused to acknowledge the one true God "became vain in their imaginations, and their foolish heart was darkened. Professing themselves to be wise, they became fools . . ." It is impossible to write a more precise evaluation of Houston Stewart Chamberlain than this. His seemingly harmless philosophizing led him and many others straight into the arms of Hitler.

> *Their throat is an open sepulcher; with their tongues they have used deceit; the poison of asps is under their lips . . . destruction and misery are in their ways: and the way of peace have they not known . . . (Romans)*

---

[1] Adolf Hitler, *Mein Kampf*, trans. Ralph Manheim (Boston 1999), p. 270.

[2] Houston Stewart Chamberlain, *The Foundations of the Nineteenth Century*, trans. John Lees (London: 1912); http://www.hschamberlain.net/index.html; accessed January 2008. www.hschamberlain.net/grundlagen/division1_chapter3.html; accessed July 2007. www.hschamberlain.net/grundlagen/division2_chapter5.html; accessed July 2007. Unnoted quotes from Chamberlain can be found by searching the relevant chapters.

[3] William L. Shirer, *The Rise and Fall of the Third Reich* (New York 1960), p. 103.

[4] Ibid., p. 108.

[5] Richard Steigmann-Gall, *The Holy Reich: Nazi Conceptions of Christianity, 1919-1945* (Cambridge 2004), p. 20.

[6] Peter Viereck, *Meta-politics: The Roots of the Nazi Mind* (New York 1965), p. 183.

[7] Shirer, p. 109.

[8] Unless otherwise stated, quotes in this section will come from chapter 5, "The Entrance of the Jews into Western History."

[9] Peter Padfield, *Himmler: Reichsfuhrer-SS* (New York 1990), p. 54.

[10] Hitler, p. 119.

[11] Richard J. Evans, *The Coming of the Third Reich* (New York 2005), p. 28.

[12] Werner Maser, *Hitler's Letters and Notes* (New York 1974), p. 237.

[13] Martin Gilbert, *The Holocaust: A History of the Jews of Europe During the Second World War* (New York 1985), p. 27.

[14] Adolf Hitler, *Hitler's Second Book: The Unpublished Sequel to Mein Kampf,* trans. Krista Smith (New York 2006), p. 233.

[15] Gilbert, pp. 27-28.

[16] Ibid., p. 28.

[17] Maser, p. 241.

[18] Hitler, p. 254.

[19] Unless otherwise indicated, all quotes in this section are from chapter 3, "The Revelation of Christ."

[20] Hitler, p. 212.

[21] Jonah Goldberg, *Liberal Fascism: The Secret History of the American Left from Mussolini to the Politics of Meaning* (New York 2007), p. 369.

Chapter 8. Haeckel

Darwin, Haeckel, and Hitler

So much of National Socialism can be found in the Folkish movement that it is not surprising two major studies have located the origins of Hitler's ideology there. Viereck's *Meta-politics: The Roots of the Nazi Mind* focuses on the ideas of Wagner. Mosse's *The Crisis of German Ideology: Intellectual Origins of the Third Reich* focuses on broader intellectual trends and currents of which Wagner was only a representative. Viereck spends more time elaborating on the Folkish roots in romanticism, especially in philosophy, while Mosse concentrates more on the spread of Folkish ideas through German society in the 19th and early 20th centuries—but in spite of their differences, both studies have a lot in common. Taken together, they provide a significant part of the explanation for Hitler.

Neither Mosse nor Viereck pay much attention to Darwin, and neither of their books lists Darwin in the index. Viereck makes only one passing reference to "social Darwinism," the belief that the Darwinian law of survival-of-the-fittest applied to people as well as to animals. Mosse devotes a few pages to social Darwinism and recognizes its importance, but asserts the fundamental incompatibility between National Socialism and Darwinism proper. He claims that the Darwinian concept of the origins of man was not acceptable to Nazi race theorists.[1] Not only (in Mosse's view) was such a humiliating ancestry unsuitable to a race of superior beings destined to rule; it also required a common origin of all races—another blow to the Aryan ego.

It might seem, then, that Darwinism as Darwin taught it is of little relevance to our study—and those who believe that Darwinism is true and beneficial will find no difficulty in detaching it from National Socialism, which was false and harmful. Apart from this basic presupposition, they have a number of other reasonable points to make against the idea of a Hitler-Darwin connection.

For one thing, there are many and great personal dissimilarities between Darwin and Hitler. For another, many people have believed in Darwin's theories without becoming Nazis, and many countries have ingested Darwinism into their cultural mainstreams without becoming fascist dictatorships. Another argument has already been presented—that a Darwinian concept of the origins of man is incompatible with Naziism. Obviously, Darwinism does not inevitably or necessarily lead to Naziism.

Those on the other hand who do not believe that Darwinism is true have no difficulty seeing a very real connection—and they too have plausible arguments. For one thing, there is Hitler's Darwinian rhetoric—rhetoric that was elaborated on at length in *Mein Kampf* and later supported by Hitler's actions (not, like a very few random comments about Christianity, contradicted by his actions).

Hitler frequently appealed to Darwinian logic. Here are a few examples from one chapter of *Mein Kampf*:

> . . . the most patent principles of Nature's rule. . .

> . . . it will later succumb in the struggle against the higher level

. . . the will of Nature for a higher breeding of all life . . .

Only the born weakling can view this as cruel, but he after all is only a weak and limited man; for if this law did not prevail, any conceivable higher development of organic living beings would be unthinkable.

In the struggle for daily bread all those who are weak and sickly or less determined succumb, while the struggle of the males for the female grants the right or opportunity to propagate only to the healthiest. And struggle is always a means for improving a species' health and power of resistance and, therefore, a cause of its higher development.

. . . since the inferior always predominates numerically over the best, if both had the same possibility of preserving life and propagating, the inferior would multiply so much more rapidly that in the end the best would inevitably be driven into the background, unless a correction of this state of affairs were undertaken. Nature does just this by subjecting the weaker part to such severe living conditions that by them alone the number is limited, and by not permitting the remainder to increase promiscuously, but making a new and ruthless choice according to strength and health.

. . . exact scientific truth . . . cold logic . . .

. . . the rigid law of necessity and the right to victory of the best and stronger in this world. [vol. I chapt. 11, "Nation and Race"]

Hitler is not angling for votes or trying to deflect opposition here. He is stating that the Darwinian struggle for survival-of-the-fittest is the fundamental law of life, and only weaklings don't accept it. As Hitler put it in his unpublished second book, ". . . life itself is a never-ending battle against death . . . and the struggle for survival, in turn, contains the precondition for evolution. . . . This development is characterized by the never-ending battle of humans against animals and also against humans themselves."[2]

This is not a question of a few cut-and-paste quotes. Hitler made many references, in speeches and in writing, to nature's elimination of the unfit as essential to progress. Moreover, in a chapter from a work in progress (*Hitler's Ethic*), historian and scholar Richard Weikart makes the useful observation that Hitler frequently used the word *Entwicklung*, and explains that the word can be translated as "development," but was also used by German biologists to mean "evolution."[3] This same source also notes that Hitler never used the word "Darwinism." I offer my own observation that this can be used to argue either that Darwin was not important to Hitler, or that Hitler saw the progress of animal species (including the human animal species) through struggle and the elimination of the unfit as a basic law of life, not as a theory presented by an English scientist.

A second argument in favor of a Hitler-Darwin connection comes from the inner logic of Darwinism itself. If Darwin's theory of the origins of man is correct, and the law of natural selection really is the ground of our being, then why shouldn't it be the basis of our ethic and philosophy? Is it reasonable, is it consistent, to posit a Darwinian origin for the human race and then arbitrarily declare an end to the age-old law of struggle now that we are comfortable with our level of development?

If some—like Hitler, but also like many other social-Darwinists in the decades prior to 1933—felt that this iron law of struggle did apply, and based their ethic on the belief that it is normal for the weak to perish and the strong to survive, why not? True, other Darwinists have objected to the attempt to apply this thinking to human society, but are they objecting on the basis of moral and ethical values that are not derived from Darwinism and in fact contradict the theory they claim to believe in? People who claim Darwinism is nothing more than a biological theory of origins need to reflect that our understanding of origins has a vast influence on how we look at life as a whole. Is it credible that there is no connection at all between the emergence of biological and racial anti-Semitism in the second half of the nineteenth century and the translation into German of the new theory of evolution? Prior to the introduction into Germany of Darwin's ideas, race was "usually defined as cultural rather than biological."[4] What caused this shift?

Thirdly, many German racist thinkers long before Hitler openly appealed to Darwin's theory and used it to justify their perverted thinking. If life evolved by natural selection, then those who are higher on the evolutionary pyramid are superior to those who are lower. People who have gone farther in their evolutionary development (white Europeans) are obviously worth more than those lower on the scale (especially Negroes, Slavs, and Asians)—and according to nature's "scientifically proven" law of survival-of-the-fittest, the more highly developed forms have the right to take what they wish and let the weak perish. We are talking here of course about people, not about finches or squirrels.

A barrier assaulted

Advocates of some sort of a Hitler-Darwin connection not only have these arguments. They can also find some holes, some rather large holes, in the seemingly impenetrable barrier their opponents have placed between Darwin and Hitler. For example, it is true that there are many obvious differences between Hitler and Darwin, yet Darwin did have a very limited concept of the value of human life. His famous *Origin of Species* is subtitled "The Preservation of Favoured Races in the Struggle for Life"—ominous words, especially when we consider that in *The Descent of Man* Darwin wrote "At some future period, not very distant when measured by centuries, the civilized races of man will almost certainly exterminate and replace throughout the world the savage races."[5]

If a right-wing fundamentalist Christian wrote about superior races exterminating the savage races, there would be anguished howls of righteous indignation from the secular anti-religious left, and the statement would be used as proof of the evil intolerance of theistic religious belief. But, if Darwin said it? It should be added that Darwin saw nothing wrong with this extermination—he saw it as natural and normal.

Darwin looked calmly on the extermination of the inferior North American savages by the superior white race—after all, it was in his mind only one more example of what had been occurring at all levels of the evolutionary scale for eons. It was the sort of conflict that was the very foundation of life on earth. If Hitler felt that the European seizure of the Americas was in essence no different from the Aryan seizure of Eastern Europe; if he thought the subjugation of inferior Slavs was justified according to the theory of survival-of-the-fittest; by what standards inherent in Darwinism can he be refuted? The strong survive, the weak die—that is what life is all about, if Darwinism is true.

It may be that Darwin himself did not speculate on the practical implications of his theory of man as in essence nothing more than a highly developed animal because he was still very much under the cultural influence of the pre-Darwinian social values he was raised with. It may be that he did see the implications of his theory clearly but kept quiet about them for tactical reasons. A detailed study of Darwin's private life and motives is far beyond the scope of this essay. Suffice it to say that Marx was very different from Lenin and Stalin, but he influenced them nonetheless. Influences can be deep and subtle, far beneath the surface of outward appearance, so pointing to differences between Darwin and Hitler does not in and of itself eliminate the possibility of at least some sort of influence, however small or indirect.

It should be pointed out that some 19th-century Darwinists did object to seeing human relationships only in terms of Darwinian struggle. They postulated that the evolution of higher consciousness and social norms had raised us above our origins—but many others disagreed. Which is more consistent with Darwin's theory—the idea that the basic law is still in place, or the idea that we have somehow transcended it?

Returning to the subject of the barrier placed between Hitler and Darwin by those who refuse to accept any connection, the second and third points are incontestably true: Darwinism does not inevitably lead to fascism and racism either on the national or on the personal levels. However, while we can agree that Darwin did not *cause* Hitler, the idea that Darwin's theory may have *contributed* to Hitler is an entirely different one—and here we need to make a very basic but insufficiently recognized point about Darwinism.

It is striking, how Darwinism can appeal to people with radically different outlooks. For example, Karl Marx endorsed Darwinism, and wrote in a letter to Engels that Darwin's *Origin of Species* "contains the foundation in natural history for our view."[6] On the other hand, American robber baron capitalists also appealed to Darwinism as a theoretical justification for the stronger dominating the weaker economically. What two world views could be more diametrically opposed? Yet believers in both appealed to Darwin to justify themselves.

One individual who believes in Darwin's theory can be a pacifist multiculturalist who abhors racism, while another can be an ardent racist, militarist, and nationalist. Atheists can appeal to Darwin for an explanation of life's origins, while some theists can accept Darwinism and say that God is directing it.

Atheists, theists, Communists, capitalists, right-wingers, left-wingers—the idea that life developed in a Darwinian fashion is amenable to a wide array of non-related and even totally contradictory world views. The reason is not far to seek. Once people eliminate God from the picture (or reduce God to an abstract concept according to their own imaginings) they are free to believe anything they wish. No longer constrained by any higher spiritual law, they are free to adopt the values they have acquired from who-knows-where—parents, friends, society, personal emotional needs, whatever. Thus, Darwinism serves as a metaphysical launching pad from which one can take off in many different directions.

Darwin wrote in his autobiography that for someone who did not believe in traditional religion, the basic rule of life was "only to follow those impulses and instincts which are the strongest or which seem to him the best one."[7] The implications of this are obvious. Those who sincerely believe in laws revealed by God will be held closer to a core of values than will those who have no higher law than survival-of-the-fittest, and follow only their own instincts. In some cases, following one's personal inclinations will lead to liberalism and pacifism. In other cases, it will not.

The question before us now therefore is not "Did Darwin cause Hitler?" It is, "Was Darwinism used to a significant extent in Germany to justify values that later became foundational to National Socialism?" We are not asking how Darwinism should be interpreted, or can be interpreted, or how it was interpreted in France, America, China, or England. We are discussing how it was interpreted by influential circles in Germany for fifty years and more prior to the advent of Hitler—and, of course, how it was interpreted by Hitler himself.

Did Hitler believe Darwin's theory?

About Mosse's argument that a Darwinian theory of human origins was incompatible with Naziism, it is theoretically plausible, but gives the Nazis too much credit for logical consistency. Hitler could be rigorously logical, but within narrow limits. We considered in chapter five his ability to selectively adopt ideas he thought were useful while ignoring others. He called this retaining the "essential" and ignoring the "non-essential." The idea of struggle as being fundamental to progress was deeply compelling to Hitler, and foundational to his world view. Confirmation by "science" added a lot of respectability and depth to what would otherwise have been mere philosophy. Darwin's concept of progress through struggle was for this reason vastly more compelling than Hegel's. Inconvenient aspects of the theory were lightly passed over. It was possible for German racial thinkers to adopt some parts of Darwin's theory without worrying about details.

H.S. Chamberlain, whose ideas were in so many ways basic to National Socialism, was ambivalent about Darwinism. He rejected the theory of entirely new forms evolving, believing that there could only be change within limits. Nevertheless, he wrote that there were two significant aspects of the theory: survival-of-the-fittest or life as struggle, and also the idea of improving species (including the human species) through selective breeding. This was of course directly related to Chamberlain's obsession with racial purity and the harmful effects of cross-breeding between incompatible human types.[8]

As in so many other areas, Hitler seems to have shared Chamberlain's attitude. In vol. I chapt. 11 of *Mein Kampf* ("Nation and Race"), he stressed natural selection as essential to the development of life, as we have seen. He was passionately devoted to the idea of progress through struggle, through the victory of the strong over the weak (an inescapable requirement of Darwinism). He also was obsessed with the effects of human breeding—yet he sidestepped the whole question of human origins thus:

It is idle to argue which race or races were the original representative of human culture and hence the real founders of all that we sum up under the word "humanity." It is simpler to raise this question with regard to the present, and here an easy, clear answer results. All the human culture, all the results of art, science, and technology that we see before us today, are almost exclusively the creative product of the Aryan. This very fact admits of the not unfounded inference that he alone was the founder of all higher humanity, therefore representing the prototype of all that we understand by the word "man."

Key aspects of Darwinian theory are applied to a situation in which human life is somehow accepted as a given, and the difficult question of human origins is avoided.

Not being a systematic thinker, Hitler was capable of being very logical, but only insofar as it suited him. Other Nazi thinkers came up with absurd speculations about the origins of the Aryan race, but Hitler prudently avoided that in *Mein Kampf*. His understanding of Darwinian law was applied to a situation in which the human race had already, somehow, come into being. As he did with other thinkers, Hitler borrowed what was useful and ignored the rest.

Darwin himself employed the same tactic of assuming a lot of things as a given and then bringing his theory into play, only he started much farther back. Matter, the earth, the solar system, scientific laws, the first emergence of life—all of these were assumed to be in existence, and then evolutionary theory was applied. Both Hitler and Darwin tried to start evolutionary law from a situation whose origins were left unexplained.

While Hitler was not clear on the exact manner in which the first humans may have emerged, there are a number of quotes in which Hitler refers to man's animal nature and origins. One of them is from vol. II chapt. 4 of *Mein Kampf* (quoted in chapter 3):

The first step which visibly brought mankind away from the animal world was that which led to the first invention. The invention itself owes its origin to the ruses and stratagems which man employed to assist him in the struggle with other creatures for his existence and often to provide him with the only means he could adopt to achieve success in the struggle . . . everyone who believes in the higher evolution of living organisms must admit that every manifestation of the vital urge and struggle to live must have had a definite beginning in time and that one subject alone must have manifested it for the first time . . . all these inventions help man to raise himself higher and higher above the animal world and to separate himself from that world in an absolutely definite way. Hence they serve to elevate the human species and continually to promote its progress.

Somehow, man emerged from the animals. Hitler leaves this unexplained (as Darwin left the first origins of life unexplained). He was sure of the event, but not of the details.

Hitler was sufficiently committed to Darwinism to offer an evolutionary explanation for the first emergence of human society—and this was not an eccentricity of Hitler's. It was a common theme of Darwinists in the decades before Hitler emerged—indeed, it is an essential question for Darwinists even today. If the human race has an evolutionary origin, then human society and its ethical values must have had an evolutionary origin as well. Hitler's explanation in *Mein Kampf*—which many Darwinists would take seriously if they did not know who said it—is as follows:

> The will to live, subjectively viewed, is everywhere equal and different only in the form of its actual expression. In the most primitive living creatures the instinct of self-preservation does not go beyond concern for their own ego. Egoism, as we designate this urge, goes so far that it even embraces time; the moment itself claims everything, granting nothing to the coming hours. In this condition the animal lives only for himself, seeks food only for his present hunger, and fights only for his own life. As long as the instinct of self-preservation expresses itself in this way, every basis is lacking for the formation of a group, even the most primitive form of family. Even a community between male and female beyond pure mating, demands an extension of the instinct of self-preservation, since concern and struggle for the ego are now directed toward the second party; the male sometimes seeks food for the female, too, but for the most part both seek nourishment for the young. Nearly always one comes to the defense of the other, and thus the first, though infinitely simple, forms of a sense of sacrifice result. As soon as this sense extends beyond the narrow limits of the family, the basis for the formation of larger organisms and finally formal states is created [vol. I chapt. 11].

In summary, it is clear that Hitler, like Chamberlain and many others of that period, accepted at least some of Darwin's theory. Just as Marx modified Hegel, so the National Socialists modified Darwin, adding of course many other things into the mix—but Marx's relationship to Hegel is a well-known fact of intellectual history, while Hitler's relationship to Darwin is not. One reason for this is that no one has much of an interest in defending Hegel anymore—he is not a popular icon like Darwin is.

A quote from *Table Talk* shows that as a boy Hitler believed in evolution. He is reported to have complained about the "absurdity" of teaching both the scientific and the biblical accounts of creation:

> . . . at 10 a.m. the pupils attend a lesson in the catechism, at which the creation of the world is presented to them in accordance with the teachings of the Bible; and at 11 a.m. they attend a lesson in natural science, at which they are taught the theory of evolution. Yet the two doctrines are in complete contradiction. As a child, I suffered from this contradiction, and ran my head against a wall. Often I complained to one or another

of my teachers against what I had been taught an hour before—
and I remember that I drove them to despair.[9]

The young Hitler not only believed in evolution—he argued with his teachers in favor of it. Yet, there is another quote, also from *Table Talk*, that has been used to show Hitler's rejection of evolution:

> Where do we get the right to believe that humanity was not already from its earliest origins what it is today? Looking at nature teaches us that in the realm of plants and animals transformations and further developments occur. But never within a genus has evolution made such a wide leap, which humans must have made, if they had been transformed from an ape-like condition to what they are now.[10]

This quote has not been as widely used as one might expect—possibly because acceptance of *Table Talk* as a source might lead to acceptance of Hitler's many attacks on Christianity as well. Nevertheless, the quote has been noticed. Does it prove Hitler did not believe in evolution? Hitler had just stated prior to these remarks that he had been reading a book about human origins. He often referred to the animal nature of man but did not have a clear concept of how the first humans might have emerged. Hence, a book might have led him to puzzle over the question of man's descent from the apes without calling his basic world view into question. There are numerous other quotes in which Hitler stated his belief in the animal origin of man.

It should be added that this is much more than just a question of Hitler's own personal views. Nazi legal experts, at least one of whom (Ernst Rudin) was on the committee that finalized the first German eugenics law of 1934, specifically mentioned Darwin as a formative influence in their published commentary on the legislation. This Law for the Prevention of Hereditarily Diseased Offspring allowed physicians and other health care administrators to forcibly sterilize people with various psychiatric problems ("including the elastic category of feeble-mindedness"). Their official comments "carefully explained that natural selection was a beneficial process that brought biological progress by causing 'inferior' people to die, while the healthy and strong reproduced."[11] This is only one instance out of many that could be given showing the ugliness of social Darwinism in Hitler's Germany—but, some would feel happier and more comfortable talking about the Inquisition or the Crusades.

Daniel Gasman's third way

The Darwinists have yet one more potent argument in their favor: that so many essential aspects of National Socialism evolved prior to and outside of any Darwinian influence. Clearly, Darwin was not to blame for the Folkish movement. To clarify this point, we need to examine the combination of Folkish ideas with German interpretations of Darwin.

Prof. Daniel Gasman has found what might be a way out of this quagmire. In his book *The Scientific Origins of National Socialism*, he asserts that it was not Darwinism, but German distortions of Darwinism, "far from the biological ideas or underlying moral and philosophical ideas of Darwin himself"[12] that contributed significantly to the formation of National Socialist ideology.

He focuses specifically on Ernst Haeckel, Wilhelmine Germany's leading advocate of Darwinism, and asserts it was his ideas, a "synthesis of romantically inclined Volkism with evolution and science" that "provided an ideological basis for National Socialism." This was "remote from the familiar naturalism of Spencer, Darwin, and Huxley."[13]

This theory, if true, accounts very well for some Darwinian rhetoric used for non-Darwinian ends. Darwin is thus removed from the discussion—one reason why Stephen Gould, a prominent Darwinist, could accept Gasman's interpretation.[14] Since Gasman sees Haeckel combining Folkish philosophy with pseudo-Darwinism, it also accounts for the importance of the entire Folkish tradition in the formation of National Socialist ideology.

There are some objections to this theory and it has been criticized from different angles. Before considering those objections, we need to examine some of Haeckel's ideas. Having done that, we can then compare and contrast them with Hitler's and consider the possibility of some kind of a relationship more effectively. Finally, we can try and determine the extent to which Haeckel's ideas did or did not follow logically from Darwinism.

The marriage of science and philosophy

Ernst Haeckel (1834-1919) started out in medicine but became more interested in zoology and earned a doctorate in that field. He taught Zoology and Comparative Anatomy at the University of Jena, and contributed significantly to the biological knowledge of his day. He was also an enthusiastic advocate of Darwinism, and became known as Germany's leading apologist for the new theory. A diligent researcher, lecturer, and author of best-selling books on science and philosophy, he achieved, in Gasman's words,

> . . . great popularity as the authoritative voice of modern science
> . . . As the recognized spokesman of Darwinism in Germany he
> was taken as the virtually incontestable and exacting voice of
> science among many of the scientists and certainly among the
> general public.[15]

Firmly committed to the "Enlightenment" principle of the sovereignty of human reason, Haeckel not only rejected but was openly hostile to traditional religion. In his most well-known book, *The Riddle of the Universe* (*Die Weltraetsel*) (1899), Haeckel ridiculed the Christian God as a "gaseous vertebrate,"[16] and asserted there was an "open and irreconcilable opposition"[17] between science and Christianity. He wrote in *The History of Creation* that "where faith commences, science ends,"[18] and in *The Riddle of the Universe* (which he had personally solved) described Christianity as "mere superstition," "incompatible with the firmest results of modern science."[19]

His ideas of Christ were not high. He saw Christ as "a noble prophet and enthusiast," "full of the love of humanity," but thought he was "far below the level of classical culture." The Gospels "were selected from a host of contradictory and forged manuscripts"[20] so it was not possible to know what Christ really taught anyway. Protestantism was a lie, Catholicism was bankrupt,[21] and the real hope for the future of mankind lay in scientific knowledge.

It says a lot about the decline of traditional Christianity in the Germany of Haeckel's day that some of his books were best-sellers. It also says a lot about the church of Haeckel's day, that he could write popular books and travel the land exalting Darwinism and attacking Christianity, yet not be expelled from the Free Evangelical Church that he had belonged to since his youth (he was probably placed on the membership roster in infancy).

When Haeckel was nearly 80, he finally decided to leave the church, explaining in an article called "My Church Departure" that he had retained his membership only "out of regard for family and friends"—he thought leaving the church would cause them "heavy sorrow and injury."[22]

What kind of church would allow such a person to remain in it? Only a church that was totally indifferent to New Testament teachings about the meaning and purpose of the church. Haeckel's family and friends should have realized, and maybe some of them did realize, that Haeckel's membership had no meaning or significance. His departure was a benefit to the church. He should have been removed from the membership roster decades earlier.

Not only was Haeckel opposed to traditional religious superstitions—he was thoroughly committed to Darwinism. So deep was his belief in the new theory that, unlike many Darwinists, he sought to rigorously and logically deduce its implications for human life. Haeckel's ideas of philosophy, war, foreign policy, government, social relations, crime, education, were based on his understanding and interpretations of Darwinism—and his understanding was deeply colored by the cultural values of his time and place.

Rejecting religious revelation and relying on human reason alone, Haeckel sought "a clear view of the world—a view that shall be based on truth and conformity to reality."[23] Relying only on "purely rational knowledge," Haeckel pursued an "honest search for truth."[24] This led him to Darwinism—and not merely to Darwinism as an easy explanation for human origins that allowed him to then go off and enjoy himself. Haeckel was far more intellectually consistent than that. Correctly reasoning that if Darwinism was true then we should think and live accordingly, Haeckel affirmed "the sovereignty of the law of evolution." There was no other higher law. Thus he claimed that "evolution dominates the entire universe" and spoke of Darwinism's "universal application," its "world-wide application."[25]

It is in the light of evolution that we need to understand everything, according to Haeckel. In this theory "we have the key to the question of all questions," and the enigma of "the place of man in nature is solved."[26] "The key" to the "cosmic problem" "is found in the one magic word—evolution."[27] Thus a theory of origins is elevated to the metaphysical, philosophical, and even (as we shall see) to the religious level—and why shouldn't it be, if it is true?

What, then, were the earthly implications of Darwinism when used (in Gasman's words) not merely as "the basis for the science of biology, but for a whole new cosmic philosophy"?[28] This question needs to be answered on two levels—the theoretical level, involving general concepts of life, death, and human nature; and the practical level, meaning questions of ethics, political science, social justice, and even foreign policy. We will consider these two levels separately, though of course each affects and is affected by the other.

To begin with, the basic law of life in Haeckel's philosophy was struggle. In his words, the "struggle for life" was "the powerful natural force which has exerted supreme control over the entire course of organic evolution for millions of years." People like us were "merely the inevitable outcome of the struggle for existence, the blind controller." [29] It is remarkable how closely this coincides with the ideas of Schopenhauer.

There was in Haeckel's view nothing above or beyond this struggle, no controlling mind, and no moral laws or features. There was "no moral feature whatever," "no trace of a moral order."[30] Haeckel claimed that "the fate of those branches of the human family, those nations and races which have struggled for existence and progress for thousands of years, is determined by the same 'eternal laws of iron' as the history of the whole organic world."[31]

Notice an essential point—in this passage Haeckel has upgraded the concept of survival-of-the-fittest to national and racial levels. Thus "victory of the stronger" is a law not only for individual organisms but for nations and for ethnic groups. Since Darwin saw the extermination of the primitive races as an example of evolution in action, he made the same connection, if not so overtly.

Given the belief that mankind emerged solely as the result of natural causes, it followed logically that man was no different from the animals—in fact, he was an animal, nothing more. This was Haeckel's conclusion: "Man has no single mental faculty which is his exclusive prerogative. His whole psychic life differs from that of the nearest related mammals only in degree, and not in kind; quantitatively, not qualitatively."[32]

Naturally, the human spirit or soul also fell by the wayside. What was traditionally thought of as a "soul" was merely the "sum of cerebral functions" and disappeared at death. The immortal soul was a superstition and the Christian idea of an afterlife was an "impossibility," "purely mythical."[33]

This led to the denial of free-will. Haeckel was completely certain that "The human will has no more freedom than that of the highest animals, from which it differs only in degree, not in kind."[34] This being so, man was inevitably and inescapably a part of nature—and what was nature? Not beautiful sunsets or meadows full of daisies, but pitiless, impersonal, and amoral struggle. As Haeckel put it in *Freedom in Science and Teaching*,

> The theory of selection teaches that in human life, as in animal and plant life everywhere, and at all times, only a small and chosen minority can exist and flourish, while the enormous majority starve and perish miserably and more or less prematurely . . . Only the picked minority of the qualified "fittest" is in a position to resist it [the process of selection] successfully, while the great majority of the competitors must necessarily perish miserably. We may profoundly lament this tragical state of things, but we can neither controvert nor alter it.[35]

In this struggle, human life was of no value. Haeckel confidently stated that human nature "has no more value for the universe at large than the ant, the fly of a summer's day, the microscopic infusorium, or the smallest bacillus."[36] This was not mere theory. Haeckel said that executing criminals was the same as "destroying luxuriant weeds, for the prosperity of a well-cultivated garden."[37]

With this attitude, it was easy to advocate killing such useless people as the insane and the incurably ill. This could be done with "some painless and rapid poison" (Gasman quotes Haeckel's ironically titled *Wonders of Life* here).[38] Weak, sickly, or deformed babies should also be killed—and why not? Relative to the infinity of the cosmos, said the professor sagely, a weak, sick, crying little baby was worth no more than an ant, a fly, or a bacillus. Haeckel praised the Spartans for killing defective babies, and thought this practice would be beneficial to society, but neglected to ask himself, "And where are the Spartans today? Did killing babies help them? Didn't they go the same way as other peoples of their day who did not have this practice?"

It should be stressed that, as an evolutionist, Haeckel thought that death was normal, ordinary, natural, and benevolent. It was death, after all, that facilitated the progress of the human race and indeed the progress of all of life by weeding out the weak, the unfit, the infirm. Prof. Richard Weikart's influential study *From Darwin to Hitler: Evolutionary Ethics, Eugenics, and Racism in Germany* elaborates at length on the shift from the Christian concept of death as the result of sin, to death as ordinary, normal, even beneficial.

In this evolutionary scenario, human life wasn't worth much, but some people were somehow still worth more than others. Haeckel had a very strong sense of hierarchy. Some animals had progressed farther and were more advanced on the evolutionary scale—and this naturally included humans. There was an evolutionary tree, and some people were higher on it than others. This was perfectly logical, given the belief of Haeckel—and of Darwin—in the "long chain of evolution which stretches unbroken from the lowest to the highest stages."[39] Robert Richards, author of a biography of Haeckel, agrees that evolutionary theory itself, as Darwin presented it, requires a hierarchy of animal species.[40] This includes human animals. There is an evolutionary tree and some people are higher on it than others, if Darwinism is true. This is why historian Laurence Rees can reasonably refer to the "overtly Darwinian ideals of Nazism, which rested on telling every 'Aryan' German he or she was racially superior . . . ."[41]

Haeckel even believed that the lowest humans on the scale were more like animals than people. In his words:

> The difference between the reason of a Goethe, a Kant, a Lamarck, or a Darwin, and that of the lowest savage, a Veddah, an Akka, a native Australian, or a Patagonian, is much greater than the graduated difference between the reason of the latter and that of the most "rational" mammals, the anthropoid apes, or even the papiomorpha, the dog, or the elephant. This important thesis has been convincingly proved by the thoroughly critical comparative work of Romanes and others.[42]

Dirty and ignorant savages were more like dogs, elephants, and apes than people—and naturally Haeckel put his own group at the top. He went even further, and claimed some people were, in his objective scientific view, worth less than dogs. To prove this, he told of "an old head-forester," a widower with no children, who lived in a "noble forest in East Prussia." He had two servants and a pack of dogs, "with whom he lived in perfect psychic communion." In his "impartial and objective estimation," his best dogs were "at a higher stage of psychic development than his old, stupid maid and the rough, wrinkled manservant."[43] This sort of attitude explains how Nazis could be more concerned about their horses and their dogs than about people. Should we be surprised when ideas have consequences? A horse or a dog after all has more utilitarian value and a higher level of consciousness than someone who is sick and dying.

This same spirit can be found in the writings of modern day evolutionists. For example, animal rights activist Peter Singer writes that "there are many nonhuman animals whose rationality, self-consciousness, awareness, capacity to feel, and so on exceed that of a human baby a week or a month old."[44] The same could be said of course of the mentally handicapped and the senile, none of whom have any special right to life and can be easily dispensed with.

The practical implications of Haeckel's ideas

Life was essentially amoral and purposeless struggle. Man was only an animal and human life was of little value. People weren't worth much, but some were worth more than others. It was nothing to be concerned about if the weak and unfit perished miserably (again, this included people, human beings, men, women, and children). Eliminating socially harmful human elements was like getting rid of some weeds.

How did someone with these views approach problems of life and society? In Haeckel's case, we find that a clear, objective, logical consideration of scientific fact led to racism, authoritarianism, militarism, and imperialism. These all made perfect sense, and make sense today—if the presuppositions described in the previous section are true.

Looking at racism, we have already seen that the evolutionary tree puts some humans higher than others, with the whites at the top. This idea, by the way, was not unheard of outside of Germany. In Haeckel's case, it led to an emphasis on racial purity. He shared Gobineau's ideas and recommended Gobineau as a source.[45]

Haeckel stressed the inferiority of Negroes, who were—after all—closer to monkeys than to geniuses like Goethe or Haeckel. Quoting Haeckel's *History of Creation*, Gasman writes that in Haeckel's view, " 'wooly-haired' Negroes were 'incapable of a true inner culture and of a higher mental development,' and he noted that 'no wooly-haired nation has ever had an important "history".' "[46]

This was more than mere dislike of Negroes. It was believed by Haeckel (and by many others with similar ideas) that the human races were naturally and rightly divided, assigned as the result of evolutionary struggle to their respective stations. The white races were in a higher position by natural right, and reached their highest perfection in the Germanic peoples. As Haeckel wrote in *The Wonders of Life*, "lower races (such as the Veddahs or Australian Negroes) are psychologically nearer to the mammals (apes and dogs) than to civilized Europeans, we must, therefore, assign a totally different value to their lives."[47]

Keeping in mind the important point that Haeckel was only the most well-known of many who advocated such views, we may want to qualify Gasman's contention that Haeckel "was largely responsible for forging the bonds between academic science and racism in Germany in the later decades of the nineteenth century,"[48] but Haeckel certainly contributed more than his share. As a result of this type of thinking, racism was upgraded from mere Folkish philosophy to objective scientific fact.

Richards seeks to defend Haeckel by saying he was just a man of his time and didn't know any better.[49] He fails to point out that the Bible teaches the fundamental humanity of all mankind. This is why countless Christians participated in or supported spiritually and financially attempts to provide supposedly inferior races with schools, hospitals, and teachings about the meaning of life. This does not deny Christians have been guilty of racism or other sins. It does show that just having lived in a certain period of time does not justify Haeckel's ugly, primitive, and ignorant understanding of life.

Haeckel also contributed to authoritarianism. The democratic traditions of England and America were unknown in Germany except as theories, and German thinkers and rulers had a long tradition of authoritarianism. Haeckel, however, made this seem scientific. He pontificated loud and long on the fact that in nature, in the conditions of permanent struggle, the strongest and the most fit prevailed. It is strength that decides in nature, not committees, elections, and parliamentary deals.

Other Darwinists advocated democracy—we recall that once one accepts the animal origins of man one can then go off and believe in anything one wishes. Haeckel, however, tried to follow the implications of Darwinism as literally as possible—this led him to the conclusion that nature was aristocratic, so human government should be as well.

This tied in perfectly with the organic theory of the state as expressed by Wagner and others. Rather than representing a voluntary association of free individuals living in harmony under agreed upon rules, human members of society were seen as subordinate to the whole. Haeckel even went so far as to compare human society to that of insects. He wrote in *Eternity,* for example, that people in a body were like cells in an organism, bees in a hive, or ants in a nest: "Each cell, though autonomous, is subordinated to the body as a whole; in the same way in the societies of bees, ants, and termites, in the vertebrate herd and the human state, each individual is subordinate to the social body of which he is a member."[50] Even today, Darwinists are still trying to understand human society by studying insects. Keith Ward's study of science and religion, *Pascal's Fire: Scientific Faith and Religious Understanding*, tells of a 1996 book that seeks to understand human virtue by studying group survival strategy of ants.[51] As Jesus said, "If therefore the light that is in thee be darkness, how great is that darkness!"

When Hitler said in a speech of 1937 that the German nation "can only exist as a nation and not as a collection of individuals,"[52] he was expressing a common sentiment of German political philosophy, and a basic belief of the Folkish movement. This "organic" concept of the state contributed to hostility to democracy. False and un-German ideas of a free press, quarreling political parties, and the democratic triumph of mediocrity were not the solution to Germany's pressing social and economic problems (it will be recalled that Germany was by this time politically unified, and the greatest industrial power in Europe). What was necessary, it was argued, was for the people to work together in unison, as one, under a strong leadership.

This is not National Socialism—but it is the hostility to democracy that helped to undermine the Weimar Republic. It is different from Darwin's democratic liberalism as well—but some form of authoritarianism does seem to me at least to be vastly more consistent with the amoral struggle for survival of the fittest. Perhaps Darwin was too much a prisoner of the pre-Darwinian conventions he was raised in. Haeckel, the product of an entirely different tradition, had no such handicap.

These ideas blended easily with imperialism and militarism. Animals take the space they need, and the weaker animals are pushed to the side. Elevating this principle to the national and the international levels provided an objective and scientific justification for imperialism—and Haeckel's imperialism is easily documented. Writing in *World War and Natural History* (*Weltkrieg und Naturgeschichte*), Haeckel wrote passionately of Germany's overpopulation problem—hence its need for *Lebensraum*.[53] He also dreamed about the territories that would be annexed by Germany after its victory in the Great War (this objective and scientific man tried to tell people about the meaning of life).

He wrote in *Eternity* about how the new territories should be "Germanized," and insisted in the same work that a great world power such as Germany needed extensive colonies. This was all, viewed scientifically, "a natural consequence of the 'struggle for existence' among the nations"[54] and hence morally justifiable (morality being derived from evolution with its iron law of struggle).

This went together with militarism like the index finger goes with the thumb. Haeckel made a few passing comments about pacifism—possibly in the belief that the European countries should divide up and rule the world without fighting among themselves—but when World War I broke out, whatever theoretical pacifism he may have had quickly disappeared. As Weikart points out, "The pacifism of many German Darwinists was paper-thin, and when push came to shove, many abandoned their pacifism."[55] Haeckel, at any rate, became an ardent supporter of German victory.

Haeckel desperately yearned for a German victory. Even in 1917 he opposed any idea of compromise for the sake of peace, and advocated the continued pursuit of victory.[56] Germany needed that *Lebensraum* after all. Believing as he did that struggle was the basic reality of life, he urged German soldiers to go into battle with "enthusiasm"; to "gladly" lay down their lives "for the preservation of the fatherland"; to be ready to sacrifice all in "the higher interests of their country."[57]

Haeckel's appeal to soldiers not to fear death shows how not religion but secularism can encourage men to fight and die. Haeckel argued that there was no life after death, that death came to everyone by chance anyway, and thus should not be feared. Soldiers should leave their fate "to blind chance, which rules the universe in the absence of a wise Providence."[58]

Noteworthy is Haeckel's hostility to England. He had viewed the English as racially akin to the Germans, and thought they should cooperate with Germany in dominating the world. This touching sentiment vanished in 1914. Writing again in *Eternity*, Haeckel blamed England for the war, and said England started it for the sake of world domination.[59] In his fury he went so far as to advocate the invasion of England and the occupation of London. He was especially upset about the racial aspect of the war. England introduced imperial troops into the conflict, soldiers from inferior races like Negroes and Asians. "Haeckel warned very seriously that this racial mixture would prove disastrous for the future of Europe."[60]

All of this was inseparably bound up with an intense nationalism, an ardent devotion to the fatherland. He wrote in *The Riddle of the Universe* that Bismarck "led us by a marvelous statecraft to the long-desired goal of national unity and power."[61] Bismarck's several wars were "marvelous" and the attainment of unity and power inflamed Haeckel with patriotic pride and the lust for domination.

One of Haeckel's correspondents, his friend Hermann Allmers, was thrilled by the German victory over France in 1870, and gushed "every people around here from near and from far will bow to the majesty of the German people." Haeckel answered, "I have followed all the victories of the newly blossoming fatherland with enthusiasm and like yourself hope for a promising future."[62]

Some have argued that Haeckel had no interest in politics or that he opposed Bismarck. They may have simply assumed that, as an advocate of objective science and rational thought, Haeckel would naturally be indifferent to nationalism, or even see it as a threat to world peace, like themselves. They may have been misled by a youthful criticism of Bismarck. Whatever the case, Haeckel's mature views were clearly stated. He did object to modern warfare as interfering with natural selection,[63] yet he still felt war was justified and necessary in the fight for survival, and was confident that the evolutionary process would continue regardless.

Haeckel's ethics

Haeckel, surprisingly, wrote in his *Riddle of the Universe* of the need for "charity and toleration, compassion and assistance."[64] He claimed there that love for one's self and for one's neighbor were good principles. The validity of these noble qualities was not derived however from God's character and laws, but rather was derived from a proper understanding of evolution, from "the solid ground of social instinct."[65]

According to Haeckel, the struggle for survival led to the evolution in human society of both egotism (necessary to preserve the self), and altruism (the self-sacrifice necessary to preserve society). Thus, the balance between duty to self and the duty to society that emerged out of blind, amoral, and pitiless struggle was "the chief and fundamental principle of our morality."[66]

Haeckel thought that the Golden Rule, "to love your neighbor as you love yourself," was a good principle. He believed, however, that the rule derived its authority not from God or from Jesus, but from a proper scientific understanding of life as struggle. Thus, the Golden Rule long preceded Christianity and had in fact been plagiarized by Christians.

What did all of this mean in human terms? It seems that the rule applied only to those united together in Darwinistic struggle. It did not apply to those on the outside—for them it was kill or be killed. Even for those within the magic circle—in this case, the superior Germans—the Golden Rule did not apply to those who were of no use or who were a hindrance in the struggle. The mentally, ill, the handicapped, the unfit, criminals, unhealthy newborns—they were not worthy of consideration and could be, should be, killed without a qualm.

How a system of ethics might be derived within an evolutionary scenario was a common topic of conversation among Darwinists trying to come to terms with the implications of their revolutionary new theory. Some thought that traditional religious ideas were false and should be done away with. Others thought traditional ethics had some truth, but should be based on reason and science, not religion.

There were different approaches to the problem of evolutionary ethics, as Weikart amply documents in his study. In Haeckel's case—and his views were common—the attempt to derive an ethical system from nature led to cruelty, inhumanity, barbarism, and the worst sort of racism, nationalism, and imperialism. All of this was from a man who fondly dreamed his ideas were objective and scientific.

The extent to which all of this was or was not consistent with Darwinism as Darwin presented it can be discussed in another section. For the present, suffice it to say that Haeckel's attempt to pull an ethical system out of his magician's hat ended in abject and miserable failure. This was inevitable. How could someone who claimed that individual human lives were insignificant, that people were worth no more than animals and sometimes were worth even less than animals, possibly have anything serious to say about ethics?

Euthanasia

Not surprisingly, given his low concept of the value of life and his belief that life was a pitiless and amoral struggle for survival, Haeckel advocated euthanasia. People who were of no use to society, useless burdens whose lives were not worth living (in his judgment), should be killed.

This has already been mentioned in the context of discussing Haeckel's low view of human life, but some of the implications of this heartless, cruel, sinister and evil philosophy are worth elaborating on. For one thing, it makes perfect sense in a Darwinist scenario. After all, that is what happens in nature—the inferior and the unfit die—and people should live according to nature.

Previous ideas of the sanctity of life in Europe were derived from the Jewish and Christian religions—once those are abandoned, traditional systems of ethics begin to disappear along with them. This occurs more swiftly and radically with some individuals, and more slowly with others. There are Darwinists whose humanity overrides their philosophy. They do not follow their beliefs through to the bitter end and still are susceptible to the appeals of human conscience. Their humanitarianism is, however, nothing more than a vague sentiment. Contrary to scientific fact—if Darwin's ugly and soul-deadening theory is true—such vague emotions cannot stand up against the driving force of ideologues who take their Darwinism more seriously.

Haeckel was the "earliest significant German advocate for killing the 'unfit,' " according to Weikart,[67] and he imagined that his policies would benefit society. He thought that killing a new-born infant was no more than killing an animal, and claimed that aversion to killing sick and defective babies was the result of illogical emotion.[68] This corruption of the soul due to the loss of God explains how murder could be increasingly accepted as something beneficial to society, or at least nothing to be too concerned about.

Not long ago someone who was attacking Christianity found a Protestant pastor who supported the Nazis' euthanasia program. This pastor was given as an example of how evil the Christians were, and of how Christianity was related to Naziism. The fact that some Darwinists had been calling for such a program long before Hitler was overlooked. In the same vein, Richard Evans mentions "Protestant charities" whose "doctrines of predestination and original sin" led them to welcome sterilization of the unfit.[69] He neglected to point out that such ideas were unheard of in preceding centuries. What reputable Christian has ever used the doctrines of original sin or predestination as an excuse for killing babies?

The worthlessness of individual human life and the denial of the immortal soul are secular concepts, not biblical ones.

Christianity never eliminated or promised to eliminate all of the evils of society (prior to Christ's return). It did assign a high value to the human soul, however—to such an extent that abortion, euthanasia, and suicide were generally regarded as wrong. It was not until the advent of the modern scientific age, and especially the advent of Darwinism, that people began to dispassionately argue for the extermination of the weak, the sick, the handicapped, the mentally ill, even new-born babies. This is perfectly reasonable—if Darwin's fiendish and devilish philosophy is true, that is.

Wilhelm Schallmeyer, a German eugenicist, called for a "rational, scientific investigation of Chinese infanticide,"[70] claiming European criticism of the practice was misguided. Nowhere is the contrast between the innate humanity of biblical Christianity and the inhumanity of secular Darwinism more evident than when we consider the contrast between this "scientific" speculation and the narrative of a Christian girl, the daughter of missionaries in China, who sought to rescue an infant that had been abandoned to die.

She had found the baby naked and lying in mud, its eyes filled with pus, covered with flies, but still alive. The child was taken to the hospital, cleaned, and fed—but the effort was too late and it died.[71] The hospital, by the way, had been built by Christian missionaries, not by Darwinists who had come to China to tell the people the good news of Darwinism. Significantly, even today some people will still point to Chinese infanticide as proof that the practice is natural. Peter Singer, for example speaks of the "sophisticated urban communities" of imperial China and ancient Greece and argues that other people killed babies, so therefore it must be right.[72]

The rise of modern eugenics shows how principles inherent in Darwinism led to attempts to improve society by elimination of the unfit, and by selective breeding. In the Nazi context, such principles are more easily seen as cruel and sinister. The extent to which such views were (and are) common in England and America as well is insufficiently appreciated. There is a library of information on this subject, documenting eerie parallels between Haeckel, Hitler, and leftist secular progressives who sought (and seek) to engineer the advancement of the human race by eliminating the unfit.

A brief overview of this too much neglected topic is found in Joshua Goldberg's *Liberal Fascism: The Secret History of the American Left from Mussolini to the Politics of Meaning.* Goldberg not only documents the broad and unmistakable similarities between fascism and liberal, democratic, progressive eugenics in America. He also states that Hitler was aware of American eugenic ideas and even influenced by them. According to Goldberg, Hitler was especially interested in a book by Madison Grant called The *Passing of the Great Race.* Hitler even wrote to the American Eugenics Society requesting a copy of *The Case for Sterilization.*[73]

Hitler found much to agree with in such books. Madison Grant believed that only people who were "useful" to the race or to the community should be valued as people—the rest should be eliminated. This was a necessity of natural law, and natural law had no place for misguided and sentimental beliefs in divine law, traditional morality, or the preciousness of human life.[74]

Haeckel's anti-Semitism

Haeckel's ethic included anti-Semitism. Hostility to Jews was not central to his philosophy, and it was only briefly mentioned in *The Riddle of the Universe*—Haeckel said that Christ's "high and noble personality" was "certainly not semitical."[75] Nevertheless, it is worth looking at briefly.

Unlike Hitler, Haeckel recommended assimilation as the solution to the Jewish problem. In a published interview on the question of anti-Semitism Haeckel said,

> It must be understood that the [German] people will no longer tolerate the strange ways of Jewish life, and their desire is to deprive the Jews of all that is specifically Jewish and to convert them to German habits and customs so that they will resemble the people among whom they live in all respects.[76]

What should have been done if the Jews did not want to assimilate is not mentioned—someone with Haeckel's low view of life would not find it hard to justify mass killing, if it were in the national interest.

Haeckel's hostility to Jews was nationally and racially rather than religiously motivated. It stemmed from his absurd exaggeration of the importance of race and Folk. Haeckel was not concerned about the wrath of an imaginary God on a people who rejected God's imaginary Son.

Yet, there was a religious aspect of a different sort to Haeckel's anti-Semitism. He could not fail to note the obvious and undeniable fact that Jewish values had influenced the West through Christianity. Since this Christian influence was in Haeckel's view harmful, the Jews could be directly blamed for having had a negative impact on all of Western civilization. Thus, in attacking the creation story in Genesis, Haeckel wrote, "The Hebrew legend of creation obtained its great influence through its adoption into the Christian faith and its consecration as the 'Word of God.'"[77]

It is one of the most important yet little-known aspects of modern German anti-Semitism, that it included hostility to the Jews for having introduced false concepts via Christianity. This can be seen in the writings of Haeckel, Wagner, and Chamberlain, and will be further documented from Nietzsche's writings. Yet, the aforementioned biographer of Haeckel, Robert Richards, argues that Haeckel was not anti-Semitic at all.

One of his arguments is surprising. He claims that "the most rabid anti-Semites during Haeckel's time were conservative Christians," and reasons that Haeckel would not have wanted to be allied with them.[78] This complete omission of secular philosophical and racial anti-Semitism calls his understanding of the issue into question. Pointing out that Haeckel had Jewish friends and even praised Jews for their contributions to German culture seems more relevant, and explains why Haeckel thought that Jews could assimilate with the Germans as stated in the quote above. Still, the Jews could not survive as a people—they had to disappear (from Germany at any rate). Whether or not the best Jews could assimilate was a debated question among secular, racial anti-Semites. What was not debated was that the Jews as a body could not be tolerated.

A family tree of the human races drawn up by Haeckel and reproduced by Richards shows the Jews at the very top, and quite close to the Germans: yet it was this high level of development that made the Jews especially dangerous.

Joseph Mengele, the famed Nazi death camp doctor, asserted that "there were only two gifted nations in the world": the Germans and the Jews. "The question is," he wondered, "which one will dominate?"[79] That the Jews were highly developed enough to infiltrate the German Folk yet were inferior nevertheless was not an impossibility to the Nazi "mind."

Richards concedes that placing the Jews on the same line as the Germans at the top of the chart did not prevent Haeckel from giving his unbiased and objective scientific view that the "Indo-German" family was the source of the "most highly developed cultural peoples."[80] Haeckel also placed the Berbers at the top, on the same plane as the Jews, the Romans (*Die Romanen*), and the Germans. This was, no doubt, because the Berbers have blue eyes.

Haeckel's idea of God

It might seem that Haeckel's concept of God would be a matter only of historical curiosity, but some of his ideas are actually rather relevant. They illustrate how the mere use of words such as "God," "the Almighty," "the Creator," could be used in a totally non-Christian context. This will help to shed some light on comments of Hitler's in a similar vein.

In works such as *Eternity* and *Monism as Connecting Religion and Science: The Confession of Faith of a Man of Science*, Haeckel strongly affirmed the existence of God—but his God was a personal invention, a strange mixture of romantic pantheism ("God is everywhere") with scientific materialism ("God is the sum of all energy and matter").[81]

Trying to imagine a God consistent with his emphasis on science, Haeckel dreamed that the entire universe was a "colossal organism" held together by a mysterious substance called a "mobile cosmic ether."[82] This sum total of all physical being he called (writing in *Generelle Morphologie*) "almighty . . . the single Creator, the single cause of all things . . . absolute perfection."[83] This strange hybrid of God and nature, of theology and materialism, operated according to scientific law and was discoverable by scientific law. Such a God was of course perfectly compatible with evolutionary theory. With this in mind, trying to foster the continued evolutionary progress of mankind by eliminating the unfit and preserving or improving the master race can be understood as "doing the will of the Lord." Comments of Hitler's to this effect refer not to biblical Christianity, but to theistic evolution.

In Haeckel's thought we can see that the idea of God has declined one step further. It was merely the sum total of "that which is," understood in scientific terms. This was a decline from Schopenhauer's blindly striving Will, which at least had an independent existence. From the Bible, to the Deists, to the romantics with their nebulous spirit, to Schopenhauer, to Haeckel—there is literally nothing left but the final descent to Nietzsche's denial of God altogether.

It is commonly assumed that since Germany was a fundamentally Christian culture, any references by Hitler to "God" should be understood in that context. This mistake derives from three sources: (a) eagerness to discredit Christianity; (b) ignorance of German cultural history; and (c) ignorance of biblical Christianity.

Haeckel's unscientific ideas

Although Haeckel was proud of his scientific objectivity, he came up with a number of ideas which had no scientific validity and in fact seem ridiculous today. This is not surprising, given the comparatively primitive state of science in his day. In the words of Michael Behe, a modern biologist, science has revealed that the cell "is tremendously more complex than Haeckel thought"[84]—and, of course, the same could be said of the cosmos, matter, and the biological processes of life.

In his simple-minded nineteenth-century complacency, it was easy for Haeckel to imagine that all of his ideas were scientific. This attitude led him further and further astray. He thus believed in spontaneous generation (the emergence of life from non-living matter) as a common and presently occurring event; that the cosmos was an organism united by "ether"; and in the doctrine of eternal recurrence. This last was described as "an eternal repetition in infinite time of the periodic dance of the worlds, the metamorphosis of the cosmos that ever returns to its starting point."[85]

Like many secularists both of his day and today, Haeckel could be quite dogmatic in presenting as facts ideas for which he had not a shred of empirical evidence. For example, he asserted in *The Riddle of the Universe* that the existence of the cosmic ether was "a positive fact." This ether was "the ultimate cause of all phenomenon," "neither gaseous, nor fluid, nor solid," "boundless and immeasurable . . . in eternal motion."[86] Hitler also referred to the "ether" in *Mein Kampf* ("this planet once moved through the ether for millions of years," vol. I chapt. 11) but this was a common concept at that time.

Haeckel also advocated sun-worship:

> Sun-worship (solarism, or heliotheism) seems to the modern scientist to be the best of all forms of theism . . . the whole of our bodily and mental life depends, in the last resort, like all other organic life, on the light and heat rays of the sun . . . in the light of pure reason, sun-worship, as a form of naturalistic monotheism, seems to have a much better foundation than the anthropistic worship of Christians and of other monotheists who conceive their God in human form.[87]

This was somehow reconciled with pantheism.

Needless to say, Haeckel's views were not always well-received even by secularists. *The Riddle of the Universe* was condemned by a contemporary, Friedrich Paulsen, who wrote "I have read this book with burning shame over the condition of the general and philosophical education of our people. It is painful that such a book was possible . . . ."[88] Erik Nordenskiold's *History of Biology* (published in 1929) describes Haeckel's book in this way:

> . . . from a scientific point of view it must be regarded as utterly valueless . . . biology takes up only one quarter of the volume; the rest is devoted to psychology, cosmology, and theology. The cosmological section gives evidence of the author's hopelessly confused ideas on the simplest facts of physics and chemistry.[89]

It is significant that Haeckel (like the Nazis) rejected Einstein's Theory of Relativity—yet, because he rejected the Bible and believed in science, he could imagine that his ideas were scientific. How many opponents of religion today are confidently making scientific assertions that will look foolish 100 years hence—if civilization as we know it still exists at that time?

A brief overview

Before discussing what relevance these ideas might have to Hitler, it seemed worthwhile to make a few general comments. First, Haeckel is an excellent example of the falsehood of the fantasy of scientific objectivity. Opponents of religion can allege the objectivity of science all they like, but Haeckel shows how scientific knowledge does not guarantee an understanding of human nature or of society. Haeckel's attempt to follow reason alone led to folly—and cruel, heartless folly at that. The myth of scientists as the sole guardians of ultimate truth is a spiritually and intellectually harmful fantasy, derived from wishful thinking and totally unsupported by (as well as contrary to) empirical evidence. Brilliant scientists like Max Planck and Nobel Prize winning physicist Werner Heisenberg were not led to denounce Hitler by their commitment to scientific truth.[90]

Secondly, Haeckel reveals how the new theory of Darwinism was interpreted in the light of the German Folkish tradition. Darwinism was, to put it another way, put to the service of a world view that Darwin himself did not have in mind. Of course, it may be argued that Christianity was similarly conformed to suit the demands of the age, and it was—with a major difference. Christians rejected, violated, and ignored all of the most basic teachings of their faith when they followed the world. This cannot be said of Darwinists who supported racism, militarism, imperialism, eugenics, and other ideas. There is nothing inherent in Darwinism to refute those views, and much to support them.

Thirdly, it has already been said but merits repeating, that Haeckel was just the tip of a great iceberg. The ideas he preached were advocated (with variations) by an increasingly significant minority of the German intelligentsia. Gasman's book shows us an individual whose ideas were in some ways close or even identical to Hitler's. Weikart's book shows us these views as they spread through much of German society. In spite of differences, the two books complement each other well.

Haeckel and Hitler

Gasman not only traces the roots of Haeckel's thought in scientific naturalism, Darwinism, and the Folkish tradition. More significantly, he makes the assertion that it was this combination of Folkish ideas with uniquely German interpretations of Darwinism that could "explain more successfully than any other theoretical framework the origin and nature of Nazi ideology." He stresses that "Other sources of Naziism were . . . also important to bear in mind," but makes the bold assertion that the essential nature of National Socialism "was most clearly apparent in the way that Haeckel had formulated his idiosyncratic *Weltanschauung*."[91]

If this is indeed true, there is some possibility that Gasman's hope for "a fundamental revision of the way in which scholars have perceived the origin and nature of National Socialism and fascism" will be fulfilled.[92] Certainly, to take two differing schools of thought—that Hitler emerged from the Folkish tradition, or that Hitler was the product of Darwinism—and combine them is, if accurate, a very significant contribution to the Hitler debate. Gasman's thesis, like any other, is open to contradiction, and some have found fault with his theory. Before examining some criticisms, it will be necessary to compare the worldviews of Haeckel and Hitler.

Both Haeckel and Hitler saw a racial kinship between Germany and England, and both thought the two nations should cooperate in ruling the world on the basis of a shared racial superiority. Both were deeply disappointed when England entered the war against Germany, and quickly changed from admiration to hostility. Both of them also put the blame on England, attributing its siding against a virtuous and innocent Germany to the basest of motives. Just as Haeckel objected to the British use of non-white colonial troops, fearing it would lead to the racial pollution of the white Europeans, Hitler objected to the French use of non-white troops during their occupation of the Ruhr.

There is clearly a deep similarity of outlook here. No one is arguing that Haeckel was identical to Hitler, and there were differences between them. Nevertheless, as we examine their basic presuppositions and world views the parallels and commonalities that emerge are deep and profound. For example, that life was essentially a struggle in which the strong triumphed over the weak was fundamental to the views of the two men. Moreover, this was an amoral struggle, void of enduring higher ethical and spiritual truths—one in which "might makes right" was the ruling principle.

Both thought that the struggle that occurred between animals in nature was also carried out on the level of societies and nations. After the passions of war blew away the cobwebs of Haeckel's theoretical pacifism, he (like Hitler) saw victory and conquest as Germany's right and destiny—a view that was totally inconceivable to the diplomats who saw peace as the desired end and war as an evil to be avoided.

Haeckel and Hitler both had a low view of human life. There was in their view nothing unique about the human soul, and the perishing of millions was an ordinary occurrence, part of natural law, unavoidable, and nothing to be concerned about. The significance of this for understanding the crimes of the Nazis cannot be overstated. The guards in the death camps who could go calmly about their business and pursue their ordinary lives off-duty viewed the whole situation as just the way life was. We recall Haeckel's statement, ". . . the great majority of the competitors must necessarily perish miserably. We may profoundly lament this tragical state of things, but we can neither controvert nor alter it."[93] Sinful qualities such as indifference, selfishness, and cruelty had now been sanctioned and approved by the latest scientific findings.

Hitler wrote in *Mein Kampf* that "Nature looks on calmly, with satisfaction in fact," [vol. I chapt. 11] while the weak and sickly succumb in the struggle for survival. It is not hard to understand how someone could arrive at this view—it is held by some Darwinists today. What is hard to understand is that it should be put into practice on a human level—but why should it be hard to understand? Are people supposed to have ideas, but not act on them? When the commandant of Auschwitz, Rudolf Hoess, wrote in his prison memoirs "I was never cruel"[94]— was he blatantly lying, as he did elsewhere? Or was he stating his sincere belief that the perishing of the weak and the unfit was not cruel at all, but only "natural"?

Richard Dawkins, a prominent Darwinist, has been quoted as saying "If there is mercy in nature, it is accidental. Nature is neither kind nor cruel but indifferent."[95] Thus it is natural to be indifferent to the weak and perishing humans or animals who have failed in the struggle for existence. It is not hard to imagine someone with that cruel and inhuman point of view over-seeing sick, starving, and dying prisoners and then going home to enjoy his off-duty domestic life as if there were nothing amiss. It would only be natural.

This is related to the view of human nature as being animal nature. A cat did not exercise free will in seizing a mouse, and it did not consider ethical questions of right and wrong—it acted according to its nature (Hitler used the cat and mouse analogy to this purpose in *Mein Kampf*). Similarly, the Germans, the lions and tigers of the world, took what they wanted. It was not a matter of ethics, but of natural law. Only "pacifist windbags" and "born weaklings," in Hitler's words, could fail to see this fundamental law of nature—or see it, but fail to apply it to human society.

That this natural law of struggle did apply to human society, and that only false religious or ethical views attempted to elevate man above the struggle, was a shared belief of both Haeckel and Hitler. Haeckel (and many others) openly blamed the Christian religion for introducing false and unnatural values into society, and advocated a return to the natural law of struggle and conflict. Hitler also blamed Christianity for introducing these values—but he had seen von Schonerer's mistake in alienating the churches, pointed it out, and was determined not to repeat it. He made a temporary agreement with the Soviet Union intending all along to destroy it, and he did the same with the churches.

Hitler did refer to the idea that "Man's role is to overcome nature"—that man was not confined to the animal level of struggle, that we should seek something higher than a cruel state of nature. He dismissed it with contempt, saying "Millions thoughtlessly parrot this Jewish nonsense and end up by really imagining that they themselves represent a kind of conqueror of Nature" [vol. I chapt. 11].

That Christianity teaches we are more than animals and far above a mere struggle for survival, and that Christianity is profoundly Jewish in its origins and outlook do not need to be documented. That Hitler wanted and needed the votes of millions of people who were either Christians or respectful of Christianity also does not need to be documented.

The belief in the animal nature of man explains some of the more bizarre and seemingly inexplicable aspects of the Holocaust. Hundreds of thousands or even millions of cattle or poultry can be legally and ethically slaughtered to prevent the spread of cattle disease or bird flu. If people are essentially animals, who—except a born weakling, a pacifist windbag, or someone who thoughtlessly parroted Jewish nonsense—would allow poetical ethical notions to interfere with the need to eliminate harmful human beings for the good of society? By the way, I could slaughter a hundred thousand chickens to prevent the spread of bird flu and then go home and enjoy a normal life with my family—and so could someone who rid the earth of some noxious and harmful subhumans.

Also, we breed better forms of cattle or horses, and there is nothing wrong with that. Himmler was being perfectly logical and reasonable in trying to breed better and more advanced types of humans—if, that is, people are essentially no more than animals as Darwinists claim. We use the hair and skin of dead animals—why not do the same with people? To waste the skin and other useful by-products of dead people makes no sense at all—if people are the same as animals.

One of the weirdest and most difficult aspects of Nazi ideology and actions to comprehend is that they followed logically from certain presuppositions. The Nazis had a clear, consistent, and coherent world-view and acted accordingly. Much of their world view—though not all of it of course—can be found in the writings of Haeckel, and of many other less prominent German social Darwinists who shared his views.

Returning to our comparison, both Haeckel and Hitler had a sense of hierarchy. Some human animals were higher than, superior to, and worth more than others. This follows logically from an evolutionary scenario—and which group of people, according to secular standards, was the most highly developed in the world? Who had the most advanced technology, and were able to dominate other groups most easily? The Europeans. And who dominated among the Europeans? The Spaniards, the Greeks, the French, the Italians had had their day. The Eastern Europeans were dismissed as backward. It was the northern Europeans, the Germanic peoples, who occupied by right the highest place on the evolutionary tree—all others were beneath them.

Haeckel and Hitler also had an authoritarian and hierarchical view of government. Haeckel never advocated National Socialism—that was (in its final form) inconceivable given the stability of the imperial government. Nevertheless, a shared philosophical hostility to democracy as unhealthy and unnatural, with a strong emphasis on the right of the stronger to dominate, is significant.

Also significant is the very similar concept of God shared by the two men. This was not the God the Judaeo-Christian tradition. It was a god that emerged out of a modern and uniquely German philosophical tradition, a god that was merely the projection of man-made ideas onto the cosmos as a whole. Hitler was not a systematic thinker outside of the limited confines of his ideology, though within those confines he was rigorously logical. Basically his concept of god was a peculiar hybrid: a combination of a Folkish spirit that advanced the human race through the instrumentality of conflict with the German people as its chosen group, and a scientific naturalist view of God as working through, and being understood by, scientific and natural law.

"God" for Haeckel and for Hitler, and for many others of that day, was thus merely an abstract and impersonal concept. It could be described with language borrowed from religion—"Almighty," "Supreme Being," "the Creator," "Providence"—but it was a god invented by human reason and working within the confines of human reason. This is clearly illustrated by Martin Bormann's concept of God.

It is worth noting how perfectly Bormann's concepts match Haeckel's. Some of those concepts are (quoting a Nuremberg document written by Bormann):

> National Socialism and Christianity are irreconcilable . . .
> National Socialism is based on scientific foundations . . .
> National Socialism on the other hand must always, if it is to

fulfill its job in the future, be organized according to the latest knowledge of scientific research . . .

. . . the concepts of Christianity, which in their essential points have been taken over from Jewry.

When we National Socialists speak of a belief in God, we do not understand by God, like naïve Christians and their spiritual opportunists, a human-type being, who sits around somewhere in space . . . The force of natural law, with which all these innumerable planets move in the universe, we call the Almighty or God.

. . . we National Socialists impose on ourselves the demand to live naturally as much as possible, i.e., biologically. The more accurately we recognize and observe the laws of nature and of life, the more we adhere to them, so much the more do we conform to the will of the Almighty.[96]

Since Bormann did not attain his position of influence by creative and independent thought, we can assume he wrote nothing here that Hitler would have taken exeception to. Hitler's actions as well as his many private comments are in perfect harmony with these ideas of Bormann's—and that Hitler valued science is insufficiently appreciated. Some quotes from his *Table Talk* could easily have been made by such apostles of the New Atheism and enemies of Christianity as Sam Harris, Christopher Hitchens, or Richard Dawkins. For example, he reportedly stated that people were attracted to religion by fear of the unknown or by intellectual simplicity, but the time would come "when science can answer all the questions."[97]

This source has many comments to that effect. Religion would "crumble" before the "advances of science"; science cannot err too much because it is non-dogmatic and self-correcting. Hitler is quoted as saying, "science postulates the search for, and not the certain knowledge of, the truth." Religious dogma was in conflict with research, and would collapse "under the battering-ram of science."[98]

One curious note in the *Table Talk* is a short passage praising the Ten Commandments. This can be explained if we interpret those commandments in the light of Hitler's definition of "God." If "God" is the sum total of nature and all of its laws, animated by a mysterious cosmic Will, then it is wise to have no other God—including the Christian one. If one discounts the subhumans and the weak who deserve to perish, then it is right that the members of the master race should not lie to, steal from, kill or defame each other.

It is unfortunate that so many people write about Lenin, Stalin, Mao, and Hitler with no real knowledge of or interest in the religious dimension. The beliefs that there was no God, no divine law, no afterlife, that we could build the ideal society here on earth and that people were only animals—these were essential to the crimes of the atheists. The concept of God as an impersonal force (German philosophy) working to effect the advancement of the human race through evolutionary conflict, as well as the beliefs that the individual was insignificant and people were only animals (philosophy plus science) were essential to the crimes of Hitler.

When Hitler in a speech of 1944 referred to "the Almighty" and stated that the "laws of his rule" were found in animals struggling to survive in nature; when he wrote in *Mein Kampf* that the Aryan race was "the work of the Lord"; when he stated that his wars, conquests, and massacres were "in accordance with the will of the Almighty Creator,"[99] he was speaking as a theistic evolutionist. Using religious language to express secular ideas was common practice in Germany from Kant to Haeckel. In this way a concept of "natural law" can be called "divine," even though in many ways similar and even identical to atheistical concepts of "natural law." Liberal Protestant pastors easily reconciled their secularized religion with Darwinism as well.

To conclude this overview of similarities between Haeckel and Hitler, it is worth looking at Gasman's analysis of *Hitler's Table Talk*, and also of his *Secret Book* (a continuation of *Mein Kampf* that Hitler never published). My essay has not in any way relied on the *Table Talk* to prove Hitler's hostility to Christianity, but the book is accepted as authentic by reputable historians. In this context, it merely serves to confirm what is already evident—that Haeckel and Hitler had a lot in common.

Remembering that the question of a direct influence of Haeckel on Hitler is not presently the issue, let us consider some of the points in *Hitler's Table Talk* (and to a lesser extent the *Secret Book*) that Gasman draws attention to:

~ that life consisted primarily of struggle, in which the will of the stronger was the final arbiter
~ that life should be lived consistently with this natural law of struggle, in obedience to the laws of nature
~ that these laws were inescapable and unavoidable
~ that the correct world view should be based on an objective and scientific study of nature
~ that people lowest on the evolutionary scale were closer to animals than to the most advanced human types
~ that Christianity had introduced false and unnatural values

There were other ideas of Hitler's identical to Haeckel's and identified in Gasman's study: admiration for the Spartan practice of killing unhealthy infants; assertions that Christ was not Jewish but Aryan; the belief that art should be realistic and follow nature (this aversion to excessive creative independence in art was shared by Stalin and by Mao); that true religious feeling was found in the contemplation of nature.

Gasman goes so far as to make the very plausible assertion that "rightly considered, a number of Hitler's conversations and the content of some of his writings emerge as an extended paraphrase and at times even plagiarism of Haeckel's *Natürliche Schöpfungsgeschichte* and the *Welträtsel*." He points to specific examples of similarities and draws the conclusion that "Hitler's views on history, politics, religion, Christianity, nature, eugenics, science, art, and evolution, however eclectic, and despite the plurality of their sources, coincide for the most part with those of Haeckel and are more than occasionally expressed in very much the same language."[100] Weikart also writes that "some of Hitler's statements about evolution could easily have been cribbed from Haeckel."[101]

Did Haeckel influence Hitler?

We can see many obvious similarities and parallels—but how much did Haeckel actually influence Hitler? Gasman is careful to state that his assertion of Haeckel's influence on Hitler is not meant

> . . . to deny the influence on Hitler of many other writers and Volkish intellectuals, for it is apparent, that Hitler's views were far too heterogeneous a compilation to be limited to a single source. Yet, the evidence does seem to show parallels and affinities between Haeckel and Hitler that so far have not been satisfactorily explored and determined.[102]

He points out that Haeckel's ideas "had been widely disseminated in Germany since the 1860's and had already become the property of countless Volkists."[103] Nevertheless, he strongly argues for a Haeckel-Hitler connection. This theory has been objected to by Richard Weikart, who correctly makes the point just mentioned, that many people had similar ideas. Weikart draws attention (with much scholarly detail) to other German thinkers who sought to base their understanding of life on the theory of evolution, and came to conclusions similar to or identical to Haeckel's. That this goes far beyond just one individual is a crucial point.

For the purpose of this study, it is sufficient to point out that such ideas have a secular origin. I can assert a profound secular influence on the development of Hitler's thought. Whether Hitler read Haeckel or only someone like him is beside the point. Nevertheless, it is interesting to speculate: if as a young man Hitler had gotten hold of Haeckel's *Riddle of the Universe*, read it, and believed it, this would have given a "scientific" basis to similar ideas picked up from Wagner and elsewhere.

That the young Hitler was an avid reader is amply attested to. That he should have been interested in a best-selling book is more plausible than not. That the entire National Socialist misosophy easily harmonizes with Haeckel's ideas is clear. That Haeckel's ideas as expressed in that book could easily be joined to an enthusiasm for Aryan supremacy and German conquest, and in no way contradicted any of Hitler's later ideas, make it plausible (though of course not proven) that Hitler's boast of having early arrived at a world view of life as evolutionary struggle that never needed modification was, in addition to his passion for Wagner, partly based on his reading of Haeckel's *Riddle of the Universe*. These would provide an intellectual basis for the popular anti-Semitic literature Hitler must have read as well (perhaps he considered it light reading).

It is thoroughly plausible that Hitler as a teenager believed that people were essentially animals; that the white Aryan race was superior; that the meaning of life was pitiless struggle; that sterilization and killing of the unfit should be used to strengthen the race. Later ideas of politics, foreign policy, anti-Semitism, or whatever would all fit easily into the greater concept of life as struggle. Some may consider this speculative—but it is not speculative that Hitler's thought contains many significant aspects of both the Folkish movement and the extreme form of social Darwinism of which Haeckel was only the most well-known representative out of many. It is also not speculative that Haeckel clearly personifies the union of those two trends. His supposedly objective science was in fact influenced by powerful philosophical, cultural, and national biases—as are the supposedly objective views of many opponents of Christianity today.

Hitler was not a man who advertised his intellectual influences. He plainly wrote of the political and tactical lessons he drew from von Schonerer and Luger in his Vienna days, and praised Wagner in a general way, but never explained his philosophy by saying "I was influenced by so-and-so," or "I got a lot of ideas from such-and-such." He referred to his having read widely in his youth, but what did he read?

In addition to Wagner's powerful influence, there are elements of Kant, Hegel, Fichte, Schopenhauer, Gobineau, Chamberlain, and Haeckel in Hitler's comments and writing. Hitler could have picked up ideas from anywhere, but he was not such a stupid idiot as many people seem to think, and could also have gotten ideas directly from original sources (or from abbreviated compilations of original sources). Yet, he did not explain who influenced him, or how, or when.

This can be attributed to the fact that Hitler was deeply self-conscious of his image as the Fuhrer, the Man of Destiny. Hitler imagined that he was the mouthpiece and the acting agent for a vast cosmic Will. As such, it would have detracted from his status and brought him down to the level of an ordinary person if he had credited particular individuals with having influenced his world view. He deliberately fostered an air of mysterious greatness, separating himself from other mere mortals. His reticence about influences was part of this.

Gasman's contribution here is I think a helpful one, yet he only mentions the importance of the Folkish influence, and could have done more to clarify how Haeckel added a pseudoscientific dimension to pre-existing trends. Wagner engaged Hitler's enthusiasm and admiration in a way that Haeckel never did, and Gasman's list of commonalities between Hitler and Haeckel, while important and illuminating, is less striking when we consider that much the same could be said of Wagner and Hitler as well. Haeckel's influence on German *Kultur* was great, and his evangelism for his version of Darwinism made racism, authoritarianism, and militarism seem much more legitimate, but those trends were already in place before Haeckel came along. Haeckel's (and Darwin's) views found such ready acceptance as the soil had been prepared well in advance. Nevertheless, Haeckel is a perfect symbol of the convergence of important intellectual currents—all of them secular, all of them contrary to the Bible, and many of them similar to what we are hearing in our own day.

Haeckel and Darwin

A fundamental question remains—did these extreme views of Haeckel's represent a perversion of Darwinism, as Gasman claims, or did Haeckel merely follow some of Darwin's principles more consistently and more logically than Darwin and his English and American supporters did? This is related to another significant question: why did social Darwinism develop in a much more extreme fashion in Germany than it did in other countries?

The Christian influence in England and America was stronger than it was in Germany. A book examining the reasons for this might well be written. Perhaps it was due to the greater dependence of the German churches on the state. This robbed the churches of their spiritual authority and integrity. Also, as stable and well-defined entities in the end of the 19th century, England and America were less wracked by the struggles of unification and industrialization that put a greater strain on German society.

Whatever the case, German Darwinists pursued the implications of their theory much more rigorously and much farther than their counterparts in other countries. To what extent did they depart from Darwinism in doing so? In rejecting traditional values derived from religion and at least attempting to establish a new ethic based solely on their 19th-century views of science, they were being logical and consistent. If human life emerged in a certain way, then our ethic should reflect that underlying reality—and ethics derived from antiquated falsehoods need to be revalued.

Attempts to apply religious values, or retain some special status for humans merely because they are the most highly developed of animals, are inconsistent. Attempts to manufacture ethical systems that do not reflect the scientific realities of human origins always fall flat. They are inherently contradictory, and do not provide anything solid for people to rest on in times of real trial.

If life is essentially survival in an impersonal, amoral struggle; if staying alive is what it is all about; then keeping one's mouth shut and looking out for number one is the rational and scientific thing to do. Altruism, self-sacrifice as a virtue that emerged out of Darwinian conflict, is a theory only that does not touch the human heart. It is a cobweb that breaks under any real pressure.

If Darwinism is true, there is no higher ethical law beyond that of survival. Attempts to invent one are not only false at bottom, weak, and unconvincing. They also betray the innate human inability of Darwinists to live consistently with what they say they believe. Their minds assert one thing, but their deeper human feelings say something that is more powerful.

Those who so far stifle human feeling as to attempt to really live according to a Darwinist ethic sink by degrees into a dark night of the soul. The strong survive, the weak die—this is their ethic, their law, and their philosophy. When they put it into practice, it becomes a criminal philosophy—one totally at odds with the vastly more enlightened and humane concept of people as presented in the Judaeo-Christian tradition.

Some have denied the existence of any such tradition. They want to claim there is no tradition derived (in the Western context) from Christianity and from Judaism involving one God, creator and governor of the world; revealed laws from God, showing us what we should and should not do; God's personal concern for our behavior as individuals; an afterlife, with heaven for the righteous and hell for the wicked; and the belief that we should so live as to please God. If anyone wants to deny that these principles have had a formative influence on Western civilization, or that they come from Christianity and Judaism, let them go their way. They are incapable of facing plain and simple facts of cultural history.

The secular, modern repudiation of this lofty and noble tradition derived from religion has had many results. In one country it led to the hideous barbarism of the Third Reich. It has also led to the hideous barbarism of the abortion Holocaust. Darwinism inevitably devalues life. The divine spark of the soul is lost, and man is reduced to mere matter. This inescapable truth of Darwinism can be interpreted and acted on in different ways. Some Darwinists still have too much humanity to really live by the principles they profess, and only use Darwinism as a metaphysical escape mechanism so they can enjoy themselves without having to come to grip with invisible spiritual realities they fear to confront. Those who, however, make a real effort to live consistently with the real essence of Darwinism, inevitably lose their better human instincts. They sink deeper into the cold, pitiless, indifferent and cruel selfishness of those who know no higher law than their own survival.

It is true, many Christians don't live by their beliefs either. If they did, the world would be a better place. If all of the world followed the teachings of Christ there would be no wars, no jails, no armies, no police, and no poverty. There would be no crime, no prostitution, no alcoholism or drug abuse, no mental illness, and no suicide. There would be no abortion, no homosexuality, no pornography. Since people would have inner peace they would be content with simpler lives, and there would be less waste of resources and destruction of the environment due to the manufacturing of innumerable trifles and superfluities.

If, however, everyone lived according to the principles of Darwinism, the world would become a hellish nightmare. Ruthless egotists would trample on the weak and consider it their moral and scientific right to do so. The death of weaker human beings through disease, famine, or strife would be considered as ordinary and natural, even beneficial and essential to progress.

There would be swift social breakdown as well. People who followed their own instincts without regard to God's law (as Darwin recommended) would become involved in all sorts of deviant social behavior. Crime and immorality would abound, and the family would disintegrate. In short, there would be much of what we see today, only more so.

A prominent Darwinist of our own day boasted that Darwinism was an acid, a universal solvent. This is true. It is a powerful acid that burns away the best and finest impulses of the human soul, and damages what makes us most uniquely human. It is no coincidence that Wilhelmine Germany's leading advocate of Darwinism was so close to Hitler spiritually, and did so much to prepare the way for horrors unimaginable in his day.

From an orthodox Darwinian point of view, there is no other reason for condemning Hitler other than that he failed. The Germans proved to be weaker in the struggle for survival, and the millions who perished were nothing more than the inevitable casualties of the cold, amoral struggle that—in the nightmarish Darwinian scenario of life—is the sole basis for our existence. Some Darwinists will disagree—but they do so on the basis of values totally inconsistent with what they say they believe is true.

One of the truly extraordinary things about Hitler was not merely his ideas— other people had them as well. Hitler's evil gift was the ability to put those ideas into practice. What others only said—often not realizing the implications of their ideas—Hitler did. No doubt his experiences in the Great War helped him to view the perishing of millions as nothing of any consequence.

The collapse of the old order in WWI and the turbulence of the Weimar era cleared the way for the emergence of new ideas. The results more than amply confirmed a remarkable prophecy made by Adam Sedgwick, a British academic who wrote to Darwin in 1859. He warned Darwin that his denial of the moral aspects of nature had the potential to brutalize humanity and "sink the human race into a lower grade of degradation than any into which it has fallen since its written records tell us of its history."[104]

Darwin postulated the theory that there is no higher moral or ethical law, that mankind evolved as the result of a purposeless and amoral struggle for survival. Is he to be completely exempt from blame if people less than a century later used this concept in ways he himself did not imagine? I think Gasman protects Darwin too much.

Hitler thought that by exterminating the weak he was acting in accordance with the laws of nature. He also thought that by eliminating false values and returning to a state of nature he would purify, strengthen, and advance the human race. He imagined his ideas were objective and based on science—a common error on the part of those who imagine man is his own master.

It is commonly stated that the discovery of the earth's rotation around the sun was deeply humbling, in that it removed man from his imaginary place at the center of the universe. Supposedly we are wiser now, since we know that our planet is no longer at the center. Like many of the arguments of the secularists, it is totally false. In fact, it is the very opposite of the truth.

Those who believed that the earth was at the physical center of the cosmos but far beneath higher invisible powers, above all under God, were far more humble and modest in their approach to life than are those who know that earth is not at the center, but wrongly believe there is no higher power to which they are subject. Those who wrongly placed earth at the center but rightly knew they were subject to higher spiritual laws were infinitely less conceited than are those who rightly know the earth is not at the center, but wrongly imagine they are their own masters, accountable to no one.

The Bible has many statements about the weakness, frailty, and insignificance of man. These are far more humane and moving than boring statistics about the vastness of space made by those who foolishly imagine they have the ability to control their own destinies. It was modern secularists (on the right and on the left) who in their ignorance of higher unchanging laws imagined that they could reshape society according to their theories. In attempting to fulfill their dreams they brought about suffering of a magnitude absolutely inconceivable before the modern age.

One of the most striking points of Weikart's book is that Hitler was more than just a criminal madman. He had an ideal, an ethic, and sought to improve the human race both racially and culturally by eliminating unclean elements. He had a utopian vision of the world in which the strong were free to dominate, to indulge their will-to-power to the maximum extent. Free from the artificial restraints of false cultural values, they would lead the elite of the human race to great heights of mastery and power, while lesser humans would either rightfully perish, or exist only to serve their betters.

In the words of a different historian, Georges van Vrekham, "If one has not read the book, one should discard once and for all the idea that *Mein Kampf* is a kind of trivial, wacko oddity, written by an illiterate maniac." After referring to the amorality, lies, sophistry, and contempt for human values, as well as the bad odor of the book, van Vrekham goes on to say, ". . . behind all that there is a vision by which Adolf Hitler had been and would continue to be driven, which was unprecedented and revolutionary, and which aimed at a new world and a new man."[105] This is illustrated by a quote from Hitler, "Anyone who interprets National Socialism merely as a political movement knows almost nothing about it . . . It is more than a religion; it is the determination to create a new man." This was one of Hitler's consistently held ideas. As he said in a speech of 1932, "It is my firm belief that in the National Socialist Youth Movement a new type is growing up."[106]

Weikart also calls our attention to a key point that is often missed: that Hitler supported some traditional values, but for non-traditional reasons. He opposed alcohol, pornography, and abortion not because of his religious values, but because he thought they would weaken the master race in its drive for domination. Weikart's documentation of the extent to which these and other related ideas had permeated an influential minority within the German intelligentsia in the half-century and more prior to 1933 is a valuable contribution to western intellectual history.

Darwin wrote in *The Origin of Species* that "from the war of nature, from famine and death, the most exalted object which we are capable of conceiving, namely, the production of the higher animals, directly follows."[107] Why should this not apply to people? From the death of the weaker, higher forms emerge. Death and the means of death (famine, illness, conflict) have been officially declared to be good, salutary, natural, and helpful to progress, essential to progress. The perishing of the weak in the death camps was merely what life was all about—and speeding up the process with the help of Zyklon B could accelerate the advancement of the human race.

This statement of Darwin's sheds more light on Naziism than many other statements, and reveals not merely the ugliness and brutality inherent in Darwinism, but also the paltriness of its vision for humanity – and this is not a question of one quote only. In the conclusion to *The Descent of Man*, Darwin also wrote:

> Man, like every other animal, has no doubt advanced to his present high condition through a struggle for existence consequent on his rapid multiplication; and if he is to advance still higher, it is to be feared that he must remain subject to a severe struggle. Otherwise he would sink into indolence, and the more gifted men would not be more successful in the battle of life than the less gifted.[108]

Hitler wrote in *Mein Kampf*, "Those who want to live, let them fight, and those who do not want to fight in this world of eternal struggle do not deserve to live. Even if this were hard—that is how it is!" [vol. I chapt. 11]. If Darwinism is true, Hitler was right—this must be the way life is. For those of us however who know that Darwinism is not true, that the human spirit comes from God and not from the lower animals and the primordial slime, it is easy to see the profoundly secular character of Hitler's words and works.

Hitler's nightmare vision of an improved humanity was, to a significant extent, modern, forward looking, and based on approved and up-to-date philosophies. If we are only animals engaged in a merciless struggle for survival, what is to prevent anyone from living out that "philosophy" to the fullest? The Nazis did nothing more than logically follow false ideas to the farthest limits. In the words of the Roman Stoic philosopher Seneca, "Natural desires are limited; those which spring from false opinions have nowhere to stop, for falsity has no point of termination."[109]

Discretion shall preserve thee, understanding shall keep thee:
To deliver thee from the way of the evil man, from the man that speaketh
forward things;
  Who leave the paths of uprightness, to walk in the ways of darkness;
  Who rejoice to do evil, and delight in the frowardness of the wicked.
(Proverbs)

---

[1] George L. Mosse, *The Crisis of German Ideology: Intellectual Origins of the Third Reich* (New York 1971), p. 103.

[2] Adolf Hitler, *Hitler's Second Book: The Unpublished Sequel to Mein Kampf*, trans. Krista Smith (New York 2006), pp. 7-9.

[3] Richard Weikart, *Hitler's Ethic: The Nazi Pursuit of Evolutionary Progress* (New York 2009), p. 36.

[4] Paul Lawrence Rose, *Wagner: Race and Revolution* (New Haven 1992), p. 80.

[5] Cited in Richard Weikart, *From Darwin to Hitler: Evolutionary Ethics, Eugenics, and Racism in Germany* (New York 2004), p. 186.

[6] Ibid., p. 4.

[7] Ibid., p. 21.

[8] Ibid., p. 124.

[9] "Excerpts from *Hitler's Table Talk*"(citing the edition by Weidenfeld and Nicolson, London 1953), Kevin's Articles on Religion; http://davnet.org/kevin/articles/table.html; accessed June 2008.

[10] Weikart, *Hitler's Ethic*; citing Hitler's *Tischgespräche im Füherhauptquartier*, ed. Henry Picker (Frankfurt: Ullstein, 1989).

[11] Richard Evans, *The Coming of the Third Reich* (New York 2005), pp. 152-154.

[12] Daniel Gasman, *The Scientific Origins of National Socialism* (London 2004), p. xxxvii.

[13] Ibid., p. xxxviii.

[14] Ibid., p. xii.

[15] Ibid., pp. xiii, xlvi.

[16] Ernst Haeckel, *The Riddle of the Universe at the Close of the Nineteenth Century*, trans. Joseph McCabe (London 1900), p. 295.

[17] Ibid., p. 317.

[18] Cited in Gasman, p. 56.

[19] Haeckel, pp. 315, 338

[20] Ibid., pp. 319-320.

[21] Gasman, p. 62.

[22] Cited in Gasman, p. 59.

[23] Haeckel, p. 2.

[24] Ibid., pp. xvi, xi.

[25] Ibid., pp. 4-5.

[26] Ibid., p. 5.

[27] Ibid., p. 238.

[28] Gasman, p. 8.

[29] Haeckel, p. 276, 275.

[30] Ibid., pp. 276, 278.

[31] Ibid., p. 277.

[32] Ibid., p. 109.

[33] Ibid., pp. 193, 200.

[34] Ibid., p. 133.

[35] Gasman, p. 112.

[36] Haeckel, p. 249.

[37] Gasman p. 96 (quoting Haeckel's *History of Creation*).

[38] Gasman, p. 95.

[39] Haeckel, p. 128.

[40] Robert Richards, "Ernst Haeckel's Alleged Anti-Semitism and Contributions to Nazi Biology"; http://home.uchicago.edu/~rjr6/articles/Haeckel--antiSemitism.pdf; accessed June 2008.

[41] Laurence Rees, *Auschwitz: The Nazis and the Final Solution* (London 2005), p. 23. Elsewhere (p. 33) Reese refers to the "quasi-Darwinian attitude" of life as struggle.

[42] Haeckel, p. 127.

[43] Ibid., p. 206.

[44] Peter Singer, *Practical Ethics* (Cambridge 2009), p. 169.

[45] Weikart, *Darwin to Hitler*, p. 108.

[46] Gasman, p. 39.

[47] Ibid., p. 40.

[48] Ibid.

[49] Richards, pp. 5-9.

[50] Cited in Gasman, p. 83. The full title of the work is *Eternity. World War Thoughts on Life and Death, Religion, and the Theory of Evolution.*

[51] Keith Ward, *Pascal's Fire: Scientific Faith and Religious Understanding* (Oxford 2006), p. 181.

[52] Adolf Hitler, *Hitler Speeches and Quotes* (London 2008), p. 39.

[53] Cited in Gasman, p. 136.

[54] Gasman, p. 128.

[55] Weikart, *Darwin to Hitler*, p. 164.

[56] Gasman, p. 24. One history of the Third Reich mentions that many Protestant pastors supported the war effort without mentioning that many Darwinists did so as well. Is that objective history?

[57] Gasman, p. 131, quoting *Eternity*.

[58] Ibid., (also quoting *Eternity*).

[59] Gasman, p. 132.

[60] Ibid., p. 134.

[61] Haeckel, p. 342.

[62] Gasman, p. 5.

[63] Weikart, *Darwin to Hitler*, p. 84. Kubizek's reference to Hitler's youthful flirtation with pacifism might refer to the evolutionary objection to modern war because it interfered with natural selection by indiscriminately slaughtering the fit and

the unfit. Hitler mentions this in his *Second Book*, stating that excessive and unnecessary wars eliminate the best racial stock of a nation (pp. 10-12). Hitler's emphasis on swift victories was thus not merely a matter of tactics, but was related to his racial misosophy.

[64] Haeckel, p. 346.

[65] Ibid., p. 358.

[66] Ibid., p. 358.

[67] Weikart, *Darwin to Hitler*, p. 146.

[68] Ibid., p. 147.

[69] Evans, p. 377.

[70] Weikart, *Darwin to Hitler*, p. 154.

[71] John Pollock, *A Foreign Devil in China* (Minneapolis 1988), p. 202.

[72] Singer, *Practical Ethics,* pp. 172-173. Singer agrees that the desire to protect the lives of infants is a "distinctively Christian attitude" (p. 172). He also believes that parents should be allowed to kill their children for up to a month after they have been born (p. 172). Many can easily see the ugliness and brutality of such cruel and inhuman misosophies.

[73] Jonah Goldberg, *Liberal Fascism: The Secret History of the American Left from Mussolini to the Politics of Meaning* (New York 2007), p. 248.

[74] Ibid., p. 445.

[75] Haeckel, p. 337.

[76] Gasman, p. 158, quoting "Antisemitism: An International Interview."

[77] Haeckel, p. 382.

[78] Richards, p. 9.

[79] Martin Gilbert, *The Holocaust: A History of the Jews of Europe During the Second World War* (New York 1985), p. 582.

[80] Richards, p. 11.

[81] Gasman, p. 65.

[82] Ibid.

[83] Ibid.

[84] Michael Behe, *The Edge of Evolution: The Search for the Limits of Darwinism* (New York / London 2007), p. 93.

[85] Haeckel, p. 381.

[86] Ibid., pp. 230, 233, 234.

[87] Ibid., pp. 287, 288.

[88] Gasman, p. 14.

[89] Cited by Gasman, p. 29.

[90] Evans, p. 424.

[91] Gasman, pp. xi-xii.

[92] Ibid., p. xxv.

[93] Ibid., p. 112.

[94] Rudolf Hoess, *Commandant of Auschwitz*, trans. Constantine Fitzgibbon (London 2000), p. 179.

[95] Os Guinness, *Unspeakable: Facing up to Evil in an Age of Genocide and Terror* (New York 2005), p. 131.

[96] J.S. Conway, *The Nazi Persecution of the Churches 1933-1945* (Vancouver 1968), pp. 383-384.

[97] "Excerpts from *Hitler's Table Talk*," see note 7 above.

[98] Ibid. In his book *A Mighty Fortress: A New History of the German People 110 B.C. to the 21st Century* (London 2004), Prof. Steven Ozment uses the *Table Talk* to document Hitler's belief in evolution and in the superiority of science over religion (p. 282). He also states that it was the decline of traditional values and the emergence of modern ideology that opened the door to Hitler (pp. 252, 276, 286).

[99] Weikart, *Hitler's Ethic*, pp. 39, 85.

[100] Gasman, pp. 159-160, 161.

[101] Weikart, *Darwin to Hitler*, p. 216.

[102] Gasman, p. 161.

[103] Ibid., p. 166.

[104] Cited in Weikart, *Darwin to Hitler*, p. 1.

[105] Georges van Vrekham, *Hitler and his God: The Background to the Hitler Phenomenon* (New Delhi 2006), p. 124.

[106] Joachim C. Fest, *Hitler,* trans. Richard and Clara Winston (New York 1974), p. 433 and Hitler, *Speeches*, p. 79.

[107] Weikart, *Darwin to Hitler*, p. 17.

[108] Charles Darwin, *The Descent of Man*; http://www.infidels.org/library/historical/charles_darwin/descent_of_man/chapter_21.html; accessed June 2008

[109] Lucius Annaeus Seneca, *Letters from a Stoic (Epistulae Morales ad Lucilium)*, trans. Robin Campbell (London 2004), p. 65.

Chapter 9. Nietzsche

The quintessentially modern man

There is, arguably, no writer who comes closer to the heart of modern and post-modern culture than Friedrich Nietzsche (1844-1900). In his emphasis on self—"Reverence for self; love of self; absolute freedom of self . . ." (Preface to *The Antichrist: Curse on Christianity*)[1]—and in his philosophy of total freedom based on denial of the Christian God and repudiation of traditional morality, Nietzsche genuinely was ahead of his time. He was the herald of a new age. Some seem to consider him a hero of spiritual freedom who has attained to nearly mythical status.

Nietzsche has been called the most influential thinker of our time, and the list of artists, poets, playwrights, and intellectuals who have been influenced by him is a long one. Heidegger, Camus, Jaspers, Foucault, Tillich, Buber, Freud, Rilke, Mann—many have been taken with (if not intoxicated by) Nietzsche's radical repudiation of traditional values. Even many who have never read his books share his ideas—ideas that seem commonplace today, but in his lifetime were daring and radical (though not always as unique to Nietzsche as is commonly assumed). Arguing not only that the conventional concept of God was dead, but also that the centuries-old traditional moral and cultural values derived from Christianity were false, Nietzsche called loudly and boldly (before he went completely insane) for a re-evaluation of all values and norms.

Nietzsche claimed in *The Antichrist* that many centuries of Christian belief were "simply a psychological self-delusion" (Section 39) and dismissed "whole millenniums" of Christianity as "lunacies" (38). Going further, he stated that in thousands of years only one man had spoken the truth—Nietzsche. As he put it, "there is one, and one only, who has said what has been needed for thousands of years—*Zarathustra*" (53). This is followed by a quote of himself.

Before looking at the strenuously contested question of Nietzsche's relationship to Hitler, more needs to be said about Nietzsche's proclamation of an entirely new system of values. One essential point is complete freedom for the self. Since there are no higher values, we invent our own virtue: "A virtue must be *our* invention; it must spring out of *our* personal need and defence. In every other case it is a source of danger" (11). The rightness of an action is determined solely by the pleasure it gives us: "An action prompted by the life-instinct proves that it is a *right* action by the amount of pleasure that goes with it" (11).

Nietzsche praised "the courage for the *forbidden*" (forbidden it will be recalled in 19th-century bourgeois culture) and called for "New ears for new music . . . A new conscience for truths that have hitherto remained unheard" (Preface). This had to do not merely with ethics—it extended to ways of thinking and reasoning. In Nietzsche's words, "*we ourselves*, we free spirits, are already a 'transvaluation of all values,' a *visualized* declaration of *war* and victory against all the old concepts of 'true' and 'not true' " (13).

It is easy to see the extent to which these ideas are prevalent in modern society. "If it feels good, do it" is a much simpler way of stating part of Nietzsche's ideas quoted above. We invent our own truths—something is true for us, but not necessarily for others (a reasonable inference from the proposition that there is no higher enduring truth). Old-fashioned morals and ways of thinking based on false and outdated religious beliefs need to be overturned and replaced by an entirely new system of values. This attitude explains why today new moral and social practices are automatically considered to be good, in and of themselves, if only they challenge long-standing conventions.

It would be foolish to blame the current popularity and increasing dominance of these ideas on Nietzsche, as if he were alone or even primarily to blame. There are many reasons behind the decline of old ways of thinking and the attempts to replace outdated values with new ones—but Nietzsche was one of the first to express these ideas, and no one articulated them more forcefully, with greater clarity, consistency, and insight than he did. The ideas that he did so much to popularize are now deeply embedded in Western society and accepted as the norm by many.

The Nazi philosopher?

What does all of this have to do with Hitler? As is the case with Darwinism, there are many who agree with Nietzsche's ideas as expressed above, yet are very far from being Nazis, and in fact sincerely repudiate Hitler with abhorrence. Moreover, as is also the case with Darwinism, it seems impossible that anyone whose ideas are at bottom true and good could have had anything to do with Hitler, whose ideas were false and bad. Thus followers of Nietzsche will from the outset refuse to consider any possibility of a connection, and consider attempts to link him to Hitler misguided, if not ridiculous—yet, defenders of Nietzsche notwithstanding, there are plenty of people who definitely link Nietzsche to Hitler. Their reasons are not difficult to understand.

For one thing, Nietzsche advocated the extermination of the weak and the unfit. He wrote, "The weak and the botched shall perish: first principle of *our* charity. And one should help them to it" (2). Kaufmann's translation reads "The weak and the failures shall perish: first principle of *our* love of man. And they shall be given every possible assistance."[2] It is not hard to see why Nietzsche's followers do not like to call attention to this passage.

In *Ecce Homo*, Nietzsche called for "the higher breeding of humanity, including the unsparing destruction of all degenerates and parasites."[3] He despised the virtues of kindness, pity, and mercy as weak and degenerate, and glorified cold and pitiless cruelty as a virtue (this will be elaborated on). He also (confining ourselves now to *The Antichrist*) described the "more valuable type" of man as "most feared," the opposite of "the domestic animal, the herd animal, the sick brute-man--the Christian . . ." (3) [for "brute-man" Kaufmann translates "human animal"]. Was not Hitler not only dreaded, but also the exact opposite of the ideal presented in the Sermon on the Mount?

Moreover, Nietzsche glorified power and war:

> What is good?--Whatever augments the feeling of power, the will to power, power itself, in man.
> What is evil?--Whatever springs from weakness.
> What is happiness?--The feeling that power *increases*--that resistance is overcome.

Not contentment, but more power; not peace at any price, but war; *not* virtue, but efficiency (2)

If we are to take this literally—and why should we not?—it means that Hitler and Stalin were the happiest of men. That this should be taken literally is supported by Nietzsche's contempt for and hatred of democracy and other modern liberal values—another point that will be elaborated on in this study. Nietzsche felt the elite (like himself) should rule, and praised the Hindu caste system: "*The order of castes*, the highest, the dominating law, is merely the ratification of an *order of nature*, of a natural law of the first rank, over which no arbitrary fiat, no 'modern idea,' can exert any influence." (57).

These are just a few of the quotes that can be pulled from Nietzsche's books— and the Nazis did not neglect them. They produced many statements by Nietzsche that, taken at face value, were in perfect agreement with their "philosophy." Hitler himself had admiration for Nietzsche. According to Shirer, he "often visited the Nietzsche museum in Weimar and publicized his veneration for the philosopher by posing for photographs of himself staring in rapture at the bust of the great man."[4] This was no small statement by the image-conscious Fuhrer.

Needless to say, those who admire Nietzsche are not lacking in responses. They argue that Nietzsche was quoted out of context and further point out that Nietzsche's unfinished works were altered by his sister after his collapse into insanity or after his death. They also stress significant differences between Hitler and Nietzsche: Hitler was a theist who strongly condemned atheism and Nietzsche was an atheist; Nietzsche was not anti-Semitic, condemned anti-Semites, said good things about Jews, and even praised the Old Testament; Nietzsche made many severe criticisms of the Germans, whom he disliked; he also disliked mass movements such as socialism.

Those who do not believe in Nietzsche's ideas, and who see him as an evil man with a disgusting philosophy, afflicted with mental and emotional problems long before his final collapse, have their responses to these responses. They claim Nietzsche was not, overall, taken out of context—he meant what he said and said what he meant. Could someone so distort John Stuart Mill's writings as to make him seem like a predecessor of Hitler? How many sisters would it take to make Kierkegaard or Dostoevsky sound like progenitors of Hitler? If (?) the Nazis did take Nietzsche out of context, he certainly gave them a lot to play with.

Advocates of a Hitler-Nietzsche connection also point to books that are full of evil ideas identical to Naziism, and that were published or prepared for publication by Nietzsche himself prior to his collapse. This simple fact makes the argument about his sister's influence totally irrelevant, and possibly nothing more than a clever evasive tactic. It may even, in some cases, be a dishonest tactic, since serious disciples of Nietzsche know which books were finished by Nietzsche before the final descent into the insanity that he had been moving toward for years.

Opponents of Nietzsche also assert that supposed differences between Hitler and Nietzsche are not significant. True, Nietzsche was an outspoken atheist while Hitler (most would agree) was some kind of a theist—but Nietzsche's atheism is almost always misunderstood. He objected to some kinds of theism, but not to all kinds. His famous statement about the death of God referred to the death of the Christian God. Nietzsche did make positive comments about other kinds of belief in God. For example, he spoke favorably of Islam: "If Islam despises Christianity, it has a thousandfold right to do so: Islam at least assumes that it is dealing with *men*. . . ." (59). The Moslems were conquering warriors and hence good in Nietzsche's eyes—not at all like the democratic, pacifist, sissy Christians.

He also spoke favorably of the original Jewish concept of God that preceded later priestly legal corruptions. He said, as we shall see shortly, that the original Jewish concept of God, while only the product of human consciousness, was the product of a healthy consciousness. After all, a concept of God that allowed for wars, conquests, and massacres couldn't be all bad. Nietzsche was by no means automatically averse to any and every concept of "god." He not only praised the Hindu Laws of Manu, saying they were far superior to Christianity. He even saw some positive aspects in Greek polytheism.

This helps to explain what would otherwise be a puzzling comment in *On the Genealogy of Morals*: ". . . even we knowledgeable people of today, we godless and anti-metaphysical people—we still take our fire from that blaze kindled by a thousand years of old belief, that faith in Christianity, which was also Plato's belief, that God is the truth, that the truth is divine . . ." (Third Essay, Section 24).[5] Nietzsche, while an atheist, could respect a concept of the divine that was not riddled with false values and allowed the unfettered pursuit of the will-to-power. He would not have objected violently to the concept of God as a philosophical abstraction in agreement with scientific law presented by Martin Bormann and discussed in the previous chapter.

Nietzsche also would not have had much trouble with Haeckel's concept of "the divine" as an abstract philosophical designation for the cosmos. He shared Haeckel's belief in the strange doctrine of "eternal recurrence," the belief in a vast and repetitive cosmic cycle (possibly he derived this from Haeckel). Whatever the case may be (and Nietzsche had other points in common with Haeckel), Nietzsche did not object because the Christians said "God is truth"—he objected because he thought they presented completely false and unnatural concepts in the guise of truth.

Apart from all of this, how much difference is there between a man who says "There is no God, so I can do whatever I want," and a man who says "There is some kind of a God, but it agrees completely with my own philosophy and understanding, so I can do whatever I want"? This explains the many profound similarities between the "theist" Hitler and the atheists Lenin, Stalin, and Mao. Someone whose concept of "god" gives him complete license to pursue his own will to power without let or hindrance is theoretically a theist, but practically an atheist. Hitler's concept of "god" endorsed and encouraged him in his pursuit of power. Jim Walker's argument that Hitler and Nietzsche could not possibly have had anything to do with each other because one was an atheist and the other was a "theist"[6] shows an extremely simplistic approach to Nietzsche's thought, and to Hitler's. Hitler, incidentally, condemned Marxist atheism, which is of course not necessarily synonymous with all atheism.

As to the issue of anti-Semitism, it is claimed that Nietzsche was not anti-Semitic, but his occasional positive statements about a few Jews he could accept need to be balanced with his vitriolic denunciations of the Jewish people as a whole. Nietzsche saw the Jews as "the most fateful people in the history of the world" (24)—Kaufmann translates "fateful" as "catastrophic"—and claimed it was the Jews, through Christianity, who had infected all of Western civilization with false values. Nietzsche's opinion of Jews as corrupters of civilization and master manipulators of decadence will be demonstrated in due course, and harmonized with positive statements about those certain types of Jews Nietzsche approved of. In this context, it will be seen that he condemned traditional, conventional, bourgeois anti-Semitism only because it was the wrong kind of anti-Semitism, itself infected with Jewish moral values. "Christian" anti-Semitism was especially offensive to Nietzsche, since Christianity came from Judaism and represented Jewish values. This will be demonstrated in detail.

Concerning Nietzsche's criticisms of the Germans, Hitler also frequently criticized the Germans. Hitler condemned the dull, complacent stupidity of the German bourgeoisie (as we have seen in the study of Wagner)—and what was the Nazi slogan "Germany Awake" if not a criticism of Germans as being asleep? Nietzsche fiercely rejected the idea that merely being a member of the German nation entitled one to feel superior, no matter how stupid he might be, no matter how wrong his beliefs—but Hitler too attacked, even imprisoned and murdered many Germans. He too recognized that ideas were more important than the mere fact of nationality—and he also had more of an international emphasis than is commonly recognized. Hitler was not concerned solely with Germany, but wanted to unite all Aryans, including the many Aryans in the Americas and throughout Europe, into a world super-state. Hitler was, to a remarkable extent, an internationalist and a globalist.[7]

Finally, Nietzsche disliked mass democratic left-wing socialism because of his elitism—but Hitler's authoritarian, elitist, right-wing socialism was unknown in Nietzsche's day (though as we have seen many of its necessary ideas were in circulation). A mass movement in which the common herd followed and obeyed their elite masters was by no means antithetical to Nietzsche's thought, and fits perfectly with the caste system Nietzsche praised in *The Antichrist*.

The question of Hitler's visits to the Nietzsche archive is disputed. It has been claimed by one of Nietzsche's defenders that Hitler visited the archive only once, and then because he was pressured by the director, Nietzsche's sister. She must have been a very powerful woman to bend the Fuhrer to her will. Different sources, however, state that Hitler visited the archive at different times—in 1932, in 1933, and in 1934. He attended Elisabeth Foerster-Nietzsche's funeral in 1935 as well. Michael Kalish (citing Ben Macintyre's, *Forgotten Fatherland: The Search for Elisabeth Nietzsche*) asserts that Hitler visited the Nietzsche archive seven times.[8]

Nietzsche's *Antichrist*

Interpretations of Nietzsche are radically diverse, and the points made above are not meant to be definitive; they are only intended to roughly draw the parameters of the discussion. To see these issues more clearly, more detailed analysis will be necessary. Nietzsche was not so obscure and ironic as to be totally incomprehensible. A careful consideration of some of his ideas from the vantage point of belief in Christianity can shed new light into much-debated questions—though the conclusions thus arrived at will be unfamiliar and disagreeable to many.

This essay will concentrate on one of Nietzsche's books—*The Antichrist*. The book was completed by Nietzsche and prepared for publication prior to his mental collapse. A slightly modified version was brought out in 1895, while he was still alive but hopelessly insane. It was toned down in a couple of places to make him seem less contemptuous of Christianity than he actually was, but the full version as Nietzsche wrote it has long since been available, thanks to modern scholarship. This is not too significant, as the few modifications in the 1895 edition did not in any way alter the main purpose of the book.

The Antichrist has a great deal of relevance for this essay, though I did wonder at one point if a book completed just before Nietzsche's mental breakdown might be dismissed by Nietzsche's admirers as not representative of his work. Since, however, parts of the book have been quoted with approval by Nietzsche fans (and even called "marvelous"); and since a reputable Nietzsche scholar, R.J. Hollingdale, has stated that ". . . the philosophical content [of *The Antichrist*] is at one with the preceding works; no new ideas are introduced, and nothing of Nietzsche's already formulated philosophy is contradicted,"[9] I feel justified in using it.

To those who object to my relying primarily on one book, this study by no means attempts to summarize or deal with all of Nietzsche's thought. It focuses on a specific aspect—one that is necessary to this study, as Nietzsche's ideas of Christianity and Judaism were to a remarkable extent identical to Hitler's. That directly contradicts many evaluations of Nietzsche by people who admire his philosophy and have been often less than accurate in their comments on *The Antichrist* (possibly out of fear for Nietzsche's reputation)—but let the reader judge for himself.

Though there are a number of lesser points that deserve comment and will be studied later, I will concentrate on three of Nietzsche's main ideas first: (a) that Christianity is false, harmful, and bad; (b) that Christianity had Jewish origins and is fundamentally and in essence Jewish; and (c) that the bloodsucking Jewish vermin devised this false philosophy so that they might weaken stronger peoples with a false slave morality and dominate them.

Having discussed these central aspects of Nietzsche's thought, we can then look at some other points, such as his ringing appeal for the extermination of the weak; his glorification of pitiless coldness and cruelty; and his contempt for traditional virtues like kindness, mercy, and pity. Some comments will also be made about another book of Nietzsche's, *On the Genealogy of Morals*. Then it will be possible to examine points of similarity or dissimilarity with Hitler.

The Antichrist—subtitled *A Curse on Christianity* in one manuscript version—has been consistently misrepresented by Nietzsche fans. Confident that few will ever bother to read the book, they claim Nietzsche had respect for Christ and that he loved the Old Testament, when in fact this book shows differently. They consistently cover up its venomous loathing of Jews and obscure the issue with evasions or misleading quotes. They are surely aware that a broader understanding of this book would not only seriously damage (if not destroy) Nietzsche's reputation. They also know that it would place Nietzsche directly at the center of intellectual and spiritual currents that converged to form the Third Reich.

The purpose here is not to refute *The Antichrist*, so many misconceptions, even falsehoods, about Christianity will be ignored or mentioned briefly. The main purpose is to shed light on the new and more virulent strain of anti-Semitism that emerged not out of Christianity, but out of the rejection of Christianity. That this same Nietzschean repudiation of traditional values led to many other Nazi-like sentiments apart from anti-Semitism will not be overlooked.

Nietzsche and Christianity

I am sure that the most ardent defender of Nietzsche will not accuse me of distorting his message or taking it out of context when I state that he despised Christianity. Since the entire book is devoted primarily to attacking Christianity, it is not difficult to find many examples.

A sneer at "Christian monotono-theism" (19) is a good starting point. The resurrection of Jesus is a lie (42), and "The vast lie of personal immortality destroys all reason" (43). Love is a delusion, "the state in which man sees things most decidedly as they are *not*. The force of illusion reaches its highest here . . ." (23), and the "religion of love" is based on fear of life's pain (30). The very idea of "conscience" is false—the inner sense of right and wrong is dismissed as nothing more than a "physiological disorder" (25). The world of the Gospels is a world of "scum," "nervous maladies," and "idiocy" (31).

Truth and religious faith are "two wholly distinct worlds of ideas, almost two diametrically *opposite* worlds" (23)—but it is enough for religious people if only they believe something is true, never mind about reality. Faith is hostile to reason, knowledge, and logical inquiry (23). Faith is "a form of sickness . . . the will to avoid knowing what is true" (52). Faith "is a need of weakness," the result "of self-effacement, of self-estrangement." Religious believers are "the antagonists of the truthful man . . ." (54). Faith "vetoes science" (47). It is not faith we need—"science makes men *godlike*--it is all up with priests and gods when man becomes scientific" (48). "Such a religion as Christianity, which does not touch reality at a single point and which goes to pieces the moment reality asserts its rights at any point, must be inevitably the deadly enemy of the 'wisdom of this world,' which is to say *science* . . ." (47). God, soul, sin, forgiveness, grace, repentance, the kingdom of God, the day of judgment, eternal life, the presence of God—this is all nothing but fiction, totally divorced from reality and based on hatred of reality (15).

Christianity is "indecent"; the concepts of the church are "sinister" and contrary to real life; "the priest himself is seen as he actually is--as the most dangerous form of parasite, as the venomous spider of life creation . . ." (38). Christianity is for failures—"Christianity has to thank precisely *this* miserable flattery of personal vanity for its *triumph*--it was thus that it lured all the botched, the dissatisfied, the fallen upon evil days, the whole refuse and off-scouring of humanity to its side"(43). "Christianity is a revolt of all creatures that creep on the ground against everything that is lofty: the gospel of the 'lowly' *lowers* . . ." (43).

Basic teachings of Christianity are nothing but lies, invented by priests to enslave people; "the concepts 'the other world,' 'the last judgment,' 'the immortality of the soul,' the 'soul' itself: they are all merely so many in instruments of torture, systems of cruelty, whereby the priest becomes master and remains master . . ."(38). Morality is nothing but a trick—"Morality is the best of all devices for leading mankind *by the nose!*" (44).

The claim of Christians to have "the truth" is "the most fatal sort of megalomania that the earth has ever seen: little abortions of bigots and liars began to claim exclusive rights in the concepts of 'God,' 'the truth,' 'the light,' 'the spirit,' 'love,' 'wisdom' and 'life'. . . " (44). I Corinthians 3:16 is dismissed with the statement "For that sort of thing one cannot have enough contempt . . ." (45). Nietzsche finds the New Testament so disgusting that he suggests people wear gloves while reading it (46). I Corinthians 7:2,9 is dismissed as "vile" (56). Nietzsche elaborates on his disgust for the New Testament, saying

> I have searched the New Testament in vain for a single sympathetic touch; nothing is there that is free, kindly, open-hearted or upright. In it humanity does not even make the first step upward--the instinct for *cleanliness* is lacking . . . Only evil instincts are there . . . (46)

Paradise, for Nietzsche, was boring (48). The purpose of Christianity is to make people sick; "Christianity finds sickness necessary . . . Christianity has the rancour of the sick at its very core--the instinct against the *healthy*, against *health* . . . Christianity remains to this day the greatest misfortune of humanity" (51).

Concepts of "guilt, punishment, and immortality" corrupt the soul (58). Christianity and alcohol are "the two *great* means of corruption" (60). For Nietzsche, in his fury, Christianity was "the greatest of all imaginable corruptions . . ."(62)—it had turned "every integrity into baseness of soul" (62). Christians were ". . . stealthy worms [Kaufmann says "vermin"] . . . cowardly, effeminate . . ."—it was they who caused the collapse of the Roman Empire (58).

When he contemplated the fall of Rome, Nietzsche reached a fever pitch of demented and impotent rage. That the Christian and the anarchist aim "only toward destruction . . . can easily be read in history"—that is, in the fall of Rome:

> The Christian and the anarchist: both are *decadents*; both are incapable of any act that is not disintegrating, poisonous, degenerating, *blood-sucking*; both have an instinct of *mortal hatred* of everything that stands up, and is great, and has durability, and promises life a future. . . . Christianity was the vampire of the *imperium Romanum*,-- overnight it destroyed the vast achievement of the Romans . . . (58).

Nietzsche was dazzled by the glory of Rome (no doubt he especially loved the slavery, the imperialistic conquests, and the gladiatorial games)—but Rome

> . . . was not strong enough to stand up against the *corruptest* of all forms of corruption--against Christians. . . . These stealthy worms, which under the cover of night, mist and duplicity, crept upon every individual, sucking him dry of all earnest interest in *real* things, of all instinct for *reality*--this cowardly, effeminate and sugar-coated gang gradually alienated all "souls," step by step, from that colossal edifice, turning against it all the meritorious, manly and noble natures that had found in the cause of Rome their own cause, their own serious purpose, their own *pride* (58).

Nietzsche had another (to him) devastating point to make against Christianity—it was to blame for democracy. "The poisonous doctrine, '*equal rights for all*,' has been propagated as a Christian principle . . . The aristocratic attitude of mind has been undermined by the lie of the equality of souls . . ." (43).

Christianity was, in Nietzsche's eyes, nothing but anarchism, since its doctrine of equality led to the breakdown of the natural hierarchy according to which superior people (like Nietzsche) were entitled to rule: "The anarchist and the Christian have the same ancestry . . . There is a perfect likeness between Christian and anarchist: their object, their instinct, points only toward destruction." (57, 58). To state it more clearly, Christianity represented equality:

> The "equality of souls before God"--this fraud, this *pretext* for the *rancunes* ["for the rancor"—Kaufmann] of all the base-minded--this explosive concept, ending in revolution, the modern idea, and the notion of overthrowing the whole social order--this is *Christian* dynamite. . . . The "humanitarian" blessings of Christianity forsooth! (62)

Nietzsche preferred the Hindu caste system, as has already been said. A few more of his comments on that are appropriate: "The order of castes, the *order of rank*, simply formulates the supreme law of life itself; the separation of the three types is necessary to the maintenance of society, and to the evolution of higher types, and the highest types--the *inequality* of rights is essential to the existence of any rights at all" (57). The three types consisted of: the masters (the elite, the strongest, the fewest); secondly the warriors, judges, and upholders of the law (the enforcers of the elite); and, lastly, the mediocre, "the great majority" (57) such as you and I, as well as all people who disagreed with Nietzsche or failed to recognize his genius. It is not surprising that elsewhere Nietzsche enthusiastically argued for the necessity of slavery. Elitist contempt for the masses is an important theme in *The Antichrist*.

Heinrich Himmler was also attracted to Hinduism. Peter Padfield's detailed biography of Himmler (*Himmler: Reichsfuhrer-SS*) states that Himmler not only believed in the Hindu doctrines of reincarnation and karma, but that he also kept a notebook with quotations from the Bhagavad Ghita. Imagine if he had done that with the Bible! The whole world would know about it. He too was, not surprisingly, attracted to the caste system—though Padfield describes not three levels but four: the rulers, the warriors, the peasants and artisans, and the serfs . . . .[10] Then there was a fifth group (or, for Nietzsche, a fourth group) not to my knowledge known to Hinduism—the sub-humans who deserved only to be destroyed. Joachim Fest states in his biography that Hitler divided his ideal society into four levels: the elite or "high nobility"; the middle class of average party members; the collective mass of Aryans; and the "subject alien nationals . . . the modern slave class."[11] This of course omits the Jews, in Hitler's demonic vision long since exterminated. Nietzsche would have approved of such extermination (not only of the Jews, but also of the handicapped, the mentally ill, chronic invalids, and the aged). His views on this subject have been quoted above, but since Nietzsche's admirer's so consistently overlook them, I can be forgiven for repeating them: "The weak and the botched shall perish: first principle of *our* charity. And one should help them to it." (2).

Nietzsche is often presented as an apostle of radical personal freedom—and what could someone like that possibly have to do with fascism? But Nietzsche's concepts of freedom were meant only for the few, the elite, the spiritually enlightened such as himself. The rest were meant only to serve—in a higher capacity, as the judges and guardians, or in a lower capacity, as serfs and menials. Remaining worthless sub-humanity was to be exterminated. People do not seem to reason that the logical, inevitable, and essential counterpart to Nietzsche's famed "overman" is the "underman"—the man who thought it was important to be kind, patient, civilized, and to live a quiet and harmless life.

Given Nietzsche's popularity today, it is worth asking if many defenders of Christianity are aware of the extent to which contemporary attacks on Christianity are motivated not by reason, logic, and evidence, but by hostility and contempt.

Nietzsche and the Jews

Nietzsche's hostility to Christianity becomes considerably more relevant to our study when we realize that he considered Christianity to be Jewish, the product of Judaism, the invention of Jews. Not content merely to reject Christianity, Nietzsche sought to understand its origins. He found them in Judaism. Correctly noting Christianity's obvious Jewish origins, he wrote: "Christianity is to be understood only by examining the soil from which it sprung--it is not a reaction against Jewish instincts; it is their inevitable product; it is simply one more step in the awe-inspiring logic of the Jews" (24). Parenthetically, "awe-inspiring logic" (*furchteinflössender Logik*) in the original, has also been translated as "frightening logic."[12] The German word for "fear" is *Furcht*.

This is not merely an inference, a subtlety, "taken out of context"—as if Nietzsche meant the opposite of what he said. Nietzsche writes on it at length and it is central to his argument. A few more examples of his understanding of Christianity's obvious Jewish origins and nature are:

> . . . the Christian church, put beside the 'people of God,' shows a complete lack of any claim to originality . . . (24).

> . . . the small insurrectionary movement which took the name of Jesus of Nazareth is simply the Jewish instinct redivivus . . . (27)

> . . . in primitive Christianity one finds only concepts of a Judaeo--Semitic character . . . (32)

> One would as little choose "early Christians" for companions as Polish Jews: not that one need seek out an objection to them . . . Neither has a pleasant smell (46).

Nietzsche saw Christians as "little super-Jews, ripe for some sort of madhouse . . . The Christian is simply a Jew of the 'reformed' confession" ["merely a Jew of 'more liberal' persuasion"—Kaufmann] (44).

How, though, did Christianity arise out of Judaism? To understand this, we need to start with a brief overview not of Jewish history, but of Jewish history as Nietzsche perceived it (such a distinction is made necessary by the fact that Nietzsche's perceptions of many subjects were often far removed from reality). This overview is provided in sections 25 & 26. Nietzsche himself attached some importance to this analysis, stating that "The history of Israel is invaluable as a typical history of an attempt to *denaturize* all natural values . . ." (25). Nietzsche attempts to show how natural values became corrupted and inverted, denied and "denatured" (made to seem unnatural) by Judaism and its offspring, the hated Christianity. An understanding of this portion of Nietzsche's book should help to dispel some of the many misconceptions of Nietzsche's attitude toward Jews.

Nietzsche believed that originally the Jews got off to a good start. Their God, though imaginary and merely a projection of human consciousness (man makes God in his image), was nevertheless the projection of a healthy consciousness: "Originally, and above all in the time of the monarchy, Israel maintained the right attitude of things, which is to say, the natural attitude. Its Jahveh was an expression of its consciousness of power, its joy in itself, its hopes for itself . . ." (25). It was, after all, a concept of God that allowed people to invade, conquer, plunder, and slaughter. It was basic to 19th-century German secular concepts of Jews, even anti-Semitic concepts, that long ago, when they had their own country, kings, and heroes, the Jews were initially not so bad, even praiseworthy. They were originally a normal people like any other.

So, the early Jewish concepts of God were acceptable and even had something to recommend them. With the passing of time, however, confronted by "anarchy within and the Assyrian without" (25), the Jews found their old primitive ideal inadequate. It could not hold up to the realities of life. At this point the Jews should, in Nietzsche's opinion, have abandoned their imaginary God—instead, however, they changed their concept: "The old god no longer *could* do what he used to do. He ought to have been abandoned. But what actually happened? simply this: the conception of him was *changed* . . ."(25).

At this time the Jewish priests invented a new concept of God: "The public notion of this god now becomes merely a weapon in the hands of clerical agitators, who interpret all happiness as a reward and all unhappiness as a punishment for obedience or disobedience to him, for 'sin' . . ." (25). The priests falsified the concept of God so as to bring people under their control. They also falsified their history. This is such an important part of Nietzsche's thought that a lengthier excerpt is necessary:

> The concept of god falsified; the concept of morality falsified;-
> -but even here Jewish priest craft did not stop. The whole history
> of Israel ceased to be of any value: out with it!--These priests
> accomplished that miracle of falsification of which a great part
> of the Bible is the documentary evidence; with a degree of
> contempt unparalleled, and in the face of all tradition and all
> historical reality, they translated the past of their people into
> *religious* terms, which is to say, they converted it into an idiotic
> mechanism of salvation, whereby all offences against Jahveh
> were punished and all devotion to him was rewarded. We would
> regard this act of historical falsification as something far more
> shameful if familiarity with the *ecclesiastical* interpretation of
> history for thousands of years had not blunted our inclinations
> for uprightness in *historicis* (26).

This religious concept made its way into philosophy:

> And the philosophers support the church: the *lie* about a "moral
> order of the world" runs through the whole of philosophy, even

the newest. What is the meaning of a "moral order of the world"? That there is a thing called the will of God which, once and for all time, determines what man ought to do and what he ought not to do; that the worth of a people, or of an individual thereof, is to be measured by the extent to which they or he obey this will of God; that the destinies of a people or of an individual are *controlled* by this will of God, which rewards or punishes according to the degree of obedience manifested.--In place of all that pitiable lie *reality* has this to say: the *priest*, a parasitical variety of man who can exist only at the cost of every sound view of life, takes the name of God in vain: he calls that state of human society in which he himself determines the value of all things "the kingdom of God . . ." (26).

Now the priests are thoroughly in control- "Supreme principle: 'God forgives those who repent'—in plain language: *those who submit to the priest*" (26).

> They went a step further: the "will of God" (in other words some means necessary for preserving the power of the priests) had to be *determined*--and to this end they had to have a "revelation." In plain English, a gigantic literary fraud had to be perpetrated, and "holy scriptures" had to be concocted--and so, with the utmost hierarchical pomp, and days of penance and much lamentation over the long days of "sin" now ended, they were duly published. (26).

This is identical to the understanding of Jewish history we have seen expressed by Chamberlain (not because Chamberlain had a sister who revised his works after his death). The Jews originally were a healthy people and some of the ideas scattered throughout the Bible are genuine and have value (Nietzsche said in the passage above that "a great part" of the Bible had been falsified, not all of it). Then, about the time of the Assyrian invasion, the Jews began to imagine themselves as a separate people. A fake scripture was invented by priests, Jewish history was falsified to make the Jews a chosen people, and concepts of sin, guilt, fear of God, and God's will were introduced that (through Christianity) had a harmful effect on European civilization.

Those ideas of Chamberlain's were expressed in a best-selling book. The ideas expressed here by Nietzsche were by no means wholly original—though he took his reasoning farther and condemned both Christianity and Judaism much more radically. Chamberlain thought that Christianity was of value if only purged of its Jewish influences. He had some respect for it and tried to salvage a part of it— whereas Nietzsche had nothing but rage, hatred, scorn, bitterness, and contempt and wanted to obliterate it entirely.

Now it is possible to see more clearly the meaning of some of Nietzsche's positive comments about the Old Testament in *Beyond Good and Evil* or in his *Nietzsche contra Wagner*. Nietzsche could find something good to say about the prophets; could object to combining the Old Testament with the New as the former was superior; could consider Christianity to be not an advance from Judaism but a decline. The original God of the Jews, though imaginary, was a

God that allowed for that exercise of the will-to-power that Nietzsche thought was the essence of life.

Nietzsche had no problem with the "heroic" Jews in their early primitive stage, and he distinguished (as did many Old Testament "scholars" of the period) between "pure" and "original" statements in the Bible on the one hand and later "corruptions" on the other. He felt that the concept of God invented by the priests at this stage was a decline from the earlier concept of God: "Formerly he represented a people, the strength of a people, everything aggressive and thirsty for power in the soul of a people; now he is simply *the good god* . . ."(16).

So, it was the Jews who introduced "the lie about a 'moral order of the world' "—a lie that infected not only Christianity but all of modern philosophy. Any philosopher such as Kant, Hegel, Chamberlain, whoever, that saw a moral order to the universe was infected with Jewish principles. Christianity in particular was the direct outcome of this Jewish falsification: "Christianity sprang from a soil so corrupt that on it everything natural, every natural value, every *reality* was opposed by the deepest instincts of the ruling class--it grew up as a sort of war to the death upon reality, and as such it has never been surpassed." (27). It was for this reason that Nietzsche stated:

> . . . the Christian church, put beside the "people of God," shows a complete lack of any claim to originality. Precisely for this reason the Jews are the most *fateful* people in the history of the world: their influence has so falsified the reasoning of mankind in this matter that today the Christian can cherish anti-Semitism without realizing that it is no more than the *final consequence of Judaism*. (24)

Nietzsche had much in common with others on these points. To give only one example, the anti-Semitic atheist Wilhelm Marr (1819-1904) also attacked Christianity as an offspring of Judaism. He saw both Judaism and Christianity as a "disease of human consciousness." He warned against the "Jewification of mankind," and his book *The Victory of Judaism over Germanism* (1879) was a best seller.[13]

This explains Nietzsche's hostility to traditional anti-Semites. Traditional "Christian" anti-Semites were idiots, making a lot of noise about the Jews when they themselves represented Jewish values and were infected by Jewish values. "Philosophical" anti-Semites such as Wagner, and others were nearly as bad. They too were full of Jewish values. Nietzsche heaped scorn on anti-Semites because they had the wrong kind of anti-Semitism—and Nietzsche was commonly scornful and contemptuous of people who disagreed with him in other areas as well. That was part of his megalomania.

It is significant that in *Nietzsche contra Wagner*—his attack on Wagner—Nietzsche mentioned Wagner's anti-Semitism briefly, in passing. What disturbed him much more, and which he elaborated on carefully, was Wagner's alleged submission to Christianity. Nietzsche saw Wagner's opera *Parsifal* as expressing Christian values—though, as was noted in the chapter on Wagner, it did nothing of the kind and Nietzsche, as usual, did not know what he was talking about. That Wagner should—in Nietzsche's eyes—be talking about anti-Semitism while being himself under the influence of Semitic values was ridiculous (I suspect Nietzsche broke with Wagner so strongly, instead of discussing things with him as a friend, because he could not endure having any deep human tie at all, but wanted to finally retreat into his own private world).

Nietzsche's hostility to conventional anti-Semitism would have especially applied to Adolf Stoecker, Kaiser Wilhelm's chaplain. Stoecker vehemently attacked the Jews, thought they were out to rule Germany, and wanted to restrict their influence—but then said Christianity was the answer to Germany's problems! This was, in Nietzsche eyes, wanting to eliminate Jewish influence so it could be replaced with Jewish influence. No wonder he hated traditional anti-Semites so deeply. In one of the demented letters written about the time of his final breakdown, Nietzsche stated that he wanted to have Stoecker eliminated (along with Bismarck and the Kaiser). He needn't have worried about Stoecker though—Stoecker was not successful and his Christian Social Party never got anywhere. That individual's traditional anti-Semitism gave way to the more virulent racial and secular variety in the same way and at the same time that the horse and buggy gave way to the automobile.

In another letter written about the time of his breakdown, in addition to the comments cited above, Nietzsche made an oft-quoted comment about having all anti-Semites shot. This is commonly used to show Nietzsche was not anti-Semitic himself—but at the same time he was writing many other delusional things. "I am just having all anti-Semites shot"[14] should be placed with his statements about having just taken possession of his kingdom and having imprisoned the Pope; claiming to be Christ; requesting a meeting with the King of Italy, and so on. If he sincerely did want to have them shot, and this letter was written in a fleeting moment of lucidity, it shows his objection to the common bourgeois form of anti-Semitism—it also shows Nietzsche's fundamental cruelty and brutality. Executing people who disagree with us is not good philosophy.

Nietzsche was able to say positive things about primitive Jews who preceded the priestly corruptions of the Old Testament, or about Jews of the Diaspora who broke completely free of their religious values and became secular free thinkers of a sort acceptable to Nietzsche. He respected some Jews like Spinoza or Heine who rejected traditional religion, and would have accepted a Jew who said "Nietzsche, you are a great thinker, and I agree with everything you say"—though if the same Jew had disagreed with him on some point, even a minor point, Nietzsche would probably have dismissed him with hostility and contempt and retreated into the proud isolation he was most comfortable with.

Nietzsche's deeper hostility to the Jewish race becomes more evident when we consider Nietzsche's theory about the emergence of Christianity. The machinations of the arch-rabbi Paul; the Jews' use of *all* forms of decadence to undermine people and so gain power for themselves (explaining how the Jews were behind *all* social evils); the racial qualities of the Jews (Nietzsche stresses "race")—an understanding of these points will make it possible to see how relevant some of Nietzsche's ideas are to an understanding of National Socialism.

It is more than a little significant that H.L. Mencken, Nietzsche's most ardent defender in America after WWI, was hostile to some Jews, but not all Jews. After muttering about Jewish plutocracy and "the intellectual cynicism of the Jew" in the introduction to his translation of *The Antichrist*, he states "The case against the Jews is long and damning; it would justify ten thousand times as many pogroms as now go on in the world."[15]

Whether some Jews could gain entrance into the German family by virtue of their spiritual assimilation or whether they were permanently barred because of race was a point German secular anti-Semites of that period disagreed on. Nietzsche scorned the idea that people were automatically guaranteed of superiority merely by being German, no matter how stupid their beliefs, and would have found a Jew like Spinoza who rejected traditional values infinitely preferable to a German who espoused Jewish values (whether in Christian or in philosophical form).

In *Beyond Good and Evil* Nietzsche even suggested breeding a few of the best Jews with the best Germans. Thus the Germans' "inherited art of commanding and obeying" could be combined with the Jewish "genius of gold and patience" (Part Eight, 251).[16] The Jews, in other words, were good with money and also at surviving hardship. This shows that a few Jews could be exempt by virtue of their special abilities. It also shows not only that Nietzsche was concerned with biological racism, but also that he was inhabiting a peculiar world of his own. That Nietzsche suggested breeding people like animals (one of Himmler's ideas as well) also shows his ignorance of (if not contempt for) common human feelings. That people should marry out of love was a foreign concept to Nietzsche—not surprisingly, since he dismissed love as a delusion.

Rose makes some useful comments on Nietzsche's anti-Semitism that will help to summarize this part of the discussion. He states that even though Nietzsche objected to Wagner's brand of anti-Semitism, he nevertheless "retained a profound antagonism to Judaism, which he furiously attacked from several directions." This statement is accompanied by a quote from *Human, All Too Human*, in which Nietzsche refers to the "disgusting" "stock exchange Jew." To quote Rose again, "the current picture of a 'gentle Nietzsche' has a little too much whitewash in it."[17] Nietzsche's condemnations of more obvious kinds of anti-Semitism do not alter the fact that he wanted to eliminate "Jewish" values for his own reasons.

Nietzsche's view of Christ

It is not necessary to say much about Nietzsche's attempts to understand the life and teachings of Christ. For Nietzsche, Christianity really began with the apostle Paul. Since, however, Nietzsche's admirers have tried to claim that he had a high opinion of Christ, and since some understanding of this is necessary to grasp Nietzsche's comments on Paul, a few comments are appropriate.

We have seen above Nietzsche's dismissal of the entire New Testament. He found no sympathetic character in the entire book except for Pontius Pilate:

> Must I add that, in the whole New Testament, there appears but a *solitary* figure worthy of honour? Pilate, the Roman viceroy. To regard a Jewish imbroglio *seriously*--that was quite beyond him. One Jew more or less-- what did it matter? . . . The noble scorn of a Roman, before whom the word "truth" was shamelessly mishandled, enriched the New Testament with the only saying *that has any value*--and that is at once its criticism and its *destruction*: "What is truth?". . . (46)

Nietzsche's understanding of Christ was rather confused, and Nietzsche confessed he had difficulty imagining what the original Christ might have been (28). Since the gospels were in Nietzsche's view falsified, and contained legends, distortions, borrowings from other religions and outright lies that were added later by the apostles, Nietzsche could only speculate as to what Christ might have really intended (we see here how close liberal textual criticism is to atheism).

Nietzsche figured out that Christ was basically a rebel against the status quo (27). He was some sort of a free spirit (32) who was opposed to the religious power structure of the Pharisees (33). Again, this is in the main identical to Chamberlain's view, and also agrees with some of Wagner's ideas (it is possible Chamberlain read *The Antichrist*). Nietzsche thought Christ was killed only because of his rebellion (27), though exactly what he hoped to accomplish was something of a mystery to Nietzsche. To the extent that the emphasis on peace, love, and forgiveness was authentic, it represented only an attempt to escape from reality by someone incapable of dealing with real life.

Nietzsche's attempts to further explore this require no elaboration because of their lack of substance. Suffice it to say that, whatever Christ may have been, his disciples distorted his teachings after his death, or so Nietzsche thought. The small Christian community created a God according to its own needs (31) and put whatever words would serve their purpose into the mouth of Christ. Nietzsche's charge (by no means an original one) that the early Christians borrowed ideas from cults of the Roman empire is commonly repeated by unbelievers today.

The gospels were so written as to get revenge on the Jews who killed Christ (this distortion of history was done by Jews, using Jewish logic and Jewish methods, as will be elaborated on when we discuss Paul). When therefore Nietzsche stated that Christ was the only true Christian (39), this was not meant to praise Christ as is often mistakenly claimed. It was meant to attack Christianity. Whatever Christ may have intended, Nietzsche thought the apostles completely distorted it.

In his earlier writings Nietzsche made at least one and possibly other positive references to Christ; however, Nietzsche also had a very high opinion of Wagner, yet later turned 180 degrees and attacked him bitterly. The fact that Nietzsche earlier said something positive about Christ or about Wagner should not be allowed to detract from or confuse our understanding of his final views. Complete consistency should not be expected of someone with Nietzsche's individualistic and highly creative concept of "truth."

Paul and the emergence of Christianity

For Nietzsche, Christianity began with Paul. The rabbi Paul, whose Jewishness is stressed by Nietzsche (25)(23), wanted only power for himself (22). To gain power, he invented a false philosophy so as to bring people under his control. This was identical to the earlier methods and motives of the Jewish priests when they fabricated the Bible (26)(29). Paul's rewriting of history to suit his own ends was a typically Jewish trick (24). In short, Paul was not only a Jew, he was "the Jew, the *eternal* Jew *par excellence* . . ." (58).

Paul then used his new doctrine to mobilize the losers, the failures, the people at the bottom, to bring down the Roman Empire. His motivation was resentment and hatred "against everything noble, joyous and high spirited on earth . . ." (43). Since Nietzsche uses the word "us" in that context, "against us," it is clear (as if evidence were needed) that Nietzsche considered himself among the spiritually favored few—indeed, elitist contempt for common people is a recurring theme of the book. In other words, Paul and the Christians set out to destroy the Roman empire just because it represented real life. If Nietzsche considered the Christian destruction of Rome as revenge for the crucifixion of Christ, that is not stated in this particular book.

In elaborating on these ideas, Nietzsche has comments referring to the Christians as vampires, parasites, and bloodsuckers (49) (58). It needs to be stressed that this included Jews and applied to Jews (except for the few independent spirits acceptable to Nietzsche). He makes this clear when he states that, although the original God of one chosen people became the God of the whole world, the democratic God, the cosmopolitan God, yet nevertheless " . . . he remains a Jew, he remains a god in a corner, a god of all the dark nooks and crevices, of all the noisesome quarters of the world!" (17).

Unlike some today, Nietzsche understood that there was such a thing as the "Judaeo-Christian moral system" (24). That there is one God, a God of moral laws and rules that we must submit to and obey; that happiness in life comes not from exaltation of the self but from obedience to God; that God is a moral God who rewards good and punishes evil—often in this life but certainly in the next—Nietzsche understood that, in the European context of his day, this came from Christianity and initially from Judaism.

Nietzsche declared war on these concepts and sought to destroy them. Although his ideas are more acceptable now, they will fail in the end—and his own personal campaign ended in his destruction. As Jesus said, ". . . whosoever shall exalt himself shall be abased; and he that shall humble himself shall be exalted." None of his contemporaries exalted themselves more highly than Nietzsche, the overman, the spiritual elitist who despised common people, the first man to speak the truth in many centuries—and none were more horribly abased (as the sordid descriptions of an insane Nietzsche amply illustrate). Howling, raging, weeping, singing, smashing windows, writing nonsense, making barking noises, groaning, raving and making wild gestures, dancing naked, uttering long incoherent monologues, roaring, begging for help, childlike and docile, silent with vacant eyes, moaning, and unable to control his bodily functions—such was the fate of this pitiful loser who thought of himself as an "overman," a superior being.

I hope no one will imagine I am gloating. I am stating the facts, and would have been much happier if Nietzsche could have repented of his sinful ideas, come to a real understanding of life, and found the happiness that always eluded him—but, Nietzsche did not want to do that. He fought against God, and he lost. I can agree with Stefan Steinberg's comment that "In a certain respect Nietzsche's tragic end is itself a metaphor . . ."—though Steinberg did not mean this in a Christian context, and explained his metaphor in a secular way.[18]

The Jewish menace to civilization

It is necessary to look at some other ideas about the Jews expressed by Nietzsche in his book. For one thing, he stressed the racial toughness of the Jews: "Psychologically, the Jews are a people gifted with the very strongest vitality . . ." (24). The Jews have "the most profound national instinct, the most powerful national will to live, that has ever appeared on earth." (27). Hitler had the same idea:

The mightiest counterpart to the Aryan is represented by the Jew. In hardly any people in the world is the instinct of self-preservation developed more strongly than in the so-called 'chosen.' Of this, the mere fact of the survival of this race may be considered the best proof. Where is the people which in the last two thousand years has been exposed to so slight changes of inner disposition, character, etc., as the Jewish people? What people, finally, has gone through greater upheavals than this one-and nevertheless issued from the mightiest catastrophes of mankind unchanged? What an infinitely tough will to live and preserve the species speaks from these facts! [*Mein Kampf* vol. I chapt. 11].

This was by no means unique to Hitler and Nietzsche. How else to explain the mysterious survival of the Jews in strictly human terms? Christians and Jews can explain the mystery as the result of the will of God and his covenant with Abraham. Let those who scoff at this try to present a more credible empirically verifiable and falsifiable alternative. They can't.

Although I have confined myself so far almost exclusively to one of Nietzsche's books for the sake of clarity and simplicity, some of Nietzsche's comments from *Beyond Good and Evil* are useful in this context. This book too, by the way, was published by Nietzsche before his collapse, so his sister's influence is not relevant. Anyway, Nietzsche says "But the Jews are undoubtedly the strongest, most tenacious, and purest race now living in Europe. They understand how to assert themselves even under the worst conditions (better even than under favourable conditions) . . ." (Part Eight, 251).[19] In the same context Nietzsche added that it was necessary for thinkers concerned about the future of Europe to "take the Jews as well as the Russians into account as, for the time being, the surest and most probable factors in the great interplay and struggle of forces" (251).

This is rather peculiar. The Jews are the strongest race in Europe? They know how to assert themselves? A sure factor in the great struggles of the day? Even before his breakdown, Nietzsche revealed himself here as a man with a very strange way of looking at things. Significantly, Nietzsche says in this same section that no more Jews should be allowed into Germany because they were a threat to the survival of Germany:

That Germany has a richly sufficient number of Jews, that the German stomach and German blood have difficulty (and will still have difficulty for a long time to come) absorbing even this quantum of "Jew" in the way the Italians, the French, and the English have absorbed them, as a result of a stronger digestive system—that is the clear message and language of a general instinct which we should listen to and according to which we must act. "Let no more Jews in! And especially bar the doors to the east (also to Austria)!" So orders the instinct of a people whose type is still weak and uncertain, so that it could be easily erased, easily dissolved away by a stronger race (251).

Nietzsche's strangeness becomes even more evident when he says "That the Jews, if they wanted to—or if people were to force them, as the anti-Semites seem to wish to do—could even now become predominant, in fact, quite literally gain mastery over Europe, is certain; that they are not working and planning for that is equally certain" (251).

The Jews could gain mastery over Europe if they wanted to? No sensible person would claim that Jewish butchers, bakers, candle-stick makers, Talmud scholars, lawyers, and teachers had the ability to gain mastery over Europe. Nietzsche is here showing an idea of the Jews that was completely divorced from reality. Within a few years he would progress in his understanding from the perception that the Jews could have the mastery of Europe but were not aiming for it, to the perception, stated in *The Antichrist*, that they were undermining European civilization to ensure their own survival.

Maybe someone who studied Nietzsche in more depth (not that I recommend this) could show how the progression of his insanity was evident in his writings. That seems to be the case, in this instance at least. Obviously, the man was not the picture of mental health one month and stark raving mad the next month. But, such speculations aside, let us examine Nietzsche's final view as expressed in *The Antichrist*. There Nietzsche wrote that the Jews used decadence to ensure their own self-preservation by undermining and weakening people who would otherwise be a threat to them:

> Psychologically, the Jews are a people gifted with the very strongest vitality, so much so that when they found themselves facing impossible conditions of life they chose voluntarily, and with a profound talent for self-preservation, the side of all those instincts which make for *decadence*--*not* as if mastered by them, but as if detecting in them a power by which "the world" could be *defied* (24).

The cunning, tricky, and devious Jews are not decadent themselves—they are, after all, "gifted with the very strongest vitality." No, they use decadence to achieve their goal of domination:

> The Jews are the very opposite of *decadents*: they have simply been forced into *appearing* in that guise, and with a degree of skill approaching the *non plus ultra* of histrionic genius they have managed to put themselves at the head of all *decadent* movements (--for example, the Christianity of Paul--), and so make of them something stronger than any party frankly saying Yes to life. To the sort of men who reach out for power under Judaism and Christianity,--that is to say, to the *priestly* class-- *decadence* is no more than a means to an end. Men of this sort have a vital interest in making mankind sick . . . (24).

Notice that the Jews are at the head of all movements of decadence. This was the view stated by Wagner, whom Nietzsche deeply admired for a long time. Democracy, a free press, socialism, bad music, capitalism, worker unrest, failure to admire Nietzsche, Christianity—anything that conflicted with an imaginary ideal could be attributed to Jewish corruption. Of course, Bolshevism was unknown in Nietzsche's day, but someone who could blame the Jews for all forms of decadence, including socialism, would have no difficulty in linking them to whatever else might come up.

Nietzsche went on to point out that the Jewish problem was a racial problem: "The whole disaster was only made possible by the fact that there already existed in the world a similar megalomania, allied to this one in race, to wit, the *Jewish* . . ."(44). All of this "is not an accident due to the chance talents of an individual, or to any violation of nature. The thing responsible is *race*. The whole of Judaism appears in Christianity as the art of concocting holy lies . . ." (44).

Defenders of Nietzsche ignore or minimize his comments about the Jews, sometimes even stating the exact opposite of the truth in this matter—whether through ignorance, or through sincere inability to recognize their hero's faults, or through deliberate deception to protect Nietzsche's reputation I won't presume to guess.

It is interesting that the Chinese Communists also saw Christianity as a trick devised to oppress people. They claimed that the American imperialists were "using the Bible to anaesthetize people in order to enslave them."[20] This does not mean that they were influenced by Nietzsche—though some Chinese intellectuals were (and are) more well informed about Western philosophical trends than many realize. That religion was used by the capitalists to keep people satisfied with their oppressed state was a basic idea of Marxism long before Nietzsche. He had a similar idea, only he blamed not the capitalists, but the Jews.

More teachings of *The Antichrist*

Misconceptions about Nietzsche's famous overman abound. Nietzsche clarifies this for us, though few seem to have read his comments here. He first refers to the overmen as individuals found "in various parts of the earth and under the most widely different cultures" He goes on immediately to explain, however, that "Even whole races, tribes and nations may occasionally represent such lucky accidents" (4).

The overman could thus be embodied in a people—but the German people? Nietzsche had, as has been said, a low opinion of them. The main reason he had for his low opinion of them, however, was their Christianity. Not only had they accepted Christianity in the Middle Ages (19) but, when Christianity was about to die, it was a German who revived it with the Protestant Reformation (61). Moreover the Germans were to blame not only for Protestantism, but because their entire philosophy from Kant to Wagner was infected with Christian values (19).

So, Nietzsche did not like the Germans—but if he could have seen them casting off their Semitic Christian influences and adopting his emphasis on strength, mercilessness, and the unrestrained pursuit of the will to power, he would have changed his mind. He would have been especially delighted to see the Germans casting off their old god and inventing a new one:

> The fact that the strong races of northern Europe did not repudiate this Christian god does little credit to their gift for religion--and not much more to their taste. They ought to have been able to make an end of such a moribund and worn-out

product of the *decadence*. A curse lies upon them because they were not equal to it; they made illness, decrepitude and contradiction a part of their instincts--and since then they have not managed to *create* any more gods. Two thousand years have come and gone--and not a single new god! Instead, there still exists, and as if by some intrinsic right,--as if he were the *ultimatum* and *maximum* of the power to create gods, of the *creator spiritus* in mankind--this pitiful god of Christian monotono-theism! (19).

A "god" that allowed for the domination of the blonde Aryan beast and the repudiation of traditional values would have struck Nietzsche as a vast improvement. Nietzsche abhorred nationalism of the conventional bourgeois sort, but he would not have condemned the emergence of a nation of overmen.

There is much more to be said about this. Nietzsche specifically advocated breeding, and willing, this higher type of man—someone "the most valuable, the most worthy of life, the most secure guarantee of the future" (3), unlike the inferior common folk far below. This was Hitler's and Himmler's project exactly—to breed and to educate a higher race. This "higher type" was, as I have already said, "the most feared," the exact opposite of the Christian (3)—and Hitler was the exact opposite of the ideal of the Christian as taught by Christ, was he not? His philosophy and practice was the extreme opposite of the standards presented by Paul in his famous passage on love in I Corinthians: love is patient, love is kind, is not puffed up, rejoices in goodness and in truth—one could not invent a better antithesis to this than Hitler if one tried.

Another related aspect is Nietzsche's emphasis on the gratification of the will to power as the whole meaning and essence of life (2)(6). This attitude helps to explain the baffling cruelty of the Nazi death camp guards. What could give a greater feeling of power than to stride like a demi-god among pitiful, sick, starving wretches, able to dispense death left and right at whim? This is the fullest development of the Nietzschean will to power.

Someone may say "Nietzsche didn't mean that." I say "He did mean it." I believe if Nietzsche could have seen a Nazi death camp he would have been thrilled. He would have said "Where do I sign up to become a guard?" Then he could have acted out his "first principle of *our* charity"—that "The weak and the botched shall perish . . . And one should help them to it" (2).

In understanding this we need to be mindful of these words of Nietzsche's:

> Pity thwarts the whole law of evolution, which is the law of natural selection. It preserves whatever is ripe for destruction; it fights on the side of those disinherited and condemned by life; by maintaining life in so many of the botched of all kinds, it gives life itself a gloomy and dubious aspect (7).

Nietzsche also said that "all imaginable horrors and vices" were less harmful than "humility, chastity, poverty, in a word, *holiness* . . ." (8). Cruelty was a virtue, and kindness was a vice—and this too helps to shed light on the ability of Nazi criminals to routinely practice the worst evil. They believed that what they were doing was good—natural, normal, healthy, and good. They were not able to do evil in the camps and then go home and enjoy normal lives because of "compartmentalisation" or psychological "discontinuities" or "a high degree of personal fragmentation,"[21] or any of the other humanistic concepts people might use. They were able to do what they did as they believed in a Nietzschean ethic in which kindness and pity were harmful, contrary to nature and to real life.

This does not mean they studied Nietzsche's books and consciously decided "I am going to do what Nietzsche says." It does mean that a repudiation of biblical Christianity as false and an emphasis on life as amoral struggle has an effect—and this was not "pseudo-Nietzschean" as someone claimed. It was pure Nietzsche, perfectly in harmony with ideas stressed repeatedly and at length in *The Antichrist* and in other books as well—and Nietzsche's ideas were plentifully spread throughout the Third Reich. This is not to blame it all on Nietzsche. There were deeper spiritual currents of which Nietzsche was only a mouthpiece. These currents would affect those who never read a line of Nietzsche—but those who set up the system knew Nietzsche, and agreed with him.

Nietzsche claimed that man was only an animal, nothing more (14). As such, man needed only to act according to his own instinct—without regard for ethics, morality, concern for others, or restraint. Nietzsche advocated total freedom for the human beast to act according to instinct alone—yet, paradoxically, this teaching of radical freedom (for, it will be recalled, the elite few only) included a denial of free will. This belief was also held by Haeckel, as well as by other social Darwinists of the period. It is interesting to speculate that Nietzsche may have been significantly influenced by Haeckel. There are many similarities between them, and it is inconceivable that Nietzsche should not have read him.

Nietzsche thought that the imaginary concept of "free will" was a product of the old religious order (14). That having been done away with, and man's animal nature having been re-established, free will was done away with as well. "Will" was nothing but response to stimuli; "consciousness," "spirit," were only "a symptom of a relative imperfection of the organism" (14). One is freed from the need to evaluate the rightness or wrongness of one's actions; one can dispense with conscience—"it is only the result of faulty vision" (9). People with clear vision need no conscience. "Pangs of conscience" are dismissed as one of the many aspects of religion that are totally divorced from reality (15). Morality is nothing but a "a physiological disorder produced by the canker worm of conscience . . ." (25). The overman is beyond such things, and does what he pleases without regard for outmoded concepts of good and evil.

In all of this, Nietzsche was not the philosophical lone ranger he is often mistaken for. Other thinkers of his day had similar ideas—and why not? If Christianity is false, then the moral values derived from it are also false. If man evolved from the animals by pitiless struggle, and still is an animal, why should he try to escape from the laws of struggle by protecting himself with false values?

This is of course intimately related to Darwinism, and Nietzsche did not accept all of Darwinism. He rejected positivism and pure scientific materialism[22]—but he did say that "Pity thwarts the whole law of evolution, which is the law of natural selection" (7).[23] He modified the Darwinian scenario somewhat, believing that creatures did not only struggle for survival in conditions of scarcity, but were driven to compete even in conditions of abundance by the will to power, the desire to dominate.[24] Nevertheless, like many people of his day, he was deeply attracted to Darwin's simple-minded idea of life as the result of an amoral conflict in which only the stronger survived.

Much of what Nietzsche wrote was compatible with Darwinism, and more than just "compatible." One of Nietzsche's German contemporaries, Josef Diner, asserted that "If one examines Nietzsche's conception of the world in terms of its results, one finds that it is wholly in accord with the more recent scientific discoveries. The teachings of Darwin and Haeckel, too, ultimately lead to the *Ubermensch*." Gregory Moore, the author from whom this quote was taken, says this response was "typical."[25] H.L. Mencken stated that Nietzsche's "plain aim" in writing *The Antichrist* was "completing the work begun, on the one hand, by Darwin and the other evolutionist philosophers, and, on the other hand, by German historians and philologians."[26]

This is very logical. If man reached his present state by a process of cold and impersonal elimination of the unfit, why should not the process continue? Are those who want to call a halt to natural law now that they are comfortable with their own level of development acting under the insidious influence of unhealthy, unnatural, and unscientific traditional values? Shouldn't we have progressed beyond outdated concepts of right and wrong and be, as Nietzsche stated in the title of one of his books, "*Beyond Good and Evil*"?

Nietzsche rejected not science but the overestimation of science. He felt that science lacked the power to create values and so could not stand on its own, but that he did value scientific knowledge in the proper context and as a weapon against religion is clear: "science makes men *godlike*--it is all up with priests and gods when man becomes scientific!" (48).

A number of other thinkers with ideas similar or identical to Nietzsche's are presented in Richard Weikart's *From Darwin to Hitler: Evolutionary Ethics, Eugenics, and Racism in Germany*. Wilhelm Schallmayer, a physician, wrote a pamphlet called *The Threatening Physical Degeneration of Civilized Peoples* (1891). In It he asserted that Christian values were contrary to natural selection.[27] Alexander Tille, a university professor, sought to synthesize Darwin with Nietzsche (not a difficult thing to do). He claimed that nature was without pity, so pity was unnatural. Man is an animal and should live like an animal. Tille also rejected love and compassion as false, even "immoral in many cases."[28]

Tille wrote a book, *From Darwin to Nietzsche* (*Von Darwin bis Nietzsche*). In it, this Einstein called for "a merciless elimination of the worst people" and argued that "this means becoming hard against those who are below average."[29] He also complained about Christian ideas of equality leading to the evils of democracy, humanitarianism, and socialism, all of which were "irreconcilable with the theory of evolution."[30] Theodor Fritsch, Alfred Ploetz, Christian von Ehrenfels and many others disapproved of the false humanity based on misguided pre-evolutionary beliefs. Whatever people may say today, many of Nietzsche's period understood him to be speaking literally—and I am tired of hearing about Nietzsche's "ironical" or "metaphorical" style. If I express myself in such a way that my ideas are commonly and routinely taken to be the opposite of what I intended, I am to blame.

More can be said about elements of National Socialism in *The Antichrist*, such as the thirst for "lightnings and great deeds" as opposed to "lazy peace, cowardly compromise" (1), or the deliberate repudiation of centuries of Western civilization. It is not surprising that, as was said in chapter 7, the Nazi ideologue

Alfred Rosenberg named Nietzsche as one of the intellectual founders of National Socialism (along with Wagner, Lagarde, and Chamberlain).[31] In Joseph Goebbel's autobiographical novel the main character carried and quoted from a copy of Nietzsche's *Zarathustra*.[32]

A brief glance at one of Nietzsche's other books—which we also have as he published it—will serve to confirm and amplify the ideas discussed above. Then it will be possible to study the dark riddle of Hitler's anti-Semitism, and conclude with some general comments about Nietzsche.

On the Genealogy of Morals

In this book (published by Nietzsche in 1887), the author attempts to explain how moral concepts arose. Needless to say, he presented not a particle of evidence for his non-falsifiable, non-empirical views. Like many atheists today, he thought that because he rejected religion, he was automatically objective. In fact, he was highly subjective, even delusional.

There are many ideas in the book that are irrelevant to this study (and to any other study for that matter) but there are some that help to confirm and sometimes even illuminate the concepts expressed in *The Antichrist*. The book is divided into three essays. Each essay has section numbers that will be indicated for reference.[33]

The First Essay refers to the conquering Aryan blonds who subdued the dark-haired original inhabitants of Italy (a common theme of Folkish thinkers). There are other references to the "blond German beast" in this essay, "splendidly roaming around in its lust for loot and victory" (11). This plainly shows that Nietzsche was not metaphorically referring to the blondness of a lion. It is significant that Nietzsche's tendency to use irony and metaphor is most conveniently appealed to when he is saying deeply embarrassing things that make him vulnerable to criticism and would be troubling to his admirers if taken too literally.

Nietzsche refers openly and repeatedly to these conquering Aryan beasts, his ideal, whom he contrasts favorably with the tame and domesticated household pets produced by Christian culture. This repudiation of modern Western civilization as sickly and unhealthy was one of Haeckel's themes as well, and helps to explain the joyful Nazi repudiation of traditional values.

Nietzsche does refer in this context to the Arabs and the Japanese as partaking of the heroic qualities of unbridled and rapacious violence. Hitler also saw martial virtues in the Japanese, and stated (in his *Table Talk*) his preference for Islam over Christianity due to its warlike qualities. This did not mean Hitler's own emphasis on blondness was only a metaphor. Hitler—and Nietzsche—could recognize fighting virtues in other races, but the blond Aryans remained the ideal.

There is talk about how evil and poisonous priests are, and more about the bad Jews and Christians (7)(8). Talk about racial blood poisoning shows Nietzsche's concern for racial purity and connects him to the biological racism that was very popular in his day (9). It also tends to confirm a statement I was unable to substantiate—that Nietzsche was enthusiastic about Gobineau's theories of the dangers of racial impurity.

Nietzsche rambles on about the "slave revolt in morality" which undermined the heroic virtues of bloodthirsty conquest and slaughter, and goes on to state that what is considered "evil" by standards of conventional is in fact "good" (11). "Tame" people are referred to in this same section as "maggots" (11). Then we

422

read about how strong and noble the Romans were (love those conquests) before they were themselves conquered by the Jews (16). After this came the Renaissance, but the Protestant Reformation spoiled it (16).

In the Second Essay we read that the evil principle of equality is hostile to life and destroys the human spirit (11)—the will to power is the essence of life (12). Then there are some thoughts on the origin of the state. Nietzsche teaches that it was the "blond predatory animals, a race of conquerors and masters," that began the whole idea of the state by organizing their subjects for war (17). This confirms Hitler's (and Chamberlain's) theory that real civilization begins with the Aryan. Nietzsche was not being original, daring, or creative here. He shared this most unphilosophical view with many other racists, fanatics, and nationalistic thinkers of the period.

In this passage Nietzsche presents a remarkably prophetic description of Hitler. Leaders and founders of states command; they are natural masters. The born leader is "violent in his actions and gestures" (we recall here Hitler's oratorical style). The natural leader does not have to be concerned with contracts or with the rightness of his actions. Far above ethical qualms, he only acts, "like fate," like lightning, "fearsome," and "sudden." His "fearsome egotism" is not burdened by "guilt" or "conscience." After all, "Bad conscience is a sickness" (19). The tyranny of this natural leader is "hateful" and "painful," but it is necessary and beneficial because it is out of his deeds that the state and civilization emerge. This natural leader is also an artist. It is highly probable that Hitler studied this passage and applied it to himself.

It is interesting to note in this context that Bertrand Russell parallels Nietzsche here. In "Icarus, or, the Future of Science," he stated that cruelty and despotism were necessary for the long-range benefit of civilization:

> I believe that, owing to men's folly, a world-government will only be established by force, and therefore be at first cruel and despotic. But I believe that it is necessary for the preservation of a scientific civilization, and that, if once realized, it will gradually give rise to the other conditions of a tolerable existence.[34]

It is not a coincidence that two famous modern atheists both endorsed present cruelty for the future benefit of "mankind." This was also the approach of Lenin, Stalin, Hitler, and Mao. What a terrible contrast to the much more modest Christian beliefs that the world is inherently sinful and we cannot introduce Utopia; that a future imaginary and unattainable ideal does not justify even one single murder; that our primary goal is not to save the human race but to serve and obey God on the personal and individual level.

The Third Essay has some praise for the Old Testament (22)—we recall that Nietzsche once praised Wagner as well, but in the end turned bitterly against him. There is a statement already referred to above about truth being "divine"—". . . even we knowledgeable people of today, we godless and anti-metaphysical people—we still take our fire from that blaze kindled by a thousand years of old belief, that faith in Christianity, which was also Plato's belief, that God is the truth, that the truth is divine . . ." (24). This shows Nietzsche's objection to the Christian concept of God, but not to every concept of God. That the conquering blond beasts who represented his ideal worshipped many gods did not bother him in the least.

Section 25 shows that Nietzsche rejected not scientific knowledge, but only the overestimation of it. In the next section we see his hostility to "the anti-Semites, who nowadays roll their eyes in a Christian-Aryan-Bourgeois way" (26). This shows that he scorned the anti-Semitism of people under the influence of Semitic values. He especially rejected the tame, domesticated, household Aryans, boasting of their race while showing none of the fierce, warlike, heroic, pagan ideals of the blond conquering beasts of the good old days. A blast against German nationalism is also found in this section (26). Nietzsche objected to a boring, democratic "Christian" Germany paralyzed by modern ideas. How surprised and delighted he would have been if he could have seen the original German spirit re-awakening, casting off alien Semitic and Mediterranean ideas, and re-emerging—proud, fierce, imperious, destructive, cruel.

Hitler's Table Talk

Those who are familiar with the published transcripts of Hitler's conversations will have no difficulty in seeing parallels between Nietzsche's ideas of Christianity and Hitler's. We read in *The Antichrist* that "Christianity remains to this day the greatest misfortune of humanity" (51). Hitler said, "The heaviest blow that ever struck humanity was the coming of Christianity."[35] A coincidence? There are many such coincidences in the *Table Talk*:

~ Christianity was an invention of the Jews.
~ The Jews mobilized the underworld to bring down the Roman empire with Christian teaching.
~ Christianity is a rebellion of the weak against the strong. It is in opposition to life.
~ Christ died in the fight against Judaism.
~ Christ's teachings were falsified by Paul.
~ Paul deliberately planned Christianity as a means of ruining the Roman empire.
~ Judaism leads to social disintegration.
~ Christianity is against natural law.
~ Centuries of Medieval Christian civilization were completely wasted.
~ Christianity is a religion for failures and losers.
~ It is scientific knowledge that matters (Hitler's repeated appeals to science are insufficiently appreciated). Nietzsche too wrote "science makes men *godlike*—it is all up with priests and gods when man becomes scientific!" (48).
~ Priests use the claim that they represent God as a means to gain power.
~ Islam is superior to Christianity

A final point of exact equivalence requires a little elaboration. Just as Nietzsche expressed admiration for the wickedness of the Renaissance Popes, and asserted that the corruptions of Cesare Borgia represented the victory of true nobility over Christianity (a positive development leading toward the death of Christianity that was ruined by Luther) (61), so too Hitler stated "But a Pope, even a criminal one, who protects great artists and spreads beauty around him, is nevertheless more sympathetic to me than the Protestant minister who drinks from the poisoned spring."[36] Nietzsche, like Hitler, even used the word "beauty" in this context, stating that the picture of a wicked Pope who denied Christianity seemed "to scintillate with all the vibrations of a fine and delicate beauty" (61).

Hitler also referred to Nietzsche directly in *Table Talk*, calling him a great man and saying "In our parts of the world, the Jews would have immediately eliminated Schopenhauer, Nietzsche, and Kant."[37]

I realize that, though *Hitler's Table Talk* is accepted by legitimate historians, some claim that Hitler's comments about Christianity were distorted by Bormann. I have not relied on *Table Talk* to clarify Hitler's relationship to Christianity, but I do accept it as genuine and think its parallels with Nietzsche are confirmed by Hitler's public expression of admiration for Nietzsche. Yet, this is not a matter of one disputed book only.

Saul Friedländer's in depth study of the Holocaust, *The Years of Extermination: Nazi Germany and the Jews 1939-1945*, quotes a Nazi official (Robert Ley) as criticizing the Jews for "the reversal of all natural values"[38]— Nietzsche's point exactly, and even in his terminology. Countless examples of such parallels and commonalities could be given. In a public speech, also quoted by Friedländer, Hitler referred to the "Jewish-democratic world enemy."[39] If one accepts Nietzsche's premises that Christianity is to blame for democracy, and the Jews are behind Christianity as well as all other movements of decadence, the belief that the democracies were serving Jewish interests makes perfect sense. That would explain why otherwise disunited countries were united in opposition to Hitler.

The belief that Christianity was related to Judaism was not merely a matter of some comments in *Table Talk* or of official propaganda statements and publications. It was also reflected in government policy. In his book *Hitler and the Holocaust: How and Why the Holocaust Happened*, Holocaust historian Robert Wistrich states:

> . . . even church passivity on the "Jewish question" was interpreted by Hitler, Himmler, Goebbels, Ley and others as proof that Christianity was irredeemably tainted by "Jewish" influences. It was no coincidence that in the reports of the SD (Security Services) the churches after 1937 figure prominently, alongside Jews and Communists, as "ideological enemies" of the regime.[40]

Wistrich also makes some very insightful comments about Hitler's reasons for hating the Jews. He writes that Hitler blamed the Jews "for having invented the very notion of a moral conscience, in defiance of all healthy, natural instincts."[41] This in turn led to Christianity and to Communism, with their dreams of peace, equality, and justice. Wistrich later states that Naziism was a rebellion "against the entire civilization that had been built on Judaeo-Christian ethics."[42] It was the Jews, Hitler believed, that were ultimately responsible for "contemporary teachings of pacifism, equality before God and the law, human brotherhood and compassion for the weak, which Naziism had to uproot."[43] Hitler's ideal required the elimination of those values, and of the people who spread them.

This explains why Hitler thought the triumph of Jewish values would lead to the end of civilization. As Nietzsche explained in the Second Essay of *On the Genealogy of Morals*, "harming, oppressing, exploiting, destroying" are not "unjust" at all. They are ordinary manifestations of life: "life essentially works that way, that is, in its basic functions it harms, oppresses, exploits, and destroys—and cannot be conceived at all without these characteristics." This being so, "partial restrictions on the basic will to live, which is set on power"— meaning those moral and ethical restrictions for which the Jews were ultimately to blame—were contrary to life. More than that, they represent "a principle hostile to life, a destroyer and dissolver of human beings, an assassination attempt on the future of human beings, a sign of exhaustion, a secret path to nothingness" (11).[44] Jewish values fatally undermined the unprincipled will to power which was essential to the struggle for survival and without which humanity would sink back into the void from which it emerged.

In this passage Nietzsche is referring specifically to Duehring's "communist cliché" of equality. This is quite significant as it shows the linkage between Christianity and Communism that Hitler saw as well. Christianity and Communism both advocated human equality—radically different sorts of equality, but such trifles were lost on Nietzsche and on Hitler. To them, this concept of equality came, as we have seen, from the Jews, and was destructive no matter how it manifested itself:

> In order to mask his activity and lull his victims, however, he [the Jew] talks more and more of the equality of all men without regard to race and color. The fools begin to believe him . . . His ultimate goal in this stage is the victory of 'democracy,' or, as he understands it: the rule of parliamentarianism. It is most compatible with his requirements; for it excludes the personality - and puts in its place the majority characterized by stupidity, incompetence, and last but not least, cowardice [*Mein Kampf* vol. I chapt. 11, "Nation and Race"].

We can now understand more clearly a concept Hitler presents in *Mein Kampf*:

> At this point someone or other may laugh, but this planet once moved through the ether for millions of years without human beings and it can do so again some day if men forget that they owe their higher existence, not to the ideas of a few crazy ideologists, but to the knowledge and ruthless application of Nature's stern and rigid laws [vol. I chapt. 11, "Nation and Race"].

If because of the teachings of crazy ideologists we forget that we owe our existence to ruthless struggle, the weak and the inferior will predominate, and the human race will decay until it eventually dies out. Hitler elaborated on this point in his unpublished *Second Book*. After stating that struggle is an essential and inescapable part of life, he elaborates: "Anyone who wishes to permanently banish this struggle from the earth might end the fighting between men, but he would thereby also eliminate the highest driving force for their development."[45]

It is significant that Hitler's ideas on these important issues were literally identical to one of the most famous and widely admired philosophers of modern times. This means two things: that Hitler's intellectual reputation should be upgraded (he did read and understand some philosophy), and that Nietzsche's reputation should be downgraded, drastically downgraded. It is also significant that such ideas were by no means unique to Nietzsche, but were a logical result of the spread of a modified Darwinian scenario of the origins and the meaning of life.

Hitler, the atheistic theist

It is commonly said that Hitler was an atheist, but his frequent attacks on atheistic Communism and numerous references to some higher power that had sent him are generally accepted as sincere by serious students of the subject. That Hitler was not an atheist and in fact opposed atheism is therefore commonly used to distance him from Nietzsche. Yet, as was pointed out earlier in this chapter, someone whose concept of God allows him to do whatever he likes is, in practice, no different from an atheist.

The significance of this can be demonstrated by presenting the deep parallels between National Socialism and Communism. One was theistic in a vague philosophical sense, the other was overtly atheistic—yet they had so much in common because they both came from the same source. That source was independent human reason following its own course without divine revelation.

Consider the following points:

~ Hitler, Lenin, Stalin, and Mao all saw themselves as the infallible interpreters of the vast impersonal historical process that lay at the root of life. Whether it was a biologically motivated conflict between races or an economically driven conflict between classes makes little difference.

~ Both world views offered paradise to their elite groups (the workers or the Aryans) after the elimination of those who hindered the historical process (capitalists, kulaks, imperialists, or Jews).

~ National Socialism and Communism both had contempt for the middle class, the bourgeoisie.

~ Both sought to create a new man, a new society, to replace the old traditional ideal.

~ Both systems accepted the use of violence, force, repression as ordinary and natural instruments of policy.

~ A personality cult based on blind devotion to the infallible leader was essential.

~ Hostility to democracy was shared by all four of these great totalitarian leaders. Lenin and Hitler both eliminated struggling democracies.

~ Totalitarian control of every aspect of life with obedience enforced by secret police, repression, terror, torture, and concentration camps was integral to their systems.

~ No moral constraints were operative. Opponents of the regime were "insects" to Lenin, "sub-human vermin" to Hitler and could be crushed without mercy by the hundreds of thousands and by the millions—for the future good of humanity. Cruelty and brutality were considered normal, even virtuous. Justice was purely relative—there were no higher objective standards. What helped the cause was "just," what hindered it was "unjust."

~ Both ideologies were hostile to traditional religion. This was expressed more openly in Communism, where the much weaker Chinese and Russian churches did not have to be dealt with so carefully—but even Stalin and Mao came to see the impossibility of just wiping out religion by force, and in the end sought, like Hitler, to bring the churches under the complete control of the state.

~ Both ideologies sought world domination.

More similarities can be mentioned, such as: hostility to modern art; violent purges of the party; love of mass parades and displays of power; pseudo-classical architecture (this applies even to China, where the Stalinist style prevailed for a time). Finally, both systems were totally false, but caused immense suffering, misery, destruction, and death before being abandoned.

Even some supposed differences were only apparent: for example, the Nazis glorified Germany while the Communists praised internationalism. This difference supposedly shows the stark black and white contrast between left and right—but the Chinese and the Russians ruthlessly pursued nationalistic policies behind a smokescreen of internationalist rhetoric, while Hitler had international ambitions for all Aryans irrespective of their national boundaries. Thus, to say that internationalism is peaceful, while nationalism in any form is dangerous and potentially fascist, is exceedingly simple-minded.

Another dramatic contrast between the Nazis and the Communists evaporates under the light of reason—imperialism. The Nazis openly advocated imperialism while the Communists condemned it—yet both the Russians and the Chinese consistently and aggressively practiced imperialism. The real difference here is only that the Communists were more skilled in camouflaging their true intentions.

Yet one more example of a supposed difference that vanishes under objective analysis is that the Nazis preached elitism while the Communists glorified the masses—but in practice the Communist system benefited only a small elite, while the masses were exploited and oppressed. Hitler did not, unlike Lenin, try to wipe out capitalism, and the industrialists profited during his regime—but he subjugated big business to the state, employed numerous economic restrictions, and was deeply socialist in his belief that economic activity should be regulated by the state. Does it need to be pointed out that Lenin backed off from his extreme attempts to eliminate capitalism and instituted the NEP? His ideology was, like Hitler's, inflexible in pursuit of its main goals, but very flexible in its short-term policies.

Given all of these points in common, we can see that the supposed differences between Hitler's theism and Communist atheism are more apparent than real. That is because Hitler's "god" was a human god that allowed Hitler—like the Communists—to pursue ideals derived from human reason alone. It is no surprise that Hitler and Stalin were able to work together in close harmony. Both men had similar aims and similar methods. Their philosophies emerged from a common spirit—that of autonomous man seeking to build a new society by the light of human reason alone. This helps to explain the hostility shared by the collectivists on the right and the collectivists on the left toward their common enemies of "liberal capitalism, with its individualism, its limited government, its separation of church and state" (that is, religious freedom, not elimination of religion) as well as the emphasis on peaceful cooperation and compromise among members of society.[46]

One of the most common and pernicious myths about Hitler is that he emerged from the "religious right." In fact, with an insufficiently recognized political genius, he skillfully combined elements from both the left and the right. He was a revolutionary with a new philosophy most closely approximated by those of Lenin, Stalin, and also Mussolini (Mussolini's origins in left wing socialism and Communism don't require documentation here).

After stating that "Communists and fascists worked together against liberalism many times in the Twenties and Thirties," Nick Cohen is on solid ground when he adds "it was a natural partnership because the similarities between communism and fascism were more important than the differences."[47] While many will find it difficult to relinquish their cherished notion that Communism and National Socialism were polar opposites, their stereotypes are based solely on outward appearances and emotional needs, not on objective analysis.

Concluding thoughts on Nietzsche

Nietzsche's thought was the final culmination of a long process. First, revelation was dispensed with and faith was placed in human reason alone. God became a Deist force, abstract and impersonal (though still divine). Then, by a law of spiritual gravity that operates just as surely as the law of gravity acts on a physical body (though much more slowly), the descent continued.

The next step was the vague "spirit" of German idealistic philosophy—considerably reduced in power and in elevation, no longer above and apart from the world, but inseparably bound up in it. From this fantasy, the next step was the impersonal, mindless, blindly striving Will of Schopenhauer. This had no pretense of divinity, and was only some kind of a force.

There are two more steps in the descent. The first was the "scientific" abstraction of Haeckel. The cosmos itself, the sum total of all energy and matter, was arbitrarily labeled "god"—a "god" that worked through scientific law and was discernible through scientific law. The following step was Nietzsche—complete and total rejection both of traditional theism and of any and all concept of higher cosmic purpose or law that might be considered as having emerged out of religion. This brought along with it the final rejection of traditional moral values based on now outdated concepts of God—a process that had been underway since the "Enlightenment" and even earlier. Initially the rejection of divinely revealed religion was more respectful, but criticisms of Christianity became more vehement as the 19th century progressed. Haeckel was scornful and contemptuous of Christianity. Nietzsche expressed hatred and malevolence.

It was with this attitude that Nietzsche called for a re-evaluation of all moral values. What had been traditionally called "good" was in fact bad. What had been traditionally called "bad" was good. Exaltation of the self to the farthest possible extent was good—even to the extent of total indifference to (and pleasure in?) the suffering of others. Denial of the self was bad—whether it came from fear of others, or from imaginary and irrational fears about the approval of a non-existent supreme being.

This removal of all moral and ethical restraint, this labeling of virtue as bad and of self-exaltation as good, had a catastrophic effect on the personalities of those already committed to militarism, imperialism, and racism. Now the deepest power of sin in the individual, the power that society seeks to restrain and that Christianity promises to subdue and ultimately destroy—this power of sin was given free reign. In this way Nietzsche expressed the last missing ingredient in our analysis of National Socialism—pure, undiluted evil; the cold inhuman cruelty that called brutality "brave," "noble," "natural," "honest," and "good"; and that called kindness, patience, modesty, humility, and fairness "weak," "cowardly," "unnatural," and "unhealthy." This blazing hatred of good and the fiendish, rapturous joy in savage and bestial cruelty was Nietzsche's contribution. First, evil is denounced; then, tolerated or ignored; then, it is denied. Soon it is accepted; finally it is embraced and loved.

Hitler deeply admired Nietzsche, studied him, tried to live by his teachings, and understood him far better than academics who like to talk about Nietzsche but are too spineless and soft to really try and live by his philosophy of power and selfish cruelty. Of course, defenders of Nietzsche will deny my comments here—which brings up a very significant point. People who reject God and traditional values, who invent their own values and seek only their own self-affirmation, can go off in many different directions from the single starting point of rejecting God. As was the case with Darwinism, some can use their commitment to Nietzschean "philosophy" as a justification for militarism, imperialism, and even—admittedly in extreme cases—for smashing babies' heads against a wall or kicking people to death for the fun of it. Others can use it to justify hedonistic lives devoted only to the most mindless enjoyment and pampered self-indulgence.

People can take the same principles and run with them in completely different directions. Too many assume that vicious evil-doers have nothing to do with Nietzsche, and cannot perceive that it is actually those vicious evil-doers who really understand Nietzsche the best, and live by his principles most consistently. Nietzsche himself would have had nothing but scorn for those who talked about his philosophy but were still in bondage to outdated humanitarian conventions that derived ultimately from Semitic sources.

Nietzsche denied the immortal soul and said that man was only an animal, and many people today agree—but there are different kinds of animals. There are the wolves, the lions, the tigers, the violent blond beasts of Nietzsche's pre-Christian Aryan ideal (one he shared with Wagner, Chamberlain, Himmler, and Hitler). Then there are the rabbits, the sheep, the chickens that are the right and lawful prey of the carnivorous beasts.

This Nietzschean "philosophy" of people as animals following only their own instincts inevitably leads to disaster. Nietzsche, like all atheists, had a completely false idea of freedom, and did not understand that his idea of "freedom" (one which he offered by the way only to the elite few) was in fact slavery: slavery to the tiny little self, to sin, to ignorance, to vice, to selfish stupidity and conceited ignorance.

True freedom is found within limits—limits that include respect for higher spiritual laws and concern for other people. Nietzsche thought he was free—strong, tough, one of the spiritual elite, an overman. In fact he was nothing but a poor, helpless, lonely, unhappy, and miserable man—and that was before his final crack-up. He claimed in *The Antichrist* to have found the way of happiness (2)—he was deceived, and all of his intellectual brilliance was completely wasted. All of his vast influence has been bad. Has anyone significantly influenced by Nietzsche ever made any positive contribution to Western culture? No. On the contrary, as Paul Lawrence Rose points out, the "megalomaniacal mood of arrogant defiance of civilized values that he [Nietzsche] fostered among German students and youth" helped to create "a climate ripe for mass warfare and mass murder well before the rise of Naziism."[48]

It has been said that Nietzsche wrote a "powerful critique" of Christianity. If someone said "Karl Marx was a Jew, and Marxism was nothing but a Jewish hoax"—would that be a "powerful critique" of Marxism? If I said "Darwinism is a Jewish plot to undermine civilization"—would that be a powerful and effective critique? Nietzsche had no real understanding of Christian history, teaching, or practice, and his critique is too wide of the mark to be effective. A vastly more effective critique of current Christianity can be found in the teachings of Christ and the apostles.

Nietzsche's ideas are to an extent identical to these assertions of Thomas Paine, made in 1794 in *The Age of Reason*: "All national institutions of religion, whether Jewish, Christian or Turkish, appear to me no other than human inventions set up to terrify and enslave mankind, and monopolize power and profit."[49] The difference between Nietzsche and Paine is that the hatred of virtue and the love of evil we find in Nietzsche would have been inconceivable to Paine. It took time, and the addition of Darwinian pseudo-science and modern philosophy, for the evil latent in Paine's ideas to reach its full fruition.

If Nietzsche were rightly understood, all decent people would turn from his books in loathing and disgust—but so many are enamored of his principle of freedom from any higher law that they refuse to see any evil in him. Because they agree with him on the deepest level, they assume he is generally in the right, and are incapable of objectively analyzing the great potential for evil that lurks in his words. I believe no single book takes us more deeply or more intimately into the heart, mind, and soul of Hitler than Nietzsche's *Antichrist*.

> *Wherefore God also hath highly exalted him, and given him a name which is above every name:*
> *That at the name of Jesus every knee should bow, of things in heaven, and things in earth, and things under the earth;*
> *And that every tongue should confess that Jesus Christ is Lord, to the glory of God the Father. (Philippians)*

---

[1] Friedrich Nietzsche, *The Antichrist: Curse on Christianity*, trans. H.L. Mencken; http://www.primitivism.com/antichrist.htm; accessed August 2008. Future quotations from Mencken's translation of *The Antichrist* will not be noted but will be followed only by "Preface" or by the section number in parentheses. The sections are all short, so quotations can easily be located. Indirect quotes will also be indicated by section numbers where a direct quote seemed unnecessary. All emphatic italicized portions of quotes are taken from the translation—no emphasis has been added. Some eccentricities of punctuation have been retained.

[2] Friedrich Nietzsche, *The Antichrist: Curse on Christianity*, trans. Walter Kaufmann, *The Nietzsche Channel*; http://www.geocities.com/thenietzschechannel/anti.htm; accessed December 2007.

[3] Cited in Richard Weikart, *From Darwin to Hitler: Evolutionary Ethics, Eugenics, and Racism in Germany* (New York 2004), p. 49. This was not an idiosyncracy of Nietzsche's, but a belief common to eugenicists who wanted to improve the race by sterilization and selective breeding.

[4] William L. Shirer, *The Rise and Fall of the Third Reich* (New York 1960), p. 100.

[5] Friedrich Nietzsche, *On the Genealogy of Morals: A Polemical Tract*, trans. Ian Johnston; http://www.mala.bc.ca/~johnstoi/Nietzsche/genealogytofc.htm; accessed January 2008.

[6] Walker, Jim. "Hitler's Christianity—Hitler Myths," *NoBeliefs*.com; http://www.nobeliefs.com/hitler-myths.htm; accessed January 2008.

[7] I am indebted to Phillip Collins for this insight (see endnote # 2).

[8] Michael Kalish, "Friedrich Nietzsche's Influence on Hitler's *Mein Kampf*"; http://www.history.ucsb.edu/faculty/marcuse/classes/133p/133p04papers/MKalishNie tzNazi046.htm; accessed January 2008. [The source he cites is Ben Macintyre, *Forgotten Fatherland: The Search for Elisabeth Nietzsche* (New York 1992)].

[9] R.J. Hollingdale, *Nietzsche: The Man and his Philosophy* (Cambridge 1999), p. 199.

[10] Peter Padfield, *Himmler: Reichsfuhrer-SS* (New York 1990), pp. 92, 402.

[11] Joachim C. Fest, *Hitler*. trans. Richard and Clara Winston (New York 1974), p. 678.

[12] Peter Myers, review of Nietzsche and Jewish Culture, Jacob Golomb ed., London and New York 1997; http://users.cyberone.com.au/myers/nietzsche.html; accessed December 2007. See also the German version of *The Antichrist* at http://www.geocities.com/thenietzschechannel/antig.htm; accessed December 2007. Kaufmann agrees with Mencken here and also says "awe-inspiring."

[13] Lowell C. Green, *Lutherans Against Hitler: The Untold Story* (St. Louis 2007), p. 113.

[14] Friedrich Nietzsche, "Nietzsche: Letters of Insanity," *The Nietzsche Channel*; http://www.geocities.com/thenietzschechannel/niletters.htm; accessed January 2008.

[15] H.L. Mencken, "Introduction to Nietzsche's Antichrist," *The Gutenberg Project*; http://www.gutenberg.org/files/19322/19322-h/19322-h.htm; accessed August 2008.

[16] Friedrich Nietzsche, *Beyond Good and Evil*, trans. Ian Johnston; http://www.mala.bc.ca/~johnstoi/Nietzsche/beyondgoodandevil8.htm; accessed January 2008.

[17] Paul Lawrence Rose, *Wagner: Race and Revolution* (New Haven 1992), pp. 100-101.

[18] Stefan Steinberg, "One hundred years since the death of Friedrich Nietzsche: a review of his ideas and influence—Parts 1–3 (Part 3)," *World Socialist Web Site*; www.wsws.org/articles/2000/oct2000/niet-o23.shtml; accessed January 2008.

[19] Nietzsche, *Beyond Good and Evil*.

[20] Stephen Wang, *The Long Road to Freedom: The Story of Wang Mingdao* (Tonbridge 2002), p. 32.

[21] Robert Wistrich, *Hitler and the Holocaust: How and Why the Holocaust Happened* (London 2002), p. 234.

[22] Weikart, p. 46.

[23] In the German Nietzsche uses the word *Entwicklung*—Mencken translates it "evolution," while Kaufmann translates it "development." See note 15 above for the link to the German original.

[24] Weikart, p. 47.

[25] Gregory Moore, excerpt from *Nietzsche, Biology and Metaphor* (Cambridge University Press Catalogue); http://www.cambridge.org/catalogue/catalogue.asp?isbn=9780521812306&ss=exc; accessed January 2008. http://assets.cambridge.org/97805218/12306/excerpt/9780521812306_excerpt.pdf; accessed January 2008. Moore mentions others who shared this view—Karl Knortz, Alexander Tille, and Kurt Bauer.

[26] Mencken, ibid.

[27] Weikart, p. 15.

[28] Ibid., pp. 82, 46.

[29] Ibid., p. 45.

[30] Ibid., p. 94.

[31] Peter Viereck, *Meta-politics: The Roots of the Nazi Mind* (New York 1965), p. 183.

[32] Ibid.

[33] Nietzsche, *Genealogy* (see note #6). All Nietzsche quotes in this section come from this source.

[34] quoted by Vox Day, *The Irrational Atheist: Dissecting the Unholy Trinity of Dawkins, Harris, and Hitchens* (Dallas 2008), p. 76.

[35] Adolf Hitler, "Excerpts from *Hitler's Table Talk*," *Kevin's Articles on Religion*; http://davnet.org/kevin/articles/table.html; accessed January 2008.

[36] Ibid.

[37] Ibid.

[38] Saul Friedländer, *The Years of Extermination: Nazi Germany and the Jews 1939-1945* (London 2007), p. 24. He is quoting Ley's book *Our Socialism: The Hate of the World (Unser Sozialismus: Der Hass der Welt)*.

[39] Ibid, p. 18.

[40] Wistrich, pp. 141-142.

[41] Ibid., p. 15.

[42] Ibid., p. 138.

[43] Ibid., p.141.

[44] Nietzsche, *Genealogy*, (see note #6).

[45] Adolf Hitler, *Hitler's Second Book: The Unpublished Sequel to <u>Mein Kampf</u>*, trans. Krista Smith (New York 2006), p. 18.

[46] Stephen R. C. Hicks, *Explaining Postmodernism: Skepticism and Socialism from Rousseau to Foucault* (Phoenix, AZ 2004), p. 105.

[47] Nick Cohen, *What's Left?* (London 2007), p. 89.

[48] Rose, p. 101.

[49] Quoted in Alister McGrath's *The Twilight of Atheism: The Rise and Fall of Disbelief in the Modern World* (London 2004), p. 114. Schopenhauer expressed a similar idea.

Conclusion

What was Naziism?

There have been many attempts to record the "what" of the Holocaust, and we can be thankful for these grim narratives and histories. Attempts to go from the "what" to the "why" are considerably less compelling. Many explorers into this realm have no real beliefs or convictions of their own; hence their explanations are necessarily shallow. Others have more firm convictions, but lack understanding of many spiritual truths and realities accessible to those who believe in the Bible and accept it as a reliable guide.

With both biblical principles and the preceding analysis in mind, we can attempt to answer some questions that have consistently occupied serious students of Hitler. Was Naziism the result of a coherent world view, or was it merely nihilistic? Was it opportunistic, the adaptation of the will-to-power to whatever means or ideas fit the circumstances? I would answer that National Socialism was all of those.

Naziism was a coherent philosophy with a logical and consistent world view derived from well over a century of respected German thought. It included a coherent concept of human nature as animal nature in need of liberation from artificial constraints of ethics and morality. There was also a metaphysic of life as a continuing ascent driven by conflict in a cosmos ruled by scientific law, yet also containing a vague and indeterminate spiritual reality that worked in the world through scientific law, and was accessible by human reason alone (the so-called Enlightenment); by science (modern secularism); and by intuition (German romanticism). This was greatly strengthened by the concept of life as an amoral struggle in which the fittest dominated by right. There was also some nihilism in that Naziism advocated, even rejoiced in, the destruction of the old moral, social, and political order. There was obviously a significant amount of opportunism as well. Merely by repeating a few simple slogans and giving unquestioning obedience, people who in normal life would never have amounted to much suddenly had the possibility of power beyond their wildest dreams. Even true believers could be opportunistic to an extent, and adapt themselves as circumstances required.

Much more could have been said about Hitler's predecessors and contemporaries. Men like Guido von List, Theodor Fritsch, Oswald Spengler, Arthur Moeller van den Bruck, and Lanz von Liebenfels, to name only a few, show that Hitler's ideas were not just his private inventions. They had an intellectual basis, and seemed respectable to many educated people before the attempt to put them into practice led to catastrophe. Rudolf von Sebottendorff of the proto-Nazi Thule Society saw life as basically struggle in which the Germans needed to prevail against their deadly enemies, the Jews.

Under all of this weird pseudo-philosophy lay the sinful will to power. Free from tedious moral laws, people were able to magnify themselves to the fullest extent; to replace God, to be their own gods, and make their own destiny; to crush the unfortunates so far beneath them, and freely wield the power of life and death like superior beings. All of this was, of course, a gigantic rebellion against the biblical God, against his laws, rules, and values, and against the boring, old-fashioned society that—though imperfect—had been so deeply influenced by those values. There was special hatred against the Jews, through whom those ideas had been introduced to the world.

This rejection of traditional religion opened the door to something new, and something worse. A new philosophy emerged out of human reason, yet with religious overtones and a deeply spiritual dimension. This "something new" offered a new chosen people, a new promised land, a new messiah, a new concept of sin (cultural and racial pollution), and a new means of salvation from sin (eliminating foreign elements). The Nazis sought "a completely experimental future."[1] Unfortunately it was all false, a clever counterfeit but a counterfeit nonetheless.

This new faith was founded on human egotism. It was a profound philosophical rationalization of the sinful human will-to-power, and it subordinated not only science, but also religion and philosophy to meet its needs. It was an attempt to replace the traditional God of revealed religion with a new god—a god that failed.

Never again

The stirring motto "Never again" is a recurring theme among those who take a serious interest in the profound questions raised by the Holocaust. The vow to make sure that "never again" will such atrocities be committed has been expressed in language as solemn and as serious as human reason can make it—but are not such resolutions idle, futile, hollow, empty, and vain, serving no other purpose than to gratify the ego?

Someone, I don't remember who, said sadly (or sarcastically?) that we can indeed be sure the Holocaust will never happen again. Never again will the Germans attempt to exterminate all of the Jews. Never again will National Socialism offer the enticing promise of world domination to a master race. Never again will there be a Second World War. Never again will we see Hitler.

The world is full of sin and evil. It has been since the fall in the Garden of Eden and will be until Christ returns. Many atrocities have taken place since 1945, though not on the scale of the Holocaust, and the world has been almost powerless to prevent them. Yet more will occur in the future, and they cannot be stopped.

These new evils will emerge in unexpected places and from unexpected directions. Those who monitor the "Christian right," mistakenly thinking that Hitler emerged from there, anxiously looking for the next Hitler in Jerry Falwell or Pat Robertson, are occupying defensive positions that will prove to be totally useless as the forces of evil that animated Hitler and his followers reappear in a different guise. Auschwitz survivor Primo Levi's comment on this is truly profound: "A new Fascism" can come "walking on tiptoe and calling itself by other names."[2] This is happening in Europe and America today.

Some lessons to be learned

The Holocaust will I believe retain its position as the symbol of ultimate evil for as long as Western civilization endures. How it will be interpreted, and what lessons will be drawn from it, are different questions altogether. Apart from the obvious insights that people who are hateful and cruel to Jews will be hateful and cruel to others as well; that people who have bizarre fantasies about the Jews will have bizarre fantasies of other sorts; that society is not automatically progressing toward higher and higher planes of civilization; that technology is not an unmixed blessing; that mankind is not basically good, what else can we conclude?

A knowledgeable writer suggested that one lesson to be gained from these horrors was the importance of resisting evil in its early stages—good advice, but he did not explain what evil was, or how we could define or recognize it, let alone resist it. The Nazis claimed *they* were resisting evil by eliminating democracy, the Jews, and Bolshevism. We have different ideas—but who are we to impose our values on others? You can talk as much as you like, but as soon as you try to really impose your concepts of right and wrong some hysterical atheist will start shrieking about the Taliban (unless your values are the same as his).

The same author just referred to also stated that the crimes of the Nazis confirm that racism and anti-Semitism should not be tolerated. Now, that is a truth with which I can whole-heartedly concur—but Lenin and Mao were not racists or anti-Semites, and they slaughtered countless millions of people. Stalin was not a racist, and the anti-Semitism that came to the fore late in his life had nothing to do with the vast majority of his evil deeds.

Those who want to fight evil first of all have to understand what evil is. They also need a firm basis for their understanding, one that is shared by enough people to make joint action possible. Secondly, they have to be prepared to fight evil— and by "fight" I don't mean only standing up for the truth, as vital as that first step is. I also mean "fight" as in war legally waged by duly appointed governments, using bombs and bullets, and requiring blood, guts, self-sacrifice, heroism, determination, perseverance, and confidence in the rightness of one's cause.

These two qualities—understanding of evil and the strength to resist it—are not in abundance in our modern western society. Those who have been brought up to believe that the supreme goods of life are pleasure, self-indulgence, passive comfort, and security, are not going to have the will to resist. Believing that "One man's terrorist is another man's freedom fighter" doesn't help. Can those who think that George Washington was no different from Yassir Arafat really be expected to fight evil?

This was one of Hitler's advantages over his opponents (both in Germany and abroad). He not only had a clear perception of his goals and values: he also had the strength of will to pursue them. Far from fearing conflict or shrinking from it, he prized it, valued it, and sought it. Like Hegel, Schopenhauer, Marx, and Darwin, he believed that conflict was a necessary, inevitable, and positive aspect of life.

One lesson to be learned from all of this, then, is that without a strong and deeply rooted understanding of right and wrong, we will not be able to recognize or resist evil—especially when it emerges in new and previously unseen forms. Where can such an understanding be found? I believe it can only be found in biblical Christianity of a sort that is very rare anywhere—though a defense of this assertion would take me far beyond the confines of this conclusion.

The role of government

Another lesson has to do with the purpose of government. Are governments supposed to save the human race? Bring paradise on earth? Establish Utopia? Secularists who have a humanly derived vision of the social ideal will answer

"Yes"—and woe unto those who stand in the way of the future happiness of mankind!

Bible-believing Christians, on the other hand, if their ideals are properly derived from Paul's Letter to the Romans, have a much more modest concept of government. They understand that evil in society is caused by evil in the human heart. They do not believe that evil will be eliminated and paradise established on earth before Jesus Christ returns. They see the purpose of government as being to restrain and punish evil so that society can function in its flawed but ordinary ways.

This minimal role of government explains why totalitarian attempts to save humanity, to introduce paradise, to radically improve society, only emerged out of secular philosophies subsequent to the turning away from religion. The difference between Christianity and secularism in this respect is the difference between Calvin Coolidge and Joseph Stalin. There were of course governmental excesses in the traditionally Christian centuries before the modern era, but they were nothing like modern totalitarianism—and they were also a deviation from the biblical role of government as explained by Paul. To force religion on people is not a divinely ordained purpose of government.

This is why Paul commanded obedience even to authorities that were persecuting Christianity—but the obedience has limits. It is not blind and unthinking. Governments have no authority to tell us what to believe, and they have no authority to force us to disobey the commandments of God.

John Calvin has been much abused in this respect. Some like to compare him to Lenin because of his alleged fanaticism and totalitarianism. If they would think more carefully about Calvin's Geneva, they might understand that Geneva was not surrounded by barbed wire, mine fields, and guard dogs. People who did not like Geneva were free to walk out of the city at any time, without passports or visas, and go a few miles down the road to another city in the same country. Not that I am a great fan of Calvin's, but comparing him to Lenin or to modern totalitarianism is unreasonable and unjustified.

It says a great deal that one man (Servetus) condemned to death by the city government of Geneva counts for more with some than tens of millions of people shot, beaten, tortured, enslaved, starved, and gassed by the forces of modern secularism. If someone does not believe in Christianity that is their choice, but those who compare Calvin to Lenin either have difficulty with rational thought on this subject, or else are propagandizing—that is, making statements they know to be false in order to achieve some other end. This means they are liars.

Returning to the subject of the role of government, the founders of American democracy may not have been Christian themselves, but their understanding of limited government emerged out of a culture in which the single most powerful and deep source of values was inarguably Christianity. This is why the erosion of Christian influence and the rise of secularism in America have been accompanied by a dramatic expansion in the size and the role of government.

In the Christian view, government is essentially a policeman—now, it has become not only a policeman, but also a nanny, teacher, guide, healer, and provider of happiness and material security. It has also become a means of steering society toward an imaginary secular ideal. The end of this process will have been reached when the government is master, tyrant, source of values, spiritual guide—and chastiser of those who do not conform. This chastisement will be done by all-knowing experts (like Sam Harris and Richard Dawkins) for the good of humanity.

This has been a dream of a certain segment of society since the days of Plato. That great philosopher, whose achievements were in many ways so impressive, foolishly imagined he could invent out of his own brain an ideal society. In this society people such as himself (naturally) would be the rulers, the elite—lesser people would have to toil in their appointed stations. Others since Plato have had a similar dream of remaking humanity according to their liking, but not until the modern era and the emergence of poisonous secular philosophies did this take place on a grand scale.

Defective human reason

This leads us to the shocking discovery that human reason by itself is not a trustworthy or reliable guide. People who reject the Bible and divine revelation can brag and boast of their rationality all day, but the fact remains that—in the case of Germany at least—it was human logic and wisdom apart from divine revelation that led to the concepts of Aryan supremacy; life as Darwinian struggle only; hostility to democracy; euthanasia; the insignificance of human life; and the belief that the Jews were deliberately undermining the Aryan race to reach their own goal of world domination.

From whence do we derive our law, our justice, our sense of good and evil, of right and wrong? If we derive these from God, as given to us in the Bible, there will be mistakes and errors. We live in a fallen world and the purpose of Christianity is not to usher in a golden age prior to Christ's return. If, however, we make ourselves into gods and rely only on ourselves, inventing our own private realities, then we are headed inevitably toward catastrophe.

It is easy to talk about the necessity of the "rule of law"—but whose law? Which law? The Nazis thought they were following the rule of law—the law of nature, which decreed that life was a harsh and amoral struggle. Some of us object to that, but on what basis? Personal feeling? Something more than that is needed.

Humanistic inspired catastrophe can take many forms. There can be disasters very different from the Third Reich in outward appearance, yet still inspired by human reason striving on its own without reference to divine truth (how the world hates those words, "divine truth"). The disasters of the Soviet Union and of Red China are well-known examples of human reason out of control. Less obvious is the disaster of liberal secular humanism and socialism. These philosophical vices are eating out the heart of the West like a malignant cancer, and sinking it to new lows of depravity, cowardice, stupid complacency, effeminacy, ignorance, and evil. The apostles of the New Militant Atheism, with their books, debates, lectures, and DVDs are leading their gullible followers to the abyss of new totalitarianisms, new evils, and—if they are successful—to the collapse of Western civilization.

This is one of the most important but little-understood lessons of Hitler: that those who thought they would usher in a better world by rejecting religion and relying on reason alone were deceived. Primo Levi wrote that one safeguard against another Holocaust is "to renounce revealed truths."[3] He did not consider that when revealed truths are renounced, people will not automatically lapse into the desired neutrality and passivity. Some will, but others will invent new replacement truths, as did Marx, Wagner, Haeckel, Hitler, Lenin, and Stalin—as does Richard Dawkins. What we need is the rediscovery of truth, the recovery of truth, not its abandonment.

The reality of evil

Not only is there such a thing as evil, but many people embrace evil and follow it enthusiastically. These dark truths should forever destroy the dimwitted liberal fantasy of human nature as being basically good—and would destroy it, were not some people irrevocably attached to their secular myths. Those who continue to hold to this fiction in our day and age are divorced from reality on a deep level. They are walking, talking, debating, and writing in their sleep.

Such unpleasant truths as the reality of evil and the sinfulness of human nature do not in any way undermine the Christian religion. Believers in the Bible know the innate sinfulness of man. We know this not only because "the Bible tells me so," but because we have experienced it in ourselves. Pride, revenge, hatred, ignorance, misunderstanding, darkness, irrationality—I have experienced all of these things in myself and know that, were it not for God's grace, there is literally no evil I would not be capable of.

Human nature being what it is, any one should have been able to predict that the end of World War II would not usher in a golden age of world peace—and what horrors has the world seen in the subsequent sixty years? Biafra, the Sudan, Cambodia, the Congo, China—not to mention the countless individual cruelties, horrors, rapes, tortures, murders inflicted throughout the world. These do not approach the rationalized and industrialized technological nightmare of the Holocaust, but they show without question that the world is a dark place. It will remain so until Christ returns.

A renowned scholar, historian, and Holocaust expert wrote of the need for vigilance—but vigilance without the ability to act is useless. What good does it do us to be alert for coming danger if, when it comes, we are too passive, weak, cowardly and immersed in our love of pleasures and vice to confront it bravely? But bravery is an old-fashioned virtue. The ability to be caring, compassionate, sensitive, and nuanced is more valued today—unfortunately, these are not qualities that are of much use when locked in a desperate struggle with openly malignant evil.

People need something to believe in

Like many today, a significant number of Germans in the 19th century saw Christianity as false—outdated, unscientific, and an obstacle to progress. They thought by eliminating Christianity they would be opening the door to a better, brighter future. In their attempts to eliminate Christianity and replace it with something better, they did indeed open a door—a door to something worse. In Germany, the loneliness of modern unbelief, and the inability to confront the black emptiness of a cosmos with no higher purpose, led people to find deeper meaning in the state. They also found it in the race, and in the nation, which they considered to be synonymous. They found it in the vision of an earthly, secular paradise freed of the distractions and cumbrances of God, divine law, sin, righteousness, the judgment, heaven and hell.

The results of this are known to all. People who think themselves to be only animals in the end become even worse than animals. The removal of divinely placed barriers leaves people vulnerable to passions and sins that not even beasts can conceive of. If people look to Christianity for guidance, there will inevitably be errors and sins, as we live in a fallen world—but there is also a real possibility of peace, harmony, and wisdom. This has been found by the countless millions of Christians who, while fallible, have been sincere enough about following the teachings of Jesus to live harmless and ordinary lives, harming no one. If, however, people reject Christianity and rely on reason alone, science alone, then disaster is certain and sure. Any real hope of finding life's higher meaning is lost, and people descend deeper and deeper into darkness as they go farther and farther from God. In so doing, they will pursue evil to its farthest limits. That is why today a woman will have her breasts cut off, why people will have sex change operations or use hormones to try and alter their gender. Unisex public restrooms are demanded for people who "feel" they are of another gender. Child pornography is considered free speech, while the condemnation of homosexuality is not. Neurotics and psychotics who do not even know if they are men or women must be protected from the contrary views of ordinary people, as if said neurotics and psychotics have the "right" to live in a world where no one and nothing makes them feel "uncomfortable." I personally do not want or expect the right to live in a world where no one disagrees with me or criticizes me.

The importance of philosophy, or, the sinister logic of evil

Many people who take more than a passing interest in the problem of National Socialism assume that German philosophy is of little or no relevance. What, after all, could a crazy man like Hitler have had to do with Kant, Hegel, Fichte, and other lesser lights of autonomous human reason? Philosophy is the attempt to understand the world by reason—and National Socialism (to judge by outward appearances) was so manifestly unreasonable as to preclude any possibility of a connection.

Most of the German philosophy that emerged out of the "Enlightenment" rejection of Christianity was totally irrelevant to the Nazis. No one claims that Hitler's storm troopers and death camp guards studied the boring absurdities of Hegelian or Fichtean metaphysics in depth. Nevertheless, some who have read German philosophy with the Third Reich in mind have detected important themes that later proved to be foundational to National Socialism. Philosophy does, over time, influence society, and themes that were first articulated in extremely isolated and sheltered academic settings made their way gradually into broader social and intellectual circles as the nineteenth century progressed. They became, in the much different context of a unified and industrialized Germany, the basis for the proto-Nazi Folkish movement. Four such concepts were: (a) a new concept of the German people; (b) the Jews as antitypes of a Germanic ideal; (c) a radically different concept of the state; and (d) concepts of ethics unheard of in previous Western history.

The new concept of the German people, their nature and their role in history, was a major stepping stone on the way to the Holocaust. In a way totally incompatible with any serious commitment to biblical Christianity, unknown in the previous 1500 years of Christian dominance, the German people were assigned, in the wisdom of philosophy, to an exalted place in the history of mankind. History was seen as progress—itself an unbiblical notion—and the Germans were placed in the vanguard. Thus, the survival, advance, and domination of the German race were beneficial to humanity, essential to humanity.

Behold how "philosophy" becomes the handmaiden of ego. German cultural purity now becomes paramount—and which alien group had most deeply infested the German body, introducing false values and contaminating the racial and spiritual purity of the Folk? Even before the much later addition of racial concepts derived from biology, the Jews were identified as a menace.

About the second point, secular thinkers were not concerned about God's wrath on the Jewish people for their rejection of the Son of God. This was not relevant to them. Their hostility to Judaism emerged from their negative perception of Torah itself, their hostility to eternal and unchanging laws that, if true, permanently nullified their entire philosophical enterprise. They saw the Jews as isolated from humanity and hence not fully human in a new sense. Kant's concept of the Jews as "materialistic" in this philosophical sense—unheard of in previous centuries, nonsensical in a Christian context, and much more serious than mere stereotypes of Jews as miserly—emerged as one of the staples of later 19th-century concepts of "the Jew." On this point Hitler followed Kant in *Mein Kampf*, not Luther.

A second aspect of this second point was hostility to the Jews for having introduced Christianity. This theme emerged with increasing virulence as Christianity became less and less respected, and more and more open to criticism. Christianity was rejected as false, unhealthy, unGermanic, alien, Mediterranean—and where did it come from? From the Jews. This essay's emphasis on Nietzsche should not obscure the point that he was by no means alone in his analysis—he was only more outspoken.

Others such as Chamberlain, Wagner, and many others who saw some merit remaining in Christianity after it had been purged of its Jewish values, distorted it beyond recognition. The Trinity, the Virgin birth, the sacrificial death and resurrection of Christ, his return as God to judge the world, an eternity in heaven and hell—these were dispensed with. What was left was the reigning secular Folkish philosophy expressed in vague religious language that sounds "Christian" to ignorant secularists with no real desire to understand Christianity.

A third contribution of "philosophy" was a new concept of the state. In a total repudiation of biblical concepts, the state was presented by Hegel (and by others) as the instrument of destiny, the agent of human progress. To submit to the state was freedom, to rebel against it was to be out of harmony with the right order of things. The state became not the means of ensuring order and keeping the peace, but the means of leading mankind on toward its higher destiny.

Numbers of scholars have related Hegel to modern totalitarianism and rightly so—but this is not to blame everything on Hegel. With the loss of God, the state inevitably loomed larger on the horizon. People looked more and more to the state for answers to life's problems and even as a source of meaning.

A fourth change was in the area of ethics. With the loss of divine creation and the denial of the immortal soul, man is inevitably devalued. Hegel's glorification of Napoleon and of war, as well as his complete indifference to countless deaths and immense suffering, were not merely personal defects of Hegel's. He articulated and encouraged, but did not of course single-handedly cause, a dramatic shift that was to become increasingly dominant as the nineteenth century progressed.

A quote from historian of philosophy Stephen R. C. Hicks is appropriate here. Writing about the popularity of National Socialism among university students before 1933, he states, "Raised in an intellectual culture in which Kant, Fichte, Hegel, Marx, Nietzsche, and Spengler were the dominant voices, National Socialism seemed to many to be a moral ideal, just as it did to many of their professors, who had been schooled in the same works."[4] Radicals on the left and on the right were rebelling against "the system." In their folly they only made things worse—much worse. This is one of the biggest problems of secularists—their inability to recognize our human limits in their rash attempts to save the world.

There were of course wars and moral indifference to suffering and death in the more traditionally Christian centuries preceding—that was due to sinful human nature. Yet, enough people were serious and informed about Christian values for death and war to be generally recognized by thinking people as evils—not as matters of indifference, or as healthy, constructive, and good. It took modern secular "philosophy" to devalue human life in a new way, to a new extent.

All of the foolish tendencies that emerged out of the "Enlightenment" were greatly inflamed by Darwinism. What was first presented only as a scientific theory of origins quickly morphed into a pseudo-scientific justification for previous ideas of racism and German supremacy. It became a fertile source for new ideas as well. Death came to be seen not as evil, but rather as normal, natural, even a means of progress. Ethics was reduced to a simple matter of survival, of might makes right. The German people were presented as the strongest and best to emerge out of a Darwinian struggle, with a natural right to dominate their inferiors (inferiority and superiority following logically from Darwinian principles). The value of human life was debased and the door was open to industrialized slaughter on a scale previously undreamed of.

The relevance for today

In a significant article, Raymond Ibrahim has pointed to parallels between Hitler's *Mein Kampf* and writing by members of Al Qaeda.[5] He notes the following similarities:

~ contempt for democracy
~ glorification of violence and a call to struggle, sacrifice, commitment
~ global ambitions of domination
~ a vision of society that has to be imposed by force for the good of the human race, in the service of a higher power
~ virulent anti-Semitism, that presents Jews as a major source of evil and calls for their elimination

Directly repudiating the dull and hamster-like secular/liberal/socialist ideal of complacent and pampered hedonism, these commonalities show that Naziism was not exclusively a German phenomenon, but had deep roots in human nature as well. At present, Al Qaeda's ambitions seem ludicrous—but then, so did Hitler's in 1922. Those who are fearless, highly motivated, and firmly committed to their goals, can achieve a great deal.

An analysis of contemporary leftist politics (*What's Left?* by Nick Cohen) also illustrates the ideological kinship between National Socialism and Islamic extremism. Back in the 1950s Sayyid Qutb (an early advocate of jihad against the decadent West) saw the Jews (in Cohen's words) "as the force behind all the secular ideas that threatened the sacred power."[6] Like Richard Wagner, Qutb had an imaginary social ideal, and he saw the Jews as the embodiment and source of everything contrary to that ideal. Some ideas expressed by Hamas about the world Jewish conspiracy are identical to Hitler's.[7]

Less easy to describe are the ways in which the spirit of falsehood that animated National Socialism has emerged and is emerging in new and different (yet closely related) forms in the Western democracies. Much more cleverly disguised behind rhetoric about "peace," "justice," and so on (though Hitler also used those words), modern secularism, like Naziism, represents a rejection of divinely revealed biblical law and an attempt to reconstruct human society by reason alone.

Consider the similarities: in both Naziism and secular liberalism, a vision of a this-worldly ideal is presented. Attainable by human reason, will, and effort without reference to divine law, the two Utopias are outwardly diametrically opposed, yet spring from the same root—the root of human folly, sin, and rebellion against God.

The Nazi vision was of Aryan domination. Inferior races were either exterminated or enslaved, and life was lived according to nature, without artificial laws and rules to prevent the deepest inner fulfillment of the master race. "According to nature" meant perpetual conflict, a struggle for domination in which the weak rightly perished and the strong rightly ruled. It sought the maximum fulfillment of the will-to-power.

Today's secular vision also seeks a life "according to nature," a life in which people are free to pursue their natural instincts without divine hindrance—but with a much different understanding of what that might mean. A "natural" life in the current context means an animal-like existence not of violent struggle but of physical comfort and pleasure, of hedonism. This includes freedom to eat, sleep, drink, enjoy oneself, and have sex without regard to moral laws and rules. As the Nazis used "Nature" to justify militarism and pitiless cruelty—"animals are not concerned with ethics and we are animals"—so the secularists use "Nature" to justify homosexuality, immorality, or a simple-minded life of pleasure or personal comfort. Animals engage in homosexual activity (it is claimed) so it is right; animals are not concerned with their eternal destiny and neither should we be.

All of this makes a lot of sense—if we accept the belief that we are in essence only animals; if we reject the divine creation of man as presented in Genesis. That we should act naturally, like animals, because we are animals can—like atheism or Darwinism—be used to justify very different kinds of activity. It can be used to justify violence, imperialism and militarism, or pacifism, hedonism, and sexual license. The parts of the plant look very different—but the root is the same.

In order to create the desired society, a new type of man was required for Naziism, and for Communism. The ideal "New Soviet Man" or the ideal "Aryan Man" were wholly and unswervingly committed to the new ideologies, indifferent to and contemptuous of conflicting traditional values—and the Ideal Secular Man? What is the ideal today's modern visionaries hope to create?

To understand this more fully we need to emphasize that the envisioners of a new society are also seeking to create a New Woman. Their goal is the complete elimination of the traditionally passive, quiet, sensitive, domestic woman. The

New Woman does not find her fulfillment in the home—she finds it in being as much like a man as possible, identical to men, even superior to them.

This New Woman is supposed to be strong, smart, tough, sophisticated, fully capable of fulfilling a man's role in every sphere—in the factory, the office, or even on the battlefield. According to this ideological ideal women are even being presented, increasingly, as superior to men—more sensitive, less egotistical, less violent, wiser, emotionally stronger. For a super-woman such as this, domestic duties are a bore and child-raising is a nuisance. The Nazis tried to create supermen, and their folly is now known to all. How long will it be before the attempt to create super-women is likewise recognized as false, evil, destructive, impossible, and absurd?

The New Secular Man is supposed to accommodate this dream of unisex. He sees himself as essentially no different from a woman, as obligated to defer to women and encourage, help, and support them in their drive to excel. He must be gentle, sensitive, compassionate, avoid doing anything that offends women, and cater to their demands and expectations. He must also never impose on the woman's total freedom to be or do whatever she wishes.

It will be readily apparent that this is the exact opposite of the Nazi ideal. The Aryan Man was supposed to be strong, warlike, proud, fierce; the Aryan woman was supposed to be traditionally feminine, occupied with her home, her husband, and her children. It is less readily apparent that both of these visions spring from the same mentality—to recreate the human personality according to a false philosophy, a false ideal, in defiance of God's plan. Both new and modern visions are (or were) unnatural. The first one failed (as did the similar Soviet fantasy); the second will fail as well.

Both National Socialism and the New Secularism were / are hostile to traditional Christianity. The reason is not far to seek. Since biblical values strongly condemn both humanistic visions, and present a radically different ideal, biblical values were/are an obstacle to be eliminated. This was done in Germany by propaganda, by preaching the new faith—especially by indoctrinating children—by repression and by persecution.

Recognizing many obvious differences between America and Nazi Germany, and dismissing as absurd allegations that Bush is like Hitler, that the American invasion of Kuwait was like the Nazi invasion of Poland, we can nevertheless see some ominous parallels. In both Nazi Germany and the modern western democracies (not only America), followers of a false philosophy seized and are now seizing power by democratic means—to be followed by repression once enough power is obtained legally.

In America we are now in the propaganda stage. Events in Europe and Canada indicate that repression is not far away. People who have invented their own new reality will strive to eliminate Christianity from the public sphere. This includes the secularization of religious holidays; increasing attacks on Christianity in the media and in the educational systems; and especially use of the educational system to indoctrinate children in the new philosophy. Christians will be condescendingly promised complete freedom to talk about Christ privately as much as they like, as long as they don't try to influence society. This happened in Germany—will it happen in America?

Many churches, pastors, theologians, bishops, and of course nominal believers will effortlessly accommodate themselves to the new philosophy, as they did in

Nazi Germany. They will accept and have already accepted feminism, gay rights, evolution (crucial to the idea that we are nothing but animals), socialism, big government—all of the essential doctrines of the New Humanism. Naturally, this is accompanied if not preceded by the abandonment of biblical authority and many or all essential doctrines. Those who disagree will be reluctant to speak out. The few who do speak out will first be dismissed as eccentrics and extremists, and then—when the secularists are strong enough to dispense with their masks and reveal their true faces—persecuted.

Using the state as a means of social engineering was the essence of National Socialism and Communism; it is the essence of secular humanism today. In the name of tolerance, dissenting views will be ridiculed and persecuted. "Freedom" will come to mean "freedom to be like everyone else," or "freedom to obey the state." False, unnatural, and destructive philosophies will be proclaimed as the norm, and those who have invented their own reality will find meaning and purpose in struggling to impose their values on others. They are on a crusade to remake the world.

There is another similarity between the two false philosophies: a fascination with the primitive. Just as the German racists enthused over the German barbarians, so the modern secularists are attracted by the primitive and violent people in the Third World or in the urban ghettoes. The reason is that such people are supposedly more authentic, closer to real life, harder, tougher, free from the burdens imposed by false traditional morality.

Of course, there are differences between these two secular visions that go in radically different directions from the same starting point of human autonomy. The modern secularists glorify not war but hedonism, an easy and passive life devoted to pleasure. Food and drink, entertainments and amusements, money, sports, sex, leisure—these are the objects of their greatest desire. They do not lift up the white male but do the exact opposite—make him an object of ridicule, inferior to women, people of color, and even to children. They advocate not nationalism, but internationalism, and actively seek to undermine the existence and even the concept of the sovereign nation state. Hitler's nationalism was, however, subordinate to his racism. He saw the German nation as a means to a global goal, not an end in itself—so this difference is not so great.

One last difference is that the forces of traditional morality are putting up a stronger fight in America (they have been completely marginalized in Europe). This resistance, though feeble, has served to retard the progress of liberal secularism somewhat, but the onward march of the new philosophy is, for the present, irresistible. I say "for the present" as at some point it will end in disaster, in catastrophe, in chaos, as other false ideologies have before it.

For now, however, the new philosophy carries all before it—slowly, irrevocably, surely, at times imperceptibly. Gay rights, feminism, Darwinism, socialism, pornography, loss of traditional liberties, the marginalization of Christians—these are increasing with gathering strength and speed. Their final triumph may be closer than anyone thinks. There are encouraging signs of increasing opposition to Darwinism because of its many inherent flaws, but the Darwinists are coming to rely increasingly on the power of the state to silence dissent and keep their views dominant.

It took a little over a century for the forces of darkness to triumph in Germany after they first emerged in the German "Enlightenment." Perhaps the next few decades or even less will see the final collapse of traditional morality in America and the emergence of a left-wing secular dictatorship that practices cruelty and oppression "for the good of humanity." Jamie Glazov's book *United in Hate* provides many examples of left-wing secularists whose concepts of morality allow for all sorts of atrocities in the pursuit of their imaginary goals of "peace" and "justice."[8]

An interesting in-depth analysis of shared characteristics between the modern secular left and fascism is found in Jonah Goldberg's book *Liberal Fascism: The Secret History of the American Left from Mussolini to the Politics of Meaning.* Goldberg elaborates at length on the spiritual kinship between the fascism of Hitler and Mussolini and the goals and tactics of modern American liberals as well as of the radical left. He gives in support of his thesis the use of government to impose a secular ideal by force, and a vision of national unity in which dissenting views are unwelcome. Other profound similarities are the emphasis on deeds and action, and the desire to replace an outdated status quo with a Utopian vision. Hence the obsession with change, even violent change.[9]

This being so—and Goldberg's points are well-documented—it is no surprise that those on the left consistently display admiration for such left-wing fascist butchers as Castro and Che Guevara. Such comments of Che's as "hatred as an element of struggle; unbending hatred of the enemy, which pushes a human being beyond his natural limitations, making him into an effective, violent, selective and cold-blooded killing machine"[10] are deeply impressive to those on the left whose own soft and spineless lives make them yearn for action, commitment, violence. They are too simple-minded to see that it is this mentality, not the mentality of Jerry Falwell, that breeds little Hitlers.

That the self-proclaimed advocates of secular tolerance might themselves be (like some theists) fully capable of killing for their beliefs is exemplified by the popular atheist author Sam Harris. In his book *The End of Faith*, he states that "Some propositions are so dangerous that it may even be ethical to kill people for believing them."[11] This statement raised so many eyebrows, even among atheists, that Harris felt compelled to give an explanation on the internet.[12] Since this attitude is directly related to the crimes of Hitler, Stalin, Lenin, and Mao, it merits some discussion.

Attempting to dispel criticisms of his remark, Harris first gives on the internet the relevant passage from *The End of Faith*. Then he concedes that he did not express himself as well as he might have—"Granted, I made the job of misinterpreting me easier than it might have been"—and goes on to claim that saying he wants to kill people for their ideas "remains a frank distortion of my views." He explains:

> When one asks why it would be ethical to drop a bomb on Osama bin Laden or Ayman Al Zawahiri, the answer cannot be, "because they have killed so many people in the past." These men haven't, to my knowledge, killed anyone personally. However, they are likely to get a lot of innocent people killed because of what they and their followers believe about jihad, martyrdom, the ascendancy of Islam, etc.

At this point we can breathe a sigh of relief—if he only wants to kill some terrorists then it's alright—and Harris (who wears a white hat) can go back to his hobby of demonizing theists (who wear black hats). A closer examination of his explanation reveals, however, a couple of difficulties.

For one thing, millions of people share Osama bin Laden's ideas. Should they be killed? If Sam Harris says "Yes," then he wants to slaughter millions of people not because they have done anything wrong, but because they might do something wrong someday. That was Lenin the atheist's reasoning in a nutshell. It's easy for people who deny the immortal soul to advocate—and do—such things. If, on the other hand, Harris says millions of people should not be killed for their ideas, but should only be killed if they put their ideas into practice, or if they enable and cause others to put those ideas into practice, then he has shifted ground considerably, and did express himself poorly.

A second problem with this is that in his aforementioned book *The End of Faith*, Harris has repeatedly identified not only Islamic extremists, but also Christians who believe in the Bible, as threats to the survival of humanity. According to him, belief in the Bible is a threat to civilization and Christians, not just Osama bin Laden, could easily be included among those whose dangerous ideas require their elimination.

Many quotes could be given to show that Harris sees theism, including biblical Christianity, as a danger.

> . . . our religious differences—and hence our religious *beliefs* [emphasis in original]—*antithetical to our survival* [emphasis added]. We can no longer ignore the fact that billions of our neighbors believe in the metaphysics of martyrdom, or in the literal truth of the book of Revelation . . .Words like "God" and "Allah" *must* [emphasis added] go the way of "Apollo" and "Baal," or they will unmake our world. "[13]

> . . . faith is still the mother of hatred . . . The only salient difference between Muslims and non-Muslims is that the latter have not proclaimed their faith in Allah, and in Mohammed as his prophet. [Harris is imprecise in his use of language here—he says "non-Muslims" when he means "non-Muslim theists like Christians and Jews," not "all non-Muslims"—but his meaning is clear from the preceding words and from the whole thrust of the chapter.][14]

Words like "the fall of civilization," "could ultimately destroy us," "driving us toward the abyss," "life-destroying gibberish" (this of both the Koran and the Bible)[15] tell us that Sam "The-sky-is-falling" Harris wants to save the human race from religion—and what might not be done if the fate of humanity is at stake? Wouldn't it be justified to kill some people to save humanity—especially if they have no immortal souls and are nothing but matter?

Harris does not just want to save humanity—he wants to "create the world anew." This requires "the building of strong communities"[16] where everyone will think the way Sam Harris wants them to. Wouldn't life be so much easier in a "unified" community where everyone marched to the beat of the same drum? That was Hitler's and Lenin's dream exactly. To achieve this secular paradise religion, especially Christianity and Islam, needs to go. It is urgent for the future well-being of humanity. Religious faith "must" disappear. "Religious tolerance . . . is one of the principle forces driving us toward the abyss." Along with this clear call for intolerance, Harris advocates "uprooting" religion, which he falsely describes as "the most prolific source of violence in our history."[17] Somehow he blames the Korean War, the Vietnam War, the War of 1812, drug related ghetto violence and World Wars I & II on religion.

Sam Harris has a strong incentive to "uproot" the ideas that "must" disappear—the salvation of the human race. Do I need to point out that the word "uproot" has connotations of violence? Sam Harris openly said people with dangerous ideas might justly be killed, and then, when questioned, said "Oh, I just meant a few terrorists." He has identified theists, including Bible believing Christians, as people with dangerous ideas that menace the human race. That Christianity is dangerous is one of the main themes of his *Letter to a Christian Nation*. What is to prevent him, or those with his "values," from believing that killing Christians, or any other believers, is necessary for the good of mankind?

"The world would be a much better place if we could just get rid of (a) the capitalists and kulaks; (b) the Jews; (c) people who believe in God. They are to blame for all our problems. They are enemies of humanity, and we are doing the world a favor by getting rid of them."

Once an atheist accused me of "paranoia" on this point—but I am not the least bit paranoid about Sam Harris. I realize he may just be talking without knowing what he is saying—though I doubt it. I realize he will probably never get his hands on the levers of power. I only want to suggest that he may, like Hitler, be pointing at other people as the source of evil when he is a source of evil himself. Certainly the atheists Lenin, Stalin, and Mao make Osama bin Laden look like a Boy Scout. Hitler also gave plausible explanations to those who were concerned about his radical statements. Furthermore, Sam Harris' ideas might be taken to extremes he does not foresee, just as the pernicious ideas of German philosophers and scientists fed the mind of Hitler. But then, maybe he does foresee extreme consequences, and intends them.

Perhaps, since the idea that bloodshed follows from secular ideas is one of the main ideas of this study, it might not be too much of a digression to look at another place where Sam Harris advocates a policy that could lead to the deaths of millions. Referring to the SARS scare that emerged out of China in 2003, Harris states that the consequences of China's irrational and politically motivated policies did not lead to catastrophe—that time. He goes on to say that it is "not difficult to imagine" a situation where inability to properly handle such a health crisis would be too dangerous for the entire world. In that case, "There is little doubt we would ultimately quarantine, invade, or otherwise subjugate such a society."[18]

This is a remarkable statement. If a truly world-threatening epidemic were to emerge from China, the Sudan, Burma, Mexico, Rumania, or some other country whose health-standards were less than adequate, Harris thinks it might be necessary to "invade" or "subjugate" such a country. Oh, he allows for the possibility of a quarantine as well, but he can calmly and rationally advocate a policy—including subjugating China or, who knows, even Russia—that would cause unimaginable suffering and slaughter.

Sam Harris has a vision of an ideal world. In this world, there would be no irrational health policies and no security threats, because everyone would have basically the same ideas (his ideas naturally). In order to attain this vision, some people will have to go. Religious people have to go, and threats to the general well-being must be subjugated, by force and invasion and full scale war if necessary. Sam Harris is a good example of how the road to secular Utopias leads through swamps, bogs, and quagmires of human blood and bones—but in the end Utopia proves to be unattainable, so all of the suffering was in vain.

Even more genuinely peaceful advocates of New Age philosophies can make ominous statements. I recently came across a book that advocated finding inner peace and harmony through the ancient wisdom of the East. Discover the hidden potential of your mind, don't allow yourself to be hampered by negative thoughts, find your true destiny—all of that sounds very innocuous. What is not so innocuous is the statement that we should shake off the shackles of reason and logic and rely only on our intuition. This was a key principle of National Socialism. It seems harmless in the American context—but if people lose their peace and prosperity and become desperate enough, angry enough, their previous abandonment of reason and logic and their devotion to intuition will leave them vulnerable to the false messiahs that will surely arise out of chaos. The basic human tendencies that underlay Hitler's success are alive and well in America today.

This brings up another lesson that should be derived from the contemplation of the Hitler catastrophe. When people who reject God and his laws sit in their studies and begin to dream up new ideals for society, becoming intoxicated by humanly derived visions previously unheard of, thinking they can remake the world according to their liking, we are safe as long as no one tries to put their ideals into practice. When people do try to put those ideals into practice—be they French revolutionaries, Russian revolutionaries, Nazis, or modern secularists with their new ideas of a global paradise—disaster is sure to follow.

Abortion

That the destruction of millions of innocent people at the hands of secularists is not merely a fantasy or a rhetorical sally on my part is evident when we consider the modern practice of baby-killing. This highlights the underlying spiritual kinship between key aspects of modern secular liberalism and National Socialist fanaticism.

Consider, if you will, the following points. In both cases we have a totally false philosophy of life: on the one hand, National Socialism; on the other, a new ideology claiming that women are supposed to be identical to men, that a woman's happiness in life requires her to be as much like a man as possible; that sex is a recreational activity, a game, a sport, to be pursued without rules or limits, and enjoyed without consequences or responsibilities.

Both of these two philosophies are totally false, contrary to human nature and centuries of human experience, and derived from secular human wisdom in defiance of plain biblical teachings that are dismissed with contempt as irrelevant. More importantly, both philosophies arbitrarily categorize entire groups of people, Jews or unborn babies, as subhumans. Jews and babies were or are obstacles to the desired goals of Aryan racial and cultural purity or total freedom for the woman. They were/are dismissed as less than fully human, and then slaughtered in the millions—callously, efficiently, legally, without a qualm, and all for the good of humanity.

To be sure, there are differences. No one claims the two situations are identical (I am familiar with the trick of pointing to some differences and then ignoring similarities). A woman chooses to murder her baby of her own free will—but then, come to think of it, the Nazis also chose to kill Jews of their own free will. Did the Jews have free choice? No. Do unborn babies have free choice? No. There is freedom for the criminal, but none for the helpless and innocent victims.

There are more parallels. Both ideologies use/used euphemisms, innocent-sounding language, to conceal the viciousness and brutality of their ugly and evil crimes. "Choice . . . resettlement . . . termination of pregnancy . . . natural reduction" (through hard labor on starvation rations without adequate medical care or housing)—these and many other verbal tricks are/were used to conceal truth and ease the consciences of the killers.

Both ideologies also rely/relied on pseudo-science to justify their crimes. Nazi racial scientists, professors with degrees and credentials, could show that Jews were not really human. In the same way, abortionists can also make their case. "Prove that a Jew or a fetus really is human"—you can't to those who are determined not to accept it. What if someone had earnestly said to an SS man, "But Jews really are human beings"?

Hopefully future ages will look with horror, disgust, and mystification on the practice of treating little babies as if they were garbage, ripping them apart, smashing their skulls, just as we today look on the crimes of the Nazis. Maybe future generations will clearly see that since the fetus is fully human in its origin, and fully human in its end, it is also human in between.

So great are the parallels between these two cases of legally sanctioned and socially approved mass murder, that I make the following assertions: someone who kills unborn babies is morally no better than someone who kicked Jews to death or shoved them into the gas chambers. Someone who participates in the abortion process even indirectly is morally on the same plane as people who didn't kill Jews themselves, but only helped the process along. Those who only approve of the killing of unborn babies, or see nothing wrong with it, are morally indistinguishable from Germans who approved of the killing of Jews, or saw nothing wrong with it.

There are those who claim that linking the ongoing abortion Holocaust to the Nazis is only a propaganda trick. Since the Nazis have become in the West an almost universally accepted symbol of evil, linking anything whatever to them is a standard polemical technique. Such an easy and light response ignores the two main points of similarity I have presented: the falsehood of the underlying motivational ideology, and the catastrophic results in terms of human life destroyed.

Bernard Nathanson, co-founder of the National Association for the Repeal of Abortion Laws (NARAL) and an early abortion rights activist, himself a Jew, came to see the abortion holocaust as similar to the Nazi Holocaust. He described it as being so vast and terrible as to be "beyond the ordinary discourse of morality and rational condemnation." He sees the slaughter in America alone of over forty million babies as "a new event, severed from connections with traditional presuppositions of history, psychology, politics, and morality. It extends beyond the deliberations of reason, beyond the discernments of moral judgment, beyond meaning itself." He refers to it as "a mystery that carries with it not only the aspect of vastness, but the resonance of terror, something so unutterably diabolic as to be literally unknowable to us."[19]

People say "Never again," but it is happening again and they don't even care. They criticize the Germans for saying nothing and they say nothing. Famed Holocaust survivor Elie Wiesel "swore never to be silent whenever and wherever human beings endure suffering and humiliation,"[20] but in his Nobel Peace Prize Address he was silent about millions of helpless people arbitrarily categorized as subhuman and then butchered efficiently, methodically, legally—for the good of society. This does not concern or trouble him, to judge by his Address—in exactly the same way that the slaughter of Jews did not concern or trouble many Germans.

Again, a question of presuppositions

How we approach the many problems involved in understanding Hitler and his crimes depends on our presuppositions. If we consider biblical Christianity to be the truth revealed by God from heaven, we can see the pitiful behavior of the vast majority of German Christians as a betrayal of biblical Christianity—or at least as a failure to live up to it. If someone else defines Christianity culturally, it is easier to miss the vast and eternal gulf separating Christianity from Hitler, and concentrate on ties between Hitler and the German churches—as if those churches defined what Christianity is or is not; as if they had not betrayed the faith they were supposed to be representing.

Our understanding of the Jews, who and what they are as a people, is critical. If we view the Old Testament as a collection of myths, then it is impossible to determine who and what the Jews are, let alone why they have suffered, and why they have survived. If, on the other hand, we view the Old and The New Testaments as the literal word of God, it is easy to see why the Jews should be a special object of Satan's malevolence, and why they should have prevailed against all attempts to eliminate them.

If we see the Pope as God's appointed leader for the church, infallible in his office, then we will try to understand his failure to more forthrightly condemn Naziism in one way. If, however, we see him as a fallible man, no holier or closer to God than anyone else, and in some cases even less so, we will interpret his actions differently. Those who do not revere the papacy can easily attribute the Pope's failure to take a bolder stand for the truth to his desire to protect the physical Catholic institution in Germany to the detriment of spiritual truth.

The silence of the Darwinists

A broad survey of Nazi-occupied Europe as a whole shows more Christian opposition to the Nazi persecution of the Jews than is commonly assumed. This was weak, sporadic, ineffectual on more than a limited scale, yet still there was some, more than many think. In France, Holland, Belgium, Norway, Bulgaria, and other countries, there were priests, pastors, and individual Christians who objected, sometimes publicly, and on explicitly religious grounds, to Nazi persecutions. This even occurred, though much more rarely, in Germany itself.

There is no instance, that I am aware of, of even one single Darwinist—let alone numbers of them in different countries—objecting to the Nazi persecution of Jews because of principles inherent in Darwinism. Of course Darwinists can be moral, sometimes even more so than professing Christians, but their morality is contrary to the amoral theory of human origins they profess to believe in. If life emerged as the result of natural selection, then survival is the basic law, the ground of our being. A coherent system of ethics cannot be derived from this, though feeble, unconvincing, and self-contradictory attempts have been made.

The solution to this debate

When Christ returns, then the nature of Hitler's ideas will be completely clarified. It will be seen that Christ's teachings of repentance, faith, and love toward God and toward man are totally contrary to the philosophy patched together by Hitler from the fantasies of a disordered lot of humanists who rejected Christ and placed their faith in human reason.

It will also be seen that those who—either out of ignorance or out of malice—sought to link Christianity to Hitler were distorting facts, and perverting history. Their false witness will be permanently erased. There will also be a complete vindication of God's justice when all of us, including the Nazis, have to give an account for our lives before God.

And many of them that sleep in the dust of the earth shall awake, some to everlasting life, and some to shame and everlasting contempt. (Daniel)

---

[1] Steven Ozment, *A Mighty Fortress: A New History of the German People (100 B.C. to the 21st Century)* (London 2004), p. 268.

[2] Primo Levi, *The Reawakening,* trans. Stuart Wolf (New York 1995), p. 229.

[3] Ibid.

[4] Stephen R. C. Hicks, *Explaining Postmodernism: Skepticism and Socialism from Rousseau to Foucault* (Phoenix, AZ 2004), pp. 133-134.

[5] Raymond Ibrahim, "The Al Qaeda Reader and Mein Kampf," *FrontPageMagazine.com*, Friday, November 09, 2007; http://www.frontpagemag.com/Articles/Read.aspx?GUID=4EDEB0E8-C6B0-4147-883D-D37738482652; accessed February 2008.

[6] Nick Cohen, *What's Left?* (London 2007), pp. 348.

[7] Ibid., pp. 348-349. Cohen refers to the 1988 edition of the Hamas "constitution." Article 22 of this less than Jeffersonian document blames the Jews for the French Revolution, the Russian Revolution, and just about everything else. A brief but detailed overview of the connections between Naziism and Islamic anti-Judaism is found in David Meir-Levi's book *History Upside Down: The Roots of Palestinian Fascism and the Myth of Israeli Aggression* (New York / London 2007).

[8] Jamie Glazov, *United in Hate: The Left's Romance with Tyranny and Terror* (Los Angeles 2009).

[9] Jonah Goldberg, *Liberal Fascism: The Secret History of the American Left from Mussolini to the Politics of Meaning* (New York 2007).

[10] Ibid., p. 194.

[11] Sam Harris, *The End of Faith: Religion, Terror, and the Future of Reason* (London 2006), pp. 52-53.

[12] Sam Harris, "Response to Controversy," http://www.samharris.org/site/full_text/response-to-controversy2/; accessed September 2008.

[13] Harris, *End of Faith*, pp. 13-14.

[14] Ibid., p. 30.

[15] Ibid., pp. 26, 26, 15, 23.

[16] Ibid., pp. 24, 21. Hitler, in a speech of 1937, stated that "Its [the National Socialist Party's] aim is to set up a strong community, to rule wisely and sensibly, to the end that it may thus make life possible for all its fellow citizens" (May 1937, *Hitler Speeches and Quotes*, p. 63).

[17] Ibid., pp. 14, 15, 27.

[18] Ibid., p. 233.

[19] David Kupelian, *The Marketing of Evil: How Radicals, Elitists, and Pseudo-Experts Sell Us Corruption Disguised as Freedom* (Nashville 2005), pp. 204-205.

[20] Eli Wiesel, "The Nobel Prize Acceptance Speech," published in *Night*, trans. Marion Wiesel (New York 2006), p. 118.

Bibliography

Amis, Martin. *Koba the Dread*. London: Vintage, 2003.

Aschheim, Steven A. *In Times of Crisis: Essays on European Culture, Germans, and Jews*. Madison, WI: University of Wisconsin Press, 2001.

Avrich, Paul. *Russian Rebels 1600-1800*. New York / London: W.W. Norton Company, 1972.

Bascomb, Neal. *Hunting Eichmann: How a Band of Survivors and a Young Spy Agency Chased Down the World's Most Notorious Nazi*. Boston: Houghton Mifflin Harcourt, 2009.

Behe, Michael. *The Edge of Evolution: The Search for the Limits of Darwinism*. New York / London: Free Press, 2007.

Bentley, James. *Martin Niemöller*. London: Hodder and Stoughton, 1984.

Browning, Christopher R. *Ordinary Men: Reserve Police Battalion 101 and the Final Solution in Poland*. New York: Harper Perennial, 1998.

Chamberlain, Houston Stewart. *The Foundations of the Nineteenth Century*; online version of *The Foundations of the 19th Century*. Translated by John Lees. London: John Lane, The Bodley Head, 1912; http://www.hschamberlain.net/index.html; accessed January 2008.

Cohen, Nick. *What's Left?* London: Harper Perennial, 2007.

Cohn-Sherbok, Dan. *Fifty Key Jewish Thinkers*. New York / London: Routledge, 2007.

Conway, J.S. *The Nazi Persecution of the Churches 1933-1945*. Vancouver: Regent, 1968.

———. Review of *Elisabeth Schmitz und ihre Denkschrift gegen die Judenverfolgung. Konturen einer vergessenen Biographie (1893-1977)*. Edited by Manfred Gailus. *Association of Contemporary Church Historians (Arbeitsgemeinschaft kirchlicher Zeitgeschichtler) Newsletter* vol. XIV, no. 11 (November 2008); http://www.calvin.edu/academic/cas/akz/akz2811.htm; accessed January 2009.

"The Cosmic Consciousness of a Dynamic Trio: The Hitler Connection," *How the Philosophy of Friedrich Nietzsche Explains the Resurrection and Eternal Return of Jesus Christ*; http://lempisophia.org/Title%20Page.htm; accessed December 2006.

Craig, Gordon A. "Enshrining the Fuhrer," *The New York Times* August 25, 1985; http://query.nytimes.com/gst/fullpage.html?res=9A07E4D7163BF936A1575BC0A963948260; accessed January 2008.

Darwin, Charles. *The Descent of Man*. The Secular Web: Library: Historical Documents; http://www.infidels.org/library/historical/charles_darwin/descent_of_man/; accessed June 2008.

"Dawkins: Religion equals 'child abuse': Scientist compares Moses to Hitler, calls New Testament 'sado-masochistic doctrine'", Faith Under Fire: *WorldNetDaily*; http://www.worldnetdaily.com/news/article.asp?ARTICLE_ID=48252; accessed May 2007.

Day, Vox. *The Irrational Atheist: Dissecting the Unholy Trinity of Dawkins, Harris, and Hitchens*. Dallas: Benbella Books, 2008.

Diephouse, David J. "Antisemitism as Moral Discourse: Theophil Wurm and Protestant Opposition to the Holocaust." Paper presented to the 30th Annual Scholar's Conference on the Holocaust and the Churches, Philadelphia, March 2000. CD-ROM Sourcebook, Philadelphia, Geneva: Vista Intermedia, 2001.

Edwards, David L. "Rudolf Bultmann: Scholar of Faith." Christian Century, September 1-8 (1976), 728-730. *Religion Online*; http://www.religiononline.org/showarticle.asp?title=1827; accessed May 2007.

Engelmann, Bernt. *In Hitler's Germany: Everyday Life in the Third Reich*. Translated by Krishna Winston. New York: Pantheon Books, 1986.

"Enlightenment: The French Revolution," *Florida Holocaust Museum*; http://www.flholocaustmuseum.org/history_wing/antisemitism/enlightenment.cfm;

accessed May 2007.

Evans, Richard J. *The Coming of the Third Reich*. New York / London: Penguin Books, 2005.

_____. "Nazism, Christianity and Political Religion: A Debate," *Journal of Contemporary History* 42, no. 1 (2007), 5-7.

"Excerpts from *Hitler's Table Talk*," *Kevin's Articles on Religion* (citing the edition by Weidenfeld and Nicolson, London 1953); http://davnet.org/kevin/articles/table.html; accessed June 2008.

Feldberg, Michael. "John Adams embraces a Jewish homeland," *Homepage for Lewis Loflin*; http://www.sullivan-county.com/id2/adams_jews.htm; accessed January 2008.

Fest, Joachim C. *Hitler*. Translated by Richard and Clara Winston. New York / London: Harcourt Brace, 1974.

Fichte, Johann Gottlieb. "Addresses to the German Nation," *Internet Modern History Sourcebook*; http://www.fordham.edu/halsall/mod/1806fichte.html; accessed January 2008. http://www.fordham.edu/halsall/mod/1807fichte1.html; accessed January 2008.

———. *Addresses to the German Nation.* Translated by R.F. Jones and G.H. Turnbull. Chicago and London: Open Court Publishing, 1922.

———. *Addresses to the German Nation.* Translated by R.F. Jones and G.H. Turnbull, Ed. George Armstrong Kelly. New York: Harper and Row, 1968.

Frank, Walter S. "Adolf Hitler: The Making of a Fuhrer (Who was Responsible?)," *Smoter .com*; http://www.smoter.com/hitler.htm; accessed January 2008.

Friedländer, Saul. *The Years of Extermination: Nazi Germany and the Jews 1939-1945*. London: Weidenfeld and Nicolson, 2007.

Gasman, Daniel. *The Scientific Origins of National Socialism*. New Brunswick USA / London: Transaction Publishers, 2004.

Gay, Peter. *Weimar Culture: The Outsider as Insider*. New York: Harper and Row, 1968.

Gilbert, Martin. *The Holocaust: A History of the Jews of Europe During the Second World War*. New York: Henry Holt and Co., 1985.

Glazov, Jamie. *United in Hate: The Left's Romance with Tyranny and Terror*. Los Angeles: WND Books, 2009.

Goldberg, Jonah. *Liberal Fascism: The Secret History of the American Left from Mussolini to the Politics of Meaning*. New York: Doubleday, 2007.

Goldhagen, Daniel Jonah. *Hitler's Willing Executioners: Ordinary Germans and the Holocaust*. New York: Alfred A. Knopf, 1996.

Golomb, Jacob and Robert Wistrich, Eds. Introduction to "Nietzsche, Godfather of Fascism? On the Uses and Abuses of Philosophy," *Princeton University Press*; http://www.pupress.princeton.edu/chapters/i7403.html; accessed January 2008.

Green, Lowell C. *Lutherans Against Hitler: The Untold Story*. St. Louis: Concordia, 2007.

Guinness, Os. *Unspeakable: Facing up to Evil in an Age of Genocide and Terror*. New York: HarperSanFrancisco, 2005.

Gundry, Stanley N. and Steven B. Cowan, Eds. *Five Views on Apologetics*. Grand Rapids, MI: Zondervan, 2000.

Haeckel, Ernst. *The Riddle of the Universe at the Close of the Nineteenth Century.* Translated by Joseph McCabe. London: Rationalist Press, 1900.

Hallie, Philip. *Lest Innocent Blood Be Shed: The Story of the Village of Le Chambon and How Goodness Happened There*. New York: Harper and Row, 1979.

Hankins, Barry. *Francis Schaeffer and the Shaping of Evangelical America*. Grand Rapids, MI: William B. Eerdmans, 2008.

Harris, Sam. *The End of Faith: Religion, Terror, and the Future of Reason*. London: The Free Press, 2006.

———. "Response to Controversy"; http://www.samharris.org/site/full_text/response-to-controversy2/; accessed September 2008.

Harrison, Paul. "Hegel: Philosophy and history as theology," *Pantheist History*;

http://members.aol.com/pantheism0/hegel.htm; accessed January 2008.

Hayek, F.A. *The Road to Serfdom*. Chicago: The University of Chicago Press, 2007.

Heer, Jeet. "Enlightened Kant Racist," Review of German Idealism and the Jew: The Inner Anti-Semitism of Philosophy and German Jewish Responses, by Michael Mack. *Adelaide Institute*; http://www.adelaideinstitute.org/Germany/kant.htm; accessed January 2008.

Hegel, G.W. *The Philosophy of History.* Translated by J. Sibree. Great Books of the Western World, *Encyclopedia Britannica*, 1952.

Hegel, G.W. *The Philosophy of Right.* Translated by T.M. Knox. Great Books of the Western World, *Encyclopedia Britannica*, 1952.

"Hegel's Philosophy of Right (Third Part: Ethical Life, iii. The State)," *Hegel by HyperText*; http://www.marxists.org/reference/archive/hegel/works/pr/prstate2.htm#PR324; accessed January 2008.

Heine, Heinrich. *On the History of Religion and Philosophy in Germany.* Translated by Howard Pollack Milgate. Cambridge: Cambridge University Press, 2007.

Henry, Matthew. "Commentary on the Whole Bible," *Christian Classics Ethereal Library*, Calvin College; http://www.ccel.org/h/henry/mhc2/MHC00000.HTM; accessed January 2008.

"The Hep! Hep! Riots," *Gates to Jewish Heritage*; http://www.jewishgates.com/file.asp?File_ID=80; accessed March 2006.

Hicks, Stephen R. C. *Explaining Postmodernism: Skepticism and Socialism from Rousseau to Foucault*. Phoenix, AZ: Scholargy Publishing, 2004.

Hitler, Adolf. *Mein Kampf*; http://www.hitler.org/writings/Mein_Kampf/; accessed July 2007.

———. *Mein Kampf.* Translated by Ralph Manheim. Boston / New York: Mariner Books, 1999.

———. *Speeches*; http://www.adolfhitler.ws/lib/speeches/text/speeches.htm; accessed April 2006.

_____. *Hitler Speeches and Quotes*. London: World Propaganda Classics, 2008.

_____. *Hitler's Second Book: The Unpublished Sequel to Mein Kampf.* Translated by Krista Smith. New York: Enigma Books, 2006.

"The Hitler No One Knows," *German Propaganda Archive,* Calvin College: from Heinrich Hoffmann, *Hitler wie ihn keiner kennt* (Berlin: "Zeitgeschichte" Verlag, 1932); http://www.bytwerk.com/gpa/hitler2.htm; accessed January 2008.

"The Hitler of *Mein Kampf*"; http://www.geocities.com/mikem2u/meinkampf.html; accessed January 2008.

Hockenos, Matthew. Review of The Reluctant Revolutionary: Dietrich Bonhoeffer's Collision with Prusso-German History, by John A. Moses; *Association of Contemporary Church Historians (Arbeitsgemeinschaft kirchlicher Zeitgeschichtler) Newsletter* vol. XV, no. 7 (July 2009); http://www.calvin.edu/academic/cas/akz/akz2907.htm; accessed July 2009.

Hoess, Rudolf. *Commandant of Auschwitz.* Translated by Constantine Fitzgibbon. London: Phoenix Press, 2000.

Hollingdale, R.J. *Nietzsche: The Man and His Philosophy*. Cambridge: Cambridge University Press, 1999.

Horne, Alistair. *The Age of Napoleon*. New York: Modern Library, 2006.

Hughes, John Jay. "A Mass Murderer Repents," *Institute for Christian Spirituality*; http://theology.shu.edu/lectures/massmurder.htm; accessed January 2008.

Ibrahim, Raymond. "The Al Qaeda Reader and *Mein Kampf*," FrontPageMagazine.com, Friday, November 09, 2007; http://www.frontpagemag.com/Articles/Read.aspx?GUID=4EDEB0E8-C6B0-4147-883D-D37738482652; accessed February 2008.

Jäckel, Eberhard. *Hitler's World View: A Blueprint for Power*. Cambridge, MA: Harvard University Press, 1997.

Jefferson, Thomas. "Syllabus of an Estimate of the Merit of the Doctrines of Jesus, Compared with Those of Others." http://www.angelfire.com/co/JeffersonBible/jeffbsyl.html; accessed January 2008.

Johnson, Paul. *Modern Times: The World from the Twenties to the Nineties*. New York: Harper Perennial, 1991.

———. *A History of the Jews*. London: Weidenfeld and Nicolson, 1987.

Johnson, Phillip E. *The Wedge of Truth: Splitting the Foundations of Naturalism*. Downers Grove, IL: InterVarsity Press, 2000.

Judaken, Jonathan. Review of From Darwin to Hitler: Evolutionary Ethics, Eugenics, and Racism in Germany, by Richard Weikart. *H-Ideas, H-Net Reviews*, June, 2005; http://www.h-net.org/reviews/showrev.cgi?path=80951126890820; accessed May 2007.

Just, Dieter. *"Ich denke—also bin ich nicht."* English summary by Herbert Renz-Polster; http://www.d-just.de/text1eng.htm; accessed January 2008.

Kalish, Michael. "Friedrich Nietzsche's Influence on Hitler's *Mein Kampf*"; http://www.history.ucsb.edu/faculty/marcuse/classes/133p/133p04papers/MKalishNietzNazi046.htm; accessed January 2008.

Kant, Immanuel. *An Answer to the Question: "What is Enlightenment?"*. Translated by H.B. Nisbet. London: Penguin Books, 2009.

Katz, Steven A. *The Holocaust in Historical Context* (Vol. 1). New York/Oxford: Oxford University Press, 1994.

Kay, James. Review of Christian Faith in Dark Times: Theological Conflicts in the Shadow of Hitler, by Jack Forstman. *Theology Today* 50, no. 4 (January 1993); http://theologytoday.ptsem.edu/jan1994/v50-4-bookreview6.htm; accessed May 2007.

Kershaw, Ian. *Hitler, 1889-1936: Hubris*. New York / London: W. W. Norton, 2000.

_____. *The Nazi Dictatorship: Problems and Perspectives of Interpretation*. London: Arnold, 2000.

Kimel, Alexander. "Holocaust and Christianity," *Holocaust Educational Digest*; http://www.kimel.net/christi.html; accessed January 2008.

Klemperer, Victor. *I Will Bear Witness: A Diary of the Nazi Years 1942-1945*. Translated by Martin Chalmers. New York: Random House / Modern Library, 2001.

Kubizek, August. *The Young Hitler I Knew*. Translated by Geoffrey Brooks. London: Greenhill Books, 2006.

Kupelian, David. *The Marketing of Evil: How Radicals, Elitists, and Pseudo-Experts Sell Us Corruption Disguised as Freedom.* Nashville, TN: WND Books, 2005.

Laqueur, Walter. *Weimar: A Cultural History*. New York: Perigee, 1980.

Levi, Primo. *The Reawakening*. Translated by Stuart Wolf. New York: Touchstone Books, 1995.

Livingstone, David. "Plato the Kabbalist," *Illuminati Conspiracy Archive*; http://www.conspiracyarchive.com/NewAge/Plato_Kabbalist.htm; accessed January 2008.

Lukacs, John. *The Hitler of History*. New York: Alfred A. Knopf, 1997.

Luther, Martin. *On the Jews and Their Lies.* Translated by Martin H. Bertram. *Humanitas International*; http://www.humanitas-international.org/showcase/chronography/documents/luther-jews.htm; accessed January 2008.

_____. *Martin Luther: Selections from his Writings*. Edited by John Dillenberger. New York: Anchor Books, 1962.

_____. *Table Talk*. Translated by Theodore G. Tappert (*Luther's Works* vol. 54). Philadelphia: Fortress Press, 1967.

_____. *The Table Talk of Martin Luther*. Translated by William Hazlitt. *Center for Reformed Theology and Apologetics*; http://www.reformed.org/master/index.html?

mainframe=/documents/Table_Talk/table_talk.html; accessed June 2009.

Mack, Michael. *German Idealism and the Jew: The Inner Anti-Semitism of Philosophy and German Jewish Responses*. Chicago / London: University of Chicago Press, 2003.

Marcuse, Harold and Werner Cohn. "Correspondence about Niemöller's Antisemitism"; http://www.history.ucsb.edu/faculty/marcuse/projects/niem/NiemAntisemCohnHMCor resp034.htm; accessed January 2008.

Maser, Werner. *Hitler's Letters and Notes*. New York: Harper and Row, 1974.

McGrath, Alister. *The Twilight of Atheism: The Rise and Fall of Disbelief in the Modern World*. London: Rider, 2004.

Mencken, H.L. "Introduction to Nietzsche's Antichrist," *The Gutenberg Project*; http://www.gutenberg.org/files/19322/19322-h/19322-h.htm; accessed August 2008.

Michael, Robert. "Theological Myth, German Antisemitism, and the Holocaust: The Case of Martin Niemoeller." *Holocaust and Genocide Studies: An International Journal*, vol. 2, no. 1 (1987), 105-22.

Montgomery, John Warwick. *In Defense of Martin Luther*. Milwaukee, WI: Northwestern Publishing House, 1970.

_____. *Tractatus Logico-Theologicus*. Bonn: Culture and Science Publishing, 2003.

Moore, Gregory. Excerpt from *Nietzsche, Biology and Metaphor*, (Cambridge University Press Catalogue); http://assets.cambridge.org/97805218/12306/excerpt/9780521812306_excerpt.pdf; accessed January 2008.

Moorhouse, Roger. *Berlin at War: Life and Death in Hitler's Capital, 1939-1945*. London Vintage Books, 2011.

Mosse, George L. *The Crisis of German Ideology: Intellectual Origins of the Third Reich*. New York: Grosset & Dunlap, 1971.

Myers, Peter. Review of Nietzsche and Jewish Culture, Jacob Golomb, ed.; http://users.cyberone.com.au/myers/nietzsche.html; accessed January 2008.

Nietzsche, Friedrich. "*Der Antichrist: Fluch auf das Christenthum*," *The Nietzsche Channel*; http://www.geocities.com/thenietzschechannel/antig.htm; accessed December 2007.

———. *The Antichrist: Curse on Christianity*. Translated by Walter Kaufmann, *The Nietzsche Channel*; http://www.geocities.com/thenietzschechannel/anti.htm; accessed December 2007.

———. *The Antichrist: Curse on Christianity.* Translated by H.L. Mencken; http://www.primitivism.com/antichrist.htm; accessed August 2008.

———. *Beyond Good and Evil*, translated by Ian Johnston; http://www.mala.bc.ca/~johnstoi/Nietzsche/beyondgoodandevil8.htm; accessed January 2008.

———. "Nietzsche contra Wagner," *The Nietzsche Channel*; http://www.geocities.com/thenietzschechannel/ncw.htm#for; accessed January 2008.

———. *On the Genealogy of Morals: A Polemical Tract.* Translated by Ian Johnston; http://www.mala.bc.ca/~johnstoi/Nietzsche/genealogytofc.htm; accessed January 2008.

"Nietzsche: Letters of Insanity," *The Nietzsche Channel*; http://www.geocities.com/thenietzschechannel/niletters.htm; accessed January 2008.

Orenstein, Phil. "Heil, Professor!" *FrontPageMagazine.com*, July 14, 2006; http://www.frontpagemag.com/Articles/ReadArticle.asp?ID=23293; accessed May 2007.

Ozment, Steven. *A Mighty Fortress: A New History of the German People (110 B.C. to the 21st Century).* London: Granta Books, 2004.

Padfield, Peter. *Himmler: Reichsfuhrer-SS*. New York: Henry Holt and Company, 1990.

Pascal, Blaise. *Pensées*. Translated by A.J. Krailsheimer. London: Penguin Books, 1995.

Pashak, Barrett. Review of German Idealism and the Jew: The Inner Anti-Semitism of Philosophy and German Jewish Responses, by Michael Mack. *Constantinbrunner.info*; http://www.constantinbrunner.info/pages/mack.htm; accessed January 2008.

Peukert, Detlev J. *The Weimar Republic: The Crisis of Classical Modernity.* Translated by Richard Deveson. New York: Hill and Wang, 1992.

Pollock, John. *A Foreign Devil in China.* Minneapolis, MN: World Wide Publications, 1988.

"Pre-1933 Nazi Posters," *German Propaganda Archive*, Calvin College; http://www.calvin.edu/academic/cas/gpa/posters1.htm; accessed January 2008.

"The Private and Political Testaments of Hitler, April 29, 1945"; http://www.ibiblio.org/pha/policy/1945/450429a.html; accessed May 2007.

Reck-Malleczewen, Friedrich. *Diary of a Man in Despair.* Translated by Paul Rubens. London: Audiogrove Ltd., 1995.

Rees, Lawrence. *Auschwitz: The Nazis and the 'Final Solution.'* London: Ebury Publishing 2005.

———. *The Nazis: A Warning from History.* New York: New Press, 1997.

Richards, Robert J. "Ernst Haeckel's Alleged Anti-Semitism and Contributions to Nazi Biology"; http://home.uchicago.edu/~rjr6/articles/Haeckel--antiSemitism.pdf; accessed June 2008.

Rose, Paul Lawrence. *German Question / Jewish Question: Revolutionary Antisemitism from Kant to Wagner.* Princeton: Princeton University Press, 1990.

———. *Wagner: Race and Revolution.* New Haven / London: Yale University Press, 1992.

Rosenbaum, Ron. *Explaining Hitler.* New York: Random House, 1998.

Rousseau, Jean-Jacques. *The Social Contract.* London: Penguin Books, 2004.

Russell, William. *Berlin Embassy.* New York: Carroll and Graf, 2005.

Ryback, Timothy W. "Hitler's Forgotten Library: The Man, His Books, and His Search For God." *The Atlantic Monthly*, May 2003; http:www.fpp.co.uk/Hitler/library/Atlantic_Monthly.html; accessed May 2007.

———. *Hitler's Private Library: The Books that Shaped his Life.* London: Vintage Books, 2010.

Sachar, Abram Leon. *A History of the Jews.* New York: Alfred A. Knopf, 1964.

Sachar, Howard M. *A History of the Jews in the Modern World.* New York: Vintage Books, 2006.

Schaeffer, Francis. *The Great Evangelical Disaster.* Westchester, IL: Crossway Books, 1984.

Schopenhauer, Arthur. *The Horrors and Absurdities of Religion.* Translated by R. J. Hollingdale. London: Penguin, 2009.

———. *Religion.* Translated by T. Bailey Saunders. *eBooks@Adelaide*; http://etext.library.adelaide.edu.au/s/schopenhauer/arthur/religion/chapter6.html; accessed May 2007.

———. *The World as Will and Idea.* Translated by R. B. Haldane and J. Kemp. *Internet Archive*; http://www.archive.org/stream/theworldaswillan01schouoft/theworldaswillan01schouoft_djvu.txt; accessed September, 2009.

Seneca, Lucius Annaeus. *Letters from a Stoic (Epistulae Morales ad Lucilium).* Translated by Robin Campbell. London: Penguin, 2004.

Shirer, William L. *Berlin Diary.* New York: Alfred A. Knopf, 1941.

———. *The Rise and Fall of the Third Reich.* New York: Simon and Schuster, 1960.

Shyovitz, David. "The Hep Hep Riots," *Jewish Virtual Library*; http://www.jewishvirtuallibrary.org/jsource/anti-semitism/hep.html; accessed May 2007.

Singer, Peter. *Practical Ethics.* Cambridge: Cambridge University Press, 2009.

Smith, James K. A. *Who's Afraid of Postmodernism? Taking Derrida, Lyotard, and Foucault to Church.* Grand Rapids, MI: Baker Academic, 2008.

Snell, John, ed. *The Nazi Revolution: Germany's Guilt or Germany's Fate?.* Lexington, Mass.: D.C. Heath, 1959.

Spengler. "Islam: Religion or political ideology?," *Asia Times Online*; http://www.atimes.com/atimes/Front_Page/FH10Aa01.html; accessed May 2007.

Stalin, Joseph. "Dialectical and Historical Materialism," *The Art Bin*; http://art-bin.com/art/ostalineng.html; accessed January 2008.

Steigmann-Gall, Richard. *The Holy Reich: Nazi Conceptions of Christianity, 1919-1945*. Cambridge: Cambridge University Press, 2004.

Stein, Leo. "Niemoller speaks!" The National Jewish Monthly May 1941; *Homepage of Harold Marcuse*; www.history.ucsb.edu/faculty/marcuse/projects/niem/njm415/NatJewMonthly415.htm; accessed January 2008.

Stein, Stuart. "Individual Responsibility of Defendants: Julius Streicher," *Nuremberg Judgment*; http://www.ess.uwe.ac.uk/genocide/Streicher.htm; accessed January 2008.

Steinberg, Stefan. "One hundred years since the death of Friedrich Nietzsche: a review of his ideas and influence—Parts 1–3," *World Socialist Web Site*; www.wsws.org/articles/2000/oct2000/niet-o20.shtml; accessed January 2008; www.wsws.org/articles/2000/oct2000/niet-o21.shtml; accessed January 2008; www.wsws.org/articles/2000/oct2000/niet-o23.shtml; accessed January 2008.

Stephens, Don. *War and Grace: Short Biographies from the World Wars*. Darlington: Evangelical Press, 2005.

Stewart, Jon. *Introduction to The Hegel Myths and Legends*; http://www.marxists.org/reference/subject/philosophy/works/us/stewart.htm; accessed January 2008.

Swan, James. "Martin Luther's Attitude Toward the Jews," *New Testament Research Ministries*; http://www.ntrmin.org/Luther%20and%20the%20Jews%20(Web).htm#a1; accessed June 2009.

Teo, Thomas. "The historical problematization of 'mixed race' in psychological and human-scientific discourses"; http://www.yorku.ca/tteo/teach/Teo2004.htm; accessed January 2008.

Thomas, Robert. "The Nature of Nazi Ideology," *Libertarian Alliance*; www.libertarian.co.uk/lapubs/histn/histn015.pdf; accessed January 2008.

Thornton, Ted. "Persecution of the Jews in Europe," *History of the Middle East Data Base*; http://www.nmhschool.org/tthornton/mehistorydatabase/christian_persecution_of_the_jew.php; accessed January 2008.

Toland, John. *Adolf Hitler*. Garden City, NY: Doubleday and Co., 1976.

"Toledoth Yeshu," *Ancient Jewish Accounts of Jesus*, [Text from Goldstein, *Jesus in the Jewish Tradition*, pp. 148-154.]; http://ccat.sas.upenn.edu/humm/Topics/JewishJesus/toledoth.html; accessed January 2008.

"The Trial of Adolf Eichmann," Session 105 (Part 4 of 4), *The Nizkor Project*; http://www.nizkor.org/hweb/people/e/eichmann-adolf/transcripts/Sessions/Session-105-04.html; accessed January 2008.

Triumph des Willens (Triumph of the Will), directed by Leni Riefenstahl; http://video.google.com/videoplay?docid=-1624809629731313480; accessed July 2007.

"The 25 Points of Hitler's Nazi Party," *Scrapbookpages.com*; http://www.scrapbookpages.com/DachauScrapbook/25Points.html; accessed January 2008.

Tyndale, William. *The Obedience of a Christian Man*. London: Penguin Books, 2000.

van Vrekhem, Georges. *Hitler and his God: The Background of the Hitler Phenomenon*. New Delhi: Rupa and Co., 2006.

Viereck, Peter. *Meta-politics: The Roots of the Nazi Mind*. New York: Capricorn Books, 1965.

von Lang, Jochen, and Claus Sibyll, Eds. *Eichmann Interrogated: Transcripts from the Archives of the Israeli Police.* Translated by Ralph Manheim. New York: Farrar, Strauss, and Giroux, 1983.

von Metternich, Prince Klemens. *Memoirs of Prince Metternich (1880—Vol. 03),* "free online text repository"; http://www.literature.at/elib/index.php5?title=Metternich_-_Memoirs_of_Prince_Metternich_-_1880_-_Vol_03; accessed July 2008.

Wagner, Richard. "Hero-dom and Christendom." Translated by William Ashton Ellis; http://users.belgacom.net/wagnerlibrary/prose/waghero.htm; accessed October 2007.

———. "Introduction to a Work of Count Gobineau's." Translated by William Ashton Ellis; http://users.belgacom.net/wagnerlibrary/prose/wlpr0155.htm; accessed October 2007.

———. "Know Thyself." Translated by William Ashton Ellis; http://users.belgacom.net/wagnerlibrary/prose/wagknow.htm; accessed October 2007.

———. "On State and Religion." Translated by William Ashton Ellis; http://users.belgacom.net/wagnerlibrary/prose/wagstarel.htm; accessed October 2007.

———. "Religion and Art." Translated by William Ashton Ellis; http://users.belgacom.net/wagnerlibrary/prose/wlpr0126.htm; accessed October 2007.

Walker, Jim. "Hitler's Christianity," *NoBeliefs.com*; http://www.nobeliefs.com/Hitler1.htm; accessed January 2008.

———. "Thomas Jefferson on Christianity and Religion," NoBeliefs.com; http://www.nobeliefs.com/jefferson.htm; accessed January 2008.

Wang, Stephen. *The Long Road to Freedom: The Story of Wang Mingdao.* Tonbridge: Sovereign World, 2002.

Ward, Keith. *Pascal's Fire: Scientific Faith and Religious Understanding.* Oxford: One World, 2006.

"Was Hitler an atheist...?" *Critical Thought and Religious Liberty*; http://www.stephenjaygould.org/ctrl/quotes_hitler.html; accessed January 2008.

Weikart, Richard. *From Darwin to Hitler: Evolutionary Ethics, Eugenics, and Racism in Germany.* New York: Palgrave MacMillan, 2004.

———. *Hitler's Ethic: The Nazi Pursuit of Evolutionary Progress.* New York: Palgrave Macmillan, 2009.

Weil, Simon. *Wagner and the Jews;* http://members.aol.com/wagnerbuch/intro.htm, accessed January 2008.

Wesley, John. *The Journal of John Wesley.* Oxford: Lion Publishing, 2003.

Whitefield, George. *George Whitefield's Journals.* Edinburgh: Banner of Truth Trust, 1998.

Wicks, Robert. "Arthur Schopenhauer," *The Stanford Encyclopedia of Philosophy*; http://plato.stanford.edu/archives/sum2003/entries/schopenhauer/; accessed January 2008.

Wiesel, Eli. "The Nobel Prize Acceptance Speech," published in *Night*, Translated by Marion Wiesel. New York: Hill and Wang, 2006.

Wistrich, Robert S. *Hitler and the Holocaust: How and Why the Holocaust Happened.* London: Phoenix Press, 2002.

Index

R

Rosenbaum, Ron, 227
  Explaining Hitler, 227
Rosenberg, Alfred, 173, 176, 177, 178,
    177–78, 182, 184, 186, 196, 197, 204,
    269, 335, 358, 422
  The Myth of the Twentieth Century,
    177, 204, 269, 358
Rousseau, 240, 297, 298, 331, 433, 459
  emphasized feeling and passion, 240
  general welfare of state greater in
    importance than individual life, 241
  influened Kant, Fichte, and Hegel, 240
Rousseau, 240
Ruhs, Friedrich, 276
Russell, Bertrand
  parallels Nietzsche's endorsement of
    cruelty for the benefit of mankind,
    423
Russell, William, 220
Russian Rebels: 1600-1800, Paul Avrich,
    232
Russian support of Hitler, 170
Ryback, Timothy, 253, 254, 255, 257, 278,
    290

S

SA (*Sturmabteilung*, storm troopers,
    Brownshirts), 101, 119, 122, 138, 145,
    147, 148, 162, 171, 190, 192, 196, 197,
    270, 440
Sachsenhausen, *See under* concentration
    camps, Sachsenhausen
Schallmeyer, Wilhelm, 379
Schelling
  On the World Soul, 259
Schemann, Ludwig, 286, 287
Schemm, Hans, 286
Schirach, Baldur von, 146
Schleicher, Kurt von, 165
Schleiermacher, Friedrich, 198, 199, 291
Schmitz, Elisabeth, 205
Schneider, Pastor Paul, 185, 189, 224
Schonerer, Georg von, 120, 160, 178, 295,
    385, 390
Schopenhauer, Arthur, 81, 117, 163, 243,
    249, 258, 272, 288, 291, 304, 305, 309,
    311, 312, 313, 336, 347, 356, 372, 381,
    390, 425, 429
  expanded and radicalized Kant's ideas,
    283
  individual has no value, 282
  Jews aliens and parasites, 283
  Judaism to be destroyed through
    assimilation, 284
  life pointless, 284
  man merely advanced animal, 283

quoted in *Mein Kampf*, 279
  Schopenhauerian Christianity, 284, 311
    blamed Christianity on the Jews,
      283
  The World as Will and Representation,
    278, 312
  ultimate Will, 280
SD (*Sicherheitsdienst*, Security Service),
    171
Sebottendorff, Rudolf von, 434
Second Book, Hitler, 224, 258, 279, 301,
    361, 395, 397, 426, 433
Security Service, *See under* SD
  (*Sicherheitsdienst*, Security Service)
Shirer, William L., 77, 98, 102, 105, 114,
    115, 116, 144, 165, 166, 167, 171, 189,
    205, 212, 268, 271, 334, 335, 401
  The Rise and Fall of the Third Reich,
    77
Sicherheitsdienst, *See under* SD
  (*Sicherheitsdienst*, Security Service)
Singer, Peter, 374, 379, 397
Social Darwinism, 49, 94, 99, 268, 287,
    292, 362, 390
Society Against Jewish Domination, 295
Solf, Frau, 171
Spandau, The Secret Diaries, Speer, 324
Spanish Inquisition, 285, *See also*
  Inquisition
Speer, 143, 324
Spinoza, 199, 246, 412, 413
SS, 20, 104, 123, 125, 180, 193, 357, 450
Stalin, Joseph, 11, 46, 76, 77, 110, 130,
    131, 133, 136, 144, 167, 170, 178, 190,
    197, 205, 219, 242, 266, 326, 357, 365,
    388, 401, 402, 423, 427, 428, 429, 436,
    437, 446, 448
Stalingrad, 261
Steffens, Heinrich, 269
Steigmann-Gall, Richard, 3, 4, 13, 22, 23,
    27, 28, 79, 80, 107, 116, 117, 118, 145,
    186, 192, 258, 272, 291, 311, 314, 315,
    335, 340
Stein, Leo, 169, 210
Stellbrink, Pastor Karl Friedrich, 175
Stephen of Sofia, 221
Stoecker, Adolf, 412
storm troopers, *See* SA (*Sturmabteilung*,
    storm troopers, Brownshirts)
Strasser, Gregor, 320
Streicher, Julius, 44, 47, 129, 152
Swedenborg, cult of, 293
Sylten, Dr., 205

476

T

V

W

www.ingramcontent.com/pod-product-compliance
Lightning Source LLC
Chambersburg PA
CBHW070858140426
R18135300001B/R181353PG42812CBX00004B/7